D1189700

NATO ADVANCED STUDY INSTITUTES SERIES

Proceedings of the Advanced Study Institute Programme, which aims at the dissemination of advanced knowledge and the formation of contacts among scientists from different countries.

The series is published by an international board of publishers in conjunction with NATO Scientific Affairs Divison

A	Life Sciences	Plenum Publishing Corporation
B	Physics	London and New York
C	Mathematical and Physical Sciences	D. Reidel Publishing Company Dordrecht and Boston
D	Behavioural and Social Sciences	Sijthoff & Noordhoff International Publishers B.V.
E	Applied Sciences	Alpen aan den Rijn, The Netherlands and Germantown, Md., U.S.A.

Series D: Behavioural and Social Sciences — No. 2

THEORETICAL ADVANCES IN BEHAVIOR GENETICS

edited by

JOSEPH R. ROYCE
Center for Advanced Study in Theoretical Psychology,
University of Alberta
Edmonton, Alberta, Canada

and

LEENDERT P. MOS
Center for Advanced Study in Theoretical Psychology,
University of Alberta
Edmonton, Alberta, Canada

SIJTHOFF & NOORDHOFF   1979
Alphen aan den Rijn   The Netherlands
Germantown, Maryland   USA

Proceedings of the NATO Advanced Study Institute on

Theoretical Advances in Behavior Genetics
Banff Centre, Banff, Alberta, Canada
September 29, October 8, 1978

also sponsored by

The Center for Advanced Study in Theoretical Psychology
The University of Alberta,
Edmonton, Alberta, Canada

ISBN 90 286 0569 X

Copyright © 1979 Sijthoff & Noordhoff International Publishers B.V., Alphen aan
den Rijn, The Netherlands.

All rights reserved. No part of this publication may be reproduced, stored in a
retrieval system, or transmitted, in any form or by any means, electronic, mechanical, photocopying, recording, or otherwise, without the prior permission of the
copyright owner.

Printed in The Netherlands

WELCOMING REMARKS

Ladies and gentlemen, welcome: not quite to the University of Alberta, but to a campus every bit as beautiful. This is an excellent time to be in the mountains, and I hope that during the next few days we will all have the opportunity of absorbing this heady environment and find ways and means of injecting it into our deliberations.

The theme of this Advanced Study Institute--Theoretical Advances in Behaviour Genetics--is a particularly significant one at this time in the history of mankind when a sense of direction --in thought and in action--is being both sought and challenged by so many, and with so many different purposes. I think it is obvious that the options which are open to society, the choices which are available, the very possibilities, form the essential material, if not the basic framework, within which the discussion of directions should be conducted. The Institute promises at least an enquiry, and perhaps some new directions.

Looking at the programme it is clear to me that the next ten days will keep us all fully occupied, and I would suggest fully stimulated, at the frontier--or should I say frontiers--of the component disciplines of behaviour genetics. The Institute brings together people, and it is of course just such human organisms which are the special interest of the enquiry. The Institute also brings together disciplines, and whereas disciplines are not organisms they are organic. Disciplines are born and do die; they evolve, responding and adapting to their circumstances, and most of all perhaps to related disciplines. Disciplines also divide in a manner which sometimes resembles mitosis and sometimes looks like divergent evolution; and they also merge in what may well be analogous to convergent evolution.

It may be too much to insist on a complete analogy between a discipline and the human organism, but yet the similarity is close enough--and significant enough--to suggest some intriguing questions. For example, does the relationship between ontogeny and phylogeny in organisms have a counterpart in disciplines? Would it be true to say, for example, that the early development of an emerging discipline recapitulates the history of knowledge? Intuitively perhaps we sense some relationship of this kind, and perhaps it is enough merely to note the connection. But I raise questions of this kind because it seems\ to me that this Institute, in bringing together the two principal disciplines of Psychology and Genetics, might contemplate a framework of enquiry which is not merely the framework of the constituent disciplines. I think it is important to recognize that, to the extent that a discipline has structure and function--and perhaps leading me back to the analogy with an organism--that structure and function, and indeed the entire makeup of the discipline, is invariably perceived from the inside. I hardly need emphasize at a gathering like this that the inside view may be privileged but it is also prejudiced. When disciplines meet it is essential to consider not only an outside view, but an <u>overview</u>.

My own experience has taught me that interdisciplinary activities are difficult to come to grips with--both conceptually and administratively. The activities at the University of Alberta which come under my jurisdiction provide many good examples of these difficulties, though I don't propose to list them here. But perhaps I might mention that the Center for Advanced Study in Theoretical Psychology is one of some eight organizational units at the University of Alberta engaged in a very wide variety of teaching, research and community related activity. The Center's principal objective, as its name suggests, is research and teaching in Theoretical Psychology, and therefore it is most appropriate for it to organize, sponsor, or otherwise participate in, advanced study institutes such as this one. This is, in fact, the fourth occasion when the Center has gathered together here in Banff distinguished workers of several disciplines and many countries. And perhaps I can take this opportunity to express my appreciation, and yours, to Dr. Royce--and to what I believe can be accurately described as his dedication and vision--for acting as the architect of this Institute. Since I know it will be a success, I have no hesitation in adding also my congratulations to the organizers in general, and to Dr. Mos in particular.

Let me welcome you then, on behalf of Interdisciplinary Studies at the University of Alberta, indeed on behalf of the entire University, if not the entire province. May the debate be incisive, and the discussion productive, and may we all emerge from the Institute wiser but hopefully not sadder. Thank you very much.

Gerald Lock
Dean of Interdisciplinary Studies
The University of Alberta

CONTENTS

J. H. F. van ABEELEN

K. IMMELMANN

PART II   MOLECULAR BIOLOGY

PART III   GENE-ENVIRONMENT INTERACTIONS

PART V METHODOLOGICAL AND CONCEPTUAL ISSUES

PART VI PSYCHOLOGICAL THEORY

PROLOGUE: The Need for Unifying Theory

J. R. Royce

KEYNOTE ADDRESS

Genes, Molecules, Organisms, and Behavior

J. N. Spuhler

PROLOGUE: The Need for Unifying Theory

Joseph R. Royce

This is the fourth of our Center-sponsored institutes on
theoretical psychology. The previous meetings dealt with the
general problem of theoretical synthesis (Royce, 1970a), the nature
of cognition and epistemology (Royce & Rozeboom, 1972), and the
relationship between multivariate analysis and psychological
theory (Royce, 1973).

For the past four years the Center has devoted a portion of
its efforts to the theme of this institute—theoretical advances
in behavior genetics. It was felt that, after some 30 years of
empirical and methodological research, it was time for an appraisal
of conceptual foundations. Such an appraisal includes attempts
to provide substantive syntheses in addition to critically examining methods, concepts, and philosophic presuppositions. The Center
program includes inviting leading contributors to the Center for
week-long seminar exchanges on foundational issues. Recent Center
visitors on the theme of this institute include P. L. Broadhurst,
H. J. Eysenck, B. E. Ginsburg, J. L. Fuller, N. D. Henderson, G.
E. McClearn, D. D. Thiessen, and W. R. Thompson.

A Banff institute provides for a final series of meetings,
with all relevant Center visitors and additional participants
brought together at one time. A generous grant from the North
Atlantic Treaty Organization permitted the invitation of the 18
major participants whose papers constitute this volume, plus providing partial financial support for the 60 additional participants
listed at the end of this volume.

We are grateful to Catherine Hardie, Manager, Conference
Division, Banff Centre. She and her able staff made our ten days
at Banff an uncomplicated event. Our thanks go, once again, to
Paul DeGroot, Department of Psychology technician, for the audio-
and video recordings of the conference proceedings. This is
Paul's fourth Center conference and his contribution is highly
valued. We thank John Wozny for preparing the subject index. We
are especially grateful to Evelyn Murison for administrative and
secretarial assistance, and Frances Rowe for typing and proof-
reading of the manuscripts.

The institute was held over a period of ten days, September
29 - October 8, 1978, at the Banff Centre in the Canadian Rockies.
Since the aims of the institute included educating the prospective researcher in his secondary field, we incorporated a one-
hour state-of-the-art lecture just prior to a two hour seminar-
in-the-round. This was in addition to our usual procedure of

pre-distributing papers, and providing highly compressed commentary following each paper. Participants in a given seminar session were limited to 250 words for the printed version of the discussion material. The official discussant, however, was allowed up to 1,000 words, and each author was allowed around 1,000 words in rebuttal.

The interdisciplinary spirit of the conference was initiated by Professor Spuhler's wide ranging keynote address under the title "Genetics, molecules, organisms, and behavior". His analysis includes the swimming behavior of E. coli at the molecular level and the neural and genetic bases of language at the molar level. He argues that behavior genetics should be viewed from a very broad evolutionary perspective--that is, a perspective which begins with the physical bases of behavior and also allows for an emergent mind and culture.

The first three lecture-seminars elaborated on the evolutionary theme. It is, of course, well established that genetic-evolutionary theory constitutes the best available biological statement on the nature of living forms. However, despite psychology's long term interest in animal-comparative psychology, we are a long way from having a full blown phylogeny of behavior (e.g., see Warden, Jenkins, & Warner, 1935, 1936, 1940; Maier & Schneirla, 1935; Munn, 1965; Aronson et al., 1970; Razran, 1970; Wilson, 1977). An evolutionary account of behavior is, of course, a large order, a problem on which science will continue to work for many decades before a satisfactory answer will be forthcoming. However, behavior genetics provides a new perspective--namely the interactions between genes, behavior, and evolution. Although Broadhurst, van Abeelen, and Immelmann develop this theme, their foci are different. Broadhurst elaborates on behavioral evolution based on within-species psychogenetic findings. For example, he reviews the experimental evidence for the following two selection effects: (1) directional selection--behavioral phenotypes (such as mating behavior and avoidance) with genotypes characterized by uni-directional dominance variation and epistasis, and (2) stabilizing selection--behavioral phenotypes (such as activity level and open-field defecation) with genotypes characterized by ambi-directional or no dominance and additive variation. Van Abeelen's and Immelmann's papers can be viewed as complementary aspects of the ethological approach to the problem. Van Abeelen provides us with a wide ranging review of how the behavior-evolutionary findings and methods of ethology can enhance behavior genetics, while Immelmann focuses on a specific example, the case of genetically determined individual differences in sexual imprinting.

The implications of behavior genetic findings for the evolution of behavior crop up throughout this book, most prominently in the section on biochemical and molecular advances. Oliverio, for example, provides us with a gene-environment interaction model for the evolution of flexible behavior. It is based on gene caused differences in brain structure and brain biochemistry. The evolutionary theme also crops up in Thiessen's paper, particularly in his analysis of the phylogeny of variability, and the importance of regulator genes for understanding behavior. Thiessen also provides a bridge to psychology in his suggestion that we take a serious look at sociobiology as the framework for psychological theory. Although it is doubtful that Wilson's speculations about human behavior will hold up in their present form, the contributions of the sociobiologists are important because of their relevance to an interdisciplinary theory of man (Royce & Powell, 1978).

In the next section Thompson and Henderson remind us that the genetic model includes environmental and gene-environment interaction terms. Thus, Thompson calls for sophistication in the analysis of environmental effects and Henderson focuses his attention on the complexities of gene-environment interactions.

In the following section the authors take up the Henderson-Thompson challenge by offering a variety of analytic methods for testing the relative weights of genetic and environmental effects. Although Fulker and Loehlin provide a wide range of examples from the research literature, Loehlin focuses his attention on how best to combine data sets from several sources and Fulker makes the case for the biometric methods. DeFries et al. provide us with equations for estimating the genetic and environmental basis for correlated phenotypes, particularly in the case of factor identified phenotypes. Their most convincing substantive example involves the spatial relations factor, which shows genetically caused correlations of .26 with the verbal comprehension factor and .31 with the visual memory factor, and an environmentally caused negative correlation of .30 with the verbal comprehension factor.

In the next section the concern for concepts and methodology is extended to foundational issues, with Fuller focused on the phenotype and Wahlsten focused on the genotype. Wahlsten raises questions about the basic concepts which have been used in behavior genetics. He points out, for example, that hereditary effects are not limited to gene effects (e.g., they include cytoplasmic hereditary effects), which is the usual assumption in behavior genetic model building. Fuller raises the question—What constitutes an adequate behavioral phenotype? The answer which emerges is that we should focus our attention on those behavioral phenotypes which have theoretical significance.

But who can divine the answer to that one? Eysenck, McClearn, and Royce give their answers in the last section. In brief, Eysenck calls for biological and differential constructs as the

best explanatory basis for behavioral phenomena, McClearn points
to the potential relevance of information processing constructs,
and Royce elaborates on the factor-gene model. That's quite a
range of recommendations. But they are not necessarily in conflict, nor do they exhaust the set of relevant possibilities. The
views of Eysenck, McClearn, & Royce, and indeed all the contributions of this institute, can best be viewed as manifestations of
the reality that advances in theory construction emerge out of the
minds of men, not as a side effect which automatically occurs as
a consequence of gathering additional data (Royce, 1970b, 1976,
1978). This means that future developments in theoretical behavior genetics will require disciplined and trained theoreticians,
and institutional and financial backing of their efforts.

This brings us to the issue of the present state of the art in
the domain of behavior genetics (see Caspari's Epilogue chapter in
this volume for more on this). In several recent analyses I have
described the state of the art in psychology as anarchistic, with
a level of sophistication in theory construction which has lagged
far behind the psychologist's competence in experimentation and
statistical-methodological analysis (Royce, 1970b, 1976, 1978). It
is my impression that the situation in behavior genetics is more
like theoretical apathy than theoretical anarchy. Because of this,
it is difficult to assess the present level of competence in theory
construction, but there is little doubt that the major concerns of
behavior geneticists for the past 30 years have also been of an
experimental and methodological nature. Perhaps the major theme
which has emerged during this institute is that behavior genetics
can be described as a solid empirical science with a potential for
becoming a more powerful, explanatory science. Scientific explanation, however, requires viable theory in addition to a sound empirical foundation.

Providing complete understanding of the causal chain from
gene to behavior is a large order. It will not be achieved over-
night, and the task of providing a conceptual framework for the
observables of behavior genetics has just begun. Nevertheless, a
pattern seems to have emerged from the deliberations of this institute. What I see on the horizon is an amalgamation of quantitative theory in genetics with differential (i.e., individual differences) theory in psychology and evolutionary theory in biology.
I am personally optimistic that significant headway toward a synthesis of psychological and genetic findings will be forthcoming
during the next few decades because of the strength of the extant
data base on the one hand, and the demonstrated explanatory power
of the currently separate theoretical strands on the other hand.

There is, however, a major weakness in our theoretical efforts to date--this is a weakness in some of the concepts of behavior genetics. These concepts must be subjected to explicit

and thorough analysis as a basis for substantive theory construction. This kind of analysis, called metatheory by the philosophers of science, includes conceptual-linguistic analysis, the attempt to clarify the meanings and implications of theoretical terms. The concern is to "unpack" conceptual complexities into their simpler components and to increase precision in the communication of intended meanings. The claim is that conceptual clarification and elaboration of the logic, language, epistemology, and ontology (i.e., the metatheory) of science has implications for the construction of theory. The strong version of this claim is that conceptual analysis can result in increments in linguistic precision, and that conceptual precision can, in turn, result in increments in theoretical (i.e., explanatory) power (Royce, 1978).

In short, the message is that astute metatheoretic analysis will sharpen the conceptual foundations of the discipline. Fuller's analysis of the behavioral phenotype constitutes an excellent example of this claim. However, other concepts, such as hereditary-environment interaction, are in need of serious metatheoretic analysis. Part of the difficulty with these concepts is the globality of such terms as heredity and environment. It is clear that further theoretical progress is dependent upon a more analytic treatment of these terms. Perhaps the most controversial foundational concept in behavior genetics is that of heritability. The informal metatheoretic analysis it has received to date indicates that it is used in at least two senses--labeled "narrow" and "broad". And Wahlsten's analysis suggests that the term is further confounded by both genetic and non-genetic sources of hereditary transmission, and by uncontrolled sources of environmental transmission as well. If we also consider the many methods for estimating heritability, it is clear that we are not referring to the same concept via this single term.

It is our hope that this first institute on the theoretical aspects of behavior genetics will be viewed for what it is--the mere beginnings of a potentially rewarding task. Although it is difficult to predict just how rewarding theoretical research will be in the domain of behavior genetics, it is clear that all advanced sciences have developed viable theory. Is this domain ready for a more conscious confrontation with its implicit theoretical structure? We believe it is. Behavior genetics has been dramatically successful in its relatively short history as an interdisciplinary science. A commitment to move in the direction of theoretical maturity does not imply a diminution in its empirical foundations. The realities are that no science can make it to maturity without a solid empirical foundation. The optimal route appears to be one that includes a continuing interaction between evolving theoretical structures on the one hand and methodologically sound data gathering on the other hand (Royce, 1978).

8

References

Aronson, L. R., Tobach, E., Lehrman, D. S., & Rosenblatt, J. S. _Development and evolution of behavior_. San Francisco: W. H. Freeman & Co., 1970.

Maier, N. R. F., & Schneirla, T. C. _Principles of animal psychology_. New York: McGraw-Hill, 1935.

Munn, N. L. _The evolution and growth of human behavior_ (2nd ed.). Boston: Houghton Mifflin, 1965.

Razran, G. _Mind in evolution_. Boston: Houghton Mifflin Co., 1971.

Royce, J. R. (Ed.). _Toward unification in psychology_. The First Banff Conference on Theoretical Psychology. Toronto: University of Toronto Press, 1970a.

Royce, J. R. The present situation in theoretical psychology. In J. R. Royce (Ed.), _Toward unification in psychology_. The First Banff Conference on Theoretical Psychology. Toronto: University of Toronto Press, 1970b.

Royce, J. R. (Ed.). _Multivariate analysis and psychological theory_. The Third Banff Conference on Theoretical Psychology. London: Academic Press, 1973.

Royce, J. R. Psychology is multi: Methodological, variate, epistemic, world-view, systemic, paradigmatic, theoretic, and disciplinary. In W. J. Arnold (Ed.), _Nebraska Symposium on the Conceptual Foundations of Theory and Methods in Psychology_. Lincoln, Nebraska: University of Nebraska Press, 1976, 1-63.

Royce, J. R. How we can best advance the construction of theory in psychology. _Canadian Psychological Review_, 1978, _19_(4), 259-276.

Royce, J. R., & Powell, A. _Toward a theory of man: A multi-disciplinary, multi-systems, multi-dimensional approach_. Proceedings of the Sixth International Conference on the Unity of the Sciences. New York: International Cultural Foundation Press, 1978.

Royce, J. R., & Rozeboom, W. W. (Eds.). _The psychology of knowing_. The Second Banff Conference on Theoretical Psychology. London and New York: Gordon and Breach, 1972.

Warden, D. J., Jenkins, T. N., & Warner, L. H. _Comparative psychology_. New York: Ronald Press, 1935, 1936, 1940.

Wilson, E. O. _Sociobiology_. Cambridge, Massachusetts: Harvard University Press, 1975.

GENES, MOLECULES, ORGANISMS, AND BEHAVIOR

J.N. Spuhler

Department of Anthropology, University of New Mexico
Albuquerque, New Mexico 87131

Sometimes we abstract
  man from environment,
Sometimes we abstract
  environment from man,
Sometimes we abstract
  both man and environment,
Sometimes we abstract
  neither man nor environment.

From Rinzai Gigen *(Lin-chi I-hsüan)*,
Chinese Zen Master, A.D. ? - 867,
(text from Dumoulin 1953:72, the
translation by Sokei-an is modified
slightly and the calligraphy is mine).

有時人境俱不奪。　有時人境俱奪。　有時奪境不奪人。　有時奪人不奪境。

　　　Professor Royce and his colleagues at the University of
Alberta Center for Advanced Study in Theoretical Psychology
invited us to this beautiful place in the Canadian Rockies to
discuss, at the leasurely pace possible for NATO Advanced Study
Institutes, the current state of Theoretical Advances in Behavior
Genetics.

　　　In writing us about the Institute he pointed out that behavior
genetics made impressive advances in the last 20 years. Empirical
research is progressing at a rapid rate. Advances in methodology
make possible increasingly sophisticated research. But he questioned that we have made impressive conceptual headway in understanding the relationship between genetics and behavior. Not
that the field lacks all theoretical unification. Not that
research publications tend to proliferate without direction.

Rather, it is that behavioral geneticists have not taken time to evaluate their findings within their largest context, giving due consideration to both sides of our hybrid discipline - genetics and behavior.

The intent of the Institute is to address the foundations and the directions of behavioral genetics rather than to present more data. The purpose of this Institute is to move toward theoretical advancement in our field. Professor Royce wants us to view things and events in their true theoretical relations, to judge their relative importance, and even to be daring.

The four statements in the opening text were written when Chinese Zen reached its peak in originality, about the middle of the Tang Dynasty, A.D. 713-905, during the flowering of the Rinzai Sect. The form of the text rests on the "Four Propositions" of Indian Buddhist logic, the meaning corresponds to the "Four Aspects of Reality" of Chinese Kegon teaching (Dumoulin 1953:22).

Sometimes in genetics we abstract formal genes in man and other organisms from environment.

Sometimes in ecology, usually in geography, often in most social sciences, we abstract environment from man and other organisms.

Nearly always in linguistics and social anthropology, especially in the symbolism of Claude Lévi-Strauss and other explicitly nonbiological human behavioral sciences, we abstract both organisms and their nonhuman environment.

Some of behavioral genetics will reach conceptual integration, if my forecast is right, by considering seriously the interaction of the triplet, the genes, the organisms, and the behavior that adapts these two and itself to environments, where neither organism nor environment is left out (the literal Chinese is "robbed").

Rinzai took the "Four Arrangements of Subject and Object" to indicate an ascending scale in the comprehension of Reality. On such a scale, pure genetics is lowest, and an integrated behavior genetics would be the highest level.

BEHAVIORAL GENETICS AND THE GENERAL THEORY OF EVOLUTION

My first suggestion for theoretical integration of behavioral genetics is to interpret the field in terms of the general theory of evolution. The suggestion is not new: Darwin stressed the evolution of behavior and Jerram Brown (1975) provides an excellent survey of the evidence since Darwin.

You may question why I look to the general theory of evolution, a field itself that is viewed with wide differences by competent biologists (even though it is probably considered to be suitably integrated by a majority of working scientists dealing with genetics and the biological aspects of behavior). For example, Pierre Grassé (1978) does not accept the synthetic theory of evolution joining population genetics, systematics, and paleontology of Haldane-Fisher-Wright, E. Mayr and G.G. Simpson; and there are quarrels between the neutralism of Muller-Crow-Kimura and the panselectionism of Dobzhansky-Ford-Mayr; and there is the different synthesis of Løvtrup (1977) as well as the biological Marxism of Lewontin in recent years.

Dissatisfied with the supposed political implications of both the classical neutral mutation – random drift (Muller) and the balanced polymorphism – panselectionist (Dobzhansky) schools of the genetic basis of evolution, Lewontin (1974:31) writes: "For Muller, human progress meant enriching the species for a few superior genotypes while for Dobzhansky it means increasing, or at least maintaining, genetic diversity. Neither view admits the possibility that genetic variation is irrelevant to the present and future structure of human institutions, that the unique feature of man's biological nature is that he is not constrained by it." Regarding the relationship between scientific knowledge and the social context within which "science" is done, Rose and Rose (1973:479) state: "A non-ideological, and hence scientific and non-oppresive paradigm, would be a version of interactionism, dialectical materialism, such a science cannot be fully realized except in a transformed society." Stronger examples of the power of ideology over objectivity could hardly be found, as King (1975) pointed out in his review of Lewontin's The Genetic Basis of Evolutionary Change. King goes on to add (1975:508n): "My own feeling is that human genetic inequality is often painful, frequently awkward, and seemingly unjust; it is not about to change, nor can it be rationalized as being for the best. We are constrained only to deal with inequality as fairly, compassionately and creatively as we can." Political philosophers of the radical left disagree strongly on the significance of biology for human behavior (see Pennock and Chapman, 1977) but active, disciplined Marxists must struggle against human behavior genetics. It is noteworthy that J.B.S. Haldane and H.J. Muller, two former Marxists who were distinguished geneticists, give up the party rather than their science. Wilson (1978:277) notes that "It is a remarkable fact that in recent years the most effective opposition to the study of human evolution has come not from the religious fundamentalists and the political right, but from biologists and other scientists who identify themselves with the radical left. The focus of these critics was initially on the inheritance of intelligence, but more recently, and significantly, it has been broadened to include virtually any kind of study that touches on the genetic evolution of human behavior."

I leave this topic by noting that other members of the political left have no quarrel with human behavioral genetics. Indeed Noam Chomsky (1975) makes an inherited capacity fundamental to language, man's most distinguishing behavior, and Herbert Marcuse (1955) recognizes that a strict environmental determinism implies that human behavior can be molded into permanent conformity by any totalitarian regime, of either the right or left. And it is interesting to observe that the XIV International Congress of Genetics organized and held in Moscow August 21-30, 1978, included sessions on human behavioral genetics.

The title of a recent paper by Dobzhansky (1973) will serve to return us to an integrative theme for behavioral genetics: "Nothing in biology makes sense except in the light of evolution."

There are three great realms of general evolution: cosmic or physical, biological, and cultural. Given the origin of life, the problems of mind - that is, of complex behavior - and of culture - that is, of symbolic language - are the great problems in the evolutionary transit through three billion years from the first genes to man. Following H.J. Muller we may define life as a system capable of replication, metabolism, and mutation, or following J.F. Crow, as a system capable of natural selection. By definition genes have these properties. By discovery, nucleic acids have them. The problem of the origin of life was greatly simplified by discovery of the genetic code, the replication, transcription, and translation of nucleic acids, as well as by the laboratory synthesis of nucleic acids, amino acids and proteins under early earth conditions.

Much of genetics is adequately and elegantly explainable on the molecular level. In bacteria we are approaching the first understanding of a stimulus-response system on that level.

I agree with Ernest Nagel that we should reduce as much of biology as is possible to molecular explanations. With reservations excluding his kind of vitalism, I agree with the geophysicist Walter Elsasser (1975) that all of organismic biology, or even of cell biology, cannot be reduced to physical chemistry. The reservations are met by the mathematical physicist, later biologist, Jacob Bronowski who shows (in 1968 and 1974 papers reprinted in 1977) that organic evolution makes biology a different kind of subject from physics. Bronowski wrote (1977:183): "When Wigner and Walter Elsasser say that there must be some biological law different from the laws of physics in order that copying in the organism shall be free from error, and the storage of the instructions which govern its exact form and development from the cell shall be perfectly accurate, they are asking for the immortality of the individual but ensuring the destruction of species. We have only to look about us to see that the evidence is against them, on both counts."

Some interpret mind, and the ability to symbolize, as an intrusion or an emergent or complete novelty unique to the human species. Others, including the geneticist Sewall Wright (1953) view mind as an aspect of reality; they see the universe as a multiplicity of minds, each with two aspects: (a) as it _is_ to itself (mind), and (b) as it _seems_ as an intrusion into the mind of another (matter). Most minds are inaccessible to scientific study.

By stressing the evolutionary continuity of mental or minding experience, Griffin (1976) has reopened the question of animal awareness. I will close my talk by mentioning the possibility that two-way communication between man and chimpanzee using American Sign Language opens a window on the minds of some apes, and touches on the validity of the notion that some non-human primates have culture in the sense we mean for man.

The main idea that underlies Elsasser's theoretical biology is that an organism is a locus of utmost complexity, a complexity not even remotely approached in the inorganic world. Almost all physical science is understandable in terms of uniformity and homogeneity. Variability and complexity are the essence of theoretical biology.

The laws of quantum mechanics, Elsasser argues, must be accepted without reserve as valid within the world of organisms. John von Neumann (1932) proved with mathematical rigor that the general, formal rules underlying quantum mechanics cannot be amended or modified without invalidating all quantum mechanics. Most living organisms contain mechanisms whose functioning can well be described by the laws of physics and chemistry. This is the overwhelming part of all biological science, including much of behavioral genetics.

Two abstractions "individuality" and "contingency" are central to much of behavioral biology and are at best marginal to the logical framework of physical science. If the laws of physics cannot be modified or extended, the only novelty we are permitted to introduce involves the interplay of mechanisms with contingencies. This mixture of mechanisms with contingencies is, in nature, irreducible. But, of course, our knowledge is incomplete.

Elsasser's semi-definite construct of finite classes can embody properties of organisms verbally described by terms such as spontaneity, creativity, and irrationality (without specifying them in the logico-mathematical system of physical science). It is impossible to disentangle contingencies from mechanisms in living matter: the world of living organisms is not only utterly complex but irreducibly so.

But as Bronowski (1977:195) argued: "The progression from simple to complex, the building up of stratified stability, is the necessary character of evolution from which time takes its direction. And it is not a forward direction in the sense of a thrust toward the future, a headed arrow. What evolution does is to give the arrow of time a barb which stops it from running backward; and once it has this barb, the chance play of errors will take it forward of itself."

Sir Karl Popper and Sir John Eccles (1973) replace Cartesian dualism with Popper's concept of three worlds:
1st World: Physical objects and states, inorganic, organic, artifactual,
2nd World: States of consciousness, emotions, dreams, all subjective knowledge and experience.
3rd World: Objective knowledge, including language, culture, and science.

Some good neurobiologists find satisfaction in trialist interactionism.

New studies on brain and language, especially the split brain findings, seem to show that consciousness is not a universal property of all things. The balance of the neurophysiological evidence favors the conclusion that consciousness is selectively localized within human and other mammalian brains and that some functionally important neural systems (cerebellum, etc.) lack consciousness. Because the stream of consciousness in a human individual can be divided into right and left realms by cutting the corpus callosum, Sperry (1975) concluded that "consciousness is an operational derivative in particular cerebral circuit systems designed expressly to produce their own specific conscious effects...with action upon as well as from neural events." Man and chimpanzee have consciousness but not bacteria or hydrogen ions.

MOLECULAR GENETICS OF A STIMULUS-RESPONSE SYSTEM

Recent rapid progress in the study of swimming behavior in flagellated bacteria suggests that bacterial chemotaxis almost certainly will become the first stimulus-response system to be understood at the molecular level (for reviews see Adler 1975, Berg 1975, Iino 1977, Koshland 1976, Hazelbauer and Parkinson 1977, and Parkinson 1977).

Escherichia coli is the best understood organism at the molecular level. It is ideal for behavior genetic study. It is haploid; under optimal conditions it reproduces every 2 hours providing large numbers of organisms of identical genotype in relatively small containers, over short periods of experimental time. It also undergoes conjugation leading to genetic recombination. It has only about 1000 genes of which the function of about 400 is known (Watson 1976). A high level of genetic engineering is possible.

Berg (1975) reviewed the literature starting in the 1880s demonstrating purposeful movements in bacteria that allow them to avoid hostile environments and to accumulate in favorable ones.

Berg and Anderson (1973) showed that E. coli swim by rotation of their stiff helical flagella, the principle of the wheel not being exemplified previously in living organisms. Silverman and Simon (1974) confirmed flagellar rotation by tethering the tip of a flagellum to a microscope slide by treatment with flagellar antibody and viewing the rotation of single cells through a phase contrast microscope recorded on videotape and transferred to photographic film.

Larsen et al (1974) showed that change in direction of flagellar rotation is the basis of the chemotactic response in E. coli and in Salmonella. For smooth translational movement, the direction of rotation of the flagellar base must be the same as the handedness of the filament. As the helix of wild-type flagellar filaments is left-handed, the base must rotate counterclockwise (CCW) looking from the tip down to the base to produce smooth swimming.

During typical wild-type swimming E. coli individuals move their rod-shaped bodies, that average 2 microns long and 1 micron in diameter, in a smooth straight line at a speed of 30 microns per second for about 8 seconds or 120 body lengths. Then they suddenly tumble and swim off in a new direction. Bacteria tumble less frequently when they swim up an attractive gradient or down a repellent one and tumble more frequently when they move into a less favorable surrounding. This chemotactic behavior transports the bacteria in a probabilistic fashion toward a more favorable setting (Keller and Segel 1971).

Sudden large changes in attractant concentration or decrease in repellent levels result in smooth swimming responses lasting for several minutes; increase in repellent concentration results in tumble swimming responses usually lasting a shorter time. Polytricherous bacteria including E. coli and Salmonella rotate in unison several flagella in a bundle during smooth swimming. The bacterial chemotactic mechanism allows response to concentration changes rather than to absolute concentration of a chemical by detecting temporal changes in chemical gradients.

The stimulus-response behavior in E. coli chemotaxis is summarized in Figure 1. Attractants increase smooth and decrease

Figure 1

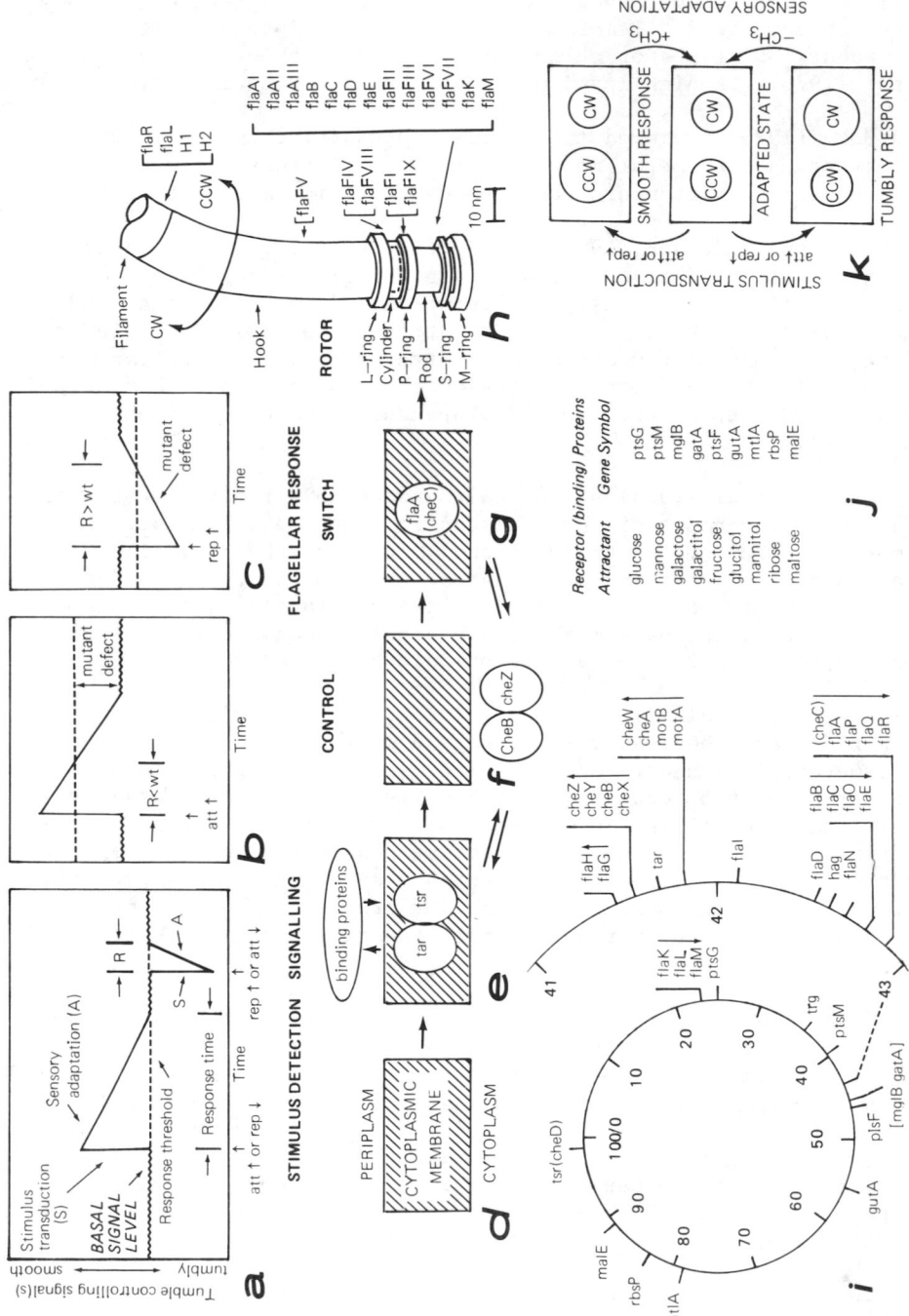

Figure 1. Parts a through k, opposite (Redrawn from Iino,
          1977, and Parkinson, 1977)

(a) Summary of behavioral changes observed in Escherchia coli.
(b) Stimulus-response of chemotaxis mutants in E. coli, showing the response of cheB or cheZ strains to attractant stimuli.
The high spontaneous tumbling rate and short response times in
these mutant strains may result from an increase in response
threshold or a decrease in the basal signal level established by
the adaptation system.
(c) Analysis of cheX mutant strains in E. coli to repellent
stimuli. The low spontaneous rate of tumble swimming and the long
response times may be caused by a defect in the adaptation system.
(d) The pathway of information flow during stimulus transduction in E. coli based on phenotypes of chemotaxis-defective mutants. The path flows from left to right through the five steps
shown in parts e, f, g, and h. Stimulus detection involves binding
protein (receptor) allels shown in part j. The order of mutants
from least to most pleiotropic is as follows: signalling trg,
tar, tsr(cheD); control cheB, cheZ; switch flaA(cheC), cheA, cheW,
cheY; rotor fla mutants, motA, motB. The receptor mutants are
least and the motility mutants are most pleiotropic.
(e) Signalling system.
(f) Control system. Flagellar response is executed by the
control, switch and rotor. See text for explanations.
(g) Switch.
(h) Rotor. Model of the basal structure of a flagellum of
Salmonella typhimurium from Iino (1977). The scale in nanometers
refers to part h (the flagellum) only. Lubrication is not a problem because the rotor is very small (Berg, 1974). The rod is connected to the relatively long filament (now shown in full) by the
hook. The torque is generated between the M ring and the S ring.
The M ring is mounted rigidly on the rod and rotates freely in the
cytoplasmic membrane. The S ring is mounted in the periplasmic
space (wall). The Salmonella gene symbols in Figure 1h indicate
the approximate morphological location where the proteins coded
by the several genes are assembled into the flagellum.
(i) Approximate linkage map positions (in minutes) of chemotaxis related loci in E. coli. Arrows to the right of gene clusters show the direction and extent of cotranscription within the
cluster. The linear order of genes within brackets is not known.
(j) Some known genes of E. coli for receptor proteins that
detect attractants.
(k) A model showing the role of a methyl-accepting chemotaxis
protein (MCP) in stimulus transduction and sensory adaptation. The
changes in MCP function by methylation-demethylation are indicated.

tumble swimming; repellents increase tumbles and decrease smooth.
The wavy line represents the basic signal level. The conversion
of stimulus information into a signal that modulates flagellar
rotation is called stimulus transduction. The response time in
return to basic signal level is slower for attractants.

Figure 1 (top) distinguishes five steps in flagellar response.
We will consider them briefly from left to right.

Stimulus Detection. Attractant and repellent stimuli are
detected by binding proteins located in the periplasmic space.
Seemingly the binding proteins are also involved in active transport of the respective ligands. The structural genes from sugar-
binding proteins involved in chemotaxis are shown on the genetic
map in Figure 1i and j. Little is known about the genetics or
biochemistry of the receptors for amino acids (8 of which are
known to act as attractants) nor of the repellents (including
aliphatic alcohols, fatty acids, hydrophobic amino acids, H^+ and
OH^- ions, indole, and divalent metal cations). It seems likely
that these receptors are also binding proteins but their characterization must await isolation of specific receptor mutants. The
two processes of chemoreception and transport are distinct although
they share a common component.

Signaling. Duration of flagellar response after stimulation
is directly proportional to change in receptor occupancy by ligands
(Figure 1a,b,c). Three known signal mutants are motile but lack
response to two or more receptors. Mutant trg does not transduce
ribose or galactose stimuli. Mutant tar is not attracted to as-
partate or maltose nor repelled by OH^- ions or divalent metal cations. Mutant tsr is not attracted to serine nor repelled by H^+
ions, fatty acids, indole, or hydrophobic amino acids. λ trans-
ducing phage with tar or tsr regions make in the host membrane
proteins of about 60,000 molecular weight. Based on complementation
tests expression of these two structural genes depends on wild-
type fla genes.

Only when a receptor is occupied by ligand is it able to
interact with common signal elements. The ribose-galactose sig-
naler may be the product of the trg locus. The tar and tsr loci
are involved in signaling at a later step than the trg locus.

The collective product of the tar and tsr genes (Figure 1e) is
a methyl-accepting chemotaxis protein (MCP). S-adenosyl methionine
is a methyl-denoting compound derived from ATP and methionine.
CH_3 groups are joined by ester linkage to glutamic acid residues
in MCP molecules (Figure 1k). Chemotactive stimuli alter the
amount of CH_3 associated with MCP: a) increase in attractant
ligands increases transfer of CH_3, suppresses tumble, resulting in
smooth swimming (CCW rotation), b) increase in repellent ligands

decreases CH$_3$, linked to MCP, and results in tumble (CW rotation).

Control. Genes for chemotaxis are termed che. Mutation in cheB and cheZ genes cause excessive tumbling (Figure 1f). Neither gene is essential for CCW rotation. Perhaps these components are control elements that interact with the switch to modulate tumbling in response to chemotactic stimuli, with cheB handling inputs from the tar component and cheZ those from tsr.

The flaA component may be responsible for establishing the relative probabilities of CCW and CW rotations. flaA seems to be a null class of cheC mutations which are nonflagellated. Other cheC mutants have normal flagella but swim without tumbling. cheB and cheZ convey receptor signals to the switch.

Switch. cheA, cheW, and cheY products may play important roles in producing CW reversals. They result in non-tumbling phenotypes in which flagellar rotation is exclusively CCW (Figure 1g). cheC in the switch interacts specifically with cheZ in control. Their loci are tightly linked.

Rotor. Intact flagella with filament, hook, and basal body have been isolated from osmotically lysed bacterial cells. Iino (1977) reviews the genetics of their structure and function. In gram-negative bacteria, including E. coli and Salmonella the basal body is composed of four rings, a rod passing through the centers of the four rings, and a cylinder filling in the space between the two outer rings (Figure 1h).

The four rings are termed L,P,S and M and are mounted by connection of their outer periphery to four layers of the cell envelope. Some bacteria that rotate their flagella lack L and P rings showing that the motor involves the S and M rings. The rod connects to the hook which joins the filament of the flagellum. Flagellar structures are made of proteins. The approximate site of assembly for 22 polypeptides coded by known Salmonella structural genes is indicated in Figure 1g. The amino acid sequences of hook and filament protein (flagellin) are known. The basal body consists of at least 7 component proteins. The proteins self-assemble to make the flagellum. Growth is from the base outward. Monomers are transmitted through the hollow flagellum to be added at the tip. Salmonella flagellin-i is composed of 470 and flagellin-fg of 386 amino acid residues.

Other flagellar genes are symbolized by fla followed by a capital letter and/or Roman numeral to designate a cystron. Several non-flagellate mutant phenotypes are available. 21 fla genes are located in the 55 min linkage group and 10 in the 47 min cluster. (See Figure 1i.)

A third category of flagellar genes (mot) control function without changing overall structure, the mutation from mot$^+$ to mot$^-$ resulting in flagellar paralysis. motA and motB are required for flagellar rotation.

The structural genes for flagellin are homologous in Salmonella (H1 and H2) and E. coli (hag) as determined by complementation tests between fla$^-$ mutants in intergeneric translocational hetero-zygotes. In Salmonella the structural H2 gene for flagellin is in the 82 min position. The relative position of the functionally homologous genes on their chromosomes is not exactly the same in these two genera, suggesting the occurrence of an inversion or translocation in the evolutionary history of these genera.

Two cistrons motA and motB are responsible for rotation of flagella in both E. coli and Salmonella. In E. coli motA, motB, and cheA are organized into one operon called Mocha. The molecular weight of motA gene product is 31,000 and that of motB 39,000. These proteins may take part in the link between the basal body and the cell membrane structures.

Larson et al (1974) found that an intermediate in oxidative phosphorylation (but not ATP) is required for flagellar rotation in E. coli. Berg (1974) suggested that one molecule moving down an electrochemical gradient through the cell membrane causes another molecule to exert a force on the S ring in a direction parallel to the face and normal to the radius of the ring. The power dissipated in spinning the rotor 10 rps is of the order 10^{-9} erg s^{-1}, and the energy gained in transit of one molecule through the membrane is of order 10^{-13} erg, 10^3 such transits could drive the rotar through one revolution. A force in the opposite direction, or from a different set, could result from a change in the coupling of these molecules.

Parkinson (1977) summarized the genetic and biochemical evidence on bacterial chemotaxis in a model of the transduction process shown in Figure 1d-h. The model proposes that chemical information detected by binder proteins on the outer surface of the cytoplasmic membrane is transmitted to the flagella by a cyto-plasmic message. The tar and tsr proteins span the cytoplasmic membrane to interact with the signalers in the periplasm and with the cheB and cheZ products that are the cytoplasmic messenger. The next link is the flaA (cheC) component, thought to be a mem-brane protein that controls direction of rotation.

Parkinson suggests that the system would work as follows: 'Both the cheC component of the switch and tar-tsr products are able to bind the B-Z complex. When B-Z is bound to the switch, CCW rotation and smooth swimming result. When the switch is free of B-Z, CW rotation and tumbling result. Thus, tumbling behavior

is controlled by the amount of B-Z available for interaction with
the switch. The transduction and adaptation systems, which act on
the tar and tsr components, can change the available supply of
B-Z by modulating the affinity of tar-tsr proteins of the B-Z complex. Tumble-suppressing stimuli or demethylation events convert
MCP (i.e. tar-tsr products) to the "CCW state" (see Figure 1k) which
must have a low affinity for B-Z. Tumble-enhancing stimuli or
methylation events convert MCP to the "CW state" which must have a
high affinity for B-Z. The role of the cheB-cheZ products is therefore analogous to the hypothetical "tumble-controlling signal" in
Figure 1b.'

The model has several implications both chemical and behavioral
that are testable and the work of testing is in progress.

Linkage maps of the flagella genes of Salmonella (S) and
Escherichia (E) shows that chemotactic behavior in the two genera
is homologous. A comparison of the two maps (from Iino 1977)
follows. The chromosomal position of each linkage group is shown
in "min" in the 138 min linkage map of Salmonella typhimurium. The
linear arrangement of the genes in parentheses is not known. An
arrow indicates the direction of transcription of an operon. A
dotted line indicates a pair of homologous cistrons:

55 min

S: his--D-B-Q-P-N-R-S-AIII-AII-AI-HI-nml-L-T-E-K-motA,B-che-C-M--tre

E: his--R-Q-P-A-E-O-C-B-N-hag-D-uvrC-I-motA,B-che-G-H---argS

I-II-(III-IV)-V-(VI-VII)-VIII-IX-hag-(X-XI)

47 min

S: trp--(FI-FII-FIII-FIV-FV-FVI-FVII-FVIII-FIX-FX)---aroE

E: trp----(M-L-K)----pyrD

82 min

S: aroF---H2---purG

Key to gene symbols:

arg: arginine	nml: N-methyl lysine
aro: aromatic amino acids	pur: purine
che: chemotaxis	pyr: pyrimidine
fla: flagellation	tre: trehalose
hag, H1, H2: flagellin	trp: tryptophan operon
his: histidine operon	(including A-E cistrons)
(including A-I cistrons)	uvr: ultraviolet light
mot: motility	sensitivity

Molecular biology is giving us detailed knowledge of the genetics and evolution of chemotactic behavior in some organisms. The behavior is relatively simple at the phenotypical level; it is highly complex at the level of genes and molecules. Let us now examine some of the things known about the genetics and evolution of a class of behavior that is exceedingly complex at the phenotypical level -- human language.

WHITAKER'S MODEL OF PERIPHERAL AND CENTRAL LANGUAGE SYSTEMS

Harry Whitaker (1971) developed a functional anatomical model of how language is represented in the brain. His is the first model that attempts to correlate brain structure and function with contemporary linguistic theory. It also includes the extremely important relationships between central and peripheral mechanisms, as well as the role of thalamic and other subcortical nuclei in the working of the central language system. This multidisciplinary model is one product of the new hybrid science of neurolinguistics. Whitaker's model is an extrapolation from a wide spectrum of data relating to brain structures and aphasic symptomology. Just as single function theories that language is solely a product of the brain's ability to associate stimuli (Skinner 1957) are overly simple (Chomsky 1959), so theories that all aphasic symptoms are due to disruption of the brain's ability to associate stimuli are likewise overly simple. Other models on representation of language in the brain are discussed by Dingwall (1978).

The model consists of peripheral and central language systems. The peripheral language system contains four structurally and functionally distinct subsystems: 1) speaking, and 2) listening systems are present in all human languages and thus are termed primary production and recognition systems, 3) writing, and 4) reading systems are absent in many languages and thus termed secondary production and recognition systems. These systems are biologically distinct because they use distinct sense receptors (eye and ear) and distinct effector nerve-muscle-support tissues (the arm/hand and the vocal tract) but the effectors may be generalized to other motor systems in man. Both primary and secondary systems link production and reception by high level feedback compatible with the meaning or semantics of the intended production (Laver 1968). These mechanisms coordinate the speaking and hearing modalities with one another where the feedback is by way of the eighth cranial (acoustic) nerve, proprioceptors being absent from the muscles of the voice box (Bonin 1963). Two types of feedback are proposed, one being peripheral and system-specific (MacNeilage 1970) and the other general to the central language system.

The speaking-hearing system is the primary production and recognition system in the sense that it is difficult to imagine speaking with an organ other than the vocal tract or hearing with an organ other than the ear, whereas one can easily substitute the foot for the dominant hand in writing in the sand, or substitute the finger for the eye in reading braille. The primary system transmits by acoustic wave and the secondary system by conventional graphic patterns received visually or tactically. In a given individual all four peripheral systems, although of separate evolutionary history, converge in being a part of the same language system. The four peripheral modalities are shown in Figure 2.

The central language system contains three or (on a different view) four linguistically distinct components collectively called the grammar: 1) semantic, 2) syntactic (or semantic/syntactic), 3) phonological, and 4) lexical. The central language system uses an appropriate set of semantic, syntactic, and phonological rules to define words (morphemes) and sentences.

Chomsky's (1965) distinction between competence (the grammar of the language, what one must know to know the language) and performance (what one actually says and hears) is of obvious heuristic value in allowing grammarians who control linguistic input to ignore "extraneous" features of output such as slips of the tongue, accents, stammers, and the like. Chomsky holds that the theory of performance is different from and irrelevant to the theory of competence, which he makes the central concern of linguistics (Hockett 1968). Other students of language, whether attracted to biology or avoiding it, find some applications of the distinction difficult, especially attempts to apply the competence/performance distinction to aphasia. These authors suggest that competence remains intact in aphasia while performance is changed, and that, if brain damage cannot affect competence, then competence is not a property of the brain.

Whitaker (1971:342) concludes that present evidence from aphasia is equivocal on the problem of anatomical separation of deep and surface linguistic structures, although the data tend to support a model with separate surface and deep components. With reservations, he provisionally avoids modeling deep and surface components of grammar. Rather grammar is modeled to contain three components: the syntactic/semantic system, the phonological system,

24

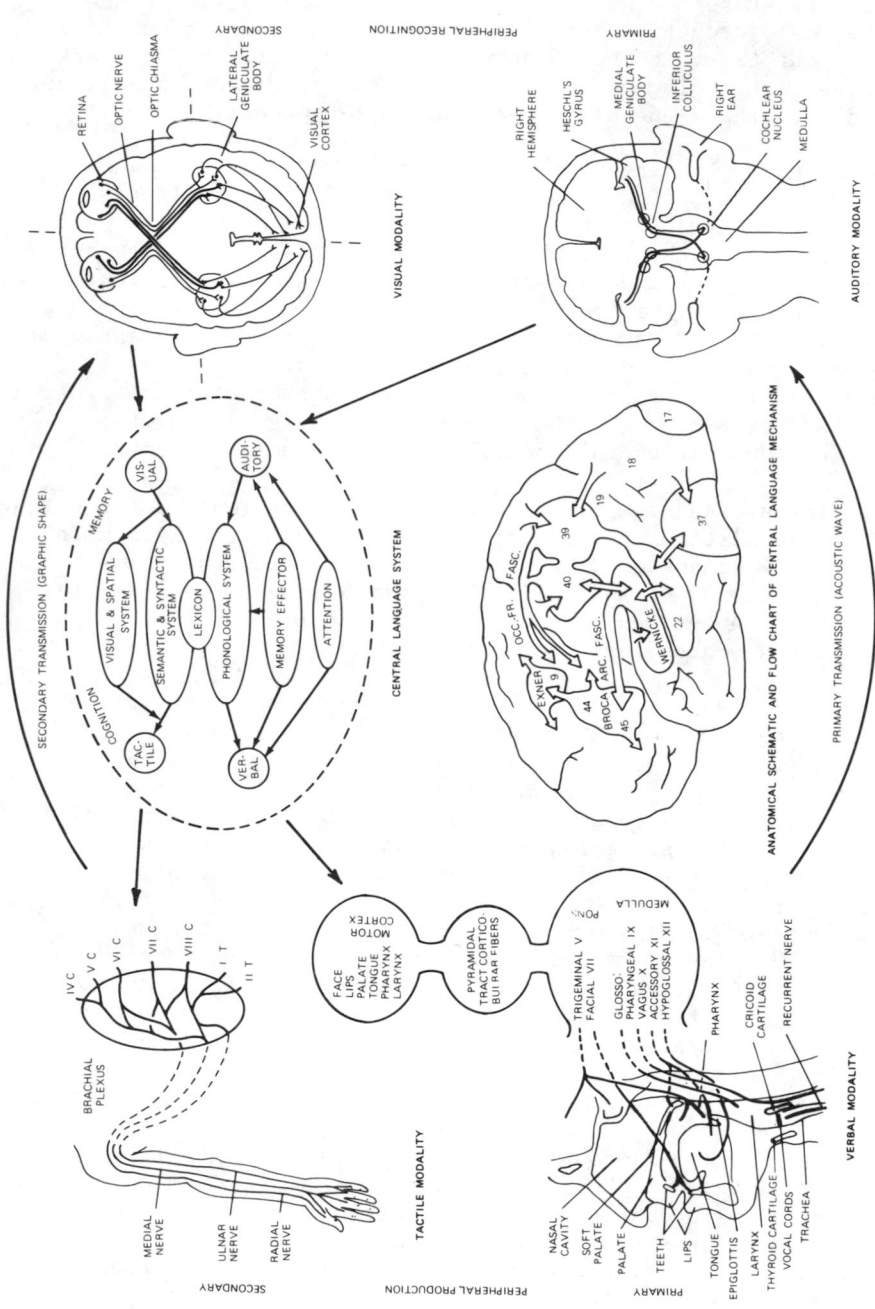

Figure 2. Peripheral and central language systems as modelled by Whitaker (from Spuhler, 1977).

and the lexicon. The grammar integrates input and output of the four peripheral language systems by employing four tracking systems (see Figure 2). A tracking mechanism (represented in Figure 2 in the four circles labelled auditory, tactile, verbal, visual) which converts linguistically motivated units into units that represent motor commands to the articulatory muscles.

Geschwind and Levitsky (1968) demonstrated that the usual lateralization of the left hemisphere for speech and language is associated with marked anatomical differences between the two sides of the brain (Figure 3) in indivuals with left hemis-pheral dominance for language. In 100 adult human brains free of significant pathology, the mean length of the outer border of the planum temporale (a part of Wernicke's area) was 3.6 ± 1.0 cm. on the left and 2.7 ± 1.2 cm. on the right (the difference being at the 0.001 level). The asymmetry of the planum is present at birth and the asymmetry has been demonstrated in several other population samples (Spuhler 1977).

The major pathways for the transfer of symbols in the central language system are well established although the detailed mechanisms of the transfer are unknown (Figures 2,4): the angular gyrus connects with the visual association cortex (area 19 of Brodmann); the supramarginal gyrus connects with somatic afferent association cortex (areas 7 and 40); the posterior part of Wernicke's area and the auditory association area connects with the association cortex surrounding Heschl's gyrus (area 42); the long fibers of the arcuate fasciculus connects parts of Wernicke's area with parts of Broaca's and Exner's centers, the long fibers of the occipitofrontal fascic-ulus connect the angular and supramarginal gyri with the precentral motor cortex (area 4).

Whitaker postulates that the regions of the cortex representing the semantic/syntactic component and the lexicon are localized in the posterior part of Wernicke's area, the auditory association area, the supramarginal and angular gyri. The numerous cortical interconnections of the inferior parietal lobe and the superior temporal lobe, and the lack of subcortical connections to these parts, led Geschwind (1972) to suggest that evolutionary reorgani-zation of this area was a prerequisite for the capacity of language in man. Paleoanthropologists have long recognized that the inferior parietal and superior temporal lobes show the greatest quantitative change in the evolution of the hominid brain (Jerison 1973).

The cytoarchitecture of the cortical language areas is clearly distinct in the different composition of the six cell layers with differing kinds of neurons and arrangements of dendrites and axons. Whitaker calls attention to the remarkable correspondence of the different Broadmann areas with the "areas" classically identified with the central language system: Broadmann's area 44 with Broca's,

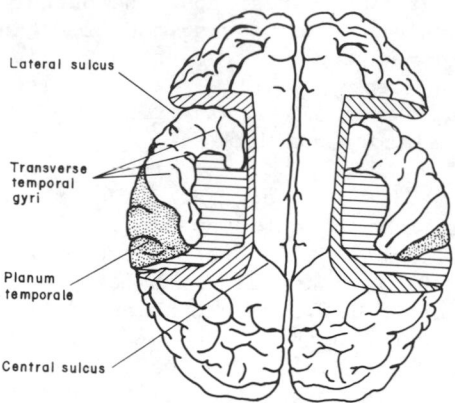

Figure 3. Hemispherical differences in the anatomy of the planum temporale, a part of Wernicke's area (from Spuhler, 1977).

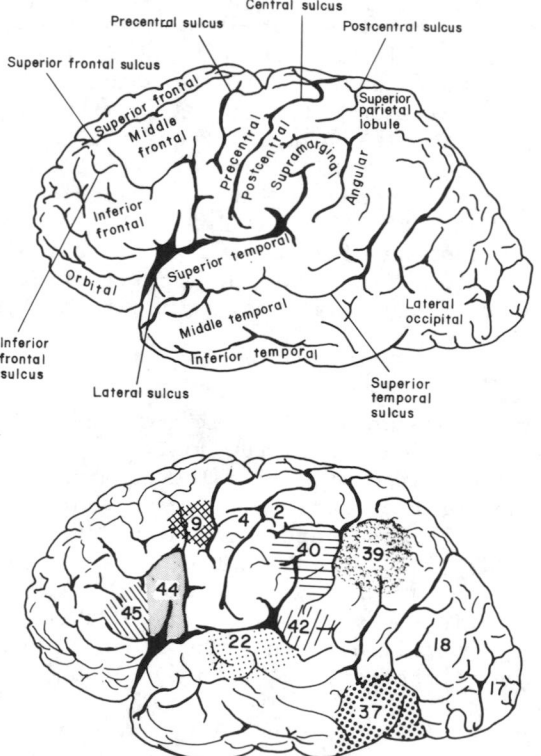

Figure 4. (Top) Sketch of the lateral surface of the left cerebral hemisphere showing the main gyri and sulci. (Bottom) Broadmann's areas related to language (Spuhler, 1977).

a part of area 6 with Exner's, the primary motor and sensory areas
with 4 and 2 respectively, the supramarginal gyrus with parts of
40 and 42, the angular gyrus with 39, Wernicke's with 42 and parts
of 22, Heschl's gyrus with 41, and the auditory association area
with the main part of 22. Because the architectonic areas of
Broadmann show less variation between individuals than the surface
topography of the cortex mapped by major ridges and grooves -- which
show considerable variation between individuals, including within
pairs of monozygotic twins (Patzig 1939), it is claimed that these
cytoarchitectonic areas are the anatomical correlates of the central
language system.

Memory is a complex of at least short- and long-term varieties
(Rozin 1976). The type of memory that is part of the central
language system may be called verbal memory. The lexicon is a
component of the central language system whether localized at the
tissue level or not.

The fact that retrograde and anterograde amnesia do not affect
current language shows that there is a memory system quite independent from language, which, in Figure 2, is simply labelled "memory."
The anatomical locus at the tissue level for this kind of memory,
if any, is also unknown although the system is located in large
part in the hippocampal gyri and adjacent limbic structures. Disruption of the short-term memory system, as in Wernicke-Korsakoff's
syndrome, with the result that the patient cannot remember things or
events for more than 15-20 minutes, affects the central language
system only to the extent that such patients cannot learn new words.
Details of the physiological and molecular basis of all memory
systems are still unknown (Rozin 1976), and, as mentioned above,
the extent of anatomical localization, if any, beyond that of diffuse
large biomolocules, is uncertain. The various forms of aphasia
strongly indicate that the memory system is functionally separate
from the language system regardless of localization.

The requirement that long-term memory of the lexicon must be
'content-addressable' in recall and not merely 'location address-
able' presents both theoretical and experimental difficulties in
supposing that long-term memory operates according to purely local
storage principles. Julesz and Pennington (1965) suggested that
certain types of composite stimulus may be stored in memory in a
holographic rather than a photographic manner. Longuet-Higgins
(1968) expounds the hypothesis that time-varying patterns can be
stored in an analogous manner, and proposed the term "holophone"
for such a system. If memorization of short sequences does involve
holophonic as opposed to gramophonic principles, the problem of
content-addressing is immediately solved and the parts of the brain
storing the memories in question should exhibit periodic response
characteristics which may be directly accessible to neurophysiological study.

Whitaker's model requires minor modification to include separate boxes for short- and long-term memories, especially as linguistic input and output to and from short-term memory and may underlie man's unusual abilities for sustained minding in prolonged situations with everchanging makeup, as in group hunting, or manufacture of complex implements (Isaac, 1976; Jerison, 1973).

The model separates the system that executes memory storage from the storage itself (Talland, 1965; Rozin, 1976). In addition to non-verbal memory, several human faculties (emotions, probably general cognition, problem solving, visual-spatial pattern processing) are independent of the major parts of the central language system, but are related to or make use of language. Aside from providing a box for "attention", Whitaker does not model the effect of emotion on the operation of the central language system because intuitively emotion is less closely related than other included systems in terms of rules, units, and components. See Grossman (1967) for details on the problem of emotion and language.

Penfield and Roberts (1959) were first to suggest that parts of the thalamus must be included in the central language system, based mostly on the observation that electrical stimulation of the left pulvinar (but not the right in individuals with left hemispherical dominance) causes anomia, and damage to other left-sided thalamic nuclei may cause aphasia. The pulvinar is phylogenetically late in evolution of the thalamus and is more specialized in man than in other primates (Le Gros Clark, 1971). Emotions influence the central language system through the frontal lobes or the thalamus (Crosby, Humphrey, & Lauer, 1962). The reticular activating system controls attention (Magoun, 1963).

The special box for the visual and spatial systems is supported by studies on brain lesions showing that a neuronal pathway between peripheral tactile and visual systems must exist independently of the central language system, because a meaningless sequence of letters can be copied without invoking any part of that system. Problem solving abilities and general cognitive functions are combined in the model as a general cognitive system labelled simply "cognition."

Kimura (1967) studied the hemispherical localization of the capacity to interpret numbers, words, non-sense syllables, and melodies by the method of dichotic (two ear) listening. Three pairs of two different sounds are presented simultaneously in rapid succession through earphones to each ear. The subject repeats all he hears. If speech is localized in the right hemisphere as determined by sodium amytal tests (Wada & Rasmussen, 1960), recall of digits is 89% for the left ear and 78% for the right ear during dichotic listening. Regardless of handedness, the ear on the side opposite the hemisphere dominant for speech is superior in dichotic listening.

The dichotic test shows that speech is hemispherically localized as early as four (4) years of age. The test indicates that boys are slower to develop speech asymmetry than girls just as they are well known to be slower on the average in the onset of speech. Dichotic listening to melodies show that the area for singing is located in the hemisphere opposite that dominant for language, providing an explanation of the observation that some individuals with severe central speech impediments can sing beautifully, and that some individuals with the left hemisphere dominant for speech who have Broca's aphasia can sing elegantly and easily.

The first physiological evidence for the localization of speech production in a specific convolution in the intact human brain was produced by McAdam and Whitaker (1971). Eight right-handed young adults with normal speech were tested. Electrodes were attached to the skin over the precentral gyri, Broca's area, the corresponding part of the third inferior frontal convolution on the right, the mastoid processes, and on the frontal bone to serve as a ground. The subjects made four sounds: spitting gestures, words of three syllables with initial "k," coughs, and words of three syllables with initial "p." Electrical potentials were recorded at a maximum over Broca's area in the left hemisphere (but not the right) when the syllables with initial "k" and "p" were produced. The electrical potentials were bilaterally symmetrical when the nonspeech spit and cough occurred.

Eimas and associates (1970) measured conditioned sucking response rates in 1- and 4-month-old infants to show that the infants not only discriminate three variations of /b/ and three of /p/ but also show categorical perception of speech sounds along the voicing continuum in approximately the same manner in which adults perceive these phonemes but with little or no differential reinforcement for speech behavior.

Speech and reading provoke increased regional cerebral blood flow in the superior, anterior, and posterior language cortices (Ingvar 1976). Localized regional blood flow in the dominant hemisphere reflects aspects of the specific physiological events underlying the way the brain handles symbolic language.

GENETICS, SPEECH, AND LANGUAGE

The living organism is not merely a mosaic of "unit characters," each representing an anatomically distinct part of the body, and each determined by a special gene. Pleiotropism or manifold effects are characteristic of most major genes. It is convenient to name major genes for an easily observed unit character, preferably an early gene product, but the named character may represent only a small sector of the total range of characters affected by the gene.

Studies on transmission genetics in family lines and twin
pairs show that a large number of major genes do in fact modify
speech and language function. Thus far, none of these have been
named "genes for language" as such. Every gene that includes a
manifold effect involving the normal structure and function of the
central language system in the brain could be called a "gene for
language." One autosomial recessive mutant gene is named a gene
for "metachromatic leukodystrophy" because of a manifold effect on
leucocytes, fibroblasts, and myelin sheaths of nerves. The basic
metabolic effect is failure to degrade the sulfate ester of galacto-
cerebroside, a structural component of the myelin sheath and of
other tissues in the body, due to lack of the lysosomal enzyme
cerebroside sulfatase. In the late infantile form of the syndrome,
developmental defects appear after the 12th to 16th month of age,
marking the onset of widespread failure of motor development, ability to walk, and loss of speech. Cognition seems to have been
normal before loss of speech. There follows a widespread increase
in sulfatides in the brain, peripheral nerves, gall bladder, testes,
liver, and pancreas, associated with progressive breakdown of membranes in the myelin sheaths. Death usually occurs two to four
years after onset of the disease. Thus the autosomal dominant
allele that codes for the enzyme cerebroside sulfatase is a gene
necessary for normal development of speech and language. Rather
than name this set of alleles "language locus x," it is better to
identify the locus by the enzyme or the primary phenotype.

The fourth edition (1975) of McKusick's catalogue of known
human major genes includes 1218 autosomal dominants, 947 autosomal
recessives, and 171 X-linked genes, a total of 2336. Hundreds of
these genes are known to be relevant to normal development of
speech and language. As expected, more major genes are known to
affect the four peripheral language modalities than the central
language system, but many major genes do have fundamental importance
for the structure and function of the central language system,
starting, for instance, with the normal alleles of genes resulting
in anencephaly, involving lack of proper development of the entire
brain, or (by probable homology with a major gene known in the house
mouse) the normal alleles of genes for congenital absence of the
corpus colosum (Grüneberg, 1943), the largest single fiber tract in
the human brain, and the many genes that control enzymes involved
in normal metabolism of the brain. Over 100 major gene loci are
known to affect each of the visual-verbal-auditory production and
recognition systems, fewer are known that specifically alter development of the tactile peripheral system. Given that all cases
of severe mental retardation are relevant to language facilitation,
well over 100 major gene loci are known to affect the central
language system (McKusick 1975, Bergsma 1973,and Slater and Cowie
1971).

Histidinemia is the best known case in which a major gene may
have a specific pinpointed effect on speech. The published critical
evidence is limited to about ten cases. This metabolic error is
inherited as an autosomal recessive genotype resulting in a defect
in the enzyme histidine α-deaminase necessary for the normal metabolism of histidine to urocanic acid. The enzyme is active in the
liver and the stratum cornium of the skin, tissues not usually
considered to be a part of the central language system. The clinical findings of histidinemia are variable. Subjects with the
recessive genotype have increased concentrations of histidine in
the blood, and urinary output of histidine exceeds twice that normal for comparable ages. Other laboratory findings include per-
sistently low glutamic acid and high α-alanine in body fluids, and
excretion of other organic acids in the urine. The sex ratio in
histidinemia is one boy to two girls. Crome and Stern (1967)
suggest that the speech defect can be prevented, if treated early,
by a diet low in histidine. As histidine is an essential amino acid
required for normal growth, it can not be eliminated from the diet
while the child is growing, but it is not necessary for protein
maintenance in adults. Most histidinemia patients have speech
difficulties, less than 1/2 show growth retardation, over 1/3 are
mentally deficient, and about 1/4 are completely free from such
symptoms. A peculiar electroencephalographic pattern is found in
some individuals with histidinemia (Witkop and Henry 1963).

Nearly all cases of histidinemia show defective speech articulation and language organization. Mispronunciations, "less" for
"yes," are accompanied by a right deviation of the tongue tip and
obicularus orus muscle (the muscle that brings the lips together
and pushes them forward) and lateral movement of the mandible during
its elevation and descent in speech. The tongue is unable to perform movements independent of the mandible -- "la,la,la" becomes
"ja,ja,ja." The tongue is not able to rise to contact the palate
in order to form a consonant while the mandible lowers to anticipate
forming a vowel. Consonants requiring independent movement of the
tongue and mandible (especially /t/, /d/, /n/, and /l/) are mis-
articulated to degree varying with the position of a syllable relative to the vowels and consonants that go before and come after.
The space in the mouth required for vowel formation is reduced
sporadically when the mandible assists or follows the tongue tip in
contacting the palate to form consonants. Histidinemia does not
alter normal hearing and normal response to a sequence of visual
signals, but children with the syndrome have an auditory scramble
resulting in inability to repeat words added one at a time, in
sequence, so that it is difficult to link words together in a
sentence. Errors occur in both syntax and noun usage. Teachers
often characterize these children as visual learners who can not
learn by auditory means because they have short auditory memory
span.

The biochemical path connecting the enzyme deficiency to the auditory and speech-production difficulties is not known, that is whether the condition results from accumulation of normal products synthesized before the metabolic block, or from the absence of metabolites normally present after the blocked step. Although the enzyme is absent throughout life, the deleterious effects of histidinemia probably are restricted to the period of prenatal and infantile development.

Genotypes that are expressed in both sexes, but in a different manner in males and females, are called sex controlled or sex modified genes. Bernstein (1925) concluded that the singing voice in adult Europeans is a sex controlled character with low bass voice in males and the high soprano in females controlled by genotype A^1A^1, the high tenor in males and the low alto in females by genotype A^2A^2, and the baritone in males and mezzo-soprano in females by heterozygote A^1A^2. Later family studies indicate that the mode of inheritance of human singing voice type is genetically more complex (Stern 1973). The differentiation of the voice box in the male "change of voice," takes place at the time of puberty under the influence of a testosterone-induced multiplication of cells in the thyroid and cricoid cartilages at about the same time as the hormone induced adolescent spurt in body length (Tanner 1962).

CULTURE IN NON-HUMAN ANIMALS?

A number of ethologists conclude that some monkeys and apes have "culture" in the sense we mean for man. Most cultural anthropologists (White 1975) and some philosophers (Langer 1967, 1972) strongly object to the conclusion, if not the idea. If we insist that culture must be mediated by symbols as used in human spoken language, then, by definition, macaques and chimpanzees, and all other non-human animals, lack culture. At best they could have complex learned social traditions.

Until recently most cultural anthropologists greatly underestimated the importance of learning and social behavior in non-human primates (e.g., Boas 1938). In his Study of Man, published in 1936 and a popular textbook during the next decade, Ralph Linton could still define culture as behavior that is learned, shared and transmitted over two or more generations in a social context. On this definition sweet potato washing by Japanese macaques and termite fishing by East African chimpanzees, and a dozen or more other primate traditions, qualify as "cultural" as do certain learned traditions observed in birds.

McGrew and Tutin (1978) give a new review of the evidence for culture in monkeys and apes. Their analysis is based mainly on two long-term studies of wild chimpanzees in western Tanzania. The

work of Jane Goodall (1968, 1973) and her colleagues at the Gombe
National Park has continued since 1960, but has been severely
curtailed after 1975 by political disturbances in the area. The
observations at Kosoge in the Mahali Mountains originally directed
by Itani and later by Nishida (1968, 1974) began in 1965 having
grown out of several exploratory projects under the direction of
Imanishi, one of the first field workers to suggest that non-human
primates had culture. These two parallel studies provide a rich
body of data collected over 18 years on the same subspecies (Pan
troglodytes schweinfurthii). The study areas are only 170 km apart
and the two groups formerly were joined in a continuous population
now disrupted by deforestation.

McGrew and Tutin analyzed a behavior pattern, the grooming-
hand-clasp, that occurs commonly at Kosoge but is absent at Gombe.
One hand from each animal joins in an overhead clasp while a free
hand is used in grooming. They define eight necessary criteria of
culture that are capable of empirical verification. The first six
were abstracted from Kroeber's 1928 paper on "Sub-human Cultural
Beginnings:" innovation, dissemination, standardization, durability,
diffusion, tradition. McGrew and Tutin added two criteria: non-
subsistence (solitary or social behaviors which transcend subsistence activities) and natural adaptiveness (living under conditions
in which direct human influences do not exceed levels exerted by
human hunters and gatherers). These last two criteria were considered essential because both the Gombe and the Kasoge chimpanzees,
and all of the major Japanese macaque study populations, have been
artificially provisioned. Despite determined efforts by Izawa (1970)
in the Kasakati Basin and by Reynolds and Reynolds (1965) and
Sugiyama (1973) in the Budongo Forest, studies on non-provisioned
free living chimpanzees have not produced consistent, prolonged,
close-up observations. (See also Itani and Nishimura 1973.)

McGrew and Tutin conclude that no available set of observations
on chimpanzees or macaques meet all eight criteria for culture, but
that the grooming-hand-clasp pattern qualifies as a social custom
by meeting the first six criteria. It is important to note that
Goodall (1964) observed termite fishing, leaf sponging, and ant
dipping, social traditions that like nest building, must be learned,
in the Gombe chimpanzees before the onset of provisioning.

Because the fact of non-human culture would be crucial for our
views on the evolution of human behavior, the caution of these two
authors is admirable. However, we should consider and test the
possibility that the non-provisioning and natural adaptiveness
criteria are too stringent. Nearly all laboratory observations
on animal behavior are on provisioned animals and many field observations are on animals liable to direct or indirect influence
of human activity from the Neolithic on.

Clearly it would be unwarranted, overly anthropocentric, and scientifically obscurantistic to allow the non-subsistence and natural adaptiveness criteria to foreclose compelling conclusions from all possible observations on culture-like behavior in higher primates. We know enough about gestural communication and free-living social behavior in chimpanzees to make the following observation plausible: a wildborn captive, artificially provisioned, sexually mature female chimpanzee repeatedly communicates in ASL to a human observer: "I won't copulate with that male chimp because he is my half brother on my mother's side." If this happens, we ought to conclude that some non-human primates have both language and culture in a sense fully meaningful and significant for human behavior.

TWO-WAY COMMUNICATION BETWEEN MAN, CHIMPANZEE AND GORILLA

Washoe, a wild-born female chimpanzee, was 8 to 14 months old in June 1966 when she arrived at the Gardner's psychological laboratory in Reno, Nevada. She was named for Washoe County, the home of the University of Nevada. Gardner and Gardner (1969, 1971) taught Washoe American Sign Language (Stokoe, Casterline, and Croneberg 1965). By the end of the first 36 months of instruction, Washoe had learned to communicate with her human companions using 85 signs of the ASL, and two signs of her own invention not included in the ASL lexicon. She knew 160 signs after five years of training (1971).

American Sign Language is a system of gestural communication used by the deaf in North America consisting of manually-produced visual symbols, called "signs," which are analogous to words used in human spoken language. Some of the signs are iconic but many are arbitrary. The signs can be analyzed into cheremes (Stokoe 1960) just as words can be analyzed into phonemes: 19 cheremes identify the position of the hand(s) making the sign (flat, tapered, pointing hand), 12 cheremes identify the body surface (lips, ear-lobe, nose, back of hand) where the sign is made, and 24 cheremes identify the action of the hand(s), for example simple contact, repeated contact, move across, circular motion, a total of 55 cheremes.

Like spoken language, ASL has syntax and lexicon but replaces the phonetic with a cheremic system. ASL possesses all of Hockett's (1959) original list of seven design features for human language except, of course, vocal-auditory channel, and possibly, cultural transmission. And, of course, other human languages also depart from the auditory channel, for example, Braille reading employs a tactile mode, and ordinary reading a visual mode.

Other pongid species demonstrate a capacity to learn sign

language (see several papers in Harnad, Steklis and Lancaster,
1976; Peng, 1978, and Rumbaugh, 1977). Francine Patterson started
sign language work 12 July 1972 with Koko, a one-year female lowland gorilla, who, separated from her mother because of malnutrition
and shibella, later recovered and thrived in the nursery at the
San Francisco Zoo. Not only has Koko shown a capacity for acquiring
a sizable vocabulary (110 signs at 42 months of age, and 224 signs
at 53 months) she has also spontaneously combined two or more
signs into meaningful and sometimes novel sentences. She uses sign
language in imaginative play, and when alone, she signs to herself
and seems embarrassed when observed doing so. She also used sign
language to tell lies, to express her emotions, and to refer to
things out of sight and touch and displaced in the past (Patterson
1978).

In the ongoing study of three recently captured pygmy chimpanzees (Pan paniscus) now housed at the Yerkes Regional Primate
Center on loan from the Zairian government, Rumbaugh, Savage-
Rambaugh, and Gill (1978) distinguished 21 hand gestures regularly
used to coordinate copulatory positions, the first well-documented
example of complex wild-type communication by hand gestures in
pongids.

The capacity to tell lies is characteristic of human symbolic
language (Mounin 1976). Linden (1974) relates the following on
Washoe's ability to prevaricate: "One day in Nevada, after some
minor squabble, Roger found himself facing Washoe across a table.
Washoe gave every evidence of having forgotten whatever it was that
earlier had made her angry. Seductively she signed, "Come, Roger."
Fouts edged around the table. As soon as he was within striking
distance, Washoe dropped her pretense and lunged at him."

Eight chimpanzees in the outdoor colony where Washoe now lives
at the Primate Center in Norman, Oklahoma, use ASL to sign with one
another (Fouts 1978). Several untutored chimpanzees have learned
signs from other chimpanzees without human intervention. Several
new signs have been invented by the chimpanzees: "fruit drink" for
orange juice, "water bird" for swan, "cry hurt food" for radish,
"candy water food" for watermelon, and new signs for "leash" and
"bib." Numerous spontaneous chimp-to-chimp conversations are on
record. Booee approached Bruno who was eating raisins:

    Booee: "Tickle Booee."
    Bruno: "Booee me food" (translation: "Don't bother me, I'm
eating.")

And, perhaps the most significant fact about chimp-man communication to date is that Washoe tells who she is and who her human
associates are (Gardner and Gardner 1978:66): A primatologist signed
to Washoe while she was looking in a mirror:

Primatologist: "Who is that?"
Washoe: "Me, Washoe."
Primatologist: "Who me?"
Washoe: "Linn."

REFERENCES

Adler, J. Chemotaxis in bacteria. Ann. Rev. Biochem, 1975, 44, 341–56.

Berg, H.C. Dynamic properties of bacterial falgellar motors. Nature, 1974, 249, 77–79.

Berg, H.C. Bacterial behaviour. Nature, 1975, 254, 389–92.

Berg, H.C., & Anderson, R.A. Bacteria swim by rotating their flagella. Nature, 1973, 245, 380–82.

Bergsma, D. Birth defects: Atlas and compendum. Baltimore: Williams & Wilkins, 1973.

Bernstein, F. Beiträge zur Mendelistischen Anthropologie. Sitzungsber. Preuss. Akad. Wiss. Phys.-Math. Kl., 1925, 5, 61–70.

Boas, F. The mind of primitive man. 2nd ed. New York: Macmillan, 1938.

Bonin, G. von. Evolution of the human brain. Chicago: Univ. Chicago Press, 1963.

Bronowski, J. A sense of the future: Essays in natural philosophy. Cambridge: The MIT Press, 1977.

Brown, J.L. The evolution of behavior. New York: Norton, 1975.

Chomsky, N. A review of Skinner's Verbal behavior. Language, 1959, 35, 26–58.

Chomsky, N. Aspects of the theory of syntax. Cambridge: MIT Press, 1965.

Chomsky, N. Reflections on language. New York: Random House, 1975.

Clark, W.E.LeG. The antecedents of man, 3rd ed. Chicago: Quadrangle books, 1971.

Crome, L. & Stern, J. Pathology of mental retardation. London: Churchill, 1967.

Crosby, E., Humphrey, T. & Lauer, E.W. Correlative anatomy of the nervous system. New York: Macmillan, 1962.

Dingwall, W.O. The evolution of human communication systems. Studies in Neurolinguistics, 1978, 4. (In press.)

Dobzhansky, T. Nothing in biology makes sense except in the light of evolution. Amer. Biol. Teacher, 1973, 35, 125–129.

Dumoulin, H. The development of Chinese Zen. New York: First Zen Institute, 1953.

Eccles, J.C. The understanding of the brain. New York: McGraw-Hill, 1973.

Eimas, P.D. et al. Speech perception in infants. Science, 1970, 171, 303–306.

Elsasser, W.M. The chief abstractions of biology. Amsterdam: North-Holland, 1975.

Fouts, R.S. Sign language in chimpanzees: Implications of the visual mode and the comparative approach. Sign language and language acquisition in man and ape: New dimensions in comparative pedolinguistics. American Association for the Advancement of Science, Selected Symposium 16, 1978.

Gardner, B.T. & Gardner, R.A. Two-way communication with an infant chimpanzee. In Behavior of non-human primates, ed. A. Schrier & F. Stollnitz, 1971, 4, 117-84, New York: Academic Press.

Gardner, B.T. & Gardner, R.A. Comparing the early utterances of child and chimpanzee. In A. Pick, ed., Minnesota Symposium on Child Psychology, 1974, 4, 3-23, Minneapolis: University of Minnesota Press.

Gardner, R.A. & Gardner, B.T. Teaching sign language to a chimpanzee. Science, 1969, 165, 664-672.

Gardner, R.A. & Gardner, B.T. Comparative psychology and language acquisition. Ann. N.Y. Acad. Sci., 1978, 309, 37-76.

Geschwind, N. Language and the brain. Sci. Amer., 1972, 226(4), 76-83.

Geschwind, N. & Levitsky, W. Human brain: left-right asymmetries in the temporal speech region. Science, 1968, 161, 186-87.

Goodall, J. Tool-using and aimed throwing in a community of free-living chimpanzees. Nature, 1964, 201, 1264-66.

Goodall, J. The behaviour of free-living chimpanzees in a Gombe Stream Reserve. Anim. Behav. Monogr., 1968, 1, 161-311.

Goodall, J. Cultural elements in a chimpanzee community. In Pre-cultural primate behavior, ed. E.W. Menzel, 1973, Symp. 4th Internat. Cong. Primatol. 1.

Grassé, P.P. Evolution of living organisms: Evidence for a new theory of transformation. New York: Academic Press, 1978.

Griffin, D.R. The question of animal awareness: Evolutionary continuity of mental experience. New York: Rockefeller Univ. Press, 1976.

Grossman, S.P. A textbook of physiological psychology. New York: Wiley, 1967.

Grüneberg, H. The genetics of the mouse. Cambridge: Univ. Press, 1943.

Hazelbauer G.L. & Parkinson, J.S. Bacterial chemotaxis. In Reception and recognition: Microbial interactions, ed. J. Reissig. London: Chapman and Hall, 1977.

Harnad, S.R., Steklis, H.D. & Lancaster, J. Origins and evolution of language and speech. Ann. N.Y. Acad. Sci., 1976, 280, 1-914.

Hockett, C.F. Animal "languages" and human language. In Evolution of man's capacity for culture, J.N. Spuhler, ed. Detroit: Wayne Univ. Press, 1959.

Hockett, C.F. The state of the art. Paris: Mouton, 1968.

Iino, T. Genetics of structure and function of bacterial flagella. Ann. Rev. Genet., 1977, 11, 161-82.

Ingvar, D.H. Functional landscapes of the dominant hemisphere. Brain Res., 1976, 107, 181-97.

Isaac, G.L. Stages of cultural elaboration in the Pleistocene: Possible archaeological indicators of the development of language capabilities. Ann. N.Y. Acad. Sci., 1976, 280, 275-88.

Itani, J. & Nishimura, A. The study of infrahuman culture in Japan. A Review. In Precultural primate behavior, ed. E.W. Menzel, Symp. 4th Int. Cong. Primatol. vol. 1. Basel: Karger, 1973.

Izawa, K. Unit groups of chimpanzees and their nomadism in the savanna woodland. Primates, 1970, 11, 1-46.

Jerison, H.J. Evolution of the brain and intelligence. New York: Academic, 1973.

Keller,E.F. and Segel, L.A. Model for chemotaxis. Journal of Theoretical Biology, 1971, 30, 225-235.

Julesz, B. & Pennington, K. Equidistributed information mapping -- an analogy to holograms and memory. J. Optic. Soc. Amer. 1965, 55, 604.

Kimura, D. Functional asymmetry of the brain in dichotic listening. Cortex, 1967, 3, 163-78.

King, J.L. Review of R.C. Lewontin, the genetic basis of evolutionary change, 1974. Annals of Human Genetics, 1975, 38, 507-10.

Koshland, D.E.,Jr. A response regulator model in a simple sensory system. Science, 1976, 196, 1055-63.

Kroeber, A.L. Sub-human cultural beginnings. Quart. Rev. Biol., 1928, 3, 325-42.

Langer, S.K. Mind: An essay on human feeling. 2 vols. Baltimore: Johns Hopkins, 1967, 1972.

Larsen, S.H. et al. Change in direction of flagellar rotation is the basis of the chemotactic response in Escherichia coli. 1974, Nature, 249, 74-77.

Laver, J. Phonetics and the brain. Work in Progress No. 2 Dept. Phonet. Ling. Edinburgh Univ. 1968.

Lewontin, R.C. The genetic basis of evolutionary change. New York: Columbia University Press, 1974.

Linden, E. Apes, men, and language. New York: Dutton, 1974.

Linton, R. The study of man. New York: Appleton-Century, 1936.

Longuet-Higgins, H.C. The non-local storage of temporal information. Proc. Roy. Soc. Lond., Ser. B, 1968, 171, 327-34.

Løvtrup, S. The phylogeny of vertebrata. London: John Wiley and Sons, 1977.

MacNeilage, P.E. Motor control of serial order of speech. Psychol. Rev., 1970, 77, 182-96.

Magoun, H.W. The waking brain. Springfield, Ill: Thomas, 1963.

McAdam, D.W. & Whitaker, H.A. Language production: Electroencephalographic localization in the normal human brain. Science, 1971, 172. 499-502.

McGrew, W.C. & Tutin, C.E.G. Evidence for a social custom in wild chimpanzees? Man, n.s. 1978, 13, 234-51.

McKusick, V.A. Mendelian inheritance in man, 4th ed. Baltimore: Johns Hopkins, 1975.

Marcuse, H. Eros and civilization. Boston: Beacon Press, 1955.

Mounin, G. Language, communication, chimpanzees. Current Anthropology, 1976, 17, 1-21.

Nagel, E. The structure of science. Problems in the logic of scientific explanations. New York: Harcourt, Brace & World, 1961.

Nishida, T. The social group of wild chimpanzees in the Mahali Mountains, Primates, 1968, 9, 167-224.

Nishida, T. Ecology of wild chimpanzees. In Human Ecology, Ohtsuka, Tanaka & Nishida, eds. Tokyo: Kyoritsu-Shuppan, 1974.

Parkinson, J.S. Behavioral genetics in bacteria. Ann. Rev. Genet. 1977, 11, 397-414.

Patterson, F. Linguistic capabilities of a Lowland Gorilla. In F.C.C. Peng, ed., Sign language and language acquisition in man and ape: New dimensions in comparative pedolinguistics. American Association for the Advancement of Science, Selected Symposium 16, 1978.

Patzig, B. Erbbiologie und Erbpathologie des Gehirns. Handb. Erbbiol. Menschl., 1939, 5(1), 233-349.

Penfield, W. and Roberts, L. Speech and brain-mechanisms. Princeton: Princeton Univ. Press, 1959.

Peng, F.C.C., ed. Sign language and language acquisition in man and ape: New dimensions in comparative pedolinguistics. American Association for the Advancement of Science, Selected Symposium 16, 1978.

Reynolds, V. and Reynolds, F. Chimpanzees of the Budongo Forest. In Primate behavior, ed. I. DeVore, New York: Holt, Rinehart & Winston, 1965.

Rose, S.P.R. and Rose, H. 'Do not adjust your mind, there is a fault in reality' -- Ideology in neurobiology. Cognition, 1973, 2 (4), 479-502.

Rozin, P. The psychobiological approach to human memory. In Neural mechanisms of learning and memory, ed. M.R. Rosenzweig, et al. Cambridge: MIT Press, 1976.

Rumbaugh, D.M. Language learning by a chimpanzee: the Lana project. New York: Academic Press, 1977.

Rumbaugh, D.M., Savage-Rumbaugh, E.S., and Gill, T.V. Language skills, cognition, and the chimpanzee. In F.C.C. Peng, ed., Sign language and language acquisition in man and ape: New dimensions in comparative pedolinguistics, American Association for the Advancement of Science, Selected Symposium 16, 1978, 137-159.

Silverman, M. and Simon, M. Flagellar rotation and the mechanism of bacterial motility. Nature, 1974, 249,73-74.

Skinner, B.F. Verbal behavior. New York: Appleton-Century-Crofts, 1957.

Slater, E. and Cowie, V. The genetics of mental disorders. London: Oxford Univ. Press, 1971.

Sperry, R.W. In search of psyche. In The neurosciences: Paths of discovery, R.G. Worden et al, eds. Cambridge: MIT Press, 1975.

Spuhler, J.N. Biology, speech and language, Ann. Rev. Anthropol., 1977, 6, 509-61.

Stern, C. Principles of human genetics, 3rd ed. San Francisco: Freeman, 1973.

Sugiyama, Y. The social structure of wild chimpanzees: A review of field studies. In Comparative ecology and behaviour of primates,

R.P. Michael & J.H. Crook, eds., London: Academic Press, 1973.

Stokoe, W.G. Sign language structure: An outline of the visual communication system of the American deaf. University of Buffalo Studies in Linguistics, Occasional Papers 8, 1960.

Stokoe, W.G., Jr. The shape of soundless language. In The role of speech in language. J.E. Kavanaugh & J.E. Cutting, eds. Cambridge: MIT Press, 1975.

Stokoe, W.C., Casterline, D. and Croneberg C. Dictionary of American Sign Language on linguistic principles. Washington, D.C.: Gallaudet College Press, 1965.

Talland, G.A. Disorders of memory. Baltimore: Penguin Books, 1968.

Tanner, J.M. Growth at adolescence. Oxford: Blackwell, 1962.

Von Neumann, J. Mathematische grundlagen der Quantenmechanik. New York: Dover Publications, 1943.

Von Neumann, J. Mathematical foundations of quantum mechanics. Princeton: Princeton University Press, 1955.

Wada, J.A. and Rasmussen, T. Intracarotid injection of sodium amytal for the lateralization of cerebral speech dominance. Experimental and clinical observations. J. Neurosurg., 1960, 17, 266-82.

Watson, J.B. Molecular biology of the gene. 3rd ed. Menlo Park: Benjamin-Cummings, 1976.

Whitaker, H.A. On the representation of language in the human brain: Problems in the neurology of language and the linguistic analysis of aphasia. Curr. Ing. Lang. Ling. Vol. 3. Edmonton: Linguistic Research, 1971.

White, L.A. The concept of cultural systems. New York: Columbia Univ. Press, 1975.

Wilson, E.O. The attempt to suppress human behavioral genetics. JGE: The Journal of General Education, 1978, 29(4), 277-287.

Witkop, C.J., Jr. and Henry, F.V. Sjögren-Larsson syndrome and histidinemia: Hereditary biochemical diseases with defects of speech and oral functions. J. Speech Hearing Disorders, 1963, 28, 109-23.

Wright, S. Gene and organism. Am. Nat., 1953, 87, 5-18.

EVOLUTIONARY THEORY AND BEHAVIOR

The Genetic Approach to Behavioral Evolution

P. L. Broadhurst

Ethology and the Genetic Foundations of Animal Behavior

J. H. F. van Abeelen

Genetical Constraints on Early Learning:
A Perspective From Sexual Imprinting in Birds

K. Immelmann

THE EXPERIMENTAL APPROACH TO BEHAVIORAL EVOLUTION

P. L. Broadhurst

Department of Psychology, University of Birmingham,
England

ABSTRACT. One consequence of the development of interest in the
study of the genetics of behavior of a single species is the insight it can be made to yield into the evolution of behavior, an
unpromising area of investigation with few obvious approaches to
its study. Of the various ways of grappling with this problem,
the one which emerges from a study of the genetic architecture of
a behavioral phenotype is preferred. The theoretical arguments
which allow inferences to be made from a knowledge of the genetic
architecture to the kind of natural selection which has operated
are discussed together with the relevant experimental evidence,
derived from experiments with <u>Drosophila</u>.

   The main conclusions from this evidence suggest that phenotypes which show strong directional dominance and the type of
epistatic interaction associated with duplicate gene action have
been subject to natural selection of a directional kind. They are
often related to the fitness qualities of the species. On the other
hand, phenotypes which have a genetic architecture showing primarily additive variation and a less well marked dominance, often of an
ambidirectional kind, are the outcome of stabilising selection.

   The further evidence allowing the extension of this approach
from the morphological characteristics from which it was largely
developed to behavioral phenotypes is reviewed, and the rest of the
paper is devoted to a survey of investigations where the technical
quality of the analysis enables some identification of the relevant
features of the genetic architecture to be made. This material is
evaluated in terms of the support it lends to the theoretical
position.

INTRODUCTION

The intention of this paper is to review the evidence supporting the major thesis that a knowledge of genetic architecture
within a species gives clues to the evolution of behavior. To this
end, a study of some of the origins of this idea, both within
genetics and psychology, will be embarked upon, together with a
review of the experimental evidence supportive of it. This review
will concentrate on behavioral phenotypes, though not to the
exclusion of other, usually morphological, character on which the
original enunciation of the proposition was based.

Essentially, the rationale is disarmingly simple. The study
of the gene action governing a behavioral or other characteristic,
by revealing the genetic architecture of the organism or species,
indicates the forces of natural selection which have moulded the
genetic architecture in the way that it is observed today. Thus
natural selection leaves its imprint on the genome and it is argued
that a sophisticated analysis of that genome in turn allows an
inferential statement about the nature of those forces. It will be
at once apparent that the substructure for this type of argument is
that of Darwinian evolutionary theory, which is so widely and so
pervasively accepted in contemporary biology that it seems hardly
necessary to argue its case.

The same, however, is perhaps less evident in contemporary
psychology, especially in relation to controversies regarding the
extent and potency of environmental determination versus genetic
influences. It is not proposed to enter this controversy, since
the standpoint of this conference is one which enables its participants to accept, if not uncritically and entirely on trust, a
general belief in the importance of biological determinants of
behavior. Thus the roots of the argument in Darwinian theory will
be assumed, and it is on this basis that the argument will proceed.

In passing, it may be noted that this theory and indeed a
similar style of inferential argument has proved to be an effective
framework for the study of behavior in another connection. The
crucial importance and the consequences of genetic relationships in
family groupings in animals, pointed out especially by Hamilton
(1964), contributed to a recent resurgence of interest as witnessed
in the rapid development of what is now generally called sociobiology (Wilson, 1975).

Alternative approaches

The approach which I shall be adopting in the present paper
is, however, one of several possibilities. At least three can be
identified: the first is what I have characterized (Broadhurst,

1968) as the approach from experimental psychology, the second from ethology and the third from psychogenetics. Bitterman's work (1965) is perhaps most characteristic of the first, the psychological approach, though an interest in comparative studies of animal "intelligence" was a feature of early animal studies at the beginning of the century and before, which became canalized into the study of learning processes and the subsequent flowering of learning theories around the 1940's. Bitterman, it will be recalled, sought to analyse the variety of species in respect of standard learning problems, spatial and visual, and to identify behavior which was either rat-like or fish-like, and hence to develop a sort of philogenetic scale in which the less complex the organism the more fish-like is the behavior. This technique of "philogenetic filtration" was a most interesting attempt to study the evolution of behavior, albeit small samples of behavior in a small sample of species, chosen, nevertheless, for their representativeness in respect of different classes and orders. But the attempt must be judged not to have succeeded: the problem is inherently so complex that a method, ingenious though it is, to unravel it through a reliance on relatively simple applications of experimental psychology without drawing on aspects of population genetics could hardly be expected to do more than provide some interesting comparisons between species.

The second approach derives from ethology and is also an interspecies study. This approach to the evolution of behavior was initially also based on species comparisons (Lorenz, 1941), but of a kind designed to utilise behavioral characteristics to illuminate and solve taxonomic problems. In this it was strikingly successful in that behavioral criteria were, in many cases (Mayr, 1958), recognised as equal in value to other, usually morphological, characteristics which differentiated the groups studied. But the involvement of the genetic process as such as an independent variable, that is, by hybridisation or cross-breeding, is essential and examples of ethological work of this kind, especially where the phenotype in question is a variation in a fixed action pattern, are of considerable interest. The contribution to the present volume by van Abeleen (1978) exemplifies some of this material.

The intra-specific approach

This brings us to the third of the alternative approaches identified and characterised as potentially leading to an increased understanding of the evolution of behavior. It seeks to analyse the behavioral phenotype into its genetic and environmental components of variation, especially seeking to divide the former into those dependent on additive, dominance and non-allelic interaction. In this way the nature of the genetic determination can be compared with that which is known to result from the operation of the forces of natural selection in the wild or original population from which sample--usually a laboratory population--is derived. Proceeding thus allows an inferential statement regarding the nature of that selection to be made and hypotheses deriving from it put to the test.

Before, however, embarking on a description of the theoretical principles which support this approach, it should perhaps be noted that a consideration of genetic architecture in terms of the additive, dominance and interaction components of variation is to some extent an over-simplification. The balancing action of many mechanisms governing the genetic structure of populations, as Mather (1973) has pointed out, is a complex end product of the action of different forces, of which selection is but one. They include the reproductive system, though this is usually sexual in respect of the behavioral phenotypes to which psychologists normally limit their attention; the mating system, broadly speaking, inbreeding versus outbreeding; and the balance of free versus potential variation in the genetic system. It is important not to lose sight of these other considerations, but for the purpose of the present discussion, attention will be concentrated on selection as such.

Natural and artificial selection

The broad basis for this kind of inferential argument from natural selection has been pioneered by Mather (1943, 1953, 1960, 1966, 1973), and demonstrated by him and his colleagues, in a series of supporting investigations. Others have developed not dissimilar points of view, deriving largely from Falconer's (1960) account of the influence of natural selection on quantitative characters, and perhaps developed most extensively in relation to behavior by Roberts (1967). Other accounts may be found, for example, in Bruell (1967). But none is as comprehensive and as fully grounded in the detailed developments of biometrical genetics as that of Mather and his school. What follows therefore is based largely on his account (Mather, 1973) and also follows closely a previous exposition (Broadhurst and Jinks, 1974).

With Mather, we recognise three kinds of selection, stabilising, directional and disruptive. These three may be distinguished by their effects on phenotypic expression in the population to which they are applied. They may move the mean phenotypic expression from a previous level which was in balanced equilibrium maintained by previous selective and other pressures of the kind referred to above. These selective pressures may result in a new optimum expression in the population and individuals which depart from that optimum are less favored in an adaptive sense and consequently leave, on average, fewer progeny--that is to say, are less fit in a Darwinian sense.

Thus there is associated with *stabilising selection* a level
of expression which is an intermediate one in respect of the phenotypic range, and departures from it will be less fit, irrespective
of whether they exceed or fall short of it, that is differ in either
a negative or a positive direction. *Directional selection* will
also result in a single optimal expression, but this optimal value
need not be the mean population value if selection has not yet
resulted in equilibrium. This value will be towards one end or the
other of the phenotypic scale, and in consequence genetic mechanisms
favored in the population will be those which tend to move the population mean towards that value. The third type of selection
distinguished by Mather, *disruptive selection*, will result in more
than one, and usually two, optima. As a result dimorphisms and
even polyphormisms may arise. These morphisms may be in a stable
equilibrium within the population, and a common and but nevertheless
striking diphormism is to be found in the existence of the two sexes
in dioecious species. Sexual reproduction is, of course, the most
important mechanism by which outbreeding populations maintain access
to potential variability which can be converted into free variability should the need arise as in, for example, a change in environmental pressures which demand a response for species survival.
Alternatively dimorphism can lead to breeding isolation and incip-
ient speciation. Behavioral examples of disruptive natural selection
are uncommon, though, of course, the effect of artificial selection
in the laboratory in creating dimorphic phenotypes is well known.
Therefore, it is the first two kinds of selection, stabilising and
directional, which result in single optima that we are at present
primarily concerned with, and we must examine the different consequences for the genetical architecture of those characters on
which they operate.

Stabilising selection

Stabilising selection will favor the average phenotype. Thus,
the balanced genotype which will be favored at the expense of those
determining extreme phenotypic values, which by definition result
from imbalance between increaser and decreaser genes and between
dominant increasers and dominant decreasers. The genetic architecture to be expected when a character subjected to stabilising
selection is analysed appropriately will therefore show dominance
variation of one of two kinds. On the one hand, the presence of
very little or almost no dominance may be revealed, so that the
dominance ratio, that is, the proportion of dominance to additive
variation, is very low. If, on the other hand, dominance is shown
to be significantly high, it will be usually of an ambidirectional
kind, with dominant increasers cancelling the effect of dominant
decreasers. However, the possibility of some small measure of
directional dominance resulting from a lack of precise coincidence
between the average phenotypic value of the character and the

optimum value from the point of view of the population's fitness
should not be overlooked. Stabilising selection will also generally
show a large additive component of variation, relative to the size
of the dominance component. Another diagnostic feature of the
outcome of stabilising selection may be the detection of linkage
of genes in the repulsion phase--that is, positive (increaser) with
negative (decreaser).

Now these are the genetic mechanisms which maximise potential
variation at the expense of free variation since free variation
causes phenotypes to arise in the population which deviate from
its mean and which are less fit because of such deviation. It
should be noted that such a trait, despite the impression of lack
of variation which it shows, will nevertheless yield a sustained
response to disruptive selection (Mather and Harrison, 1949),
especially of a bi-directional kind which will allow recombination
to break the repulsion linkages which previously held increasers and
decreasers together in balance. Recombinants having predominantly
increasing or decreasing effects will thus come to exert their
effect at the phenotypic level.

Directional selection

Directional selection, as we have seen, is identified as that
which increases the fitness of phenotypes towards one extreme of
the distribution. The consequence of this kind of natural selection
is a genetic architecture with some important features. First,
directional dominance may be found, so that if selection has been
for an increase in the character--a higher mean score--then the
increasing alleles will be the dominant ones. Similarly, and not
to be overlooked, if selection has been for a decrease, then
decreasers will be dominant. Therefore a high level of dominance
variation is to be expected, relative to the additive variation.
This latter may well be small, and not constitute a reservoir of
potential variation. Second, directional selection may result in
a type of epistasic interaction involving duplicate genes. This
form of non-allelic (between gene) interaction differs from allelic
or within gene interaction, normally referred to as dominance.
Duplicate gene interaction leads to a greater number of different
genotypes each having an optimal phenotypic effect. Thus a greater
proportion of possible genotypes attains the most appropriate level
of expression for maximising fitness. Consequently more pathways
are provided whereby the genotype is optimally expressed, so that
the most important characteristics are overdetermined genetically.
From the point of view of survival it is not surprising that
genetic architecture of this kind is often found for fitness
characters such as viability and fertility. These fitness characters, unlike characters subject to stabilising selection, do not
show a large response to artificial selection, since the optimum

achieved is under constant pressure from natural selection. A response in a direction <u>away</u> from that optimal level of expression may, of course, be expected.

Under certain circumstances, notably when selection pressure, as in artificial selection, has been especially heavy and is recent and is concentrated on the identification of just a few individuals in a population for their use as parents, directional selection may be supported by a different type of interaction, complementary interaction. This arises when two non-allelic genes jointly have a greater phenotypic expression than the sum of their individual effects. It could perhaps be argued that the detection of this element in the genetic architecture might be used as an indicator of the recency of the selection process, as opposed to duplicate gene interaction which bespeaks a long standing effect whereby a relatively large proportion of the population is well adapted from a fitness point of view compared with the relatively few who are poorly adapted and comprise the tail end of the distribution. Thus selection may not only leave its imprint on genetic architecture, but it may also give a clue to the period in the evolutionary history of the species when it operated, and, specifically, whether it was natural or artificial.

Experimental evidence

While these are essentially theoretical statements, based on Mather's formulations, they are the outcome of a series of experiments using the fruit fly which underpin them, and it is to this material that we must now turn. Breese and Mather (1960) studied the genetic architecture governing two characters, viability and the number of abdominal bristles in *Drosophila melanogaster*. Bristle number is known to show intermediate expression, when considered in terms of the range possible when selected artificially for either high or low scores, and numbers about 18-20 in unselected populations. Viability, the other character studied, is a fitness character *par excellence*. Clearly, the number of progeny individuals leave is in general a direct measure of the adaptive success of the genotype they represent. In accordance with the theory, Breese and Mather found a genetic architecture for viability which was characterised by unidirectional dominance (for higher viability) together with duplicate gene interaction. The significance of the directional dominance is clear; genes governing high viability show dominance, and, on the average, complete dominance, over those governing low viability.

In contrast, bristle number, the second character which Breese and Mather invesitgated on the same population, yielded a quite different genetic architecture. While some degree of dominance was detected, it was less than in the case of viability, and moreover, was less complete. No duplicate interaction of genes was detected. But for bristle number there is not an immediately obvious valid-ation for assuming a selective advantage as is the case with a viability measure. It therefore becomes necessary to demonstrate that the intermediate phenotypic expression detected has in fact arisen as a result of selection. The next step in supporting Mather's argument was provided by Kearsey and Barnes (1970, Barnes and Kearsey, 1970) who used a procedure designed to mimic natural selection, but in a laboratory setting. They employed population cages in which the eggs of not laboratory but of wild populations of *Drosophila* were sampled over time. These populations were main-tained for a considerable period--over six months--which allowed a number of generations to be studied, since each matures in approx-imately two weeks. These samples of eggs, taken at intervals, were allowed to hatch and the emerging flies reared in standardised manner. They were then scored for the two characters, bristle number and viability of progeny. It was quite clear that the flies having intermediate scores in respect of bristle number had the greater viability.

It should be noted that the large dominance variation typically associated with fitness measures leads to their having a low herit-ability of the "narrow" kind. This may seem paradoxical, until it is recalled that dominance variation is excluded from the numerator in calculating a narrow heritability ratio, leaving only the additive component representing the genetic variation to be compared with the total (genetic plus environmental) variation. The numer-ator is consequently considerably less than is the case in calculat-ing the broad heritability ratio, or "degree of genetic determination" as it is sometimes called, in which dominance is included in the numerator. This discrepancy between the two ratios calculated in this way could be taken as a mark of a fitness character. Also, additive variation itself will tend to be small, with the result that the narrow heritability index will be depressed for this reason as well. The additive genetical variation has already been fixed for fitness characters since large variation between labor-atory strains in this respect would not be expected, the unfit strains having been eliminated during the process of domestication.

The duplicate gene interaction, which Mather and Breese demon-strated to be characteristic of *Drosophila* viability in reinforcing the selective effect of directional dominance, has the further effect of reducing variance by making different genotypes all share the same phenotype (Mather, 1967). Accordingly, a fitness charac-ter can be recognised experimentally by the kind of the genetic architecture revealed by a biometrical analysis.

Moreover, this effect was also subject to the influence of environmental pressure of a kind likely to be encountered in natural conditions. The relationship was more marked when Kearsey

and Barnes imposed crowded conditions which caused an increased
density of egg laying, thus heightening the severity of the competition between flies for the available resources. Thus a character not directly related to fitness can also show the effects of
natural selection, but in this case it can be demonstrated to have
been of the stabilising kind.

Further support for the position comes from investigations by
Kearsey and Kojima (1967) who studied two similarly contrasting
characters, the hatchability of eggs and live body weight, also in
Drosophila melanogaster. Again the techniques involved enabled the
analysis of the effects of not only different chromosomes but also
different chromosomal segments. The results are in good accord
with the previous findings: the character more directly related
to fitness, egg hatchability in this case, was shown to have a
genetic architecture which featured strongly directional dominance
for high yield, interaction effects of a duplicate gene kind, together with relatively insignificant additive effects. Body weight,
on the other hand, showed primarily simple additive effects indicative of stabilising selection.

APPLICATIONS TO BEHAVIOR

The next step in the inferential process relates to considering the extent to which these notions can be applied not to morphological phenotypes but to behavioral ones. To those of us who
have long accepted the view that the application of biological
techniques of analysis such as biometrical genetics to behavioral
measures presents no insuperable conceptual problems, the task may
seem to be one of supererogation. Nevertheless, experiments have
been performed which serve to link to the two main classes of
phenotypes distinguished and their impact will now be assessed.

A relatively early application to behavior of the principles
inherent in the argument as rehearsed above was that of Fulker (1966)
in his analysis of mating speed in the male fruit fly, *Drosophila
melanogaster*. He used a diallel cross breeding technique in which
six lines of flies which differed in the number of observed copulations were completely intercrossed to give a diallel table of mean
values. The behavior thereafter was then inferred since the measure
used was the number of females impregnated during a given time. He
was able to demonstrate significant directional dominance for speedy
mating, though there was no evidence of interactive effects. A
subsequent re-analysis using a simplified version of the triple-test
cross breeding technique (Kearsey and Jinks, 1968) gave the same
results (Fulker, 1972). But perhaps more important was the evidence,
additional to the intuitively obvious association of speed of mating
with fitness, that Fulker was able to present that the flies that
copulated fastest were those that achieved more fertilisations of

females and subsequently produced more offspring, so that the relationship between speed and copulation as an important component of fitness was unequivocally established for this behavior.

Using a time-sampling technique, Hay (1972) studied the trait of reactivity to disturbance occurring after mechanical stimulation, also in the fruit fly. Directional dominance for high reactivity, combined with epistasic interaction of the duplicate gene kind, pointed strongly to such activity as an important fitness trait. Hay also related this genetic architecture to viability by studying the various strains he used under less optimal environmental conditions. He allowed flies to remain in their original bottles without fresh medium (food) and assessed the extent of mortality occurring. He found that the greater mortality occurred among the less reactive flies which confirms the identification of reactivity as being an important component of fitness.

Angus (1974b) extended these studies to the genetic architecture of two further traits in *Drosophila*, spontaneous activity and the incidence of preening. Preening can be clearly observed in this species and is usually regarded as a form of cleaning behavior, though there may be displacement activity elements. Both were observed by time-sampling techniques, and the response to a shadow stimulus caused by interrupting the light falling on the flies was also assessed. This latter technique was designed to provide some of the stimulus elements involved in the predation to which this species is subject in the wild. The measures of activity and of preening before stimulation showed directional dominance for a high level and the presence of genic interactions of a duplicate kind. After stimulation, the genetic architecture indicated dominance for a decrease in both activity and preening, suggestive of selective advantage of the kind expected. The next step was the demonstration by Angus (1974a) of the fitness component of spontaneous activity, including preening. He did this by using the technique of simulating natural selection in population cages as used by Barnes and Kearsey and succeeded in showing that natural selection for increased spontaneous activity in a crossbred population of *Drosophila* had in fact operated after they had been maintained in cages for a long--11 months--period. These results, taken with the finding of the directional dominance and duplicate gene interaction for a high level of spontaneous activity and preening and the evidence for dominance for a decrease in both in response to shadow stimulation, lend powerful support to the propriety of making inferences from genetical architecture to natual selection.

In this way the adaptive significance to the species of a quantitative trait which is studied in a laboratory population of it can be demonstrated by knowing the genetic architecture and relating it to the level of expression of the trait which is observed. Furthermore, we can accept that these properties apply

equally to behavioral traits as to the morphological ones on which
they were originally demonstrated.

A SURVEY OF THE GENETIC ARCHITECTURE OF ANIMAL BEHAVIOR

Early attempts

It seems worthwhile, therefore, to devote some attention to a
short attempt to survey the development of the ideas in the context
of their applications to behavior as elucidated by biometrical
genetics. An early adumbration of the methodology is to be found
in Broadhurst's (1960) account of the first behavioral analyses
using the diallel cross method (Broadhurst, 1959). A 6 x 6 diallel,
completely intercrossing six different strains of laboratory rat,
produced subjects which were measured in the open-field test for
emotional defecation and ambulation. A strain having brown coat
color, nearest of all those used to that of the wild Norway rat,
was shown to have the highest proportion of dominant to recessive
genes governing its ambulatory behavior. It was also shown to be
intermediate in respect of its ambulation score which lead to a
"speculation regarding the part natural selection might play in
determining optimum ambulation behavior in a strange situation.
Perhaps "Curiosity killed the cat" is valid for species other than
the feline!" (Broadhurst, 1960, page 97). Subsequent, more refined
analysis (Broadhurst and Jinks, 1966), was able to make the point
more precisely, by showing that ambulation was determined by a
genetical architecture in which the dominance shown was ambidirectional and favored an intermediate phenotypic score. The stabilising selection thus hinted at in the first descriptions of this
early application of the diallel cross technique to behavioral
phenotypes was thus supported. Similarly, directional dominance
for a lowering of emotional defecation with increasing experience
of the test situation, which is only mildly stressful, strongly
suggested a history of natural selection for low, rather than high,
expression of this trait. Once again we have an example of different characters, measured on the same material and the same experiment, as in the *Drosophila* examples cited above, yielding different
genetic architecture and pointing to a different evolutionary
history for the two aspects of behavior studied.

Heritability

Comparisons with other analyses which permitted some resolution
of the genetic architecture and made around this time were however
not especially encouraging. They were made in terms of heritability
ratios and, while consistency was noted in the two measures of the
open-field test, in that heritability in the narrow sense fell with

increasing experience of the test, this consistency contrasted with
a re-analysis of Vicari's (1929) data which showed (Broadhurst and
Jinks, 1961) an increment in heritability during maze learning and
Fuller and Thompson's report (1960, page 92) of random fluctuations
in heritability ratios of the performance of dogs with practice.
Leaving aside for the moment the problem created by comparisons of
different phenotypes, since it surely would be naive to expect
different behaviors in different species to have necessarily similar
genetic architecture, the reliance on heritability estimates as a
method of comparison both within and between experiments was at that
time, and still is, for that matter, misplaced. A heritability
ratio serves merely as a summary statement of the genetic architecture and is no substitute for a detailed knowledge of the additive,
dominance and interactive components which constitute it, to say
nothing of the other balancing force which hold a population in
equilibrium.

Construction of the present survey

The situation today, however, is very different and the number
of investigations which have used some form of biometrical approach
to behavioral phenotypes is quite considerable. The rest of this
paper will, therefore, be devoted to a necessarily brief survey,
supported by extensive tabulations of such investigations. It should
be noted, however, that no attempt is made to cover every investigation in which cross-breeding of a kind which, in principle, could
have given rise to a satisfactory analysis of genetic architecture.
The intention is to include as many as possible of those reports
for which an analysis which is deemed to be technically satisfactory
in the way described has been undertaken, that is, gives some unmistakable evidence of dominance, and its direction. It is often
difficult to distinguish unequivocally dominance from *potence*, that
is, the mere phenotypic resemblance of an F_1 to one of its parental
strains, which for polygenic traits is not satisfactory evidence of
a corresponding degree of dominance, since it does not guarantee
that that parental strain carries all or even most of the dominant
alleles. While there are many data in the literature which are
susceptible of such analysis, biometrical techniques have been
applied to only a minority of them. Nor is there any present
attempt at systematic re-analysis of such data, though some instances,
deriving especially from the papers of Broadhurst and Jinks (1961)
and Fulker (1972) will be included. For these reasons the survey
does not attempt an exhaustive coverage, and moreover there is some
concentration on more recent rather than older studies, except where
they have been the subject of re-analysis in the way mentioned.

The format of the Tables is based on the one presented by
Kearsey and Kojima (1967), in which the genetic architecture of
different morphological characters of *Drosophila* was succinctly

summarised in such a way as to indicate the extent to which it
provided evidence for the kind of selection, directional or
stabilising, which controlled the phenotypes in question. The
present tables are confined to non-human behavioral phenotypes but
seek to summarize the evidence in the same way. In each case the
direction of expression of any dominance listed is to be understood
to be in the logically positive direction, that is, for the behavior
given in the "Phenotype" column.

In tables condensed in the way these must be, it is not possible
to do justice to the richness of material available, and attention
must perforce be concentrated on those aspects to which the theory
can be applied, to the exclusion of many other interesting facets
of the investigations surveyed. An attempt has, however, been made
to indicate the extent of the material on which the conclusions are
based. This will be found in the "Method" column, where "crosses"
indicates first and sometimes second, filial crosses only, usually
between more than a single pair of inbred strains, "back-crosses"
indicates more extensively derived generations, "diallel" refers
to the method of complete intercrossing of usually three or more
strains, with "½ diallel" indicating the absence of reciprocal
crosses and "partial" signifying that some at least of the
requisite crosses were not bred. But, as has been noted elsewhere,
(Broadhurst, 1977, page 290) "the diallel cross as a breeding
design must be sharply distinguished from the diallel analysis for
which this design has been extensively employed in biometrical
genetics (Mather and Jinks, 1971)", and few of the analyses presented adequately exploit its possibilities. Indeed, in many cases
there has been hardly any attempt beyond the inferential to investigate and to specify genetic dominance, merely relying on potence,
that is, *phenotypic* dominance as an indicator for the purpose.
Where some attempt has been made, the entry "+ analysis" has been
added. Such an analysis may, however, range from a complete
Hayman (1954) Anova together with the analysis of Jinks' (1954)
covariance.variance (W.V) diagrams, through the former--or some
part of it--without the latter, to a Griffing (1956) Anova which,
while giving some indications of additive and dominance variation
through its general and specific combining abilities terms respectively (Broadhurst and Jinks, 1966, page 454), is more a statistical
model approach rather than a genetical one, and less suited to the
fine-grain analyses requisite for the complete specification of
genetic architecture. Even simpler approaches, such as comparing
parental and F_1 mean values have been recognised in this way also.
Fortunately the few applications of the triple-test cross technique
so far reported do not share these failings...at least, not as yet.

Features of the present survey

As will be observed, the Tables are organised in a rough

progression from what might be deemed to be primary fitness characters associated with reproduction and the like and hence likely to be governed by strong directional dominance for expression in an adaptive direction to ones less markedly so for which stabilising selection might have operated to achieve an approximate intermediate expression. But before the extent to which these expectations have been realised are considered, some general points may be made. First, it is striking what preponderance there is of analyses shown in the tables, successful or otherwise, which derive from investigations reporting the use of the *diallel cross* method. It perhaps fulfills the prophecy of Chung, Morton and Yasuda who wrote in 1966 that "The methodology of the diallel cross is only a generation old. It is now ready to pass from the hands of experimental geneticists into the mainstream of . . . . biology" (page 684), a view which seemed unduly optimistic at the time. However, it may still appear so when the missing word which I omitted is restored. It was "human"! But insofar as biologically oriented psychologists are concerned, the situation which Chung *et al.* described, which referred of course not to experimental studies with animals but the analysis of inter-racial crosses in Hawaii, may now be with us, since the diallel method, as may be seen, has been put to increasing use in recent years.

From the point of view expressed in the present paper, this reliance on diallels is perhaps to some extent unfortunate, since the diallel analysis, though well able to reveal the presence of non-allelic interactions, is not especially sensitive in distinguishing the type of interaction, a requirement central to present concerns. Newer methods, such as the triple-test cross (Jinks, Perkins and Breese, 1969), and the subsequent developments of it, for example, that of Chahal and Jinks (1978), are more successful for application to laboratory material for the detection of the type of epistasis.

A second point relates to *scaling*, a word about which is also in order: as Kearsey and Kojima (1966) point out "It is well known that a change in the scale of measurement often alters the picture of interactions considerably. The proposed theory assumes that the genotypes are measured in the same scale as that in which selection is acting. However, one is usually ignorant of what this natural scale is, and normally uses the simplest, most conventional or most convenient scale for data analyses. One must then assume that the observed genetic effects are so gross that the dominance relationships between homozygotes and heterozygotes are maintained approxiamtely whatever 'reasonable' scale is used." (page 34).

Thirdly the rationale developed can, of course, be applied to *survival behavior* directly, that is by concentrating on traits having an obvious *a priori* claim to be a fitness character in that they have direct consequences for individual and hence, for species

survival, in the way pointed out by Roberts (1967). An example is
seen in Angus's work on the simulation of predation among fruit
flies, described above (1974b). A start has also been made along
these lines by investigators working with rodents. As may be seen
in Table 2 by Wilcock (1972), for example, who studied the genetic
architecture of escape from water among weanling rats, explicitly
emphasized this trait's survival value, as did Festing (1974) in
his study of learning to escape from water in mice. Such claims
are noted in the tabulation of their and others' findings. Moreover,
it is possible to make predictions from a knowledge of a species'
behavior and, perhaps more importantly, a knowledge of the behavior
of its known predators or other environmental hazards, to a specification of the likely genetical architecture which will be found on
an adequate investigation. This approach can be most explicitly
observed in Henderson's (1978) success (Table 7B) in demonstrating
dominance and hence the operation of natural selection for low
activity in infant mice as opposed to the higher expression characteristic of adults. As has been noted elsewhere (Broadhurst and
Jinks, 1974, pages 59-61), there are several other areas which are
obviously ripe for the application of this methodology, sexual and
reproductive behavior generally being perhaps one of the more obvious
examples.

Conclusions from the present survey

The first impression the reader may derive from a perusal of
the tables is that it has been possible to accumulate a deal of
evidence which appears to bear on the Matherian hypothesis relating
genetic architecture to natural selection. The evidence is, in
fact, surprisingly massive, even though this survey is doubtless not
exhaustive and some further examples may have been missed. But the
second impression may be one of regret at the numerous query marks
which the absence of satisfactorily hard information has made it
necessary to insert in all-too-numerous entries. Why is this? The
main reason lies, in my view, in the relatively small-scale nature
of many of the studies that have been completed in biometrical
genetics by psychologists. One of the numerous details which had
to be omitted from the table for fear of overloading it was the
size of the investigations noted. Despite the difficulties of working with other than plant material, and the bulk of the entries
relate to mammals, particularly mice and rats, it still seems to be
assumed that relatively small investigations can somehow be made to
yield definitive findings. What can be extracted from, to take but
one example, an incomplete half diallel cross, is limited indeed.
The message therefore must surely be that if investigators wish to
study genetic architecture in the detail necessary to allow inferences to be made to natural selection, then researches must be invest-
ed with greater resources.

The second point relates to the quality of the analyses applied to what data have been collected, which, here again, it was not possible to indicate in detail in the tables, and which might, in any case, have been invidious to judge even if there had been room! This point has already been touched on and so will not be labored further. Nevertheless, it is clear that the simplicity of detecting merely additive variation, which can be done by strain-difference studies, is not matched by the more difficult task of identifying dominance which needs at the very least some classical Mendelian crosses. Thus there are relatively few entries which on examination can do more than give broad indications of directional dominance for behaviors of a putatively adaptive kind even though they find place in the antepenultimate columns of the tables. Finally, the frequency of breeding designs and analyses capable of revealing the subtleties of the effects of non-allelic interactions of an epistatic kind which would support the inference of even directional, much less stabilising selection, are conspicuous by their absence from the penultimate columns.

Accordingly, for studies illustrating stabilizing selection, the picture is even more depressing. As long ago as 1967, Kearsey and Kojima wrote "Perhaps the weakest link between the theory and its evidence as it exists at present, is the lack of knowledge of proved cases of stabilizing selection" (Kearsey and Kojima, 1967, page 33). Mather (1973) makes a similar point (page 145) but notes that " ... in the case of sternopleural chaeta number in *Drosophila* there is now ample evidence that it is in fact under the stabilizing selection that its genetic architecture would suggest (Kearsey and Barnes, 1970)." Thus the morphological evidence, as is so often the case, has outstripped the behavioral, though the demonstration (Table 8A) by Belyaev *et al.* (1977) that reproductive success appears to be associated with an architecture featuring an inter-mediate response to stress suggests such evidence is, in principle, available and may be more readily available in the not-too-distant future. Nevertheless, it is still a matter of some regret that such little progress has been made in these matters. Indeed, I cannot resist the temptation to re-quote (Broadhurst, 1960, page 4-5) from one of my teachers, Stone, who wrote in 1947 as follows: "To many of us who have worked for a long time in the field of comparative psychology it is a matter of shame and regret that only an amateurish beginning has yet been made by psychologists in the utilization of pure lines of animals in fundamental research in the nature-nurture area (1947, page 344)". In my view, this criticism, trenchant though it may seem, still has some force today, and only by dint of recog-nizing the need for large-scale studies, adequately analysed and expertly interpreted against the background of the solid achieve-ments of population and biometrical genetics can substantial progress be made in several areas, of which the one I have been concerned with in the present paper--that of inferences to the evolution of behavior--is after all only part.

Table 1: Genetic architectures of mating behaviors

Reference Author(s)	Year	Species	Phenotype	Methods	Dominance Present	Dominance Direc of expr.	Inter-action	Remarks
Kessler	1969	D. pseudo-obscura	mating	Selection, crosses + back-crosses	Yes	Hi	No	
Parsons	1964	D. melano-gaster	mating	Diallel	Yes	Hi	?	
Jakway	1959	Guinea pig	mating behaviors	Crosses + back-crosses	No	-	-	
			- male circling					
			investigate		Yes	Lo	No	
			mount		Yes	Lo	No	
			intromission		Yes	Hi	No	
			ejaculation		Yes	Hi	Yes	Complementary: log scale abolishes
Goy & Jakway (re-analysed Broadhurst & Jinks 1961)	1959		- female estrus latency		Yes	Lo	No	
			estrus duration		Yes	Hi	No	
			lordosis		Yes	Lo	Yes	? type: log scale abolishes
			mounts		Yes	Lo	No	

Table 1 (continued)

Reference Author(s)	Year	Species	Phenotype	Methods	Dominance Present	Direc of expr.	Interaction	Remarks
McGill	1970	Mouse	mating behaviors – male intromission latency	Crosses + back-crosses	No	–	?	
			ejaculation latency		No	–	?	
Vale & Ray	1972	Mouse	mating behaviors – male: various (17)	Diallel	Yes	Hi	?	
Cook, Siegel & Hinkelmann	1972	Chicken	mating behaviors – male: matings	Diallel	Yes	Lo	?	
Dewsbury	1975	Rat	mating behaviors – male	Diallel	Yes	Hi	?	
Festing	1975	Mouse	reproduction – various measures	Diallel + analysis	Yes	Hi	No	

Table 1 (continued)

Reference Author(s)	Year	Species	Phenotype	Methods	Dominance Present	Direc of expr.	Inter-action	Remarks
Schüler & Borodin	1976	Mouse	Nubility in females - various measures	Diallel + analysis	Yes	Hi	?	
Kuse & DeFries	1976	Mouse	Social dominance	Crosses	Yes	Hi	?	Enhanced by females

Table 2: Genetic architectures of water escape behavior

Reference Author(s)	Year	Species	Phenotype	Methods	Dominance Present	Dominance Direction of expression	Interaction	Remarks
Winston	1964	Mouse	water escape	½ diallel	Yes	Hi	?	
Smith Smith & Connor	1972 1974	Mouse, + wild	underwater escape	½ diallel + analysis	Yes	Hi	No	Interacts with environment
Wilcock	1972	Rat	water escape	crosses	Yes	Hi	?	"fitness" character
Festing	1974	Mouse	water escape	Diallel + analysis	Yes	Hi	No	"fitness" character
Hyde	1974	Mouse	water escape	Diallel	Yes	Hi	?	
Royce, Holmes & Poley	1975	Mouse	underwater – swimming factor	Diallel + analysis	Yes	Hi	?	

Table 3: Genetic architecture of geotaxis behavior

Reference Author(s)	Year	Species	Phenotype	Method	Dominance Present	Direction of expression	Inter- action	Remarks
Walton	1968	Droso- phila melano- gaster	geotaxis	Diallels + analy- ses	Yes	Hi	No	

Table 4: Genetic architectures of nesting activities

Reference Author(s)	Year	Species	Phenotype	Method	Dominance Present	Direc of expr.	Inter-action	Remarks
Barnett & Scott	1964	Mouse	nest building gnawing (wood or food)	Incomplete diallel	Yes Yes	Hi Hi	? ?	
Van Oortmerssen & Beardmore	1967	Mouse	paper fraying	Crosses	No	-	?	
Lynch & Hegmann	1972	Mouse	nest building	Partial ½ diallel + crosses	Yes	Hi	?	
Lee	1973	Mouse	nest building	Crosses, backcrosses + diallel	Yes	Hi	?	"Adaptive signifi-cance"
Royce, Holmes & Poley	1975	Mouse	tunneling factor	Diallel + analysis	Weak	Hi	No	

Table 5: Genetic architectures of consummatory activities

Reference Author(s)	Year	Species	Phenotype	Method	Dominance Present	Direc of expr.	Inter- action	Remarks
Manosevitz & Lindzey	1967	Mouse	food hoarding	Crosses + backcrosses	No	–	No	
Henderson	1970b	Mice	food seeking	Diallel + analysis	Yes	Hi	Yes	
Wilcock & Bush	1972	Rat	drinking after air blast	½ diallel + analysis	Yes	Lo	Yes	
Connor & Winston	1972	Mouse	food approach lat- ency	½ diallel + analysis	Yes	Hi	No	
			contact time		No	–	No	
			eating time		Yes	Hi	No	
Vale & Vale	1973	Mouse	water intake	Diallel + analysis	Weak	No	?	

Table 6: Genetic architectures of sleep behaviors

Reference Author(s)	Year	Species	Phenotype	Method	Dominance Pre-sent	Direc of expr.	Inter-action	Remarks
Vesell	1968	Mouse	Hexobarbital sleep time	Incomplete diallel	No	–	?	
Friedmann	1972	Mouse	Sleep	Diallel				
			total		Yes	Hi	?	
			long epis-odes		Yes	Hi	?	"Contribute to over-all fitness"
			paradoxical		Yes	Lo	?	
			diurnal ratio		Yes	Lo	?	

Table 7: Genetic architectures of activity: A. Spontaneous Activity

Reference Author(s)	Year	Species	Phenotype	Method	Dominance Present	Direc of expr.	Interaction	Remarks
Brody (re-analysed Broadhurst & Jinks 1961)	1942	Rat	wheel running	Crosses + backcrosses	No	-	Yes	j-type
Bruell	1962 1964b	Mouse	wheel running	Crosses + backcrosses	Yes	Hi	?	
Bruell	1964a 1964b	Mouse	wheel running	Crosses	Yes	Hi	?	
Bruell	1967	Mouse	wheel running	Diallel	Yes	Hi	?	
Oliverio, Castellano & Messeri	1972	Mouse	wheel running	Diallel + analysis	Yes	Hi	No	
Messeri, Oliverio & Bovet	1972	Mouse	wheel running	As above extended	Yes	Hi	No	
Smith Smith & Connor	1972 1974	Mouse, + wild	wheel running	½ diallel + analysis	Yes	Hi	No	

Table 7: B. Situational Activity

Reference Author(s)	Year	Species	Phenotype	Method	Dominance Present	Direc of expr.	Interaction	Remarks
Dawson (re-analysed Broadhurst & Jinks 1961)	1932	Mouse	runway activity	Crosses + back-crosses	Yes	Hi	Yes	j-type
Kerbusch	1974b	Mouse	diurnal activity e.g. 16-1800 e.g. 06-0800	Diallel + analysis	No Yes	- Lo	Yes Yes	
Kerbusch	1974a 1974b	Mouse	dark preference	Diallels + analyses	No Yes	- Hi	No No	
Royce, Holmes & Poley	1975	Mouse	"freezing" factor activity factor	Diallel + analysis	No No	- -	No No	
Henderson	1978	Mouse	infant activity	Simplified triple-test cross	Yes	Lo	No	

Table 7: C. Activity-modified

Reference Author(s)	Year	Species	Phenotype	Method	Dominance Present	Direc of expr.	Inter-action	Remarks
Henderson	1968	Mouse	conditioned suppression	Diallel + analysis	Yes	Hi	?	
			activity extinction		No	-	No	Develops after trial 9
Newell	1970	Mouse	activity	Crosses, backcrosses, diallel + analysis	No	-	No	
			shock elicited		No	-	Yes	
Connor & Winston	1972	Mouse	conditioned suppression	½ diallel + analysis	Yes	Hi	No	
			bar press rate		?	?	Yes	
			recovery rate		No	?	No	
Kerbusch	1974a 1974b	Mouse	shock escape learning	Diallel + analyses	Yes	Hi	No	
			runway		Yes	Hi	Yes	Develops after trial 3
			T maze		Yes	Hi	Yes	Develops after trial 4
Anisman	1976	Mouse	activity after shock	Diallel	No	-	?	
			after amphetamine		No	-	?	
					No	-	?	
			after scopolamine		weak	Lo	?	

Table 8: Genetic architectures of emotional responsivity. A: Open field

Reference Author(s)	Year	Species	Phenotype	Method	Dominance Present	Direc of expr.	Interaction	Remarks
Broadhurst	1960	Rat	Open-field defecation	Diallel + analyses	No		No	
			ambulation		Weak	Mid	No	
(re-analysed Broadhurst & Jinks	1966)		stability of defecation		Yes	Hi	No	"Advantageous"
			change in defecation		No	–	No	
			change in ambulation		Yes	Mid	No	Increases over days
(also Fulker	1972)		defecation	+ simplified triple-test cross	No		No	
			ambulation		No		No	
Fuller & Thompson (re-analysed Broadhurst & Jinks	1960 1961)	Mouse	Open-field ambulation	Crosses + backcrosses	Yes	Hi	Yes	j-type
Henderson	1967	Mouse	Open-field defecation	Diallels + analyses	Yes	Lo	No	
			ambulation		Weak	Lo	No	

Table 8.A (continued)

Reference Author(s)	Year	Species	Phenotype	Method	Dominance Present	Direc of expr.	Inter- action	Remarks
Bruell	1969	Mouse	Defecation	Diallel	Weak Weak	Hi Lo	? ?	for males for females
Newell & Yates	1969	Mouse	Emotionality factor after frust- ration	Diallel + analysis	No Yes	– ?	No ?	
Rose & Parsons	1970	Mouse	Open-field elimination exploration	½ diallel	Yes Yes	Lo Hi	? Yes	
Fulker, Wilcock & Broadhurst	1972	Rat	Combination low defecation high ambula- tion, avoid- ance	Diallel + analysis	Yes	Hi	?	
(partial re- analysis) Fulker	1972)	Rat	Avoidance 2-way intertrial crossings	Diallel + analysis, simplified triple-test cross	No No	– –	No No	

Table 8.A (continued)

Reference Author(s)	Year	Species	Phenotype	Method	Dominance Present	Direc of expr.	Inter-action	Remarks
Smith Smith & Connor	1972 1974	Mouse + wild	Open-field activity defecation wall seeking emergence	½ diallel + analysis	No No No Weak	– – – Hi	? ? ? ?	
Kerbusch	1974a	Mouse	Open-field ambulation home cage emergence	Diallels + analyses	Weak No	Mid –	Yes Yes	Other exploratory behaviors similar
Halcomb, Hegmann & DeFries (re-analysed Hewitt, Fulker & DeFries 1977)	1975	Mouse	Open-field defecation ambulation	Diallel + analysis	No No	– –	No No	
Goodrick	1976	Mouse	Emotionality defecation	Partial ½ diallel	Yes	Hi	?	
Borodin, Schüler & Belyaev	1976	Mouse	Open-field ambulation measures (various)	Diallel + analysis	Yes	Hi	?	

Table 8.A (continued)

Reference Author(s)	Year	Species	Phenotype	Method	Dominance Pre-sent	Direc of expr.	Inter-action	Remarks
(Belyaev, Schüler & Borodin	1977)		defecation		Weak	Lo	?	Correlates with re-productive fitness measure

74

Table 8: B. Exploration, Emergence and Descent

Reference Author(s)	Year	Species	Phenotype	Method	Dominance Present	Direc of expr.	Inter-action	Remarks
McClearn	1961	Mouse	Maze explora-ation	Crosses + backcrosses	Yes	Hi	?	
(re-analysed Newell	1970)				No	–	Yes	j-type
(also Jinks & Broadhurst	1974)				No	–	Yes	j-type
Bruell	1962	Mouse	Maze explor-ation	Crosses + backcrosses	Yes	Hi	?	
	1964b		pole descent		Weak	?	–	
			emergence		Weak	?	–	
Bruell	1964b	Mouse	Maze explor-ation	Crosses	Yes	Hi	?	
Bruell	1965	Mouse	Pole descent emergence	Crosses	Weak	?		
					Weak	?		
Newell	1969	Mouse	Exploration factor after frust-ration	Diallel + analysis	Yes	?	?	
					Yes	?	?	
Royce, Holmes & Poley	1975	Mouse	Acrophobia factor	Diallel + analysis	No	–		

Table 9: Genetic architectures of learning. A: Avoidance

Reference Author(s)	Year	Species	Phenotype	Method	Dominance Present	Direc of expr.	Inter-action	Remarks
Collins	1964a	Mouse	Avoidance extinction	Diallel	Yes	Hi	?	
Collins (re-analysed Wilcock 1969)	1964b	Mouse	Avoidance 2-way	Diallel + analysis	Yes	Hi	No	Major gene?
Stasik Stasik & Kidwell 1969	1970	Mouse	Escape learning	Diallel	Yes	?	?	Abolished by LSD
Owen	1970	Rat	Avoidance 1-way	½ diallel	Yes	Hi	No	
Rose & Parsons	1970	Mouse	Avoidance 2-way	½ diallel	Yes	Hi	Yes	
Wilcock & Fulker	1971	Rat	Avoidance 2-way	Diallels + analyses	Yes	Lo→Hi	?	Reverses after 15-20 trials
Royce, Yeudall & Poley	1971	Mouse	Avoidance	Diallels + analyses, crosses, backcrosses	Yes	Hi	Yes	

Table 9.A (continued)

Reference Author(s)	Year	Species	Phenotype	Method	Dominance Present	Direc of expr.	Inter- action	Remarks
Oliverio, Castellano & Messeri	1972	Mouse	Avoidance 2-way	Diallel + analysis	Yes	Hi	No	
Messeri, Oliverio & Bovet	1972	Mouse	Avqidance 2-way	As above extended	Yes	Hi	No	
Owen	1972	Rat	Avoidance 2-way intertrial crosses	½ diallel + analysis + simplified triple-test cross	Yes Yes Yes Yes	Lo→Hi Lo→Hi Lo Lo	Yes } Yes } Yes Yes	Reverses after 20 trials
Smith Smith & Connor	1972	Mouse + wild	Avoidance 2-way	½ diallel	No	–	?	
Holmes, Aksel & Royce	1974	Mouse	Avoidance	Diallels + analyses	Yes	Hi	Yes	Duplicate, especially males
Kerbusch	1974a 1974b	Mouse	Avoidance passive passive	Diallels + analyses	Weak Weak	Mid Mid	No Yes	

Table 9.A (continued)

Reference Author(s)	Year	Species	Phenotype	Method	Dominance Present	Direc of expr.	Inter-action	Remarks
Anisman	1975	Mouse	Avoidance 1-way 2-way passive (inhibitary avoidance)	Diallel Diallel Diallel	Yes Yes Weak	Yes Yes -	No ? ?	
Stavnes & Sprott	1975	Mouse	Avoidance jump up	Crosses + backcrosses	Yes	Hi	?	Major gene?
Hewitt & Fulker	1978	Rats, including wild	Avoidance learning 2-way	Triple-test cross	Yes	Lo→Hi	Yes	Duplicate genes: Reverses after 20 trials
Owen	1978	Rat	Avoidance 2-way	Triple-test cross	Yes	Lo→Hi	Yes	Duplicate genes: Reverses after 30 trials

Table 9: B. Maze and other learning

Reference Author(s)	Year	Species	Phenotype	Method	Dominance Present	Direc of expr.	Interaction	Remarks
Vicari (re-analysed Broadhurst & Jinks 1961)	1929	Mouse	Maze learning	Crosses	Yes	Hi	Yes	Increases with trials
Tryon (re-analysed Broadhurst & Jinks 1961)	1940	Rat	Maze learning	Crosses	Weak	Hi	?	
Winston	1964	Mouse	Maze learning	½ diallel	Weak	Hi	?	
Oliverio, Castellano & Messeri	1972	Mouse	Maze learning	Diallel + analysis	Yes	Hi	No	
Henderson	1972	Mouse	Maze learning	Diallel + analysis	No	–	Yes	
			reversal		Yes	Hi	?	
			Visual discriminations		Yes	Hi	No	
			improvement		Yes	Hi	Yes	
Hyde	1974	Mouse	Maze learning	Diallel	Weak	?	?	

Table 9: C. Detour Learning

| Reference Author(s) | Year | Species | Phenotype | Method | Dominance | | Inter-action | Remarks |
					Pre-sent	Direction of expression		
Scott & Fuller (partial re-analysis Broadhurst & Jinks 1961)	1965	Dog	Barrier test	Crosses	No	–	Yes	
Kiker, Siegel & Hinkelmann	1976	Quail	Detour response speed	Diallel	Yes	Hi	?	

Table 10: Genetic architectures of memory

Reference Author(s)	Year	Species	Phenotype	Method	Dominance		Inter-action	Remarks
					Present	Direction of expression		
Graves & Siegel	1968	Chicken	Imprinting	Diallels	Yes	Hi	?	
Henderson (re-analysed Fulker 1972)	1970a	Mouse	Alternation	Diallel + analysis	Yes	Hi	Yes	
				Triple-test cross	Yes	Hi	Yes	
Carran	1972	Mouse	Reversal learning	Diallel + analysis	No	-	No	
Heinze	1974	Rats	Ether amnesia	½ diallel	Yes	Hi	?	

Table 11: Genetic architectures of alcohol preference

Reference Author(s)	Year	Species	Phenotype	Method	Dominance Present	Direc of expre.	Inter- action	Remarks
McClearn & Rodgers (also Rodgers & McClearn 1962) (re-analysed Brewster	1961 1968)	Mouse Mouse	Alcohol pref- erence Alcohol pref- erence	Crosses + backcrosses Crosses + backcrosses	Yes No	Lo –	? No	
Fuller	1964	Mouse	Alcohol pref- erence	Partial diallel + analysis	Yes	?	Yes	
(partial re- analysis Brewster	1968)	Mouse	Alcohol pref- erence	½ diallel + analysis	Yes	Mid	–	
Fuller & Collins	1964	Mouse	Alcohol pref- erence	Crosses + backcrosses	Yes	Hi	Yes	
Brewster	1968 1969	Rat Rat	Alcohol pref- erence	Diallel + analysis	Yes	Ei	?	
Thomas	1969	Mouse	Alcohol pref- ernece	Crosses + backcrosses	Yes	?	?	

Table 11 (continued)

Reference Author(s)	Year	Species	Phenotype	Method	Dominance Present	Direc of expr.	Inter-action	Remarks
Eriksson	1971	Mouse	Alcohol preference	Crosses + backcrosses	Yes	Lo	No	
Whitney	1972	Mouse	Alcohol preference	Crosses + backcrosses	Yes	Lo	?	
Drewek	1978	Rat	Alcohol preference	Simplified triple-test cross	Yes	Lo	No	Males only

Table 12: Genetic architectures of audiogenic phenomena

Reference Author(s)	Year	Species	Phenotype	Method	Dominance Present	Direction of expression	Inter-action	Remarks
Romanova	1975	Rat	Audiogenic seizure	Diallel + analysis	Yes	Lo	No	Major gene?
Royce, Holmes & Poley	1975	Mouse	Audiogenic reactivity factor	Diallel + analysis	Yes	Hi	No	

Table 13: Genetic architectures of morphine effects

Reference Author(s)	Year	Species	Phenotype	Method	Dominance Present	Direction of expression	Interaction	Remarks
Eriksson & Kiianmaa	1971	Mouse	Morphine addiction	Crosses + back-crosses	Yes	Hi	Yes	Scalar problems
Castellano & Oliverio	1975	Mouse	Response to morphine activity analgesia	Crosses + back crosses	Yes	Hi	?	
					Weak	?	?	

REFERENCES

Angus, J. Changes in the behaviour of individual members of a Drosophila population maintained by random mating. Heredity, 1974a, 33, 89-93.

Angus, J. Genetic control of activity, preening, and the response to a shadow stimulus in Drosophila melanogaster. Behavior Genetics, 1974b, 4, 317-329.

Anisman, H. Effects of scopolamine and d-amphetamine on one-way, shuttle, and inhibitory avoidance: A diallel analysis in mice. Pharmacology, Biochemistry and Behavior, 1975, 3, 1037-1042.

Anisman, H. Effects of scopolamine and d-amphetamine on locomotor activity before and after shock: A diallel analysis in mice. Psychopharmacology, 1976, 48, 165-173.

Barnes, B. W., & Kearsey, M. J. Variation for metrical characters in Drosophila populations. Heredity, 1970, 25, 1-10.

Barnett, S. A., & Scott, S. G. Behavioural "vigour" in inbred and hybrid mice. Animal Behaviour, 1964, 12, 325-337.

Belyaev, D. K., Schüler, L., & Borodin, P. M. Problem'i genetiki stressa soobshchenie. III. Differentsial'noe vliyane stressa na plodovitost' myishei razn'ikh genotipov. [Problems of stress genetics: III. Differential effect of stress on the fertility of mice of different genotypes.] Genetika, 1977, 1, 52-58.

Bitterman, M. E. Phyletic differences in learning. American Psychologist, 1965, 20, 396-410.

Borodin, P. M., Schüler, L., & Belyaev, D. K. Problem'i genetiki stressa soobshchenie. I. Geneticheskii analiz povedeniya myishei v stressiruyushchei situatsisii. [Problems of stress genetics: I. Genetic analysis of mice behaviour in stress- ful situation.] Genetika, 1976, 12, 62-71.

Breese, E. L., & Mather, K. The organisation of polygenic activity within a chromosome in Drosophila: II. Viability. Heredity, 1960, 14, 375-399.

Brewster, D. J. Genetic analysis of ethanol preference in rats selected for emotional reactivity. Journal of Heredity, 1968, 5, 283-285.

Brewster, D. J. Ethanol preference in strains of rats selectively bred for behavioral characteristics. Journal of Genetic Psychology, 1969, 115, 217-227.

Broadhurst, P. L. Application of biometrical genetics to behaviour in rats. Nature, 1959, 184, 1517-1518.

Broadhurst, P. L. Experiments in psychogenetics: Applications of biometrical genetics to the inheritance of behaviour. In H.J. Eysenck (Ed.), Experiments in personality: (Vol. 1. Psychogenetics and psychopharmacology). London: Routledge and Kegan Paul, 1960.

Broadhurst, P. L. Experimental approaches to the evolution of behaviour. In J.M. Thoday & A.S. Parkes (Eds.), Genetics and environmental influences on behaviour. (Eugenics Society Symposia: Vol. 4). Edinburgh: Oliver & Boyd, 1968.

Broadhurst, P. L. Pharmacogenetics. In L. L. Iverson, S. D. Iverson, & S. H. Snyder (Eds.), Handbook of psycho-pharmacology, Vol. 7. New York: Plenum Press, 1977.

Broadhurst, P. L., & Jinks, J. L. Biometrical genetics and behavior: Re-analysis of published data. Psychological Bulletin, 1961, 58, 337-362.

Broadhurst, P. L., & Jinks, J. L. Stability and change in the inheritance of behaviour: A further analysis of statistics from a diallel cross. Proceedings of the Royal Society, Series B, 1966, 165, 450-472.

Broadhurst, P. L., & Jinks, J. L. What genetical architecture can tell us about the natural selection of behavioural traits. In J.H.F. van Abeelen, (Ed.), The genetics of behaviour. Amsterdam: North Holland Publishing Company, 1974.

Brody, E. G. Genetic basis of spontaneous activity in the albino rat. Comparative Psychology Monographs, 1942, 17, 1-24.

Bruell, J. H. Dominance and segregation in the inheritance of quantitative behavior in mice. In E. Bliss (Ed.), Roots of behavior. New York: Harper Bros., 1962.

Bruell, J. H. Heterotic inheritance of wheelrunning in mice. Journal of Comparative and Physiological Psychology, 1964a, 58, 159-163.

Bruell, J. H. Inheritance of behavioral and physiological characters of mice and the problem of heterosis. American Zoologist, 1964b, 4, 125-138.

Bruell, J. H.   Mode of inheritance of response time in mice.   Journal
of Comparative and Physiological Psychology, 1965, 60, 147-148

Bruell, J. H.   Behavioral heterosis.   In J. Hirsch (Ed.), Behavior-
genetic analysis.   New York: McGraw-Hill, 1967.

Bruell, J. H.   Genetics and adaptive significance of emotional
defecation in mice.   Annals of the New York Academy of Science,
1969, 159, 825-830.

Carran, A. B.   Biometrics of reversal learning in mice: II.
Diallel cross.   Journal of Comparative and Physiological
Psychology, 1972, 78, 466-470.

Castellano, C., & Oliverio, A.   A genetic analysis of morphine-
induced running and analgesia in the mouse.   Psychopharmacologia, 1975, 41, 197-200.

Chahal, G. S., & Jinks, J. L.   A general method of detecting the
additive, dominance and epistatic variation that inbred lines
can generate using a single tester.   Heredity, 1978, 40,
117-125.

Chung, C. S., Morton, N. E., & Yasuda, N.   Genetics of interracial
crosses.   In J. Brožek (Ed.), Biology of human variation.
Annals of the New York Academy of Science, 1966, 134, 666-687.

Collins, R. L.   Heterosis in avoidance-conditioning extinction in
twenty-five genotypes of mice.   American Psychologist, 1964a,
19, 520 (Abstract).

Collins, R. L.   Inheritance of avoidance conditioning in mice.
Science, 1964b, 143, 1188-1190.

Connor, J. L., & Winston, H.   Genetic analysis of conditioned
emotional responses in the mouse (Mus musculus L.).   Journal
of Comparative and Physiological Psychology, 1972, 81, 37-44.

Cook, W. T., Siegel, P. B., & Hinkelmann, K.   Genetic analyses of
male mating behaviour in chickens.   II.   Crosses among selected
and control lines.   Behavior Genetics, 1972, 2, 289-300.

Dawson, W. M.   Inheritance of wildness and tameness in mice.
Genetics, 1932, 17, 296-326.

Dewsbury, D. A.   A diallel cross analysis of genetic determinants
of copulatory behavior in rats.   Journal of Comparative and
Physiological Psychology, 1975, 88, 713-722.

Drewek, K. J. A psychopharmacogenetic investigation of alcohol
preference in selected strains of rats. Unpublished doctoral
dissertation, University of Birmingham, England, 1978.

Eriksson, K. Inheritance of behaviour towards alcohol in normal
and motivated choice situations in mice. Annales Zoologicae
Fennici, 1971, 8, 400-405.

Eriksson, K., & Kiianmaa, K. Genetic analysis of susceptibility to
morphine addiction in inbred mice. Annales Medicinae Experi-
mentalis et Biologiae, 1971, 49, 73-78.

Falconer, D. S. Introduction to quantitative genetics. Edinburgh:
Oliver & Boyd, 1960.

Festing, M. F. W. Water escape learning in mice. III. A diallel
study. Behavior Genetics, 1974, 4, 111-124.

Festing, M. F. W. Effects of marginal malnutrition on the breeding
performance of inbred and F_1-hybrid mice--A diallel study.
In Th. Antikatzides, S. Erichsen, & A. Spiegel (Eds.), The
laboratory animal in the study of reproduction, (6th ICLA
Symposium, Thessaloniki, 1975). Stuttgart: G. Fischer Verlag,
1976.

Friedmann, J. K. Genetics of sleep (Doctoral dissertation,
University of Florida, 1971). Dissertation Abstracts International, 1972, 32, 6028B-6029B. (University Microfilms No.
72-12, 469)

Fulker, D. W. Mating speed in male Drosophila melanogaster: A
psychogenetic analysis. Science, 1966, 153, 203-205.

Fulker, D. W. Applications of a simplified triple-test cross.
Behavior Genetics, 1972, 2, 185-198.

Fulker, D. W., Wilcock, J., & Broadhurst, P. L. Studies in genotype-environment interaction. I. Methodology and preliminary
multivariate analysis of a diallel cross of eight strains of
rat. Behavior Genetics, 1972, 2, 261-287.

Fuller, J. L. Measurement of alcohol preference in genetic experiments. Journal of Comparative and Physiological Psychology,
1964, 57, 85-88.

Fuller, J. L., & Collins, R. L. Ethanol consumption and preference
in mice: A genetic analysis. Annals of the New York Academy
of Science, 1972, 197, 42-48.

Fuller, J. L., & Thompson, W. R. Behavior genetics. New York: Wiley, 1960.

Goodrick, C. L. Mode of inheritance of emotionality in the mouse (Mus musculus): Sex differences and the effects of trials and illumination. Psychological Reports, 1976, 39, 247-256.

Goy, R. W., & Jakway, J. S. The inheritance of patterns of sexual behaviour in female guinea-pigs. Animal Behaviour, 1959, 7, 142-149.

Graves, H. B., & Siegel, P. B. Chick's response to an imprinting stimulus: Heterosis and evolution. Science, 1968, 160, 329-330.

Griffing, B. A generalised treatment of the use of diallel crosses in quantitative inheritance. Heredity, 1956, 10, 31-50.

Halcomb, R. A., Hegmann, J. P., & DeFries, J. C. Open-field behavior in mice: A diallel analysis of selected lines. Behavior Genetics, 1975, 5, 217-232.

Hamilton, W. D. The genetical evolution of social behaviour. I. Journal of Theoretical Biology, 1964, 7, 1-16.

Hamilton, W. D. The genetical evolution of social behaviour. II. Journal of Theoretical Biology, 1963, 7, 17-52.

Hayman, B. I. The analysis of variance of diallel crosses. Biometrics, 1954, 10, 235-244.

Hay, D. A. Genetical and maternal determinants of the activity and preening behaviour of Drosophila melanogaster reared in different environments. Heredity, 1972, 28, 311-336.

Heinze, W. J. Genotype influences on ether-induced retrograde amnesia in rats. Behavioral Biology, 1974, 11, 109-114.

Henderson, N. D. Prior treatment effects on open-field behaviour of mice--A genetic analysis. Animal Behaviour, 1967, 15, 364-376.

Henderson, N. D. Genetic analysis of acquisition and retention of conditioned fear in mice. Journal of Comparative and Physiological Psychology, 1968, 65, 325-329.

Henderson, N. D. A genetic analysis of spontaneous alternation in mice. Behavior Genetics, 1970a, 1, 125-132.

Henderson, N. D. Genetic influences on the behavior of mice can be obscured by laboratory rearing. Journal of Comparative and Physiological Psychology, 1970b, 72, 505-511.

Henderson, N. D. Relative effects of early rearing environment and genotype on discrimination learning in house mice. Journal of Comparative and Physiological Psychology, 1972, 79, 243-253.

Henderson, N. D. Genetic dominance for low activity in infant mice. Journal of Comparative and Physiological Psychology, 1978, 92, 118-125.

Hewitt, J. K., & Fulker, D. W. The genetic control of active avoidance learning in wild rats. Submitted to Science, 1978.

Hewitt, J. K., Fulker, D. W., & DeFries, J. C. Open-field behavior in mice: Generality of results from a diallel analysis of replicate selected lines. Behavior Genetics, 1977, 7, 441-446.

Holmes, T. M., Aksel, R., & Royce, J. R. Inheritance of avoidance behavior in Mus musculus. Behavior Genetics, 1974, 4, 357-372.

Hyde, J. S. Inheritance of learning ability in mice: A diallel-environmental analysis. Journal of Comparative and Physiological Psychology, 1974, 86, 116-123.

Jakway, J. S. The inheritance of patterns of mating behaviour in the male guinea-pig. Animal Behaviour, 1959, 7, 150-162.

Jinks, J. L. The analysis of continuous variation in a diallel cross of Nicotiana rustica varieties. Genetics, 1954, 39, 767-788.

Jinks, J. L., & Broadhurst, P. L. How to analyse the inheritance of behaviour in animals--the biometrical approach. In J. H. F. van Abeelen (Ed.), The genetics of behaviour. Amsterdam: North Holland Publishing Company, 1974.

Jinks, J. L., Perkins, J. M., & Breese, E. L. A general method of detecting additive, dominance and epistatic variation for metrical traits. II. Application to inbred lines. Heredity, 1969, 24, 45-57.

Kearsey, M. J., & Barnes, B. W. Variation for metrical characters in Drosophila populations II. Natural selection. Heredity, 1970, 25, 11-21.

Kearsey, M. J., & Jinks, J. L. A general method of detecting additive, dominance and epistatic variation for metrical traits. I. Theory. Heredity, 1968, 23, 403-409.

Kearsey, M. J., & Kojima, K. The genetic architecture of body weight and egg hatchability in Drosophila melanogaster. Genetics, 1967, 56, 23-37.

Kerbusch, J. M. L. A diallel study of exploratory behaviour and learning perfomances in mice. In J. H. F. van Abeelen (Ed.), The genetics of behaviour. Amsterdam: North Holland Publishing Company, 1974a.

Kerbusch, J. M. L. Genetic analysis of exploratory behaviour, simple learning behaviour and cerebral AChE and ChE activities in mice by means of the diallel method. (Doctoral dissertation, Catholic University of Nijmegan) Nijmegan: Schippers, 1974b.

Kessler, S. The genetics of Drosophila mating behavior. II. The genetic architecture of mating speed in Drosophila pseudo-obscura. Genetics, 1969, 62, 421-433.

Kiker, J. T., Siegel, P. B., & Hinkelmann, K. Genetic analysis of behaviors related to the solution of detour learning task Behavior Genetics, 1976, 6, 315-326.

Kuse, A. R., & DeFries, J. C. Social dominance and Darwinian fitness in laboratory mice: An alternative test. Behavioral Biology, 1976, 16, 113-116.

Lee, C. T. Genetic analyses of nest-building behavior in laboratory mice (Mus musculus). Behavior Genetics, 1973, 3, 247-256.

Lorenz, K. Vergleichende Bewegungsstudien an Anatiden. [Comparative studies of movement in Anatides.] Journal für Ornithologie (Suppl.), 1941, 89, 194-294.

Lynch, C. B., & Hegmann, J. P. Genetic differences influencing behavioral temperature regulation in small mammals. I. Nesting by Mus musculus. Behavior Genetics, 1972, 2, 43-53.

Manosevitz, M., & Lindzey, G. Genetics of hoarding: A biometrical analysis. Journal of Comparative and Physiological Psychology, 1967, 63, 142-144.

Mather, K. Polygenic inheritance and natural selection. Biological Reviews, 1943, 18, 32-64.

Mather, K. Genetical control of stability in development. Heredity, 1953, 7, 297-336.

Mather, K. Evolution in polygenic systems. Accademia Nazionale dei Lincei, 1960, 47, 131-152.

Mather, K. Variability and selection. Proceedings of the Royal Society, Series B, 1966, 164, 328-340.

Mather, K. Complementary and duplicate gene interactions in biometrical genetics. Heredity, 1967, 22, 97-103.

Mather, K. Genetical structure of populations. London: Chapman and Hall, 1973.

Mather, K., & Harrison, B. J. The manifold effect of selection. Heredity, 1949, 3, 1-52; 131-162.

Mather, K., & Jinks, J. L. Biometrical genetics: The study of continuous variation (2nd ed.). London: Chapman and Hall, 1971.

Mayr, E. Behavior and systematics. In A. Roe, & G. G. Simpson (Eds.), Behavior and evolution. New Haven: Yale University Press, 1958.

McGill, T. E. Genetic analysis of male sexual behavior. In G. Lindzey & D. D. Thiessen, (Eds.), Contributions to behavior-genetic analysis: The mouse as a prototype. New York: Appleton-Century-Crofts, 1970.

Messeri, P., Oliverio, A., & Bovet, D. Relations between avoidance and activity: A diallel study in mice. Behavioral Biology, 1972, 7, 733-742.

McClearn, G. E. Genotype and mouse activity. Journal of Comparative and Physiological Psychology, 1961, 54, 674-676.

McClearn, G. E., & Rodgers, D. A. Genetic factors in alcohol preference of laboratory mice. Journal of Comparative and Physiological Psychology, 1961, 54, 116-119.

Newell, T. G. Three biometrical genetic analyses of activity in the mouse. Journal of Comparative and Physiological Psychology, 1970, 70, 37-47.

Newell, T. G., & Yates, A. Personal communication, 1969.

Oliverio, A., Castellano, C., & Messeri, P. Genetic analysis of avoidance, maze, and wheelrunning behaviors in the mouse. Journal of Comparative and Physiological Psychology, 1972, 79, 459-473.

Owen, V. A. A 3 x 3 half-diallel cross to investigate the interaction of genotype with two methods of one-way avoidance
conditioning. Unpublished undergraduate honours thesis,
University of Birmingham, England, 1970.

Owen, V. A. The inheritance of two-way avoidance behaviour in
rats: An introduction to the triple-test cross. Unpublished
Master's thesis, University of Birmingham, England, 1972.

Owen, V. A. The genetic control of shuttle avoidance behaviour in
laboratory rats: A triple test-cross investigation.
Doctoral thesis to be submitted, University of Birmingham,
England, 1978.

Parsons, P. A. A diallel cross for mating speeds in Drosophila
melanogaster. Genetica, 1964, 35, 141-151.

Roberts, R. C. Some evolutionary implications of behavior.
Canadian Journal of Genetics and Cytology, 1967, 9, 419-435.

Rodgers, D. A., & McClearn, G. E. Alcohol preference of mice.
In E. L. Bliss (Ed.), Roots of behavior. New York: Harper
Bros., 1962.

Romanova, L. G. Geneticheskoe ieuchenie pov'ishennoi
chuvstyitel'nosti k evuku u kr'is. [Genetic studies of
susceptibility to audiogenic seizures in rats.] In
V. V. Ponomarenko (Ed.), Aktual'nye problem'i genetiki
povedeniya. [Current problems in genetics of behaviour.]
Leningrad: Izdatel'stobo "Nauka", 1975.

Rose, A., & Parsons, P. A. Behavioural studies in different
strains of mice and the problem of heterosis. Genetica, 1970,
41, 65-87.

Royce, J. R., Holmes, T. M., & Poley, W. Behavior genetic analysis
of mouse emotionality. III. The diallel analysis. Behavior
Genetics, 1975, 5, 351-372.

Royce, J. R., Yeudall, L. T., & Poley, W. Diallel analysis of
avoidance conditioning in inbred strains of mice. Journal of
Comparative and Physiological Psychology, 1971, 76, 353-358.

Schüler, L., & Borodin, P. M. Die Geschlechtsreife bei der
weiblichen Maus--Eine genetische Analyse mit Hilfe der
diallelen Kreuzung. [Puberty in the female mouse--a genetic
analysis by means of the diallel cross.] Zeitschrift für
Versuchstierkunde, 1976, 18, 296-302.

Scott, J. P., & Fuller, J. L. Genetics and the social behavior of the dog. Chicago: University of Chicago Press, 1965.

Smith, R. H. Wildness and domestication in Mus musculus: A behavioral analysis. Journal of Comparative and Physiological Psychology, 1972, 79, 22-29.

Smith, R. H., & Connor, J. L. The inheritance of behavioral wildness in house mice (Mus musculus L.). Animal Learning and Behavior, 1974, 2, 249-256.

Stasik, J. H. Inheritance of T-maze learning in mice. Journal of Comparative and Physiological Psychology, 1970, 71, 251-257.

Stasik, J. H., & Kidwell, J. F. Genotype, LSD and T-maze learning in mice. Nature, 1969, 224, 1224-1225.

Stavnes, K. L., & Sprott, R. L. Genetic analysis of active avoidance performance in mice. Psychological Reports, 1975, 36, 515-521.

Stone, C. P. Methodological resources for the experimental study of innate behavior as related to environmental factors. Psychological Review, 1947, 54, 342-347.

Thomas, K. Selection and avoidance of alcohol solutions by two strains of inbred mice and derived generations. Quarterly Journal of Studies on Alcohol, 1969, 30, 849-861.

Tryon, R. C. Genetic differences in maze-learning ability in rats. Yearbook of the National Society for the Study of Education, 1940, 39, 111-119.

Vale, J. R., & Ray, D. A diallel analysis of male mouse sex behavior. Behavior Genetics, 1972, 2, 199-209.

Vale, J. R., & Vale, C. A. Diallel analyses of water intake, body weight, and percent hemoconcentration in male mice. Behavior Genetics, 1973, 3, 187-192.

van Abeelen, J. H. F. Ethology and the genetic foundations of animal behavior. Paper prepared for the NATO Advanced Study Institute on Theoretical Advances in Behavior Genetics, Banff, Alberta, September - October, 1978.

van Oortmerssen, G. A., & Beardmore, J. A. An age factor affecting variance of a behavioural character in F_1 hybrids between inbred lines of the house mouse. Experientia, 1967, 23, 328-333.

Vesell, E. S. Genetic and environmental factors affecting hexo-
barbital metabolism in mice. Annals of the New York Academy
of Sciences, 1968, 151, 900-902

Vicari, E. M. Mode of inheritance of reaction-time and degrees of
learning in mice. Journal of Experimental Zoology, 1929, 54,
31-88.

Walton, P. D. The genetics of geotaxis in Drosophila melanogaster.
Canadian Journal of Genetics and Cytology, 1968, 10, 673-687.

Whitney, G. Relationship between alcohol preference and other
behaviors in laboratory mice. In O. A. Forsander &
K. Eriksson (Eds.), International Symposium Biological Aspects
of Alcohol Consumption, Helsinki, September 1971. The Finnish
Foundation for Alcohol Studies, 1972, 20, 151-161.

Wilcock, J. Gene action and behavior: An evaluation of major gene
pleiotropism. Psychological Bulletin, 1969, 72, 1-29.

Wilcock, J. Water-escape in weanling rats: A link between behaviour and biological fitness. Animal Behaviour, 1972, 20,
543-547.

Wilcock, J., & Bush, M. A. Heterosis for punishment-induced inhibition of drinking in laboratory rats. Life Sciences, 1972,
11, 403-412.

Wilcock, J., & Fulker, D. W. Avoidance learning in rats: Genetic
evidence for two distinct behavioral processes in the shuttlebox. Journal of Comparative and Physiological Psychology,
1973, 82, 247-253.

Wilson, E. O. Sociobiology: The new synthesis. Cambridge,
Mass.: Belknap Press, 1975.

Winston, H. D. Heterosis and learning in the mouse. Journal of
Comparative and Physiological Psychology, 1964, 57, 279-283.

COMMENT BY N. D. HENDERSON

It is particularly appropriate that Professor Broadhurst begin this conference with a broad survey of experimental research and related issues concerning the relationship of genetic architecture and evolution of behavior. In 1959-60 Broadhurst introduced biometrical genetic techniques to investigators of animal behavior. Judging from the considerable number of studies published from the mid 60s through the present that used these techniques, his efforts have obviously borne fruit. His tables demonstrate that not only have a large number of studies been carried out in a variety of behavioral domains, but that by and large the results of most of these studies are rather consistent despite a variety of minor flaws in design, genetic sampling, and measurement procedures.

Later in the conference several papers will be exploring one or more of the issues raised by Broadhurst, and I believe that explanations for some of the few anomalies found in his tables will be forthcoming. This morning I would like to comment on a few points he has raised with respect to understanding the forces of natural selection through the study of gene action governing a behavioral characteristic.

My first point concerns the relationship of additive and dominance variance to directional and stabilizing selection. It seems to me that we still have a rather large blind spot with respect to interpreting the results of many genetic experiments in terms of natural selection. These are situations in which little or no directional dominance is observed, and most genetic variation is of the additive kind. This genetic architecture may be indicative of prior stabilizing selection, but it will also occur for "biologically neutral" characters, having little direct relationship to fitness components. There are probably no characters truly biologically neutral, but many behavioral measures, particularly those derived by experimental psychologists not always sensitive to the lack of correspondence between an animal's normal behavioral repertoire and the responses they require in the laboratory, may be only weakly related to fitness components through complex biological and behavioral chains.

I suspect there are several clues which might help us to determine if we are dealing with a character only weakly related to fitness or one strongly related to fitness which is under stabilizing selection. I believe the latter is more likely to be the case if: (1) a large degree of bidirectional dominance and epistasis is present; (2) intermediate scoring strains are those showing the most dominance; (3) there is considerably more between- and within-family variance among inbred than among F_1

hybrid subjects; (4) linkage exists in a repulsion phase. Unfortunately, our current data base is not very substantial on this point.

Professor Broadhurst reminds us that biometrical genetic methods hold the possibility of even helping us determine whether selection pressures on a character have been steadily exerted for a long period of time (resulting in duplicate gene interaction), or whether selection has been fairly recent and especially heavy, as in the case of artificial selection (resulting in complementary gene interaction). In theory this is true, but two practical issues face investigators doing behavioral research with mammals. First, selection pressures are likely to vary considerably over time and are particularly likely to change during domestication. Selection pressures may be steadily exerted on a particular character in a wild population, leading to duplicate gene interaction, but upon domestication, considerably increased selection pressure may work on the character for a short period of time, which should result in complementary interaction. In such circumstances, it is difficult to speculate what the resulting genetic architecture for the trait would look like. A second, more practical, issue involves the ability to detect subtle duplicate or complementary gene interaction effects. Without extensive sampling of genotypes, careful scaling, and a powerful genetic design, the specific nature of an epistatic interaction is difficult to detect.

I am particularly pleased that Professor Broadhurst chose to review the experimental evidence concerning bristle number in drosophila which relate to Mather's formulations. We should all remember that gathering this evidence required three stages:

(1) Determining the genetic architecture through a breeding study. In the case of bristle number the data indicated largely additive genetic variance with little directional dominance.

(2) Determining whether the intermediate phenotypic expression detected has risen as a result of selection by carrying out an experiment designed to mimic natural selection. The results indicated that flies having intermediate bristle numbers had the greater viability.

(3) Determining the relationship between viability and bristle number under varying environments. The advantages of intermediate bristle numbers were greatest under more severe competition.

Together these three steps provide a model for genetic research concerned with evolutionary processes. Unfortunately, there is a considerable difference in the time and resources required to

carry out such studies with drosophila and simple behaviors or
morphological characters and carrying out studies with laboratory
mammals and complex behavioral phenotypes. Hopefully this will
not prevent at least some work of the latter type being carried
out following this general model. On the whole, however, I'm
afraid that much of this area of behavior genetics will have to
be done using rapidly reproducing insect species.

Several other issues and examples presented by Broadhurst
mesh nicely with points to be brought up later in this meeting,
particularly his discussion of GE interactions and his concern
that our reliance on heritability estimates may be misplaced.

Finally, I would like to warn readers that, although a great
deal of consistency appears to exist among the studies tabulated
by Broadhurst, a close look at the original reports will reveal
that these data are not as "clean" as one might like. This should
hardly be surprising for behavioral research and perhaps we should
be pleased that at least some consistent patterns have emerged.
On the other hand, the animal research in this field has raised a
number of questions concerning methods and assumptions in behavior
genetics and evolution. Hopefully, many of these issues will be
discussed during this conference

COMMENT BY J. H. F. van ABEELEN

In his interesting discussion of natural selection and the
genetic architecture of behavioral phenotypes, Broadhurst seems
to agree with the conclusion arrived at by Angus (1974b) that the
directional dominance for high level of preening in Drosophila,
observed before stimulation, indicates a history of directional
selection with regard to this behavior. This is a surprising
conclusion. In terms of fitness, one would predict moderate
levels to be most advantageous: A low level of preening will be
maladaptive in view of its function in cleaning and, possibly,
communication, whereas a high preening level will be maladaptive
because of predation. One would therefore expect to find indications of a history of stabilizing selection rather than of directional selection. Moreover, Hay (1972) found either no dominance
or dominance for low level of preening in Drosophila. He used
mechanical stimulation in his experiments, though (see also
Angus, 1974b).

COMMENT BY K. IMMELMANN

The first part of Dr. Broadhurst's paper provides an excellent example of the amount of relevant information about the genetics and evolution of behaviour which can be obtained from studying one single species, in this case the fruit-fly (Drosophila melanogaster).

In the second part he gives a critical discussion of the rather different situation with regard to the study of behaviour genetics of vertebrates in which many studies have been carried out with the rat, mouse, or chicken. Quite expectedly such studies have frequently yielded different and often contradictory results. The reason for this becomes apparent by looking at the relevant tables which have been compiled by Dr. Broadhurst--the research involves the use of small and often undetermined samples.

Unfortunately this also occurs in my own field of research, the study of imprinting. Many conclusions about sensitive phases or about the degree of stability of imprinting have been drawn from studies with small numbers of individuals and have afterwards been refuted and replaced by other statements based on new studies that have used slightly different methods and slightly different animals, again in small numbers. Considering the large amount of individual variation which is characteristic of imprinting (see my own chapter, this volume), the value of some of these conclusions and statements remains unknown. The same probably applies to other studies on learning in animals. Dr. Broadhurst's critical commentary, therefore, is most welcome.

COMMENT BY D. A. HAY

Professor Broadhurst is to be congratulated on his synthesis of an enormous range of the literature; a contribution which should be very useful to future investigators. For example, I hope that someone will take the time to add to his tables the details of directional dominance in genotype-environment interactions. While it has sometimes been found that dominance is for low variability on every environmental measure, from micro-environmental effects to major treatment effects (Hay, 1973), Fuller and Thompson (1978, p. 79) point out this is not always the case.

There are two limitations I can see, however, to Professor Broadhurst's views on the relationship between genetic architecture and the evolution of behaviour, and these I shall illustrate from work on nest-building behaviour. I was relieved to see from Table 4 that Van Oortmerssen reports no dominance for one aspect of this

behaviour, paper-fraying, since this is one of the few cases where
stabilizing selection has been demonstrated and not just inferred.
Van Oortmerssen (1970) reported low fertility in both high and low
'paper frayers'. This leads to my first query, the specificity
of the behaviours we study and the limited range of environments
in which they are studied. One might have anticipated that nest-
building, or at least some aspect of maternal care, would have a
selective advantage and would therefore show directional dominance.
While paper-fraying is important in making a good spherical nest,
the absence of dominance compared with the rest of Table 4 makes
it clear that we must specify precisely which measure of nest-
building we refer to if we are to talk about directional or stabilising selection for this trait. It is also obvious that the
environmental conditions are vital--good nest-building may be irrelevant in the normal, warm laboratory whereas Barnett and his
students have shown things may be very different at -3°C.

While this first issue is a general problem in all behavioural
research, the second is more serious and more specific to the
genetic architecture argument. This argument assumes that there
is a common set of evolutionary pressures on, say, all the strains
in a diallel cross. However (to refer again to Van Oortmerssen,
1970), his suggestion, backed up by fairly convincing data of the
hole- and surface-dwelling origins of different mouse strains,
would argue both against the concept of a general evolutionary
strategy in nest-building and against the study of hybrids where
the co-adapted complexes of behaviour would be broken down. While
quibbles can be raised over some of Van Oortmerssen's conclusions,
the points still create valid objections to the immediate inference
of evolutionary pressures based on genetic architecture.

References

Angus, J. Genetic control of activity, preening, and the response
    to a shadow stimulus in Drosophila melanogaster. Behavior
    Genetics, 1974b, 4, 317-329.
Fuller, J. L., & Thompson, W. R. Foundations of behaviour genetics.
    St. Louis: Mosby, 1978.
Hay, D. A. Genetical and maternal determinants of the activity and
    preening behaviour of Drosophila melanogaster reared in dif-
    ferent environments. Heredity, 1972, 28, 311-336.
Hay, D. A. Genotype-environmental interaction in the activity and
    preening of Drosophila melanogaster. Theoretical and Applied
    Genetics, 1973, 43, 291-297.
Van Oortmerssen, G. A. Biological significance, genetics and evo-
    lutionary origin of variability in behaviour within and be-
    tween inbred strains of mice: A behaviour genetic study.
    Behaviour, 1970, 38, 1-92.

ETHOLOGY AND THE GENETIC FOUNDATIONS OF ANIMAL BEHAVIOR

J.H.F. van Abeelen

Department of Zoology, University of Nijmegen,
Nijmegen, The Netherlands

INTRODUCTION

This chapter discusses some methodological problems pertinent to
the genetic analysis of behavior, it points to the relevance of
ethological concepts and accomplishments to the field of research
that is called Behavior Genetics, and, conversely, it indicates
some ways in which ethological work may benefit from behavior-
genetic studies.

THE NATURALISTIC APPROACH

As its students put it, ethology is the objectivistic, biological
study of behavior. It is carried out either in the field under
natural circumstances or in the laboratory under semi-natural
conditions and its first purpose is to obtain a total picture of
the behavior of organisms by using the technique of direct
observation of species-specific behavior patterns. Ethograms are
then constructed. In this and in other respects, European
ethology has differed greatly from North-American comparative
psychology, which has occupied itself with learning performances
in a few species under controlled but impoverished testing
conditions. Integration of the two approaches has progressed to a
certain extent however, particularly since Hinde's book of 1966.

INNATE BEHAVIORAL DIFFERENCES

In the early times of ethology the emphasis rested on the innateness of behavior or, rather, of the behavioral differences between

species. It is characteristic of behaviors that have been called innate that they are executed more or less uniformly by the members of a particular species. This notion of innateness is embodied in the concept of *Erbkoordination*, which means inherited motor co-ordinations. This would seem to imply that the fixed patterns of acts and postures are in some way genetically encoded in the physical substrata of behavior and that they are entirely or largely independent of experience. Stated otherwise, they show developmental stability, that is, their development is channeled along restricted pathways through the programmed construction of a nervous system. It is noteworthy, however, that a *pur sang* ethologist like Eibl-Eibesfeldt (1963), in his work on various behaviors in rats and squirrels, demonstrated the importance of previous experiences and practice for the sequence and orientation of the behavioral components involved. Imprinting is another example of experiential factors influencing later behavior.

The well-known heredity-environment controversy will not be discussed in the present paper. The distinction between innate and acquired behavior, as it was formulated, is devoid of meaning. The point has been dealt with by Hebb (1953), Lehrman (1953), Verplanck (1955), Anastasi (1958), Hirsch (1967; p.419), and, more recently,by Wilson (1975, p.26). It is realized that behavior is a phenotype, showing variability, and it is now generally accepted that the individual differences in behavior result from variation in genetic factors, variation in environmental factors, and their covariation and interaction.

STEREOTYPED BEHAVIOR

There is no denying, however, that there exist behaviors which are difficult to modify. They convey the impression of being rigidly encoded in the brain, as can be seen, for example, from the way in which Dilger's (1962) F_1 hybrid parrots (*Agapornis* spec.) carried their nest-material to the nest-site. A similar rigidity can be observed in the components of the "language" of foraging honeybees; even "dialects" can be discerned in the round-, sickle-, and waggle dances of different races and hybrids (von Frisch, 1962). Not only insects or birds, but also mammals may show all different kinds of stereotyped acts; note for example the very characteristic way of face cleaning, a component of self-directed grooming, in rodents (Northup, 1977).

CAUSATION

Brown (1969) defines instinct as "the collection of mechanisms through which the effects of evolution on behavior are mediated". Defined in such a way, the use of the concept of instinct seems acceptable and legitimate. It covers both aspects - the ontogenetic and the phylogenetic - of the question of the causation of behavior and of behavioral differences which, in fact, has always been the central theme in ethology.

The term causation can thus be used in two senses: that of mechanism (proximate causation) and that of evolution (ultimate causation). Firstly, behavior depends on the development, structure, and chemistry of the nervous system, the blood circulation, endocrinological factors, the perceptual capabilities of the sense organs, and the motor functions of the muscles. All these physiological mechanisms are subject to the action of the genetic information contained in the DNA and to influences from the environment during ontogeny. One might also call this the phenogenetic aspect of causation and I shall return to it presently. Secondly, the behavior of organisms has its evolutionary roots. To understand its causation, it is necessary to trace the origins of the genetic content which controls the specific properties of the physical substrata of behavior.

CHOICE OF PHENOTYPES

It is unfortunate that ethology has to a large degree neglected the actual genetic analysis of behavior. In spite of this consideration, this field of investigation can claim great merits and behavior genetics can profit from them. Ethology has provided most valuable methods of observation and experimentation, and concepts such as: key stimuli, social releasers, conflict behavior, displacement activities and other derived behaviors, and ritualization, with their social, ecological, and evolutionary implications (see Baerends, 1975). It is the present author's opinion that in future work behavior genetics should direct more efforts towards the analysis of the genetic underpinnings of the specific rigid behavior patterns - rigid in the sense that they are difficult to modify - and should show perhaps a little less preoccupation with the more global behavioral categories such as emotionality, activity level, or learning ability. One might observe that "learning" seems declining now as the organizing idea of behavioral science. We should not, of course, disregard the fact that learning abilities are also products of evolution and are dependent on - and limited by - genetic programming.

The rigid, stereotyped behavior patterns seem to represent the "appropriate" or "good" behavioral phenotypes, as Vale (1973) calls them, but he regards them as relatively rare. However, to mention only one possibility, it would seem very worthwhile and feasible to subject the behavioral components of von Frisch's honeybees to more detailed genetic analysis.

BEHAVIOR GENETICS AT THE POPULATION LEVEL

Mutation, selection, breeding structure, migration, and genetic drift determine the genetic composition of a population and this, in turn, determines the behavior of its individual members. Conversely, the behavior of the organisms, which interact with changing environmental conditions, affects, by virtue of the adaptive value of the underlying genes, the frequency distribution of alleles in the gene pool of the population. These two problems are, of course, not completely distinct but interrelated (Haldane, 1960). Behavioral evolution can be very rapid; examples of this are given by Wilson (1975; p.145).

In investigating behavior at the population level, the naturalistic methods of ethology offer rich opportunities for studying the processes which in the course of evolution have led to phenotypic differences in behavior within and between species and for studying the role of behavior in directing evolution. Evidently, these opportunities have not yet been fully exploited. An answer to these problems requires an understanding of the function (selective advantage) of the behavior in the animal's natural surroundings.

COMPARATIVE AND HYBRIDIZATION STUDIES

In the comparative method, behavioral similarities and differences between existing related species are studied and explained in terms of phylogeny. Until now, this approach has, by itself, thrown but little light on the genetic foundation of behavior patterns specific for species or races. Although crossing experiments with related species are often difficult to carry out, they are by no means impossible, as appears from the work on mating behavior of different species of swordtails (*Xiphophorus* spec.) by Clark, Aronson, and Gordon (1954) and Franck (1974) and from work on various behaviors in two cricket (*Gryllus*) species by von Hörmann-Heck (1957). Both polygenic and monogenic control of traits has been detected.

Within the wild-caught groups to be studied, mutations are rare occurrences but sometimes behavioral variants can be discovered if one searches for them, offering excellent prospects for research. For example, when investigating and crossbreeding four populations of three-spined sticklebacks (*Gasterosteus aculeatus* L.), Sevenster and 't Hart (1974) obtained evidence for unifactorial control of a particular component of nestbuilding, a characteristic which differentiates the races.

BIOMETRICAL APPROACHES

In connection with the foregoing, it should be pointed out that considerably more sophisticated methods are now available for the genetic analysis of such behavioral variables. These are the bio-metrical genetic techniques described by Falconer (1960) and Mather and Jinks (1971); their applicability to behavioral characteristics has been made clear, for instance in recent publications by McClearn and DeFries (1973) and Broadhurst and Jinks (1974). Within the framework of biometrical methodology, monogenic control of behavioral or other variables may be studied by attempting to isolate responsible polygenes through appropriate crossing and selection techniques. In my own work on the exploratory component "rearing" in house mice, which is a typical fixed action pattern, a single locus affecting rearing frequency in a novel environment could be identified (van Abeelen, 1975). Such an isolation of individual members of a polygenic system controlling a metrical behavioral trait goes beyond what, sixteen years ago, Broadhurst and Jinks (1963) conceived as possible.

As Fulker (1972) and Broadhurst and Jinks (1974) suggest, another biometrical approach, the triple-test cross method, might prove very fruitful. It involves the mating of a single animal, that may have been captured in the field and may be a non-inbred one, to three laboratory tester stocks, that is, to two different inbred strains and their F_1 hybrid, and the observation of the behavioral phenotypes of the offspring thus produced. We do not need interspecific hybrids in these approaches; intraspecific crossings would be sufficient. Important advances may be hoped for if the biometrical genetic techniques were applied to the behavior patterns described in the ethologists' earlier attempts to reconstruct evolutionary history.

ETHOLOGICAL BARRIERS

A case in point is the study of ethological isolating mechanisms. These are behavioral phenomena such as mating preferences or habitat preferences which can lead to the avoidance of hybridization and hence to the separation of gene pools. With regard to this, much work has been done in *Drosophila* by Spieth (1951), Manning (1967), and Parsons (1973), to mention but a few.

Of the utmost importance in the isolating processes are those behavior patterns that are used in communication between animals (Scott, 1976). These signal movements, called ritualized displays and presumed to originate from ambivalent behaviors, displacement activities, and other conflict behaviors, have been amply documented in many species (see Brown, 1975, chapters 13-19, and Wilson, 1975, chapter 8, for surveys), and many of them would seem quite amenable to genetic analysis. Apart from differences in communicative behavior, differences in seasonal mating cycles can also be a cause of reproductive isolation (Tauber, Tauber, and Nechols, 1977).

AGGRESSIVE BEHAVIOR AND SPACING

Another aspect of behavioral evolution that can be studied at the population level is social spacing, a phenomenon in which behavioral characters are clearly involved. It is adaptive to have population density kept within limits set by the availability of food, cover, nesting sites, etc. Agonistic social interactions may, through this, contribute to the perpetuation of the species' gene pool.

Particularly interesting in respect of social spacing are mice and other rodents which, under natural conditions, tend to live in small, relatively closed groups: the demes. Thiessen's chapter in this volume contains an extensive discussion on this subject. Although one advantage of using inbred mouse strains for investigating this problem is their replicability (see also Gould, 1974), a drawback is that we do not have much information about the natural environmental conditions under which the ancestors of our inbreds were living in the past. It has been found, however, that in inbreds the dominance order of males can account for over 90 percent of the variation in male reproductive success (DeFries and McClearn, 1970). In their work on the ecological genetics of aggressive behavior in house mice, Busser, Zweep, and Van Oortmerssen (1974) distinguish, on the basis of their attack latencies, two types of males among laboratory mice as well as feral mice: tolerant ones and aggressive ones showing differential fertility which depends on population density and spacing. Genetic analysis of such types would seem to be very worthwhile.

PHENOGENETICS

The developmental and physiological genetics of behavior is concerned with proximate causation, that is, with the action of genes upon regulatory mechanisms at the biochemical and physiological levels during ontogeny. Important steps on the road to the elucidation of the primary effects of mutant genes on neuronal functions have recently been taken by Hotta and Benzer (1972) and Homyk (1977), Brenner (1973), and Bentley (1975), using, respectively, the fruit fly *Drosophila*, the nematode *Caenorhabditis*, and the cricket *Teleogryllus*. Chemical induction of mutations altering behavior has been achieved in *Drosophila* (*e.g.* von Schilcher, 1977). The study of the developmental aspects in genetic mosaics may open interesting perspectives for other species as well, for instance in mice. Chimaeric, also called "allophenic" mice (Markert and Ursprung, 1971, p.158; Mintz, 1971; Mintz and Illmensee, 1975) may provide valuable experimental material for these purposes.

SINGLE-GENE STUDIES

A gene usually has more than one phenotypic effect. Guide lines for investigations into the nature of the intermediate pathways between genotype and behavior may be offered by the method of gene substitution, in which the behavioral effects of single "major" genes are traced. This approach, that has been strongly advocated by Thiessen (Thiessen, Owen, and Whitsett, 1970), has been criticized by Wilcock (1969) who dismisses the results of much work along these lines as cases of what he calls trivial pleiotropy. It is the present author's opinion, however, that this is an over-critical position; the gene-substitution method does not become less valuable just because no great intellectual effort is required to explain a number of the behavioral consequences of these single genes. It still seems to be worthwhile to analyze, for example, pigmentary mutations, to look for accompanying changes in as many items of the ethogram as is practicable, and to look for changes in the underlying perceptual processes, central co-ordination and motivation, and motor functions.

NEUROPHYSIOLOGICAL CORRELATES

To make phenogenetic sense of the detection of the behavioral effects of "major" or "minor" genes, the physical correlates must be examined. Firstly, the elements of the behavioral repertoire may be manipulated indirectly through different kinds of breeding schemes and the concomitant changes in neurotransmitter levels, enzyme activities, and electroencephalographic patterns can be observed. But, secondly, these behaviors can also be affected more directly by lesioning (see Donovick, Burright, Fuller, and Branson, 1975; Oliverio, Castellano, and Messeri, 1973), by electrical stimulation, or by drug administration (see van Abeelen, 1974; Green and Meier, 1965), preferably under (semi-)natural conditions. The latter types of neuro-ethological experimentation should thus always utilize animals of different genotypes to take into account or, better still, control the genetic variable (see also Isaacson and McClearn, 1978). Unfortunately, research along these lines is still rare.

SUMMARY AND CONCLUSIONS

The main points of this theoretical-methodological chapter
concern matters of research strategy:
1. In my view, more attention could be paid by behavior-
geneticists to behaviors that are important to the animal under
natural conditions, looking at as many elements of the ethogram
as is feasible. Often, developmentally stable, rigid patterns
would then be chosen as the phenotypes to study.
2. Doing this, attempts should be made to analyze both the
ultimate, phylogenetic causes and the proximate, phenogenetic
causes of the behaviors chosen.
3. As far as their evolutionary history is concerned, analysis of
genetic architecture by means of biometrical-genetic techniques
seems most appropriate and useful. In many cases one shall need
as tools controlled genotypes, obtainable by inbreeding and/or
selection.
4. As for the ontogenetic factors and neurophysiological
mechanisms that may be regulated by genes, diverse manipulative
and measuring techniques are available which could also be applied
in situations that mimic natural environments. In the framework
of investigations into single-gene effects upon behavior, the use
of chimaeric organisms may be singled out for mention.

   In the opening sentence I called Behavior Genetics a field of
research, avoiding the use of the term discipline. Whether or not
behavior genetics should be considered as a distinct discipline
seems a rather immaterial question. As a field of investigation it
has no sharp boundaries, but it has a purpose of its own, namely
the study of the genetic correlates of behavior in both an
evolutionary and a gene-physiological sense.

ACKNOWLEDGEMENT

I wish to thank Mrs Marianne van Bakelen-Suurmeijer for typing the
manuscript.

REFERENCES

Abeelen, J.H.F. van Genotype and the cholinergic control of
     exploratory behavior in mice. In J.H.F. van Abeelen (Ed.),
     The genetics of behaviour. Amsterdam: North-Holland; New
     York: American Elsevier, 1974, pp.347-374.

Abeelen, J.H.F. van Genetic analysis of behavioral reponses to
     novelty in mice. Nature, 1975, 254, 239-241.

Anastasi, A. Heredity, environment and the question "how"?
Psychological Review, 1958, 65, 197-208.

Baerends, G.P. An evaluation of the conflict hypothesis as an
explanatory principle for the evolution of displays. In
G. Baerends, C. Beer, & A. Manning (Eds.), Function and
evolution in behaviour. Essays in honour of Professor Niko
Tinbergen, F.R.S. London: Oxford University Press, 1975,
pp.187-227.

Bentley, D. Single gene cricket mutations: Effects on behavior,
sensilla, sensory neurons, and identified interneurons.
Science, 1975, 187, 760-764.

Brenner, S. The genetics of behavior. Advances in Molecular
Genetics, 1973, 29, 269-271.

Broadhurst, P.L., & Jinks, J.L. The inheritance of mammalian
behavior re-examined. Journal of Heredity, 1963, 54, 170-176.

Broadhurst, P.L., & Jinks, J.L. What genetical architecture can
tell us about the natural selection of behavioural traits.
In J.H.F. van Abeelen (Ed.), The genetics of behaviour.
Amsterdam: North-Holland; New York: American Elsevier,
1974, pp.43-63.

Brown, J.L. Neuro-ethological approaches to the study of
emotional behavior: Stereotypy and variability. Annals of
the New York Academy of Sciences, 1969, 159 (3), 1084-1095.

Brown, J.L. The evolution of behavior. New York: Norton, 1975.

Busser, J., Zweep, A., & Oortmerssen, G.A. van Variability in the
aggressive behaviour of Mus musculus domesticus, its possible
role in population structure. In J.H.F. van Abeelen (Ed.),
The genetics of behaviour. Amsterdam: North-Holland; New
York: American Elsevier, 1974, pp.185-199.

Clark, E., Aronson, L.R., & Gordon, M. Mating behavior patterns
in two sympatric species of xiphophorin fishes; their
inheritance and significance in sexual isolation. Bulletin of
the American Museum of Natural History at New York, 1954, 103,
135-226.

DeFries, J.C., & McClearn, G.E. Social dominance and darwinian
fitness in the laboratory mouse. American Naturalist, 1970,
104, 408-411.

Dilger, W.C. The behavior of lovebirds. Scientific American,
1962, 206, 88-98.

Donovick, P.J., Burright, R.G., Fuller, J.L., & Branson, P.R. Septal lesions and behavior: Effects of presurgical rearing and strain of mouse. Journal of Comparative and Physiological Psychology, 1975, 89, 859-867.

Eibl-Eibesfeldt, I. Angeborenes und Erworbenes im Verhalten einiger Säuger. Zeitschrift für Tierpsychologie, 1963, 20, 705-754.

Falconer, D.S. Introduction to quantitative genetics. New York: Ronald Press Cy, 1960.

Franck, D. The genetic basis of evolutionary changes in behaviour patterns. In J.H.F. van Abeelen (Ed.), The genetics of behaviour. Amsterdam: North-Holland; New York: American Elsevier, 1974, pp.119-140.

Frisch, K. von Dialects in the language of the bees. Scientific American, 1962, 207, 78-87.

Fulker, D.W. Applications of a simplified triple-test cross. Behavior Genetics, 1972, 2, 185-198.

Gould, J.L. Genetics and molecular ethology. Zeitschrift für Tierpsychologie, 1974, 36, 267-292.

Green, E.L., & Meier, H. Use of laboratory animals for the analysis of genetic influences upon drug toxicity. Annals of the New York Academy of Sciences, 1965, 123, 295-304.

Haldane, J.B.S. Mind in evolution. Zoologische Jahrbücher, 1960, 88, 117-124.

Hebb, D.O. Heredity and environment in mammalian behavior. British Journal of Animal Behaviour, 1953, 1, 43-47.

Hinde, R.A. Animal behaviour. A synthesis of ethology and comparative psychology. New York: McGraw-Hill, 1966.

Hirsch, J. Behavior-genetic analysis. In J. Hirsch (Ed.), Behavior-genetic analysis. New York: McGraw-Hill, 1967, pp.416-435.

Homyk, T., Jr. Behavioral mutants of Drosophila melanogaster. II. Behavioral analysis and focus mapping. Genetics, 1977, 87, 105-128.

Hörmann-Heck, S. von Untersuchungen über den Erbgang einiger Verhaltensweisen bei Grillenbastarden (Gryllus campestris L. ∿ Gryllus bimaculatus De Geer). Zeitschrift für

Tierpsychologie, 1957, 14, 137-183.

Hotta, Y., & Benzer, S. Mapping of behaviour in *Drosophila* mosaics. Nature, 1972, 240, 527-535.

Isaacson, R.L., & McClearn, G.E. The influence of brain damage on locomotor behavior of mice selectively bred for high or low activity in the open field. Brain Research, 1978, 150, 559-567.

Lehrman, D.S. A critique of K. Lorenz's theory of instinctive behavior. Quarterly Review of Biology, 1953, 28, 337-363.

Manning, A. Genes and the evolution of insect behavior. In J. Hirsch (Ed.), Behavior-genetic analysis. New York: McGraw-Hill, 1967, pp.44-60.

Markert, C.L., & Ursprung, H. Developmental genetics. Englewood Cliffs, N.J.: Prentice-Hall, 1971.

Mather, K., & Jinks, J.L. Biometrical genetics. The study of continuous variation (2nd ed.). London: Chapman and Hall, 1971.

McClearn, G.E., & DeFries, J.C. Introduction to behavioral genetics. San Francisco: Freeman, 1973.

Mintz, B. Genetic mosaicism in vivo: Development and disease in allophenic mice. Federation Proceedings, 1971, 30, 935-943.

Mintz, B., & Illmensee, K. Normal genetically mosaic mice produced from malignant teratocarcinoma cells. Proceedings of the National Academy of Sciences of the USA, 1975, 72, 3585-3589.

Northup, L.T. Temporal patterning of grooming in three lines of mice: Some factors influencing control levels of a complex behaviour. Behaviour, 1977, 61, 1-25.

Oliverio, A., Castellano, C., & Messeri, P. Genotype-dependent effects of septal lesions on different types of learning in the mouse. Journal of Comparative and Physiological Psychology, 1973, 82, 240-246.

Parsons, P.A. Behavioural and ecological genetics. A study in *Drosophila*. Oxford: Clarendon Press, 1973.

Schilcher, F. von A mutation which changes courtship song in *Drosophila melanogaster*. Behavior Genetics, 1977, 7, 251-259.

Scott, J.P. Genetic variation and the evolution of communication. In M.E. Hahn & E.C. Simmel (Eds.), Communicative behavior and evolution. New York: Academic Press, 1976, pp.39-58.

Sevenster, P., & 't Hart, M. A behavioural variant in the three-spined stickleback. In J.H.F. van Abeelen (Ed.), The genetics of behaviour. Amsterdam: North-Holland; New York: American Elsevier, 1974, pp.141-165.

Spieth, H.T. Mating behavior and sexual isolation in the Drosophila virilis species group. Behaviour, 1951, 3, 105-145.

Tauber, C.A., Tauber, M.J., & Nechols, J.R. Two genes control seasonal isolation in sibling species. Science, 1977, 197, 592-593.

Thiessen, D.D., Owen, K., & Whitsett, M. Chromosome mapping of behavioral activities. In G. Lindzey & D.D. Thiessen (Eds.), Contributions to behavior-genetic analysis: The mouse as a prototype. New York: Appleton-Century-Crofts, 1970, pp.161-204.

Vale, J.R. Role of behavior genetics in psychology. American Psychologist, 1973, 28, 871-882.

Verplanck, W.S. Since learned behavior is innate, and vice versa, what now? Psychological Review, 1955, 62, 139-144.

Wilcock, J. Gene action and behavior: An evaluation of major gene pleiotropism. Psychological Bulletin, 1969, 72, 1-29.

Wilson, E.O. Sociobiology. The new synthesis. Cambridge, Mass.: Belknap/Harvard University Press, 1975.

COMMENT BY P. L. BROADHURST

It is perhaps paradoxical that in offering my compliments to Dr. van Abeelen on his interesting paper I should emphasize something which is absent from his paper rather than present. Doing so epitomizes the advance in ethological thinking since comparative psychologists started, some 25 years ago, to feel constrained to respond to the impact of ethological thought. In van Abeelen's paper the problems associated with the so-called isolation experiment are not rehearsed and, indeed, it is not mentioned at all. To recapitulate briefly, it had been widely held by ethologists, including Lorenz (1966), that in order to discover the importance of genetic influences upon adult behavior it suffices to take an organism and rear it in an environment in which it is deprived of the normal sign stimuli which might elicit innate reaction mechanisms throughout its early development. The extent to which its adult behavior is affected by such deprivation treatment, usually administered in the form of isolating the animal from its fellows for relatively prolonged periods, may be taken as evidence of the strength of innate determinants of behavior.

Modern biometrical approaches have demonstrated the fallacy of this way of thinking. Behavior is a phenotype, like any other, and susceptible to both genetic and environmental influences, either of which can be manipulated in experimental situations. The clearest answers to experimental problems are thus achieved by holding one of these major classes of variables constant while manipulating the other. Perhaps the best example of this approach is selective breeding since, typically in a selection experiment, all aspects of the environment which can be appropriately controlled by laboratory methods are kept constant, and the outcome of selection is achieved by mating extreme exemplars of the phenotype which it is desired to study, allowing their genotype to be maximally influential. But the isolation experiment does not achieve any such outcome. Rearing animals under deprivation, that is to say in a grossly abnormal environment, does not achieve the similar result of allowing the genetic influences to become manifest against a uniform environmental background. All that is achieved is the measurement of a grossly abnormal phenotype, which is the outcome of the interaction of the genotype and the unusual environment imposed by the typical procedures of the isolation experiment, and which will inevitably be distorted to a degree which renders it possibly unrecognisable phenotypically. Its failure is guaranteed by the absence of any involvement of the genetic process of meiosis and chromosomal reassortment as an independent variable in the experiment. Clearly, only in this way can we hope to establish a satisfactory genetic analysis of the behavior chosen for study, and I am glad to see Dr. van Abeelen is of decidedly the same view.

I strongly endorse his suggestion that the behavioral components of von Frisch's work on directional communication in honeybees might be subjected to more detailed genetic analysis. Considering their economic importance, the analysis of honeybee behavior has been strangely limited. Rothenbuhler's (1964) analysis
of hygienic behavior in bees is deservedly often cited as an
elegant piece of major-gene analysis, but selection for phenotypes
of economic importance is also clearly a possibility. The work of
Nye and Mackensen (1970, 1965, 1968; Mackensen & Nye, 1966, 1969)
on breeding honeybees for overcoming their low preference for collection of alfalfa pollen is of importance in this connection in
that by the fifth generation of selection (S_5) the average percentage of pollen collected had increased to 85% from a value typically
of the order of 30%.

It is surprising that the interest of ethologists in hybridization studies, exemplified in van Abeelen's contribution, has not
resulted in a larger volume of genetical analyses. The utility of
a biometrical approach, such as the diallel cross, may be emphasized in this connection. In this breeding design the analyses
achieved by measurement of derived generations do not go beyond
the F_1 level, in contrast to the classical Mendelian methods involving F_2 and back-crosses. Given several species, which are
only partly inter-fertile in that the F_1 between them are sterile,
then a method such as this which only requires one generation of
inter-species breeding would seem apposite for further behavioural
analysis. Thorpe's work on the pattern of song in different species
of doves might point in this direction (Lade & Thorpe, 1964).

Finally, van Abeelen modestly placed little emphasis on his
own experimental work of a psychopharmacogenetic kind (van Abeelen,
Smits & Raaijmakers, 1971; van Abeelen, Gilissen, Hanssen & Lenders, 1972) in which he succeeded in demonstrating the importance
of a cholinergic mechanism governing exploratory activity in the
mouse. His ingenious research strategy includes the use of drugs
having a central acting effect on exploratory behaviour in two
strains of mice, together with quaternary congeners of them which
do not pass the blood-vein barrier, and then manipulating this
latter effect by direct hippocampal injection. Using this elegant
method the drug-strain interaction was teased apart in a most
satisfactory way.

COMMENT BY K. IMMELMANN

Dr. van Abeelen's article gives an interesting and important
overview of the possible contribution of ethological research to
behaviour genetics. It also points to those fields in ethology
where more intensive studies are highly desirable as they will

probably be able to provide new insights into the mechanisms of behaviour genetics.

The article also describes some recent developments within the field of ethology. This refers above all, to the degree to which the so-called "innate" or "inherited" behaviour patterns are open to environmental influences of different kinds (e.g., social and non-social experience). In the early literature on comparative ethology, as Dr. van Abeelen points out, the modifying role of external factors had been considered to be rather small, a notion, that resulted in the term Erbkoordination and led to the extensive and sometimes rather polemic discussion of the nature-nurture problem. With more information having become available it has become increasingly clear that even in the development of genetically encoded behaviour patterns, especially during early stages, the environment may exert crucial and sometimes long-lasting effects. In order to give credit to these insights and to stress the fact that inherited behaviour patterns are far less "fixed" than the term fixed action pattern (F.A.P.) suggests, Barlow (1968) proposed to replace the original expression with the new term "modal action pattern (M.A.P.)", a term now frequently used in the literature.

Another example of the close interaction between genetic basis and environmental influence mentioned by Dr. van Abeelen has to do with the determination of sensitive phases for imprinting. Experimental studies in different species of birds have clearly shown that the duration of sensitive phases involves two aspects: a static aspect, because the outer limits of that period, which can only be determined experimentally using a large number of individuals, seem to be largely species-specific, and a dynamic aspect, because even within a species different individuals, depending on rearing conditions, social environment, etc., become imprinted at different ages. Obviously, therefore, the genome determines at which period during development in a given species imprinting is possible, whereas the environment (e.g., the amount and kind of social contact) decides at what age during this period imprinting actually does take place in the individual (Immelmann, 1972).

These examples show that ethological research may provide a tool to arrive at a better understanding of some general aspects of the interaction between genes and the environment.

COMMENT BY D. THIESSEN

Dr. van Abeelen's crisp discussion of the interaction between ethology and behavior genetics is a welcome opportunity to assess the links between two often disparate disciplines. Both areas can gain from the other. This is particularly true when analyses are focused on traits with narrow phenotypic canalization.

I would only add the suggestion that behavior genetics could profit by additional attention to reproductive fitness. Perpetuation of the genotype is the bottom line of natural selection, hence the characteristics of greatest interest may turn out to be those with the closest relationship to reproductive efforts. A research strategy revolving around reproduction has the advantages of cutting across conceptions of innate and acquired behaviors and blurs the distinctions between classical ethology, comparative psychology, behavior genetics and general biology.

COMMENT BY A. OLIVERIO

I strongly agree with the general idea underlying van Abeelen's paper--that Behavior Genetics should not become an isolated, autonomous discipline. Van Abeelen argues that both behavior genetics and ethology are moving in the direction of studying neurobiological mechanisms. For example, he shows that within the field of animal behavior (1) behavior genetics has been used to indicate the rigidity and encoding of a number of instinctive (paleocephalic) mechanisms, (2) behavior genetic analyses and methods provide replicable animal material for the laboratory, thereby permitting the assessment of a number of biological correlates, (3) by using inbred strains, artificial selection, or inbreeding it has been possible to work on "models" of instinctive behaviors, such as feeding behavior in bees and nesting behavior in sticklebacks.

Thus, I agree with van Abeelen that the most important value of psychogenetics is not related to biometric analysis or to tracing gene effects, but rather, to study the neurophysiological and neurochemical correlates of behavior.

COMMENT BY D. A. HAY

This paper is very broad in scope and raises many issues. The point on which I would like to focus is the feasibility of connecting ethology and behaviour genetics or, more specifically, the behaviours in which ethologists are interested and the methods employed by behaviour geneticists. Even though there is an increasing awareness among ethologists that their 'fixed action patterns' are by no means as fixed as was once thought (Schleidt, 1972), I still remain sceptical about the practicality of breeding studies.

especially the biometrical approaches discussed by van Abeelen.
Even when present variability is limited in such behaviours and,
to obtain significant results, exceptionally large sample sizes
would be needed for any breeding program. The feasibility of
this is even further reduced when one bears in mind the time it
can take to obtain quantitative records of some of these ethological traits such as detailed grooming patterns, when compared with
things such as the Drosophila taxes or rodent open-field ambulation
and defecation, the behaviours first studied in modern behaviour
genetics. More importantly, the search for genetic variation in
such stereotyped behaviours is surely missing the point. Certainly
one may find some variability, but statistical significance need
not imply that genetic differences are important in evolutionary
terms. Perhaps Drosophila courtship and mating are the best instance of this. While one can carry out diallel crosses (Fulker,
1966) or selection experiments (Manning, 1963) on specific aspects
of courtship and mating, one could justifiably argue that the large
species differences in behaviour (Manning, 1959) and song (Ewing
& Bennet-Clark, 1968) have told us far more about the evolution of
these behaviours and their ethological importance than the demonstration of genetic variation within species.

A final point is that ethologists are often interested in sequences of behaviour, especially songs, and a great many statistical techniques are now available to demonstrate sequential dependence among the components. Almost without exception, however, one
cannot use these statistics to compare different sequences and,
until this mathematical problem is solved, our ability for genetic
analysis of behaviour sequences will be very limited (Guttman,
Lieblich & Naftali, 1969).

REPLY TO D. A. HAY

J. H. F. van Abeelen

I disagree with Hay's line of reasoning pertaining to the
feasibility of connecting the behaviors in which ethologists are
interested and the methods employed by behavior geneticists. Indeed, I am less sceptical about the feasibility of such research
than he is. Application of biometrical-genetic techniques of
analysis to differences in stereotyped behavior observed between
and within populations of feral animals still seems to me most
useful and practicable, for example, in the cases referred to in
my chapter concerning subspecies of honeybees (von Frisch, 1962),
races of sticklebacks (Sevenster and 't Hart, 1974), and populations of house mice (Busser, Zweep, and van Oortmerssen, 1974).

References

Barlow, G. W. Ethological units in behavior. In D. Jugle (Ed.),
The central nervous system and fish behavior. Chicago:
University of Chicago Press, 1968.

Busser, J., Zweep, A., & Oortmerssen, G. A., van. Variability in
the aggressive behaviour of Mus musculus domesticus, its
possible role in population structure. In J. H. F. van
Abeelen (Ed.), The genetics of behaviour. Amsterdam: North-
Holland; New York: American Elsevier, 1974, pp. 185-199.

Ewing, A. W., & Bennet-Clark, H. C. The courtship songs of Drosophila. Behaviour, 1968, 21, 288-301.

Frisch, K. von. Dialects in the language of the bees. Scientific
American, 1962, 207, 78-87.

Fulker, D. W. Mating speed in male Drosophila melanogaster.
Science, 1966, 153, 203-205.

Guttman, R., Lieblich, I., & Naftali, G. Variations in activity
scores and sequences in two inbred mouse strains, their hybrids and backcrosses. Animal Behaviour, 1969, 17, 374-385.

Immelmann, K. Sexual and other long-term aspects of imprinting
in birds and other species. In D. S. Lehrman, R. A. Hinde,
& E. Shaw (Eds.), Advances in the Study of Behavior (Vol. 4).
New York: Academic Press, 1972, pp. 147-174.

Lade, B. I., & Thorpe, W. H. Dove songs as innately coded patterns
of specific behaviour. Nature, 1964, 202, 366-368.

Lorenz, K. Evolution and modification of behaviour. London:
Methuen, 1966.

Mackensen, O., & Nye, W. P. Selecting and breeding for collecting
alfalfa pollen. Journal of Apicultural Research, 1966, 5,
79-86.

Mackensen, O., & Nye, W. P. Selective breeding of honeybees for
alfalfa pollen collection: Sixth generation and outcrosses.
Journal of Apicultural Research, 1969, 8, 9-12.

Manning, A. Selection for mating speed in Drosophila melanogaster
based on the behaviour of one sex. Animal Behaviour, 1963,
11, 116-120.

Nye, W. P., & Mackensen, O. Preliminary report on selection and
breeding of honeybees for alfalfa pollen collection. Journal
of Apicultural Research, 1965, 4, 43-48.

Nye, W. P., & Mackensen, O. Selective breeding of honeybees for
alfalfa pollen: Fifth generation and backcrosses. Journal
of Apicultural Research, 1968, 7, 21-27.

Nye, W. P., & Mackensen, O. Selective breeding of honeybees for
alfalfa pollen: With tests in high and low alfalfa pollen
collection regions. Journal of Apicultural Research, 1970,
9, 61-64.

Rothenbuhler, W. C. Behavior genetics of nest cleaning in honey
bees. IV. Responses of F_1 and backcross generations to
disease-killed brood. American Zoologist, 1964, 4, 11-123.

Schleidt, W. How 'fixed' is the fixed action pattern? <u>Zeitschrift</u>
    <u>fur Tierpsychologie</u>, 1974, <u>36</u>, 184-211.
Sevenster, P., & 't Hart, M. A behavioral variant in the three-
    spined stickleback. In J. H. F. van Abeelen (Ed.), <u>The</u>
    <u>genetics of behavior</u>. Amsterdam: North Holland; New York:
    American Elsevier, 1974, pp. 141-165.
van Abeelen, J. H. F., Smits, A. J. M., & Raaijmakers, W. G. M.
    Central location of a genotype-dependent cholinergic mechanism
    controlling exploratory behaviour in mice. <u>Psychopharmacolo-</u>
    <u>gia</u>, 1971, <u>19</u>, 324-328.
van Abeelen, J., Gilissen, L., Hanssen, Th., & Lenders, A. Effects
    of intrahippocampal injections with methylscopolamine and
    neostigmine upon exploratory behaviour in two inbred mouse
    strains. <u>Psychopharmacologia</u>, 1972, <u>24</u>, 470-475.

GENETICAL CONSTRAINTS ON EARLY LEARNING:
A PERSPECTIVE FROM SEXUAL IMPRINTING IN BIRDS

Klaus Immelmann

Department of Ethology, University of Bielefeld,
West Germany

At first sight, it may seem curious to many readers to find
a chapter on imprinting in a book dealing with theoretical advances in behavioral genetics: Firstly, publications dealing
with imprinting, the present one included, are mostly based on
empirical data, and secondly, rather little attention has been
paid to the possible genetic basis of imprinting except perhaps
for some discussions about the possible influence of unlearned
preferences on the imprinting process. I will try to show, however, that the study of imprinting, now a well-established concept,
has something to offer to the field of behavioral genetics and
that even without selection and hybridization studies by looking
at individual differences in imprintability interesting principles
may be elucidated.

One of the recent trends in animal behavior sciences is the
increasing attention given to intraspecific variation in behavior.
This development has been influenced by sociobiological thinking
which stresses the importance of individual differences as a tool
in evolution. It seems also to be a result of the increasing
amount of interdisciplinary dialogue with human psychology where
the main interest has always been in the individual. In ethology
many of the early studies concentrated on species-specific behavior and paid comparatively little attention to intraspecific
variation, and if they did it was more to differences between
different strains and other categories within the species than
to individual differences. At present, knowledge about individual
particularities in animal behavior is still rather small. A number
of studies which have followed up individual differences, however,
show that even outside of the more highly developed mammals and
birds, such variation is indeed present and often much greater

than expected (see reviews in Alcock, 1975; Eibl-Eibesfeldt, 1970; Immelmann, 1977).

SEXUAL IMPRINTING IN ZEBRA FINCHES

One example of the need to focus on individual differences is provided by the study of imprinting in birds. The characteristics of imprinting, like onset and duration of sensitive phases have been regarded as typical species-specific phenomena, and many data and discussions are available on species differences (Klopfer, 1959; Mattson & Evans, 1974; Schutz, 1965; Schutz, 1970). Much less information is on hand about the range of variation within a species, perhaps because many imprinting studies have been carried out with rather small numbers of animals and thus have provided little opportunity for the detection of such variation.

With the Australian Zebra Finch, we have been lucky enough to have found an animal which enables us, for several different reasons, to do laboratory research on sexual imprinting with large numbers of individuals. Altogether, we have been able to study the sexual preferences of more than 2000 birds, for all of which we have kept complete qualitative and quantitative records of individual social experience.

The need for a great amount of information became apparent when the data from two pilot studies started to come in. They revealed such an unexpectedly high degree of various individual differences that, in order to arrive at any general conclusions, one had to work in each experiment with a large number of birds.

I would like now to give a brief description of some of our experiments, in order to demonstrate the character of such intraspecific variation. This will serve as a basis for speculation about its function and possible genetic basis.

In the first study, Zebra Finches were raised by another species of estrildid finches, the Bengalese Finch. The young Zebra Finches were separated from their foster parents when they had reached nutritional independence, i.e., when they were able to feed by themselves and no longer needed to be fed by their foster parents, and were then isolated from all other birds. When they became sexually mature, the males were tested in a series of double choice experiments with a conspecific female and a Bengalese Finch female. All Zebra Finch males in this study courted the Bengalese females almost exclusively, and there were no apparent individual differences in the strength of this preference (Immelmann, 1969).

In the second study, foster-reared Zebra Finch males were

deprived of any further visual and acoustic contact with the foster parents' species after weaning, but they were provided with a conspecific female and with nesting facilities. Most of these males eventually mated with the female and jointly raised one or several broods. After several months or years, they were separated from their conspecific mates and were tested again in a double choice situation. The results of these tests revealed the same preference for the Bengalese Finch females as was observed before the period of intraspecific contact. This means that the brief contact with the foster parents early in life clearly exerted a longer-lasting influence than did social contact of long-term duration during adult life. It can be concluded that in adult Zebra Finches sexual imprinting is characterized by a degree of stability that justifies the term "irreversible", an expression which has been used in the early literature on imprinting but has frequently been criticized and at present is not commonly used. Again no apparent individual variation was found in this series of experiments, as all males tested retained their primary preferences (Immelmann, 1972).

At this stage, an interesting detail has to be added: If tested in a double choice situation very briefly after separation from the conspecific female, some of the Zebra Finch males (about 20%) preferred to court the Zebra Finch female (although a strange female and not the bird's previous mate was offered) and paid less attention to or ignored the Bengalese Finch female. However, subsequent daily tests revealed that such preferences gradually decreased and finally disappeared, whereas the original preference for the foster species reappeared and increased again. After a number of days or weeks, the Bengalese Finch females were again courted preferentially or exclusively, just as they had been before the Zebra Finch male's period of intraspecific contact (Immelmann, unpublished data). It follows that even in individuals with "irreversible" preferences, a new preference can be established in adult life. The point is, however, that the "new" preference will be lost in the absence of continual exposure or reinforcement, whereas the original preference established during the sensitive phase is retained indefinitely even without any further reinforcement. Similar results have recently been obtained in filial imprinting in quails by Bateson and Cherfas (unpublished data).

It can be concluded from these experiments that even in a seemingly "classical" case of irreversibility in the old Lorenzian sense, no complete buffering against subsequent acquisition of new social signals is always observed. Instead, for some adult ♂♂ it has been found that a primary preference can be superimposed by a secondary one. This does not mean, however, that the first one has been lost. On the contrary, after disappearance of the social object that caused the change in preference, the old preference comes back again unchanged.

At this stage of the investigation, the great amount of individual differences became apparent for the first time: In 80%
of the males tested, no change in preference was to be observed
at all, and the old preference for Bengalese Finch females was
present even immediately after separation from the brood mate,
i.e., as soon as the male was given a choice again. Within the
20% of males which did show a transient change in preferences,
however, the way and speed with which the primary preference came
back again was also different. In some of the males, the "new"
preference had disappeared completely after only three days,
whereas in others some indications of this new preference were
still to be seen even 70 days after separation (fig. 1). Obviously, therefore, the degree of resistence against subsequent
change found in "irreversible" imprinting is different in different
individuals.

It has to be added that the conditions under which the animals were kept and tested, the age of the males during intraspecific contact as well as the duration of such contact were kept
as constant as possible. Environmental variables which could be
responsible for the individual variation observed in the degree
of preference stability have thus not become apparent.

TERMINATION OF SENSITIVE PHASES

A third study investigated whether the same degree of irreversibility observed in adult birds can also be demonstrated in
adolescents. Zebra Finches were again foster-raised by Bengalese
Finches, but instead of being kept isolated after separation from
the foster parents, they were first given intraspecific experience
by being put into a cage with several Zebra Finch females. Four
series of experiments were run with, 3, 7, 30, and 60 days of
intraspecific contact, respectively. The age at which the birds
were transferred from Bengalese foster parents to Zebra Finch
females varied from the 27th to the 73rd day of age.

The results of this study can be summarized as follows. For
adolescent males, in contrast to adults, it is still possible to
alter a previously established preference and to "re-imprint" the
birds of their own species. The success of such attempts, however, depends on two variables, the age of the bird and the duration of social contact with its own species. If only 3 or 7 days
of intraspecific contact are permitted, such contact must begin
no later than the 40th day of life in order to have any permanent
effect on subsequent sexual preferences. On the other hand, if
30 or 60 days of contact are provided, changes of preference are
still possible when the bird is placed together with the

FIGURE 1

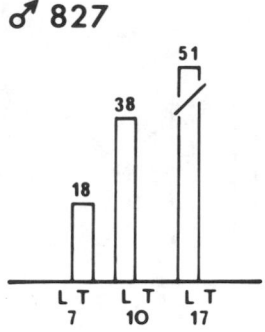

♂ 827

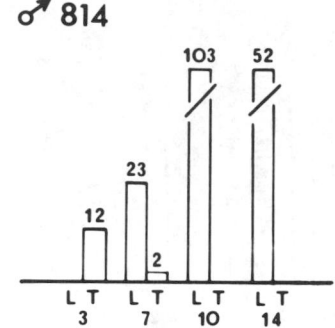

♂ 814

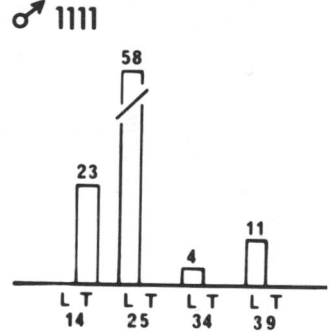

♂ 1111

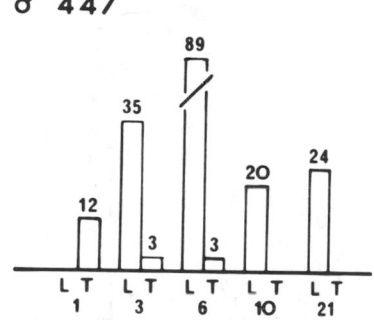

♂ 447

Fig. 1. Transient preference for Zebra Finch females displayed by
Zebra Finch males "misimprinted" on Bengalese Finches following intraspecific breeding contact. The numbers on
top of the blocks represent the number of courtship sequences directed toward the Bengalese Finch female (L)
or the Zebra Finch female (T) respectively. The numbers
below the line give the date of the double-choice experiments (in days after separation from the conspecific female).
♂ 827, ♂ 814, ♂ 1111, ♂ 447: examples of males which after
separation courted only the Zebra Finch female but returned
to the primary preference for Bengalese Finches after a
number of days. ♂ 666, ♂ 140, ♂ 326: examples of males
which courted both females with a preference either for the
Zebra Finch or for the Bengalese Finch female and also returned to the primary preference. ♂ 189: example of a male
that retained the primary preference for Bengalese Finch females from the first day after separation. This is representative of ca. 80% of all males tested.

FIGURE 1 (continued)

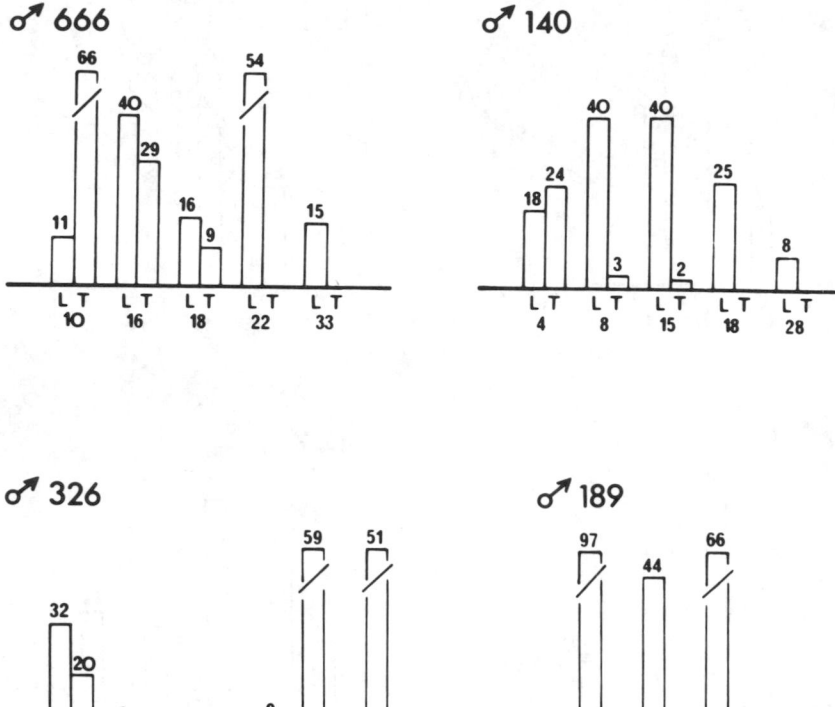

Fig. 2.   Sexual preference of male Zebra Finches reared by Bengalese Finch foster parents and subsequently exposed to
conspecific females for 3, 7, 30, or 60 days. The left
column gives the age (in days) of transfer from the foster parents to the conspecific females. A stroke represents an individual which had retained the preference for
Bengalese females; a star represents a male which showed
a preference for Zebra Finch females on a 70% or 90%
basis respectively.

FIGURE 2

70%

d 3		d 7		d 30		d 60	
25		25		25		25	
26		26		26		26	
27		27		27		27	
28	*/ /	28	*//////	28	/	28	
29	////	29	////	29	*	29	
30	*//	30	/////	30	//	30	*
31	///	31	*//	31	///	31	**/
32	///	32	///	32	//	32	*
33	*//	33	**/	33	*/	33	*/
34	//	34	*/	34	*///	34	*/
35	//	35	///	35	//	35	*
36	//////	36	//	36	//	36	*/
37	///	37	*//	37	*	37	**
38	////	38	////	38	**/	38	*
39	//	39	///	39	//	39	///
40	**//	40	//	40	*/	40	//
41	//	41	//	41	*//	41	//
42	////	42	//	42	*///	42	**/
43	////	43	/	43	/	43	//
44	////	44	///	44	//	44	/
45	//	45	///	45	///	45	*//
46	///	46	///	46	//	46	///
47	//	47	//	47	///	47	//
48		48	//	48	//	48	*
49		49	//	49	*//	49	//
50	////	50	//	50	//	50	///
51		51	//	51	///	51	*//
52		52	//	52	//	52	//
53		53	/	53	*/	53	//
54		54	/	54	///	54	//
55		55	/	55	//	55	/
56		56		56		56	*///
57		57		57	*//	57	*//
58		58		58	//	58	//
59		59		59	//	59	//
60		60		60		60	*/
61		61		61	/	61	//
62		62		62	///	62	*/
63		63		63	///	63	//
64		64		64	///	64	///
65		65		65	//	65	**/
66		66		66	//	66	
67		67		67		67	/
68		68		68		68	///
69		69		69		69	*/
70		70		70		70	///
71		71		71		71	*//
72		72		72		72	//
73		73		73		73	///
74		74		74		74	
75		75		75		75	
76		76		76		76	
77		77		77		77	
78		78		78		78	
79		79		79		79	
80		80		80		80	

FIGURE 2 (continued)

90%

d 3		d 7		d 30		d 60	
25		25		25		25	
26		26		26		26	
27		27		27		27	
28	*/ /	28	///////	28	/	28	
29	////	29	////	29	*	29	
30	///	30	/////	30	//	30	*
31	///	31	///	31	///	31	**/
32	///	32	///	32	//	32	*
33	*/ /	33	*/ /	33	*/	33	*/
34	//	34	//	34	*///	34	*/
35	//	35	///	35	//	35	*
36	//////	36	//	36	//	36	*/
37	///	37	///	37	*	37	**
38	////	38	//	38	*/ /	38	/
39	//	39	///	39	//	39	///
40	*///	40	//	40	*/	40	//
41	//	41	//	41	*/ /	41	//
42	////	42	//	42	////	42	**/
43	////	43	/	43	/	43	//
44	////	44	///	44	//	44	/
45	//	45	///	45	///	45	*/ /
46	///	46	///	46	//	46	///
47	//	47	//	47	///	47	//
48		48	//	48	//	48	*
49		49	//	49	*/ /	49	//
50	////	50	//	50	//	50	///
51		51	//	51	///	51	*/ /
52		52	//	52	//	52	//
53		53	/	53	//	53	//
54		54	/	54	///	54	//
55		55	/	55	//	55	/
56		56		56		56	*///
57		57		57	///	57	*/ /
58		58		58	//	58	//
59		59		59	//	59	//
60		60		60		60	*/
61		61		61	/	61	//
62		62		62	///	62	*/
63		63		63	///	63	//
64		64		64	//	64	///
65		65		65	//	65	**/
66		66		66	//	66	
67		67		67		67	/
68		68		68		68	///
69		69		69		69	*/
70		70		70		70	///
71		71		71		71	*/ /
72		72		72		72	//
73		73		73		73	///
74		74		74		74	
75		75		75		75	
76		76		76		76	
77		77		77		77	
78		78		78		78	
79		79		79		79	
80		80		80		80	

conspecific females as late as 57 or 71 days, respectively. This means that the older the adolescent bird is, the more social contact is necessary to change a previously established social preference. In other words, with increasing age the social effort, i.e., the amount of social contact, necessary to establish new preferences becomes greater, and this process, as a comparison of the 4 series indicates, is a gradual one. Therefore, the sensitivity to those social stimuli responsible for establishing permanent social preferences decreases by degrees and comes to its definite end gradually rather than abruptly.

Other data in the literature also point to a gradual close of certain sensitive phases. Guinea Pigs, for example, are more sensitive to olfactory imprinting during the period from 1 to 3 days of age than during later 3-day exposure periods (Carter & Marr, 1970). (For review of further examples, see Fabricius, 1964; Sluckin, 1973.)

The most interesting point here is the great amount of individual variation that was again found in this study: For example, some males proved to be so strongly imprinted on the species of their foster parents that at the early age of only 31 days even 60 days of intraspecific contact produced no change in their subsequent preference for Bengalese Finches, whereas in others, such preferences could still be reversed with only 3 days of intraspecific contact at as late an age as 40 days (see fig. 2). This means that some individuals must have developed a very high degree of permanence, i.e., of resistance against subsequent social influences, very early, whereas others remained "open" for a longer period of time. Such distinction between "early imprinters" and "late imprinters", however, certainly does not refer to two different categories but rather to extremes in a continuum of possibilities. Again the experimental conditions under which these birds were bred, kept, and tested were identical for all individuals.

DISCUSSION

Due to the fact that during the course of the study, all environmental variables, non-social and social, were kept constant, the possibility of explaining the large amount of individual variation as being an artifact of laboratory conditions can be more or less excluded. Rather, this variation has to be seen as a real phenomenon that, with all probability, also exists in nature.

Although, as mentioned in the beginning, the amount of data on intraspecific variation in imprintability is still rather small, there is some evidence that individual differences are also to be found in other species: In a laboratory study on filial imprinting in Pekin ducklings, Reinherz (1979) found pronounced differences in the degree to which the following response can be elicited (see also Gottlieb, 1961; Klopfer & Gottlieb, 1962). Under semi-wild field conditions, Schutz (1965) found differences in the strength of sexual imprinting in several species of ducks. And even under natural conditions such differences have been described: In a colony of the dimorphic Lesser Snow Goose, Cooke (1978) found that mate selection as a rule is based on familial plumage colour, but that approximately 11% of the population chose a mate of the opposite colour. It follows that the degree to which pre-pairing experience influences subsequent mate selection must be different in different individuals. Such evidence, together with our own data, warrants a discussion of the possible biological function of intraspecific variation and of the mechanisms by which they are being controlled.

If individual differences do occur under natural conditions there must be a selection pressure having given rise to and maintaining the observed degree of variability. Before speculating about the possible biological significance one should recall where individual differences in sexual imprinting are to be found: For the Zebra Finch, the relevant information is available. Here, individual differences are not at all important for the general occurrence of imprinting to another species in a cross-fostering situation nor for the permanence of early preferences to the foster species which remain stable even in the face of very extended subsequent experience with conspecific individuals. Where one does find individual differences, however, is in the degree of resistance of primary preferences to subsequent transient changes and in the duration of "openness", i.e., in the maximum age at which new preferences can still be established and will remain permanent. Altogether, individual variation does not refer to the existence or non-existence of permanent sexual imprinting but rather to very subtle characters of the imprinting process.

It is these attributes which point to the possibility that individual variation may be correlated with a function of sexual imprinting which has recently been discussed by Bateson (1979), and which seems to be slightly different from the general notion accepted so far.

According to the traditional assumption, sexual imprinting plays a role in species recognition, which--since it leads to an automatic shift in preferences if the bodily appearance of a species changes during the course of evolution--provides a much more adaptive mechanism than any genetically determined ("innate") recognition of species-specific characters, and, therefore, may be of special advantage in any rapidly evolving group of species.

Bateson argues that imprinting may also serve to enable the

young bird to recognize its close kin and may thus contribute to achieving an optimal balance between inbreeding and outbreeding within a given population. Working with Japanese quail, he found that his birds preferred to mate with an individual which is slightly different but not too different from its parents and siblings. Such preference for "optimal discrepancy" may lead to matings which preserve local adaptations of the population, since the individuals involved are closely enough related to each other, but which also maximise heterozygosity as they do not involve immediate kin.

Such a function of sexual imprinting which probably should not be regarded as an alternative to the "classical" function of species recognition but rather as an addition to it, might also be involved in sexual imprinting in Zebra Finches. The mechanism, however, by which the optimal balance between inbreeding and outbreeding is achieved through sexual imprinting seems to be slightly different from the one described by Bateson. It seems to be closely correlated with the two kinds of individual variation described above, the differences in the duration of sensitive phases and the differences in the strength of the results of early imprinting. Those males which establish early and strong preferences would, it is to be assumed, try to mate with a partner as similar as possible to their own mother. Those individuals, on the other hand, who remain "open" a little longer, i.e., up to an age when they have left their parents could still make small changes to their primary preference due to social interactions with other birds. These birds might prefer to mate with individuals slightly different from their own mother.

A mechanism like this would be well adapted to the reproduction strategy of the Zebra Finch which breeds in loose colonies ("neighborhoods") where the young come into contact with other birds as soon as they leave the nest (Immelmann, 1962). It might also be more flexible and might thus be superior to the "optimal discrepancy" principle described by Bateson, i.e. to a general preference for mates slightly different but not too different from the male's mother.

It has to be stated here that, for methodological reasons, almost all experiments have been carried out with male Zebra Finches and no general conclusions are as yet available about the possible occurrence of similar functions of sexual imprinting in females. With regard to acoustic recognition, however, some results are indeed available which point in the same direction. In a recent study, D. Miller (1978) conducted simultaneous auditory choice tests with female Zebra Finches presenting them with tape recordings of the song of the female's own father and the song of another adult male. He found that when the strange song is dissimilar from the father's song, the female prefers the latter.

When the strange song is similar, however, the preference for father's song is greatly attenuated and some females prefer both songs equally, but there is <u>no</u> distinct preference for the strange song. On the other hand, the preference for one particular song demonstrates a remarkable long-term memory for a familiar stimulus as a consequence of early exposure, and it seems quite likely that under natural conditions, song is involved in mate selection. So again, individual differences in the duration of sensitivity could provide a mechanism that would allow for the existence of both individuals with strong and with weak preferences for the familiar song-type of the father.

It can be concluded that the great amount of individual variation found in the duration and stability of early experience in Zebra Finches may have a biological function and may serve to achieve the optimal balance of inbreeding and outbreeding, which is necessary to preserve local adaptations of the population without the genetical risks of continuous inbreeding (Bateson, 1978). It seems plausible that in other species, intraspecific variation in imprinting may also be of biological significance.

No evidence about the control of individual variation is available yet. Due to the above-mentioned fact that laboratory conditions have been kept as constant as possible it can be argued that such differences are, at least in part, genetically determined. Experiments are planned, therefore, to select "early imprinters" and "late imprinters" and, at a later stage, to breed hybrids between the two lines.

Hopefully, such experiments will provide evidences as to whether there is a real genetic basis to the unexpectedly high degree of individual variation found in sexual imprinting of Zebra Finches. If this is indeed the case, it may help to explain many of the frequent contradictions and controversies which have accompanied imprinting research from its very beginning.

REFERENCES

Alcock, J. <u>Animal Behavior</u>. Sunderland, Mass.: Sinauer Ass., 1975.
Bateson, P. Sexual imprinting and optimal outbreeding. <u>Nature</u>, 1978, <u>273</u>, 659-660.
Bateson, P. How do sensitive periods arise and what are they for? <u>Anim. Beh.</u>, 1979, in press.
Carter, C. S., & Marr, J. N. Olfactory imprinting and age variables in the Guinea-Pig, Cavia porcellus. <u>Anim. Beh.</u>, 1970, <u>18</u>, 238-244.
Cooke, F. Early learning and its effect on population structure. <u>Z. Tierpsychol.</u>, 1978, <u>46</u>, 344-358.

Eibl-Eibesfeldt, K. Ethology, the biology of behavior. New
York: Holt, Rinehart and Winston, 1970.
Fabricius, E. Crucial periods in the development of the follow-
ing response in young nidifugous birds. Z. Tierpsychol.,
1964, 21, 326-337.
Gottlieb, G. The following response and imprinting in wild and
domesticated ducklings of the same species. Behavior, 1961,
18, 205-227.
Immelmann, K. Beiträge zu einer vergleichenden Biologie austra-
lischer Prachtfinken. Zool. Jb. Syst., 1962, 90, 1-196.
Immelmann, K. Über den Einflub frühkindlicher Erfahrungen auf
die geschlechtliche Objektfixierung bei Extrildiden. Z.
Tierpsychol., 1969, 26, 677-691.
Immelmann, K. The influence of early experience upon the develop-
ment of social behavior in estrildine finches. Proc. XV
Int. Ornith. Congr., The Hague 1970, 316-338, 1972.
Immelmann, K. (Ed.). Grzimek's Encyclopedia of Ethology. New York:
Van Nostrand Reinhold, 1977.
Klopfer, P. H. An analysis of learning in young Anatidae.
Ecology, 1959, 40, 90-102.
Klopfer, P. H., & Gottlieb, G. Learning ability and behavioral
polymorphism within individual clutches of wild ducklings.
Z. Tierpsychol., 1962, 19, 183-190.
Mattson, M. E., & Evans, R. M. Visual imprinting and auditory
discrimination learning in young of the Cauvasback and semi-
parasitic Redhead (Anatidae). Con. J. Zool., 1974, 52,
421-427.
Miller, D. Beyond sexual imprinting. Proc. XVII Int. Ornith-
ology Congr., Berlin, 1978, in press.
Reinherz, L. Behavioral polymorphisms and imprinting: Some
evolutionary and naturalistic considerations, in preparation.
Schutz, F. Sexuelle Prägung bei Anatiden. Z. Tierpsychol.,
1965, 22, 50-103.
Schutz, F. Zur sexuellen Prägbarkeit und sensiblen Phase von
Gänsen und der Bedeutung der Farbe des Prägungsobjekts.
Verh. Zool. Ges. Würzburg, 1969, 301-306, 1970.
Sluckin, W. Imprinting and early learning. Chicago: Aldine
Publ. Comp., 1973.

COMMENT BY J. L. FULLER

Immelmann's paper differs from all others presented at the Institute in the absence of reference to genetic experiments in the usual sense. There are no diallel crosses, parent-offspring correlations or even simple Mendelian crosses. Nevertheless his contribution has major significance for behavior geneticists working with many problems. It deals with persistent problems of behavioral development. What aspects of development can be considered to be genetically programmed? What is the role of experience? How do the roles of genes and ambient stimulation change during the course of development? How rigid is the behavioral structure imposed early in life by genotype-environment synergy? These questions can be raised for most of the organisms that we study.

The paper concentrates on a series of experiments on sexual imprinting in estrildid finches. Many publications on imprinting have appeared but little attention has been given to its variability among individuals. It is not surprising that variability exists; individual differences are a prerequisite for producing strain differences by selection or inbreeding. For Immelmann imprinting is a form of learning that occurs most effectively during a limited part of the life span (generally early) and which is relatively permanent. Thus he looks in his male Zebra finches for variability in the duration of the sensitive period for sexual-partner imprinting upon female Bengalese finches, and later for differences in the stability of mating preference following sexual experience with a conspecific female. The design is both simple and powerful; parametric studies make it possible to find answers to the questions listed in the first paragraph. The experiments are still incomplete but the existence of individual variability is well established. Immelmann explains this variation in terms of the degree of "openness" of the imprinting process over a period of at least 70 days.

He contrasts his concept with Bateson's theory of optimal discrepancy. Both hypotheses seem plausible to me. Considering Bateson's view first: assume that successful mating requires an intermediate level of general excitation. A prospective partner exactly like the imprinting model could produce less arousal (and thus be less attractive) than a partner differing in small details. A small amount of ambiguity in the stimulus would potentiate the courtship. A prospective partner extremely different from the model would fail to elicit sexual advances and might even become a target for agonistic behavior. Immelmann's hypothesis is somewhat simpler; it requires only quantitative differences in the duration of the sensitive period and in the stability of the original imprinting. To me it seems more readily testable, but I do not consider the two hypotheses as necessarily contradictory.

Immelmann wisely does not claim that the individual differences he finds are genetic in origin. Although rearing procedures
of the finches are standardized there is no way to eliminate small
differences in life history that might have subtle effects on imprinting and its duration. What is certain is that he has a rich
opportunity to combine ethological and genetic techniques in his
studies of the sexual preferences of these finches. I wish him
well.

COMMENT BY P. L. BROADHURST

Professor Immelmann's paper fully lived up to its title in
that it gave us a new "perspective" on a developmental phenotype
which has been of considerable interest to behavioral workers for
some time. I would wish to raise only two points in connection
with it; the first is the possibility which his own work clearly
provides of directionally selecting for onset of imprinting in
zebra finches. Such an artificial selection experiment could concern itself with late versus early imprinting and, if successful--
which one has no reason to doubt in view of indications of an important genetic component in the determination of the phenotype as
described by Professor Immelmann--then some advance in our understanding of the nature of the genetical control would be obtained.
This would not, of course, be an appropriate substitute for a fine-
grain genetic analysis which it is not, in my view, in the nature
of selection experiments to provide, but it would yield strains of
late versus early imprinters which could be of considerable value
for further analysis.

The second point relates to the possibility of employing the
concept of supranormal stimuli in further behavioral analysis; it
might, for example, be possible to expedite a selection experiment
of the kind described by the use of such stimulation.

COMMENT BY J. N. THOMPSON, Jr.

The study described by Immelmann is exciting both for its
elegance and completeness and for the report it makes on individual differences in imprinting. As he points out, sociobiological
theory stresses the importance of individual differences in evolution, but seldom has such a potentially powerful system been identified for genetic analysis.

The simple fact that some components of the complex character "imprinting" are genetically variable is an interesting observation in itself. It has self-evident significance for evolutionary change. It is particularly striking since fitness of such a trait is not necessarily measured by fitness of the individual, but rather by the inter-individual interactions which are its function.

The genetic analysis of this variation can take several directions. As suggested above, the evolutionary genetic implications are fascinating. But a more efficient approach would probably be to analyze the character variation with the goal of identifying simpler components that might eventually be amenable to more precise genetic and physiological study. The fact that brief contact has longer lasting influence than long-term social contact suggests something akin to a permanent social "search image" or behavior promoter, to borrow an idea from developmental biology. Such a promoter might be mappable in the nervous system by a variety of techniques such as those applied to similar mapping of sensory processing in mammals. Physiological correlates might also be suggested by identifying correlations with such things as memory facility, specificity of pattern sense, and maturation rate. But there is certainly no doubt that further reports of this study will be awaited eagerly.

A Genetic Approach to Behavioral Plasticity and Rigidity

A. Oliverio, C. Castellano, and S. Puglisi-Allegra

Biological Trends in Behavior Genetics

D. Thiessen

A GENETIC APPROACH TO BEHAVIORAL PLASTICITY AND RIGIDITY

A. Oliverio, C. Castellano and S. Puglisi-Allegra

Istituto di Fisiologia Generale, University of
Rome and Laboratorio di Psicobiologia e Psico-
farmacologia, CNR, via Reno 1, 00198 Rome, Italy

1. A COMPARATIVE APPROACH TO BEHAVIORAL SPECIALIZATION AND GENERALIZATION

The mammalian nervous system may be subdivided
into three functional components, the spinomedullary,
paleocephalic and neencephalic, three structures which,
in agreement with Altman (1966) and MacLean (1975), control three separate classes of behavioral functions.
This tripartite organization of activities is distributed
within a continuum ranging from stereotyped innate activities to individual and acquired behaviors. The
spinomedullary activities control a number of neuromus-
cular functions which are dependent on morphogenetic
processes; that is, the activities are reflex innate
capacities which are resistant to modification by experience. The paleocephalic nuclei, through the mesence-
phalon, the diencephalon, and the limbic system, control
a major class of activities which have been defined as
recurrent catering or servicing activities. These include a number of appetitive, consummatory, agonistic
and affiliative behaviors, and the control of circadian
energy-deployment processes. The purposes of these activities - which may be defined as instinctive - are
set by inborn needs and dispositions: however their
mode of execution is guided and may be altered through
interaction with the environment. Finally, the

neencephalic functions consist of novel, variable, and
highly adaptive behaviors that individuals display in
response to unique situations or to new problems raised
by the environment. These activities cannot be directly
programmed by inborn mechanisms, but are developed by
the individual within a given environment. In other
words, they are acquired capacities. By way of summary,
the structural subdivision of the mammalian brain
corresponds to a functional subdivision which is responsible for classes of behavioral activities ranging
from species-specific innate and stereotyped behaviors
to acquired and unique individual-specific behaviors.

This short evolutionary foreword makes the point
that the behavioral abilities of different species may
be determined in more rigid or more plastic terms
depending on their level of encephalisation. At the
lowest level protochordates, such as amphioxus, are
characterized by a spinomedullary nervous system and
by "reflex" activities. At the intermediate level pro-
tovertebrates, such as amphibia or reptiles, depend on
paleocephalic mechanisms and on "instinctive" processes.
At the highest level protomammals and mammals are en-
dowed with neencephalic structures and respond with
individual "intelligent" behaviors. However, within
mammals the role of "instinctive" or of "intelligent"
processes may be more or less relevant, depending on
the importance of paleocephalic or neencephalic mechanisms. There are species which are characterized by
fixed action patterns and species which are more plastic
and rely on flexible strategies. At one extreme the
nervous structure, and the behavior which it allows,
confine the specialist animal to a relatively narrow
niche. At the other end of the continuum the structure and behavior are more flexible and versatile,
and allow the animal to exploit a greater array of environmental situations. These broad niched animals
are known as generalists.

What are the advantages of these two conditions?
In a slowly changing environment of low variability
behavioral specialization probably represents an advantage for the specialist. However, there is the evolutionary risk that the environment might deviate too

rapidly for the individual to adapt. On the other
hand, the generalist organism, with a reduced number
of behaviors which are organized with a minimum of
personal experience, spends his entire life solving
problems that the specialist's genetic background has
solved for it. While specialist species rely on fixed
action patterns and other behaviors that are more structurally determined, generalist species are more flexible, depend on individual experience for acquiring
useful behaviors, and are able to temporarily link diverse responses in new ways in order to solve new problems (Mayr, 1974; Parker, 1974).

    The distinction between specialist and generalist
species is not only based on cerebral evolutionary
correlated, but also the different mechanisms which
may produce response variability. In addition to brain
development, security for predators, or living in a
non-agonistic social framework (defined as a hedonic
mode by Chance, 1975), is conducive to the generation
of variable behaviors. Other mechanisms which have
been related to the production of behavioral variability
are 1) living under relaxed motivational pressures
(Parker, 1974), 2) play behavior, and 3) paradoxical
sleep. The latter mechanism has been related to the
evolutionary level of different species, and it has
been indicated that paradoxical sleep occupies a more
important role in the most evolved mammals (Jouvet,
1976; Rojas-Ramirez & Drucker-Colin, 1977). Of course
the possession of a diverse behavioral repertoire must
not be passively connected with the level of adaptive
behavior or intelligence, but that repertoire (and
behavioral plasticity) represents the necessary starting
point.

2. BRAIN MATURITY AT BIRTH AND BEHAVIORAL RIGIDITY
    OR PLASTICITY

    In addition to their relationships with the level
of encephalisation, behavioral rigidity or plasticity -
specialisation or generalisation - may also be considered from another point of view, the maturity at birth
of mammals. In the precocial species (such as guinea

pigs or ruminants) sensory and motor maturation at
birth allows for immediate identification with the
mother and the establishment of social and mother-
offspring relationships which resemble imprinting in
birds (Scott, 1958; Sluckin, 1965). On the contrary,
in non-precocial (altricial) mammals, which form a
heterogeneous group ranging from rodents to carnivores,
primates and man, the immediate postnatal period is
characterized by great maternal dependency, by a later
onset of primary and social relationships, and by immaturity of sensory and motor abilities.

From an evolutionary point of view, precocity at
birth may be regarded as a characteristic of behavioral
specialisation while immaturity at birth is characteristic of behavioral plasticity and generalisation. The
precocial species have the advantage that the ontogeny
of the CNS is realized during the fetal period and that
the newborn organism is practically mature for independent life soon after birth. The behavioral adaptation
of a precocial species is set, in large part, through
innate mechanisms (Sedlacek, 1974). The immaturity of
behavioral functions in the altricial neonate, at birth
and during the first days - or months and even years -
of postnatal life, is compensated for via parental behavior. The immature brain passes through critical developmental periods under different influences of the
external environment which may have positive (or negative) effects on brain and behavioral maturation. In
other words while precocial species have the advantages
of the "specialist" and rely to a greater extent on innate patterns, altricial species have the advantages
of the "generalist", and are more flexible and open to
the effects of the environment.

These different points are summarized in a tentative
model in Fig 1 where the various mechanisms leading to
behavioral rigidity or plasticity are considered in relation to infancy and adulthood. Different maturational
and behavioral patterns during infancy lead to specific
interactions with the environment; similarly, the stimulating or detrimental effects of the environment have a
more pronounced effect on those species which reach their
maturity at a later age. Whether an adult animal is a
"specialist" or a "generalist" depends upon these early
mechanisms and behavioral categories, upon the type of
interaction with the environment, and finally, upon the
evolutionary genetic mechanisms which set the types of

species-specific or individual cerebral and behavioral
organization.

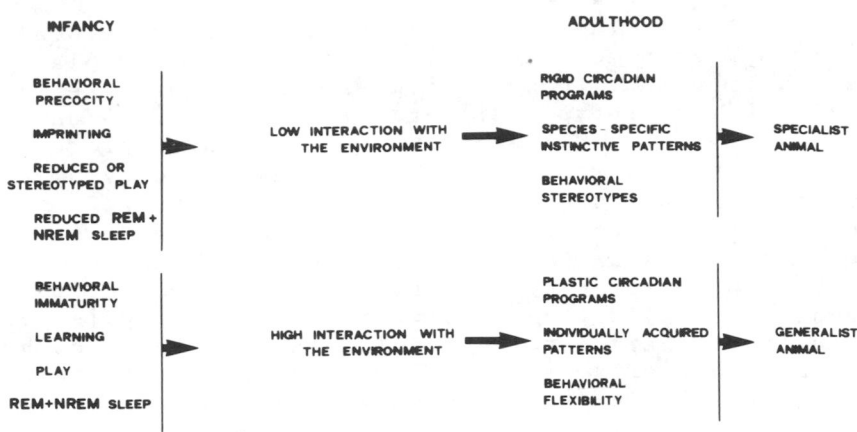

Fig. 1. Behavioral rigidity (specialization) or plasti-
        city (generalization) in relation to a number
        of factors acting during infancy or adulthood.

3. A GENETIC APPROACH TO BEHAVIORAL INDIVIDUALITY

What is in fact the relevance of a genetic approach
to the problem of behavioral rigidity or plasticity and
to their psychobiological correlates ? A number of programmatic studies of the phylogeny of learning have been
conducted by using different procedures by varying the
conditions under which the different species try to solve
specific problems (Bevitashvilii, 1971; Bitterman, 1965).
However, these types of contributions only indicate the
existence of species-related differences in specific
learning tasks and it is rather difficult to equate the
experimental procedures or to correlate behavioral differences to specific brain characteristics. In order to
understand the mechanisms of behavioral evolution,
within-species comparisons seem more fruitful than the

interspecific approach. As pointed out by Schneirla
(1966) the existence of outstanding individual differences within the same species must be regarded as a powerful tool for these studies. Within the same species there
are differences between individual lines, such as precocity or immaturity at birth, behavioral rigidity or
plasticity, specialisation or generalisation.

Within the framework of a theoretical behavioral
genetic approach to the problem of rigidity and plasticity it is important to work with a species characterized
by 1) clear phenotypic differences at the brain and behavioral level, 2) differences in relation to precocity
and maturity at birth and 3) behavioral rigidity or plasticity in relation to a number of paleocephalic - instinctive - or neencephalic - adaptative - patterns.
From an analysis of the data available, the mouse seems
to represent "a prototype" (Lindzey and Thiessen, 1970;
Oliverio, 1977a) for any behavior genetic analysis. Some
inbred lines characterized by different patterns of behavioral plasticity or rigidity may represent a useful
model in this type of analysis. We will examine these
findings as a basis for a tentative theoretical model.

4. PHENOTYPIC DIFFERENCES AT THE BRAIN AND BEHAVIORAL
   LEVEL.

A very large number of strains of mice are now
available (Green, 1966; Medvedev, 1958; Staats, 1972),
their genetic homozygosity resulting from a number of
studies based on different immunological methods.Thirty-
-nine strains have also been characterized by alleles
involving as many as 16 polymorphic loci. The variability
among these strains is at least as great as in any single
feral population, a large group of inbred strains with
unique alleles and no overlapping pedigrees, and the best
group available to screen for a hoped-for variant (Roderick et al., 1971). The existence of clear, intraspecific, phenotypic differences of the peripheral and central
nervous system has also been assessed.

A search of the literature up to 1978 indicates a
total of 107 reports, 71 dealing with a number of biochemical or enzymatic difference at the peripheral level
(nerves, ganglia and organs) and 36 with differences at
the brain level. It is important to note that most of the
estimates at the brain level deal with four strains: in
particular, 55 biochemical estimates have been conducted
on C57BL/6 mice, 55 on DBA/2 mice, 20 on BALB/c mice and

Table 1

Biochemicals	C57/BL/6	DBA/2	SEC/1Re
	S T R A I N S		
Glutamic acid decarboxylase	II 20 13 18 I 21	I II	
GABA transaminase	II 21	I	
GABA	I 15	II	III
Monoamine oxidase	I 20 7 II 12 13	II I	
Catechol-O-methyl transferase	I 20	II	
Tyrosine hydroxilase	II 1 I 2	I II	
pons + medulla	I 19	II	
Tyrosine hydroxilase hypothalamus	II 19	I	
Cyclic AMP	III 14	I	II
Noradrenaline pons + medulla	I 5	III	II
hypothalamus	I 5	II	III
cortex	II 5	I	III
Noradrenaline amygdala	II 21	I	
frontal cortex	II 21	I	
hypothalamus	II 21	I	
hippocampus	I 21	II	
Dopamine	II 5	I	III
Serotonin	I 5	III	II
Aromatic-L-amino acid decarboxilase	III 12 13	I	II
Choline acetylase	II 20	I	
Choline acetylase frontal	II 3 9 10 11	I	III
temporal	III 3 9 10 11		
Acetylcholine esterase total	III 20 13 3 9 10 11	I	II
frontal	II 3 9 10 11	I	III
temporal	III 3 9 10 11	I	II
Choline esterase	I 12 13	II	
Na$^+$ K$^+$ ATlase	II 16	I	
Taurine, aspartine, glutamic acid	I 15	III	II
GABA	I 15	II	III
Serine, arginine	III 15	II	I
Histidine	II 15	III	I
Polyribosome/ribosome	I 6	II	
Synaptic membranes	I 4	II	
Hypoxanthine--guanine phospo ribosil transferase	II 17	I	
S100 protein	II 8	I	

14 on the SEC/1ReJ strain. By contrast, there are just
40 estimates dealing with 11 other strains. These figures indicate that 1) there are strains in which a number of biochemical estimates are conducted because of
their interesting behavioral patterns, and 2) there is
value in concentrating on the most thoroughly investigated strains in order to determine the significance of
findings already available. With this approach in mind
brain level biochemical differences for three strains
(C57BL/6, DBA/2 and SEC/1Re) are reported on Table 1.
A number of estimates dealing with the gabaminergic, noradrenergic, dopaminergic, serotoninergic and cholinergic systems or with aminoacids and protein synthesis
were considered. Due to the different technical procedures used by various authors the differences evident between these strains were expressed by using a ranking
procedure. The results indicate that the three strains
clearly differ in their brain biochemistry and in a number of possible behavioral-biochemical correlates.

C57 mice are characterized by lower brain weight
(Roderick et al., 1971), lower thickness of brain cortex and corpus callosum (Gozzo et al., 1978) higher a-
mounts of maternal care (D'Udine, 1978) and aggressive
behavior (Puglisi-Allegra et al., 1978; Southwick and
Clark, 1966), higher exploratory, locomotor, and wheel
running activity (Oliverio et al., 1972; van Abeelen,
1966; Malorni et al., 1975; Oliverio and Castellano,
1977), more pronounced circadian wheel-running and sleep

Table 1. Biochemical differences between three inbred
strains of mice. The roman numbers refer to the
ranking order between the three strains (ranking
I indicates the highest observed value for a
given characteristic) while the arabic numbers
refer to the authors.
Authors: 1 Ciaranello et al., 1972; 2 Diez et
al., 1976; 3 Ebel et al., 1973; 4 Gurd et al.,
1972; 5 Kempf et al., 1974; 6 MacInnes and
Schlesinger, 1971; 7 MacPike and Meier, 1976;
8 Malup and Sviridov, 1978; 9 Mandel et al.,
1973; 10 Mandel et al., 1974; 11 Oliverio et al.
1974; 12 Pryor, 1968; 13 Pryor et al., 1966;
14 Sattin, 1975; 15 Simler et al., 1977; 16
Stefanovic et al., 1974; 17 Suran, 1973; 18
Sze, 1977; 19 Tiplady et al., 1976; 20 Tunnicliff et al., 1973; 21 Wimer et al., 1973; 22
Wong et al., 1974.

rhythmicity (Malorni et al., 1975), and lower levels of passive and active avoidance, and maze learning (Bovet et al., 1969; Oliverio et al., 1972; Sprott, 1971). Finally, the time spent in non REM and REM sleep is lower in the C57 than in the other two strains (Valatx et al., 1972).

It is obviously difficult to summarize in a short space the large number of findings available. However, it is possible to indicate two main points: 1) The three strains considered are characterized by sharp phenotypic differences at the brain and behavioral level. 2) Within the framework of the classification proposed by Altman (1966), it is hypothesized that the behavioral patterns

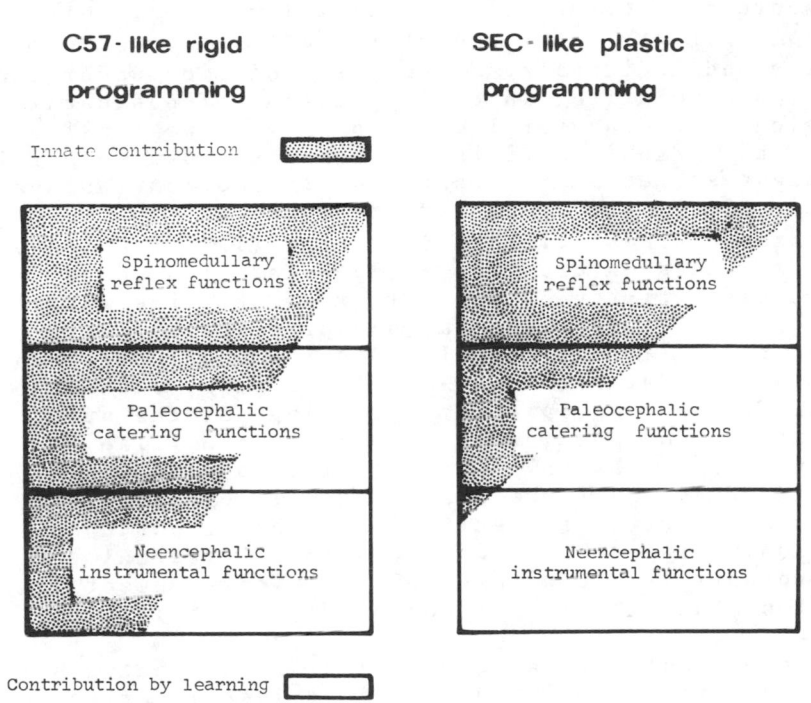

Fig. 2. A theoretical model for the role of innate contribution or of learning in the reflex, catering and instrumental functions of two strains of mice (C57BL/6 and SEC/1Re).

of C57 mice are primarily determined by paleocephalic or instinctive processes (circadian patterns, locomotor ac-

tivity, maternal behavior, emotional and aggressive behavior), while the behavioral patterns of SEC and DBA
mice are primarily determined by neencephalic processes
or individual adaptation (escape and avoidance behavior,
visual discrimination, maze learning etc.). This view is
expressed via a tentative theoretical model which depicts
the two strains in terms of innate versus learned sources
of behavior (see Fig. 2).

5. A GENETIC APPROACH TO BEHAVIORAL MATURITY AT BIRTH.

It was previously noted that maturity at birth is
an important point in evolutionary terms since the behavior of precocial species is hypothesized to be related
to innate mechanisms while altricial species, which attain a later brain and behavioral maturation, are more
plastic and modifiable. The strains of mice under consideration also differ in their patterns of postnatal neurological and behavioral development. If we consider ele-
ctrocorticographic activity, which was shown to parallel
different stages of maturation of the cortex (Kobayashi
et al., 1963), there are strains (such as C57 mice) which
are more mature at birth and strains (like SEC mice)
which are less mature. For example, at eight days of age
electrical activity of the cortex of SEC mice was similar to the C57 strain on day one of postnatal life (Oliverio et al., 1975a). Similar developmental differences
are also evident for a number of reflexes, such as cliff
aversion, righting, placing, grasping, or the startle
response which appeared at an earlier age (also 3-4 days
in advance) in the C57 strain (Oliverio et al., 1975b).
These findings indicate that there are clear genetic differences in the intraspecific patterns of postnatal maturation, a fact which suggests that individual genetic
make-up sets limits within which the environment is able
to affect the patterns of postnatal maturation.

It may well be, as a matter of fact, that a strain
which is more precocial at birth is less reactive to environmental differences 1) because its behavior is more
"rigidly" determined, and 2) because precocial brain maturation leaves less room for the stimulating or/and detrimental effects of environmental situations (see again
in this respect the model represented in Fig. 1). Independently of the mechanisms implicated, it was shown
that the effects associated with an early improverished
or enriched environment were less evident in the C57
strain than in the SEC mice. In fact SEC mice reared
postnatally in an enriched or impoverished environment

later attained a higher or lower performance in different
learning tasks, whereas the effects of the two environmental situations were not statistically significant in
the C57 strain (Oliverio, 1977b).

In short, a number of biochemical and morphological
differences at the brain level characterize strains which
are also different in their patterns of postnatal and
adult development, including behavior.

6. BEHAVIORAL RIGIDITY OR PLASTICITY.

The paleocephalic activities control, as previously
noted, a number of circadian, energy-deployment processes. For example, it was shown that C57 mice are characterized by clear-cut differences between the circadian
patterns of sleep while no sharp differences are evident
in the SEC strain (Valatx et al., 1972). Furthermore,
recent data indicate that free-running rhythms of sleep
and activity may be plastic or rigid depending on genetic factors involved in the expression of circadian rhythmicity. Under 12hours-12hours light-dark (L-D) schedules
it was shown that the external synchronizer induces well
defined activity phases at night and lower activity levels during the hours of light in C57 and SEC mice. However when the running activity of the strains was assessed under constant light (L-L) or darkness it was shown
that C57 mice (and other strains) conserve a pronounced
circadian rhythm while SEC mice (and other strains as
BALB/c) do not (Malorni et al., 1975; Oliverio, 1977b).

A clearer demonstration of the importance of genetic factors in modulating the plasticity or rigidity of
these two (and others) strains was evident by studying
wheel running and sleep under L-D schedules shorter than
12hours-12hours. The effects of 12-12h, 6-6h, 3-3h and
1-1h L-D cycles, and of constant light (L-L) were studied in C57 and SEC mice (Oliverio and Malorni, 1978).
Wheel running activity and sleep were inhibited by light
and enhanced by darkness; however, in the C57 strain the
L-D induced changes were less pronounced and superimposed on a clear circadian rhythm. Under the subsequent
L-L schedule clear patterns of daily rhythmicity were
evident in the C57 strain but not in the SEC strain
(Fig. 3). A second finding was rather interesting. SEC
mice experimentally shifted from a short L-D schedule to
a condition of constant light retain for a short time
the experience of their previous rhythmic performance
(e.g. they present a rhythmic behavior similar to that

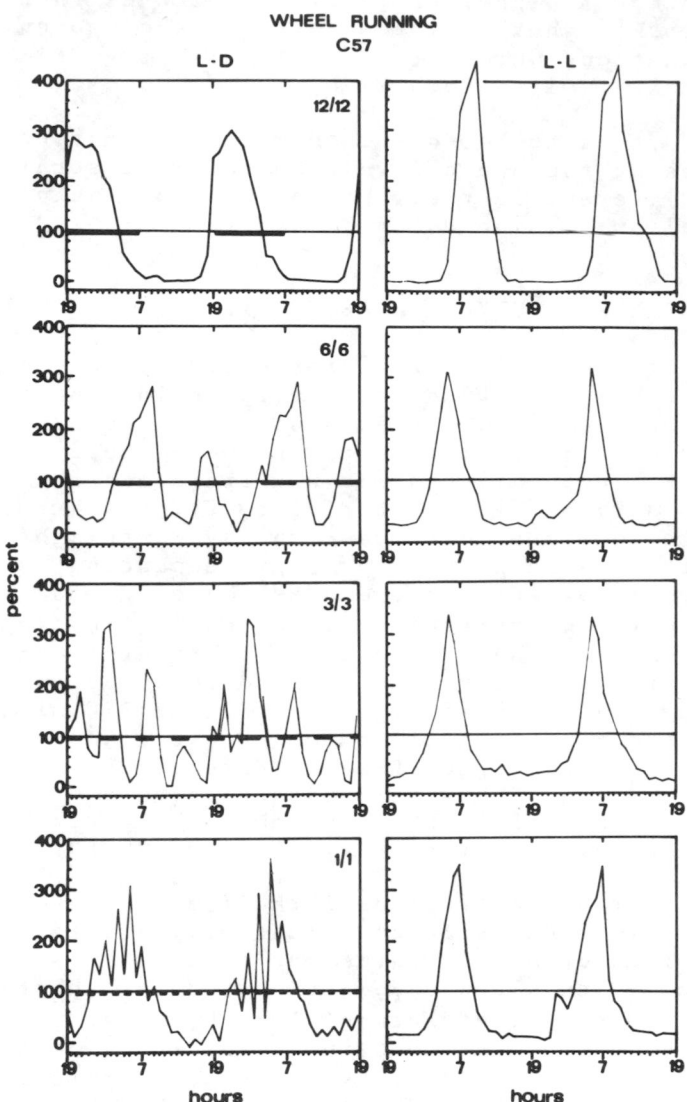

Fig.3a. Wheel-running behavior of different groups of
C57 subjected to different L-D schedules (12-12h,
6-6h, 3-3h and 1-1h; left column) and subsequently to a L-L schedule (right column). The parameters are plotted as mean percent deviations
from the average 24h activity (100% level) for
successive 1-h periods. The black bars superimposed to the 100% performance line indicate the
dark periods.(from Oliverio and Malorni, 1978).

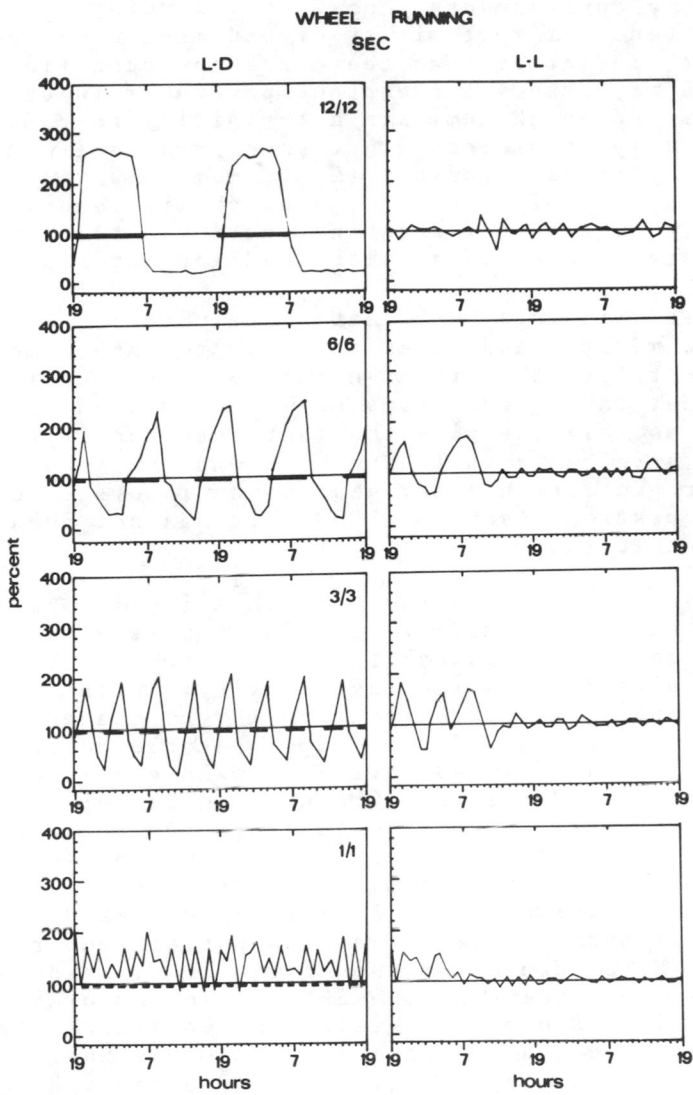

Fig.3b. Wheel running behavior of SEC mice (from Oliverio and Malorni, 1978) (see Fig. 3a).

induced by the previous L-D schedule), a fact which suggests that a pacemaker is able to "memorize" a rhythm
determined by environmental cues. This finding, combined
with the absence of rhythmicity of SEC mice under constant light, indicates that there are non specific structures which may assume a transient pacemaker function
when the circadian rhythms are not rigidly programmed.
It seems likely, therefore, that some strains are more
influenced by the environment (i.e., more plastic), not
only for a number of acquired "neencephalic" behavioral
activities, but also for such instinctive, paleoencepha-
lic behavioral processes as sleep and locomotor activity.

Do these findings mean that these patterns of circadian rhythmicity respond essentially to inborn mechanisms ? Generally, this is assumed; however, our findings
indicate that these mechanisms may be modulated by early
experience as well. Despite the fact that the rhythms
of animals have been studied under a wide range of conditions for generation after generation in order to answer this question (Aschoff, 1960), it has not been possible to settle the issue.

A number of findings indicate that imprinting-like
mechanisms may play a role in circadian rhythms and that
rearing in constant light or imprinting to 12-12h L-D
cycles can affect wheel running activity. In fact, as
previously noted, a clear circadian rhythm characterizes
adult C57 mice reared under 12-12h L-D cycles when their
activity rhythm is allowed to free run in continuous
light while no evidence for circadian rhythmicity is evident in the SEC strain. On the contrary adult C57 and
SEC mice reared under constant light do not present a
clear pattern of daily rhythmicity under continuous light
while C57 mice imprinting to 12-12h L-D cycles during
days 15 to 18 show a clear circadian pattern under constant light. No evidence for the imprinting-like phenomenon was instead evident in the SEC strain (Malorni and
Oliverio, 1978). A number of relations between early experience and sexual preferences in the mouse have been
assesses by Mainardi et al. (1965) and recently discussed
by Bateson (1978). Within this field, it was also shown
that in the C57 strain - but not in SEC mice - imprinting-
-like phenomena play also an important role in relation
to sexual preferences (Alleva et al., 1978)

In general, the findings reported in this section
underline the existence of rigid or plastic behavioral
pattern, presumably correlated with paleocephalic mechanisms and genetic make-up. Again,it is hypothesized that

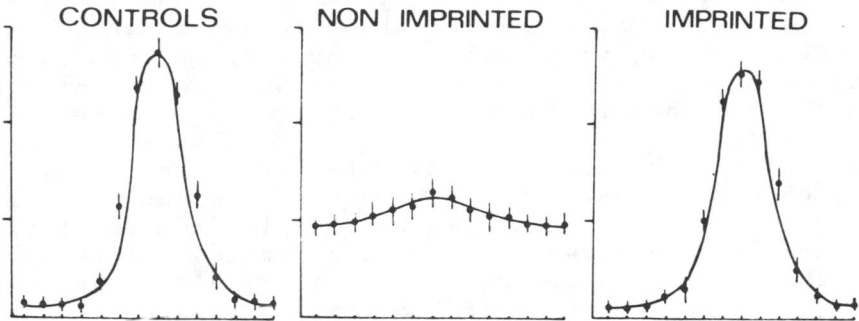

Fig. 4. Daily wheel running rhythms of three groups of
C57 mice in continuous light. Control mice were
reared under a 12-12h L-D schedule. Non imprinted
mice were reared in continuous light. Imprinted
mice were reared in constant light but were subjected to a 12-12h L-D schedule during days 15
to 18 after birth. The lines indicate the fitted
theoretical curves. The dots indicate wheel running activity expressed as a percentage ($\pm$ S.E.
M.) of daily mean level. Scale: ordinates 100%;
abscissae 2 h. (from Malorni and Oliverio, 1978).

cerebral precocity or maturity at birth is associated
with behavioral specialization or generalization.

7. CONCLUSIONS - A THEORETICAL APPROACH TO BEHAVIORAL
   PLASTICITY

In this section we will link together all the findings presented within the framework of this genetic model and look at its possible implications. The advantages
of a genetic approach to the problem of behavioral adaptation are not mainly connected to the crude application
of simple or complex biometric techniques. In fact, tracing gene - behavior pathways may represent a possible

direct approach: however, it is questionable that quantitative genetic techniques might be helpful to solve the problem of the psychobiological - neurochemical, neurophysiological, etc. - correlates of the adaptive mechanisms. On the contrary, behavior genetics may be used in order to assess the study of neurophysiological correlates of a number of instinctive or individually adaptive behaviors, of different patterns of behavioral ontogenesis and, in general, of more "rigid" or "plastic" behaviors. This approach may appear as a longer strategy than a straightforward one but may prove to be rewarding.

In order to see the advantages of an indirect, more comprehensive genetic model, and before entering into its details, let us consider an example from the field of learning and memory. One or two decades ago the approach to this field aimed at the study of simple animal models, different types of learning being studied in their simplest forms in monocellular organisms or in invertebrates with the purpose of finding the general laws of this behavior. From a biochemical point of view the approach to learning and memory was also rather straightforward. It was based on the analysis of macromolecular storage, chemical transfer, neurotransmitters, and the effects produced by a number of chemical or physical agents interfering with learning or memory consolidation. This large array of studies and the number of findings reported in the literature indicate that the problem is very complex and that there are a number of systems or sub-systems to be investigated. This conclusion is exemplified in a recent review by Will (1977), who analyses the main correlational studies between learning and neurochemistry. Many findings indicate correlations with the cholinergic system, or with adrenergic, serotoninergic or dopaminergic mechanisms. Other studies analyse the role of proteins and nucleic acids (see Table 2).

It is difficult to state whether all the chemicals listed in Table 2 exert a main or a secondary role in learning, or whether a given biochemical response is stimulation-related, acquisition-related, or experience--related. In short, the correlational approach must be supplemented by more experimentally controlled strategies (e.g., see Entingh et al., 1975), such as neurophysiological and neurochemical analyses of inbred strains. For example, there are strains which present a number of phenotypic differences at the brain level, which are behaviorally more precocial or less precocial at birth, and which are more rigid or plastic in relation to a number of environmental situations. Thus we are hypothesizing

that the existence of large individual (or strain) differences at the brain level represents the necessary condition for different adaptive behavioral mechanisms.

Parameter	Number of studies
Cholinergic system	29
"Enzymes"	28
Serotoninergic system	10
Noradrenergic system	8
Proteins + nucleic ac.	8
Dopaminergic system	5

Total studies on inbred mice 12

Table 2. Correlational studies between learning and neurochemistry (summarized from Will, 1977).

Independently of whether this biochemical diversity represents the starting point for behavioral diversity or
depends on selection pressure which exploits some "useful" behavioral differences, there are outstanding differences in the levels and the turnover of biochemical
mediators in specifiable area of the brains of different
strains of mice.

When we consider the genetic model proposed in this
paper it is possible to observe, as suggested by Mandel
and his coworkers (Ebel et al., 1973; Kempf et al., 1974;
Mandel et al., 1973, 1974), that the strains which are
more behaviorally aroused and present more "stereotyped"
exploratory activities (such as C57 mice) are characterized by more active noradrenergic mechanisms or by lower
levels of serotonin at the level of the pons and medulla.
On the other hand cholinergic turnover is higher in the
temporal cortex (which is associated with memory processes) in the SEC and DBA strains. Similarly lower levels
of protein synthesis in the C57 strain is associated with
low performance on a number of learning tasks. These are
just a few examples of the biochemical basis of observable variations in behavior.

It is worth noting that differences in cholinergic activity or/and in protein synthesis may also be relevant to the dramatic morphological differences between the brains of C57 and SEC mice. The latter strain is characterized by a greater thickness of second, third, and fifth layers of the temporal cortex, a thicker corpus callosum, and higher values of gray matter coefficients in the frontal region (Gozzo et al., 1978). The lower neuronal density in the cortex of C57 mice results in a reduced number of synaptic connections within each hemisphere and between the two hemispheres, as suggested by the decreased thickness of the corpus callosum in relation to the SEC strain.

The higher neuronal density in the cortex of SEC mice is a possible morphological correlate for their greater behavioral flexibility. A second possible basis for behavioral plasticity or rigidity are the variations

Fig. 5. Photomicrographs of sections of cerebral cortex (top and middle) and corpus callosum (bottom) of SEC (left column) and C57 (right column) strains. Toluidine blue staining. The circled areas, which correspond to the 4th layer, are enlarged in the middle pictures (from Gozzo et al., 1978).

in the pattern of postnatal maturation. It is possible that the genetic "programs" which lead to maturational differences also involve differences in the role of the instinctive or of the individual adaptation processes. In other words, as previously suggested, there are strains which are similar to precocial species and strains which are similar to altricial species. Furthermore, it is hypothesized that those strains which are characterized by slower maturational patterns are more sensitive to the effects of the environment and have more opportunities and needs to invoke individual adaptive strategies.

This model, represented in Fig. 6, tends therefore to indicate that species, strains, or individuals are different for a number of behavioral, neurophysiological, and maturational processes which determine the mode of organismic interaction with the environment. Within the same species different strategies, such as instinctive processes, imprinting-like processes, and learning, constitute different mode of survival and adaptation. The

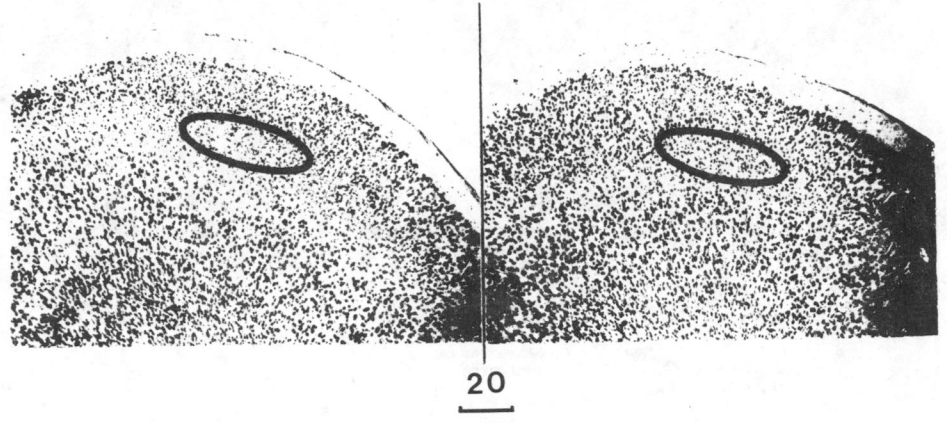

20

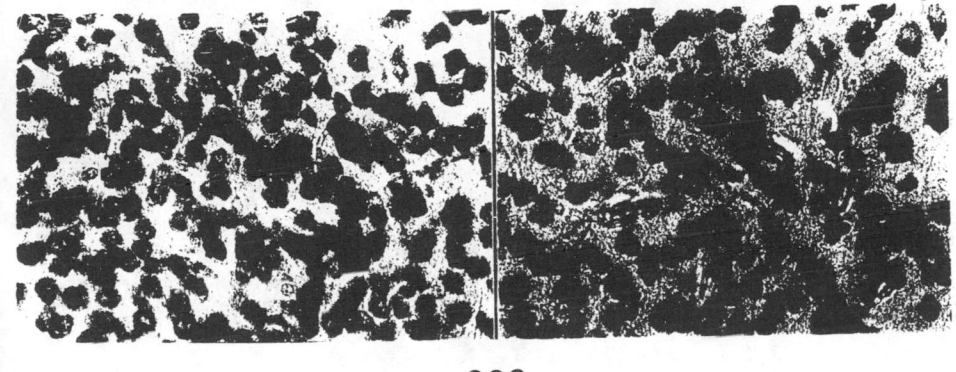

200

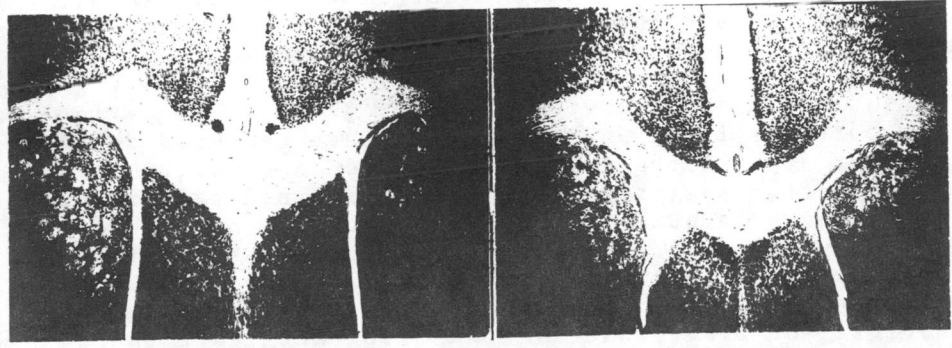

SEC $\frac{300}{\mu}$ C57

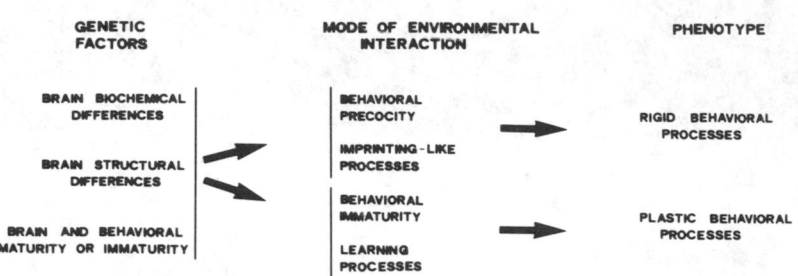

Fig. 6. A theoretical model for the role of genetic and
     environmental factors related to behavioral ri-
     gidity or plasticity.

analysis of a number of behavioral patterns (such as
sleep, early experience, play, aggression, reactions to
new stimuli, neophobia, perseveration, and response variability)and their biological correlates should result
in a better understanding of behavioral specialization
and rigidity) and generalization (and plasticity).

     In conclusion, we view behavior genetics as having
evolved from a first and necessary phase centered on the
choice of appropriate genetic tools (selection, inbreeding, biometric analyses, recombinant inbreeding) to the
application of a number of genetic tools to psychobiology
and neurophysiology. Through these techniques (applied
primarily to drosophila and rodents) it was possible to
show that the genetic make-up modulates a wide range of
behaviors and also, what is most important, that the environment is the ultimate architect of the genetic variance of the phenotype. However, behavior genetics went
through a process of "reification" regarding behavioral
categories as fixed properties of an individual rather

than emerging from a situation. This type of approach
was particularly evident in human behavior genetics where
intelligence and its different components were considered only as a property of different individuals or races,
thereby omitting the relationship of that individual or
population to the surrounding natural and social environment. In addition, even if we stick to mice or rats, we
observe that, while it is possible to control a specifiable behavior by appropriate genetic techniques or to indicate that one or more genes contribute to its variance,
it is also obvious that the environment stipulates phenotypic parameters independently of wide genetic differences.

What about the future of behavior genetics ? The
most secure prediction we can make is that the availability of strains, lines, and mutations represents a powerful approach to the study of the biological (biochemical.
hormonal, neurological, etc.) mechanisms of behavior.
More specifically, we are optimistic about the possibilities of a genetic approach to the study of brain - be_
havior relationships. We see this as more promising and
meaningful than the current propensity for determining
the number of genes which may affect a given behavior,
or assessing the sociobiological implications of behavior
patterns.

8. SUMMARY

A number of findings are reviewed suggesting that
species, strains, or individuals are different for a number of behavioral, neurophysiological, and maturational
processes which determine the mode of organismic interaction with the environment. Within the same species,
different strategies, such as instinctive processes, imprinting-like processes, and learning, constitute different modes of survival and adaptation.

The analysis of a number of behavioral patterns
(such as circadian activity, sleep, early experience,
play, aggression, reactions to new stimuli, perseveration,
and response variability) and their biological correlates, allows a better understanding of the different environmental situations which produce new responses, and
therefore the passage from behavioral specialization and
rigidity to generalization and plasticity.

A genetic approach to behavioral rigidity or plasticity is proposed, based on a number of data available on

different strains of mice. The roles of neurological and
behavioral maturity at birth, and of various biochemical
and morphological differences at the brain level, are a-
nalysed in relation to different patterns of adaptive
behavior.

It is suggested that the main interest of animal
behavior genetics .is connected to the application of a
number of genetic tools (inbreeding, mutations etc.) to
psychobiology and neurophysiology. In other words behavior genetics is mostly a tool for understanding brain-
-behavior relationships rather than being a self-suffi‾
cient science or a way for assessing the meaning of be‾
havior from an evolutionary and sociobiological standpoint.

REFERENCES

Alleva, E., Renzi, P., & Oliverio, A. Rearing in presence of acoustic rhythms affects circadian locomotor rhythmicity of adult mice. Submitted to Neuroscience Letters, 1978.

Altman, J. Organic foundations of animal behavior. New York: Holt, Rinehart & Winston, 1966.

Aschoff, J. Exogenous and endogenous components in circadian rhythms. Symposium on Quantitative Biology, 1960, 25, 11-27.

Bateson, P.P.G. Early experience and sexual preferences. In J.B. Hutchinson (Ed.), Biological determinants of sexual behaviour. London: Wiley, 1978.

Beritashvilii, I.S. Vertebrate memory. Characteristics and origin. New York: Plenum Press, 1971.

Bitterman, M.E. Phyletic differences in learning. American Psychologist, 1965, 20, 396-410.

Bovet, D., Bovet-Nitti, F. & Oliverio, A. Genetic aspects of learning and memory in mice. Science, 1969, 163, 139-149.

Chance, M.R.A. Social cohesion and the structure of attention. In R. Fox (Ed.), Biosocial anthropology. New York: Wiley, 1975.

Ciaranello, R.D., Barchas, R., Kessler, S. & Barchas, J. D. Strain differences in biosynthetic enzyme activity in mice. Life Sciences, 1972, 11, 565-572.

Diez, J.A., Sze, P.Y. & Ginsburg, B.E. Genetic and developmental variation in mouse brain. Tryptophan hydroxylase activity. Brain Research, 1976, 109, 413-417.

D'Udine, B. Behavioral differences in maternal care in two different strains of mice. Submitted to: Animal Behavior, 1978.

Ebel, A., Hermetet, J.C. & Mandel, P. Comparative study of acetylcholinesterase and choline acetyltransferase enzyme activity in brain of DBA and C57 mice. Nature-New Biology, 1973, 242, 56-57.

Entingh, D., Dunn, A., Glassman, E., Wilson, J.E., Hogan, E. & Damstrat, T. Biochemical approaches to the biological basis of memory. In H.S. Gazzaniga & C. Blakemore (Eds.), Handbook of psychobiology. New York: Academic Press, 1975.

Gozzo, S., Renzi, P. & D'Udine, B. Morphological differences in cerebral cortex and corpus callosum are genetically determined in two different strains of mice. International Journal of Neuroscience, 1979, 9,

Green, E.L. Biology of laboratory mouse (2nd ed.), New York: McGraw-Hill, 1966.

Gurd, R.S., Mahler, H.R. & Moore, W.J. Differences in protein patterns on polyacrylamide-gel electrophoresis

162

of neuronal membranes from mice of different strains. Journal of Neurochemistry, 1972, 19, 553-556.

Jouvet, M. L'Histoire naturelle du rêve. Paris, France: Institut de France, 1976.

Kempf, E., Greilsamer, J., Mack, G. & Mandel, P. Correlation of behavioural differences in three strains of mice, with differences in brain amines. Nature, 1974, 247, 483-485.

Kobayashi, T., Inman, O., Buno, W. & Himwich, H.E. A multidisciplinary study of changes in mouse brain with age. Recent Advances in Biological Psychiatry, 1963, 5, 293-308.

Lindzey, G. & Thiessen, D.D. Contributions to Behavior-Genetic Analysis. The Mouse as a Prototype. New York: Appleton-Century-Crofts, 1970.

Mac Innes, J.W. & Schlesinger, K. Effects of excess phenylalanine on in vitro and in vivo RNA and protein synthesis and polyribosome levels in brains of mice. Brain Research, 1971, 29, 101-110.

MacLean, P.D. The imitative-creative interplay of our three mentalities. In H. Harris (Ed.), Astride the two cultures. London: Hutchinson, 1975?

MacPike, A.D. & Meier, H. Genotype dependence of monoamine oxidase in inbred strains of mice. Experiencia, 1976, 32, 979-980.

Mainardi, D., Marsan, M. & Pasquali, A. Causation of sexual preferences of the house mouse. The behaviour of mice reared by parents whose odour was artificially altered. Atti della Società Italiana di Scienze Naturali, 1965, 104, 325-338.

Malorni, W. & Oliverio, A. Imprinting to light-dark cycles or rearing in constant light affect circadian locomotor rhythm of mice. Neuroscience Letters, 1978, 9, 93-96.

Malorni, W., Oliverio, A. & Bovet, D. Analyse génétique d'activité circadienne chez la souris. Comptes Rendus des Séances de l'Académie des Sciences, Paris, 1975, 281, 1479-1484.

Malup, T.K. & Sviridov, S.M. Neurospecific S-100 protein content in brains of different mouse strains. Brain Research, 1978, 142, 97-103.

Mandel, P., Ayad, G., Hermetet, J.C. & Ebel, A. Correlation between choline acetyltransferase activity and learning ability in different mice strains and their offspring. Brain Research, 1974, 72, 65-70.

Mandel, P., Ebel, A., Hermetet, J.C., Bovet, D. & Oliverio, A. Etudes des enzymes du système cholinergique chez les hybrides F1 des souris se distinguant par leur aptitude au conditionnement. Comptes Rendus des Séances de l'Académie des Sciences, Paris, 1973,

276, 395-398.

Mayr, E. Behavior programs and evolutionary strategies. American Scientist, 1974, 62, 650-659.

Medvedev, N.N. On the breeding of the laboratory strain mice. Biulletini Moskoskogo Obestva Ispitateki Pri-rodvi, 1958, 63, 117-133

Oliverio, A. Genetics, environment and intelligence. Amsterdam, North Holland:Elsevier, (1977a).

Oliverio, A. La maturation de l'E.E.G. et du sommeil: Facteurs génétiques et du milieu. Revue de Electroen-cephalographie et Neurophysiologie, 1977b, 7, 263-268.

Oliverio, A. & Castellano, C. Postnatal brain maturation and learning in the mouse. In A. Oliverio (Ed.), Gene-tics, environment and intelligence. Amsterdam, North Holland: Elsevier, 1977.

Oliverio, A., Castellano, C., Ebel, A. & Mandel, P. A genetic analysis of behavior: a neurochemical approach. In: E. Costa, G.L. Cessa & M. Sandler (Eds.), Serotonin new vistas. Advances in Biochemical Psychopharmacology, 1974, 11, 411-418.

Oliverio, A., Castellano, C. & Messeri, P. A genetic analysis of avoidance, maze and wheel running behaviors in the mouse. Journal of Comparative and Physiological Psychology, 1972, 79, 459-473.

Oliverio, A., Castellano, C. & Renzi, P. Genotype or prenatal drug experience affect brain maturation in the mouse. Brain Research, 1975, 90, 357-360.

Oliverio, A., Castellano, C. & Puglisi-Allegra, S. Effects of genetic and nutritional factors on post--natal reflex and behavioral development in the mouse. Experimental Aging Research, 1975, 1, 41-56.

Oliverio, A. & Malorni, W. Wheel running and sleep in two strains of mice: plasticity and rigidity in the expression of circadian rhythmicity. Brain Research, 1978, in press.

Parker, C.E. Behavioral diversity in ten species of non human primates. Journal of Comparative and Physiologic-al Psychology, 1974, 87, 930-937.

Pryor, G.T. Postnatal development of cholinesterase, acetylcholinesterase, aromatic L-amino acid decarboxy-lase and monoamine oxidase in C57BL/6 and DBA/2 mice. Lice Sciences, 1968, 7, 867-874.

Pryor, G.T., Schlesinger, K. & Calhoun, W.H. Differences in brain enzymes among five inbred strains of mice. Life Sciences, 1966, 5, 2105-2111.

Roderick, T.H., Ruddle, F.H., Chapman, V.M. & Shows, T.B. Biochemical polymorphisms in feral and inbred mice, Mus musculus. Biochemilcal Genetics, 1971, 5, 457-466.

Rojas-Ramirez, J.A. & Drucker-Colin, R.D. Phylogenetic correlations between sleep and memory. In R.R. Drucker-

Colin and J.L. McGaugh (Eds.) Neurobiology of sleep and memory. New York: Academic Press, 1977.

Sattin, A. Cyclic Amp accumulation in cerebral cortex tissue from inbred strains of mice. Life Sciences, 1975, 16, 903-913.

Schneirla, T.C. Behavioral development and comparative psychology. Quarterly Review of Biology, 1966, 41, 283-302.

Scott, J.P. Animal behavior. Chicago, University of Chicago Press, 1958.

Sedlacek, J. The significance of the perinatal period in the neural and behavioral development of precocial mammals. In G. Gottlieb (Ed.), Aspects of neurogenesis. New York: Academic Press, 1974.

Simler, S., Randrianarisoa, H., Koehl, C., Cielsielski, L. & Mandel, P. Pool des acides aminîs libres du cerveau de souris de lignées consanguines présentant des différences d'aptitude à l'apprentissage. Comptes Rendus de la Société de Biologie, Paris, 1977, 171, 942-946.

Sluckin, W. Imprinting and early learning. Chicago: Aldine, 1965.

Sprott, R.L. Inheritance of avoidance learning. The Jackson Laboratory's Annual Report, 1971, 42, 78.

Staats, J.L. Standard nomenclature for inbred strains of mice: fifth listing. Cancer Research, 1972, 32, 1609-1646.

Stefanovic, V., Ebel, A., Hermetet, J.C. & Mandel, P. NA+K+-Aptase activity in brain regions of C57 and DBA mice. Journal of Neurochemistry, 1974, 22, 1139-1141.

Suran, A.A. Hypoxanthine-guanine phosphoribosyl transferase in brains of mice. Regional distribution in seven inbred mouse strains. Life Sciences, 1973, 13, 1779-1788.

Sze, P.Y. Genetic variation in brain L-Glutamate decarboxylase activity from two inbred strains of mice. Brain Research, 1977, 122, 59-69.

Tiplady, B., Killian, J.J. & Mandel, P. Tyrosine hydroxylase in various brain regions of three strains of mice differing in spontaneous activity, learning ability and emotionality. Life Sciences, 1976, 18, 1065-1070.

Tunnicliff, G., Wimer, C.C. & Wimer, R.E. Relationships between neurotransmitter metabolism and behaviour in seven inbred strains of mice. Brain Research, 1973, 61, 428-434.

Valatx, J.L., Bugat, R. & Jouvet, M. Genetic studies of sleep in mice. Nature, 1972, 238, 226-227.

Wahlsten, D. Heredity and brain structure. In A. Oliverio (Ed.), Genetics, environment and intelligence. Amsterdam

North Holland: Elsevier, 1977.

Will, B.E. Neurochemical correlates of individual differences in animal learning capacity. Behavioral Biology, 1977, 19, 143-171.

Wimer, R.E., Norman, R. & Eleftheriou, B.E. Serotonin levels in hippocampus, striking variations associated with mouse strain and treatment. Brain Research, 1973, 63, 397-401.

Wong, E., Schousboe, A., Saito, K., Wu, J.Y. & Roberts, E. Immunochemical studies of brain glutamate decarboxylase and GABA-transaminase of six inbred strains of mice. Brain Research, 1974, 68, 133-142.

COMMENT BY D. D. THIESSEN

Dr. Oliverio has provided us with a broad and potentially useful evolutionary model within which to study genetic variation. The time-honored phylogenetic view of the brain, first crystallized by Hughlings Jackson, Charles Sherrington, and others, is extended toward the understanding of genetic variation within a single species, <u>Mus</u> <u>musculus</u>. In Oliverio's terms the architectural ascendency in complexity of the brain proceeded through evolutionary time from spinomedullary (showing innate capacities) to paleocephalic (with energy-deployment processes) to neencephalic (demonstrating highly flexible and adaptive functions). The classic paradigm is then applied to behavioral and genetic variations among inbred strains of mice. The interesting argument is that strain differences in maturation, circadian persistence, and reaction to stimuli and learning ability reflect relative degrees of development and utilization of this tripartite brain system. In a sense the phylogenetic roots of behavior are seen to be encapsulated in the individual variations of development, the notion that ontogeny recapitulates phylogeny.

How successful this extrapolation will be, from phylogeny to ontogeny, remains to be seen. It does seem evident that the phylogenetic stratification of the vertebrate nervous system parallels a functional hierarchical distribution of innate, stereotypical, and modifiable behaviors. But does it follow that individual and strain differences in behavior reflect a similar variation in brain stratification? Dr. Oliverio courageously says yes. Since I hope he is correct, I can only offer encouragement tempered by reservations that he may have already considered. First, I would like to address some problems that appear in the patterns of behavior among the three strains of mice tested, and then bring up some broader theoretical points. Hopefully Dr. Oliverio will respond to these points and share additional ideas with us.

The C57 inbred line, when compared to other strains, seems to be characterized by precocial development, high aggressivity, persistence of circadian activity, diminished brain cortical thickness, and reduced learning ability. All of these traits are consistent with a paleocephalic behavioral dominance, and support Dr. Oliverio's notion that genetic variation between strains can duplicate phylogenetic progression in brain stratification.

However, there are some questionable traits in the C57 strain that do not seem to fit into the expected phylogenetic pattern. For example, this line shows higher amounts of maternal care, a characteristic that might be expected in an altricial species, where cortical development and learning predominate.

Moreover, C57 animals are highly active and exploratory, characteristics usually considered to be indicative of flexible, adaptive strategies. Finally, with respect to learning ability, the C57 strain appears to do quite well under some stimulus circumstances.

The point is that the total pattern of behavior of this mouse strain is not entirely consistent with the evolutionary model. Of course inconsistencies do not summarily invalidate the generality, but they do impose a theoretical inconsistency that must be considered. Not all pieces of behavior found among laboratory animals are inevitably homologous with taxonomic groups found in their natural environments. For instance, high exploration in the mouse is not necessarily the same adaptation as found in a series of carnivores. In fact it may be an artifactual emergence of the inbreeding process. If that is the case, then the incongruous finding of high exploration in C57 is of no theoretical consequence for the major emphases of the phylogenetic model. But the point is that we simply do not know the adaptive significance of exploratory behavior in the laboratory mouse. So how do we classify it with respect to evolution? Unfortunately the same ignorance exists for those C57 traits that seem to be consistent with the model, such as low cortical weight, precocial development, and all the rest. What are the adaptive qualities of these traits and are they homologous with those found in natural ecologies where natural selection is acting full force? Until we can answer these questions it will be difficult, I think, to use genetic populations of laboratory stocks to study physiological or behavioral mechanisms of evolution.

This brings me to a broader theoretical issue. The major adaptive strategies that differentiate fish, amphibia, reptiles, and mammals represent genetic revolutions that were acquired over 500 million years of vertebrate evolution. With such major differences in ecologies and genetic architectures it is not too surprising that these taxonomic groups generally conform to an evolutionary progression from spinomedullary to paleocephalic and neencephalic dominance. The brain complexity certainly has increased across this phylogenetic trajectory. Nevertheless, even teleost fish show an unexpected amount of modifiable behavior, and there are wide species differences in adaptation without any obvious differences in brain organization. Intuitively it seems improbable that micro variations within a species, such as with inbred mice, could ever duplicate a phylogenetic trend, even if the structural differences in the brain could be found and measured.

Moreover, we must also consider species adaptations which uniquely program organisms to their ecologies. Many of these adaptations are so imperative that they override phylogenetic

trends. Precocity, for example, may in some cases be associated
with adaptation to predation rather than with a narrow sensitivity
to environmental perturbations. There may not be a close correlate with decreased cortical complexity, since these same organisms may also be adapted to complex foraging and sexual strategies. Obviously there are multitudes of species adaptations
which can be integrated in numerous ways. The only criteria
natural selection impose are successful survival and reproduction.

The above comments are not meant as a criticism of an evolutionary conception of genetic variations between populations of a
single species. On the contrary, I believe that this approach can
be fruitful. Dr. Oliverio is to be congratulated for his efforts.
At the very least the genetic variation can be used to establish
links between physiology and behavior which may eventually demonstrate the organismic constraints of natural selection.

BIOLOGICAL TRENDS IN BEHAVIOR GENETICS

D. Thiessen

Department of Psychology, University of Texas
Austin, Texas

The phenomenal advances in theoretical biology during the last two decades are triggering renewed interest in the genetic study of behavior. Concurrently, there has been an almost explosive interest in behavior genetics. All biological traits are influenced by genes and most genes may have a behavioral consequence; hence it is now common to find behavior geneticists working in cytogenetics and biochemistry, pharmacology and neurobehavior, and child development and personality (Ehrman & Parsons, 1976; McClearn & DeFries, 1973). Behavior genetics is rapidly becoming a ubiquitous tool for unraveling the complexities of behavior from the DNA molecule to social organization.

This critique offers what I view as recent biological trends in behavior genetics. Of necessity the presentation is incomplete and only illustrates what appear to be prominent research thrusts. The major trends can perhaps be summarized in three ways: (1) There is evidence of a growing interest in individual differences that underlie adaptive responses as well as preadaptations that are necessary for natural selection to occur. Behavior has evolved to serve individual needs and is tightly linked to the phylogenetic history of the organism and its ecological constraints. (2) There is a surge of appreciation that the differential expression of genes in behavior is regulated by intracellular and extracellular events. Behavioral variation is often a cause of these regulatory shifts in genetic transcription as well as its consequence. (3) A new theory of sociobiology is emerging which will influence how every aspect of behavior is viewed. Sociobiology is the logical intrusion of evolutionary principles into the investigation of social organizations from the single cell to man.

Hopefully a general view of each one of these trends will reinforce the ties that behavior genetics has already established with biological theory, and will at the same time suggest additional avenues of interaction. In keeping with the designated goals of this conference, I have not hesitated to be speculative and conjectural.

INDIVIDUAL DIFFERENCES, PREADAPTATIONS AND BEHAVIOR

Genetic variation is so extensive that with the exception of asexually cloning organisms and monozygotic twins every individual is unique. Electrophoretic studies of proteins from serum and body tissue bear this out (Brewer, 1970; Johnson, 1973). This rather simple technique of screening structural and functional proteins provides a rough approximation of the total variation in an individual or a population. Assuming that this technique gives an accurate index of genetic variation, it has been demonstrated in the horseshoe crab, <u>Drosophila</u>, mouse and man that approximately 30 to 40 percent of all genetic loci thus far investigated are polymorphic for an average of 3 to 4 alleles (Selander, 1971; Selander & Johnson, 1973). Even this estimate is considered minimal, as only a fraction of the actual variability can be detected by electrophoretic techniques. Nevertheless, it is indicative that all species and most individuals carry an abundance of alternative alleles and biochemical programs.

Humans show extensive variation in ABO blood groups, serum proteins and blood cell enzymes. Of the approximate 60 thousand structural genes, 20 thousand (fully one third) are probably polymorphic (Omenn & Motulsky, 1971; Scriver, Laberge, Clow & Fraser, 1978). This indicates that the prevalence of genetic polymorphism per locus is around 6.3 percent. The likelihood, therefore, of finding two persons with identical genotypes is on the order of one chance in three billion. Parenthetically, it is of interest to speculate that each of us has a least one identical genetic counterpart in a world with over four billion people.

Chromosomal variation in humans is nearly as extensive as gene variation (Scriver, et al., 1978). Variations have been noted in about 50 percent of aborted human fetuses, and in about 5 percent of stillbirths and in early infant deaths. Approximately 12 percent of pediatric hospital admissions suffer a chromosomal or multifactional disease. In total there are about 5000 new disorders appearing each year involving fetal chromosomes (Omenn, 1978). In addition to these there are the well known conditions of Down syndrome, trisomy 13 and 18, and the variety of sex chromosome supernumeraries or absences. Even though these chromosomal variations are clearly deviant, their sheer numbers suggest that even a greater proportion goes undetected.

Obviously it is easy to make the point that genetic variation is the general rule in sexually reproducing individuals and populations. What is more difficult, but clearly a task for behavior geneticists, is to determine the significance of this variation. The clinical importance of understanding major gene and chromosomal effects on behavioral diseases is most evident but what of the significance of genetic diversity _per se_? I will try to make the point here that genetic variants are much like paint strokes on a canvas - some provide the broad outlines of form and function, while others add nuances to the basic style, and still others go undetected.

Gene Canalization and Behavioral Polymorphism

A question of major concern to investigators is whether or not most of the observable genetic variation has an influence on behavioral processes, or, as has been claimed by some, is functionally neutral with respect to phenotype. The answer will determine whether our attention is directed more toward the genotype or the phenotype, and perhaps whether we concentrate on individual differences or on more uniformly expressed traits.

Undoubtedly some of the genetic variation found in populations is not of major significance to behavior, nor is even expressed in the phenotype (Mayr, 1970; 1976). Homeostatic mechanisms, gene canalization during development, redundant DNA sequences and environmental constraints reduce the expression of the genome and act to stabilize the phenotype. Moreover, some variation is cloaked by dominant and epistatic gene effects. Gene variation may be a ubiquitous quality of most species, but at least a part of this variation may be neutral with respect to physiological functioning and behavior at any particular moment.

Even at the molecular level, polypeptides, the messages of the genome, can vary substantially in amino acid residues apparently without altering their primary function (Johnson, 1973; King & Jukes, 1969). Last, perhaps as little as 10 percent of nuclear DNA is ever active at any one time (Beerman, 1965), and adjacent genes are often spaced by untranscribed or untranslated DNA base sequences, leaving only a relatively small number of functional genes (Ohno, 1972).

Arguments like these permit two first order inferences. First, behaviors that are critical for individual survival are likely to be narrowly canalized regardless of the overall genetic diversity of the organism. Second, "silent genes" offer a reserve of genetic material upon which selection could act at some future time.

It should be emphasized that the coefficient of variation will be reduced for survival traits that have undergone many generations of honing by natural selection. Consider the different ways in which human biochemical processes occur. Many metabolic pathways have alternative modes of operation - if one enzyme is blocked the metabolic sequence will proceed in another direction. Polymorphism of gene function is probably the rule in these cases. However, some processes, especially those dealing with energy acquisition and expenditure in the brain, are rate limiting and share few alternative metabolic pathways. Significantly, these latter vital processes lack genetic variability. Glycolysis, the metabolic pathway for glucose utilization in the brain, is a case in point. Omenn and Motulsky (1971) (also see Omenn, 1976) have examined all enzymes in this pathway from hexokinase to lactate dehydrogenase in some 135 human brain specimens and have found almost no enzymatic variants. The implication is, of course, that mutant forms in this critical metabolic system never survive long enough to be measured.

The environment is the ultimate architect of the degree of genetic variance and canalization of the phenotype. One can therefore imagine all sorts of relationships. For example, a behavior like feeding could be rigidly programmed by neonatal or even prenatal imprinting, even though genetic variability is extensive. Or, the same behavior could be directly correlated to the amount of genetic variability, or even inversely correlated. In the final analysis, the phenotype is the result of historical processes of natural selection and contemporary influences of the environment. Whether or not genes are expressed, relative to an environmental influence, depends upon a host of organismic factors related to individual fitness.

Powell (1971), in an interesting experiment with behavioral implications, has related genetic polymorphism in <u>Drosophila willistoni</u> to environmental complexity. Thirteen populations of this species were maintained in cages differing in three levels of complexity involving temperature and food media. After forty-five weeks of this treatment and the birth of several generations twenty-two enzyme loci were studied for variations. In the natural populations individual heterozygosity was about 19 percent; in the most varied laboratory environment this was reduced to about 13 percent, and in the most constant environment individual heterozygosity was only about 8 percent. The number of alleles per locus varied in a similar manner with environmental complexity. Complex environments may demand complex genotypes.

Heterogeneous environments therefore may account for a great deal of existing polymorphisms. Classic examples include light and dark morphs in many species of moths subjected to differential bird predation in light and polluted environments, environmental mimicry of shell color and banding patterns in the land snail, Cepaea nemoralis, seasonal changes in the frequencies of inversions in Drosophila and perhaps frequency dependent mating in Drosophila and other species (Ehrman & Probber, 1978; Hedrick, Ginevan & Ewing, 1976). Thus environmental pressures across geographical space or over time can act as "balancing selection" to match the genetic variability with environmental variations. It is not established that all genetic variation is of this kind, and indeed we have seen how it can be silent, but at least simple polymorphisms with major effects on the phenotype may reflect ecological demands.

While I have emphasized situations in which the genetic differences find expression in the phenotype, there are at least an equal number of cases in which the environment stipulates the phenotypic parameters independently of wide genetic differences. Table 1 gives some recent examples where chemosignals are dependent on the diet of the individual or population. In all cases the quality of the pheromones changes with diet, quite independent of genetic differences.

In one extreme case Porter & Doane (1977) cross fostered pups of Acomys cahirinus (spiny mice) and Mus musculus where the foster mother experienced different diets. When the pups were later tested for olfactory preferences, they preferred the odors from mothers on diets that their foster mothers had experienced, regardless of the species of the mother. Obviously, the pups demonstrated assortative affiliation because of environmental rather than genetic reasons.

The importance of genetic variability will obviously differ under a variety of circumstances. Whether or not it is expressed or remains in silent service of the organism will depend on the necessity of its expression in heterogeneous environments and the degree to which the environment can canalize an adaptive behavior without regard to existing variability. The more general problems revolve around understanding which forces in the environment cause genetic differentiation and expression and which do not. Even in cases where genetic variation percolates into the phenotype we must ask the difficult questions about its origin and consequences. The phylogenetic history of an organism

TABLE 1
Mammalian Chemosignals Determined by Diet

Chemical Source	Behavioral Effect	Reference
Guinea pig urine	Male attraction to females	Beauchamp, 1976
Rat milk	Choice of diet by pups	Galef & Clarke, 1972; Galef & Henderson, 1972
Rat Fecal Material	Attraction of pups to mother	Leon, 1974, 1975
Gerbil ventral scent gland excretions	Attraction of pups to mother	Skeen & Thiessen, 1977
Spiny mouse body odors	Attraction of pups to mother	Porter & Etscorn, 1975, 1976
Human palm odors	Individual recognition	Wallace, 1977

may limit gene variation, genetic drift or natural selection may stabilize the genotype, the environment may obscure gene differences, and some genetic variation may simply be non-functional. The tasks of the behavior geneticist are to classify these instances and derive relationships between gene-environment interactions and the functional qualities of the organism.

The Evolution of Sex and Variability

The task I set for myself in this section is to outline the current thinking about the origin of genetic and phenotypic variability and suggest how the study of patterns of reproduction can facilitate the goal of behavior geneticists to link behavior to gene action. Of necessity the discussion will be abbreviated and more general than I would prefer, given more time.

Gene mutation is commonly seen as the ultimate cause of variation, and so it may be in extant species. However, it is also recognized that increases in organismic complexity require more than natural selection acting on existing variants (Charles & Knight, 1970; King, 1977; Margulis, 1976; Spiegelman, 1971). Mutation and genetic recombination seem insufficient to account for many of the qualitative leaps in evolution including that to higher forms of reproduction. To get at this problem we must seek answers to the questions of how organisms acquire large amounts of variability and how such variability is transmitted to successive generations. In short, we must know a great deal about the evolution of sex.

Sex is assumed to be an evolutionary adaptation similar to any other evolved trait. Its specificity differs among taxonomic groups and in a very direct way relates to the ecological demands imposed on organisms during the course of natural selection. Sex is in a very direct sense the _sine qua non_ of survival for complex species - evolution's grandest scheme of gene survival.

Despite our bow to the significance of sex it has been asserted by E. O. Wilson (1975) and others that sex is actually an antisocial force in evolution. The problem with sexual reproduction is that there is a 50 percent loss in an individual's genotype with each offspring; that is, there is a 50 percent decrease in genetic relatedness with each gametic reduction division. George C. Williams (1975) calls this "meiotic loss". As a consequence of meiosis only one half of an organism's genes are passed on with each reproductive effort. From the point of view of an animal's attempt to maximize reproductive fitness it is obvious that complete genetic replication as in cloning or budding would be more advantageous.

Sex is genetically costly in another sense. Segregation of genes during meiosis and recombination with the formation of a unique zygote can break down coevolved genetic arrangements and introduce epistatic (non-additive) interactions among loci that may reduce viability and reproductive capacities. We can refer to this second sexual cost as a "recombination load," a genetic burden that must be carried by the sexual recombinant.

Obviously in sexually reproducing species if adaptation and evolution progress through sexual reproduction the meiotic loss and recombinational load must be compensated for by some major advantages. Here, then, is the basic question we face in the understanding of sexual reproduction and associated social mating systems. If, as Wilson asserts, sexual reproduction occurs in spite of sociality and not because of it, we must understand why sex seems so maladaptive on the surface yet appears to be the supreme result of natural selection.

Part of the answer lies in the understanding of the origins of organismic complexity and in knowing when asexual and sexual reproduction are advantageous. The point to start, perhaps, is with the evolution of eukaryotic cells and the exchange of genetic information. Much of this discussion follows that of Brown (1975), Ghiselin (1974) and Wilson (1975).

Williams (1975) believes, at odds with current dogma, that the union of particles and cellular components lies at the basis of asexuality as well as sexuality. Rather than sexual reproduction arising directly from asexual reproduction, asexual reproduction is seen as resulting from a variety of forms of particle conjugation and in itself a primitive form of sex. Indeed, current thinking in biology emphasizes that early forms of particle assemblage preceeded the importance of mutation and even the genetic code. Such mutually beneficial interactions of organic particles, that is, symbiosis, propelled species to increased size and complexity, setting the stage for the divergence of asexual and sexual strategies.

King (1977) outlines an ingenious notion that during evolutionary history the steady depletion of nutrients and recycled metabolic materials allowed the differential replication of assemblages, where mutually advantageous exchanges of metabolic materials were facilitated by close and integrated associations. Once an interdependency was established among particles it would be likely to continue because the conditions for the recycling of exchanged materials would likely persist (depleted environmental nutrients) and the internal concentration of recycled and accessible materials would remain higher with the symbiotic association. The result of symbiotic unions was a qualitative jump in organismic size and complexity, completely without mutations. It now seems evident that plastids, mitochondria and possibly other particles and organelles found in eukaryotic cells originated as free-living prokaryotes which found permanent shelter as symbiotic elements. The ability to incorporate and maintain endosymbionts is a distinctive biological attribute of eukaryotes - a basic form of sex.

King goes on to speculate that early life stages favored symbiosis, and that the genetic DNA code was an emergent property of the union of simple elements, such as nucleotide bases. As the ecological nutrients were depleted the "coefficient of symbiosis" decreased favoring mutation and later recombination as mechanisms of evolutionary progression. At some point no more symbionts were formed and processes involving the genetic code began. Natural selection acting on mutated variants would actually result in simpler (more efficient) organisms, but gene recombination and gene duplication would reverse this tendency by introducing "cooperative units of inheritance." It is possible to imagine that the recombination due to prokaryotic interaction might well have established a trend toward highly differentiated and obligatory sexual systems found in more advanced organisms.

Whatever the bases for the original conjugations of elements into symbiotic unions, it left two major forms of genetic transmission, haploidy and diploidy. The evolution of eukaryotes passed through sexually reproductive forms that were somatically or vegetatively haploid. In unicellular forms (algae, fungi, protozoa, bacteria) haploidy is the general rule throughout the life cycle. Asexual reproduction is accomplished usually by fission.

Some cells, such as bacteria, may display facultative diploidy, where only a part of the genome is occasionally exchanged between haploid individuals ("mermixia"). The primary reproductive strategy remains asexual. Haplo-diplo species represent the next evolutionary advance, where haploid asexual reproduction may be the usual vegetative state, but where there is periodic cellular union with a resulting diploid organism. In the diploid state there is fusion of genetic material from the two cells, followed by meiosis, cellular dissociation and the reversion to a haploid asexual state. Higher fungi and the highest forms of invertebrate social species which form colonies or aggregations, such as sponges, coelenterates and tunicates, are often haplo- diplo and reproduce both asexually and sexually. Still, the primary reproductive strategy is asexual.

Diploidy, as a fundamental vegetative system, is recognized only in eukaryotic organisms. Almost all vertebrates, with the exception of parthenogenetic species (some fish, amphibia and reptiles) follow this pattern. The shift from haploidy to diploidy as the somatic vegetative state is an extremely important evolutionary advance. Note here, however, that haploidy still occurs as the result of meiosis. Apparently no species has circumvented haploidy, or its equivalent, as part of the fundamental reproductive strategy.

The restriction of haploidy to simple and primitive forms and the almost universal presence of diploidy in more highly advanced forms argue strongly that the diploid condition often confers significant biological advantages. There is no definitive answer as to why diploidy has had such a selective advantage, but several reasons have been advanced:

1. Cell for cell, the diploid organism contains twice the amount of genetic information. For paired alleles at n loci a haploid contains 2n genotypes, the diploid contains 3n alleles. In a one locus system with two alleles, A and B, a haploid can either carry A or B, but the diploid can carry AA, AB, or BB.

2. Additional amounts of DNA may allow for expression of alternative alleles at the same locus, genetic redundancy and the fine-tuned regulation of structural gene expression.

3. Heterozygotes can transmit neutral genes into subsequent generations (a significant source of preadaptations) and limit the effects of deleterious recessive alleles.

4. There may at times be an advantage for the diploid population (the Baldwin effect), whereby the diploid condition allows for phenotypic accomodation of the population in suboptimal conditions until a genetic adjustment can be made in the population (comparable to Waddington's "assimilation").

5. H. J. Muller (1932) suggested that evolution will favor sexual reproduction, and hence the diploid system, because the rate of evolution is facilitated. For a haploid the generation of variability depends upon successive mutations. To get the favored combination a'b', at two loci a must mutate to a' and b must mutate to b'. With sexual reproduction, however, a'b' can result either because of successive mutations or because of recombination between two individuals, ab' and a'b. The process is speeded in small populations where social containment on individuals enforces inbreeding, or where mating occurs between sympatric populations in which each population includes one of the two variants. This process has been considered to be the long-term advantage of sexual reproduction.

6. Williams (1975), on the other hand, proposes that sexual reproduction has an immediate advantage of producing diverse organisms that can adapt to unpredictable environments. Sex, according to Williams, is an adaptation to special situations. We will trace this argument below.

In summary, the asexual and sexual modes of reproduction have distinct advantages under particular circumstances. The advantages of haploidy and asexual propagation in primitive forms are prolific reproduction of mitotically uniform types within a stable environment. The genotype is optimally adapted as long as the environment remains constant. Because of the short life cycle cloning can quickly fill a niche to capacity without meiotic loss or recombinational load. Genetic relatedness, so necessary for sociality, is high.

In contrast, and of utmost significance for natural selection, sexual reproduction in diploid systems has the advantage of quickly producing variants of the most complex form. Fewer individuals will be optimally adapted to the parental environment, but more will be preadapted for unique environments. Another way of saying this is that sex produces novel genotypes and an unusual number of extreme phenotypes. These extreme miotically diversified offspring are referred to as "sisyphean genotypes." These are the genotypes that offer the raw material for natural selection and the ones that behavior geneticists are usually concerned with. Genetic relatedness among individuals is slight and hence sociality is low.

The distinctions summarized above are heuristic but simplified. The reference has been to asexual mitotically standardized organisms or to sexual meiotically diversified organisms subjected to a variable environment. There is another important organismic distinction that can be made which will limit our original distinction. Species can be roughly classified as r-selected or K-selected species. The former refers to those with rapid density-independent growth with wide dispersal; whereas the latter refers to those with slow density-dependent growth. There are other important correlated characteristics, including degrees of sociality, some of which are listed in Table 2.

TABLE 2
Some Correlates of r and K Selection *
(After Pianka, 1970)

Attribute	r-Selection	K-Selection
Geophysical condition	variable and unpredictable	constant and predictable
Mortality	catastrophic and density independent population size variable	directed and density dependent population size constant
Intraspecific and inter-specific competition	variable, often lax	usually keen
Population number	low to high, variable	low constant
Length of life	short (less than one year)	long (more than one year)
Colonizing ability	large (random dispersal)	small (directed migration or movement)

Emphasis in energy utilization	productivity	efficiency
Attributes favored by selection	1. high reproduction 2. early reproduction 3. rapid development 4. small size 5. semelparity (single mating)	1. low reproduction 2. late reproduction 3. late development 4. large size 5. iteroparity (repeated mating)
Behavioral response to environment	adapts by genetic change, stereotyped	adapts by physiological adjustments and behavior
Social behavior	weak, schools, herds, aggregations and colonies	frequently well-developed

* Generally, r-selected species are comprised of insects, invertebrates, and lower vertebrates. Among mammals are small rodents (deer mice, house mice, voles). Social tolerance of a species has evolved to match the optimal population density and population structure. All demographic, morphological, physiological and behavioral features are coadapted. None is of more obvious importance. Dispersion is a constraining force in evolution. Small movement = small population size, greater inbreeding and loss of genetic variability (K strategists).

Now the interesting fact is that K-selected species are diploid, sexual in reproductive strategy and genetically diverse, yet they behave more like cloning organisms than they do like sexual r-selected species. Table 3 shows the similarities and contrasts both the sexual and asexual r-selected species with K-selected species. It is as if the most complex species showing K-selected traits have reassumed asexual phenotypic characteristics despite the overwhelming genetic preadaptation inherent in the genotype. Apparently a high level of organismic complexity is often associated with a standardized phenotype. As we shall see in a moment, these diverse reproductive strategies have implications for the genetic study of behavior.

TABLE 3

Expected Differences Between Asexually and Sexually Produced Offspring (Based on Williams, 1975)

Asexual (mitotically standardized offspring)	Sexual (r-selected) (meiotically diversified offspring)	Sexual (K-selected) (meiotically diversified offspring)
1. large initial size	small	large initial size
2. produced continuously	seasonally limited (semelparity)	produced continuously (iteroparity)
3. develop close to parent	widely dispersed	develop close to parent
4. develop immediately	delayed development	delayed development
5. develop directly to adult	develop through a series of diverse embryos and larvae	develop directly to adult
6. environment and optimum genotype predictable from those of parent (genetic relatedness is high)	environment and optimum genotype unpredictable (genetic relatedness is low)	environment and optimum genotype predictable from those of parent (genetic relatedness is high)
7. low mortality rate	high mortality rate	low mortality rate
8. natural selection mild	natural selection intense	natural selection mild

Before we argue the case for behavior genetics one point need be stressed about the haplo-diplo mode of reproduction. Williams (1975) speculates that haploid individuals will opt for sexual reproduction only when the niche becomes filled or the environment changes, requiring new adaptations which are only possible through genetic recombination. In other words, under threat from the environment mitotically standardized individuals will shift to an r-selected mode of reproduction. Some of the resulting sisyphean genotypes relocate in a stable and permissive environment and once again begin a haploid existence. Aphids, rodifers and many parasites fit this pattern.

With all of the above variations in reproductive strategies and with differences in genetic diversity and phenotypic stability, nature has provided the behavior geneticist with the natural laboratory for the investigation of genes and behavior. All aspects of individual survival and reproduction should follow from the modes of reproduction and the conditions of the environment. Several predictions are possible, none of which has been tested systematically. Here are just a few:

1. Asexual species should be uniform genetically and phenotypically, except during environmental changes when many of these should shift to an r-selected sexual strategy. Sociality should change accordingly, being high during asexual phases and low during sexual phases.

2. r-selected species should generate sisyphean genotypes, only a few of which survive. Those that do, however, should show an extremely close relationship between genetic variation and environmental heterogeneity. Sociality should be low.

3. K-selected species should be relatively uniform phenotypically but show a wealth of genetic variation, most of which is silent with regard to behavior. Selection pressures should nevertheless operate effectively to reconstruct the phenotype, as it does in r-strategists and in primitive species undergoing the diploid phase of reproduction. Sociality will normally be high except when phenotypic diversity manifests itself under new pressures of the environment. Then, genetic differences are expressed and the degree of phenotypic relatedness among individuals will be reduced.

Most of these predictions can be tested in the natural environment using a comparative approach. But they can also be studied in the laboratory by subjecting a few species and individuals to a variety of environments and selection pressures. Theoretically, one should be able to specify the optimal mix between gene variation, environmental demands and reproductive strategies.

Genetic Variance as Tools of the Trade

Aside from the theoretical importance of determining the impact of genetic variation on behavior, genetic variance has the very practical use of providing the investigator with units of genetic material which can be manipulated and studied. Individual mutants backcrossed onto inbred backgrounds has become a common method to isolate single genetic units in order to study physiological processes and behavior. Many other related techniques are being developed. None of these would be possible if it were not for the inherent polymorphism within and between individuals and the high penetrance of many genetic units into the visible phenotype.

Single genes and chromosomal variants have already allowed us to complete yeoman-like tasks in the elucidation of normalities and abnormalities in human pedigrees, perceptual and motor systems, and neurological processes. More generally, in the service of biology, single genetic units are providing information about individual fitness and reproductive performance. My emphasis is here.

Gene markers can illustrate the genetic architecture of a population and can be used to show the dynamics of the population over time and under a variety of environmental pressures. One can theoretically fathom from these analyses behavioral and environmental processes that produce the genetic constitution of a population and act creatively for their change.

Behavior geneticists might well attend to work being conducted by Krebs and his colleagues (Krebs & Myers, 1974). Using genetic polymorphisms in the serum protein, albumins and transferrins, these investigators have pointed out striking gene frequency changes in populations of <u>Microtus</u> (voles) associated with changes in population density, dispersal and differential migration.

In two studies of <u>M</u>. <u>ochrogaster</u> there was found a positive correlation between the frequency of the transferrin TfE allele and the changes in population density. This was due to the better survival of heterozygotes (TfE TfE) during the population decline. In other populations studied dispersing animals at peak densities appeared to be genetically dissimilar to those remaining in the population. In <u>M</u>. <u>pennsylvanicus</u> the animals with the highest reproductive capacity (young females) were dispersing, and could be identified as having a different frequency of a transferrin allele.

Krebs and his associates have speculated that animals surviving peak densities and those that disperse are different genetically, physiologically and behaviorally. The marking experiments provide examples of the different classes of animals which can be studied in order to determine the mechanisms of survival and migration. It may be that aggression, growth potential and some other phenotypes are responsible for the demographic and genetic characteristics of the population. Certainly here is a beautiful opportunity to employ genetic markers in the field and the laboratory in order to unravel the relationship between genes, behavior, and reproductive fitness.

Indeed there is growing evidence to suggest that rates of evolutionary change in morphology and other traits are related to the type of social system displayed (Bush, 1975; Wilson, Bush, Case & King, 1975). In the lineage of fish, amphibian, reptile and mammal, there is a corresponding increase in the karyotic changes in chromosome number and the average number of chromosome arms. Changes in chromosome number usually involve fission or fusion events, whereas changes in arm number are associated with inversions or gain or loss of heterochromatin. These characteristic changes are highly correlated with morphological changes, body size and the degree of inbreeding displayed by the species. Briefly, the more complex the species karyotype the more advanced it's morphological evolution. The larger the species the less rapidly it evolves. And the more socially confined a species the faster it evolves. Small placental species, like rodents, are the most rapidly evolving species of any studied.

The rationale for these correlations are as follows. Placental mammals, requiring a great deal of parental care, usually have small, sedentary and interbreeding populations. Often the breeding group never exceeds 10. When a genetic reorganization occurs, such as a change in chromosome or arm number, it quickly spreads through the breeding pool and becomes fixed in a homozygous state. If the new genetic constitution is adaptive at the phenotype it may become fixed in two or three generations.

Loosely organized species, such as lower vertebrates and marine organisms, on the other hand, lack strong barriers against gene flow between populations. As a result chromosomal rearrangements are fixed less rapidly, which is another way of saying that evolution is slower. Similarly, larger animals with wider foraging ranges and greater mobility inbreed less and evolve less rapidly. For example, primates evolve more slowly than rodents, presumably because the former are more mobile and inbreed less. And bats and whales which travel long distances evolve more slowly than primates or rodents.

There are large mobile animals, however, that do evolve rapidly. Horses (<u>Equus</u>) exemplify how a coherent family system can override mobility effects. Their chromosome numbers range from 2n = 32 in <u>E</u>. <u>zebra</u> of southwestern Africa to 2n = 66 in the Eurasian <u>E</u>. <u>przewalskii</u>. This extensive karyotypic evolution is associated with a family system which consists of one dominant stallion, several mares which remain with the stallion for life, and the young of the stallion (Klingel, 1975). The young leave the family at two to four years of age to form bachelor groups or new family units. When a member of the original group dies it is replaced by nearby younger members that appear to be related. Thus even though the home range may be as large as 200 square kilometers, the breeding units remain intact permitting the rapid spread of chromosomal variants among the related members. Socially tight knit groups such as this have been noted throughout placental mammals and may account for rapid evolutionary shifts in behavior, even in highly mobile species.

These exciting findings are possible because of our ability to karyotype organisms and identify inversions. Genetic markers such as these, even though relatively gross, provide a powerful approach to the study of behavior and reproductive fitness. I suspect that the use of genetic markers will serve the behavior geneticist in a number of other important ways. An investigator can now hope to operationally code the genotype and interrelate genetic variations and behavior to reproductive fitness and processes of natural selection.

DIFFERENTIAL EXPRESSION OF GENES IN BEHAVIOR

A second major area of growing importance in behavior genetics and biology, and perhaps one of the most crucial for the understanding of how gene action is translated into behavior, is molecular biology. It is a recognized fact that DNA is the life-stuff of most species and often varies in quantity in a parallel fashion with increasing complexity of the organism (Britten & Davidson, 1969; see previous section). A certain proportion of this DNA, that which is responsible for the most fundamental biochemicals of life, is common to most species. In the basic energy system of <u>E</u>. <u>coli</u>, mouse and man, the DNA-biochemical relations appear to be the same (Dobzhansky, 1974; Sturtevant, 1965).

It is necessary to know, then, just what function the additional amounts of DNA perform in physiological and behavioral processes and why this DNA increases in amount in more complex species. For example, in man only about 2 percent of the existing 3 million genes act as enzyme-producing genes. These are the genes commonly known as structural genes (Omenn &

Motulsky, 1971). The remaining 98 percent of the genes apparently do not produce fundamental enzymes directly but act as regulator genes, or they are neutral in their effects during some part of the life cycle.

Inherent in this notion is the suggestion that a great proportion of phenotypic variance, including behavioral variance, in man and other animals is probably due to regulator genes rather than structural genes - genes that activate, deactivate or otherwise alter the expression of a finite number of structural genes.

The best known model for gene regulation is that proposed by Jacob & Monod (1961) where it was determined with the bacterium E. coli that the synthesis of the enzyme galactosidase by a structural gene is under the control of a single regulator gene responsive to the amount of galactoside in the cytoplasm. When galactoside increases in the cytoplasm the structural gene for galactosidase activity is stimulated, and the reverse occurs when galactoside falls. A more complicated feed-back model has been proposed by Britten and Davidson (1969) which may have more relevance for gene regulation in complex species. The generalization emerges that gene transcription is open to modification by environmental factors. Thus a dynamic character is added to gene action sufficient to account for variable behavior expression and homeostatic reactions. At this point it is believable that much of the DNA of higher species is of this regulatory type, although the details of regulation may differ widely.

Certainly evidence exists for this variable gene expression and environmental control in single cells, insects, and mammals. The molting pattern of Diptern species like Drosophila is a classic example (Clever, 1964; see also Schmidt-Nielsen, 1975). Here, under the influence of the inductor hormone, ecdysone, the entire life style of the organism changes abruptly during metamorphosis from a worm-like creature to a fully developed fly. When strained properly the giant polytene chromosomes of these species show extensive puffing of specific DNA bands during critical periods of development. The puffs which occur in a specified order presumably represent new DNA and RNA activity related in time and sequence to the overall event of the metamorphosis. The chromosome effect and metamorphosis can be facilitated by the early injection of ecdysone, and puffing and development can be inhibited by tying up DNA with the antibiotic actinomycin-D. These data are highly compatible with the concept that genes are active or quiescent depending on regulatory actions from the environment and other gene units.

Extensive investigation of the slime mold <u>Dictystelium</u> <u>discoideum</u> by J. T. Bonner (1971), Konijn (1973) and others (see Thiessen, 1977) has revealed an extremely complex chemical interaction among eukaryotic cells, based in great part on environmental induction of gene activity. This work is particularly important, as the life cycle of the mold bridges the gap between single-cell and multicellular nuclear organisms - between isolated cells and social colonies.

<u>D</u>. <u>discoideum</u> has two distinct life phases: the first consists of a vegetative phase during which single cells grow, synthesize DNA, and divide; whereas the second consists of a dynamic developmental phase in which the unicellular bodies stream together to form a differential multicellular slug which has great mobility.

The slime mold plays an important role in the balance of soil bacteria. The single cells seek out and consume bacteria by following a bacterial trail of cyclic AMP and possibly another chemical which appears to be folic acid. During this vegetative phase the mold cells are kept apart by a secretory product which may be ammonia, a degradative product of normal cellular metabolism. When the feeding site is depleted of bacteria the "spacing" substance is inhibited and the cells begin to pulse the chemical attractant cyclic AMP, bringing the individual cells together within 6 to 8 hours. They then form a differentiated mass which can both move away from the depleted feeding site (attractions toward light and heat) and form stalk cells which release spores, any one of which can start a new generation. Only a few cells of the slug ever become reproductive. This remarkable cellular "cooperation" and aggregation suggests that sacrificial cells share a great many genes in common with those that go on to form reproductive spores.

For our immediate purpose it is important to note that differentiation of the slug is accompanied by increased trehalose 6-phosphate synthase activity, an increase in cellular glycogen, and increased specific activity of glycogen phosphorylase and uridine diphosphoglucose pyrophosphorylase (Garrod & Ashworth, 1973). Each of these changes occurs in a proper metabolic sequence and is due to shifts in structural gene activity. For every specific enzymatic change noted there is a limited period of sensitivity to the protein inhibitor, cycloheximide. This is compelling evidence that there is precise regulatory timing of the various phases of metamorphosis and that each metabolic phase, including chemosignal formation and emission, involves genetic transcription and translation.

Even more spectacular are cases in which not only does the
environment induce cellular changes in enzyme activity but where
receptor mechanisms are formed under environmental impact in
order to deal with surrounding pertubations. For example, in
many well-studied prokaryotic and eukaryotic systems, the
chemical environment of the cell (as with nutrient molecules)
induces the necessary enzymatic changes. When new species of
sugar are introduced as a carbohydrate source to bacteria, new
enzymes are induced which enable the cells to take up and
metabolize the new sugars (Hochachka & Somero, 1973). The
catabolic by-products of this enzymatic shift may then act as
pheromones to proximal organisms.

Adler (1973) and Adler, Hazelbaur and Dahl (1973) have shown
that at least nine membrane chemoreceptors exist for sugars in E.
coli: galactose, glucose, N-acetylgluco-samine, fucose, maltose,
mannitol, ribose, sorbital and trehalose receptors. All these
sugars can act as chemoattractants when distributed along
gradients of increasing concentration. What is truly remarkable
is that, with the exception of the glucose receptor, all of the
chemoreceptors for sugars are inducible, that is, they are formed
on the membrane surface only in the presence of the specific
sugars. For instance, a bacterium in a medium containing ribose
responds by forming ribose receptors. An induced receptor will
respond to all sugars that have sufficient molecular
similarities. Thus, not only do cells form enzymes to utilize
new foodstuffs, they actually build new membrane structures that
respond to unique environmental chemicals. Since Adler and his
colleagues have demonstrated that membrane receptors are under
genetic control, one can tentatively conclude that chemicals in
the media induce gene action necessary for the processing of
environmental signals. Certainly our attention should be drawn
to the possibility that behavior is more closely related to
regulatory processes than to structural genes.

There is little reason to think that pheromonal
changes within an organism involve all-or-none shifts in
structural gene function (Kolata, 1975). But there is
greater reason to posit that the link between the
environment and pheromones is mediated by genomic regulatory
mechanisms (Tomkins, 1975). Structural genes and their
protein products are relatively stable across a wide
phylogenetic continuum. These rather common genes show
little correlation with alterations in morphology or
behavior, and they show little variation between species
that differ widely in their phenotypes. For example,
Mary-Claire King and Allan Wilson (1975) found that human
proteins are on the average identical to those in
chimpanzees for about 99% of those sampled. This means that
humans and chimpanzees share as many structural genes as

kindred species (those primate species which are not totally sexually isolated), suggesting that the major morphological and behavioral differences are due to changes in gene regulation rather than changes in structural genes. Genetic similarity among structural genes is probably widespread across phylogenetic lines, as the basic DNA-RNA code and the fundamental energy system are nearly identical in all species. But regulatory genes shift rapidly with selection pressure and may even account for the major evolutionary divergences in the fossil record. (Valentine & Campbell, 1975). (Thiessen, 1977, page 177)

In our own laboratory we are finding that activation of ventral scent marking in the Mongolian gerbil is induced by androgens acting in the preoptic area of the brain. The hormone probably stimulates or inhibits gene activity, since antibiotics that prevent DNA activity or disrupt protein formation attenuate the hormone effect (Thiessen, Yahr, & Owen, 1973). Yahr (1977) has been able to detect immunological changes in hypothalamic proteins correlated with ventral scent marking and testosterone levels, substantiating a regulatory gene function.

Dr. Andrew Clancy (unpublished), working in my laboratory, studied the developmental interaction between hormone levels and ventral scent marking in the Mongolian gerbil. The intent was to specify a range of behavioral modifiability based on the chromosomal characteristics of the animals and their differential sensitivity to testosterone.

It proved possible to rank order animals from the various treatment groups on their behavior. Males marked significantly more than females, animals exposed to neonatal androgens marked significantly more than nonexposed gerbils, and adult testosterone maintained gerbils marked significantly more than nonmaintained animals. Further, males were significantly more sensitive than females to both neonatal and adult androgens as evidenced by their higher marking frequencies. Finally, gerbils exposed as neonates to androgens were significantly more responsive to adult testosterone than nonexposed animals. These results suggest, but do not prove, that the hormonal variations specified by the Y chromosome influence gene activity related to the behavior.

These experiments support the notion that the development of specific patterns of hormone or enzyme activity are predetermined by the sex chromosomes and are implemented by gonadal androgen in early postnatal life. Sex behavior, and its development, may depend upon similar enzymatic programming in neural tissue and during neonatal life. Analyses like those of Yahr and Clancy will help specify the molecular events that predetermine the course of behavioral development and expression. Certainly this is an exciting line of research in the study of gene regulation of behavior, and will undoubtedly have its sharp impact on the study of any dimorphic trait under chemical control.

There are several implications for the study of genes and behavior. Of foremost importance is the notion that the environment can specify and directly determine the impact of genes on behavior. Interestingly, behavior genetics arose in part as a counter force to an extreme environmentalistic position. Now, paradoxically, we are witnessing a return to this position, albeit indirectly. Only the environment can be the ultimate driving force of evolution and the arbitrator of gene function.

Obviously the environment and genes influence all behaviors and usually in complimentary ways. However, in my thinking the explanation of behavioral processes will come from an understanding of how the environment shapes the genome, physiology and behavior. With today's technology the behavior geneticist can help unravel the pathways between environmental influence, gene transcription and behavior.

A second point that I would make is that the behavioral variation that we are so accustomed to seeing, regardless of what that behavior may be, is not necessarily the result of a great deal of polymorphism. The environment, in its vissicitudes, may lend variability to the phenotype when it does not exist in the structure of the genotype. A malleable behavior may be one of nature's primary adaptations to unpredictable environments. Behaviors to meet all possible contingencies obviously cannot be programmed into a finite amount of DNA, but natural selection can provide the regulatory mechanisms for response flexibility, namely gene inducibility.

We are keenly aware of the wide range of effects of experience on behavior, due in part to the learning tradition in psychology, and in part to the psychoanalytic influence. These conceptual attacks on understanding behavior have been, and still are, extremely important. They have not, however, readily meshed with genetic explanations of behavior, and unfortunately led to decades of debate over which was more important in the determination of behavior, genes or environment. Now, perhaps, molecular biology can provide the essential links between experiential effects on behavior and gene influence.

The environment obviously does effect behavior, but it must do so through neurophysiologic and genetic change. Even at the level of the neuron it is reasonable to postulate that environmental stimuli may alter the conductive state of that neuron by way of genetic transcription. Like the action of hormones and other biochemicals, sensory input may modulate genetic and hence subsequent physiological and behavioral actions. This may not be true for rigidly programmed behaviors, but it is reasonable to guess that it is with the ontogeny of any associative behavior. In any case, I think we can now begin to envisage how environmentalistic and genetic notions are converging at the interface of the environment and gene transcription.

Unfortunately, and this may be the immediate and practical problem for behavior geneticists, it is difficult to isolate and identify regulatory genes for behavior in complex species. There have been attempts, but in my opinion the outcomes are not satisfactory. How does one distinguish a regulatory gene from a structural gene, or from a modifier gene? Is an intra-allelic interaction a regulatory effect in the sense I have used in this chapter? And what about threshold effects, epistatic interactions, canalization of the phenotype or catastrophic shifts in ongoing behavior? What may be a structural gene under one circumstance may be a regulatory gene under another. We actually know so little about the mechanisms of classic genetics that it is difficult to make the technical and conceptual leap to regulatory models.

This may not be as pessimistic as it first sounds, since powerful inferential methods of studying regulatory processes are available. DNA transcription, RNA production and protein synthesis are easiy measured in the cell, and can be done in parallel to the observations of behavior and the manipulation of the environment. The work discussed on chemotaxis in E. coli, aggregation of slime mold and metamorphic transformation of larva into adults are examples of how gene regulation can be distinguished and studied. Immunological, pharmacological and hormonal techniques are immediately applicable.

SOCIOBIOLOGY, A FRAMEWORK FOR BEHAVIOR GENETICS

Perhaps the most striking advance in biology which will ultimately affect the character of behavior genetics is the application of natural selection principles to the study of social behavior. I am of course referring to the newly emerging discipline of sociobiology. Sociobiology has been defined as the study of the biological basis of all social behavior (Wilson, 1975). It assumes that all underlying processes of behavior of

all animal species are in service of reproductive fitness
(Barash, 1977; Brown, 1975; Daly & Wilson, 1978). According to
this notion natural selection has programmed the individual to
either fulfill his selfish genetic destiny directly through
reproduction, or indirectly by helping his relatives reproduce
(Hamilton, 1963, 1964).

The theory is of great interest because of its breadth of
application and boldness. No species is immune from its
application:

> Some sociobiologists go so far as to suggest that there
> may be human genes for such behavior as conformism,
> homosexuality, and spite. Carried to an extreme,
> sociobiology holds that all forms of life exist solely to
> serve the purpose of DNA, the coded master molecule that
> determines the nature of all organisms and is the stuff of
> genes. (Time, August 1, 1977, page 54)

While this interpretation is extreme, it is true that
sociobiology has been embraced enthusiastically and applied
widely by those who seek universal explanations for behavior at
any level. Little wonder that this intellectual adventure has
been met with suspicion and derision - sociobiology, according to
its critics, promises to "geneticise" all behavior from the
single cell to man. It is seen to ennoble the gene and degrade
learning and culture. According to Washburn (1978):

> Sociobiologists are now repeating many of the errors of
> the past. The laws of genetics are not the laws of
> learning, and as long as sociobiologists confuse their
> radically different mechanisms, sociobiology will only
> obstruct the understanding of human social behavior. (page
> 416)

A similar point has been made by Sahlins (1977):

> In sum, the sociobiological reasoning from evolutionary
> phylogeny to social morphology is interrupted by culture.
> (page 11)

Actually the sociobiological application of neo-Darwinian
principles to social behavior would not be especially remarkable
if it were not for its implications for human behavior. Few
scientists disregard phylogeny in the understanding of behavior;
almost everyone accepts the principles of natural selection; and
most researchers view animal populations and their demography as
the outcome of differential reproduction. What is remarkable is
the reticence of even biologists to extent their evolutionary
logic to human behavior.

My task, it seems to me, is not to defend sociobiology or even outline its purview. Others have done that admirably. Rather, I would like to begin by assuming that there may be substance in some of its notions and suggest points of interaction between sociobiology and behavior genetics. Behavior genetics, through its systematic methodology, can add credibility to the theoretical structure of sociobiology, or at least set out predictions that can be tested in the field or the laboratory.

Proximate Versus Ultimate Causes of Behavior.

The source of greatest controversy in sociobiology is whether or not genes determine the character of adaptive phenotypes, or if the environment shapes the phenotypes. Once again we see the emergence of the nature-nurture question. The environmentalists believe that if there is flexibility to behavior (if there is learning and choice behavior), then the strict interpretation of behavior given by the sociobiologists cannot be true.

But this is an unwarranted dichotomy and ignores the possibility that natural selection can impose flexibility on an organism for the very purpose of allowing adaptive responses under conditions of change or uncertainty. Whether or not behavioral flexibility exists cannot be used to judge the degree to which genes determine behavior or the extent to which the phenotype has been selected for adaptive qualities. The bottom line of organismic success is reproductive fitness, however imposed.

Mayr (1976) believes that the ambiguity reflected in the nature- nurture question results from our inability to separate levels of causation and at the same time to see their interrelatedness. As an example Mayr reflects on why the warbler migrates south from New Hampshire in the early fall. The answers will differ depending upon our level of analysis. There is first an ecological cause. The warbler is an insect eater and cannot remain in New Hampshire in the winter when the insects disappear. Second, there is a genetic cause, in that through natural selection the warbler has acquired the genetic constitution which induces it to respond appropriately to the environmental changes associated with food availability. Third, there is an intrinsic physiological cause that stimulates the warbler to respond to a decrease in day length with migratory tendencies. This involves hormonal changes in response to photoperiods. Finally, there is an extrinsic physiological cause that triggers the flight behavior. This may be a sudden drop in ambient temperature or a seasonal change in wind direction.

Now, if we look over the four causations of the
migration of this bird once more, we can readily see that
there is an immediate set of causes of the migration,
consisting of the physiological condition of the bird
interacting with photoperiodicity and drop in temperature.
We might call these the proximate causes of migration. The
other two causes, the lack of food during the winter and the
genetic disposition of the bird, are the ultimate causes.
(Mayr, 1976, pages 362-363)

The tendency has been for an investigator to concentrate on
one of these levels of explanation without regard to the other.
Each level can be studied successfully, and many questions
resolved, yet they are all interrelated in that all have been
structured to optimize the possibility that reproduction will be
accomplished. More exactly, the warbler that reproduces will be
the one that responds appropriately to its ecology with regard to
its genotype, its physiology and the contingencies of the
environment. All other response patterns enter the log book of
the genetically damned.

And so it is with learning and the most complex neuromotor
reactions. Rats may well evidence classical or instrumental
conditioning, and humans may use language and conceptual skills,
but their application and variability will still correlate with
reproductive fitness; they have not been freed of their
evolutionary history. It is difficult to imagine that a skill,
however complex, will not have a bearing on gene transmission and
hence be subject to natural selection. K-selected species, in
particular, who must adjust to environmental and social
contingencies, should have the necessary flexibility to adapt to
changing conditions. Those that do not simply do not reproduce.

Sociobiology stresses the distinction between proximate and
ultimate causes for good reason. The proximate causes are the
immediate and most evident mechanisms of behavioral adjustment,
whereas the ultimate causes are the phylogenetic and ecological
driving forces of those mechanisms. Researchers may elect to
investigate the proximate causes of behavior, but they should not
lose sight of the possibility that their expressions are in
service of the ultimate causes.

Behavior genetics has traditionally been a discipline of
"proximate causation". It has been of interest to specify the
immediate genetic determinants of a behavior and elucidate their
physiological mediation. These pursuits can uncover a great
deal, but it must be admitted that the proximate orientation is
constraining. One could, perhaps, determine all proximate forces
acting on warbler migration without any insight into the cause of
genetic variation or the reasons why warblers migrate. If we

combine the proximate and ultimate approaches our questions will be more relevant and our investigations more direct. Consideration of the ultimate causes of behavior (the why questions) can focus our investigations on those qualities of behavior that relate to individual survival and reproduction.

The Evolution of Mating Strategies.

The diversity of mating strategies is one of the most evident facets of survival in the animal kingdom. There is no more important social behavior, since gene transmission directly follows mating.

The type of mating system used within a species will be determined in large measure by historical ecological pressures that preset the range of behavioral and physiological possibilities. Whatever the strategy, all existing systems depend upon earlier successes of reproduction. In simplistic terms, animals will protect their genetic investment to the degree necessary to insure that offspring attain reproductive status. Where cooperation between mates is essential, as when offspring survival depends upon foraging by both parents, permanent or temporary monogamy will occur. But if one parent can provide the necessary care and protection to the offspring then polygamy may develop.

Behavioral genetic analyses can decipher the potential variability of mating strategies within and between species and determine the conditions under which monogamy or polygamy will occur. For instance, there is no clear understanding why birds are primarily monogamous (90%) while mammals are essentially polygamous (97%). The environmental conditions for both forms of mating have not been clearly determined, although certain basic features seem to hold for each. Similarly, for mammals and birds, it is not certain if monogamy or polygamy are always obligatory or shift from one to the other should the environment dictate. Again, behavior genetic analyses can help determine the interactive consequences of genetic variability, behavioral plasticity and environmental change. It is a matter of asking the right questions.

At the root of differential mating strategies is the evolution of sexual dimorphism and division of male and female parental investments. We normally think of sexual dimorphism as a phenotypic difference in courtship and parental strategies or a difference in aggressive behaviors. Basic to these dimorphic traits, however, is the evolution of dimorphism in gamete structure and function. An abbreviated discussion of this evolutionary process may illuminate areas where behavior genetics can contribute to the understanding of mating strategies.

Surprisingly few theories have attended to gamete dimorphism and its evolutionary origins. The question does not arise in prokaryotic systems where mitosis is the major reproductive strategy, and it does not arise with primitive invertebrates or vertebrates where the shedding and union of isogamous (identical) gametes occur in media external to the organisms. It is a major question, however, where anisogamy (nonidentity of sexual gametes) is the rule - where sex chromosomes carry different genetic information and where internal fertilization is the mating strategy.

Parker, Baker and Smith (1972) have proposed a comprehensive theory of the evolution of gametic dimorphism that has implications for mating strategies. They suggest that there are two fundamental and opposing forces of natural selection - one for an increase in gametic number to maximize the opportunities of fertilization and one for zygote fitness once fertilization has occurred. Assuming that a finite energy can be devoted to gamete formation, the number of gametes can be increased by stripping nutritive (cytoplasmic) materials from the DNA and concentrating on DNA production. Gametic fitness, in contrast, is enhanced by producing few gametes, but each with a large store of nutritive material.

In sexually reproducing species it can be demonstrated that the optimal strategy of gamete production is for one sex to produce many small gametes (sperm) and the other to produce few large gametes (ova). Suppose that zygote size alone determines fitness and that individuals produce equal numbers of different sized gametes, say in that increasing size range of 1, 2, and 3. It is obvious that the union of 3 x 3 will be favored. However, if zygotes must have an optimal size (say 4) then it is evident from a checkerboard matrix that 1 x 3, 2 x 2, and 3 x 1 unions will be favored. If all unions are equally probable, then the union of 1 x 3 (small and large gametes) is the favored combination by 2:1. This probability matrix will differ depending on how many of each type of gamete can be formed and the costs involved, but in all cases modeled the outcome is sexual dimorphism of gamete production, that is, the evolution of males that produce sperm and females that produce ova. The conclusion from these models is that sexual dimorphism at the level of gamete production is nearly inevitable and will occur in widely different taxonomic groups.

The consequences of this divergence in gametes are many and set the stage for the evolution of sexually dimorphic mating strategies:

1. Many more sperm than ova can be produced from the same physiological investment.

2. Gametic wastage is not as critical for males as it is for females.

3. Smaller gametes are likely to be more active, or at least more readily transported by wind, water currents or host vectors.

4. Mobile sperm are better able to "search" for immobile ova, than the reverse.

5. Sperm fecundity associated with meiosis results in greater variability in male gametes and the production of more sisyphean gametes.

6. As a result males are under more intense selection pressure than females and contribute disproportionately to changes in gene frequency.

7. Not only will sperm competition be greater than ova competition, but male-male competition will also be greater. From this one can envisage higher orders of differential genetic strategies, reflected in behavioral competition and parental investment.

Parker (1970), in another landmark paper, has suggested that internal fertilization has arisen through male competition to eject sperm as near as possible to the female ova. The male that does this successfully reproduces at the expense of his competitors. This became especially important in flight species, such as insects and birds, and in terrestrial organisms, where individuals move about widely. Interestingly, copulation seems to have evolved later as the most efficient means to deposit sperm close to ova. The evolutionary sequence can be seen in insects.

In the primitive arthropod, _Trombicula_ _splendens_, the male drops encased sperm (spermatophore) which the female later picks up to inseminate herself. In _Lepisimatidae_ the male reacts similarly, but in addition spins signal threads on the ground to guide the female to the spermatophore. In _Machilids_ the sequence is elaborated by the male depositing the spermatophore on a thread extending from his abdomen. He then twists his body around the female, in this way guiding her genitalia to the spermatophore. Finally, in most complex species of insects the spermatophore has been dispensed with and the free sperm is introduced directly into the female during copulation.

The evolutionary sequence was apparently from external fertilization, more typical of marine forms, to internal fertilization on land with spermatophores, to internal fertilization with free sperm during copulation. Intrasexual competition arises from the large disparity of male-female reproductive potential and the associated greater genetic variance among males. Sperm compete with sperm and males compete with each other for access to females. The female is not isolated from intrasexual competition and may adjust her strategies depending on the number of females present. In some cases she may elect to terminate her pregnancy for some later advantage, or even murder her offspring. In any case, terrestrial life conferred an advantage on close-contact insemination, copulation (leading to internal gestation of the embryo) and high levels of sexual selection.

Sexual selection among males and polygamous mating systems have been further strengthened by the evolution of lactation and thermoregulation in mammals. Apparently it was a short step to female lactation from genetic sexual dimorphism and internal fertilization (Hopson, 1973; Pond, 1977). High rates of metabolism associated with endothermy permitted the constant production of milk. More importantly, perhaps, nursing capabilities freed the female from long periods of gestation and allowed the developmental period to be extended outside the body. This reinforced the social bond between mother and offspring and allowed for long periods of socialization.

At the same time the relative investment of the male decreased. The female's investment became so critical that she was forced to make fine discriminations among potential mates and males were selected for those traits that she desired in her offspring. For whatever ultimate reasons, sexual dimorphism was established in the phenotype and resulted in differential male-female parental investments (Trivers, 1972).

Given the biasing of anisogamy, internal fertilization and lactation, it perhaps seems odd that monogamy evolved at all in mammals. Yet a surprising number of species show at least some degree of monogamy. There is no apparent phylogenetic trend. Monogamous species may range from herbivores to carnivores. Their breeding may be seasonal or at any time of year. They may be large or small or marine or terrestrial. And their activity may be nocturnal, diurnal or crepascular (Kleiman, 1977). Some of the most obvious examples include the honey possum (marsupial), the elephant shrew (insectivore), the horseshoe bat (chiroptera), the common marmoset (primate), the deer mouse (rodentia), the bowhead whale (mysticeti), the wolf, coyote, and Cape hunting dog (carnivore), the badger (mustelidae), the dwarf mongoose (viverridae), the common seal (pinnepedia), and the grey duiker (artiodactylea). Obviously it is not going to be easy to find a common denominator among all of these variations.

Wilson (1975) has suggested that there are three conditions at work to move species in the direction of monogamy: (1) if the territory contains a scarce and valuable resource two adults may band together to protect it, (2) if the physical environment is harsh and requires two adults to cooperate in order to insure offspring survival then monogamy will result, and (3) monogamous pairs may have an advantage by breeding early, thus outcompeting non-monogamous pairs. It might be added for birds that if a great share of the embryological development is outside the female's body in the form of an egg, then male investment is more likely and monogamous bonds can form.

Kleiman (1977), in surveying the literature, sees other potentially biasing factors. For example, monogamy is correlated with a low reproductive rate and a long maturation period for the young. Under these circumstances greater care of existing offspring may be imperative.

More important is the availability of resources and the requirements of the female for male participation. Interestingly, the ratios of litter weight to maternal weight in monogamous primates is relatively high, suggesting that the greater biomass of the young necessitates more paternal investment.

Another interesting correlate of monogamy is reduced sexual dimorphism in all features of the organism. This is not a universal finding but is a significant trend (Ralls, 1977). In marmosets, the dwarf mongoose, beaver and dik-dik the female may be as large as or even larger than the male and in some species the females are more aggressive. Apparently the decrease in sexual selection among males and near equal commitments in courtship and parental investment reduce differences among males and females. As a general rule, when the male can be certain of his parentage, monogamy is more likely.

Mating and parental strategies are especially important for behavior genetic analyses. Sexual selection in polygamous species implies large differences in male genetic fitness and great sensitivity in females for the choice of mates, at least in cases where females are exposed to several potential mates. Genetic analyses could determine the kinds of traits related to fitness and the degree to which they are genetically programmed. Since mate choice in polygamous and monogamous species involves communication between males and females, it is obviously important to be able to decipher the communication codes and determine how signals are coordinated with fitness parameters.

The theories dealing with polygamy and monogamy are rough approximations at best. There are few cases in which it is definitely known what ecological features specify a mating or parental strategy. Why is sexual selection so evident in some species while monogamy occurs in others? And what aspect of the environment can overwhelm the biases toward sexual selection and lead to monogamy? A great deal must be discovered about gene-environment interactions before we can feel secure with our answers.

Altruism and Inclusive Fitness

The entire structure of sociobiology rests on its ability to explain altruistic acts. If natural selection favors individual genetic fitness, why do animals show cooperative acts and engage in high risk behaviors that favor other individuals? Sacrificial acts are so common in the animal world that a general principle must be operating.

The answer appears so obvious that it seems surprising that it emerged so late in the study of behavior. The apparent key is found in the relatedness of an individual with other members of the population or his cultural affiliations. What may appear to be a senseless individual act of sacrifice may be quite reasonable when we consider the total impact of the behavior. Parents and leaders defend their offspring and others because individual genetic immortality has been weighed against genetic immortality achieved by helping others who share genes in common, or those who can benefit relatives who do.

Two studies are sufficient to illustrate the sociobiological principle of genetic altruism. In the first, by Watts and Stokes (1971), it was found that only a very small percentage of wild turkeys in Texas ever reproduced. Of the 170 males observed, only 6 mated with the available hens, suggesting that only these males pass their genes to the next generation. However, it was also observed that brothers band together to help each other so that one of the brothers becomes dominant and can mate. Only the dominant brotherhoods, and the dominant male of each sibling group, ever mate. Without this mutual assistance none of the males have a chance to mate; single males are totally excluded from the reproductive population. The point is that one male of each brotherhood represents the others and passes the family genes on. The dominant male shares 50 percent of his genes with his siblings, so that multiple matings can compensate for the meiotic loss experienced by the brothers who never mate.

In a more rigorous investigation of Belding's ground squirrels in the Sierra Nevada mountains of California Sherman (1977) found that auditory alarm calls given when predators were in the area occurred only when near relatives might benefit by the signal. The females normally live independently of adult males in territories with their relatives. When a ground predator approaches the adult females emit a segmented alarm call in the 4 to 6 kHz range. Now the interesting finding was that the likelihood of a female giving the first alarm call was correlated with her being reproductive and living with close relatives, such as daughters, granddaughters or sisters. A female without relatives in the population, or a transient female, rarely emitted signals. Males who lived independently of relatives also demonstrated infrequent alarm calls.

Sherman was able to demonstrate that alarm signaling did not directly benefit the caller. It did not divert the predator's attention, discourage pursuit, reduce the likelihood of subsequent attacks nor encourage reciprocal signaling. Nor did the alarm appear to help the group as a whole. Apparently the signal was given only in situations where near relatives could potentially benefit from the information about an approaching predator.

The insight into genetic altruism was suggested in a rare moment when the renowned geneticist, J. B. S. Haldane, declared to the distinguished biologist John Maynard Smith that he was prepared to lay down his life in order to save two brothers or eight cousins. The essence of this notion was rigorously formulated some years after Haldanes' remark by W. D. Hamilton (1963, 1964) and has been extended by Trivers (1972) and Wilson (1975). The upshot of this theorizing is the principle of kin selection, which says that genes for altruistic behavior will be selected when $k > 1/r$, where k is the ratio of the benefit provided a recipient to the cost of the altruistic act, and r is the coefficient of relatedness between the altruist and the recipient. In the case of brothers, where r is 50 percent, k must be greater than two in order for altruism to evolve. The generalization is that individuals strive for "inclusive fitness," not merely individual fitness, which is saying that an individual strives to pass his genes into the next generation by personally reproducing and/or by increasing the reproductive chances of his relatives who carry copies of a fraction of his genes. Inclusive fitness is therefore defined as the net genetic fitness of an individual and all of his relatives.

Obviously this rather simple mathematical formulation does not account for many altruistic behaviors directed at non-relatives. Instances abound where individuals risk their own reproductive fitness for nonrelatives. Trivers (1971) refers to this behavior as reciprocal altruism, implying that individual DNA is spared by mutualistic interactions that benefit all parties. Crudely put, reciprocal altruism is based on the philosophy that, "If you scratch my back I'll scratch yours." It does not suggest a non-genetic interpretation of altruism, but a genetic advanture of the individual based on the probability that altruistic acts will be countered by similar ones.

Clearly reciprocal altruism is difficult to defend on genetic grounds, simply because it is often mediated by proximate social codes that have been learned. One must again suggest that the proximate mechanisms, however complex, must still be in service of the ultimate end product of evolution, reproduction. The difficulty, of course, is in tracing the development of a social code for reciprocal altruism and associating it with reproductive gain. It will take the combined efforts of biologists, behavior geneticists, and social scientists to uncover the well-disguised links.

Assortative Mating

As a final heuristic example of how behavior genetics might contribute to this effort, I would like to consider the sociobiological implications of assortative mating. The excellent and extensive work already accomplished by behavior geneticists may afford rich hypotheses for the testing of some aspects of altruism and inclusive fitness.

Assortative mating on the basis of phenotypic traits suggests that individuals choose each other as mates because of similarities or differences in genetic, physiological and behavioral processes. If we assume that the product of natural selection is a physiological and behavioral system capable of maximal genetic reproduction, then assortative mating must be viewed as a part of the mating strategy to enhance inclusive fitness. No evidence bears directly on this hypothesis, although the work with humans and other animals can certainly be interpreted from this sociobiological perspective. Here I will construct the argument that humans consciously or unconsciously select mates on the basis of gene commonality in order to maximize the number of genes that they share in common with their offspring. The proximate cues used in mate strategy are those aspects of the phenotype which reflect gene homology. I will call this process "assortative narcissism."

There are two recognized forms of assortative mating: (1) positive assortative mating (what I am calling assortative narcissism), where individuals demonstrate similarity of traits, and (2) negative assortative mating (sometimes called complementarity mating), where individuals show characteristics that are opposite in nature. Both types cause a departure in panmixic assortment of genes and an increase or decrease, respectively, in the overall variance of the population. Positive assortative mating (also called <u>homogamy</u>) may involve degrees of inbreeding, depending upon the extent to which the similar characteristics are based on homologous genes.

Assortative mating has been extensively studied and reviewed (Jensen, 1977; Spuhler, 1968; Susanne, 1977; Vandenberg, 1972; Johnson, Park, DeFries, McClearn, Mi, Rashad, Vandenberg & Wilson, 1976). Commonly what is found is that homogamy is the rule in human marriages, and that complementarity is the exception. Most people marry individuals who are roughly of the same age, intelligence, socioeconomic status, religious affiliation and ethnic background. There is also evidence of positive assortative mating on personality traits and morphological features.

For age, weight, ethnic status and intelligence the assortment among mates can be substantial, sometimes approaching correlations (r) of 0.50 to 0.99. Generally the extent of homogamy is much lower and statistically insignificant, averaging around 0.10 to 0.20. Despite the average low correlation between mates, there is a great deal of consistency in the direction of the correlations. In 290 traits tabulated by Spuhler (1968), 86 percent were correlated positively between mates and only 14 percent were negative. In similar studies reviewed by Vandenberg (1972) up to 92 percent were positive. Typically, then, husbands and wives show similarity among a wide array of traits, ranging from middle finger length to expressions of neurotic tendency and social dominance.

Apparently, assortative narcicism occurs prior to marriage and not after marriage. For example, couples reported to be closer to marriage than others agree more on family values and other matters. There may be, as Vandenberg suggests, a filtering process which occurs during courtship to eliminate unions of disassociative traits. First there is a wide window filter based on socioeconomic, ethnic and religious characteristics. Second, there is a medium- sized window based on general intelligence, attitudes and beliefs. And third, there is a narrow window which focuses on highly specific morphological and personality traits. Courtship, as practiced in monogamous societies such as ours, serves the purpose of assuring that "like mates with like" and that plenty of time exists for the successive stages of phenotypic filtering.

The importance of assortative narcicism is not immediately obvious and has been little investigated. It has been found by Cattell and Nesselroade (1967) that among couples, some of whom were undergoing marriage counseling, negative correlations were more common among couples with unstable marriages (50%) than those with stable marriages (6%). From an evolutionary point of view, there is some evidence that fertility is correlated to assortative mating (see Vandenberg, 1972). For 19 anthropological characters sampled, 17 (89%) show a low but consistent relationship between the degree of assortative mating and the fertility of the couples. The range of positive correlations is from 0.01 to 0.12. One cannot conclude from these fragmentary data that gene frequency in the population is being influenced substantially, but the consistency of the trends is intriguing and worthy of further investigation. Certainly most of the traits referred to show significant heritability and could be involved in natural selection processes.

With this background information I can now speculate on the genetics of assortative narcicism and how it may be related to inclusive fitness. One need only assume that individuals are genetically programmed to maximize the number of their genes in subsequent generations by selecting mates with homologous genes. If assortative mating has this effect, then the offspring will be related to each parent by the expected 50 percent consequent on meiosis plus the degree to which the couples mate assortatively. Inclusive fitness is thereby increased without an additional reproductive effort.

One need not even assume that the traits in question have adaptive consequences, and they may occasionally have long-term maladaptive effects on reproduction. The situation may be akin to sexual selection where gene frequency is increased by differential mating, but sometimes at the expense of adaptive qualities. A flashy male paradise bird may mate frequently but still be subject to high predation. The fact that there is minimal evidence that assortative mating is related to fertility suggests that the evolutionary momentum is toward increasing gene commonality among relatives and not toward directional selection of certain types.

Now, if homologous matings are at a premium, then inbreeding must be occurring. One can guess, pending evidence one way or the other, that assortative narcicism is the genetic compromise between consanguinity and outbreeding. Assortative mating among nonrelatives will still increase genetic similarity of parent and offspring while at the same time avoiding the inbreeding depression that occurs with mating among close relatives (Lindzey, 1967). The small degree of assortative mating for most traits, accounting for only about 1 to 4 percent of the variance, would be expected if inbreeding is being avoided.

Finally, let me consider the assortative filtering model within this framework. The highest degrees of assortative mating occurs for wide-window traits, such as age (r = 0.76), weight (r = 0.32), ethnic background (87.9% homogamy) and religious faith (r = 0.77), where culture is a heavy determining factor. Once prospective mates have passed through this decision framework, they make selections on intelligence (r = .44), neurotic tendencies (r = 0.16) and other very specific characteristics (r = 0.05 - 0.20). The literature and subsequent research may show that the heritability of these traits increases through these three choice stages. It is as if individuals show high assortative narcicism for low heritability traits that will not increase inbreeding significantly and low assortative narcicism for high heritability traits that would increase inbreeding substantially. Humans strive to maximize genetic homogamy while minimizing inbreeding.

I have emphasized assortative mating because it is an obvious mating strategy that has defied evolutionary explanation. One can see, however, that a sociobiological approach can redefine the problem and lead to new experiments and interpretations. Perhaps a great deal of otherwise inexplicable data will yield to this approach. For example, one might also ask if adopting parents attempt to choose offspring who share phenotypes and hence, genes. Or, one might test the possibility that reciprocal altruism is more evident among individuals who share homologous genes. Reciprocal altruism may in part be a minor form of kin selection in disguise.

Testing of these and similar notions is possible because of our abilities to assess heritability and determine genetic homology using linkage measures, electrophoretic screening and karyotyping. Sociobiology, when coupled with these techniques, offers the rationale and method for an entirely new thrust of behavior genetics into the understanding of the genetics of social behavior.

SUMMARY

Behavior genetics, as a biological discipline, is moving toward a broad application of theories and techniques for the understanding of behavior. Three general thrusts were noted in this chapter: (1) a concern for the origins and adaptive function of genetic variation and individual differences, (2) a growing recognition that phenotypes are effected by regulatory genes and processes, and (3) an integration of sociobiological theory into the fabric of behavior genetics. Genetic variance is

206

a fact of life and can be best understood within the context of adaptation, regulatory processes and evolutionary theory. Human assortative mating, well-researched by behavior geneticists, is presented as an example of a universal phenomena which can be understood in terms of sociobiological notions.

REFERENCES

1.   Adair, L. B., Wilson, J. E., Zemp, J. W. & Glassman, E. Brain function and macromolecules, III. Uridine incorporation into polysomes of mouse brain during short-term avoidance conditioning. Proceedings of the National Academy of Sciences, 1968, 61, 365-373.
2.   Adler, J. Chemotaxis in Escherichia coli. In J. Perez-Miravete (publication coordinator). Behavior of Microorganisms. 1973, Oxford: Plenum Press, 1-15.
3.   Adler, J. Hazelbaur, G. L. & Dahl, M. M. Chemotaxis towards sugars in Escherichic coli. Journal of Bacteriology, 1973, 115, 824-847.
4.   Barash, D. P. Sociobiology and behavior. New York: Elsevier-North Holland, 1977.
5.   Beauchamp, G. K. Diet influences attractiveness of urine in guinea pigs. Nature, 1976, 263 (5578), 587-588.
6.   Beerman, W. Cytological aspects of information transfer in cellular differentiation. In E. Bell (Ed.), Molecular and cellular aspects of development. New York: Harper, 1965, 204-212.
7.   Bermant, G. & Davidson, J. Biological bases of sexual behavior. New York: Harper & Row, 1974.
8.   Bonner, J. T. Aggregation and differentiation in the cellular slime molds. Annual Review of Microbiology, 1971, 25, 75-92.
9.   Brain, P. F. Hormones and aggression. (Vol. 1), Annual Research Review, Montreal, Quebec: Eden Press, 1977.
10. Brewer, G. J. An introduction to isozyme techniques. New York: Academic Press, 1970.
11. Britten, R. J. & Davidson, E. H. Gene regulation for higher cells: A theory. Science, 1969, 165, 349-357.
12. Brown, J. L. The evolution of behavior. New York: Norton, 1975.
13. Bush, G. L. Modes of animal speciation. In R. F. Johnston (Ed.), Annual Review of Ecology & Systematics, 1975, 6, 339-364.
14. Cattell, R. B. & Nesselroade, J. R. Likeness and completeness theories examined by sixteen personality factor measures on stably and unstably married couples. Journal of Personality & Social Psychology, 1967, 7, 351-361.

15. Charles, H. P. & Knight, C. J. G. Organization and control in prokaryotic and eukaryotic cells. Twentieth Symposium of the Society for General Microbiology, Imperial College, London, April 1970. London: Cambridge University Press, 1970.

16. Clever, V. Actinomycin and puromycin effects on sequential gene activation by ecdysone. Science, 1964, 146, 795-796.

17. Daly, M. & Wilson, M. Sex, evolution and behavior. North Scituate, Massachusetts: Duxbury Press, 1978.

18. Defries, J. C. & McClearn, G. E. Behavioral genetics and the fine structure of mouse populations: A study in microevolution. In T. Dobzhansky, M. K. Hecht & W. C. Steere (Eds.), Evolutionary biology. New York: Appleton-Century-Crofts, 1972, 279-291.

19. DeFries, J. C. & McClearn, G. E. Social dominance and Darwinian fitness in the laboratory mouse. American Naturalist, 1970, 104, 408-411.

20. Denef, C. & DeMoor, P. Sexual differentiation of steroid metabolizing enzymes in the rat liver: Further studies on predetermination by testosterone at birth. Endocrinology, 1972, 91, 374-384.

21. Dobzhansky. T. Chance and creativity in evolution. In F. J. Ayala & T. Dobzhansky (Eds.) Studies in the philosophy of biology. Berkeley: University of California Press, 1974, 307-338.

22. Ehrman, L. Omenn, G. & Caspari, E. Genetics, environment, and behavior. New York: Academic Press, 1972.

23. Ehrman, L. & Parsons, P. The genetics of behavior. Sunderland, Massachusetts: Sinauer, 1976.

24. Ehrman, L. & Probber, J. Rare Drosophila males: The mysterious matter of choice. American Scientist, 1978, 66 (2), 216-222.

25. Feeny, P. In L. E. Gilbert & P. H. Raven (Eds.), Coevolution of animals and plants. Austin, Texas: University of Texas Press, 1975, 3-19.

26. Galef, G. B. & Henderson, P. W. Mother's milk: A determinant of the feeding preference of weanling rat pups. Journal of Comparative and Physiological Psychology, 1972, 78 (2), 213-219.

27. Galef, G. B. & Clark, M. M. Mother's milk and adult presence: two factors determining initial dietary selection by weanling rats. Journal of Comparative and Physiological Psychology, 1972, 78 (2), 220-225.

28. Gaito, J. Macromolecules and behavior (2nd ed.) New York: Appleton-Century-Crofts, 1972.

29. Garrod, D. & Ashworth, J. M. Development of the cellular slime mold Dictyostelium discoideum. (Symposium of the Society of General Microbiology, Cambridge). Microbiological Differentiation, 1973, 23, 407-435.

208

30. Ghiselin, M. T. The economy of nature and the evolution of sex. Berkeley: University of California Press, 1974.
31. Hamilton, W. D. The evolution of altruistic behavior. American Naturalist, 1963, 97, 354-356.
32. Hamilton, W. D. The genetical evolution of social behavior. I, II. Journal of Theoretical Biology, 1964, 7, 1-52.
33. Hedrick, P. W., Ginevan, M. E. & Ewing, E. P. Genetic polymorphism in heterogeneous environments. In R. F. Johnston, P. W. Frank, D. E. Michener (Eds.), Annual Review of Ecology and Systematics, 1976, 7, 1-32.
34. Hochachka, P. W. & Somero, G. N. Strategies of biochemical adaptation. Philadelphia: Saunders, 1973.
35. Hopson, J. A. Endothermy, small size, and the origin of mammalian reproduction (Letter to Editor). The American Naturalist, 1973, 107, 446-452.
36. Horn, J. Aggression as a component of relative fitness in four inbred strains of mice. Behavioral Genetics, 1974, 4 (4), 373-382.
37. Jacob, F. & Monod, J. Genetic regulatory mechanisms in the synthesis of proteins. Journal of Molecular Biology, 1961, 3, 318-356.
38. Jensen, A. R. Genetic and behavioral effects of nonrandom mating. In R. T. Osborne, C. E. Noble & N. Weyl (Eds.), Human variation: Biopsychology of age, race and sex. In press.
39. Johnson, G. B. Enzyme polymorphism and biosystematics: The hypothesis of selective neutrality. In R. E. Johnston, P. W. Frank, & C. E. Michener (Eds.), Annual Review of Ecology and Systematics, 1973, 4, 93-116.
40. Johnson, R. C., Park, J., DeFries, J. C., McClearn, G. E., Mi, M. P., Rashad, M. N., Vandenberg, S. G., & Wilson, J. R. Assortative marriage for specific cognitive abilities in Korea. Social Biology, 1976, 23 (4), 311-316.
41. King, G. A. M. Symbiosis and the evolution of prokaryotes. BioSystems, 1977, 9, 35-42.
42. King, J. L. & Jukes, T. H. Non-Darwinian evolution. Science, 1969, 164, 788-798.
43. Kleiman, D. G. Monogamy in mammals. The Quarterly Review of Biology, 1977, 52, 39-69.
44. Klingel, H. Social organization and reproduction in equids. Journal of Reproduction and Fertility, 1975, 23, 7-11.
45. Konijn, T. M. Chemotaxis and aggregation in slime molds. In A. Perez-Miravete (Publication coordinator), Behavior of microorganisms. London: Plenum Press, 1973, 48-61.
46. Krebs, C. J. & Myers, J. H. Population cycles in small mammals. Advances in Ecological Research, 1974, 8, 267-399.

47. Leon, M. Maternal pheromone. _Physiology and Behavior_, 1974, _13_, 441-453.

48. Leon, M. Dietary control of maternal pheromone in the lactating rat. _Physiology and Behavior_, 1975, _14_, 311-321.

49. Lindzey, G. Some remarks concerning incest, the incest taboo, and psychoanalytic theory. _American Psychologist_, 1967, _22_ (12), 1051-1059.

50. Margulis, Lynn. Genetic and evolutionary consequences of symbiosis: A review. _Experimental Parasitology_, 1976, _39_, 277-349.

51. Mayr, E. _Populations, species and evolution_. Cambridge: Harvard University Press, 1970.

52. Mayr, E. _Evolution and the diversity of life_. Cambridge: Harvard University Press, 1976.

53. McClearn, G. E. & DeFries, J. C. _Introduction to behavioral genetics_. San Francisco: Feeman, 1973.

54. McKusick, V. A. _Mendelian inheritance in man_. Baltimore: Johns Hopkins University Press, 1966.

55. Money, J. & Ehrhardt, A. A. _Man and woman, boy and girl_. Baltimore: Johns Hopkins University Press, 1972.

56. Muller, H. J. Some genetic aspects of sex. _American Naturalist_, 1932, _8_, 118-138.

57. Ohno, S. So much "junk" DNA in our genome. In H. H. Smith (Ed.), _Evolution of genetic systems_ (Vol. 22). New York: Gordon and Breach, 1972, 366-370.

58. Omenn, G. S. Inborn errors of metabolism: Clues to understanding human behavioral disorders. _Behavior Genetics_, 1976, _6_ (3), 263-284.

59. Omenn, G. S. Prenatal diagnosis of genetic disorders. _Science_, 1978, _200_, 952-958.

60. Omenn, G. S. & Motulsky, A. G. _Biochemical genetics and the evolution of human behavior_. Office of Education: Rye, New York, October 3-8, 1971.

61. Parker, G. A. Sperm competition and its evolutionary consequences in the insects. _Biological Reviews_, 1970, _45_, 525-567. (Biological Reviews of the Cambridge Philosophical Society).

62. Parker, G. A., Baker, R. R., Smith, V. G. F. The origin and evolution of gamete dimorphism and the male-female phenomenon. _Journal of Theoretical Biology_, 1972, _36_, 529-553.

63. Pianka, E. R. On r- and k-selection. _American Naturalist_, 1970, _104_, 592-597.

64. Pond, C. M. The significance of lactation in the evolution of mammals. _Evolution_, 1977, _31_, 177-199.

65. Porter, R. H. & Doane, H. M. Dietary-dependent cross-species similarities in maternal chemical cues. _Physiology and Behavior_, 1977, _19_, 129-131.

66. Porter, R. H. & Etscorn, F. A primacy effect for olfactory imprinting in spiny mice. (_Acomys_ _cahirinus_). _Behavioral_ _Biology_, 1975, _15_, 511-517.

67. Porter, R. H. & Etscorn, F. A sensitivity period for the development of olfactory preference in _Acomys_ _cahirinus_. _Physiology_ _and_ _Behavior_, 1976, _17_, 127-130.

68. Powell, J. R. Genetic polymorphisms in varied environments. _Science_, 1971, _174_, 1035-1036.

69. Ralls, K. Sexual dimorphism in mammals: Avian models and unanswered questions. _American_ _Naturalist_, 1977, _111_ (981), 917-938.

70. Sahlins, M. _The_ _use_ _and_ _abuse_ _of_ _biology_. Ann Arbor, Michigan: University of Michigan Press, 1977.

71. Schmidt-Nielsen, K. _Animal_ _physiology_. New York: Cambridge University Press, 1975.

72. Scriver, C. R., Laberge, C., Clow, C. L. & Fraser, F. C. Genetics and medicine: An evolving relationship. _Science_, 1978, _200_, 946-951.

73. Selander, R. K. Genetic variation in natural populations. In V. G. Dethier, R. C. Lewontin & M. Lloyd (Eds.), _Topics_ _in_ _animal_ _behavior,_ _ecology_ _and_ _evolution_. New York: Harper & Row, 1971, 147-154.

74. Selander, R. K. & Yang, S. Y. Biochemical genetics and behavior in wild house mouse populations. In G. Lindzey & D. D. Thiessen (Eds.), _Contributions_ _to_ _behavior-_ _genetic_ _analysis_. New York: Appleton-Century-Crofts, 1970, 293-334.

75. Selander, R. K. & Johnson, W. E. Genetic variation among vertebrate species. In R. F. Johnston, P. W. Frank & C. D. Michener (Eds.) _Annual_ _Review_ _of_ _Ecology_ _and_ _Systematics_, 1973, _4_, 75-92.

76. Sherman, P. W. Nepotism and the evolution of alarm calls. _Science_, 1977, _197_, 1246-1253.

77. Skeen, J. T. & Thiessen, D. D. The scent of gerbil cuisine. _Physiology_ _and_ _Behavior_, 1977, _19_, 11-14.

78. Soule, M. E., Yang, S. Y. & Weiler, M. G. W. Island lizards: The genetic-phenetic variation correlation. _Nature_, 1973, _242_, 191-192.

79. Spiegelman, S. An approach to the experimental analysis of precellular evolution. _Quarterly_ _Reviews_ _of_ _Biophysics_, 1971, _4_ (2 & 3), 213-253.

80. Spuhler, J. N. Assortative mating with respect to physical characteristics. _Eugenics_ _Quarterly_, 1968, _15_ (2), 128-139.

81. Sturtevant, A. N. _A_ _history_ _of_ _genetics_. New York: Harper, 1965.

82. Susanne, C. Heritability of anthropological characters. _Human_ _Biology_, 1977, _49_ (4), 573-580.

83. Tata, J. R. Cell structure and biosynthesis during hormone-mediated growth and development. In M. Hamburgh & and E. J. W. Barrington (Eds.), Hormones in development. New York: Appleton-Century-Crofts, 1971, 19-40.

84. Thiessen, D. D. A move towards species-specific analyses in behavior genetics. Behavior Genetics, 1972, 2, 115-126.

85. Thiessen, D. D., Yahr, P. & Owen, K. Regulatory mechanisms of territorial marking in the Mongolian gerbil. Journal of Comparative and Physiological Psychology, 1973, 82, 382-393.

86. Thiessen, D. D. Thermoenergetics and the evolution of pheromone communication. In J. Sprague & A. N. Epstein (Eds.), Progress in psychobiology and physiological psychology. New York: Academic Press, 1977.

87. Thiessen, D. D. & Sturdivant, S. Female pheromone in the black molly fish (Mollinesesia latipinna): A possible metabolic correlate. Journal of Chemical Ecology, 1977, 3, 207-217.

88. Trivers, R. L. The evolution of reciprocal altruism. Quarterly Review in Biology, 1971, 46, 35-57.

89. Trivers, R. L. Parental investment and sexual selection. In B. G. Campbell (Ed.), Sexual selection and the descent of man 1871-1971. Chicago: Aldine Publishing Company, 1972.

90. Vale, J. R., Ray, D., & Vale, C. A. Interaction of genotype and exogenous neonatal androgen: Agonistic behavior in female mice. Behavioral Biology, 1972, 7, 321-334.

91. Vandenberg, S. G. Assortative mating, or who marries whom? Behavior Genetics, 1972, 2 (2/3), 127-157.

92. Wallace, P. Individual discrimination of humans by odor. Physiology and Behavior, 1977, 19 (4), 577-579.

93. Washburn, S. L. Human behavior and the behavior of other animals. American Psychologist, 1978, 33, 405-418.

94. Watts, C. R. & Stokes, A. W. The social order of turkeys. Scientific American, 1971, 224 (6), 112-118.

95. Williams, G. C. Sex and evolution. Princeton, New Jersey: Princeton University Press, 1975.

96. Wilson, A. C., Bush, G. L., Case, S. M. & King, M. C. Social structuring of mammalian populations and rate of chromosomal evolution. Proceedings of the National Academy of Science, 1975, 72 (12), 5061-5065.

97. Wilson, E. O. Sociobiology. Cambridge, Massachusetts: Belknap Press of the Harvard University Press, 1975.

98. Yahr, P. Central control of scent marking. In D. Muller-Schwarze and M. M. Mozell (Eds.), Chemical signals in vertebrates. New York: Plenum Press, 1977, 547-562.

212

Reference Note

Clancy, A. N. Hormonal differentiation of ventral gland
marking in the Mongolian gerbil (Meriones unguiculatus).
Ph.D. dissertation submitted to the University of Texas at
Austin, Austin, Texas, July 1978.

COMMENT BY J. H. F. van ABEELEN

In his provocative contribution, Thiessen covers a lot of ground and it is of course impossible to provide an in-depth critique of the entire paper within a relatively limited space. Therefore, I shall restrict myself to a few critical remarks.

What I particularly liked in Thiessen's paper is his account of the "Differential Expression of Genes in Behavior". His suggestion that a great proportion of phenotypic variance, including behavioral variance, must be attributed to regulator genes (which are involved in repression and derepression of structural gene activity) rather than to structural genes, seems plausible in the light of the evidence he describes. In this connection Thiessen summarizes his own research on the genetic regulation of scent marking in gerbils--research that I found just fascinating.

The point about genes remaining quiescent for a long time might be related to some ideas expressed earlier in the paper. For example, in his section on "Gene Canalization and Behavioral Polymorphism", Thiessen (on the basis of some of Mayr's notions on the significance of genetic variation in behavior) argues that "silent genes" offer a reserve of genetic material upon which selection could act at some future time, especially in so-called K-selected species. It might be interesting to mention in this connection the work of Markel and Borodin (1978), of the Institute of Cytology and Genetics at Novosibirsk, USSR, on stress reactions in mice as a factor in selection and evolution. (However, mice constitute an r-selected species.) Animals may respond with stress reactions to drastic and unfavorable changes in environmental conditions, and these reactions may depend upon the genotype. Markel and Borodin claim that stressful situations induce genetically-controlled changes in the reproductive capacity (fitness) of female mice in their experimental populations. Under stress genetic variability manifests itself to a larger extent in the phenotype; in such cases selection will be more effective than under normal conditions. Thus, stress may be instrumental in the action of natural selection. Most importantly, the effects of Thiessen's "silent genes", which are kept in reserve, also seem to be testable.

In the Introduction of the paper, three major biological trends in behavior genetics are distinguished: first, interest in individual differences that underlie adaptive responses as well as preadaptations in the context of the organism's evolutionary history and its ecological constraints; second, interest in intracellular and extracellular processes connected with genic regulation of behavior; and third, interest in sociobiological viewpoints and hypotheses. I do not quite understand why Thiessen is setting the first and the third trend apart from each other. This does not seem entirely logical, especially since they are so closely related. And the section on "Sociobiology, A Framework for Behavior Genetics" is too polemical for my taste. Moreover, I would have agreed with Thiessen had he posed the possibility that natural selection can result in flexibility of organisms, leading to the capability of executing adaptive responses under conditions of change, instead of posing the possibility that ". . . natural selection can impose flexibility on an organism for the very purpose of allowing adaptive responses . . . ." In my view, which is a biologist's view, natural selection can have and will have effects but it cannot have a purpose, or, alternatively, flexibility can have a function but it cannot have a purpose. A similar stance has been elaborated by Dawkins (1976).

Incidentally, I find it difficult to follow the reasoning by which Thiessen arrives at the speculation that each of us has at least one identical genetic counterpart in a world with over 4 billion people. If we assume the presence of just one allelic difference per pair of chromosomes, then the number of possible types of gametes is $2^{23} = 8,388,608$ (over 8 million), and the number of possible genotypes is $3^{23} = 94, 143, 178, 827$ (over 94 billion). Thiessen makes some remarks on this point in the section on "The Evolution of Sex and Variability", but he expresses himself somewhat vaguely there.

As a final remark, I must say that I found the first two paragraphs and the title of the chapter a little difficult to digest. Genetics is part of biology, not of psychology or sociology. It is my personal bias that behavior genetics--which is defined by the phenotype it deals with--is biology. Its "trends" are therefore biological ones. Moreover, since we are dealing with organisms, are not all traits biological traits in the last analysis? I would like Thiessen to define behavior genetics, as he sees it, unambiguously.

COMMENT BY J. R. ROYCE

This paper puts forward provocative generalizations which have the potential for bringing genetics, evolution, biology, and environmental analysis to bear on psychological phenomena. I found Monod's concept of regulatory genes of particular interest because of its obvious implications for behavior. Further elaboration of the functioning of regulator genes, particularly as they might relate to the decision/control aspect of information processing, would constitute a theoretical advance of the first magnitude.

COMMENT BY J. N. THOMPSON, Jr.

The comprehensive paper by Thiessen makes two major contributions: it discusses sociobiology, probably the central theoretical construct for current studies in behavior genetics, and it discusses behavior from a developmental-physiological perspective.

Thiessen's discussion of biological trends suggests several questions that deserve further attention. One of these involves the role that genetic variation and polymorphism might play in behavior. As he points out for physiological traits, genetic heterogeneity is a significant determinent of uniformity (developmental homeostasis or canalization). For example, two alleles of the gene producing the enzyme alcohol dehydrogenase in Drosophila melanogaster differ both in the enzyme activity in the breakdown of harmful alcohols in the fermenting fruit environment and in the sensitivity of the enzyme to temperature extremes. A genetically heterozygous individual is better adapted than either homozygote in dealing with alcohol and temperature variation. Behavior is also a response to variation. One might argue, however, that behavioral flexibility, not uniformity, is the more appropriate parallel to developmental homeostasis, and an understanding of its genetic basis would be a significant contribution.

On the negative side, potential confusion arises from the discussion of regulator genes in behavior. The distinction between control and regulator genes is a precise one and involves specific genetic criteria that cannot be determined from a simple examination of the phenotype. Although it is tempting to consider behavioral responses in terms of gene action initiated by control genes, it is an hypothesis that is potentially more restrictive than informative and should be analyzed with care.

COMMENT BY A. OLIVERIO

While I am not contending the accuracy of Thiessen's findings, I do disagree with their meaning and on the way these results are organized into the proposed conceptual framework. I am in agreement with Thiessen when he says, "the complexity and flexibility of higher species, including our own, suggest not less genetic control than for lower species but more genetic control since many modifications of behavior may be mediated by genes triggered into play by environmental events" (original text). However, the point is not whether more or less genetic control is required for more or less complex forms of specific behaviors, but that the genes may modulate the type of wiring and let the environment do its job. This is an important point since many sociobiological theses rest on it and on the labeling (reification) of specific units of behavior which presumably account for fitness.

There is a sentence from Time magazine (August 1, 1977) suggesting that "Some sociobiologists go so far as to suggest that there may be human genes for such behaviors as conformism, homosexuality, and spite". Although Thiessen pays lip service to this interpretation as extreme, he argues that behavior genetics should add credibility to this "intellectual adventure."

I have recently read the text of a BBC conversation on socio-biology by Steven Rose (1979) in which he shows the weak points of sociobiological theory. The first point has to do with extra-polations from animal studies to humans. It begins with the pro-cess of labeling or reifying a given behavior. For example, wife-beating, fights between rival groups of football fans, guerilla war, and the superpower arms race are all taken as manifestations of an abstract "property" called aggression. After labeling one can then introduce quantification and use some biometric techniques in order to arrive at a genetic model. As Rose shows, much of this quantification and speculating is based on biological "evidence" from animal studies. However, most of these analogies are very naive and anthropomorphic--for example, the presumed parallelisms between aggressive rats or ants and student unrest or guerilla war. The point is that such labeling and quantification consti-tute (at best) biased assumptions.

I find many of these biases in Thiessen's paper. For example, he explains (p.200) that the entire structure of sociobiology rests on its ability to explain altruistic acts. Why are sacrificial acts so common in the animal (and human) world? It is obvious! In order to achieve genetic immortality we sacrifice our own lives and help others who share genes in common. Examples are given by referring to wild turkeys and ground squirrels: the more closely related the animals are the more altruistically they behave. Thus, it is possible to hypothesize "coefficients" of kin selection and altruism. What is the relevance of this interpretation to human behavior evolved (historically) from tribal societies? Are we more altruistic in relation to our first cousins than to our second cousins? What about grandparents? Where would a wife or a husband stand in the scale of the altruistic behavior of his partner if they are not related by kinship? And what about in-fanticide (in different cultures and historical ages) or patri-cide? Do they represent genetic diseases?

A second, and even more astonishing, weakness of sociobiological theory is related to sexual choices which may result in marriage, or what is called "assortative mating". What are the principles regulating the choice of a marriage partner? An example is assor-tative mating of the narcissistic type, where partners choose mates who show a high similarity in traits (and genes). This happens just to increase the overall variance in the population. But what is even more astonishing is that a number of findings

indicate that "it is as if individuals show high assortative
narcissism for low heritability traits that will not increase inbreeding significantly and low assortative narcissism for high
heritability traits that would increase inbreeding substantially.
Humans strive to maximize genetic homogamy while minimizing inbreeding" (p.205). Let us disregard the meaning of "intelligence",
"neurotic tendencies" and other behavioral labels, and therefore
the meaning of their heritability. Within the framework of these
theories how would one explain the high divorce rate evident in
some cultures (like the U.S.) or historical ages in psychobiological or genetic terms? Is divorce a genetic disease? What is its
evolutionary meaning? It may well be that one has to embrace
sociobiology enthusiastically in order to "seek universal explanations for behavior at any level" (p.192). However, to me it
sounds more like a religion or faith than a scientific theory.

References

Dawkins, R. The selfish gene. New York and Oxford: Oxford University Press, 1976.
Markel, A. L., & Borodin, P. M. Stress phenomenon: Genetical and
evolutionary approach. Abstracts of Symposia, XIVth International Congress of Genetics, Moscow, 1978, p. 106.
Rose, S. Its only human nature: The sociobiologists' fairyland,
in press.

<u>GENE-ENVIRONMENT INTERACTIONS</u>

Familial Likeness: Etiology and Function

W. R. Thompson

Adaptive Significance of Animal Behavior:
The Role of Gene-Environment Interaction

N. D. Henderson

FAMILIAL LIKENESS: ETIOLOGY AND FUNCTION[1]

William R. Thompson

Department of Psychology, Queen's University,
Kingston, Ontario, Canada

In the early days of Behavior Genetics, the possibility of demonstrating Mendelian modes of transmission for psychological characters seemed an exciting prospect. Before the 1950s, very few people had even attempted this and there were few links between genetics and psychology. These were as yet to develop through the contributions of people like Fuller & Scott, Beach, Calvin Hall, and others. By the early 1900s, however, the field had started to grow, and the demonstration of strain and breed differences and the fitting of genetic models to hybrid cross data had become relatively commonplace. Likewise, we have seen an analogous burgeoning of knowledge on heritability of every conceivable kind of behavior in human subjects. Thus, today we have an impressive amount of data. Even the summary of it recently attempted by Fuller and myself (1978) involves over 1500 citations. Had we more time and energy, this number could probably have been doubled or tripled.

However impressive the sheer quantity and degree of sophistication of all this work may be, it is still not very clear exactly where it is taking us, particularly in relation to our allied disciplines of psychology and biology. It seems imperative, at this point in time, that we should examine our aims rather closely and attempt to delineate problems that are likely to kindle the primary interest both of "main-line" psychologists and "main-line" biologists. In the view of this writer, we have not yet been able to achieve this.

---

[1] This paper is based on the author's Presidential address to the 1978 Annual meeting of the Behavior Genetics Association, Davis, California.

The typical program in behavior genetic research proceeds as follows: first, the selection of some behavior--mostly on the basis of general interest, such as personality, or of practical importance as, say, schizophrenia, or sometimes because its simplicity seems likely to yield simple genetic results--as audiogenic seizures in mice or chirping in crickets. The second step involves substantiation of a heritable component for the behavior. The third step, when possible, focuses on mechanisms of transmission; and the final steps, if we get that far, entail locating the relevant gene or genes on particular chromosomes and the establishing of biochemical paths between these genes and the trait. There is little question that in recent years enormous advances have occurred in this area thanks to the development of techniques like DNA-RNA hybridization (Omenn, 1975) and somatic cell genetics (McKusick & Ruddle, 1977). I have little doubt that, within the next few decades, we will commence to see the exact mapping of behavior on chromosomal material just as we have seen the analogous mapping of behavior on brain areas, on specific neurons and on neurochemical pathways.

However, particularly for those human behaviors in which most scientists in allied fields have some interest, for example, IQ or schizophrenia, we seldom get beyond the second step of establishing some heritability estimate. And, as most behavior geneticists know, even doing that is not without its problems. Thus, in the case of IQ, we learn from Kamin (1974, p. 1) that "no prudent man can accept the hypothesis that IQ test scores are in any degree heritable"; while we note the whimsical rejoinder of DeFries and Plomin (1978) that "a prudent person has no alternative but to reject the hypothesis of zero heritability (of mental ability)" (1978, p. 501).

The rift between hereditarians and environmentalists is still a deep one. It has often led us into the dazzling (but often empty) statistical pyrotechnics of critics like Lewontin, Layzier, Goldberger and others, and, often, into much bitter political polemicizing.

In my view, both need to be avoided since they only serve to obscure fruitful research and theorizing about the problem which is really fundamental to the field of behavior genetics, namely the etiology and function of familial likeness. In the final analysis, this problem is unique to our field and virtually defines it.

This may seem an obvious and even trivial point. Yet if one examines most of the work in behavior genetics, one will find it deals precisely with this topic; and, likewise, if one looks at most of the work in other fields such as psychology and biology, I think one will find that little effort is given directly or primarily to the matter of familial resemblance and how it comes about. Yet, clearly, subareas of these fields have some interest in it--social and cultural psychology and sociobiology being obvious examples.

It can be claimed, of course, that formal genetics deals exactly with the problem. To a large degree this is true. However, geneticists have understandably concentrated on genetically rather than environmentally-produced familial resemblance and genetic rather than cultural modes of transmission.

Up until quite recently, most of us, with a few notable exceptions, have tended to follow these emphases. And I think it is for this reason that we have not attracted the interest of more psychologists and biologists. Certainly, it is obvious that the main goal of much of psychology is the understanding and control of behavior change. Thus, many psychologists will necessarily show antipathy to a position which seems to ignore if not deny their major interest. Likewise, the main goal of much of biology is the understanding of the function of some structure or behavior. Hence we cannot afford to ignore this feature either.

The idea that behavior genetics (or sociobiology for that matter) is dedicated to establishing iron-clad mechanistic biological imperatives for all behavior is of course false. Nevertheless, it is true that we have given too little attention to the cultural and environmental aspect of familial transmission. And since it does not seem that our critics are going to offer us much in this regard, perhaps we should do more both on the empirical and theoretical side. This is particularly true in the case of continuous behavior traits for which it is so often necessary to postulate polygenic inheritance. Multi-factor models, especially when coupled with the notions of penetrance and expressivity, have a remarkable explanatory flexibility. Indeed, one may fairly wonder whether they are heuristically superior to the equally broad concepts of "environmental factors" so often invoked by anti-hereditarians.

In any case, both genetic and cultural transmission mechanisms need full and detailed analysis. This point has been emphasized by Cavalli-Sforza and Feldman (1973), by Morton (1974), by Eaves (1976), and by Plomin, DeFries and Loehlin (1977). However, with the possible exception of the latter authors, these workers have mainly confined themselves to statistical model building with only occasional hints about the psychological mechanisms by which family or cultural groups homogenize or heterogenize their members, and what biological goals these mechanisms serve. Let me now turn directly to this problem.

There is little question that family members resemble each

other in many ways--for example, in IQ, personality, interests in attitudes and psychopathology. This appears to be a strong empirical fact that I think not even Kamin (1974) would deny. No doubt he is correct in concluding that in many cases the fact that genetic models may fit family data is not decisive, since environment has seldom been rigidly controlled. Yet we can as easily reverse this criticism and claim that we have few instances where environmental models also fit the data well and where a genetic etiology can be ruled out. That is to say, we have few studies that specifically demonstrate resemblance between genetically disparate individuals reared in similar circumstances. The human adoption studies, of course, spring to mind, but at least in respect to IQ we know that different people inspecting apparently the same data can arrive at quite disparate conclusions (Kamin, 1978; Munsinger, 1978). In the area of psychopathology, analogous studies are generally supportive of a hereditarian position. But, again, environment clearly cannot be ruled out altogether.

In the animal literature, we again find very few studies which deal in a systematic way with the etiology of family resemblance. We have much information on such social interactions as sexual behavior, epimeletic and et-epimeletic behavior, for example, but we do not really know whether these interactional processes actually make animals resemble each other more or less in behavior characteristics. Probably the data are in the literature but I do not think they have been looked at quite in the way I am suggesting.

Our knowledge about cultural transmission is thus at a fairly primitive level. However, we do have some studies both with humans and animals which at least illustrate the kinds of paths we might follow. I will now discuss these.

ENVIRONMENTAL MODELS OF FAMILY TRANSMISSION: HUMAN DATA

McAskie and Clarke (1976) in a critical review of family studies on IQ have noted that "most psychologists have been too canny to be explicit" on the matter of environmental models (p. 245). However, they suggest that two models are at least implicit in the relevant literature; these are an exposure model and an identification model. Depending on the constitution of the family structure, these can generate differential correlational predictions about familial likeness. For example, an exposure model should predict, for the traditional family arrangement, $r_{mo} > r_{fo}$. An identification model, however, would predict $r_{md} = r_{fs} > r_{ms} = r_{fd}$. Combining the two models might generate such an order as $r_{md} > r_{ms} > r_{fs} > r_{fd}$, both the order and relative magnitude depending on the particular values of exposure and identification parameters. In any case, it is likely that the predictions would be quite different from those generated by most genetic models.

These two models deal mostly (though not exclusively) with parent–offspring transmission. However, the latter is only one of the components affecting familial likeness. We may also consider sibling interactions—especially of those of like age and sex. As Eaves (1976) has pointed out, these may be cooperative or competitive and may accordingly dampen or amplify resemblance in respect to some traits.

By and large, most of the directly relevant family studies fail to support either uniquely or very strongly any particular genetic or environmental model. However, some support for a modified exposure model comes from some quite different data, namely those dealing with the relation between IQ, family size, and birth order. These do not bear directly on family resemblance. But they do permit the observation of variation of ability under systematically different environmental conditions with the genetic contribution largely excluded.

In their large Dutch sample, Belmont and Marolla (1973) reported a decline in Raven scores with increasing family size and, independently, a decline in ability with birth order. Their findings are in accord with those of many other workers as far back as Galton and Havelock Ellis and more recently of Davis, Cahan, and Bashi (1977). However, what is of more interest in the present context is the model put forward by Zajonc and Markus (1975) in explanation of these data. They have labelled this a confluence model. Without specifying exact mechanisms involved, the model postulates that a child's ability is at least partly the outcome of the total familial intellectual climate to which he or she is exposed (including his own contribution). Thus a first-born child will be exposed to a higher level of intellectual stimulation than the later born children. Likewise, the larger the family, particularly with minimal spacing between births, the lower will be the general intellectual level during most of the developmental history of that family.

The model fits the available data remarkably well, particularly when a number of quite plausible subsidiary assumptions are made. Furthermore, as Zajonc (1976) has noted, it can be explicated in a number of interesting ways. For example, it can nicely explain "Cattell's paradox" relating intergenerational stability of IQ, family size, and IQ level of parents. If a low IQ is, in fact, partly an environmental effect of large family size, then, obviously no prediction of any large dysgenic effect is necessary. Again, many ethnic and racial IQ differences may be at least partly explicable by the model. Thus, in American Blacks, according to Zajonc (1976), family size has tended to be larger, there has been a higher incidence of paternal absence, first maternal parity has been earlier, and spacing between children has been shorter. In the confluence model, every one of these factors is hypothesized to produce lowered test performance.

A final deduction from the model is worth emphasizing in the context of this discussion, namely, the distortion that may be produced in <u>magnitudes of familial correlations</u> (and hence h^2 estimates) by ignoring family size, relative ages of sibs and other parameters of the model. I think that this is clearly an admonition which behavior geneticists embarking on family studies might well keep in mind.

In my view Zajonc has made a major positive contribution to the heritability of IQ controversy. I would agree strongly with the following statement made by him (1976, p. 234):

Clearly, on the basis of empirical evidence now available, we cannot evaluate the relative importance of the two factors (heredity, environment), and the controversy will not be resolved until we know precisely how these factors influence intellectual development. Hereditarians lack information about genetic loci that might transmit intelligence, and environmentalists have not been able to identify the critical features of the environment that generate intellectual effects. And the two groups suffer equally from ambiguities about what abilities intelligence tests are assumed to measure in different populations. Generally, the environmental case has relied more on attacking the inadequacies of the genetic position than on positive evidence that would establish the role of environmental factors in intellectual development. Moreover, the hereditarian view has the advantage of a formal model - the polygenic model of parent-offspring resemblance - while up to now there has been no parallel formalization of environmental effects.

Zajonc has made a good start in such a formalization. However, several limitations of his model should be mentioned. First, the <u>range of ability</u> it attempts to explain is only about 10 IQ points. Second, the concept of exposure or confluence may work for IQ but it is difficult to apply it in the case of a quite different variable--<u>stature</u>--which appears to bear similar relations to family size and birth order as does ability (Belmont, Stein & Susser, 1975). Thirdly, there is no allowance made for prenatal effects--particularly in respect to birth-order data. The fact that these are operating has been made evident by an ingenious application of the adoption method by Horn, Loehlin, and Willerman (personal communication with L. Willerman, 1978). Thus, if we are to build on Zajonc's model, we need to incorporate into it some genetic and prenatal parameters, and also we need to analyze much more closely the mechanisms of cultural or environmental transmission which can hardly be the same for such disparate characters as IQ and height. The former of these kinds of extensions needs little elaboration. Much work has been devoted to formalizing the nature of genotype-environment interactions and correlations in human behavior starting perhaps first with Cattell (1960) and more recently by Plomin, DeFries and Loehlin (1977) among others. The second problem of mechanisms of transmission has been studied much less, however. In the case of human personality and ability, I think this is partly because of the fact that we have measured these traits in rather coarse ways. The tests we use describe the structure but not the processes underlying what we label personality and IQ. Until we start to analyze these domains in terms of temporal information-processing, I think we will have little hope of understanding how they are transmitted with family groups. A good start has been made by Hunt (Hunt, Lunneborg & Lewis, 1975; and McClearn, in this volume) towards relating the notion of tested IQ to the more molecular concepts of cognitive psychology. However, our theorizing is still at a primitive stage.

There is another related reason why we do not fully understand cultural transmission. This has to do with the fact that whatever may be transmitted by some agent (like a parent) will be filtered by the recipient according to his capacities. The latter will be determined not only by genes but also by age. Thus, the residuals of some transmitted message are likely to be sharply different at different developmental periods. The concept of confluence is a start in the right direction. But it is very broad and clearly requires refinement. To see how this might be achieved, I will next consider some relevant animal studies.

ENVIRONMENTAL MODELS OF CULTURAL TRANSMISSION: ANIMAL DATA

We have available a vast amount of data demonstrating the great plasticity of laboratory animals to environmental manipulations such as handling, shock, temperature change, enriched or impoverished rearing and the like. Thus it is clear that the potential amount of cultural or environmental transmission can be very large. However, such radical treatments probably seldom occur in nature, and are very far from the amount of stimulation normally provided by parental care. Thus, the early experience studies may not be very useful in reflecting what actually is happening in animal groups, even though they may tell us much about the mechanisms involved in environmental transmission.

To the knowledge of the writer, data on the aspects of maternal (and less commonly, paternal) care that promote or decrease familial likeness are meager. Care-taking has not really been examined in this functionalist context. However, I can offer a study carried out by McElroy and myself (Thompson & McElroy,

1962) which was specifically aimed at examining maternal-influence in animals. The study was a very simple one that merely scored open-field ambulation of young rats run in the presence or in the absence of their biological mothers. The data obtained (see Figure 1) showed clearly that when mother and offspring were tested together they were more alike than when tested apart. That is to say, high-active mothers potentiated offspring activity by their presence, whereas low-active mothers attenuated it. On two trials, mother-pup correlations for subjects run together were 0.61 and 0.56 (both significant) and for subjects run separately 0.10 and 0.31 (neither significant). Thus, when measured in a group situation, family members may be more alike than when measured individually.

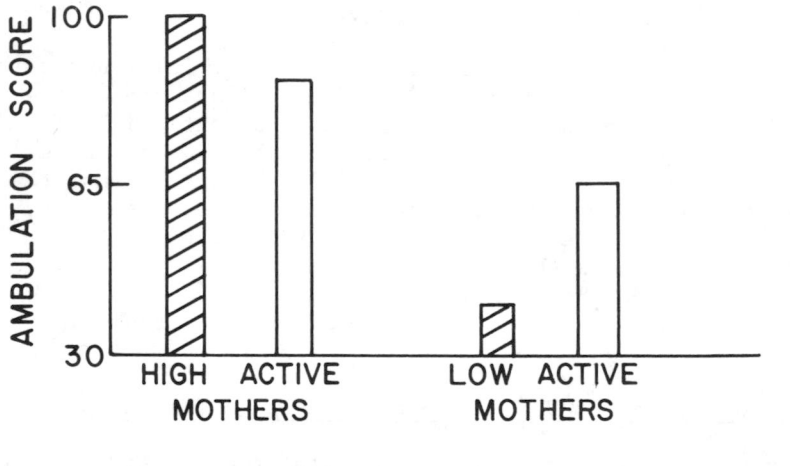

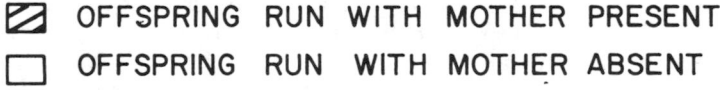

Figure 1. Effects of maternal presence on activity-levels of young mice. Note increased difference between offspring of high- and low-active mothers when run with mothers present as compared with offspring run alone. (Thompson & McElroy, 1962)

Since the study was a minor one and lacked complete controls, it should not be taken too seriously. However, it does at least illustrate a strategy by which we may directly examine parent-offspring interactions and measure the effects these have on familial resemblance.

Such descriptive work is, of course, only a prelude to analysis of precise mechanisms of transmission. As I have already emphasized there must be complex and probably vary radically with the developmental age of the recipient. With sufficiently mature offspring, whether human or lower animal, it has been not uncommon to invoke such processes as imitation, social learning, observational learning, and the like. Mainardi and his colleagues at Parma were, in fact, able to demonstrate in house mice the cultural transmission of problem-solving ability apparently by observational learning (Mainardi & Pasquali, 1968). Some of their data are shown in Figure 2. The authors concluded that "in our opinion, the way of overcoming obstacles by learning from a more experienced or cleverer member of the group . . . rather than responding to new stimuli with rigidly fixed and phylogenetically acquired behaviors is an alternative which may be particularly advantageous to those animals not specialized for a well defined way of life but which very frequently have to face new and unexpected situations" (p. 150-151).

The work of Mainardi and his colleagues has more recently been confirmed and extended with much tighter controls by Collins (1976) who has demonstrated not only improved acquisition of a preference (at least in males) for the paw used by the teacher on the manipuldum.

Remarkable as such results are, they must be viewed with caution. In the first place, we do not know to what extent they occur in nature; and secondly, and more important, there must be much cultural transmission which occurs in the development of offspring at ages when they are simply not mature enough to profit from observation, example, or even reinforcement. I would like to illustrate this latter point by reference to some other data of my own. They underline the obvious fact that the term "cultural transmission" pertains not merely to cognitive and intellectual material but also to dispositions of personality and temperament as well.

Today we have a considerable body of literature on the origin of the depressive illnesses. There seems little doubt that genetic dispositions are involved, although the exact nature of these is yet to be worked out. However, we also find numerous explanations in terms of environmental etiology, these often centering on events occurring in the family during the early life of the patient. One explanation offered has been the "learned helplessness" model of Seligman (1975). This hypothesizes that depression reflects and results from a learned inability to cope with the contingencies of reality--a kind of "give-up-itis" as it were. Thus, if the early family situation is such that cues for action usually

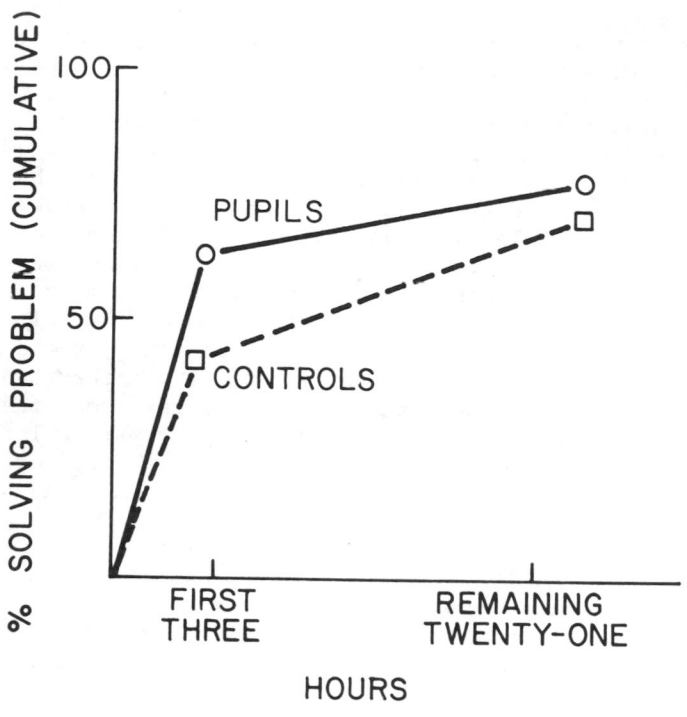

CULTURAL TRANSMISSION IN MICE
(MAINARDI AND PASQUALI 1968)

Figure 2.   Observational learning in mice. Performance of
pupils (mice which observed trained animals) compared with controls. (Mainardi & Pasquali, 1968)

occur in non-contingent ways (irrelevance) or such that actions
never produce predictable results (helplessness) the result is
what is usually described as depression.

The theory is attractive not only because it has a common-
sense quality about it, but even more because it can be articulated
in precise terms of S-R theory and tested with animal models.
Some students and I at Queen's (Niemi & Thompson, 1978; Thompson
& Davis, 1978) have attempted to examine a central proposition in
Seligman's argument--namely that an irrelevance or helplessness
regime produces greater effects if applied early in life than if
applied later. Without going into detail, rats of different ages
were subjected first to cues plus non-contingent or contingent

inescapable shock. At intervals following this treatment they
were tested for ability to acquire a free-operant avoidance
(Sidman) response--a deficit in this capacity being taken as an
index of helplessness.

Results of two independent studies showed a clear gain in
free-operant acquisition by young, but a loss in adult groups.
This occurred both with brief and with longer treatment-test intervals and also with different loci of shock (foot or tail).
Summaries of these general results are shown in Figures 3 and 4.

Thus early treatment, far from producing greater helplessness
(and by inference more depression) actually produced greater competence. This surprising result must be due to the fact that the
salient aspects of the treatment are not uniform across ages. What
was being changed in young animals probably had to do with emotionality or temperament via simply the amount of stimulation they received. Whereas in older animals what was being changed must have
been their cognitive habits of processing incoming stimulus inputs
and the contingencies between them.

Applied to naturally occurring family situations, these data
strongly indicate that any attempt to specify mechanisms of cultural transmission must take account of the age of the recipients,
of the information being transmitted, and the input and output
capacities these have for processing this information. What may
look like identical transmissions may have totally different effects at different ages.

Unless we keep in mind this fact, I think we will find it difficult merely to establish that some systematic cultural transmission is occurring and even harder to specify what its lasting
effects will be. I do believe that early experience must have effects. Likewise I believe that similar treatments early in life
must have some bearing on the later behavioral likeness of family
members--particularly for traits estimated to have a high environmental loading. Loehlin and Nichols (1976) appear to share
my faith, in spite of their own paradoxical twin data. One of
their conclusions is worth quoting, viz.:

> . . . In exploring the relationship between personality
> and the environment in view it develops, we suspect that
> better means of assessing both will be critical. But we also
> suspect that improvement in measurement will go stepwise with
> improvement in understanding the phenomena involved. In the
> absence of some good ideas about what to measure, the most
> sophisticated psychometric methods are worthless. (p. 95)

I would agree with this conclusion, and would suggest in
line with some of the work I have discussed, that one route to a

232

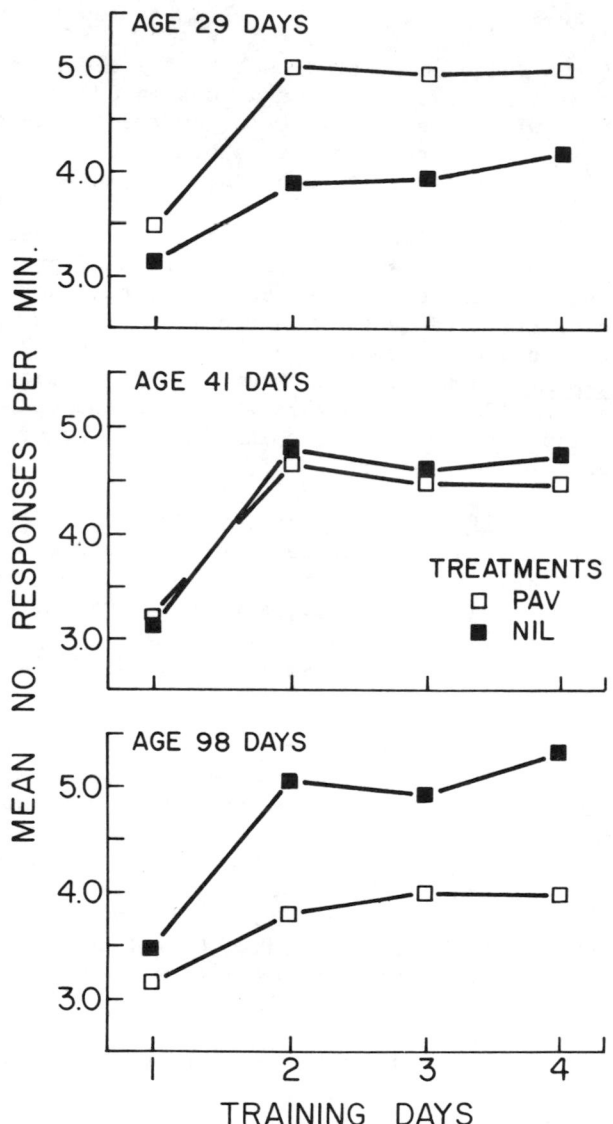

Figure 3. Effects of "helplessness" training ("PAV") on
Sidman avoidance in rats of three ages.
(Niemi & Thompson, 1978)

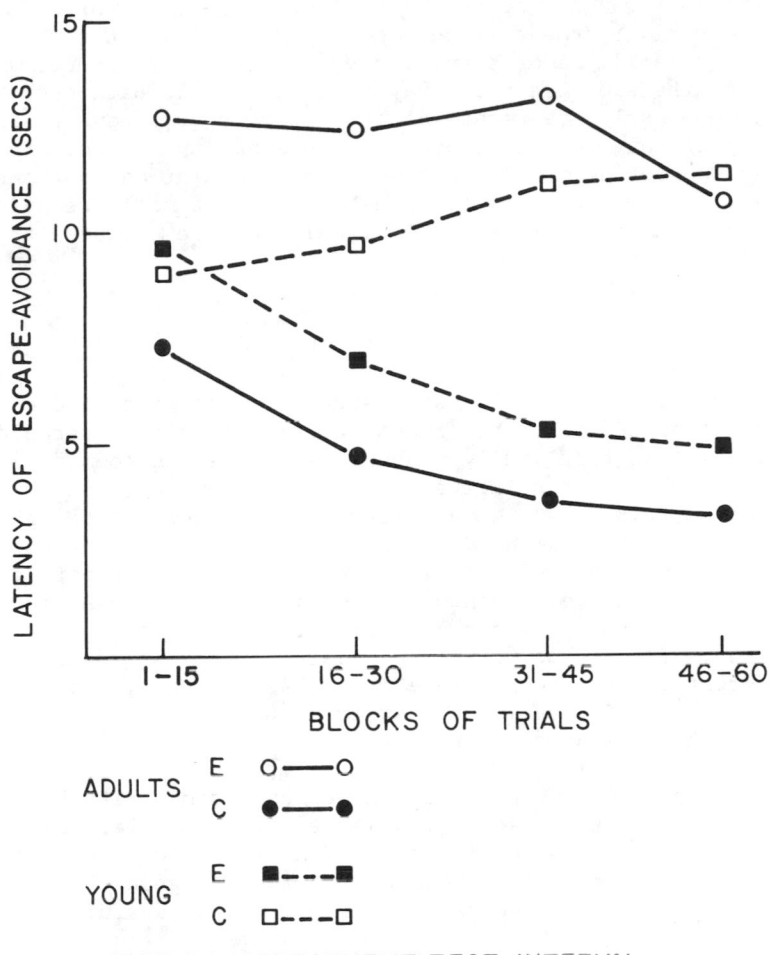

Figure 4. Effects of inescapable tail-shock on escape
avoidance latencies in young and adult rats.
E = group given inescapable shock treatment.
C = controls. Note reversal of effect in
young as compared with adults. (Thompson
& Davis, 1978)

better understanding of the relation between behavior and early
environment is through a greater attention to developmental change.
An environmental treatment at one age may radically alter the behavior of two family members and increase their resemblance; at
another age, the same treatment may have no effect whatsoever.
Likewise, some early treatments at certain ages may leave residuals in respect only to some aspects of personality and not others.
Only if we can refine our definition of environment and personality
and ability will we become able to establish systematic relations
between them, and to build sensible models for the cultural transmission of familial resemblance.

FUNCTION

Up to a point, familial resemblance needs no telenomic explanation. To the extent that genes determine various characters,
and, to the extent that family members have genes in common, it
follows inexorably that relatives will, on the average, be more
alike than non-relatives. Nevertheless, an examination of the
patterns of similarity among different family members--for example,
parent-offspring as against siblings--may allow us to separate
dominance from additive components of variation; and this, in turn,
can tell us much about the evolutionary-genetic function of that
trait. Thus, if for some trait, the likeness of sibs to each
other is greater than their likeness to their parents, then this
tells us that certain levels of that trait have been selected for
because they have fitness value.

Note, however, that the bald fact of high similarity between
siblings for a character cannot itself be said to reflect any
genetic function. It is merely an incidental biproduct of the
manner in which selection has been and is operating on the trait.
The similarity itself has no particular purpose or usefulness.

What can we say about environmentally-produced similarity
between family members? Obviously, especially for plastic behavior traits, culture can change phenotypic likeness. Is it possible to specify any rules as to when and how increases or decreases
occur and the possible functions that such alterations in either
direction may have?

Unfortunately, there are few data bearing on these points.
However, in their large-scale twin study, Loehlin and Nichols
(1976) have found that twins, at least, do tend to get treated
alike by parents and MZ pairs more so than DZ pairs. This has
suggested to them the operation of "a law of least parental effort
in twin rearing, which, in the absence of specific policy to the
contrary, ensures that, unless twins act differently, they will
get treated pretty much alike." It seems likely that such a

principle may guide the behavior of most parents in respect to their offspring whether twins or ordinary sibs. From the standpoint of parental investment it is clearly easier to manage a family unit by using one set of rules and by homogenizing its members as far as possible.

Such a policy should be expected to have at least two consequences. The first is that greater environmental constraints should be placed on genetically more deviant members. This prediction appears to be borne out by the data of Cattell, Stice, and Kristy (1957) showing predominantly negative heredity-environment correlations for personality traits. They formalized this finding as reflecting a biosocial law of "coercion to the biocultural norm."

A second somewhat loose consequence might be that in families in which the mother is the main agent of cultural transmission, similarity of offspring to her should be greater than to the father. Again, at least in the realm of personality, there is a fair amount of data to support this prediction. Not only some older studies (e.g., Hoffeditz, 1935; Crook & Thomas, 1934; Crook, 1937; Sward & Friedman, 1935), but some more recent ones (e.g., Coppen, Cowie & Slater, 1965; Insel, 1974) have shown markedly elevated mother-offspring correlations for a variety of personality dimensions. In quite different domains, for example, handedness (Annett, 1973) and stuttering (Kidd, Records, & Kidd, 1978) we also find evidence for a sex-related type of transmission.

It should be noted that for intelligence, neither of these predictions appear to hold up. However, this is perhaps not too surprising if we grant that intelligence is less plastic than personality and is also less readily influenced by precept, example or deliberate training. No doubt similar exceptions may be found for many other behavioral traits. Thus generalizations may prove to be precarious and will have to be preceded by a good deal of empirical work simply specifying patterns of likeness for different characters in differently structured familial units both in human beings and in lower animals. Only when we have gathered such data will we be properly able to address ourselves to the more elusive questions of function and purpose. This has clearly been the strategy of sociobiology which has thereby given some meaning and coherence to a mass of particularized data on social behavior in the animal kingdom.

CONCLUSION

In conclusion, it seems to the writer to be a central task of behavior genetics to address itself to the kinds of questions discussed above. Family studies are often considered to be out

of style. However, the problems they are thought to entail only
really arise if we remain obsessed with the need for educing single
heritability coefficients and specifying their exact magnitudes.
As we all know, these are bound to be imprecise except with in-
ordinately large samples and, in addition, only to serve to divert
attention from the complex processes involved in biological and
cultural transmission. There is no doubt that family members are
alike in respect to a multitude of characters. We have well worked
out genetic models as to why this should be so. But aside from
the few explanatory concepts I have discussed, we have a paucity
of theory and empirical data relating to environmental transmission.
As I suggested already, complex biometrical models will not be
enough. It will be necessary at some point to give substance to
the mathematical-statistical abstractions they entail by translat-
ing these into empirically manipulable variables.

If we can successfully accomplish this, not only will we be
serving a useful scientific end but we will also establish firmer
links both with psychology and population biology. In addition,
we will also demonstrate clearly to the world that we as behavior
geneticists are not committed to an ultra-conservative belief in
implacable genetic determinism, but are willing to consider all
variables by which information is transmitted across and within
generations.

REFERENCES

Annet, M. 1973. Handedness in families, Ann. Hum. Genet. 37:
93-105.

Belmont, L., and F.A. Marolla. 1973. Birth order, family size
and intelligence. Science 182: 1096-1101.

Belmont, L., Z.A. Stein, and M.W. Susser. 1975. Comparison of
associations of birth order with intelligence test score
and height, Nature. 255: 54-56.

Cattell, R.B. 1960. The multiple abstract variance analysis
equations and solutions: for nature-nurture research on
continuous variables. Psychol. Rev. 67: 353-372.

Cattell, R.B., G.F. Stice, and N.F. Kristy. 1957. A first
approximation to nature-nuture ratios for eleven primary
personality factors in objective tests. J. Abnorm. Soc.
Psychol. 54: 143-159.

Cavalli-Sforza, L., and M.W. Feldman. 1973a. Cultural versus
biological inheritance: phenotypic transmission from parents
to children (a theory of the effects of parental phenotypes
on children's phenotypes). Am. J. Hum. Genet. 25: 618-637.

Collins, R.L. 1975-76. Mice may learn right from left by observing
other mice. 47th Annual Report, The Jackson Laboratory, Bar
Harbor, Maine.

Coppen, A., V. Cowie, and E. Slater. 1965. Familial aspects of "neuroticism" and "extraversion." Br. J. Psychiatry 111: 70-83.

Crook, M.N. 1937. Intra-family relationships in personality test performance. Psychol. Rec. 1: 479-502.

Crook, M.N., and M. Thomas. 1934. Family relationships in ascendance-submission. Publ. Univ. Calif. Educ. Philos. Psychol. 1: 189-192.

Davis, D.J., S. Cahan, and J. Bashi. 1977. Birth order and intellectual development: the confluence model in the light of cross-cultural evidence. Science. 196: 1470-1472.

DeFries, J.C., and R. Plomin. 1978. Behavior genetics. Ann. Rev. Psychol. 29: 473-517.

Eaves, L.J. 1976. The effects of cultural transmission on continuous variation. Heredity. 33: 41-57.

Fuller, J.L., and Thompson, W.R. 1978. Foundations of Behavior Genetics. C.V. Mosby. St. Louis.

Hoffeditz, E.L. 1934. Family resemblances in personality traits. J. Soc. Psychol. 5: 214-227.

Horn, J.M., J.C. Loehlin, and Willerman. 1978. (Personal Communication).

Hunt, E., C. Lunneborg, and J. Lewis. 1975. What does it mean to be highly verbal? Cognitive Psychology. 7: 194-227.

Insel, P. 1974. Maternal effects in personality. Behav. Genet. 4: 133-144.

Kamin, L.J. 1974. The science and politics of I.Q. John Wiley & Sons, Inc. New York.

Kamin, L.J. 1978. Comment on Munsinger's review of adoption studies. Psychol. Bull. 85: 194-201.

Kidd, K.K., M.A. Records, and J.R. Kidd. 1978. Sex effects and severity in stuttering. Annual Meeting, Behavior Genetics Assoc. Davis, California. Abstract.

Loehlin, J.C., and R.C. Nichols. 1976. Heredity, enviroment and personality: a study of 850 sets of twins. University of Texas Press, Austin, Texas.

Mainardi, D., and A. Pasquali. Cultural transmission in the house mouse. Estratto dagli Atti della Societa Italiana di Scienze Naturali e del Museo Cevico di Storia Naturale di Milano. 1968. 15: 147-152.

McAskie, M., and A.M. Clarke. 1976. Parent-offspring resemblances in intelligence: theories and evidence. Br. J. Psychol. 67: 243-273.

McKusick, V.A., and F.H. Ruddle. 1977. The status of the gene map of the human chromosomes. Science 196: 390-405.

Morton, N.E. 1974. Analysis of family resemblance. I. Introduction Am. J. Hum. Genet. 26: 318-330.

Munsinger, H. 1978. Reply to Kamin. Psychol. Bull. 85: 202-206.

Niemi, R. and W.R. Thompson. 1979. Pavlovian excitation, internal inhibition, and their interactions with free operant avoidance as a function of age in rats. Devel. Psychobiol. In Press.

238

Omenn, G. Genetic mechanisms in human behavioral development. Ch. 5 in Schaie, K.W., Anderson, V.E. McClearn, G.E. and Money, J. (Eds.) Developmental Human Behavior Genetics. Lexington, Mass. D.C. Heath and Co. 1975.

Plomin, R., J.C. DeFries, and J.C. Loehlin. 1977. Genotype-environment interaction and correlation in the analysis of human behavior. Psychol. Bull. 84: 309-322.

Seligman, M.E.P. 1975. Helplessness. San Francisco, W.H. Freeman Co.

Sward K., and M.B. Friedman, 1935. Jewish temperament. J. Appl. Psychol. 19: 70-84.

Thompson, W.R., and R. Davis, R. 1978. Immediate and long-term effects of inescapable tail-shock administered to weanling and adult rats. Unpublished manuscript. Queen's University.

Thompson, W.R., and L.R. McElroy. 1962. Effects of maternal presence on offspring emotionality in young rats. J. Comp. Physiol. Psychol. 55: 827-830.

Zajonc, R.B. 1976. Familiy configuration and intelligence, Science 192: 227-236.

Zajonc, R.B., and G.B. Markus. 1975. Birth order and intellectual development. Psychol. Rev. 82: 74-88.

COMMENT BY R. E. STAFFORD

It is with considerable enthusiasm that I undertake the discussion of Dr. Thompson's paper, because he has enunciated so
very clearly the growing vague uneasiness over the past few
years that I have felt concerning the trend of behavior genetics.
My suspicion was that behavior geneticists originally had to overcome an almost pathological resistance by most psychologists to
even entertain the notion that heredity might be involved in the
explanation of behavior, and that they subsequently concentrated
on the genetic aspect to such an extent that they are now ignoring the environmental aspect. Perhaps the pendulum had to swing
to one extreme to call attention to such a neglect in psychology;
but over the last fifteen years this singular emphasis has not
brought behavior genetics into the mainstream of psychology. In
my view this paper has correctly called attention to the need to
study both environmental and hereditary effects and their interaction as proper mechanisms for the explanation of behavior.

I might point out here that "familial likeness" is not a new
thrust of behavior genetics but rather a revisit to what was once
its origin. Indeed, the "father" of behavior genetics, Sir Francis
Galton, devoted much of his time to such investigations and his
associate, Karl Pearson, derived the correlation coefficient to
quantify familial likeness in terms of regression. In the United
States such workers as Starch (1915), Cobb (1917), and Willoughby
(1927) were also investigating the degree of family similarities
for various cognitive functions.

However, it is true that we now have more sophisticated models
of both environmental and genetic effects, examples of the former
being the exposure model (with its emphasis on the greater maternal contribution compared to the paternal) and the identification model (with its psychoanalytic undertones). It is entirely
possible that a combination of these two could give rise to
Thompson's $r_{md} > r_{ms} > r_{fs} > r_{fd}$ model.

Of course, there are undoubtedly other environmental models
that could be proposed. Indeed, in my review of the hereditary
and environmental effects on quantitative reasoning (Stafford,
1973) I reported such influences as family attitude, father absence, ordinal position, gender, child rearing practices, sex
role identification, and various interactions of these environmental influences, as the bases for the family sources of variation
on quantitative reasoning.

One of the pragmatic problems of fitting data to such models,
whether they be environmental or genetic, is the fact that almost
all are based on correlations, and correlations are subject to a

host of influences (such as choice of statistical technique, reliability of measurement, and restriction of range of test scores).
For example, although the highest correlation reported on a spell-
ing test was between fathers and daughters (r = +.45; Stafford,
1963), a reanalysis of the data by Willerman & Stafford (1972)
indicated that 50% of the mothers exceeded the fathers' scores for
children scoring 1 SD below the mean and 71% of the mothers' scores
exceeded the fathers' scores for children scoring 1 SD above the
mean. In other words, two different modes of analysis of the same
data yielded two different interpretations, the correlational
method suggesting that the paternal effect was the greater while
the comparative score method emphasized the maternal effect.

Perhaps one of the most exciting newer developments described
in Thompson's paper is the "confluence" model of Zajonc and Markus,
which accounts for much heretofore unexplained data pertaining to
family size and intelligence. I wish that some other measure of
intelligence had been used instead of such an ambiguous and global
concept because it could have provided a great deal more information on the actual mode of familial transmission. However, it
does promise new and more fruitful lines of investigation.

Although most genetic models of family likeness yield results
similar to environmental models, traits influenced by a gene on
the X chromosome would show a unique family correlation such that:
$$r_{fd} = r_{ms} > r_{md} > r_{fs} = r_{fm} = 0$$
There is some evidence that spatial visualization shows this pattern (Stafford, 1961). It is also interesting to note that Galton
apparently observed this X linked characteristic of spatial visualization. Since spatial visualization is often found among natural
scientists, he noted that they do not seem to have as many eminent
fathers as do men in other occupations, but he attributed this to
an environmental influence by saying "Scientific men owe much of
their training to their mothers. . . it therefore, appears to be
very important to success in science that a man should have an
able mother" (Galton, 1869). Of course, the X linked mechanism
was not fully comprehended at that time. Another trait showing a
familial pattern corresponding to an X linked gene is that of
quantitative reasoning (Stafford, 1973).

In exploring the concept of cultural transmission Thompson
has cited animal studies which suggest several rather provocative
leads to follow, especially the concept of age specificity in the
development of the depressive syndrome from a learned helplessness
model.

In his conclusion Thompson has rightly underscored the need
for investigating all means of transmission of family similarities,
both between and within generations. Thompson's paper also serves

as a reminder that behavior geneticists must broaden their investigations to include environmental effects and interaction effects.

COMMENT BY S. G. VANDENBERG

Professor Thompson has put his finger on a very important point, which is that the environmental aspect of familial transmission may become the responsibility of behavior genetics by default. But I am in disagreement about the confluence model of Zajonc. I am willing to accept that parental time spent with children is an important factor; what bothers me is the mathematical model used. When all adults are given a value of 100, this suggests a concept similar to IQ which is independent of age and tends to be constant. On the other hand, a baby is given a value of zero, which seems to be more like a mental age. The model does not allow for parental differences in IQ due to socioeconomic status or age, nor does it allow for differences among the children in a family other than the newborn. The original idea seems of sufficient interest to warrant further exploration, but conceiving the familial influence on a baby as all or none (i.e., 100 or zero) is not consistent with the concept of intelligence. As Professor Thompson points out, the same decrease with increasing family size is found for stature, where the effect can hardly be due to time spent by parents with the child. For example, it would surprise me if there was a systematic difference between children of working and nonworking mothers.

Returning to a broader theoretical issue, it seems of crucial importance to know whether parental styles of disciplining really make a difference. It seems almost certain that the extremes have an effect, but what about styles within the normal range? This is very difficult to determine, of course. The use of reports by parents or children may be of limited validity. Even when observations of behavior are made, an adoption design may be necessary in order to avoid confounding hereditary and environmental factors and to eliminate possible effects of genotype-environment interaction.

COMMENT BY J. C. LOEHLIN

I thoroughly agree with Thompson that the explanation of familial resemblance is interesting and important; however, it might also be worth noting that, especially in the area of personality, the real challenge may lie in explaining the many family correlations of less than .2, i.e., the relative lack of familial resemblance in many traits for which, a priori, one might suppose that both shared environmental and genetic factors were important.

On a different point, I am not overly impressed by the power of the Zajonc model to explain U.S. black-white differences in mean IQ test scores. The mean difference in family size between U.S. blacks and whites is on the order of half a child or less. For the Belmont and Marolla data, half a child translates to something like one thirtieth of a standard deviation of IQ, or about half an IQ point of a 15 point difference. Father absence could add something, but the rest of the factors cited would already largely be accounted for in the family size differences.

References

Cobb, M. V. A preliminary study of the inheritance of arithmetic ability. Journal of Educational Psychology, 1917, 8, 1-20.

Galton, F. Hereditary genius. (Orig. ed. 1869). New York: Appleton, 1880.

Stafford, R. E. Sex differences in spatial visualization as evidence sex-linked inheritance. Perceptual and Motor Skills, 1961, 13, 428.

Stafford, R. E. An investigation of similarities in parent-child test scores for evidence of hereditary components. Research Bulletin 63-11. Princeton, N.J.: Educational Testing Service, 1963.

Stafford, R. E. Hereditary and environmental components of quantitative reasoning. Review of Educational Research, 1973, 42, 183-

Starch, D. The inheritance of abilities in school studies. School and Society, 1915, 2, 608-610.

Willerman, L., & Stafford, R. E. Maternal effects on intellectual functioning. Behavior Genetics, 1972, 2, 321-325.

Willoughby, R. R. Family similarities in mental test abilities Genetic Psychology Monographs, 1927, 11, 234-277.

ADAPTIVE SIGNIFICANCE OF ANIMAL BEHAVIOR: THE ROLE OF
GENE-ENVIRONMENT INTERACTION

Norman D. Henderson

Oberlin College, Oberlin, Ohio   USA

ABSTRACT. Because of several subtle differences between most
morphological and most behavioral measures, heritability estimates
in animal behavior research are often of little use. A limited
set of outcomes involving the relative magnitude of different
sources of genetic variation can provide insight concerning the
relationship of behavior to Darwinian fitness, if the following
conditions are met: (1) there is extensive genetic sampling,
preferably including wild genotypes; (2) complex behaviors are
measured in several different ways, with the genetic analysis
based on composite behavior scores; (3) animals are reared in at
least two different environments, if environmental complexity, diet,
or prior stress influence the behavior of interest. A strong test
of the adequacy of animal behavior genetic methods and assumptions
concerning genetic variation and evolution is the ability to predict interactions of experimental variables and age with genetic
architecture, based on an understanding of the dependent variables
used in light of a species ethogram.

1.   INTRODUCTION

1.1   The shift in emphasis in quantitative behavior genetics

The year 1960 signaled the end of an era for behavioral genetic
research with animals. Fuller and Thompson (1960) had aptly
summarized work of the previous forty years, which consisted largely
of selection studies, simple breeding experiments, strain difference
studies, and some beginning work on single-gene effects using
coisogenic lines and mutants. The year 1960 was also the date of

publication of Falconer's Quantitative Genetics and Broadhurst's introduction of the biometrical genetic approach of the Birmingham group to behavioral psychologists (Broadhurst, 1960). Although behavior geneticists have adopted most contemporary methods used in genetics to study behavior variables, the quantitative genetic approach has been most prevalent for the study of behavior since 1960. The methods described by Falconer (1960) and the more extensive biometrical approaches summarized by Mather and Jinks (1971) are found regularly in the literature of animal behavior. The use of more sophisticated breeding designs and analyses was due not just to the access to new methods, but to the realization that they were necessary to move beyond simple descriptive systems in order to attain insight into the possible evolutionary significance of behaviors of interest.

The shift from simple descriptive studies of strain differences or response to selection was not without pitfalls. The genetic material investigators had to work with was not ideal, both in terms of the origin of the founding populations and the effects of years of domestication in laboratories. Furthermore, most of the methodological contributions to quantitative genetics were developed largely from the point of view of agricultural production, where the emphasis often tended to be on breeding potentials and the expected usefulness of selection procedures for characters of interest and thus tended to emphasize heritability and additive genetic variance and covariance. To be sure, some contributors to this field, particularly Mather (1949), Lerner (1954, 1958), Robertson (1955, 1956) and Falconer (1960) had discussed the relationship of genetic architecture to natural selection, but their discussions were broad and theoretical and dealt primarily with morphological characters. In the move to more sophisticated genetic analyses of behavior investigators began to generate estimates of various genetic parameters for a variety of behaviors often without regard for the profound differences in the nature of behavioral versus morphological characters, possible constraining effects of laboratory environments and the arbitrary and often inappropriate choice of genetic material for research.

The preoccupation with heritability measures in conjunction with the above problems resulted in a great deal of data which are of marginal use for the understanding of the evolutionary significance of the behaviors examined. I think it is fair to say that much of what has been done with respect to elaborate genetic analyses of behavior in the '60s and early '70s was done primarily to demonstrate that even complex behavioral characters can be analyzed using sophisticated genetic techniques. The fact that the outcomes themselves may often be sufficiently distorted to be of little use in understanding a natural history of the behavior in the species studied is unfortunate but understandable.

1.2 Representative design as a strategy for behavior genetics research

Several years ago I suggested that the frequent occurrence of nonadditive effects of treatment, test, age, and genetic variables would necessitate research efforts which sampled and examined multiple levels of each of these classes of variables simultaneously in rather elaborate factorial multivariate designs (Henderson, 1969). I used the term "representative design" taken from Brunswik (1956) to describe this procedure mainly because the approach stresses the use of multiple variable experiments with a large sampling of variables of biological relevance. In the decade since writing that paper, results of subsequent research have not only reinforced my convictions about the necessity of this approach, but have suggested to me that the study of the interaction of genotype with age, environment, and test parameters may be the only way that quantitative genetic analyses of behavior can shed light on the natural history of behavior. Furthermore, prior prediction of specific interactions with genotype provides the most powerful test of the adequacy of our measures and research designs for understanding animal behavior.

I shall begin by describing the genetic indices most useful for understanding the relationship of the behavior to fitness in a natural situation, including reasons why heritability estimates are of relatively little use to behavior geneticists, progress to a discussion of the genetic sampling required for adequate behavior genetic research, then on to the nature of behavioral measurement and its effect on genetic outcome, finally on to the role of age and other environmental variables in behavior genetic research.

Although this paper deals with broad theoretical issues concerning the relationship of laboratory research results to evolutionary history, these issues are dealt with through a discussion of the "nitty-gritty" aspects of laboratory research with animals. Not only do such methodological details influence data which are used for theory building, but there are important theoretical reasons why only certain strategies involving the sampling of genotypes, dependent variables, and environmental experience are appropriate for behavior genetic research on animals. I have not attempted to provide a comprehensive review of the literature in the several areas of behavior genetics discussed in this paper. Several areas, such as the genetics of animal learning, gene-environment interactions, and the effects of domestication on animal behavior, have been amply reviewed elsewhere (Wahlsten, 1972a; Erlenmeyer-Kimling, 1972; Boice, 1973). I have limited examples to a few studies, which are used repeatedly through the paper to illustrate certain points. Finally, although the paper is broken into separate sections concerning genotypes, dependent

variables, and environmental variables these three aspects of behavior genetics research are so interwoven that placement of some
issues within this framework is rather arbitrary.

2. GENETIC ARCHITECTURE AND ITS RELATIONSHIP TO NATURAL SELECTION

2.1 The difficulty with heritability as a major parameter of in-
terest in behavioral studies

There have been many attempts to compare heritability
estimates of behaviors across a variety of studies which have used
different genotypes, testing procedures and methods of analysis.
I believe that little insight can be obtained from such exercises
with respect to behavioral variables for a variety of reasons,
most of which serve to emphasize some of the differences in the
application of quantitative genetic methods to behaviors and to
the application of these methods to morphological and physiological characters of interest to animal and plant breeders.

Let us begin with the issue of reliability of measurement.
The measurement of most morphological characters such as body
weight in mice, abdominal bristles in drosophila, or number of
grains per ear in wheat can be made with exceedingly high reliability or repeatability. Most such morphological characters
can be measured with reliabilities in excess of .9 over the short
term, whereas most individual behavioral measurements are likely
to show test-retest reliabilities in the .3 to .8 range. Given
the wide range and often low reliabilities of behavioral measures,
measurement error often has a profound effect on heritability
estimates of behavioral characters whereas they are usually of
minor consequence for morphological characters. Furthermore,
repeated measurements of individuals can substantially increase
the reliabilities of behavioral measures whereas they will do
little to change the already high reliabilities of morphological
measurements. As a result, the investigator who, for example,
records the activity level of each animal on three separate five-
minute trials will likely report a higher heritability estimate
for the behavior than an investigator who uses identical measurements and populations, but records activity on only a single
five-minute session. Unlike the field of human behavior genetics,
where standardized measuring instruments with established reliabilities are often used, allowing for adjustments for differential
reliabilities, such adjustments cannot easily be made in animal
research.

In addition to arbitrary decisions on the part of an investigator with respect to the duration of measurement or number of repeated measurements taken, a number of other methodological decisions

influence between-subject variation and consequently heritability
estimates. In agricultural research the different genotypes are
usually replicated across plots, seasons, or both, thus providing a more or less typical range of environmental variation
under which the phenotypes are produced. In animal behavior research, on the other hand, the degree of control of extraneous
variables is to a considerable degree an arbitrary decision made
in the laboratory. An experiment may extend over several seasons
or be compressed into a short time period; environmental variables
within the laboratory such as temperature, humidity, lighting conditions and animal caretaking may be tightly or loosely controlled;
litters may or may not be culled to uniform size; testing may be
done under varying degrees of control or constancy of conditions
with respect to time of day, controls over odor and other sensory
cues and uniformity of handling of subjects. Depending on the
behavior being measured each of these factors is likely to
occasionally have some influence on variability between individuals
and between families. I am not here referring to differences in
experimental outcomes with respect to overall genetic architecture
as a function of different environmental conditions within different laboratories (i.e., Genotype X Macroenvironment interactions),
but to Genotype X Microenvironment interactions, expressed as
differential degrees of within-genotype environmental variability
across experiments. The former can change the entire genetic
architecture of a character and, as we shall see later, should
best be described as the study of multiple characters with varying
degrees of genotypic correlations between them. The latter primarily influences the degree of genetic versus environmental
variance (i.e., heritability estimates) and has considerably less
influence on the relative size of additive and non-additive genetic
effects.

Another factor influencing the relative magnitude of genetic
and environmental contributions to phenotypic variance and therefore heritability, concerns the individual unit of analysis used
to estimate within-genotype environmental variance. Again, in
agricultural research such units are often chosen in terms of their
connection to units of economic importance such as variation between
litters or bushels. Heritability estimates in the behavioral
literature can be found to be computed variously from replicate
cell means, family or litter means, between-litter mean squares,
and occasionally a composite of between- and within-litter mean
squares resulting from the computation of simple within-genotype
variances composed of several litters. Obviously the same data
analyzed using each of these methods to compute within-genotype
variance will result in a different heritability estimate. Each
of course is interpretable in its own right, but hardly comparable
to other heritability estimates unless all are adjusted to a common
unit of analysis. There are few attempts to make such adjustments
when comparing heritabilities across studies, and at this point I

doubt that such an exercise would be worthwhile.

Obviously the genetic architecture of a character obtained through the analysis of one population is likely to differ from that of a second population where gene frequencies differ considerably. Heritability estimates are particularly likely to shift considerably under such circumstances. As a result, the choice of subjects in behavior genetic studies has had strong influence on the heritabilities observed. Parental stocks have sometimes been chosen randomly from those available, sometimes semi-randomly in that closely related strains are not used, and occasionally an attempt is made to use parental lines differing maximally on the character of interest. Such a choice has an obvious effect on the additive genetic variance obtained for the character in question. Inadvertent inclusion of a parental line with a sensory or motor deficit can also artificially increase between-line variance and thus heritability. Finally, I suspect if we were regularly to partition out from between-strain variance on behavior the proportion of variance due to differences between albino and non-albino strains, we would find that much additive genetic variance could be attributed to albinism effects.

With commonly used mus musculus, the amount of genetic variation represented in standard laboratory inbred lines is only a fraction of that available to the species as a whole (Selander & Yang, 1970). Insofar as the restriction in genetic variability may reduce additive genetic variance of behavioral characters in a population, laboratory estimates of heritability may be biased on the low side for some characters. In addition, because of less environmental buffering of homozygotes, heritability estimates based on variance between inbred strains relative to within-strain variance may often be lower than would be the case in a heterozygous population. Conversely, additive genetic variance when computed from variance between inbred lines will be inflated if variance due to maternal effects is present. More appropriate estimates of additive genetic variance for purposes of computing heritability ratios can be obtained by using an adjustment for between-line maternal effects if an estimate is   available (Walters and Gayle, 1977). Given the above considerations, it should be evident that heritability estimates in animal behavior research have little meaning.

2.2 The relationship of additive and non-additive genetic variance

To a large degree, difficulties associated with using heritability estimates are considerably reduced when we move away from emphasis on genetic versus environmental contributions to phenotypic variability and focus on the relative magnitudes of different genetic components of variance. Problems associated with differential reliability of measures, and the choice of subject unit used to estimate environmental variance and problems concerning distortion due to choice of genotypes are greatly reduced when the relative magnitude of genetic effects becomes our major interest.

Clearly it is the relationship of additive to non-additive genetic effects which we should be concerned with since certain relationships, in particular those situations where strong directional dominance is observed, do provide us with strong evidence that the behavioral character showing such dominance has a functional relationship with Darwinian fitness.

In this respect the most useful estimates at present are the index of average dominance across all effective genes, or $(H/D)^{\frac{1}{2}}$, using Mather's notation, and mean directional dominance, h^2. The former ranges from 0, when gene action is additive across loci involved, through 1.0, signifying complete dominance, to values greater than one in cases of overdominance. If a high proportion of the genetic variance of a behavioral character can be attributed to dominance and if this dominance is largely directional in nature, one is probably dealing with a behavioral character functionally related to fitness (Mather, 1949; Robertson, 1955; Falconer, 1960). Basically, directional selection pressures have reduced the proportion of additive genetic variance, relative to non-additive genetic variance brought about through gene interaction at either a single locus (dominance) or across several loci (epistasis). Data on morphological and physiological characters obtained from both laboratory studies and agricultural research strongly support the dominance-fitness hypothesis (Lerner, 1958; Falconer, 1960).

Despite a number of experimental design problems, there is a tendency for animal behavior data to follow an at least intuitively logical pattern with respect to directional dominance and class of characters being measured. In general, directional dominance or heterosis appears strong in mating and maternal behaviors, moderate on a number of learning measures, and weaker on general measures of ambulation and activity less obviously related to fitness. The trend is only a general one, however, and there is considerable variation in the degree of directional dominance found in each of these classes of behavior, as seen in the tables prepared by Professor Broadhurst in this volume. Some critics have taken these exceptions as evidence that the present methods used in animal behavior genetics are not capable of shedding much light on the adaptive significance of the characters we study in the laboratory, despite the strong theoretical arguments connecting dominance and fitness. I believe this is only partially correct. With some modifications and extensions, current strategies can be highly useful in this regard, as I hope to demonstrate shortly.

Before leaving this point, I believe we should clarify what I mean by strong directional dominance effects relative to additive genetic variance for behavioral characters. Obviously, statistical significance should not be used as an index. In most modern genetic designs, such as the diallel, the tests for hybrid versus parent means are exceedingly powerful and even a slight deviation of F_1s from the mid-parent average is likely to be statistically significant. Since nearly all behaviors we study involve the use of sensory and motor systems, which have at least a remote connection with fitness, the failure to find any significant difference between inbred and hybrid animals is likely to be the exception. Hegmann et. al. (1973), for example, has demonstrated a hybrid vigor effect for a general neural conductivity factor which may be related to a large class of behaviors likely to be studied. It would indeed be surprising not to find some difference between inbreds and hybrids, however small, on most behavioral characters. Until we understand the relationship of selection to gene action more fully and our experiments meet the demands of sampling and scaling more adequately, only in cases where dominance appears nearly complete or where heterosis due to overdominance or epistatic interactions is demonstrated, should we consider that the character being studied has a strong functional relationship to fitness.

Although directional dominance may be the only case in which we can safely infer some relationship to fitness, this does not mean that in situations where genetic variance is largely additive or dominance variance is ambidirectional, the characteristics reflected in the behaviors being measured are neutral with respect to natural selection. Many characters may, for example, be subjected to stabilizing selection. Often intermediate expression of a character is optimal either due to the character itself or because of limitations imposed by the environment such as in the relationship of litter size and food supplies. Depending on the nature of the stabilizing selection, its effect on the genetic architecture may vary. In most cases one would expect to find relatively large degrees of additive genetic variance, relatively little directional dominance, and an uncertain degree of ambidirectional dominance. In addition to cases involving stabilizing selection, a population may show a great deal of additive genetic variance for a character which has a strong positive relationship to one component of fitness and a negative relationship to a second component of fitness. Any further reduction in additive genetic variance would only serve to reduce overall fitness with respect to the two components. It is thus inappropriate to conclude that characters showing little directional dominance have relatively little evolutionary importance to the organism or, as Thiessen (1972) labeled such characters, "genetic junk".

I think, then, we have been guilty in overstating our case with respect to relating the genetic architecture of a character

to its natural history. In only a limited number of cases can we
make such statements and a great number of possible genetic outcomes are still uninterpretable to us from an evolutionary standpoint. This is indeed unfortunate since modern biometrical genetic
techniques allow us to estimate many parameters of genetic architecture which, in turn, allow estimates of mean proportions of
dominant and recessive genes across all loci influencing the
character, the ratio of the total numbers of dominant to recessive
genes in all parents, the constancy of dominance effects across
loci, the number of groups of genes exhibiting dominance which
control the character and some indication of the presence of gene
association or dispersion in the parent lines. In cases of non-
allelic interaction, complementary and duplicate gene interactions
can be detected. Similarly, although effects of stabilizing, disruptive, and fluctuating selection pressures on gene frequencies
are reasonably understood (e.g., Robertson, 1956; Berry, 1978)
their relationship to additive and non-additive genetic variance
and other parameters estimated using biometrical genetic methods
is not clear. Investigators should estimate all parameters available in a breeding design in anticipation of further understanding
of the relationship of some of these parameters to natural selection,
but at present only findings of substantial directional dominance
relative to additive genetic variance can be interpreted in terms
of fitness to the organism.

It is important to examine one of the criticisms made concerning the use of laboratory organisms of unknown and possibly
diverse origin as the raw material for breeding studies in behavior genetics in light of the discussion above. An underlying
assumption of the methods used in these studies is that parent
population has been derived from a common founding population
subject to more or less uniform selection pressures prior to inbreeding. Let us examine briefly the consequences of the viola-
tion of this assumption by taking an extreme example--one in
which the inbred parent lines have been derived from two distinct
populations subject to opposing selection pressures for the behavioral character being measured. If we were able to identify
the origin of each of our inbred parent strains, thereby grouping
them according to original base population and then we carried out
two separate genetic analyses, we would find that in one case strong
directional dominance for the positive expression of the trait
would occur and in the second case a strong directional dominance
for negative expression of the trait would occur. In comparison,
if all parent strains were pooled without regard to origin and a
breeding study carried out, we would obtain a considerably lower
proportion of dominance variance relative to additive variance than
in either original analysis, and what dominance was expressed would
be largely ambidirectional. A plot of the mean degree of dominance
for each of the parent lines as a function of mean score on the
character being measured would reveal a U-shaped relationship--

extreme scoring parent lines would appear to have the largest
proportion of dominant genes influencing the behavior.

From the above example it should be evident that, with respect
to the only situation in which we can confidently make statements
concerning adaptive significance, directional dominance, a vio-
lation of assumptions concerning common selection pressures of
our base population can only serve to make our results inconclusive. In heterogeneous base populations involving less extreme
circumstances effects on attenuating directional dominance will
be less, but in all cases violations of assumptions will lead to
a lower probability of incorrectly stating that a character has a
positive functional relationship to fitness. Furthermore, a simple
examination of the results of each of the crossing combinations in
a breeding design, along with the usual scaling tests and an
examination of the relationship between dominance and mean phenotypic values for parent lines, will usually result in the detection
of situations where parental lines have been derived from populations under differing selection pressures. In the absence of such
clues I suspect that results obtained with laboratory lines at
least crudely mirror those which would be obtained under circumstances more closely meeting the assumptions of the genetic analysis.
Despite this, with respect to rodent research in behavior genetics,
we can probably considerably improve our selection of genotypes
in future research, as I shall suggest below.

3. SAMPLING GENETIC MATERIAL

3.1 The sampling of laboratory strains

Investigators have frequently made less than judicious choices
in establishing breeding lines for behavior genetic research. In
rodent research the overuse of albino lines and the frequent inclusion of inbred lines with retinal degeneration or other sensory
deficits, for example, has probably often biased genetic estimates
because the experimental gene pool was so unrepresentative of that
found among wild populations. Although this work did demonstrate
the feasibility of applying various genetic procedures to behavioral
variables much of the research did little else. To interpret
genetic results in terms of evolutionary principles one must have
a broad representative sampling of genotypes, preferably derived
from a gene pool of local interbreeding populations. Breeding
research which begins with two or three inbred strains, no matter
how intensive, is unlikely to provide the diversity of genotypes
to provide even a rough picture of gene action with respect to
behavior of interest. Miniature diallels and other breeding designs are not economical shortcuts to understanding genetic
architecture. In many cases the results of such studies are simply

confusing or misleading. McGill (1970) has illustrated this nicely
in his review of some of his early work on sexual behavior of male
mice.

McGill originally analyzed 14 measures of male sexual behavior in C57 and DBA inbred strains of mice and in their F_1 hybrid
cross (McGill & Blight, 1963). Several years later he replicated
this experiment using the same 14 measures, but substituting the
AKR strain for the C57 strain (McGill & Ranson, 1968). The common
strain in both experiments, DBA, was inconsistent with respect to
being the dominant or recessive parent on several measures across
the two experiments. Furthermore, on some measures such as mount
latency, dominance for short latencies appeared in the first experiment and dominance for long latencies appeared in the second.
Taken as a pair of mini-experiments on the behavior genetics of
male sexual behavior, the results on only three of the 13 dependent
variables showing significant genetic variation were consistent
across the two experiments. Yet, if one combines the data of the
two experiments into an incomplete 3 X 3 diallel, the results are
not particularly confusing. Several measures showed directional
dominance or heterosis, and other measures showed partial directional dominance, bi-directional dominance, or primarily additive
genetic variance. As a single analysis with somewhat wider genetic
sampling, the results make at least intuitive sense. Variation in
mount latency and time of intromission was primarily a function of
additive and bidirectional dominance, suggesting that extreme
scores on these characters may not be of particular selective
advantage. It is easy to see why intermediate expression of such
characters may be of relatively greater advantage than extremely
low or high scores. Testing was done under normal room illumination in a relatively unprotected arena with clear plastic walls.
Some hesitancy in mounting and intermediate intromission times
could well be optimal for reproduction under such conditions. On
the other hand, intromission latency is probably closely related
to reproductive fitness and short latencies are probably adaptive under
any testing circumstance. Evidence of significant overdominance
toward short intromission latencies is clear in the composite
analysis. Taken individually, the two experiments shed little
light on the genetic architecture of several aspects of male
sexual behavior in mus musculus, but taken together, a reasonable
picture begins to emerge. Unfortunately, slight changes in experimental conditions and an incomplete set of F_1 crosses greatly
limit the weight one can place on the interpretation of these data.
A single experiment, with more extensive genetic sampling and testing under different levels of environmental conditions, would have
been preferable and more efficient for determining the genetic
architecture of these behaviors than several smaller studies.

Although I am pleased to see more attention being paid to the
genetic variable in animal behavior research, the increase in number

of studies casually sampling a limited number of genotypes is not
likely to serve behavior genetics very well. Such limited genetic
sampling is likely to be responsible for a number of incorrect
generalizations concerning the mode of inheritance and adaptive
significance of various behaviors. Except in cases of nearly
complete additive genetic variation, one must necessarily expect
considerable fluctuation in the outcome of individual pairs of
crosses making up a large breeding design. This fluctuation is
an inherent part of the genetic architecture of the character and
it can only be detected with extensive genetic sampling. When only
two or three lines and their crosses are tested, these individual
fluctuations become the basis for genetic conclusions. Although
gross errors in conclusions about the mode of inheritance can
probably be avoided by sampling even a modest number of parental
strains, the probability of occurrence of spuriously correlated
gene distributions among parent strains is still reasonably high
even when 5 or 6 strains are used. The presence of such correlations alters estimates of additive genetic variance, and consequently the dominance ratio $(H/D)^2$, with particularly serious inflation of this ratio when gene dispersion and uni-directional
dominance exists (Hayman, 1954). The lesson should be clear with
respect to the use of laboratory inbred parent lines for behavior
genetics research--extensive sampling from a carefully chosen pool
of strains is a must. Laboratory strains, however, comprise only
part of the genetic sampling necessary for behavior genetic research
which is designed to understand evolutionary history.

3.2 The use of wild populations

In addition to the issue of how widely one must sample parental
genotypes, it is expected that such genotypes represent a reasonable
approximation of those found among non-laboratory members of the
species. The large proportion of albino strains and strains with
sensory or motor deficits used for behavior genetic research pushes
us far from this ideal of representative sampling. Beyond such
obvious discrepancies, however, what is a "representative sample
of the gene pool"? Because of varying selection pressures in
different ecological niches it is probably inappropriate to speak
of "the" gene pool of a species. More than a decade ago Bruell
(1967) reminded investigators about these constraints and pointed
out that we know very little about the natural environmental conditions under which the founders of most laboratory strains evolved.
If selection pressures differed considerably among the original
wild populations from which laboratory lines were ultimately derived, intercrossing these lines would produce results of little
interpretive value. This is undoubtedly true, although I have
argued above that, in cases where unambiguous directional dominance
or heterosis is obtained, it is unlikely that selection pressures on
the character of interest differed substantially among the ancestors

of the different inbred parent lines used.

In addition to their unknown origin, Bruell also reminded investigators that inbred laboratory strains cannot be representative of natural populations because inbreeding guarantees the loss of recessive lethal genes and probably some semi-lethal genes. He suggested that an effort be made to study animals drawn from local wild populations which evolved under distinct and well known environmental conditions. The argument is compelling and insightful, but the paucity of data of the type advocated which has been generated during the past 10 years attests to the difficulty of carrying out such research.

The basic point of Bruell's comments was not missed however, and, taken with the increasing concern about the use of domesticated animals as models for understanding "natural" species behavior, a number of investigators began to take up and elaborate criticisms of research based on domesticated laboratory populations. Lorenz (1965) had already proclaimed that "geneticists have correctly emphasized that wild animals cannot, strictly speaking, be propagated in captivity, because captivity changes all hitherto effective selection factors in so profound a manner that serious changes must be expected in the genome of the stock after only a few generations". Specifically addressing the research of psychologists, Lockard (1968) argued that the albino rat "is rapidly evolving, and it is only a matter of time until it is recognized as a separate species."

Three questions must thus be raised with respect to the appropriateness of using inbred laboratory strains as a starting point for behavior genetic research: (1) were selection pressures for behavioral characters of interest uniform among the ancestors of the inbred parent lines to be used? (2) have the loss of lethal and semi-lethal genes and other effects of inbreeding severely distorted the gene pool of the parent populations used in breeding studies? (3) have major changes in selection pressure during domestication, other than those resulting from inbreeding, altered the gene pool influencing behavior of interest?

The answer is probably Yes to all three questions. It is highly likely that our present strains are from populations of different origins with somewhat differing selection pressures, and inbreeding and domestication have undoubtedly altered the gene pool. The work of Selander and Yang (1970), studying isoallelic variation in 10,000 mice collected from over 300 different mus musculus populations, as well as from a number of inbred laboratory strains, demonstrated conclusively that the gene pool of inbred strains was hardly representative of that found among wild mice. For many polymorphic loci studied, more alleles were represented in wild populations in Texas alone than in all of the inbred strains

Selander and Yang studied. The genetic variation represented in
inbred strains apparently is only a fraction of the total variation
in the species as a whole.

There are then several reasons to expect that the gene pool of
laboratory animals used for behavior genetic research is not quite
appropriate when the objectives of the research are to understand
something about the evolutionary significance of the behavior.
Despite this, blanket condemnations of the use of laboratory populations for behavior genetic research, or for any behavioral research for that matter, are not likely to be defensible. There
are probably many behaviors which are under considerably differing
selection pressures across different ecological niches, but there
are also likely to be many behaviors where selection pressures are
similar across niches. I suspect that behaviors of the latter type
are more likely to be of interest to psychologists and ethologists,
at least at this early stage of understanding of animal behavior,
because of their uniformity across the species. Similarly, laboratory domestication undoubtedly alters some behaviors by selecting against certain behavioral phenotypes such as finger biters,
cage escapers, food wasters, and poor breeders. Alternatively,
selection pressures are undoubtedly relaxed for a number of characters
under strong selection in natural situations. In addition, there
are no doubt many behavioral phenotypes on which selection pressures
in the laboratory and in natural ecological niches are similar.
Statements about the appropriateness or inappropriateness of laboratory animals for research therefore have meaning only with respect
to a specific behavioral phenotype.

General criticisms of the use of laboratory populations are
less constructive than attempts to derive procedures which allow
empirical estimates of the consequences of possible gene pool dis-
tortions for behaviors of interest. I have already suggested that
in some case the results of a breeding design itself will provide
clues that such distortion exists, particularly in the case of inbred parent populations which originated from populations under
radically differing selection pressures. The detection of problems
resulting from inbreeding itself or domestication can best be detected by the use of laboratory reared offspring of captive wild
animals.

There is considerable work already published on differences
between laboratory and wild groups of animals, but many of these
reported differences cannot directly be attributed to domestication
effects because rearing environments have usually differed considerably between the two groups. In reviewing the large number
of domestication studies, Boice (1973) found only one early study
(King, 1939) that attempted to analyze genetic changes accompanying
domestication of a wild population. Most other work involves
comparison of differences between recently captured wild and

domestic animals. Notable recent exceptions have been studies by
Smith (1972), Connor et al (1973), and Connor (1975) comparing
laboratory mice to wild house mice. The latter study was particularly germane to the issue of domestication, since domestication of a wild house mouse population was analyzed to assess
separately the relative contributions of genetic and environmental
alteration on a number of behaviors. The effect of domestication
was evaluated by measuring the emerging behavioral differences
between a population breeding under laboratory conditions and
one breeding in a simulated natural environment.

Connor's results provide little support for the notion that
natural selection in the laboratory produces striking and rapid
behavioral changes in increasingly domesticated populations. The
behaviors studied were the types one might expect to change rapidly,
such as ability to escape, resistance to handling, and investigation of intruders. Statements of Lorenz, Lockard, and others
about domestication effects may have been too strong, considering
that after ten generations, Connors' wild mice seemed to have
changed little as a result of laboratory rearing. Connor and Smith
have continued to examine other behaviors and continued to find
relatively small behavioral changes in mice after domestication.
In addition, Boice (1977) has demonstrated that differences in
wild and domestic rats were minor in terms of burrows dug, either
in the laboratory or in outdoor pens. Feralization of domestic
rats produced behaviors highly similar to those of wild Norway rats
in his study. These limited results suggest that, when reared
under similar circumstances, differences between wild and domesticated
rodents may not be substantial for many behaviors. Nevertheless,
the possibilities of selection, inbreeding, mutation, migration,
and genetic drift which can occur during domestication (Price &
King, 1968) provide a strong argument for determining the effects
of domestication on behaviors of interest in genetic research.

I have recently suggested one such test which can be applied
when strong directional dominance has been found to exist for a
given behavior and maternal influence appears to be small (Henderson,
1978). Although these are limiting conditions, they are the same
conditions under which we can have confidence that behavior we
have been measuring has been under selection pressure. The test
involves a comparison of the relative performance of inbred parent
strains (P), the mean of their hybrid crosses (F), and the mean of
one or more samples from different populations of wild subjects (W)
that have been maintained in the laboratory for no more than a few
generations.

If no directional selection pressure has been exerted on a
particular phenotype in a wild population, inbred derived lines from
the population should exhibit no inbreeding depression on the
character being studied and thus the mean performance of many such

inbred lines should equal that of the mean of the wild populations. On the other hand, if selection pressure is exerted on this original wild base population during laboratory domestication prior to the completion of inbreeding, inbred-hybrid differences should emerge in subsequent genetic tests. Therefore, a comparison of original wild populations with laboratory animals should result in the wild populations appearing similar to laboratory inbreds rather than all possible crosses between inbreds. A ratio of the differences between wild and parent means to that of crosses versus parent means should approach zero (i.e., $(W-P)/(F-P) \approx 0$).

If directional selection pressure has been exerted on a particular behavior in a natural setting and this selection pressure is maintained at the same level through many generations of laboratory rearing, the wild population mean should approximate that obtained from a multiway hybrid cross among inbred animals. In the case of extensive breeding designs such as the diallel or triple test cross, the means of all crosses should approximately equal the mean of all wild populations in which inbreeding is not high, while both should differ significantly from the mean of the inbred parent lines; thus $(W-P)/(F-P) \approx 1$. If selection pressures for a character are greater in the laboratory than in natural settings, the mean wild phenotype should fall between inbred and hybrid laboratory stocks producing an index of relative directional selection pressure (RDS) between zero and one. If selection pressures are stronger in natural settings, the wild population mean should deviate further from the inbred parent than from the F_1 mean; thus the RDS ratio should exceed one. Table 1 presents a summary of these relationships for several values of W relative to P and F.

Table 1. Expected relation between mean scores of several inbred strains (P), all their possible crosses (F) and many wild lines (W) when there has been selection pressure in favor of higher scoring phenotypes in laboratory environments. Copyright 1978 by the American Psychological Association. Reprinted by permission.

Score		Condition of occurrence	$(W-P)/(F-P)$
+			
F >	<W	When positive selection pressures are stronger in the natural environment than in the laboratory (N > L)	RDS > 1
	<W	When selection pressures on the phenotype are equal in laboratory and natural environments (N = L)	RDS = 1
	<W	When positive selection pressures are stronger in the laboratory environment than in the natural environment (N < L)	0 < RDS < 1
P >	<W	When there is no selection pressure toward higher or lower scoring phenotypes in natural environments (N = 0, L > 0), or when (L > 0 > N), as below	RDS = 0
	<W	Possible if selection pressures favor low scoring phenotypes in natural environment, but strong positive selection has occurred during laboratory domestication (L > 0 > N)	RDS < 0
−			

Notes: RDS=relative selection pressure. F includes both F_1 hybrids and inbreds generated from all crosses. In terms of inbred (P) v. F_1 hybrid (H) means, $F=(nH-H+2P)/(n+1)$ in an n X n diallel table.

By testing animals from several different wild populations, an indication of the consistency of the RDS ratio can be obtained. Small differences between wild lines, relative to average inbred-hybrid differences, would suggest that overall directional selection pressures were approximately uniform across different demes for the phenotype in question. In such cases general statements concerning relative selection pressures in natural and laboratory settings are meaningful, even without knowledge of the genetic relationship between the tested laboratory and the wild lines. In cases in which wide variations of different wild lines would lead to a wide variation in RDS ratios, statements about relative selection pressures or about the appropriateness of studying inbred derived laboratory versus laboratory reared "wild lines" lose their meaning.

There are two limitations which prevent the RDS ratio from being anything other than a rough estimate of changes in selection pressure during laboratory domestication. First, even in the absence of maternal effects assessed by reciprocal differences among females of inbred strains, possible differential maternal influences may exist between inbred laboratory females and genetically heterogeneous wild females, which could alter the RDS ratio. Second, the degree of inbreeding within some of wild populations sampled may be high relative to the heterozygosity of the laboratory generated F_1s, which would have the effects of lowering the RDS ratio. To determine if a high degree of inbreeding depression exists among the wild populations, crosses between them may be necessary. Despite the limitations of the RDS ratio, our limited experience thus far has failed to turn up a situation where results were counterintuitive or illogical. Clearly, however, the approach is only a start and more sophisticated measures, as well as more data comparing a range of laboratory genotypes, possibly including F_2 generations with wild populations, is desirable.

Use of one or more wild lines in conjunction with standard laboratory lines should not, of course, preclude further empirical investigations which involve both domestication and inbreeding studies of wild populations, as well as an examination of the outcome of breeding studies using animals of a common base population.

4. SAMPLING DEPENDENT VARIABLES

4.1 Characters, sub-characters, and super-characters

I have suggested that there are several differences in the nature of morphological and behavioral variables which affect the outcome of genetic experiments. Low and variable reliability coefficients of behavioral measures make estimates of relative genetic and environmental influences nearly unique to each experiment, a problem rarely encountered with morphological measures. Other characteristics of behavioral measures can also lead to differences in the outcome of studies using behavioral rather than morphological data.

The characters for which biometrical genetic procedures were developed are usually clearly defined and, with respect to agricultural research, often are of intrinsic value. They also form part of a hierarchical organization. Characters such as plant yield can be broken into a number of specific sub-characters contributing to yield which may also be subject to genetic analysis. Experience in plant breeding has suggested that the analysis of sub-characters does not simplify the methods used in genetic analysis of the polygenic system mediating variation in yield, but that analysis of sub-characters can often point out different routes to improve overall plant yield (Mather & Jinks, 1971). The relationship of sub-characters to a character is fixed, in that the character is definable and measurable as a specific product of its sub-characters.

In agricultural research different characters may be combined arbitrarily to define a super-character of interest. One might combine yield with disease resistance and other characters related to food quality to produce a super-character which might be called overall merit. Super-characters thus do not have a fixed relationship to characters, but are defined in terms of the goals of the analysis. If we are concerned with natural populations, the constitution of the population can be understood only in terms of major components of Darwinian fitness, which can be regarded as super-characters, as can a composite of these components which define fitness itself. Darwinian fitness as a super-character is quite different from a super-character defined largely in terms of economic considerations. In the latter case the combination and weights of various characters is established arbitrarily whereas, with components of fitness as super-characters, we are usually trying to determine what the relationship of a character is to various super-characters of fitness. The hierarchical relationship of sub-characters, characters, and super-characters can be expanded to include several levels of super-characters and sub-characters in any genetic analysis. The hypothetical relationship between these levels for agricultural and behavioral data is illustrated in Figure 1.

It is not difficult to see that the hierarchical model could be used to define behavioral variables reasonably well. Molecular elements of behavior such as attention, arousal, and sensory-motor responses in specific situations combine in various ways to influence characters more global in nature, such as "black-white discrimination learning in a swimming maze", or "approach latency

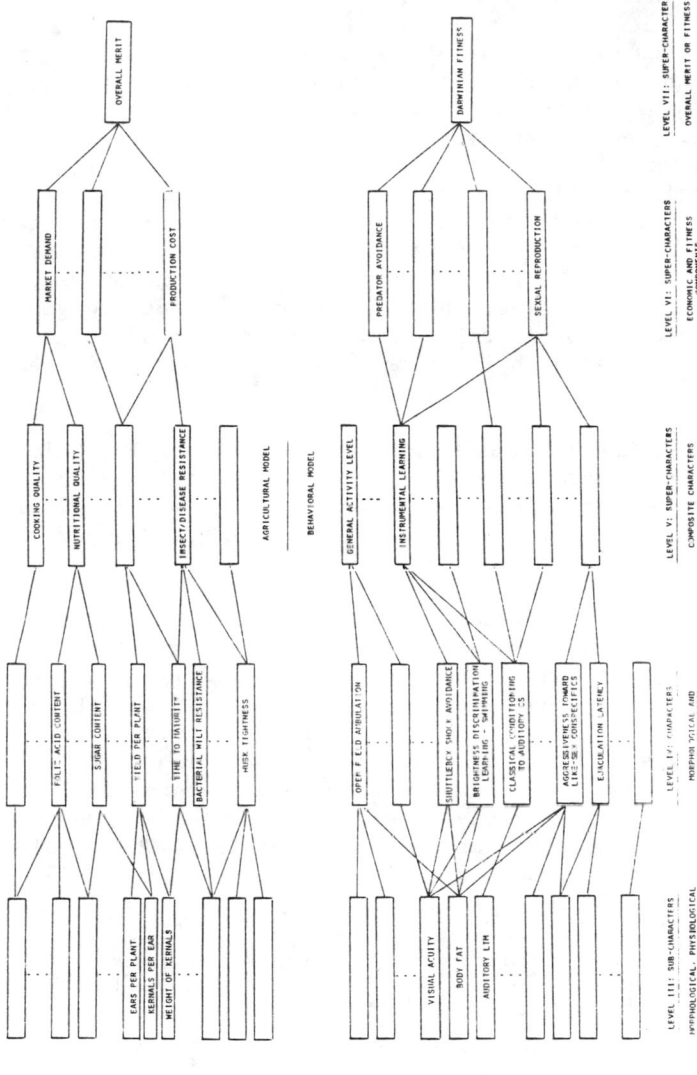

Fig. 1. A comparison of the hypothetical relationships between sub-characters, characters and super-characters in an agricultural and in a behavioral situation. Relationships between levels can vary as a function of the environment. Components within each level may be correlated because of common influences at a lower level. Level II sub-characters correspond to neural and chemical factors and level I refers to primary gene action. Examples shown are for illustration only.

to a strange male in the neutral territory of a test arena". These characters in turn may be combined in various arbitrary ways to form even more global constructs such as discrimination learning, avoidance learning, aggressive behavior, exploratory behavior, and so on, usually depending on the correlations between variables and the variables analyzed.

Genetic analyses of sub-characters can be carried out in both the agricultural and behavioral situations depicted in Figure 1, whereas all levels of super-characters can be analyzed only in the agricultural case. Genetic analysis cannot be carried out at Levels VI and VII when these super-characters deal with Darwinian fitness, since their relationship to lower levels is unknown. In addition, in the agricultural model, Level VI super-characters can have a wide range of genetic correlations between them, whereas major components of fitness are likely to have low or negative correlations between them, since the only remaining additive genetic variance in characters closely related to fitness must be due to plieotropic gene effects which influence two components of fitness in opposite directions.

Although most behavioral research is done at Level IV, this is probably the least appropriate level to concentrate on with respect to understanding natural selection and behavior. Analysis of sub-characters at Level III or an analysis of Level V super-characters is likely to be more fruitful.[1]

In choosing a behavioral measure we usually try to select one which is reliable, of interest to us, and taps at least some elements of behavior which are important to the organism under natural conditions. If we have some knowledge of both the etho-gram of the species and the nature of the demands of our experi-mental task, we may succeed in devising a measure which tests to a large degree the behavioral elements which have natural sig-nificance to our subjects. On the other hand, if we use some test apparatus designed for another purpose but conveniently available in the laboratory, performance scores may reflect very few under-lying elements of behavior of relevance to the organism in natural circumstances. Most of the time our theoretical predilections probably lead us to measuring behaviors falling somewhere in between these extremes.

Genetic variance of a behavioral character can be attributed

---

[1] One might choose to work at more reductive Levels I and II, but without the ability to connect this research to behavioral ele-ments at Level III or higher, it falls outside the realm of behavior genetics.

to a series of Level III sub-characters, some of which are related
to the organism's behavior in natural situations, and some of
which are related only to the peculiarities of the laboratory
testing situation. Some of the biologically relevant sub-
characters are likely to be monotonically related to fitness and
therefore exhibit a genetic pattern of directional dominance, but
the remaining sub-characters, involved only with behaviors peculiar
to the laboratory, must necessarily have no direct relationship
to fitness and will thus exhibit primarily additive genetic
variance. It is for this reason that many behavioral characters
which we intuitively think should be strongly connected with fitness exhibit fairly high proportions of additive genetic variance.

Our many studies of the genetics of learning provide a good
example of this. In reviewing a number of studies several years
ago, Wahlsten (1972a) expressed concern that learning ability,
which should at least intuitively have strong connections with
fitness, should demonstrate such high heritabilities. I suspect
the answer is that the measures in most of these learning studies
tapped a large number of sub-characters, such as variability in:
capacitance effects caused by different motor responses and foot-
pad thicknesses on a metal grid delivering a 1 ma of constant
current scrambled shock; willingness to make a U-turn and run
back into a small compartment which only 10 seconds before was
the location of a painful stimulus; reinforcing properties of being
snatched by the tail from the correct goal arm of the swimming
maze; the ability not to be distracted by ultrasounds, odor cues,
or a number of other stimuli normally important to the subject,
but disregarded by the experimenter. The presence of such
"laboratory noise" as part of most learning measures probably
guarantees the generation of systematic genetic variance which
has no direct relationship to fitness and thus must necessarily
be largely additive.

Studying Level III sub-characters is likely to produce more
clear effects with respect to dominance ratios and the relationship of the sub-characters to fitness. Two things occur when we
measure fairly narrow sub-elements of more complex behaviors.
First, these measures are most likely to be basic sensory, motor,
or physiological measures or fundamental prerequisites to learning
such as orienting responses which are likely to be rather consistent over a wide range of environmental testing conditions.
Second, it is likely that in studying these more basic units of
behavior (or biological systems closely related to behavior) investigators will focus on sub-characters that are at least intuitively building blocks for more complex behaviors of significance, rather than sub-characters which contribute to the
irrelevant aspects of experimental situations. Unfortunately,
even if one could identify all the individual sub-characters
which contribute to a more complex behavior such as performance

scores in a shock avoidance shuttlebox, there is some question as to the efficiency of carrying out a genetic analysis of each of these sub-characters, as might be done with sub-characters influencing crop yield. The difficulty with studying behavioral units as sub-characters is that their numbers may be large, they will often not be genetically independent, and each may influence many different complex behavioral characters of interest.

Let us now move from sub-characters to higher level behavioral constructs based on composites of several behavioral measures derived from factor analysis, the favorite tool of psychologists for empirically examining such constructs. Intuitively one might expect that, by taking a large number of Level III sub-characters measured on many genotypes and carrying out a hierarchical factor analysis on genetic correlations between the sub-characters, we would derive factors corresponding to each of the higher levels shown in Figure 1. This is unlikely to be the case, however, since there is no reason to expect that the Level III sub-characters contributing to a Level IV character have any particular pattern of correlations between them. Using an example from Figure 1, shuttlebox avoidance learning may be a function of visual acuity, thickness of body fat and several memory components, among other things, but there is no reason to expect these elements to be correlated among themselves. A factor analysis at Level III, therefore, would only tend to identify clusters of sub-characters possibly having common influences at Level II, creating a genic correlation between them.

A similar situation exists when one begins at Level IV, the level of most data in behavioral genetic research. Several measures of learning may show positive genetic correlations with each other, as would several activity measures, or measures of sexual behavior and so forth. Factors derived from genetic correlations between these measures will represent Level V super-characters such as general avoidance learning capacity, exploratory behavior, and sexual aggressiveness, some of which may be highly correlated with various components of fitness at Level VI, whereas others may show little or no relationship to fitness super-characters. Factors derived from factor analysis will thus be little different from Level IV characters in terms of their range of genetic effects. Although an analysis of genetic correlations between measures has many useful purposes in terms of understanding how joint selection may work on two characters, and perhaps tell us something about the nature of our measures themselves, factor analytic procedures applied to these data will not automatically produce factors that are all more biologically relevant or closely related to fitness components.

Factor analytic procedures might, however, help clarify certain behavioral constructs and allow us to bypass several difficulties with some Level IV behavioral characters. Suppose an investigator has measured a large number of complex learning behaviors and, in addition to analyzing each dependent variable, a number of general learning factors obtained from a factor analysis are subjected to a genetic analysis. Assuming a large and varied number of learning measures were included in the analysis, some of the extracted factors will probably represent general learning constructs, such as speed of reaction to a stimulus, retention of a learned response, speed of visual discrimination learning, and so forth, which cut across specific test situations. In addition the factor analysis is likely to identify specific situational, and "instrument factors". In terms of genetic variance, the factors reflecting largely laboratory peculiarities will exhibit largely additive variance whereas several of the more general learning factors are likely to exhibit high proportions of dominance variance In essence, the factor analysis decomposes behavioral characters of intermediate complexity and helps identify common sources of variance among them which is largely due to the more elemental Level III sub-characters making up each of the behaviors. All contributing sub-characters will not be identified as separate factors in such an analysis but clusters of correlated sub-characters are likely to appear as factors. An example of this is shown in Figure 2.

In essence, then, the investigator who, through a logical analysis, breaks down performance in a certain test situation into component sub-characters, determines the relationship between the sub-characters and then analyzes genetically these groups of sub-characters, is likely to be doing very much the same thing as the investigator who derives a number of factors from an extensive series of behavioral measures and genetically analyzes them. In both cases genetic variation of a behavioral variable which represent a complex mix of more elementary behavioral and biological sub-characters is broken down into correlated groups of factors allowing a separate analysis of both the biologically relevant and the irrelevant "laboratory-specific" factors involved in the behavior. It is often the amalgam of biologically relevant and irrelevant characteristics which produces relatively large proportions of additive genetic variance along with directional dominance in behavioral characters which intuitively should be related to fitness.

4.2 The use of composite behavior measures

The ability to generate a large number of noncontingent behavioral variables to be subject to correlation and factor analytic procedures is relatively easy when dealing with human populations and paper-and-pencil testing, but exceedingly laborious with animal populations. In conjunction with extensive breeding designs, large multivariate studies in behavior genetics are beyond the scope of

266

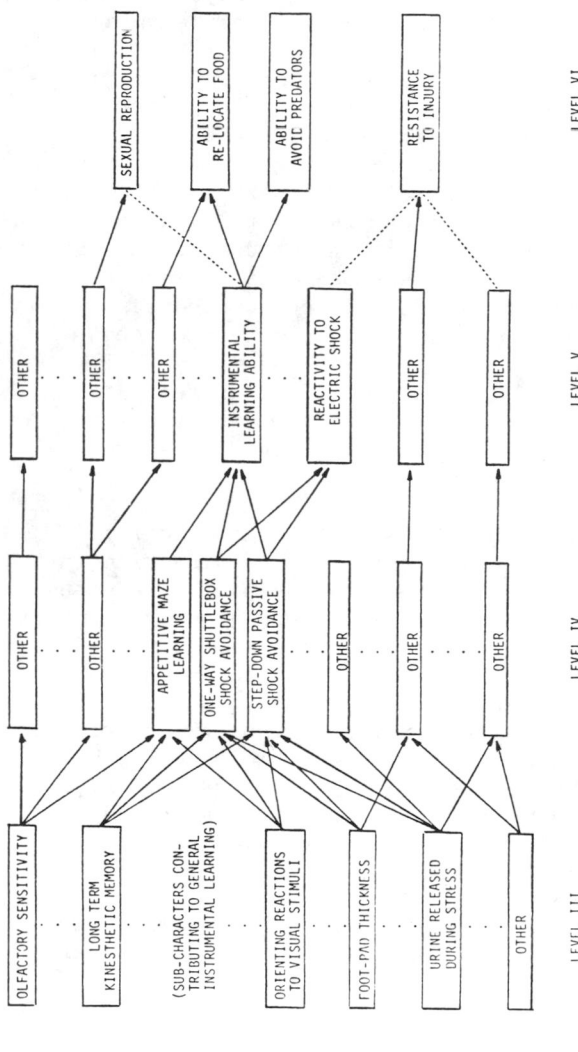

Fig. 2. Illustrative relationships between Level III, IV, V and VI factors. At level III many, sensory, motor and cognitive sub-characters influence performance on most instrumental learning tasks (Level IV), whereas other sub-characters such as olfactory sensitivity and foot-pad thickness influence only specific measures of learning. A factor analysis of many instrumental learning measures may reveal a general learning factor along with several specific test factors (Level V). The general learning factor may be strongly related to one or more components of fitness, whereas specific instrument factors may not be. Despite this, because Level III sub-characters may be related to fitness through alternate routes, some spurious correlations (indicated by dotted lines) may appear to exist between composite measures and fitness. For example, because foot-pad thickness may be related to a fitness component such as resistance to injury, reactivity to electric shock might appear to have some relationship to fitness. Unidirectional influences from lower to higher levels pertain only to genetic correlations. Phenotypic relationships between levels would require feedback loops between many factors at Levels II, III and IV.

most laboratories. Similarly, identifying and subjecting each sub-character of a more complex behavior to genetic analysis is a task unlikely to be carried out very often. Fortunately, there is an easier way to proceed and I shall use it to demonstrate that phenotypic variance in behavior on a laboratory task is produced in part by factors peculiar to the laboratory test situation, and that this portion of the variance is primarily additive genetic and environmental.

If one measures the same behavioral construct, let us say black-white visual discrimination learning, in two or more ways where the particulars of the testing situation differ widely--for example, different types of appetitive and escape learning tasks-- one will minimize the common laboratory factor variance between tasks. A composite score, based on performance summed across all tasks, will thus be more heavily loaded on the "non-laboratory" elements of black-white discrimination learning since laboratory-specific variance would be uncorrelated across measures. As a result, a composite score should give a truer picture of the mode of inheritance of a broad behavioral construct than any of its specific individual measures. If, in our example, black-white discrimination learning is related to fitness, directional dominance should be more pronounced on a composite measure of several black-white discrimination measures than on the individual tasks. The essentials of this argument are summarized in Table 2, in terms of a common factor variance model.

I shall demonstrate the above relationships using data from a 6 X 6 diallel analysis of several discrimination learning tasks carried out in our laboratory several years ago (Henderson, 1972). Two of the visual discrimination tasks studied used highly similar test equipment and procedures--swimming mazes having choice arms painted either black-white, or with vertical-horizontal stripes. Another measure, left-right discrimination, was tested in a shock escape T-maze under low red light illumination. Thus it differed considerably from the swimming mazes in terms of sensory cues and motor responses involved. Significant nonadditive genetic effects were found on both visual discrimination swimming mazes and on reversal learning in the shock escape T-maze. From the argument above, we should expect quite different results from a genetic analysis of each of the three possible composite measures that can be derived from a combination of a pair of these variables. Because of the high similarity of testing situations in the two swimming maze tasks, additive genetic variance due to the "irrelevant" laboratory aspects of swimming maze testing is likely to increase, as will common factors which do tap biologically relevant behaviors found in natural conditions. As a result, the genetic architecture of a composite score based on these two swimming mazes should not be very different from that expected from the average of these individual characters.[2] On the other hand, a

Table 2. The breakdown of phenotypic variance of a behavioral character into n factors related to behavior in natural situations and k factors related only to laboratory test situations.

VAR A =	VAR C1 + VAR C2 + . . . + VAR Cn	+ VAR Cn+1 + . . . + VAR Cn+k	+ VAR S +	VAR E
(phenotypic variance)	n common factors having some relationship to behavior in natural situations	k common factors related to laboratory environment only	specific variance	error variance
additive variance	Low to high (depends on relationship of each factor to components of fitness)	High	High	none
non-additive variance	Low to high (depends on relationship of each factor to components of fitness)	Low	Low	none
phenotypic variance of A+B where A & B measured under widely different test conditions	High (common factor loadings will result in increased variance of these factors on composite score, thus increasing non-additive genetic variance on composite measure)	Low (because test situations differ there will be few common factor loadings, thus variance of composite measure will not increase appreciably beyond the sum of the original variances, thus decreasing additive genetic variance on composite measure)	Low	no effect

genetic analysis of a composite measure formed by pairing a swimming maze task with the shock escape task is likely to produce a
different outcome from that above, since there are probably fewer
common test specific situational factors involved in these composite
measures. If a good deal of the additive genetic variance found
on the original measures is due to the specific circumstances of
testing, the relative proportion of additive genetic variance should
drop in these composite measures.

   Table 3 summarizes the obtained values of several genetic
parameters for the original three learning measures, converted to
a scale which would allow approximately equal weighting of each
task when composite measures were formed. The table also shows
the estimates of several genetic parameters obtained from a
variance-covariance analysis of the diallel tables generated for
the three composite measures. It can be seen that additive
variance, dominance variance, and mean directional dominance
variance were all significant for the three original measures and
that the dominance ratio, $(H/D)^{\frac{1}{2}}$, indicated overdominance for the
two visual discrimination tasks and dominance for T-maze reversal
learning. The composite score consisting of the sum of the two
visual discrimination tasks acts as predicted for two tasks with
highly similar testing conditions--D is approximately double the
sum of the original Ds--signifying a near perfect additive genetic
correlation between the two swimming discrimination tasks, whereas the composite H_1 is somewhat less than the sum of the original
measures, suggesting a lower correlation between nonadditive
genetic components. The resulting dominance ratio is slightly less
than that expected from a simple average of the two tasks. Mean
directional dominance (h^2) is also twice the sum of the original
h^2s, a direct consequence of both tasks having directional dominance
in the same direction and approximately equal values of h^2.[3] The

---

2 If performance on these two measures was due largely to biologically irrelevant factors, the proportion of additive genetic variance could become somewhat higher in the composite task than in
  the individual measures. Given the high degree of directional
  dominance found for both original tasks, however, one would not
  expect a large increase in additive genetic variance in the
  present case.

3 The general relationship is $h^2_{A+B} = h^2_A + h^2_B + 2r(h^2_A \times h^2_B)^{\frac{1}{2}}$,
  with r = +1 when dominance is in the same direction on A and B;
  r = -1 when dominance is in opposite directions. When there is no
  directional dominance on one or both measures $2r(h^2_A \times h^2_B)^{\frac{1}{2}} = 0$.
  Similar relationships exist for D and H parameters but in these
  cases, r can take any decimal value from -1 to +1.

Table 3. Estimates of genetic parameters for three learning measures and composite scores

Genetic Parameter*	Bl.-Wh. Discrimination (swimming maze)	Vertical-Horizontal Discrimination (swimming maze)	Left-Right Reversal Learning (shock-escape T-maze)
D	.60 ± .19	.19 ± .20	1.34 ± .14
H_1	2.48 ± .49	2.83 ± .53	1.31 ± .36
H_2	1.87 ± .44	2.42 ± .47	1.28 ± .32
h^2	5.20 ± .30	5.61 ± .32	1.07 ± .22
F	.21 ± .47	-.29 ± .51	.08 ± .35
$(H/D)^{\frac{1}{2}}$	2.0	3.8	1.0

Parameter	BW + VH	BW + T-MAZE	VH + T-MAZE
D	1.35 ± .68	1.87 ± .45	1.74 ± .42
H_1	8.47 ± 1.73	5.70 ± 1.13	6.33 ± 1.06
H_2	7.68 ± 1.55	5.74 ± 1.01	6.06 ± .95
h^2	21.64 ± 1.04	11.92 ± .68	12.10 ± .64
F	-1.02 ± 1.67	-.84 ± 1.09	-.98 ± 1.02
$(H/D)^{\frac{1}{2}}$	2.5	1.8	1.9
$(\Sigma H/\Sigma D)^{\frac{1}{2}}$	2.8	1.4	1.6
r_D	1.01	-.04	.22
r_H	.60	.53	.57

*Notation of Mather (1949): $D = 2$ X Additive Var; $H = 4$ X Dominance Var; $h^2 =$ Mean directional dominance; $F =$ Index of unequal gene frequencies. $(\Sigma H/\Sigma D)^{\frac{1}{2}}$ is expected dominance ratio assuming $r_D = r_H$. Data is based on standard-cage reared animals only. Variance between cell means set equal to unity prior to analysis.

relationship of additive variance to mean directional dominance is
essentially the same as that which would have been obtained by a
simple summing of the original parameter estimates.

When the composite measure involves two tasks measured in
different test situations, however, the results show a marked
shift from that just described. When T-maze performance is
combined with either black-white or vertical-horizontal discrimination, the resulting estimates of D are no longer greater than the
sums of the original estimates. On the other hand, composite
estimates of H_1 are both considerably larger than the original
H_1 estimates, thus the dominance ratios for the composite tasks are
both greater than that expected from a simple summation of individual parameter values. The magnitude of the directional dominance terms, h^2, relative to D has also increased considerably in
the composite scores. Despite these data being far from ideal,
the results in this example are as expected, a shift toward greater
dominance variance in composite measures based on different test
situations and a slight decrease in dominance variance of composite
measures using highly similar test situations.

The above results are a direct consequence of the magnitude
of various genetic correlations between measures. While genetic
correlations due to dominance effects were all moderately large,
an extremely high additive genetic correlation existed between the
two visual discrimination measures, whereas there were low additive
genetic correlations between performance in each of the swimming
mazes and in the T-maze. In general, anytime the overall genetic
correlation between two characters exceeds the additive genetic
correlation, one can expect greater relative dominance on a
composite measure than the average obtained from the original
measures. Since the closer two characters are related to fitness,
the more likely their additive genetic correlation is to approach
a low or a negative value, composites of measures having some relationship to fitness should generally show increased dominance
ratios.

The relationship between a genetic variance parameter of a
composite character and its original pair of characters is VAR A +
VAR B + 2COV AB and the relationship of Difference scores for two
measures A and B is VAR A + Var B - 2 COV AB. It follows, then,
that if one uses difference scores of two behavioral measures taken
in the same apparatus or under highly similar conditions, composite
additive genetic variance should be reduced substantially relative
to nonadditive variance. As a result, difference scores taken in
the same test situation may often show considerably higher dominance
ratios than the original measures. Essentially, variance due to
common apparatus factors is cancelled out when difference scores
are used, and since genetic variance due to apparatus factors should
be primarily additive, the proportion of additive to dominance

variance should drop. This expectation is confirmed by the analysis of transfer of training in the two visual discrimination swimming mazes. Since subjects were run in a counterbalanced order, by subtraction we were able to obtain an unbiased estimate of the improvement in performance on the second swimming task for each genotype. Dominance variance increased considerably and additive variance decreased on the improvement measure, relative to the values of these parameters on the original swimming measures (Henderson 1972).

Obviously, composite measures need not be limited to two scores. One could carry out a large multivariate design, sampling many behavior domains and deriving composites based on factor loadings. It is more efficient, however, simply to define a behavioral domain, generate several different behavioral measures sampling the domain, and analyze the composite score based on the measures. The behavioral domain can be fairly narrow (i.e., visual discrimination learning) or broad (i.e., instrumental learning), since the complexity of the genetic analysis does not change, only one's interpretation of results changes. For this reason, it probably makes the most sense to define a construct which has some logical meaning based on the ethogram of the species to be studied. Although such constructs are likely to be less elegant and precise than those often used by behavioral scientists, they may be more relevant from a genetic point of view.

Take, for example, the ability of an organism to "size up" an environment, then use this information to its advantage in the future. As a behavioral construct this is both vague and broad, yet intuitively a behavior pattern of this type would seem to be highly adaptive. One can attempt to measure this construct by using different test situations, demanding very different responses from the subjects, within the limits of keeping the test situations and required responses somewhat natural for the organism. At this point the construct has been operationally defined in terms of the test situation used. A pattern of dominance toward effective use of each environment should be observed but a stronger pattern of dominance should be found on a composite measure across test situations.

I have limited my examples using composite scores to those based on only two variables, even though a multivariate procedure would usually be more appropriate for defining a behavioral construct. The same relationships of course hold for second order genetic statistics derived from the sum of a variance-covariance matrix of several measures. I have also only briefly mentioned the relationship of the factor analytic decomposition of variance and the expected decrease in additive variance to the relationship of additive genetic correlations in characters related to fitness. As with the issue of comparisons of wild and domesticated popula-

tions, a full discussion of genetic correlations and composite
measures demands considerably more space than is allotted here.
I hope, however, that I have made the basic conceptual point,
stated here in three different ways: (1) Most behavioral measures
in animal research are similar to single items on personality or
aptitude tests. Each contains a considerable amount of unique
genetic and environmental variance irrelevant to the broader construct being measured. When several such items are combined,
however, to produce a composite score, a clear picture of the behavioral construct emerges. (2) A single behavioral measure is
likely to be an amalgam of variance due to several sub-characters
involved in natural behaviors and variance reflecting atypical behaviors brought on by an unusual testing situation. Genetic
variance due to the latter will be primarily additive, thus
estimates of the relationship to fitness of the construct measured
in our single task will be attenuated. (3) If one chooses highly
different test situations in which to measure behavioral constructs
of interest, common genetic variance due to irrelevant laboratory
conditions (which will primarily be additive) will be greatly reduced.

The only way we can get an adequate picture of the genetic
architecture of behavioral characters of interest (i.e., somewhat broader than those obtained in a specific apparatus under
specific circumstances) is to measure the behavior in several
different ways and analyze the composite performance of our subjects. The examination of a series of separate genetic studies
each involving one or two dependent variables measuring the same
behavior domain will not result in a true picture of the genetic
architecture of the behavior domain.

5.   SAMPLING STRATEGIES FOR REARING ENVIRONMENTS

5.1   Rearing environments and genetic architecture

The genetic architecture of any character, sub-character, or
composite of several characters is, of course, relevant only to
the population on which the measurements are taken. If the test
population is "typical" of most natural populations, its genetic
architecture may also be typical of that found in most natural
populations. Unfortunately, the rearing environment of the laboratory is hardly typical of that found in nature, and since environment inevitably co-acts with genotype, the genetic architecture
observed in laboratory-reared populations may differ considerably
from that of populations reared under other circumstances. One
should regard a character measured in two different environments
as two separate characters with a genetic correlation between
them. Physiological mechanisms and consequently the genes required

for high or low performance of the behavior may differ in different environments. The problem of different environments is similar to that concerning the genetic make-up of laboratory versus wild populations. A blanket attack on the use of animals reared in laboratory environments is no more appropriate than an attack on the use of "laboratory genotypes". The appropriateness of a given research population is always a function of the dependent variables to be studied.

A large body of research done in the '50s and '60s on early experience effects made it clear that many sensory, motor, and more complex behavioral responses develop fully in many species after only nominal environmental stimulation. For such characters, laboratory environments are probably quite adequate for the behavior to be exhibited, and the pattern observed among different groups of subjects is essentially invariant under differing levels of environmental stimulation. Other characters are likely to be greatly influenced by the level of nutrition, environmental enrichment or stress imposed on the subject prior to testing. In these cases different genotypes are likely to respond differentially to such stimulation and thus the genetic architecture observed may differ considerably as a function of rearing environment. In addition to the increase in brain size occurring in animals reared in enriched environments (e.g. Rosenzweig, 1971; Henderson, 1973), dominance variance, directional toward large brains, is considerably more pronounced when animals are reared in more enriched environments (Henderson, 1970b, 1973).

The ability to locate food in a large test box is also enhanced among animals reared in enriched environments. Different genotypes respond to enrichment differentially however, thus genetic variance in performance was found to be considerably greater among animals reared in enrichment than it was among animals reared in standard laboratory cages (Henderson, 1970a). Subsequent work (Henderson, 1976) suggested that this differential increase in performance across genotypes did not require long term rearing in enrichment. As little as six hours exposure to a complex environment was sufficient to substantially increase genotypic variation in food location ability. This was probably a case where certain prerequisite skills, which apparently required a relatively short time to develop, were necessary before subjects could exhibit systematic differential performance on a behavioral character. If the development of prerequisite skills is blocked through restricted rearing, genetic or experimental manipulation influences on the behavior may not be observed. Other short term interventions, such as the administration of stress, can differentially alter the response of various genotypes in subsequent mildly stressful test situations (e.g., Henderson, 1966, 1967).

A review of the animal research literature indicates that

gene-environment interactions occur with regularity when both
classes of variables have been studied simultaneously. The situation is becoming similar to that found with respect to strain
difference research, where significant effects are the rule rather
than the exception (e.g. Erlenmeyer-Kimling, 1972).

5.2 Understanding the nature of gene-environment interaction

The frequent occurrence of significant interactions between
genotypes and prior experience does not in itself constitute
grounds for rejecting the results of genetic research based on
laboratory reared animals. Many of the interactions reported
accounted for a relatively small proportion of the experimental
variance, and usually the interactions were ordinal in that the
general ranking of genotypes stayed more or less the same under
different environmental conditions. In these cases the underlying
genetic architecture probably would have been found to be similar
if it had been analyzed for each of the environments used. Often
gene-environment interactions are simply a function of ceiling and
floor effects on the behavioral measures used and are often eliminated by an appropriate transformation of percentage scores used
on the data. The frequently reproduced results of Cooper and
Zubek (1958) involving enrichment effects on maze bright and
maze dull rats, for example, look quite different when rescaled
using transformed proportions of errors.

Some precautions should nevertheless be observed when using
laboratory reared animals in an attempt to understand the evolutionary significance of certain behaviors. Knowledge of the
existing psychological and ethological literature on the species
can be of considerable help in this regard. If a particular behavior has previously been shown to be rather resistant to change
under differing environmental circumstances in random bred populations, both in terms of mean score and variance on the character,
one can probably proceed, at least initially, with laboratory
reared animals. It is possible to run into difficulty in that,
within a genetically heterogeneous population, some genotypes may
react to a certain environment by decreasing performance while
other genotypes react to the same environment with an increase in
performance in such a way that neither the population mean nor
variance differs in the two different environments. While the
presence of disordinal interactions between genotype and environment have been posed to explain the apparent lack of environmental
influence on certain characters such as IQ (Feldman & Lewontin,
1975; McGuire & Hirsch, 1975), it is exceedingly difficult to find
unequivocal evidence that many disordinal interactions exist
between genotype and previous environmental experience.

In the few cases where disordinal interactions have been

reported they can often be attributed to differential construct validity of the character for different genotypes. For example when Fuller's terriers emerged from isolation they showed an increase in activity level as exhibited by their skittery behavior, whereas his beagles tended to freeze upon emergence (Fuller, 1967). Isolation resulted in an increase in activity for one breed and a decrease for the second, yet knowledge of the behavior of these breeds led to a simple interpretation of the data. Fearful terriers become skittery and fearful beagles freeze, thus the effect of isolation in terms of the broader concept of fearfulness or emotionality, was the same in the two breeds. The relevance of this kind of finding to Section IV above concerning the sampling of test situations should be obvious.

Wilcock and Fulker (1973) have provided us with a nice example of how understanding the components of a complex behavior can often explain a disordinal interaction between genotype and previous experience. Early in avoidance training inbred rats appear to make more avoidance responses than hybrids, but as training progresses this situation reverses itself. One might conclude that inbreds are superior to hybrids in early learning and inferior in later learning, a disordinal interaction between level of inbreeding and previous experience on the learning task. Yet, with some knowledge of the two-factor process of avoidance learning and some knowledge of the behavioral reaction of the rat to conditioned fear, the results are exactly what one would expect if hybrid rats are superior learners to inbreds. The first phase of the avoidance learning process involves classically conditioned fear to the CS. In rats, this fear is usually exhibited as freezing behavior, thus after a few trials the hybrids in Wilcock & Fulker's experiment began to freeze, indicating that they were already developing a conditioned fear to the CS. As a result of freezing their avoidance performance was inferior to that of the inbreds, who were still scrambling around on the grid more or less randomly during these trials. Once established however, the CS provided adequate motivation for escape and subsequently avoidance behavior, thus hybrids soon began to outperform the inbred parent strains.

One would not expect to find such an interaction between inbreeding and number of previous trials in an avoidance learning situation if the conditioned response to a CS is heightened activity rather than freezing behavior. Interestingly enough, mice do not usually establish a conditioned emotional response manifested by freezing behavior, but respond with increased locomotor activity (Henderson; 1964, 1965, 1968a). With mice therefore one should not find a shift occurring from dominance toward low avoidance to dominance toward high avoidance across succeeding trials. To my knowledge such interactions have not been observed in mice - hybrids are apparently consistently superior to inbreds throughout learning (e.g. Collins, 1964; Wahlsten, 1972b).

Another situation in which disordinal interactions are occasionally reported involves 2x2 factorial experiments, where two genotypes are each exposed to two different prior experiences which result in a reversal of their behaviors on some subsequent test. The few instances of such G X E interactions have usually involved behaviors which are probably influenced in a non-monotonic fashion by the intensity or degree of previous experience, and with more extensive sampling of the levels of prior stimulation orderly relationships are likely to be found (Henderson, 1968b).

In cases where previous environmental experiences have been shown to have large effects on a behavior of interest and the differences in environment are reflective of differences which might exist between laboratory and natural environments, there is a risk of generating a picture of genetic architecture on laboratory subjects which has little relationship to that which would be obtained from populations reared under more natural conditions. Under such circumstances a genetic experiment should be replicated under more than one environmental level with some of these environments designed to approximate different aspects of natural rearing conditions. If genetic architecture shifts systematically in one direction as rearing conditions approach more natural environments, one can obtain at least some idea of what the genetic architecture of the character may be like outside of the laboratory. Sampling environments is of course as formidable a task as is broad sampling of genotypes. On the other hand, even the most sophisticated genetic analysis of a laboratory population will be of little use in understanding the natural history of an organism if there is little genetic correlation between the characters measured under laboratory and natural circumstances.

6. PREDICTING INTERACTIONS WITH GENOTYPE

6.1 The power of GE predictions

Although the presence of GE interactions suggests the unhappy prospect of larger and more complex research designs in behavior genetics, the potential existence of such interactions provides an opportunity to make powerful tests of the adequacy of research methods, assumptions concerning dominance - fitness relationships, and our understanding of the biological importance of certain behavior patterns.

Until recently most behavior genetic research on laboratory animals was largely descriptive in nature. Hypothesis testing centered around the simple question of the presence or absence of genetic influences on behavior. Occasionally slightly stronger hypotheses were made, involving predicted genetic correlations between two or more behaviors, or predicting dominance or heterosis based on an intuitive belief that the behavior being measured would be adaptive to the organism. In most cases however, genetic data were analyzed and post hoc interpretations made. This procedure provides sufficient latitude in interpretation to allow a great deal of data to be "explained" in terms of evolutionary principles. Hybrids explored more, learned better, built bigger nests, etc. because "these behaviors are adaptive and there is a relationship between directional dominance and directional selection." Similarly, "buffering against minor environmental influences such as emotional reactivity to the stress of handling is adaptive," while at the same time, "behavioral or neural plasticity such as shifts in brain weight as a function of environmental stimulation is adaptive." Such after-the-fact interpretations, however reasonable, hardly constitute convincing evidence that the genetic designs and populations used are truly providing us with insight concerning evolutionary history. Furthermore, general predictions concerning inbred-hybrid differences are hardly more convincing considering the frequency with which such differences occur.

Genetic designs are natural group designs rather than experimental designs in which subjects are assigned randomly to treatment groups. Unlike experimental designs, natural group designs pose major problems concerning the establishment of cause-effect relationships (e.g. Underwood & Shaughnessy, 1975). Hypotheses concerning cause and effect relationships can be considerably strengthened in natural group designs when one can predict specific interactions between natural groups and experimental variables which are based on a theory about a process influencing performance. Ideal experiments are those in which predicted interactions occur which other hypotheses would be hard pressed to accommodate. The ability to accurately predict, through prior analysis of the survival value of behaviors in natural settings, the genetic architecture of a specific behavior is a test for the adequacy of current behavioral genetic methodology. A more powerful test involves behaviors for which the optimum level of phenotypic expression differs with age or under different environmental circumstances, thus leading to differential genetic predictions for the same type of behavior under various conditions. Unfortunately, failure to obtain predicted results could be due to an inappropriate choice of genotypes or dependent variables, or to an inaccurate ethogram of the species. Thus negative results are inconclusive. Despite this, early results using this approach have been encouraging.

6.2 Beginning research efforts in predicting interactions with genotype

Although most studies of locomotor behavior in adult mice have

demonstrated intermediate inheritance or dominance toward high
activity (e.g., Halcomb, Hegmann, & DeFries, 1975), there is
reason to believe that this should not be the case in very young
animals. Infant mice less than one week of age have limited visual
and auditory sensitivity. Their locomotor coordination is poor,
which often results in a tendency for animals to travel in erratic,
circular paths. When young animals are removed from the nest, a
high rate of locomotor activity is likely to be maladaptive. Such
activity increases the probability of predator attack, as well as
of falling from ledges or elevated areas on which the nest may be
built. More adaptive would be low activity and dependence on the
highly efficient maternal retrieval response of mice. We predicted, then, that a breeding study of infantile activity would
result in low heritability and genetic dominance favoring low
activity, rather than intermediate heritability and partial
dominance toward high activity, typically found in older animals.
This predicted interaction between genotype and age was tested in
an experiment using four day old mice.

Two technical problems arise when studying traits likely to
show low degrees of genetic influence. First, large samples are
required to provide sufficient power to detect small genetic effects.
Second, the measure used must be shown to be sufficiently reliable
to detect experimental effects, since highly unreliable measures
would necessarily result in estimates of low genetic variance. The
latter problem is most effectively solved by including some systematic sources of environmental variation to provide benchmarks
against which to assess the reliability of the behavioral measure.
Two naturally occurring benchmarks--maternal effects, and the
normal microenvironmental variation occurring between litters--
were used in the infant activity study. A total of 2,080 house
mice from eight inbred strains and 36 F_1 hybrid crosses between
tester lines were used. Because two tester lines (C57BL/10 and
LP/J) were extremes on infantile activity, scores from crosses of
these lines could be analyzed using the TTC method. The dependent
variable was the number of squares the four day old mouse crossed
on a plastic grid during a 1-minute test period.

The results supported the prediction that locomotor behavior
of these young animals would show directional dominance towards
low activity in contrast to that found with adult mice. In
addition, both genetic homeostasis and low heritability were observed as expected. In addition to supporting the predictions, the
experiment demonstrated that powerful biometrical genetic techniques
can be successfully applied to crude or simple behaviors occurring
very early in life. In terms of understanding behavior from an
evolutionary point of view, such studies are valuable for several
reasons. The previous experience and the environment of young
rodents is far more similar to wild members of the species than
is the case with older laboratory animals. Early life is also a

period of rapid change for the organism, thus systematic behavioral changes can easily be observed over a short time interval. Mortality risks are also high, a fact which suggests that selection pressures are probably strong at this stage of development. From a practical standpoint, although the testing of wild mice in the laboratory is often exceedingly difficult, this is not the case with very young animals. In addition, although larger n̲s may often be necessary, animals need not be maintained in the laboratory for many weeks prior to testing. This combination of advantages suggests that further behavior genetic research on infant or very young animals may be quite valuable.

A second attempt to predict a change in genetic architecture as a function of the environmental circumstance focused on the test environment. If 10- to 11-day-old animals are moved 10 - 15 cm. from the maternal nest, they will usually turn and crawl back to the nest on their own if not immediately retrieved. Intuitively, the ability to return rapidly to the home nest would appear to be adaptive for mice at this age. Within range of the nest, where olfactory, thermal, and other cues can guide its return, loco-motor activity directed toward the nest might therefore be expected to have a significant dominance component. On the other hand, if mice of this age are removed from the nest and placed in a totally new environment, away from any guiding cues for nest location, it is unclear how locomotor activity would be related to fitness. Basically, the animal would be in a "nonsense" test situation-- one that would rarely if ever exist under circumstances in which natural selection would take place. One might expect therefore that an activity measure in such a test situation would produce a smaller ratio of dominance to additive genetic variance, than a measure of locomotor activity in nest return within home cages would produce.

To test this prediction, we carried out two experiments. The first involved an extended TTC design identical to that used to study infant locomotor activity described above. Except for the age of the mice, the testing situation was also identical to the locomotor activity study. At 10 - 11 days of age an animal was removed from its home cage and placed on a plastic floor marked in a grid of 2.5 cm. squares. The number of squares crossed in a 1-minute test period was the primary dependent variable. The results of the TTC analysis indicated significant additive genetic variance, but no significant dominance variation. Activity levels were essentially intermediate.

The second experiment involved an 8 X 8 diallel, using the same parent strains as those used in the TTC above. The diallel was chosen because of its greater capacity for estimating maternal effects, which we felt would be important because of differing nest odor cues. Testing involved removing parents from the home cage and then placing one pup 15 cm. from the nest. The number of seconds required for the pup to return to the nest was recorded and the pup set aside. The procedure was repeated for a total of four pups per litter. In each case at least three pups remained in the home nest during the testing of other pups. As expected, the genetic analysis of time required to return to the home nest produced markedly different results from that found when pups of this age were tested in a neutral open field. In the field no significant genetic dominance was detected relative to additive genetic variance. Not only did overdominance exist, but all significant dominance variation was directional toward fast nest-return times.

The results of these two experiments are satisfying not only from the point of view of accurately predicting a GE interaction based on an analysis of the test situation, but also because they emphasize the importance of measuring dependent variables in reasonably meaningful situations for the species. When test situations are used which have little correlation with any situation under which natural selection would take place, one should expect that genetic variance, if significant, will be largely additive.

Our final attempt to predict a differential genetic pattern under differing environmental circumstances was also successful but produced more subtle results than the studies of activity in young or infant mice. Over the years we have accumulated considerable genetic data on exploratory activity in a number of test situations, including an open field, an exploratory maze, and a test apparatus with different compartments containing various visual stimuli. This original data was collected during the latter half of the light cycle, usually from noon to 4:30 p.m. Our results typically indicated that, although dominance variance was often significant in activity measures, a large proportion of the dominance variance was bi-directional (i.e., some genes were dominant towards high activity and others towards low). The proportion of dominance variance directional toward high activity was usually relatively small. Since mice are nocturnal, we reasoned that high activity levels may not necessarily be an advantage to these animals during the light cycle, especially under lighted testing conditions. On the other hand, the disadvantages of high activity probably diminish at night, at least with respect to predation. We reasoned therefore that a greater proportion of genetic variance in activity measures made during the night cycle under low illumination should be due to direction dominance for high activity than we found in daylight activity. We therefore carried out a TTC study of night activity, using some of the same test apparatus used in our diallel cross studies run during daylight hours.

Increases in directional dominance did occur in two of the three test situations examined. In a test apparatus involving multiple rooms, normally used under moderate illumination, the proportion of genetic variance attributed to directional dominance increased from 15% to 20%. In an exploratory maze normally tested under low illumination, directional dominance increased from 2% to 13%, and in an open field, normally tested under bright illumination, the proportion of directional dominance was an identical 12% under day and night test conditions. The results are not as clear cut as those in the study on infantile activity, and our predictions were born out in only two of the three test situations used. After we had completed this study, I discovered that Jon Kerbusch, in his doctoral dissertation, had reported data directly pertinent to our work. Kerbusch (1974) had monitored in-cage activity of four inbred strains of mice and their F_1 crosses throughout the diurnal cycle. He found that directional dominance toward high activity did occur during the first few hours of the dark period but that inbred-hybrid differences decreased and eventually reversed during the last hours of the dark period. These results not only provide additional support for the predicted interaction between genotype and test situation, but also suggest why greater directional dominance effects were not found in my own study. Apart from the novelty of the test situations, we had recorded behavior several hours after the dark cycle had begun, a time when inbred-hybrid differences had already begun to decrease in Kerbusch's experiment.

The results of the experiments described above are encouraging. It appears that one can make moderately accurate guesses about differences in genetic architecture which should occur as a function of differing age or environmental parameters. This suggests that at least for some behavioral characteristics laboratory lines may be adequate genetic material for study.

Other work involving interactions between illumination levels and genotypes showing more pronounced effects can already be found in the literature. The work of McClearn (1960) and DeFries et al (1966) demonstrated an interactive effect of albino versus pigmented strains and illumination level on open field activity. The results suggested a single gene effect, mediated by the visual system, on open field activity. Apparently illumination levels can have major influences on the outcome of a genetic experiment. Earlier, I described the work of McGill on sexual behavior in male mice. Behaviors such as mount latency showed ambidirectional dominance toward intermediate latencies. I suggested that intuitively some, but not excessive, caution in initiating sexual behavior in a strange, lighted, test arena might be an optimal course of action in terms of fitness. Suppose however this sexual activity had been observed during the night cycle, when these mice were more alert and under less fearful and unprotected circumstances resulting from bright illumination. Under these test conditions less hesitancy to begin sexual behavior might be expected to be optimal in terms of fitness, thus dominance toward short mount latencies might be observed. This is indeed what happens. Using McGill's measures, but recording sexual behavior during the dark cycle under red light, Vale and Ray (1972) found substantial directional dominance toward low mount latencies using a 3 X 3 diallel which contained two of McGill's strains.

Each of the GE interactions described above involved subtle changes in the test environment which altered the genetic outcome. Obviously, designing such experiments and predicting differences in genetic architecture under different test conditions provides not only a test of our genetic methods and assumptions, but it also may sensitize investigators to the subtleties of testing situations and how these can influence results. The differences in test illumination and diurnal cycle during testing differed only incidentally in the laboratories of McGill and of Vale. The discrepancies in genetic patterns of several behaviors was not even acknowledged, no less attributed to differing test conditions - an example of the tendency to report behavior genetic results in largely descriptive terms, with little critical analysis or attempts at integration with other information.

The above examples involve age or environmental-test variables interacting with genotype. Environmental variables involving rearing conditions or previous early experiences have not, to my knowledge, been studied, where predictions were made concerning changes in genetic architecture as a function of prior rearing. Such predictions are difficult, since the role of most early environmental variables on subsequent behaviors is not well understood, nor are detailed developmental ethograms available for most species. The data base in these areas of animal research is too unreliable to build on, paradoxically, because investigators too often ignored genetic factors, subtle erroneous influences of the testing environments, and the biological relevance of the responses studied. As a consequence, except in cases of rather extreme rearing environments, investigators will have some difficulty deriving a basis for specific GE predictions involving early stimulation such as stress or enrichment. Some reliable effects do exist however, which could be used as a basis for such predictions, and clever hunches on the part of insightful investigators might generate still others.

7. CONCLUSIONS

There are several goals in animal behavior genetic research, only one of which is the attempted understanding of evolutionary history of complex behaviors. To achieve this goal is a formidable task. A heavy expenditure of effort is required to provide adequate genetic material, rearing conditions and testing situations to make such research worthwhile. Demands are sufficiently great that it is unlikely that many studies will be totally adequate, and attempts to piece together an understanding of genetic architecture for complex behaviors from separate small studies will continue. Unfortunately, with respect to understanding the evolutionary history of behavior patterns of animals, the whole can be quite different than the sum of its individual parts, and limited efforts may be more misleading than helpful.

BIBLIOGRAPHY

1. Berry, R. J. Genetic variation in wild housemice: Where natural selection and history meet. American Scientist, 1978, 66, 52-60.
2. Boice, R. Domestication. Psychological Bulletin, 1973, 80, 215-230.
3. Boice, R. Burrows of wild and albino rats: Effects of domestication, outdoor raising, age, experience, and maternal state. Journal of Comparative and Physiological Psychology, 1977, 91, 649-661.
4. Broadhurst, P. L. Experiments in psychogenetics. In Experiments in Personality (H. J. Eysenck, Ed.) Vol. 1 London: Routledge & Kegan Paul, 1960, p. 3-43.
5. Bruell, J. H. Behavioral heterosis. In J. Hirsch (Ed.) Behavior-genetic analysis. New York: McGraw-Hill, 1967.
6. Brunswik, E., Perception and the Representative Design of Psychological Experiments Second Edition, 1956, University of California Press, Berkeley, Calif.
7. Collins, R. L. Inheritance of avoidance conditioning in mice: a diallel study. Science, 1964, 143, 1188-1190.
8. Connor, J. L. Genetic mechanisms controlling the domestication of a wild house mouse population (Mus musculus L.) Journal of Comparative and Physiological Psychology, 1975, 89, 118-130.
9. Connor, J. L., Winston, H. D., & Bradford, H. The effects of domestication, environmental familiarity, and opponent familiarity on dominance in the mouse (Mus musculus L.). Behavior Genetics, 1973, 3, 339-354.
10. Cooper, R. M., & Zubek, J. P. Effects of enriched and restricted early environments on the learning ability of bright and dull rats. Canadian Journal of Psychology, 1958, 12, 159-164.
11. DeFries, J. C., Hegmann, J. P., & Wier, Morton W. Open-field behavior in mice: evidence for a major gene effect mediated by the visual system. Science, 1966, 154, 1577-1579.
12. Erlenmeyer-Kimling, L. Gene-environment interactions and the variability of behavior. In L. Ehrman, G. Omen & E. Caspari

(Eds.) Genetics, Environment and Behavior. New York: Academic Press, 1972.

13. Falconer, D. S. Introduction to quantitative genetics. New York: Ronald Press, 1960.

14. Feldman, M. W. & Lewontin, R. C. The heritability hang-up. Science, 1975, 190, 1163.

15. Fuller, J. L. Experiential deprivation and later behavior. Science, 1967, 158, 1645-1652.

16. Fuller, J. L. & Thompson, W. R. Behavior genetics. New York: John Wiley & Sons, 1960.

17. Halcomb, R. A., Hegmann, J. P., & DeFries, J. C. Open-field behavior in mice: A diallel analysis of selected lines. Behavior Genetics, 1975, 5, 217-231.

18. Hayman, B. I. The theory and analysis of diallel crosses. 1954, Genetics, 39, 789-809.

19. Hegmann, J. P., White, J. E. & Kater, S. B. Physiological function and behavior genetics. II. Quantitative genetic analysis of conditioned velocity of caudal nerves in the mouse, mus musculus. Behavior Genetics, 1973, 3, 121-131.

20. Henderson, N. D. A species difference in conditioned emotional response. Psychological Reports, 1964, 15, 579-585.

21. Henderson, N. D. Acquisition and retention of conditioned fear during different stages in the development of mice. Journal of Comparative Physiological Psychology, 1965, 59, 439-442.

22. Henderson, N. D. Inheritance of reactivity to experimental manipulation in mice. Science, 1966, 650-652.

23. Henderson, N. D. Prior treatment effects on open field behaviour of mice--a genetic analysis. Animal Behavior, 1967, 15, 364-376.

24. Henderson, N. D. A genetic analysis of acquisition and retention of a conditioned fear in mice. Journal of Comparative Physiological Psychology, 1968, 65, 325-330.

25. Henderson, N. D. The confounding effects of genetic variables in early experience research: can we ignore them? Developmental Psychobiology, 1(2): 146-152, 1968.

26. Henderson, N. D. Prior treatment effects on open field emotionality: The need for representative design. Ann. N.Y. Acad. Sci., 1969, 159, 860-868.

27. Henderson, N. D. Genetic influences on the behavior of mice can be obscured by laboratory rearing. Journal of Comparative and Physiological Psychology, 1970, 72, 505-511.

28. Henderson, N. D. Brain weight increases resulting from environmental enrichment: A directional dominance in mice. Science, 1970, 169, 776-778.

29. Henderson, N. D. Brain weight changes resulting from enriched rearing conditions: A diallel cross analysis. Developmental Psychobiology, 1973, 6, 367-376.

30. Henderson, N. D. Short exposures to enriched environments can increase genetic variability of behavior in mice.

Developmental Psychobiology, 1976, 9, 549-553.

31. Henderson, N. D. Genetic dominance for low activity in infant mice. _Journal of Comparative and Physiological Psychology_, 1978, 92, 118-125.

32. Kerbusch, J. M. L. _Genetic analysis of exploratory behavior, simple learning behavior and cerebral AChE and ChE activities in mice by means of the diallel method_. (Doctoral dissertation, Catholic University of Nijmegan) Nijmegan: Schippers, 1974.

33. King, H. D. Life processes in gray Norway rats during fourteen years in captivity. _American Anatomical Memoirs_, 1939, 17, 1-72.

34. Lerner, I. M. _Genetic Homeostasis_. New York: Wiley, 1954.

35. Lerner, I. M. _The Genetic Basis of Selection_. New York: Wiley, 1958.

36. Lockard, R. B̄. The albino rat: A defensible choice or a bad habit? _American Psychologist_, 1968, 23, 734-742.

37. Lorenz, K. _Evolution and modification of behavior_. Chicago: University of Chicago Press, 1965.

38. McClearn, G. E. Strain differences in the activity of mice: Influences of illumination. _Journal of Comparative and Physiological Psychology_, 1960, 53, 142-143.

39. McGill, T. E. Genetic analysis of male sexual behavior. Contributions to _Behavior genetic analysis- the mouse as a prototype_. Edited by : Gardner Lindzey & Delbert D. Thiessen. Appleton-Century-Crofts, 1970.

40. McGill, T. E. & Blight, W. C. The sexual behavior of hybrid male mice compared with the sexual behavior of males of the inbred parent strains. _Animal Behaviour_, 1963, 11, 480-483.

41. McGill, T. E. & Ransom, T. W. Genotypic change affecting conclusions regarding the mode of inheritance of elements of behaviour. _Animal Behaviour_, 1968, 16, 88-91.

42. McGuire, T. R. & Hirsch, J. General intelligence (g) and heritability (H^2, h^2) In: Uzgiris, I. C. & Weizmann, F. (eds.) _The Structuring of Experience_, New York: Plenum Press, 1977.

43. Mather, K. _Biometrical Genetics_ (1st ed.), Methuen, London, 1949.

44. Mather, K. & Jinks, J. L. _Biometrical Genetics_ (2nd ed.), Ithaca, N.Y.: Cornell University Press, 1971.

45. Price, E. O. & King, J. A. Domestication and adaptation. In E. S. E. Hafez (Ed.), _Adaptation of domestic animals_. Philadelphia: Lea & Febiger, 1968.

46. Robertson, A. Selection in animals: Synthesis. _Cold Spring Harbor Symposia on Quantitative Biology_. 1955, 20, 225-229.

47. Robertson, A. The effect of selection against extreme deviants based on deviation or on homozygosis. _Journal of Genetics_, 1956, 54, 236-248.

48. Rosenzweig, M. R. Effects of environment on the development of brain and of behavior. In E. Tobach, L. Aronson, & E. Shaw

(Eds.), The biopsychology of development. New York: Academic Press, 1971, 303–342.

49. Selander, R. K. & Yang, S. Y. Biochemical genetics and behavior in wild house mouse populations. In G. Lindzey & D. D. Thiessen (Eds.) Contributions to behavior-genetic analysis: The mouse as a prototype. New York: Appleton-Century-Crofts, 1970.

50. Smith, R. H. Wildness and domestication in Mus musculus: A behavioral analysis. Journal of Comparative and Physiological Psychology, 1972, 79, 22–29.

51. Thiessen, D. D. A move toward species-specific analyses in behavior genetics. Behavior Genetics, 1972, 2, 115–125.

52. Underwood, B. J. & Shaughnessy, J. J. Experimentation in Psychology. New York: Wiley, 1975.

53. Vale, J. R. & Ray, D. A diallel analysis of male mouse sex behavior. Behavior Genetics, 1972, 2, 199–209.

54. Wahlsten, D. Genetic experiments with animal learning: A critical review. Behavioral Biology, 1972, 7, 143–182.

55. Wahlsten, D. Phenotypic and genetic relations between initial response to electric shock and rate of avoidance learning in mice. Behavior Genetics, 1972, 2, 211–240.

56. Walters, D. E. & Gale, J. S. A note on the Hayman analysis of variance for a full diallel table. Heredity, 1977, 38, 401–407.

57. Wilcock, J. & Fulker, D. W. Avoidance learning in rats: Genetic evidence for two distinct behavioral processes in the shuttle box. Journal of Comparative Physiological Psychology, 1973, Vol. 83, No. 2, 247–253.

COMMENT BY D. WAHLSTEN

The suggestion "that the only way we can get an adequate picture of the genetic architecture of behavioral characters of interest . . . is to measure the behavior in several different ways and analyze the composite performance of our subjects" should give rise to even larger scale experiments than Dr. Henderson has already bequeathed upon the literature. These will make a positive contribution, provided that the published reports include full details of the individual components of behavior as well as the "composite performance". A study which analyzes modes of inheritance for higher-level characters or super-characters, perhaps in the form of factor loadings, will be of little worth unless actual scores on individual tests are fully summarized and presented for the scrutiny of the reader.

No mathematical techniques, no matter how sophisticated, can reveal the presence of characters with great adaptive significance unless the individual tests that measure the crude behaviors do indeed measure such characters. In this regard, a qualification should be added to Dr. Henderson's assertion that "the investigator who, through a logical analysis, breaks down performance in a certain test situation into component sub-characters, determines the relationship between the sub-characters and then analyzes genetically these groups of sub-characters, is likely to be doing very much the same thing as the investigator who derives a number of factors from an extensive series of behavioral measures and genetically analyzes them." The two investigators will necessarily arrive at comparable conclusions only if the "series of behavioral measures" studied with factor analysis are precisely those which are necessary for "a logical analysis" of "performance in a certain test situation." It is easy to compose "an extensive series of behavioral measures", and such test batteries have been reported in the literature. However, "logical analysis" is much more difficult, and consequently it is a rare commodity, even in a popular area such as behavioral genetics and animal learning. "Logical analysis" by the dissection of performance using direct manipulations of the task itself is far more convincing than factor analysis which uses statistical dissection of an array of numerical scores on disparate tasks, because statistical correlation does not necessarily imply causation.

The investigation of "genetic architecture" of such characters using comparisons of inbred, hybrid and wild-derived populations should provide interesting data. Whether it will truly unravel the intricacies of "fitness" remains to be seen. It is imperative that any conclusions about the Darwinian fitness of some behavioral character of animals be _directly_ verified by assessing whether animals that differ in the character do indeed differ in their propensity to increase their relative numbers in a population. The positive relationship between "directional dominance" and "fitness" is an hypothesis to be subjected to experimental verification. "Directional dominance" cannot be regarded a priori as a direct measure of "fitness".

It would be useful to distinguish clearly between the immediate causes, the physiological mechanisms, of hybrid vigor, and the historical causes, the evolutionary mechanisms, of this phenomenon. Hybrid vigor is the mirror-image of inbred languor or depression, and those characters which show substantial directional dominance, overdominance in particular, will be resistant to inbreeding-produced homozygosity and loss of fitness. Positive physiological consequences of heterozygosity provide the basis of evolutionary advantage, but adaptation and evolutionary change may entail numerous processes in addition to directional dominance. There is clearly much work that can and needs to be done in the laboratory to study physiological mechanisms of hybrid vigor, but prospects for illuminating the principles of evolutionary change do not seem so bright.

When one considers the virtual absence of reports of single locus over-dominance for any behavior in mice, for example, and at the same time considers the ubiquity of hybrid vigor when inbred strains differing in many components of heredity are crossed, the spectre arises of inter-locus interaction or epistasis rather than intra-locus interaction as the physiological basis for the difference between inbred and hybrid mice.

Could it not be the case that complex behaviors in general suffer most from inbreeding, perhaps because inbreeding disrupts developmental homeostasis, especially the spatio-temporal coordination of different parts of the nervous system, and thereby renders more difficult the integration and co-ordination of simpler units of behavior? If so, then almost any complex behavioral character should yield hybrid vigor, even though it might not possess a high survival value or reproductive advantage in a particular environment. This would have to be assessed by a direct test of "fitness".

Concerning comparisons of wild-derived (W), laboratory F_1 hybrids (F) and their inbred parents (P), the ratio $(W-P)/(F-P)$ has doubtful validity. It appears to be virtually impossible to sample wild mice today from the same populations from which the common laboratory strains must have been derived many years ago. Furthermore, a wild population is almost certainly more comparable to an F_2 hybrid cross than an F_1 hybrid cross or a mean of F_1 hybrids.

An alternative approach would be to establish two random-breeding laboratory populations: one derived from wild-trapped

animals and one derived from an eight-way cross of inbred laboratory strains. Then form a number of inbred strains using full-
sib matings from litters randomly chosen from each population.
The average rate of decline in behavioral characters should
give some indication of the relative importance of directional
dominance for wild-derived and laboratory-derived populations,
whereas the dispersion of the inbred strains should give a rough
indication of additive variation. It seems likely that epistasis
would contribute to both the decline of fitness and increased
dispersion of lines.

Finally, Dr. Henderson's attempt to minimize the significance
of "disordinal interactions" is not at all convincing. For
example, he cites Fuller's finding that isolation increased the
activity of terrier dogs and decreased activity of beagles, which
is an apparent "disordinal" genotype-environment interaction; the
effect of environmental isolation on activity depended strongly
upon the breed of dog. Then he states that isolation had a comparable effect on "fearfulness" in the two breeds, and that a
greater "fearfulness" increases activity of terriers and decreases
activity of beagles. Raw motor activity shows genotype-environment
interaction, but "fearfulness" does not. According to Henderson,
this leads to "a simple interpretation of the data," but it is
"simple" only vis-a-vis "fearfulness". There still remains the
strongly "disordinal" interaction between activity-change induced
by increased "fearfulness" and breed of dog. Why the two breeds
respond in opposite ways to the hypothetical construct "fearfulness" remains unexplained. To analyze a "disordinal" interaction
does increase our understanding of the behavior in question, but
it certainly does not make the interaction itself disappear. Dr.
Henderson's apparent wish that the problem of disordinal genotype-
environment interaction could be banished cannot be fulfilled by
this kind of ad hoc analysis.

COMMENT BY J. L. FULLER

There is an interesting relationship between Henderson's
Figure 2 and my distinction between ostensible and inferred psychophenes. The items placed by Henderson at level III (subchar-
acters), level IV (characters) and level VI (supercharacters) are
potentially observable and are ostensible psychophenes in my
terminology. His level V supercharacters are clearly inferred
psychophenes whose values and limits are dependent upon the choice
of lower components used to define them.

It is curious and perhaps unexpected that the inferred psychophenes of level V should be bounded in both directions by
ostensible psychophenes; on the one side the scores for standardized tests of performance, on the other the raw data of behavior

related to fitness. Perhaps this is why level V is the very core
of psychology. Here is where the action is.

Looking at matters from this viewpoint raises an interesting
point with respect to the reductionist approach to explanation.
In Henderson's Figure 2 the process of reductionism runs from
right to left. This involves first a reductionist explanation of
fitness characters (potentially directly measured from vital
statistics) in terms of inferred general behavioral traits. Reduction of these traits brings us back again to observable behavior. A radical behaviorist would opt to delete level V. I
disagree, but feel that behavior geneticists should be aware of
its inferential status and of possible arbitrary judgment in the
definition of its members.

COMMENT BY G. WHITNEY

There is a common thread which runs through much of this
conference that addresses broad issues of explanatory theory in
behavior genetics, and is nicely illustrated by Dr. Henderson's
work on infant behavior. My point is that when theoreticians
stay closest to Darwinian biology for concepts and variables results are consistent and lend themselves to elegant explanatory
power. In direct proportion to the extent one digs into the
closet of psychology for concepts and variables things start getting murky. Even in other areas of psychology evolutionary approaches are paying off. Although we all pay lip-service, we tend
to go to the attic of non-Darwinian psychology too often.

The gene-environment interaction approach to understanding
behavior, although employing different terminology, seems theoretically very close to the emphasis in evolutionary biology on
the benefits of viewing behaviors as essentially flexible strategies rather than as specific traits.

If behaviors are often on the cutting edge of evolution and
are capable of fast response to microenvironmental shifts, as
emphasized in theory, then an emphasis on their additive genetic
variance and heritability may not be misplaced. An apparent
paradox was dealt with by Falconer's emphasis that any trait
other than (inclusive) fitness will respond to selection as a
correlated character. It follows that the additive genetic covariance between the trait and fitness is important, and that most
behaviors are probably not truly linear components of fitness and
could have substantial additive genetic variance along with substantial directional dominance of gene influence.

COMMENT BY D. A. HAY

Although I agree completely with Dr. Henderson's persuasive arguments that we should use a wider range of genotypes, this must depend to some extent upon the questions we are asking. If we are concerned with general issues of genetic architecture and evolution then obviously the more genotypes the better. On the other hand, we may learn far more about specific behaviours, brain structures or physiological or biochemical processes by concentrating on a few genotypes. Will (1977) and the paper by Oliverio at this conference illustrate this latter approach clearly. On this point, one could hardly call the Maudsley, Roman or Tryon selection lines representative of the range of rat genotypes, but this hardly means we should disregard them or the extensive literature based around them (Broadhurst, 1977). However, even with this more specific approach there are situations where a few genotypes can be misleading, as evidenced for example by the work of Batty (1978) which followed from McGill's sexual behaviour research discussed by Dr. Henderson. In a range of three strains and their reciprocal F_1's, Batty found a clearcut negative relationship between plasma testosterone level and male sexual behaviour, but this broke down completely when she came to analyse segregating generations.

As well as emphasising more inbred genotypes, Dr. Henderson advocates more use of wild rodents. I think it is the recent work on social structure of wild populations that provides the greatest flaw in his argument that unambiguous evidence of directional dominance implies similar selection pressure among the ancestors of the inbred parental lines. In particular, the work of Busser, Zweep and van Oortmerssen (1974) suggests there might be different genetic pressures acting on different subgroups within the one population and as Dr. van Abeelen points out in his conference paper, detailed genetic analysis of such types could be very worthwhile. Suppose only one sub-group of any population sought refuge in the experimenter's traps or consistently moved round the perimeter of the colony. Then, no matter how many populations are sampled, one might well find unambiguous dominance, but the point would be that one could infer that selection pressures were uniform for that fraction of the various populations, not for the total population.

Dr. Henderson suggests some changed selection in the laboratory might explain the reduced variability among laboratory compared with wild rodents, but my point is that only a very selective fraction of the wild population might ever reach the laboratory. It is possible to obtain more random samples of natural populations than by conventional trapping with its inherent biases by, e.g., Dr. Fulker's digging out of entire rat nests or the hand-catching by one of my students of mice when a farmer removes the bottom layer of a haystack. My objection to Dr. Henderson's argument is purely a hypothetical one and I would be relieved if data obtained from such more realistic samples were to prove me wrong.

COMMENT BY P. L. BROADHURST

Dr. Henderson's wide-ranging paper covers many areas of contemporary interest in comparative psychogenetics in exemplary fashion. His measured "Conclusion" stressing the need for programmatic efforts of considerable size for solving the manifold problems in this area is one which deserves the most general support.

I would like to underline his views on the important problem of heterosis, about which confusion continues in the behavioral literature. Heterosis, defined strictly, is the occurrence of an F_1 phenotype which transgresses the metrical limits set by the mean scores of the parental populations. It is often referred to loosely as "overdominance". But there are at least three ways of regarding such "overdominance", and the first two of them are essentially pseudo-overdominance, and only by a knowledge of the gene action based on an adequate genetic analysis, can they be identified. The first case is where epistasis is causal, that is, the overdominance is not allelic, but non-allelic in origin. The second case is familiar in the behavioral literature from the widespread use of inbred strains, and results from extreme dispersion in parental lines of dominance for increasers and decreasers. The release of this potential variation into its free expression on crossing gives rise to heterotic filial generations. Thirdly, phenotypic overdominance may in fact be genuine in the sense that it is mediated by the action of allelic effects but its occurrence will be relatively rare. It may, for example, be detected in situations in which a filial generation is better buffered against negative environmental effects than the parental generations, and hence may be detected after crossing.

REPLY TO COMMENTS

N. D. Henderson

The discussants bring up several points which expand and round out issues raised in my paper. John Fuller has been helpful in pointing out the relationships between his taxonomy of psychophenes and my discussion of various levels of characters, sub-characters and super-characters. Viewed in this light, Fuller's discussion of the choice of psychophene becomes a particularly relevant supplement to my presentation.

Glayde Whitney adds another important reason to be cautious about inferring that a character showing high heritability is not important for the survival of the organism. My concerns about focusing on heritability are that it is often done without regard to other components of genetic architecture and that heritability estimates in animal behavior research are often heavily influenced by rather arbitrary decisions concerning experimental methodology and analysis.

David Hay reminds us that extensive genetic sampling is not necessary for all experimental purposes. Often specific genotypes are ideal for certain types of research because they possess certain characteristics particularly relevant to the research issues involved. As Dr. Hay points out however, even in these cases eventual replication with other genotypes may be advisable.

Dr. Hay brings up an interesting point with respect to the collection of wild animals for eventual use in laboratory studies. In theory, subpopulations within a population may differ genetically and only certain subtypes within the population may end up in the laboratory. I am afraid I see no way around this, other than using trapping or capturing procedures which result in the capture of most members of a given population. Trapping may result in obtaining a biased subsample of a population, but so may locating nests, which are likely to vary in accessibility. Almost any method we can think of to capture a small fraction of a given population could hypothetically produce a biased sample. It would be difficult to argue against the position that initial biases in the sampling of wild populations have resulted in nearly all laboratory populations being genetically different from them. All investigators of biological and behavioral phenomena using laboratory animals face this problem. It is an empirical question whether these sampling biases lead to faulty or ungeneralizable conclusions. I would be reluctant to recommend the abandonment of such research on the grounds that possible biases in sampling could occasionally lead to misleading results.

Douglas Wahlsten makes a good point when he argues in favor of dissecting performance into sub-characters using "logical analysis" and the direct manipulation of independent variables in preference to correlational methods involving characters or supercharacters. In some cases logical analysis is likely to be more efficient and, as he points out, more likely to illuminate causal effects. The problem is that we often lack the knowledge or ability to engage in logical analysis in a particular area of research, and that in such cases a multivariate approach using factor analysis with factor overdetermination may be the only recourse. Royce (1964) has argued that the latter approach is necessary for the identification of composite measures of theoretically useful constructs in most complex situations.

Dr. Wahlsten reminds us that any conclusions about Darwinian fitness should be directly verified by assessing reproductive fitness in a natural situation and relating it to the behavioral variable of interest. This is step 2 in the ideal model for genetic research on natural selection that I referred to in my commentary on Peter Broadhurst's paper. Alas, despite its apparent simplicity, such an experiment is enormously difficult to do on mammalian behavior. One would be forced to carry out a rather major study over many generations in several environments in order to balance out short term and microenvironmental selection pressures which would not necessarily accurately reflect the evolutionary history of the organism. At the same time one would have to devise a methodology which would prevent both the behavioral measurements from contaminating the natural selection process and the sampling of subjects for testing during selection from being biased. It was for these reasons that I suggested in my commentary on Professor Broadhurst's paper that further verification of the hypothetical relationship between dominance and fitness will have to come largely from research on rapidly reproducing non-mammalian species. We must not lose sight of the fact, however, that substantial empirical support for the dominance - fitness hypothesis already exists, some of which was reviewed by Broadhurst. Further support, involving a variety of species and phenotypes is certainly desirable, but isn't there a point at which we can say that it is no longer imperative to directly verify the results of breeding experiments with natural selection studies? If not, the intraspecific approach to the study of behavioral evolution in mammals has little future.

I disagree with Dr. Wahlsten concerning the ubiquity of hybrid vigor in behavioral research, if he means by this directional overdominance. A large number of behavior genetic studies show that hybrids differ significantly from midparent averages. A large proportion of these studies, however, show only complete or partial dominance for the behavioral characters involved. Overdominance which must be attributed to epistasis is sometimes found in behavioral studies, but his poses little problem for the genetic architecture - natural selection argument, as can be seen in Professor Broadhurst's discussion of directional selection. Mather (1973) argued that the effects of directional dominance will be enhanced by duplicate gene interactions, and the Drosophila data of Kearsey and Kojima (1967) on egg hatchability and body weight, and Hay (1972) on reactivity to mechanical stimulation, are in accord with this position. Dr. Wahlsten's suggestion that inbreeding may disrupt the spatio-temporal coordination of different parts of the nervous system is nevertheless intriguing, and well worth investigating.

Wahlsten's concern about the inadequacy of my RDS ratio seems to be based on his failure to distinguish between hybrids derived from a pair of inbred strains and those derived from multiple

crosses between strains. He feels that "a wild population is almost certainly more comparable to an F_2 hybrid cross than an F_1
hybrid cross or a mean of F_1 hybrids". This statement only makes
sense if one believes in the highly unlikely possibility that a
wild population is similar to an F_2 cross between a single pair of
inbred strains. In any multiway cross between a number of strains
F_1 and F_2 means will be equal; F_2's produced by random mating among
a large number of different crosses have the same inbreeding coefficient as the F_1. A demonstration of this phenomenon can be
seen in Figure 1, which shows the results of a study on brain size
I reported a number of years ago (Henderson, 1970). Brain weights
for mice reared in either enriched or standard laboratory cages are
averaged for six inbred parent strains, and their 30 possible F_1
crosses and F_2 mice from ten 4-way crosses selected to represent
parental lines in approximately equal proportions. Brain weights
of F_1 and F_2 4-way crosses are highly similar to each other in both
rearing environments. Naturally, variation within genotypes is
somewhat greater for 4-way crosses than for F_1 hybrids because of
differences in genetic heterogeneity. The ability of the diallel
cross to reproduce the original random mating population while
maintaining genetic homogeneity within groups (Griffing, 1956) is
a point often overlooked.

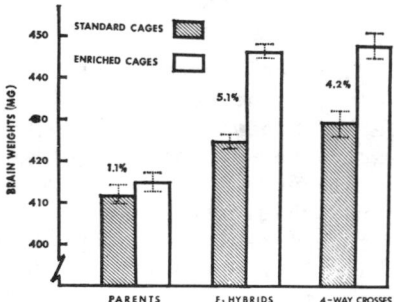

Figure 1. Averaged brain weights of the six inbred strains and
their F_1 and F_2 hybrid progeny reared in either standard cages or enriched environments. Small dotted bars
indicate standard errors of each mean. (Reprinted from
Henderson, 1970. Copyright 1970 by the American Association for the Advancement of Science.)

I did indicate that maternal effects can cause a distortion of
the RDS ratio and that inbreeding within wild populations could
bias the ratio toward low values. However, these potential

confounding effects are readily detectable. Several procedures can be used for assessing maternal effects, and one can get at least a rough index of inbreeding depression effects within wild populations by crossing animals from different demes captured in the same geographic location.

The final comment made by Dr. Wahlsten concerns what he feels is an unconvincing "attempt to minimize the significance of disordinal interactions". The issue is complex and requires considerably more space than I allotted to the problem to cover all the ramifications and issues involved. Frankly, I did not devote more space to this section simply because so few GE interactions reported are disordinal. From the point of view of generalization, disordinal interactions are troubling since their presence greatly reduces the generality of the main effects involved in the interactions. In behavior genetics disordinal GE interactions would rule out statements about overall genetic or environmental influences on a given behavior. Just as I might be accused of trying to sweep these troubling data under the rug by persons who see disordinal GE interactions as a major obstacle in behavior genetic research, such individuals might also be characterized as throwing unreasonable doubt on a large body of research because of the occasional occurrence of disordinal interactions between genotype and environment.

Let us examine in a little more detail the two examples of disordinal GE interactions I presented. The first dealt with a differential responsiveness of two breeds of dogs to emergence from long term isolation. In terms of motor behavior the two breeds' response upon emergence appeared to be in opposite directions, with terriers becoming active and beagles tending to freeze. I suggested that the knowledge that these are the respective responses of these two breeds when nervous or afraid permitted a rather simple interpretation of the effects of emergence from isolation - that it is stressful for the organism. Fuller went on to suggest that this was probably the case for many species which have been isolated prior to testing and cited data supporting this argument. The consistency across genotypes with respect to the construct of fearfulness does not, of course, eliminate the fact that the motor responses of the two breeds differed. For the purposes of Fuller's analysis this was irrelevant, but the question still remains as to why these breeds show differential motor responses in a fearful situation.

There is a striking parallel between this and the other example I described involving differences found between rats and mice in terms of their conditioned emotional response to shock. Rats show a suppression of activity during the CS after a few pairings with shock, whereas mice show an increase in locomotor activity, often approaching frantic running behavior. In the CER example we have two species showing opposite motor responses in similar CER paradigms, and in the dog example two breeds, undoubtedly subjected to rather different selection pressures, showing opposite motor responses in a fear inducing situation.[1] The parallel in these two examples includes the fact that the genotypes compared had been under different selection pressures and the fact that in both cases testing involved a typical "flight or fight" situation for the organism. Just as minor variations in an experimental set-up can lead to changes in the likelihood of flight or freezing in response to a fearful stimulus, variations in genotype apparently can do the same. It would be an interesting exercise to determine what proportion of disordinal interactions reported in the literature involve motor activity in emotionally arousing test situations using subjects which were likely to have been subjected to somewhat different selection pressures or which differ considerably in degree of inbreeding.

Contrary to Dr. Wahlsten's assertion, I would certainly hope that disordinal GE interactions are not "banished". Rather, I suggest that a priori predictions of GE interactions provide a powerful test for the adequacy of current behavioral genetic methodology and theory. Predictions of disordinal interactions with genotype are even more striking than predictions that genotypes will respond in differing degrees to a particular experimental manipulation. The verification of my prediction that directional dominance for activity should be reversed in very young mice was particularly satisfying because it did involve the prediction of a disordinal interaction between level of inbreeding and age on activity.

In reviewing both my paper and the discussants' comments, I am struck by how critical behavior geneticists are concerning genetic samples, the manipulation of independent variables, and the nature of dependent variables. We often make it appear that it is next to impossible to gather data that is worthwhile for understanding evolutionary history or most other issues concerning the inheritance of behavior. This may be an unfortunate consequence of our critical sophistication outstripping our data base. The work of early psychologists and ethologists often appears quite naive from a contemporary methodological standpoint. Nevertheless, these fields did advance, however haltingly. Less than perfect experiments often add "noise" to the system and frequently allow alternate

---

[1]On a post hoc basis, the CER results are not particularly surprising. Freezing behavior in the presence of a fearful stimulus might be the best strategy for a wild rat, whereas running may be a better strategy for a small and fast, but less vicious, wild mouse.

explanations for the outcomes observed. Progress in a scientific field cannot proceed however if, given the choice between imperfect experiments which occasionally lead us astray and no experiments, investigators choose the latter course.

References

Griffing, B. A generalized treatment of the use of diallel crosses in quantitative inheritance. _Heredity_, 1956, _10_, 31-50.

Hay, D. A. Genetical and maternal determinants of the activity and preening behavior of _Drosophila melanogaster_ reared in different environments. _Heredity_, 1972, _28_, 311-336.

Henderson, N. D. Brain weight increases resulting from environmental enrichment: A directional dominance in mice. _Science_, 1970, _169_, 776-778.

Kearsey, M. J. & Kojima, K. The genetic architecture of body weight and egg hatchability in _Drosophila melanogaster_. _Genetics_, _56_, 23-37.

Mather, K. _Genetical structure of populations_. London: Chapman and Hall, 1973.

Royce, J. R. Factors as theoretical constructs. _American Psychologist_, 1963, _18_, 522-528.

GENETIC MODELS

Combining Data From Different Groups in Human Behavior Genetics

J. C. Loehlin

Some Implications of Biometrical Genetical Analysis
for Psychological Research

D. W. Fulker

Genetic Correlations, Environmental Correlations, and Behavior

J. C. DeFries, A. R. Kuse, and S. G. Vandenberg

COMBINING DATA FROM DIFFERENT GROUPS IN HUMAN BEHAVIOR GENETICS*

John C. Loehlin

University of Texas at Austin

INTRODUCTION: TWO STRATEGIES

Perhaps the most fundamental formulation in psychology is that
behavior is a function of an organism and its environment. And
perhaps the first step forward from this is the realization that
these two variables are badly confounded. For, obviously, what
an organism is today may depend on what its environment was yester-
day, and, more often overlooked, what its environment is today may
very well depend on behaviors that the organism engaged in on some
prior date. One of the attractions of behavior genetics to at
least some psychologists is that it cuts the organism side of the
organism-environment tangle neatly into two parts: the genes--
the information carried in the DNA--and the environment, the total
effects of its milieu on the organism from conception until the
moment at which we view it. In practice, of course, the "moment"
at which we view it is an extended one: the "present" characteristics of the organism are typically assessed over some period of
time--often a quite considerable period of time--via some sort of
average or other cumulative record of behaviors. The greater the
variety of situations over which this averaging is done, other

* I am indebted to my colleagues in the Texas Adoption Study,
  Joseph M. Horn and Lee Willerman, for permitting the use of the
  data presented in the last section of the chapter. The gather-
  ing of those data was supported by grant MH-24280 from the
  National Institute of Mental Health. I am grateful to A. S.
  Goldberger and to Willerman, Horn, and the discussants at the
  Banff conference for suggestions and comments concerning an
  earlier version of this chapter.

things equal, the greater is likely to appear the relative influence of the genes, as an increasing amount of environmental variation gets treated in the measurement process as internal error. But I must leave the pursuit of this particular point to another occasion.

It would be attractive, of course, to be able to specify exactly how an individual organism's genes and environment interact to make it behave in just the way it does. For most complex behavioral characteristics, at least in humans, we are nowhere near being able to do this. Indeed, the kind of questions we are mostly asking today (and having a lot of trouble answering, I might add) concern crude averages for populations of individuals: what, roughly speaking, are the relative influences of genetic variation and environmental variation on trait X in population Y? Answers to such questions about the "heritabilities" of particular traits in particular populations are, like answers to questions about the means or standard deviations of particular traits in particular populations, rarely of much general scientific interest in themselves. But they become the essential building blocks of further knowledge when we can make comparisons among such values--comparisons for different populations, or for a single population at different historical times, or for different traits in the same population, or for populations of individuals at different points in their life span.

I do not plan to review in detail the limited substantive knowledge we have so far achieved concerning the heritability of complex human behavioral traits such as general intelligence or extraversion. Some of this is done in other chapters of this volume. Rather I propose to sketch out two strategies whereby genetic theory and environmental theory may be jointly employed to yield knowledge of the sort just described, and then say a bit more about one of these strategies.

Let me begin with the claim that any method capable of telling us anything useful along the lines mentioned must incorporate both a genetic theory and an environmental theory (either possibly quite rudimentary). Thus, estimating the heritability of a trait by doubling the parent-child correlation is in effect selecting a simple but specific model of the operation of the environment, namely that its effects are random with respect to family membership, and a moderately complex model of the operation of the genes (by Fisher out of Mendel, with the specific constraints of genetic equilibrium, random mating, and genetic additivity). If the environment were entirely responsible for individual differences in the trait, the environmental model alone would be relevant, and it predicts that the parent-child correlation should be zero. If the genes were entirely responsible for individual differences in the trait, only the genetic model would be relevant, and it predicts a value of .5 for this correlation. Values in between tell you how much relative effect each model is having. If the effects are equal, you should observe a correlation midway between 0 and .5, or .25; if the genes predominate 2 to 1 in their influence on the trait, the correlation should be two thirds of the way toward .5, or .33; if the environmental influence predominates 4 to 1, the correlation should be .10, and so on. If the genes and environment operate independently and additively, one need only double the observed correlation to obtain the proportion of phenotypic variance that is genetic in origin.

To take another example, estimating heritability by doubling the difference between monozygotic and dizygotic twin correlations employs the same genetic model as the preceding, but a different environmental model--one which allows for shared environmental influences among family members so long as these are equal for the two types of twin. More complex models, both on the genetic and the environmental sides, can be constructed; some examples will be given later. One can also postulate various relations between the genetic and the environmental models in their influence on traits: genes and environment may be correlated positively or negatively with each other, or they may interact (cf. Eaves et al., 1977a; Plomin et al., 1977a).

There are several ways in which one may be mistaken in an enterprise of this sort. First, there may be errors in the model: for example, random mating may be assumed when assortative mating is in fact characteristic of the population. Second there may be errors of measurement, either random or systematic, in assessing the trait empirically in the individuals being measured. And third there may be sampling error--the characteristics of any sample of measured individuals cannot be expected to reflect exactly the corresponding characteristics of the population from which they are drawn. Thus one might mistakenly estimate a true heritability of .60 to be .40, from an observed correlation of .20 in 100 parent-child pairs, solely because of model error (the model assumes no environmental correlation, but there was actually a negative environmental correlation present), or solely because of measurement error (which has attenuated a true correlation of .30 to an observed correlation of .20), or solely because of sampling error (the correlation of .20 in the sample differs from the population value of .30 because of chance in the selection of this particular set of individuals to measure). On any given occasion, it probably doesn't matter too much why one is wrong: the mistake is made and that's it; however, for improving one's performance the discrimination among these three potential sources of error is crucial, since each prescribes a different remedy. For a behavior genetic theoretician, the minimization of errors two and three is vital, since only then can he see clearly through to the fit or misfit of his theoretical model of genetic and environmental influence upon the trait.

Assuming that good measurement and large random samples have brought errors two and three under a reasonable degree of control, the human behavior geneticist may follow either of two strategies in looking for error one, i.e., in assessing the fits of models. One strategy is to divide and conquer. A series of independent experiments is carried out that purport to estimate the same parameter. One might, for example, estimate the heritability of a given trait from a comparison of identical and fraternal twins, then from a parent-child regression, then from a comparison of natural and adoptive siblings, and so on. If all these estimates agree (and the models employed are mutually compatible), excellent: one has substantial confidence that one is on the right track. And if they don't, the particular pattern of disagreement may help suggest what is wrong.

Let me illustrate this strategy with a hypothetical example. Suppose for trait X the correlations of MZ and DZ twins are .90 and .50, respectively. Given the model mentioned earlier (and more formally specified in the left-hand column and footnote to Table 1), we estimate the heritability h^2 to be twice the difference between these correlations, or .80. Suppose further that in a study of parents and their offspring, based on the same general population, the correlation between father or mother and a child for trait X is .40. If we assume no relevant shared environment between parent and child, and random mating, as in the middle column of Table 1, we estimate h^2 again to be .80. If we go on to measure natural and adoptive siblings in this population, and find them to be correlated .50 and .10, respectively, we can apply the model in the right-hand column of Table 1, again getting h^2 = .80. We begin to take our results seriously.

On the other hand, suppose the MZ and DZ correlations had instead been .82 and .60, with the others the same. We would have found h^2 to be .44 in the twin study, and .80 in the other two: something is wrong. Examination of the equations suggests that a nonzero p might help. Let us suppose that we have some external grounds for being suspicious of the random mating assumption. This is readily checked, since parental measurements are required in any case for the parent-child correlation. We compute the correlation between spouses, and indeed it is not zero, let us suppose that in fact it is .40. Now a new set of models are appropriate, which do not assume p = 0, and appear in the middle row of Table 1. Substituting into the equations for twins and solving for h^2, we obtain a value of .57. Proceeding on, we find that with a p of .40 the parent-child and the sibling studies yield h^2 values of .57 and .64, respectively, which may be suffi-cient to satisfy us that the heritability of trait X in this popu-lation is about .6. Or we may proceed to consider still further

Table 1

Estimating heritability from three designs under different assumptions

Twin design	Parent-offspring design	Natural and adoptive siblings
$r_{MZ} = c_1^2 + h^2 + d^2$	$r_{PO} = c_3^2 + \frac{1}{2}h^2(1+p)$	$r_{OO} = c_4^2 + \frac{1}{2}h^2(1+h^2p) + \frac{1}{4}d^2$
$r_{DZ} = c_2^2 + \frac{1}{2}h^2(1+h^2p) + \frac{1}{4}d^2$		$r_{OU} = c_5^2$
if $c_1 = c_2$ and $d = 0$	if $c_3 = 0$	if $c_4 = c_5$ and $d = 0$
$r_{MZ} - r_{DZ} = h^2 - \frac{1}{2}h^2(1+h^2p)$	$r_{PO} = \frac{1}{2}h^2(1+p)$	$r_{OO} - r_{OU} = \frac{1}{2}h^2(1+h^2p)$
if also $p = 0$	if also $p = 0$	if also $p = 0$
$r_{MZ} - r_{DZ} = \frac{1}{2}h^2$	$r_{PO} = \frac{1}{2}h^2$	$r_{OO} - r_{OU} = \frac{1}{2}h^2$
$h^2 = 2(r_{MZ} - r_{DZ})$	$h^2 = 2r_{PO}$	$h^2 = 2(r_{OO} - r_{OU})$

Note: c^2 refers to shared environments, h^2 to shared additive genes, d^2 to shared dominance deviations, and p to phenotypic spouse correlation. General assumptions: polygenic trait, genetic equilibrium, no genotype-environment correlation or interaction, negligible epistasis, phenotypic assortative mating, no selective placement.

assumptions or to test our results in new studies of MZ twins reared apart, MZ twin families, second-degree relatives, or the like.

A strategy of this kind has much to commend it. It is straightforward and relatively easy to apply and to understand, and conforms (more or less) to the historical development of human behavior genetics, as different investigators carried out their twin and adoption and family studies in more-or-less comparable populations in America and Europe. But there is a second strategy that has recently come into some vogue, which involves the simultaneous consideration of data from twins, adoptees, and so on. I will say a little more about its historical antecedents shortly, but first let me illustrate the procedure with the same simple example used for the first strategy.

Table 2 presents the essentials. The five equations of the three separate designs of Table 1 are taken as a single set, with a sixth equation for the spouse correlation. As written, there are 6 equations in 8 unknowns, and no solution is possible. However, by imposing the constraints listed at the bottom of Table 2, which are those used in the separate experiments of Table 1, the number of unknowns is reduced to 4, namely, h, c_1, c_4, and p, and solution of the equations becomes possible. Since we have reduced the number of unknowns to less than the number of equations, we cannot expect to fit the data perfectly, but we thereby gain the possibility of a statistical test of the goodness of the fit of the model to the data. I have used Rao, Morton and Yee's procedure (1974), which obtains an approximate maximum likelihood solution by minimizing the sum of weighted squared discrepancies between z-transformed observed and theoretical correlations. The solution obtained is $c_1^2 = .23$, $c_4^2 = .12$, $p = .40$, and $h^2 = .59$. Arbitrarily assuming 200 pairs per group, the χ^2 with 2 df for goodness of fit is .22. This is an excellent fit to the data. The chances of sampling fluctuation alone yielding a worse fit are about 9 out of 10. In short, the assumptions about the operation of the genes and the environment that are incorporated into this model do an excellent job of accounting for the data, and our intuitive conclusion from the individual experiments that the heritability is about .6 is well supported. Furthermore, this procedure solves explicitly for the additional environmental parameters that are implicit in the designs of Table 1 but not often actually reported in the literature: namely, the shared environments of twins, accounting for about 23% of the variance, and the shared environments of siblings that differ in age, accounting for some, but less, namely 12%.

This approach also lets us pit one set of gene-environment models against another, and thus test directly the question of whether a simpler model mightn't fit the data well enough (allowing

Table 2

The simultaneous estimation of parameters using
information from several groups

$$r_{MZ} = c_1^2 + h^2 + d^2$$

$$r_{DZ} = c_2^2 + \tfrac{1}{2}h^2(1 + h^2 p) + \tfrac{1}{4}d^2$$

$$r_{PO} = c_3^2 + \tfrac{1}{2}h^2(1 + p)$$

$$r_{OO} = c_4^2 + \tfrac{1}{2}h^2(1 + h^2 p) + \tfrac{1}{4}d^2$$

$$r_{OU} = c_5^2$$

$$r_{PP} = p$$

restrictions: $c_3 = 0$, $c_1 = c_2$, $c_4 = c_5$, $d = 0$

---

for sampling error) to obviate the necessity of using a more complex one. In the example of Table 1, where random mating was
assumed, the discrepancy between a heritability estimate of .44
and two heritability estimates of .80 led us to question our
assumptions. Should it have? Could these values just reflect
chance sampling fluctuation from some intermediate population
heritability value? We can examine this question by specifying
random mating, i.e., $\underline{p} = 0$, in the first five equations of Table
2, and again obtaining a solution. The χ^2 is now 5.92, based
on solving 5 equations for 3 unknowns, and thus still with 2 df.
The chances are only about 1 in 20 that a fit this poor would be
yielded by chance sampling fluctuation, which one might or might
not accept as plausible, depending on one's views of where parsimony lies in this situation. (If the solution is deemed acceptable,
the best-fit values are $\underline{c_1^2} = .20$, $\underline{c_4^2} = .15$, and $\underline{h^2} = .63$.) Now of
course in our earlier example we had an external reason for pre-
ferring the assortative mating to the random model: a phenotypic
correlation of .40 between spouses. If the random-mating model is
extended to encompass this correlation as well, by including all
six equations in Table 2 but setting $\underline{p} = 0$, we would clearly
reject the model: the χ^2 is 41.28 with 3 df, and the probability
of doing this badly by chance is much less than one in a thousand.
A direct statistical test of the difference between the goodness
of fit of the two solutions of the six equations--the models with
and without the assumption of random mating--can be obtained from
the difference between their respective χ^2s and dfs, i.e., as a
χ^2 of 41.06 with 1 df--once again a difference to be expected from
random sampling much less than one in a thousand times.

In short, in consolidating the three experiments into one by following the second major strategy we gain two major advantages: a single solution that best fits all the data, and a statistical test of how well that solution fits, or how it compares with another. (I should mention, by the way, that although my hypothetical example used equal-sized groups, this is not at all a requirement of the method, which is entirely flexible in this regard.) One cost of the unified strategy is that the computations are considerably more demanding: the three separate solutions of Table 1 can readily be done by pencil on the back of an envelope, but solving the set of six nonlinear simultaneous equations in four unknowns in Table 2 is a job better suited for a computer. However, the _idea_ of doing this is simple enough, and the computer program handles the actual computational labor.

SOME HISTORY: MODELING IQ

I can bring up some of the issues that arise in the application of the unified strategy to actual behavioral data by sketching in a bit of the history of a particular case: the estimation of genetic and environmental influences on IQ. I will not attempt to treat the evolution of the statistical methods as such, or related developments in other fields, such as the structural equation models of econometrics. A start on such matters may be got in Goldberger (1972) and Goldberger and Duncan (1973).

Our story begins with Sewall Wright's 1931 paper entitled "Statistical methods in biology." Wright wanted to illustrate his procedure of "path analysis," which for our purposes is just a way of representing a causal model in a diagram that greatly facilitates writing a set of equations to express it. For an audience of statisticians he chose "a case dealing with heredity in man, as perhaps of more general interest than those dealing with such animals as guinea pigs" (p. 158). His case was the intelligence-test correlations of Barbara Burks (1928) based on her studies of adoptive and matched control families in California. He presented two different models, one with eight equations and one with twelve. The first model lumped together additive and nonadditive genetic effects, while the second distinguished between them (although it placed the nonadditive effects into a miscellaneous residual category). The first model allowed for heredity-environment correlation, but the second provided a causal model of it by a two-generational representation in which the parents' genotypes influenced both the child's genotype and (via the parents' IQs) the child's environment.

Wright's analysis is not free of difficulties. First, it is not clear why he used Burks' "culture index" rather than her "Whittier index" as his environmental measure--the latter, which Burks preferred for her own analysis, is a better socioeconomic

index, and less confounded with parental IQ. Second, a deduction
Wright makes in going from foster to natural families is hard to
square with the actual standard deviations involved, and suggests
that he may have failed to notice that the foster and control
children's IQs were of equal variability in Burks' data. (Fortunately, this did not have a large effect on his results.) Finally,
the twelve-equation model gave trouble, and Wright provides only
an approximate solution. His heritability values for children
were about .8 for the first model (which yields broad heritability)
and .5 for the second (narrow). In the second model, he obtained
a lower value for narrow heritability in the parental generation,
about .3. Estimates for heredity-environment correlation were in
the range .20 to .24 in both models. Despite its problems, Wright's
pioneering paper introduces many themes we will encounter repeatedly in later studies.

Four years later the psychologist Frank Shuttleworth (1935)
took a further step toward a unified strategy by undertaking a
path analysis based jointly on twin data from Holzinger (1929)
and the adoption and control family data from Burks. Actually,
he made use of only three empirical correlations (all corrected
for attenuation): Holzinger's correlation for MZ twins reared
together, .967 after correction, and Burks' two multiple correlations of child's IQ with environmental measures, .42 and .61 in
foster and control families, respectively. With these he was able
to solve for the effects of heredity, $\underline{h}^2$ = .63; common family
environment, $\underline{c}^2$ = .18; intra-family environment, $\underline{u}^2$ = .03; and the
correlation $\underline{r}_{hc}$ = .24 (my symbols, not his). He was able to get
four values from three empirical correlations by the added
assumption that $\underline{h}^2 + \underline{c}^2 + \underline{u}^2 + 2Cov_{hc}$ totaled to 1.00. He went
on to adjust these figures a bit for the fact that the control
group was selected specifically to match the foster group; we need
not go into the details here, but merely note his awareness of the
implications that selection in sampling had for the estimates
obtained.

Our story picks up again some 18 years later with R. B.
Cattell. In 1953 he published a description of his multiple
variance analysis (later called multiple abstract variance analysis, or MAVA). This consisted of a series of equations, each
dealing with an observed variance within or among pairs of individuals in a specified relationship (such as MZ twins reared together,
sibs reared apart, etc.). In each equation, the observed variance
was expressed as a function of various theoretical ("abstract")
variances and correlations (genetic variance between families,
heredity-environment correlation within families, etc.). A set
of such equations could then be solved simultaneously to yield
values for the unknown theoretical parameters. Cattell was quite
explicit concerning the theoretical virtues of his scheme: "the
more radical methodological advance that is being proposed here

is, as stated above, to go beyond handling variances in pairs and to solve for all of them simultaneously by bringing data on all into a related set of equations" (p. 84).

Cattell applied his method to data from six groups: MZ and DZ twins, siblings reared together and apart, and unrelated children reared together and apart, using both questionnaire and objective test measures of his personality factors (Cattell et al., 1955, 1957). One of the measures in the 1957 report was his "Culture-free" test of intelligence. Nominally, in this study he used five equations and solved for within- and between-family hereditary and environmental variances, and the heredity-environment correlation in the between-family variation. He got rough estimates of the within-family heredity-environment correlation as well by arbitrarily setting this correlation to various values, solving for the other parameters, and picking the most plausible of the solutions in the light of several internal and external criteria. However, in practice he appears to have proceeded somewhat more flexibly: in the case of the Culture-free test he seems not to have used one of the groups at all (sibs reared apart, which had an anomalously high correlation), and instead to have set the between-family r_{he} arbitrarily to .25 on the basis of prior data on the association of Culture-fair IQ and social class. Also, he made a systematic mistake throughout in correcting for errors of measurement, which I have discussed elsewhere (Loehlin, 1965). Taking his solution procedure, but modifying it to reflect a more appropriate correction for measurement error, I get results as follows (expressed as proportions of the total variance): environmental variance within families, .07; environmental variance between families, .13; hereditary variance within families, .33; hereditary variance between families, .36; and between-family heredity-environment covariance, .11. Note that Cattell's design differs from the others reported so far in being one-generational. All his data were in fact obtained from children within a limited age range, 10-15 years, a procedure that has certain advantages: the heritabilities of traits can differ at different ages, at least in principle, and the comparability of measurement across different ages or generations is always a thorny issue. Also, Cattell's data are independent of those used in the other analyses described in this section, but yield reasonably concordant results.

At about the same time Cyril Burt also presented a mode of analysis based on multiple groups, and illustrated it with IQ data from his own studies (Burt and Howard, 1956). Burt's approach was based on the correlations in four groups--MZs reared apart, parents and their offspring, siblings, and spouses--plus the reliability coefficient of the test. His procedure had some odd features. First, he used Fisher's formulas based on the assumption that all environmental factors were random to divide the trait variance into four parts: additive genetic expected under random mating, additive genetic due to assortative mating, nonadditive genetic, and random environmental. He then compared the genetic part of this, the sum of the first three components, with his correlation for MZ twins reared apart. He might plausibly have taken the difference as an estimate of systematic environmental effects in ordinary families, and readjusted values on this basis. But he didn't. Instead he rescaled all his four components downward until the genetic part matched the MZA correlation, subtracted error of measurement from what was left, and took the remainder as an estimate of systematic environmental effects. This in effect counts a good share of random environment twice, both as random environment and as measurement error, so Burt's procedure would seem to underestimate systematic environmental effects. As Burt says of his method: "It is, however, admittedly a makeshift... The use of simplified models inevitably invites attack from armchair critics" (Burt and Howard, 1956, p. 125n). At any rate, his results (for unadjusted group tests) were: total additive genetic, 60%; nonadditive genetic, 17%; systematic environment, 11%; random environment, 6%; and error, 6%. The alternative method would have given estimates of 16% for systematic and 1% for random environment.

A decade and a half later, Jinks and Fulker (1970) subjected Burt's data on IQ to several different analyses based on their own version of the Fisherian equations. Of most interest to our developing story is their emphasis on estimating genetic and environmental parameters from over-determined models, that is, with more equations than unknowns, and obtaining not only the best overall fit of the model to the data, but a statistical test of the goodness of that fit. By fitting models with more or fewer parameters, they attempted to seek the simplest models consistent with the data. They used a weighted least squares fitting procedure leading to an approximate maximum-likelihood solution and a large-sample χ^2 test of goodness of fit. To illustrate their procedure they solved six equations for three unknowns. The equations dealt with the observed correlations for MZ twins reared apart and together, for DZ twins and ordinary sibs reared together, and for siblings reared apart and unrelated children reared together by virtue of adoption, all from Burt's data (for adjusted assessments). The three unknown parameters solved for were G_2, genetic variance shared by siblings; G_1, genetic variance differing between siblings; and E_2, environmental variance shared by siblings. (A fourth parameter, E_1, environmental variance within families, was obtained at the end by subtraction.) After dropping one equation which proved to be anomalous (that for unrelated children reared together), they obtained a good fit to Burt's data, with the estimates G_1 = .40, G_2 = .47, E_1 = .07, and E_2 = .06. Jinks and Fulker did not include parent-child and spouse correlations in this particular analysis, but they have in later ones (Fulker, 1973; Jinks and Eaves, 1974).

In Appendix A of the book Inequality by Christopher Jencks and his associates (Jencks et al., 1972), path analysis reappeared on the scene for the analysis of IQ correlations based on multiple groups—in this case, correlations compiled from previous studies in the literature. I won't go into details about Jencks' procedure here; I have done some of this elsewhere (Loehlin et al., 1975, Appendix I; Loehlin, 1978). All that is necessary for our present purposes is to note that Jencks proceeded in a stepwise fashion, fitting part of the data at a time; that he fitted his models informally, rather than by a single all-over procedure with statistical tests; that he made a couple of mistakes in his path models, which, as it happened, tended pretty much to cancel each other out (Loehlin, 1978); that he leaned in the direction of including many parameters rather than few (e.g., separate parameters for the environmental resemblances of MZ and DZ twins); that he was sensitive to issues of range restriction and errors of measurement; and that he ended up with lower estimates of heritability than yielded by the previous methods we have discussed. Jencks' estimates were about .45 for heredity, .35 for environment, and .20 for gene-environment correlation (Jencks et al., p. 315).

More recently, Rao and Morton and their associates at the University of Hawaii (Morton, 1974; Rao et al., 1974, 1976, 1977, in press) have undertaken several path analyses based on Jencks' IQ compilations and other IQ data from the literature, engaging in the process in something of a running controversy with the Birmingham group of Jinks and Eaves and their colleagues (e.g., Jinks and Eaves, 1974; Eaves, 1975, 1977; Eaves et al., 1977a). The main methodological points at issue seem to be: (1) Covariances versus z-transformed correlations. The Birmingham group prefer to fit their models to variances and covariances on the grounds that they contain more information than correlations, and have simpler expectations. The Hawaii group favor z-transformed correlations, on the grounds that they are more likely to meet the normality assumptions underlying the statistical tests, especially with small samples. However, the use of correlations entails some special maneuvering when variances differ (e.g., for adopted children). (2) Path models. Hawaii uses them, Birmingham does not. In principle, this should be immaterial. Provided one writes equations that correctly and consistently embody one's intended assumptions, it does not matter whether they are arrived at via the heuristic of a path diagram or not. In practice, both groups have had their troubles doing this (Goldberger, 1978a, b, in press; Loehlin, 1978). (3) Environmental measures. The Hawaii group has tended to include indices of the IQ-relevant environment in their models, such as measures of socioeconomic status or Burks' more refined indices—they follow Wright here (and Shuttleworth). The Birmingham group's models typically treat environment as they do the genes, in the abstract, following the tradition of Fisher (and Burt and Cattell). (4) Assortative mating.

The Birmingham group normally assumes assortative mating to be based on phenotype for IQ, i.e., that mates select each other for intelligence. The Hawaii group usually assumes matching of spouses for childhood environments only. (5) Genetic dominance. The Hawaii group tends to favor models with genetic additivity. The Birmingham group typically finds a large variance component due to genetic dominance. (6) Equality of generations. The Birmingham group makes the assumption of comparability across generations for heredity and environmental parameters. The Hawaii group does not make this assumption for genetic and environmental paths, although they do seem willing to make it for gene-environment correlation (which is a little curious). Their solutions, like Wright's, have typically yielded lower heritabilities in the parental than in the offspring generation. With their other assumptions and the data they use they statistically reject the hypothesis of equal parameters in both generations. I have argued elsewhere (Loehlin, 1978) that adding the assumptions of phenotypic assortative mating and dominance to their path models would permit a satisfactory fit with the same parameters for both generations. This does not, of course, guarantee that these assumptions are correct.

Obviously, there are still differences of opinion on how best to pursue the unified strategy of combining data from different groups in a single analysis, but equally obviously there is interest in doing this, and some consensus on the broad outlines of the strategy: fitting overdetermined models to the data to arrive at best estimates of parameters and statistical tests of goodness of fit. Both the Honolulu and the Birmingham camps have directed at least a few coy glances recently in the direction of Jöreskog's methods (Rao et al., 1977, Appendix I; Eaves et al., 1977b; Martin and Eaves, 1977), but whether these represent the wave of the future in this area is yet to be determined.

MODELING ASSORTATIVE MATING AND ERRORS OF MEASUREMENT

The models discussed in the preceding section of the paper take differing approaches to handling assortative mating. Several of them also take measurement error into account, for example, by carrying out analyses on correlations corrected for attenuation. In this section, I would like to commend to you the principle that if you want your equations to act right, you should incorporate explicitly into your model the assumptions you intend to make concerning these matters.

Consider Figure 1. The left-hand part of the figure shows a path diagram representing the fact that fathers' genotypes and environments affect their IQs and educational levels in the manner and to the degrees specified. (The right-hand part makes identical assumptions for the mothers.) We are not given precise definitions of $\underline{G}$ and $\underline{E}$, but the figure shows that they are taken

316

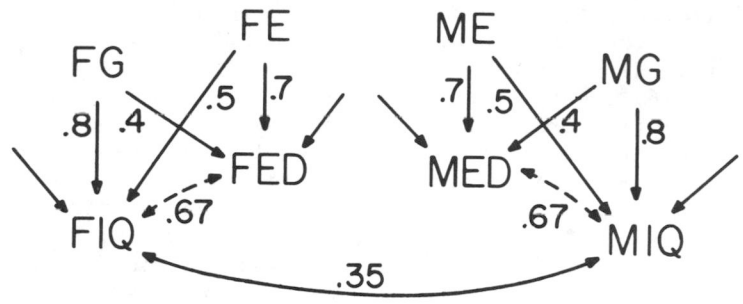

Figure 1. Assortative mating under two assumptions. Key: F = father, M = mother, G = genotype, E = environment, IQ = IQ, ED = years of education. $r_{FIQ,FED} = r_{MIQ,MED} = .8 \times .4 + .5 \times .7 = .67$.

if matching was on IQ:

$r_{FED,MED} = .35 \times .67^2 = .16$

$r_{FG,MG} = .8^2 \times .35 = .22$

$r_{FE,ME} = .5^2 \times .35 = .09$

if matching was on ED:

$r_{FED,MED} = .35/.67^2 = .78$

$r_{FG,MG} = .4^2 \times .78 = .12$

$r_{FE,ME} = .7^2 \times .78 = .38$

to be uncorrelated with one another and not exhaustive of the influences on IQ and education. As shown below the diagram, we can deduce a correlation of .67 between father's IQ and his educational level. The same holds for mothers. At the bottom of the diagram, the curved arrow indicates that father's and mother's IQs are correlated to the extent of .35 in this population. On the left-hand side below the diagram are shown the implications of one assumption often made about assortative mating, that it is phenotypic for IQ, that is, that the mating process matches spouses directly on the trait itself. On the right-hand side are shown the implications if assortative mating in fact takes place by matching spouses for a different but correlated trait, educational level, with the IQ correlation merely an incidental byproduct. Obviously, the two assumptions have quite different implications in this case. The correlations between spouses' genotypes enter into expectations concerning sibling correlations, so the correct representation of the assortative mating process could make a difference for the fit of the model to data. Incidentally, if these were real data, one would be inclined to prefer the right-hand over the left-hand model, since the observed correlation between spouses' educational levels typically exceeds that between their IQs--though seldom by quite as much as in the example.

Aficionados of path diagrams will notice that Figure 1 violates some of the canons of the genre. A more orthodox representation would have the arrow between FIQ and MIQ dotted rather than solid, and would add a series of curved arrows interconnecting the independent variables at the top of the diagram. Under phenotypic assortative mating, FE, FG and the unlabeled residual arrow would each be correlated with all three of the equivalent variables on the mother's side. The magnitude of these correlations would depend on the spouse correlation and the correlation of each with IQ, along the lines of the equations below the diagram. Figure 1a shows such an orthodox diagram for the case of phenotypic matching on IQ, and may suggest to the reader why I have preferred the representation used in Figure 1. If still dubious, he or she might wish to skip ahead a few pages to Figure 3, and imagine the same situation, multiplied manyfold, among the variables at the top of the figure, since both assortative mating and selective placement will induce a host of correlations of this sort. The representation used, however, while more readable, does necessitate some care in deriving equations from the diagram, since it is to the full diagram, not to the condensed version, that Wright's rules apply.

Figure 1 ignores errors of measurement. Let us bring these into the picture in Figure 2. This shows the IQ part of Figure 1, but now makes a distinction between the true intelligence of an individual, labeled I in the diagram, and the obtained test score, T. The reliability of the IQ test is assumed to be .80; its square root, .89, is taken as the value of the path from true score to test score. The observed correlation of .35 is of course

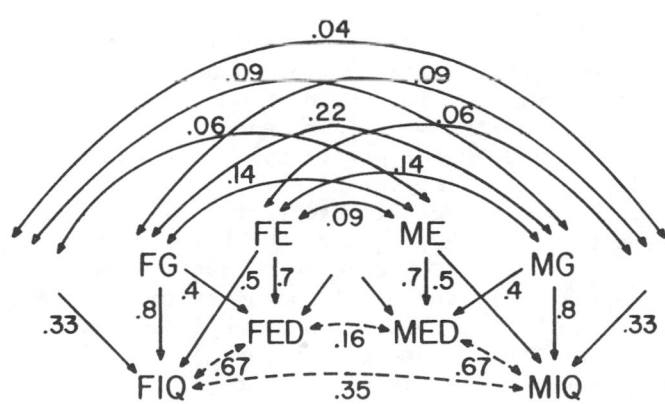

Figure 1a. Alternative representation of Figure 1, showing correlational paths explicitly, for the case of phenotypic selection based on IQ.

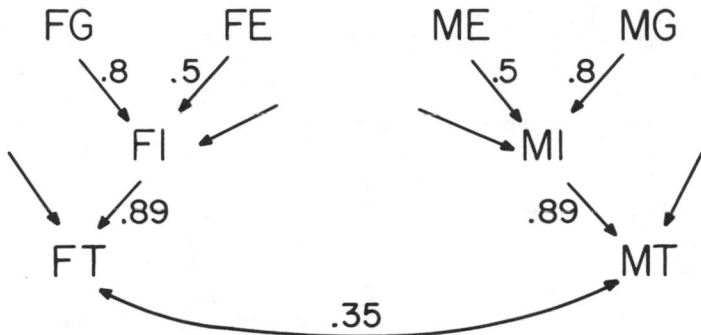

Figure 2. Assortative mating and measurement error. Key: F = father, M = mother, G = genotype, E = environment, I = actual intelligence, T = intelligence test score.

if matching was on T:

$$r_{FI,MI} = .35 \times .89^2 = .28$$
$$r_{FG,MG} = .8^2 \times .89^2 \times .35 = .18$$
$$r_{FE,ME} = .5^2 \times .89^2 \times .35 = .07$$

if matching was on I:

$$r_{FI,MI} = .35/.89^2 = .44$$
$$r_{FG,MG} = .8^2 \times .44 = .28$$
$$r_{FE,ME} = .5^2 \times .44 = .11$$

based on the test score. As can be seen below the diagram, taking the fallibility of the measurement into account makes a difference in one's expectations concerning the other correlations. If one treats phenotypic assortative mating as though it were based on the fallible measure (left) when the proposed mechanism involves the actual trait (right), one could be appreciably in error. In this particular example, one could alternatively proceed by correcting the observed correlation for attenuation and then using the simple model. But on the whole, it seems preferable to incorporate the assumptions made about error explicitly. And from the standpoint of proper statistical inference, it seems clearly better to test the fit to actual observations of a model incorporating measurement error, than to test the fit to adjusted numbers of a model that does not. These comments apply equally, of course, to all correlations in the model, not just those involving assortative mating. In brief, to treat observations known to contain error by a model that assumes its absence seems clearly a poor strategy, though the practice is not unheard of. The only guilty party I will single out by name is Loehlin (1978), though no doubt he would plead mitigating circumstances in that particular case, having to do with explicitly following the procedure of predecessors.

AN EXAMPLE FROM THE TEXAS ADOPTION STUDY

As a final, realistically-scaled example of the use of the unified strategy in combining data from various groups, I will apply a version of it to some data from the Texas Adoption Study. The details of this study are being reported elsewhere (Horn, et al., in press), so I will merely summarize a few of the relevant features here. The study involved 300 families who had adopted one or more children through a private, church-related home for unwed mothers in the southwestern United States. All adoptions were permanent, and placement was made within a week of birth. The unwed mothers had been given an intelligence test (and other tests) for counseling purposes while in residence at the home, and the adoptive parents and all available children, adopted and natural, were tested at the time of our study, usually by a local psychologist. About 40% of the adoptive families had one or more natural children. The study thus affords a number of potentially instructive correlations: between adoptive parents and their adopted and their natural children; between the unwed mothers and their adopted-away children; between the unwed mothers and other natural and adopted children in the homes into which their child was adopted; between natural and adoptive siblings; and so on. Table 3 gives correlations for twenty-one such combinations and the number of pairings on which each is based. It should be mentioned that some of these Ns are inflated: for example, a parent with two adopted children enters twice into the parent-adopted child correlations. The IQs given in Table 3 for adults are from the Revised Beta Examination, a nonverbal pencil-and-paper test which was the IQ test usually given to the unwed mothers at the agency. For children, the IQs are Performance IQs from the age-appropriate Wechsler test—in most cases the WISC, but for children over age 16, the WAIS. The Performance IQ is used, rather than the Full Scale IQ, because the Beta appears to measure abilities very similar to those measured by the Wechsler performance scales. Among the adoptive parents, who were given both tests, the correlation between Beta IQ and WAIS Performance IQ is nearly as high as the respective reliabilities of the tests permit.

Table 4 gives correlations of IQs in various groups with a socioeconomic index of the adoptive home. This index is an equally-weighted combination of father's and mother's education and father's occupation.

Figure 3 is a path model, from which the equations given in Table 5 are derived. Variables in the model are identified by paired capital letters, the first identifying the individual concerned, and the second the variable. A subscript is used if necessary to distinguish two individuals in the same class. Thus NG_1 is the genotype of the first of two natural children in the

Table 3

Correlations of Revised Beta IQs (adults) with Wechsler Performance
IQs (children) from the Texas Adoption Study

	Correlational Pairing	Correlation[a]	Pairs[b]
1.	Father and natural son	.260	75
2.	Father and natural daughter	.323	69
3.	Mother and natural son	.223	75
4.	Mother and natural daughter	.191	68
5.	Father and adopted son	.177	219
6.	Father and adopted daughter	.038	186
7.	Mother and adopted son	.236	217
8.	Mother and adopted daughter	.045	184
9.	Unwed mother and her son	.309	161
10.	Unwed mother and her daughter	.224	136
11.	Unwed mother and other adopted son[c]	.116	115
12.	Unwed mother and other adopted daughter[c]	.212	87
13.	Unwed mother and natural son[c]	−.148	77
14.	Unwed mother and natural daughter[c]	.284	66
15.	Adoptive father and mother	.240	292
16.	Unwed mother and adoptive mother	.140	337
17.	Unwed mother and adoptive father	.110	339
18.	Adopted children in family	.051	132
19.	Adopted and natural child	.240	159
20.	Natural children in family	.330	40
21.	Two unwed mothers[d]	.066	67

[a]Pearson rs, except 18, 20, and 21, calculated as intraclass
correlations, and 19 as a similarly calculated interclass
correlation.

[b]In 1–8 and 11–14 equals the number of children; in 16–17, the
number of unwed mothers; in 18–21, the number of df within
families.

[c]Refers to other children in the family into which her child
was adopted.

[d]Whose children were adopted into the same family.

___

family constellation portrayed, which consists of a mother, a
father, two natural children, two adopted children, and the biological mothers and fathers of the adopted children. Variables
representing observed quantities--IQ test scores and the socioeconomic index--are circled in the diagram. In the diagram, the
intelligence of each person (I) is represented as influenced by
four factors (not all always shown): the additive effects of the
genes (G), the effects of dominance deviations (D), common family

Table 4

Correlations of IQs with an index of the socioeconomic status[a] of
the adoptive family, Texas Adoption Study

	Group	Correlation	Pairs
1.	Adoptive fathers	.363	295
2.	Adoptive mothers	.322	293
3.	Natural sons	.086	75
4.	Natural daughters	.378	69
5.	Adopted sons	.155	222
6.	Adopted daughters	.179	184
7.	Unwed mothers	.323	342

[a]SES index an equally weighted sum of coded scores for mother's
education, father's education, father's occupational level. The
internal-consistency reliability of the index is .792 (Cronbach
alpha).

---

environment shared with his or her siblings (C), and unique environment (U)--the last is handled as a residual term, and thus also
includes any effects of genetic epistasis or gene-environment
interaction. U is by its definition uncorrelated with the other
three; D is by definition uncorrelated with G, and is taken to be
uncorrelated with C as well, since gene-environment correlations
in the model are assumed to arise from the transmission of both
genetic and environmental factors from parent to child, and
dominance deviations are not transmitted across generations.
However, C and G for a given individual reared in his natural
family will be correlated to an extent represented by a. The
paths ½ from parent's to offspring's additive genotype and the
correlation ¼ between the dominance deviations of siblings are
as specified by genetic theory. The values of paths i, j, k, and
l are set at the square roots of the internal-consistency reliabilities of the respective measures (Cronbach alphas based on the
correlations among subscales). The assumption is made of equivalence across generations, so that the parental parameters y and z
are equated to the childhood parameters c and h; and a in the
childhood generation (shown by dotted lines) to a in the parents'
generation. We will also consider a solution in which z and y
differ from h and c. Consistency is assumed across all members
of a given generation for the value of paths designated by the
same letter, and equivalence across the two sexes. Environmental
transmission is represented in the model as occurring in two ways:
via a path x representing the direct effect of a parents' phenotype on the environment shared by his or her children, and a path
f from the social and economic advantages of the home (E) to the
children's common environment (C).

322

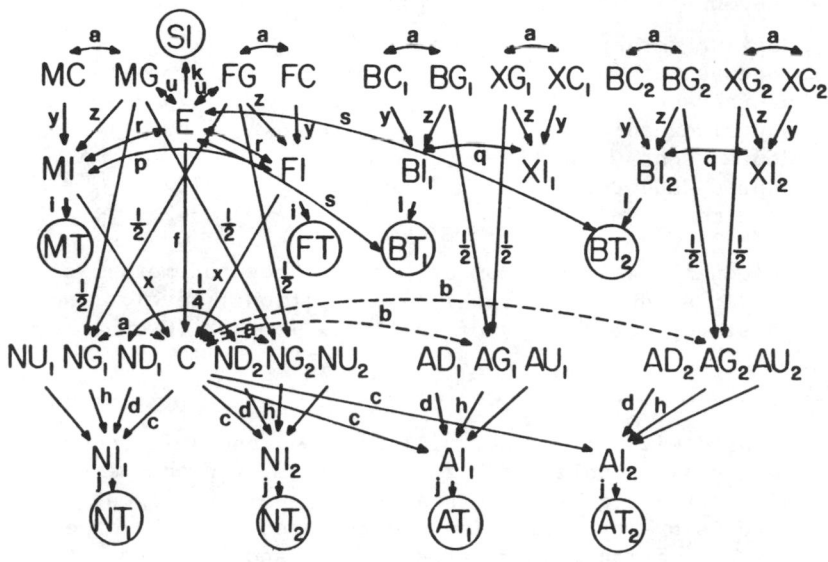

Figure 3. Path diagram for Texas Adoption Study analysis.
Key: F = father, M = mother, B = biological mother of adopted
child, X = unknown biological father, N = natural child in
adoptive family, A = adoptive child, G = additive genotype,
D = dominance deviations, C = common environment, U = unique
environment (residual), I = true intelligence, T = IQ test
score, E = social and economic advantages of the home, SI =
socioeconomic index. $y,z,x,f,h,d,c,i,j,k,l,\frac{1}{2}$ = paths; $a,b,p,q,$
$r,s,u,\frac{1}{4}$ = correlations. U and D not shown for parental generation. Residual paths not shown except for U's. Circled symbols
are empirically-observed measures.

Table 5

Equations for Texas Adoption Study analysis

Parameters solved for: h, c, d, f, x, p, r, s, u

Restrictions imposed: z=h, y=c, q=p, i=.877, j=.783, k=.890, 1=.835

Derived correlations:

$$r_{MI,MG} = g = z + ya$$

$$r_{NG,C} = a = xg(1+p) + fu$$

$$r_{E,C} = v = f + 2rx$$

$$r_{AG,C} = b = \tfrac{1}{2}g(1+q)1sv$$

ratio of natural to adopted child std. dev. =

$$t = 1/(1-2hca + 2hcb)^{\frac{1}{2}}$$

Equations for observed correlations:

$$r_{M,N} = r_{F,N} = [xc(1+p) + rfc + \tfrac{1}{2}gh(1+p)]ij$$

$$r_{M,A} = r_{F,A} = [xc(1+p) + rfc + \tfrac{1}{2}gh(1+q)1sr]tij$$

$$r_{B,A} = [\tfrac{1}{2}gh(1+q)1 + svc]tj$$

$$r_{B,N} = [svc+suh]j$$

$$r_{B,O} = [svc + \tfrac{1}{2}gh(1+q)1s^2]tj$$

$$r_{N,N} = [c^2 + \tfrac{1}{4}d^2 + 2hca + \tfrac{1}{2}h^2(1+pg^2)]j^2$$

$$r_{N,A} = [c^2 + hca + hcb + \tfrac{1}{2}gh(1+q)1suh]tj^2$$

$$r_{A,A} = [c^2 + 2hcb + \{\tfrac{1}{2}gh(1+q)1s\}^2]t^2j^2$$

$$r_{M,F} = p1^2$$

$$r_{M,B} = r_{F,B} = rsi$$

$$r_{B,B} = s^2$$

$$r_{S,M} = r_{S,F} = rik$$

$$r_{S,B} = sk$$

$$r_{S,N} = [vc + uh]kj$$

$$r_{S,A} = [vc + \tfrac{1}{2}gh(1+q)1s]tkj$$

Note: symbols as in Figure 3, except that terms entering observed correlations abbreviated to their first letter. O = other adopted child in family adopting own child, e.g., B_1 vs A_2.

Selective placement (s) is shown as occurring via matching of the measured IQ of the unwed mothers and the socioeconomic conditions of the adoptive home. This is intended to reflect the placement practices of this particular agency: they had the girls' IQ scores available, as well as considerable information on the social, educational, and economic condition of the prospective adoptive parents, and they appear to have used this information (along with other factors, such as physical characteristics, which are presumably irrelevant here) in arriving at a decision about a suitable placement.

Assortative mating is expressed as a correlation (p) between the intelligence of the two adoptive parents. Two assumptions are examined concerning the assortative mating of the unwed biological parents of an adopted child: one that it is the same (q = p), and one that it is less (q = ½p). We do not have test scores for the unwed fathers, but we do have educational information for many of them, and the correlation of the unwed parents for educational level is about the same as that of the adoptive parents. However, interpretation of this is somewhat complicated by the fact that many of the younger unwed parents were still in school, so we have also considered the alternative that assortative mating is lower in this group, as suggested by the results of Plomin et al. (1977b). The equations given in Table 5 are derived on the assumption that assortative mating is based on intelligence itself, but we will also examine the alternative possibility that assortative mating is based on a correlated trait that is more closely related to environment and less closely related to genotype than is IQ.

A correlation u is shown in the diagram between socioeconomic advantages E and parents' genotypes, MG or FG, and a correlation r between E and the natural parents' phenotypes.

The equations of Table 5 were solved for the nine parameters h, c, d, f, x, p, r, s, and u, using the 28 empirical correlations in Tables 3 and 4. The solution procedure was the one that I have used elsewhere (Loehlin, 1978). It involves setting the gene-environment correlation a to various values, solving the equations, and retaining the solution which yields a consistent value for a across generations.

Solutions under four assumptions are given in Table 6. In column 1 is shown the solution under the assumptions as given in Table 5 and described above. The χ^2 of 23.24 with 19 df implies a passable but not sensational fit of the model to the data. Taken at face value, it would mean that the odds are something like 1 in 5 that a fit this poor or worse would result from sampling error alone. I.e., we can't confidently reject it, but we shouldn't cheer very much either. Furthermore, the obtained χ^2 should not be taken strictly at face value--it provides at best

Table 6

Solutions of equations of Table 5 for data in Tables 3 and 4, under
four assumptions

Parameter	Table 5 assumptions	$q=\frac{1}{2}p$	$r_{GM,GF}=\frac{1}{2}pg^2$	$z=y=.5$
	(1)	(2)	(3)	(4)
h	.62	.63	.62	.72
c	.43	.44	.43	.43
d	.34	.26	.42	.00
f	.28	.32	.28	.29
x	.14	.12	.14	.14
p	.31	.31	.31	.31
r	.44	.44	.44	.44
s	.36	.36	.36	.36
u	.24	.22	.24	.20
Derived rs				
a	.19	.18	.19	.17
b	.05	.05	.05	.05
g	.70	.71	.70	.58
v	.40	.42	.40	.41
Fit				
χ^2	23.24	23.81	23.24	23.23
df	19	19	19	19
p	.20-.30	.20-.30	.20-.30	.20-.30

only a rough indication, for two reasons. First, as previously
noted, some of the Ns are inflated, which will tend to elevate
the χ^2. Second, the various correlations are not independent of
each other, since the same individuals enter into several correlations. This will tend to lower the χ^2 (Rao et al., 1977). One
would not expect these two errors to compensate each other exactly,
but they may justify our assuming that the goodness (or poorness)
of fit is at least somewhere in the vicinity of that shown.

Of perhaps as much interest as the overall fit of the model
is the question of where the shoe pinches. In Table 7 are shown
the observed and expected z-transformed correlations, and the
individual contributions to χ^2, for the solution in column 1 of
Table 6. This is a weighted fit, and the χ^2 values reflect both
the sizes of the discrepancies and the number of pairs on which

they are based.

Two of the three largest contributions to χ^2 involve cases where there is no reason to suspect other than chance factors to be responsible, namely, deviations among correlations of the unwed mother with children other than her own in the adoptive family. Thus it is probably unwise to do much interpreting of the other large discrepancies, such as the higher-than-expected correlation of the adoptive mother and her adopted son, for which one can more readily come up with plausible post hoc scenarios.

If we accept the model as a whole as constituting an acceptable fit to the data, we may consider its implications for a heritability analysis along traditional lines: $h^2 = .38$, $\underline{d}^2 = .12$, $\underline{c}^2 = .19$, $2\underline{hca} = \text{cov}_{hc} = .10$, and unique environment, epistasis, and gene-environment interaction $= .21$. The broad-sense heritability is .50, the independent effect of environment is .40 (or less, depending on epistasis, etc.), and the correlated effect of genes and environment accounts for .10 of the variance.

The second column of Table 6 shows that the model is not very sensitive to the assumption about assortative mating in the unwed parents. Lowering the assortative mating to half the value of that between the adoptive parents changes the results very little. The fit to the data is if anything a little worse under this assumption, although obviously not significantly so.

The third column asks about the assumption concerning the basis of assortative mating. The column 1 solution assumes that mate selection is based on phenotypic IQ. But suppose that the spouse correlation for IQ were merely a byproduct of matching spouses on another variable or variables correlated with IQ, such as education or socioeconomic status. Most of the equations in this particular model depend on the spouse correlation itself and are indifferent to how it is brought about. But for the natural sibling equation, it can make a difference. The term $\underline{pg}^2$ in parentheses is the implied correlation between spouses' additive genotypes, if the assortment is on intelligence itself. If the actual basis of assortment is on some variable less highly correlated with genotype, this correlation should be lower. The solution in column 3 of Table 6 is with this correlation reduced by half. As can be seen, this has an effect in only one place-- it increases the estimate of $\underline{d}$ (and hence the estimate of the broad heritability to .55). The parameter $\underline{d}$ appears only in the equation for natural sibs reared together, so it automatically absorbs any discrepancy of this correlation from the rest. And it appears as $\frac{1}{4} \underline{d}^2$, greatly magnifying any errors in its estimation. Furthermore, the empirical correlation for natural siblings is based on the smallest $\underline{N}$ in the table, giving it the largest sampling error. So $\underline{d}^2$ estimates from this study should be regarded with

Table 7

Discrepancies between z-transformed correlations expected under the
model with the parameter values of column 1 in Table 6, and those
actually observed

Correlational grouping	z-transformed correlation			
	Expected	Observed	Pairs[a]	χ^2
Adoptive father, natural son	.29	.27	75	.04
Adoptive father, natural daughter	.29	.34	69	.13
Adoptive mother, natural son	.29	.23	75	.30
Adoptive mother, natural daughter	.29	.19	68	.62
Adoptive father, adopted son	.12	.18	219	.76
Adoptive father, adopted daughter	.12	.04	186	1.22
Adoptive mother, adopted son	.12	.24	217	3.12
Adoptive mother, adopted daughter	.12	.04	184	1.01
Unwed mother, own son	.25	.32	161	.85
Unwed mother, own daughter	.25	.23	136	.04
Unwed mother, other adopted son	.07	.12	115	.20
Unwed mother, other adopted daughter	.07	.22	87	1.67
Unwed mother, natural son in family	.09	−.15	77	4.22
Unwed mother, natural daughter in family	.09	.29	66	2.58
Adoptive father and mother	.24	.24	292	.00
Unwed mother, adoptive mother	.14	.14	337	.01
Unwed mother, adoptive father	.14	.11	339	.23
Among adopted children	.15	.05	132	1.26
Between natural and adopted children	.17	.24	159	.83
Among natural children	.34	.34	40	.00
Between biological mothers	.13	.07	67	.24
SES of home and father's IQ	.35	.38	295	.21
SES of home and mother's IQ	.35	.33	293	.12
SES of home and natural son's IQ	.23	.09	75	1.44
SES of home and natural daughter's IQ	.23	.40	69	1.91
SES of home and adopted son's IQ	.19	.16	222	.22
SES of home and adopted daughter's IQ	.19	.18	184	.01
SES of home and unwed mother's IQ	.33	.34	342	.02

[a]See explanation in Table 3

considerable skepticism.

The fourth and final column of Table 6 shows the consequences of relaxing the assumption of equality of h and c across generations. A direct separate solution for z and y proved impossible: their values are not uniquely determined by the equation set. However, the effect of a lower heritability in the parent generation was assessed by setting z and y arbitrarily both to .5 and then solving for the other parameters. The results, given in column 4 of Table 6, do not suggest that moving in this direction will improve the fit of the model. The childhood estimate of h^2 rises (to .52), about enough to compensate for the parental decrease (to .25). One of the most conspicuous differences between this and the other solutions is the drop of the d parameter to zero, but we gave reasons earlier why estimates of this particular parameter should be regarded with some skepticism.

Another thing that this general strategy allows us to do is to test particular hypotheses about parameters. Thus we can set individual parameters in the model to zero, and see whether the fit of the model to the data becomes significantly worse. The difference in χ^2 can itself be tested as a χ^2 with 1 df (Rao et al., 1974).

Table 8 shows some examples. Setting h, c, p, r or s to zero leads to a significant deterioration in fit. Setting d, f, x or u to zero does not. This is so for the environmental transmission parameters f and x merely because either can stand in for the other--setting both to zero leads to a significant increase in χ^2 ($\chi^2 = 10.55$, 2 df). Deleting all the genetic relationships from the model (h = d = u = 0) clearly worsens the fit; deleting the environmental paths (c = f = x = 0) does too. Finally, at the bottom of Table 8, are considered a few hypotheses dealing with parameter values other than zero. The test of d = 1 suggests that the present data will be unable to reject any hypothesis about dominance within its possible range (values of d near 1 can, however, be rejected on other grounds, since they lead to negative residual variance). The two hypotheses for h correspond to two values for the narrow heritability of IQ quoted in the literature (by Loehlin et al., 1975, p. 84, and Jensen, 1973, p. 178). Neither agrees with the present data. We may push this approach a step further, and find the range within which tolerable values of a given parameter lie. For example, values of h below .42 and above .77 produce increases in χ^2 of more than 3.84 above the best-fit value, and hence correspond to a 95% confidence interval for this parameter. If we employ a double criterion based on significant increase in χ^2 or presence of negative residual variance we may set limits of acceptability for d of 0 to .58, for c of .34 to .58, and for h of .48 to .77, respectively, for the data of the present study.

Table 8

Some tests of hypotheses about particular

parameters, for the model of Table 5

Hypothesis	Increase in χ^2	df	p
h = 0	13.63	1	<.001
c = 0	15.67	1	<.001
d = 0	.01	1	.90<p<.95
f = 0	1.15	1	.20<p<.30
x = 0	1.59	1	.20<p<.30
f = x = 0	10.55	2	<.01
p = 0	17.07	1	<.001
r = 0	84.49	1	<.001
s = 0	54.15	1	<.001
u = 0	1.61	1	.20<p<.30
h = d = u = 0	14.76	3	<.01
c = f = x = 0	15.67	3	<.01
d = 1	.68	1	.30<p<.50
h = $\sqrt{.64}$	5.33	1	.02<p<.05
h = $\sqrt{.71}$	8.22	1	<.01

Another interesting possibility is to examine the sensitivity of the model's parameter estimates to variations in the input correlations. For example, the present model has been run with each of the z-transformed input correlations alternatively increased and decreased by .20 from its original value. Space does not permit a complete tabulation of the results, but a few examples are presented in Table 9.

Looking down the columns of the table, it will be seen that the parameters differ in how they respond to variation in the input. Some, like p and s, are virtually unaffected by changes in most correlations, but sensitive to the one or two that enter most directly into their determination. Thus p, the parameter for spouse correlation, is almost entirely a function of the observed spouse correlation MF, and s, the selective placement parameter, is strongly related to the correlation SB between the SES of the adoptive home and the unwed mother's IQ. The parameter r is also a member of this category, but the correlations that most affect it, SM and SF, happen not to be included in Table 9. At the other extreme is a parameter such as d that is highly unstable, swinging from zero to large values (even impossible ones like 1.09) in response to changes in many different input correlations.

Intermediate are the substantively interesting parameters h, c, x, f, and a, which respond with relatively modest shifts

Table 9

Sensitivity of parameter estimates to variations

in individual input correlations

Parameters

Input z	h	c	r	p	s	d	u	x	f	a
Original data	.62	.43	.44	.31	.36	.34	.24	.14	.28	.19
MF = .445	.56	.44	.44	.54	.36	.48	.26	.11	.30	.19
MF = .045	.69	.42	.44	.06	.36	.00	.22	.19	.23	.21
FSA = .379	.55	.42	.44	.31	.36	.42	.25	.29	.18	.30
FSA = -.021	.68	.46	.43	.31	.35	.24	.24	-.02	.37	.07
MDN = .393	.64	.42	.43	.31	.35	.00	.26	.17	.21	.22
MDN = -.007	.58	.45	.44	.31	.36	.51	.22	.10	.34	.16
AA = .251	.60	.56	.43	.31	.36	.00	.21	.11	.24	.15
AA = -.149	.62	.28	.44	.31	.36	.73	.27	.22	.39	.31
NN = .543	.62	.43	.44	.31	.36	1.09	.24	.14	.28	.19
NN = .143	.59	.40	.43	.31	.36	.00	.24	.15	.32	.21
BSA = .519	.73	.43	.44	.31	.36	.00	.22	.07	.32	.14
BSA = .119	.49	.44	.43	.31	.35	.68	.27	.20	.25	.22
SB = .535	.61	.43	.41	.31	.49	.40	.26	.16	.20	.20
SB = .135	.62	.44	.45	.31	.21	.21	.22	.12	.34	.18

to a variety of different changes in input correlations, but to some more than others. The common environment parameter c is more sensitive to changes in adoptive sibling correlations, for example, than to changes in parent-child correlations. The additive genetic parameter h, on the other hand, responds more to variation in parent-child correlations than to variations in sibling correlations. In Table 9, h shows more sensitivity to changes in BSA, the biological correlation between an unwed mother and her adopted-away child, than it does to changes in the biological correlation MDN in the adoptive family. This partly reflects the fact that MDN is one of four such correlations in the data set (FSN, FDN, MSN, and MDN), whereas BSA is one of only two (BSA and BDA); the alteration of a single correlation would be expected to have greater effects in the latter case.

The parameters a, x, and f show a similar pattern of some variation in response to a number of input changes--more for some than for others. However, the most striking general feature of Table 9, and the larger table from which it was abstracted, is that most of the parameter estimates, except for d, tend to be reasonably stable in the face of the sort of fluctuation to be expected from sampling variation in samples of these sizes (recall that .20 represents about 2 standard errors for a low correlation based on 100 pairs). For instance, h exceeds c, and both exceed f, x or a, under nearly all the conditions in Table 9, even though each of these parameters shows variation in response to input.

I do not wish to suggest that this implies that the value of h^2 or c^2 or a from this study should unhesitatingly be applied to the general population. There are other questions, such as the representativeness of this sample of adoptive families, that need to be considered before taking such a step. But in any case, the purpose of this chapter is not to ascertain a "correct" value for the heritability of IQ (or any other trait). It is to consider a particular approach to embodying genetic and environmental (and psychometric) theory into models that can be fit simultaneously to a variety of pieces of data.

SUMMARY AND CONCLUSIONS

In this chapter, two strategies were considered for fitting gene-environment models to data from various kinship groups. One is to estimate parameters separately in different portions of the data, and compare the results. The other is to fit a single over-determined model to all the data, with an overall statistical test of goodness of fit. These two strategies were illustrated by simple hypothetical examples, and then the second was examined in more detail: first in the historical perspective of estimating genetic and environmental influences on IQ; secondly with respect to particular assumptions about assortative mating and measurement error; and finally as applied illustratively to data from the Texas Adoption Study.

In conclusion, I should reemphasize that my concentration on the second of the two strategies in this chapter is not meant to downgrade the first. Calculations that can be carried out on the backs of envelopes have considerable appeal, and with reason. But I do suspect that the second strategy is here to stay. Something like this strategy, I am persuaded, will continue to be attractive to many human behavior geneticists. The precise form it will come to take, and whether it sweeps the field against other strategies, remain to be seen.

REFERENCES

Burks, B. S. The relative influence of nature and nurture upon mental development. 27th Yearbook of the National Society for the Study of Education, 1928, Part 1, 219-316.

Burt, C., and Howard, M. The multifactorial theory of inheritance and its application to intelligence. British Journal of Statistical Psychology, 1956, 9, 95-131.

Cattell, R. B. Research designs in psychological genetics with special reference to the multiple variance analysis method. American Journal of Human Genetics, 1953, 5, 76-93.

Cattell, R. B., Blewett, D. B., and Beloff, J. R. The inheritance of personality. American Journal of Human Genetics, 1955, 7, 122-146.

Cattell, R. B., Stice, G. F., and Kristy, N. F. A first approximation to nature-nurture ratios for eleven primary personality factors in objective tests. Journal of Abnormal and Social Psychology, 1957, 54, 143-159.

Eaves, L. J. Testing models for variation in intelligence. Heredity, 1975, 34, 132-136.

Eaves, L. J. Inferring the causes of human variation. Journal of the Royal Statistical Society, 1977, Series A, 140, 324-355.

Eaves, L. J., Last, K., Martin, N. G., and Jinks, J. L. A progressive approach to non-additivity and genotype-environmental covariance in the analysis of human differences. British Journal of Mathematical and Statistical Psychology, 1977, 30, 1-42. (a)

Eaves, L. J., Martin, N. G., and Eysenck, S. B. G. An application of the analysis of covariance structures to the psychogenetical study of impulsiveness. British Journal of Mathematical and Statistical Psychology, 1977, 30, 185-197. (b)

Fulker, D. W. A biometrical genetic approach to intelligence and schizophrenia. Social Biology, 1973, 20, 266-275.

Goldberger, A. S.   Structural equation models in the social
    sciences. Econometrica, 1972, 40, 979-1001.
Goldberger, A. S.   The non-resolution of IQ inheritance by path
    analysis. American Journal of Human Genetics, 1978, 30,
    442-445. (a)
Goldberger, A. S.   Models and methods in the IQ debate: Part I
    (revised) (mimeo). Social Systems Research Institute,
    University of Wisconsin-Madison, 1978. (b)
Goldberger, A. S.   Pitfalls in the resolution of IQ inheritance,
    in N. E. Morton and C. S. Chung (Eds.), Genetic epidemiology.
    Academic Press, New York, in press.
Goldberger, A. S., and Duncan, O. D. (Eds.), Structural equation
    models in the social sciences. Seminar Press, New York, 1973.
Holzinger, K. J.   The relative effect of nature and nurture
    influences on twin differences. Journal of Educational
    Psychology, 1929, 20, 241-248.
Horn, J. M., Loehlin, J. C., and Willerman, L.   Intellectual
    resemblance among adopted and biological relatives: The
    Texas Adoption Project. Behavior Genetics, in press.
Jencks, C., Smith, M., Acland, H., Bane, M. J., Cohen, D., Gintis,
    H., Heyns, B., and Michaelson, S. Inequality: A reassessment
    of the effect of family and schooling in America. Basic
    Books, New York, 1972.
Jinks, J. L., and Fulker, D. W.   Comparison of the biometrical
    genetical, MAVA, and classical approaches to the analysis of
    human behavior. Psychological Bulletin, 1970, 75, 311-349.
Jinks, J. L., and Eaves, L. J.   IQ and inequality. Nature, 1974,
    248, 287-289.
Loehlin, J. C.   Some methodological problems in Cattell's Multiple
    Abstract Variance Analysis. Psychological Review, 1965,
    72, 156-161.
Loehlin, J. C.   Heredity-environment analyses of Jencks's IQ
    correlations. Behavior Genetics, 1978, 8, 415-436.
Loehlin, J. C., Lindzey, G., and Spuhler, J. N. Race differences
    in intelligence. Freeman, San Francisco, 1975.
Martin, N. G., and Eaves, L. J.   The genetical analysis of covari-
    ance structures. Heredity, 1977, 38, 79-95.
Morton, N. E.   Analysis of family resemblance. I: Introduction.
    American Journal of Human Genetics, 1974, 26, 318-330.
Morton, N. E., and Rao, D. C.   Quantitative inheritance in man
    (mimeo). Population Genetics Laboratory, University of
    Hawaii, 1978.
Plomin, R., DeFries, J. C., and Loehlin, J. C. Genotype-environment
    interaction and correlation in the analysis of human behavior.
    Psychological Bulletin, 1977, 84, 309-322. (a)
Plomin, R., DeFries, J. C., and Roberts, M. K. Assortative mating
    by unwed biological parents of adopted children. Science,
    1977, 196, 449-450. (b)
Rao, D. C., and Morton, N. E.   IQ as a paradigm in genetic
    epidemiology, in N. E. Morton and C. S. Chung (Eds.),
    Genetic epidemiology. Academic Press, New York, in press.

Rao, D. C., Morton, N. E., Elston, R. C., and Yee, S. Causal analysis of academic performance. Behavior Genetics, 1977, 7, 147-159.

Rao, D. C., Morton, N. E., and Yee, S. Analysis of family resemblance. II. A linear model for familial correlation. American Journal of Human Genetics, 1974, 26, 331-359.

Rao, D. C., Morton, N. E., and Yee, S. Resolution of cultural and biological inheritance by path analysis. American Journal of Human Genetics, 1976, 28, 228-242.

Shuttleworth, F. K. The nature versus nurture problem. Part II. The contributions of nature and nurture to individual differences in intelligence. Journal of Educational Psychology, 1935, 26, 655-681.

Wright, S. Statistical methods in biology. Journal of the American Statistical Association, 1931, 26, 155-163.

COMMENT BY D. W. FULKER

    I am very pleased to be the official discussant for Dr. John Loehlin's paper, having admired his timely and original research in behaviour genetics for many years. During this time he has, amongst other things, pioneered multivariate analysis, clarified Cattell's MAVA, written with sensitivity and insight on the question of race and intelligence and most recently developed the application of path analysis in behaviour genetics, becoming the leading authority on the subject. It is an application of path analysis to familial data on intelligence that forms the subject of the present paper.

    The first part of the paper discusses the logic of model fitting by contrasting piecemeal approaches, such as that used by Christopher Jencks in his book "Inequality", with the approach involving the simultaneous estimation of parameters from the data set as a whole. It concludes that although the former approach is quite adequate for some purposes and much simpler computationally, the latter provides the best all round evaluation of the suggested model, since it leads to statistical tests of some of the underlying assumptions especially when the model is well overdetermined.

    This conclusion is one the present discussant can wholeheartedly agree with, the overall approach having also been advocated by the Birmingham School, for the same reasons, since the early 1970s. However, there is a difficult statistical problem involved in this approach where the data points are not independently determined, as in the case of an extensive path analysis from a single study such as the one Dr. Loehlin uses to illustrate the approach in the final section of his paper. The problem is acknowledged, but I would like to take the opportunity to draw attention to the potential solution using the pedigree approach of Lange, Westlake and Spence (1976) which can be used to estimate genetic and environmental parameters for irregular pedigrees by the method of maximum likelihood solely on the assumption of multivariate normality of the original data. The procedure is quite difficult to program for the computer and time consuming to run. However, it appears to be entirely feasible, quite robust and conceptually straightforward from my own experience of it. It has the advantage of yielding proper χ^2 goodness of fit tests and standard errors for the parameter estimates in just such situations as the present one.

    The paper briefly discusses the points of contact and differences between various biometrical schools, with the general implication with which I would also, in general, agree, that it doesn't much matter which approach one uses so long as assumptions are made clear and the method is correctly applied. One small point I would like to take up, though, concerns the use of covariances and variances as against the use of correlations as basic data in fitting biometrical models. The Rao et al. approach via z-transformed correlations is certainly an excellent one where raw data is not available, say in the re-analysis of published data, which nearly always appears as correlations. However, where raw data is available, as for example in the adoption study discussed in the present paper, I can see no advantage in working with correlations. In fact, there is a distinct disadvantage, since with variances and covariances the inequality of variance between adopted and non-adopted individuals, expected on many of the models, can be estimated from the data in a much more direct manner. In the correlation approach this difference in variance enters only indirectly as an additional parameter. The correlational approach thus throws away information. Incidentally, the Lange et al. pedigree approach previously advocated not only has the advantage statistically over the z-transform approach but also deals directly with variances and covariances.

The paper contains an excellent discussion of the importance of being clear about the assumptions made concerning assortative mating and error of measurement in model building, showing how the mechanism of assortative mating affects the genetic correlation among siblings to quite a considerable extent.

The final section of the paper presents an elaborate and very elegant path analysis of intelligence test scores in the Texas Adoption Study which involves both natural and adopted children of natural and adoptive parents. The analysis sets a very high standard for the treatment of adoption data, utilising a variety of data on test scores and measures of the environment. In all, some 28 correlations are used to estimate the 9 basic parameters of the model, this high degree of overdetermination providing a powerful test of the underlying assumptions. The discussant looks forward with great interest to a promised, much fuller account of this analysis.

Reference

Lange, K., Westlake, J., & Spence, M. A. Extensions to pedigree analysis. III. Variance components by the scoring method. Annals of Human Genetics, 1976, 39, 485-491.

SOME IMPLICATIONS OF BIOMETRICAL GENETICAL ANALYSIS FOR PSYCHOLOGICAL RESEARCH

D. W. Fulker

Department of Psychology, Institute of Psychiatry
De Crespigny Park, London

Introduction

Behaviour genetics is capable of offering a number of insights to the theoretical psychologist, these being based on information of two kinds. In the first place it can provide information concerning the general nature of the influences that determine behavioural variation; whether or not there are genetic influences and, if so, what their basis might be, what kinds of environmental influences there are and whether these genetic and environmental influences interact. At a qualitative level, identifying these sources of variation helps focus on the type of explanation a theoretical account of the behaviour should provide, steering the psychologist away from some kinds of theories and steering him towards others. At a quantitative level, the extent of the different influences will impose limits on the relative importance of the constructs that make up the theory. The second kind of information behaviour genetics provides is less concerned with the immediate causes of behavioural variation and more with the ultimate ones that have shaped its evolution and led to its present form, that is with the forces of natural selection and the adaptive significance of the behaviour. Thus, behaviour genetics offers the psychologist an aid to the development of plausible theories as well as a more general conceptual framework in which they may subsequently be placed. It is the purpose of the present paper to discuss these ideas from the point of view of biometrical genetics, drawing on illustrative material from studies of humans and laboratory animals.

I. STRAIN STUDIES

(i) Genotype-environment interaction

Establishing that behavioural variation is determined by genetic as well as by environmental influences immediately raises the question of how general we can expect a theoretical explanation to be. Given polygenic control of behaviour, which is the rule rather than the exception, even though the individual is genetically unique he may be phenotypically indistinguishable from many others. Unfortunately for the theoretician, he cannot, therefore, expect individuals, even when they may appear to be of similar type, to respond to situational stimuli in the same way. A satisfactory theoretical explanation for the behaviour of one individual may be quite unsatisfactory for another.

A small pilot study carried out in collaboration with Martin Seligman, concerning his theory of "learned helplessness" as the cause of depression, illustrates the point. Seligman's (1975) theory is that inescapable aversive stimulation has the effect, eventually, of causing the individual to believe that many other aversive situations are inescapable, too, even when they are not. The individual learns to be helpless, displaying the unhappiness and apathy characteristic of depression. The theory was developed using dogs as experimental subjects and electric shock as an aversive stimulus. However, there was considerable difficulty in demonstrating the effects in the laboratory rat (Seligman and Beagley, 1975). Casual observation of rats from the Roman Low Avoidance strain (RLA) selectively bred at Birmingham for poor performance in the shuttle box (Broadhurst & Bignami, 1965) suggested that they might be prone to heplessness in strongly aversive situations. Animals from this strain, together with those from their sister strain selected for high performance, the Roman High Avoidance strain (RHA) were divided into inescapable pre-shock and unshocked control groups. Subsequently the two groups were scored for failure to escape during avoidance training in a shuttle box, which resulted in the marked RLA pre-shock effect shown in Figure 1. Inescapable pre-shock had very little effect on RHA escape behaviour and what effect there was rapidly disappeared. RHA rats appear to be practically immune to helplessness. RLA rats, on the other hand, showed an extreme reaction to inescapable pre-shock, becoming increasingly unable to escape as triels progressed, even though they were not markedly different from the RHA strain under control conditions.

Since the two strains are both capable of learning to escape under normal control conditions, the study suggests an explanation of the pre-shock effect will require constructs in addition to those of learning theory, in which terms Seligman's explanation is exclusively couched. These constructs would have to be

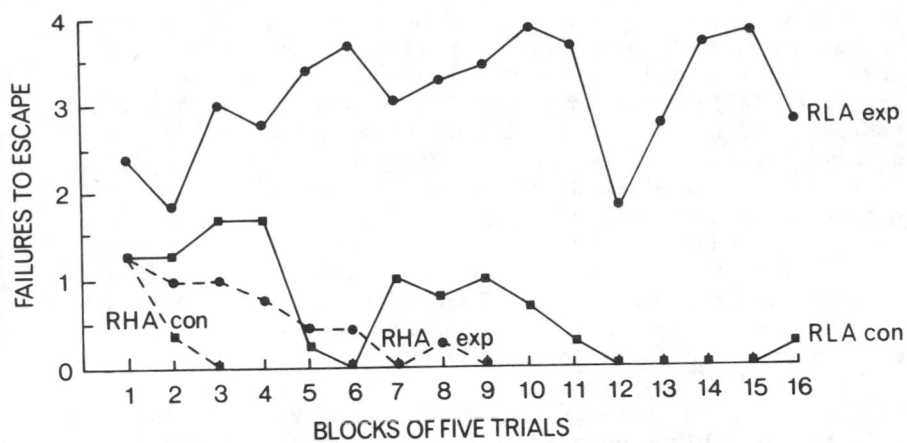

Figure 1. The effect of prior uncontrollable shock on performance
during escape-avoidance conditioning: non-escapes.
RHA rats are only slightly affected by inescapable
shock. RLA control rats show some non-escapes but
eventually learn to escape on every trial. RLA experimental rats are affected by inescapable shock a
great deal and appear to become progressively worse as
training proceeds. The divergence between RLA experimental and control groups is highly significant (p<.001).

consistent with a strong element of constitutional predisposition.
From what we know of the RLA strain and its motor responses under
stress, the alternative theory of Weiss (Weiss & Glazer, 1975) involving changes in brain biochemistry and corresponding motor
deficits resulting from inescapable shock, is more plausible than
the theory of learned helplessness. The lack of general applicability demonstrated for Seligman's theory, combined with our knowledge of the strains involved, points to the need for a different
kind of theory.

This problem of generalisability is, formally, one of genotype-
environmental interaction, which has received considerable attention from Broadhurst and colleagues in the U.K. (Broadhurst &
Jinks, 1966; Fulker et al., 1972) and from Henderson (1968, 1970a,
b) in the USA. Henderson's studies have been concerned mainly
with the developmental effects of stress, infantile stimulation,
environmental enrichment and the like, and are particularly relevant
in the present context. Typically, he has found that different
genotypes respond in quite different ways to these environmental
variables and therefore any theory that omitted to consider genetic
predisposition would have little generality.

340

(ii) Genetic correlations

The strain study just described demonstrates an interesting genotype-environmental interaction and illustrates the value of developing a behavioural theory within a genetic framework. However, it is deficient in two important respects. Firstly, it involves only two strains. Thus not only do we have a limited idea of how general the pre-shock effect might be, but neither are we able to relate established differences between the two strains to the observed effect with any degree of certainty, since with only two strains such relationships might simply be fortuitous. When we include more strains, or other distinct genotypes in a study, multivariate techniques can be used to explore the structure of the genetic correlations to see how the behaviour is organised at a constitutional level.

Even the simplest form of multivariate analysis can shed light on the likely mechanisms underlying behavioural variation. For example, Rick et al. (1971), using 8 strains of rats, looked at the correlations between additive effects for measures of activity, in the open field and in the shuttle box, avoidance learning and emotional defecation and a bio-chemical measure, the concentration of the inhibitory transmitter Gamma Amino-butyric Acid (GABA) in the rat cortex. Both phenotypic and genetic correlations between GABA and the behavioural measures are shown in Table 1.

Table 1

Correlations for GABA in rat cortex and measures
of learning, activity and emotional defecation

	Phenotypic	Genetic
AV30	-.37	-.85
ITC	-.44	-.96
Ambulation	-.19	-.55
Defecation	+.20	+.20

AV30 is total avoidance score during 30 trials in a shuttle box. ITC is the frequency of intertrial crossing in the shuttle box. Ambulation and defecation are total scores over 4 days of 2-minute testing in the open field.

Phenotypic correlations are weak and fail to demonstrate convincingly any marked relationship. The genetic correlations,

on the other hand, clearly identify a strong negative relationship
between activity and GABA. In fact for inter-trial crossing in
the shuttle box (ITC) the rank correlation for the 8 additive effects was precisely -1.0, indicating a perfect relationship. However, while GABA is clearly related to activity, it is hardly related at all to emotional defecation. A relationship between GABA
and activity has recently been replicated by Gaitonde and Festing
(1976) using a similar approach involving 12 strains of mice.
Thus even very simple approaches to genetic correlations such as
these enable us to "freeze" phenotypes and identify constitutional
relationships. More sophisticated multivariate techniques which
will be discussed when we consider human behaviour would allow a
more effective investigation of these relationships.

(iii) Crossbreeding, gene action and adaptive significance

The second deficiency of the simple two strain study lies in
the lack of information it provides concerning the gene-action
underlying phenotypic variation, information which we need if we
are to gain insight into the adaptive significance of the behaviour. In order to obtain this information a crossbreeding design
must be employed, followed by an appropriate biometrical analysis
of the data. The aim of this kind of analysis is to partition the
phenotypic variation into various genetic and environmental components, the genetic ones indicating the main features of the
gene-action underlying the phenotype.

Fairly simple biometrical designs, involving inbred strains,
can be used to determine whether the genes act in an additive
fashion or non-additively as with dominance and epistasis, whether
the non-additivity is uni- or ambi-directional, and whether a few
or many genes are involved. The gene-action revealed by these designs will be a vestigial form of that present in the natural populations from which the strains were originally obtained. Mather
(1953) has argued that this information will allow us to make inferences about the history of natural selection and learn something of the adaptive significance of the trait in question. In
general, it is argued, phenotypes controlled by directional
dominance or gene interaction which results in extreme expression
of the trait in hybrids will also have been subject to natural
selection for an extreme, the gene-action having evolved to maintain this optimal level in the population. This kind of gene-
action indicates the adaptive superiority of an extreme level of
the phenotype. However, those traits controlled by additive genes
will have been subject to natural selection for an intermediate
optimum, this being the adaptively superior phenotypic expression.
In Drosophila, for example, viability, which is necessarily a component of fitness, is controlled by directional dominance and epistasis for extreme expression (Breeze & Mather, 1960) as is an

obvious behavioural component of fitness, male mating speed
(Fulker, 1966). The number of sternoplural chaeta, on the other
hand, a phenotype known to be subject to stabilising selection
for an intermediate optimum (Kearsey & Barnes, 1970; Linney et al.,
1975), has been shown to be controlled exclusively by additive
genes.

The main value of this approach, however, lies in the information it provides when the adaptive function of the behaviour is
far from obvious. In this case it can be used to classify traits
into those with high, low or intermediate optima. Often the approach can provide surprising information. For example, recently
Quinn, Harris and Benzer (1974) demonstrated that Drosophila can
readily acquire a complex odour discrimination shock avoidance response. One of our students at the Institute of Psychiatry,
Christina Lewis, has been looking at this response within a biometrical framework. She took nine wild-type strains of Drosophila
known to differ in avoidance performance and produced a 9 x 9
half-diallel cross, that is the nine strains were crossed in all
possible combinations, ignoring the possibility of reciprocal
crosses. The resulting 45 genotypes were tested in the standard
paradigm.

The result we expected to find was one of mainly additive
gene-action and little or no dominance, based on the hunch that
the ability to learn a complex discrimination task would be of
little adaptive value to a fast breeding, short lived species like
Drosophila. The results we actually obtained are in Figure 2,
which shows, diagrammatically, the scores of all 36 F_1 crosses in
relation to those of their respective parental strains. The results are quite clear cut. Of the 36 F_1s, 31 scored above the
mean for the two parents, indicating a consistent dominance for a
high level of performance. The Anova in Table 2 confirms this
directional dominance and the W/V graph in Figure 3, although
indicating epistasis by its apparent departure from a straight line
of unit slope, can be shown by a constrained optimisation technique
to be consistent with a simple additive dominance model. Components of variation were calculated and suggest that at least 4
loci control performance, probably corresponding to the 4 chromosomes of Drosophila, that there is a complete level of dominance
and, on average, equal gene frequencies. We concluded that, contrary to our expectations, avoidance learning does form an important
component of reproductive fitness in Drosophila.

One frequently voiced criticism levelled at arguing about
adaptive significance from the results of diallel crosses, or
other breeding designs such as the classical F_1, F_2 and backcrosses, is that the strains employed seldom come from a clearly
defined base population. Strictly speaking, inference from gene-
action to adaptive significance would seem to need this condition

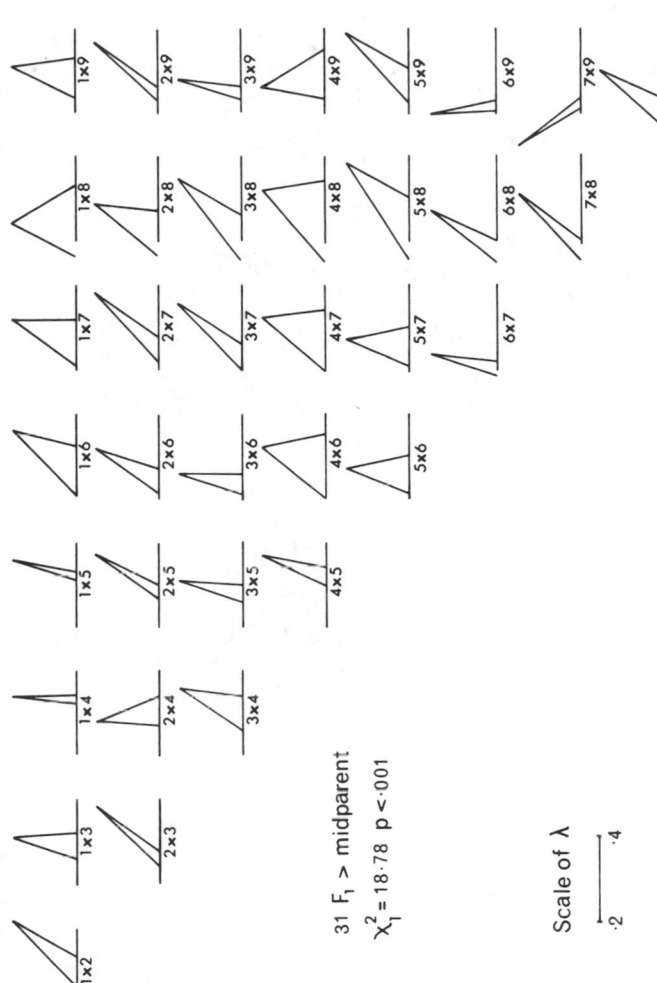

31 F_1 > midparent
$\chi^2_1 = 18.78$ p < .001

Scale of λ

.2 —— .4

Figure 2. 36 F_1s in relation to their parental strain in a 9 x 9 diallel cross of learning in Drosophila.
The base of each triangle represents the learning index (λ) for the two parental strains going into each F_1 hybrid. The apex of the triangle represents the F_1. The scale at the base of each triangle represents λs from .2 to .4. The general tendency for the triangle to lean to the right implies directional dominance for a high rate of learning. Strain key: 1. 6C1, 2. Samarkand, 3. Wellington, 4. Edinburgh, 5. Canton special, 6. Texas, 7. Florida, 8. Inhaca, 9. Oregon.

Table 2

9 x 9 half diallel analysis of variance
of avoidance learning in <u>Drosophila</u>

Item

General Combining Ability	8	0.02506	4.38[**]	$\sigma^2 + 33\sigma_1^2$
Specific Combining Ability	36	0.00910	1.63[*]	$\sigma^2 + 3\sigma_2^2$
Directional Effects	1	0.06658	11.91[**]	
Unequal Effects	8	0.00530	1	
Residual Effects	27	0.00810	1.45	
Environmental Influences	90	0.00559		

[**]p<.001
[*]p<.05

$\sigma_1^2 = 0.00059$

$\sigma_2^2 = 0.00117$

$\sigma^2 = 0.00559$

Narrow heritability = 14.86%
Broad heritability = 29.60%

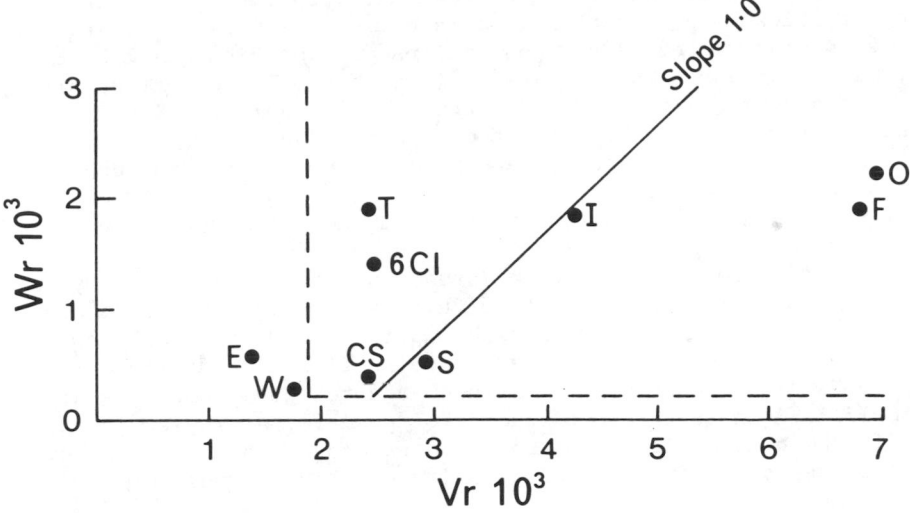

Figure 3. Variance: covariance graph of 9 x 9 diallel cross for learning in Drosophila.

The pecked axes are corrected for environmental variation. The straight line of unit slope was obtained by
a constrained optimisation technique that allowed a
proper statistical test of departure from a straight
line. The apparent departure was non-significant
(p = .3) justifying interpretation of the results of
the diallel cross in terms of a simple additive
dominance model.

Strain Key: 6Cl   —
             Samarkand   S
             Wellington   W
             Edinburgh   E
             Canton special   CS
             Texas   T
             Florida   F
             Inhaca   I
             Oregon   O

to be met. If the strains are not of common origin, in what sense can we claim that a gene pool has been influenced by natural selection? And yet plausible results are usually obtained where the adaptive significance of the phenotype is obvious. In part, I feel, the answer is that different sub-populations of a species still have very many loci in common and are subject to similar selection pressures, especially with respect to traits of fundamental importance to survival. Consequently, a set of inbred lines drawn from several populations might approximate to a set drawn from any one of them. Were this not so we might expect to find quite bizarre genetic interactions to result from combining non-co-adapted gene complexes in our breeding experiments. The uniformity of the F_1 response in the Drosophila learning study, which is typical in my experience, is in marked contrast to this expectation and lends credence to the validity of the general approach. Occasionally one does find studies in which marked ambidirectional epistatic effects occur and which do suggest that non-co-adapted gene complexes are responsible. In the present study, for example, a single cross (7 x 9) in the bottom right hand corner does appear to show epistasis for low expression in contrast to all the other crosses.

In a series of studies carried out at Birmingham University and the Institute of Psychiatry in London, we have been able to demonstrate the robustness of our biometrical techniques in relation to the conditioned avoidance response (CAR) in rats. An 8 8 diallel cross (Fulker et al., 1972; Wilcock & Fulker, 1973) established that CAR was under the control of genes dominant for low performance early in the learning sequence, changing over to dominance for high performance as learning progressed. Tentatively we took this as supportive evidence of a two process learning theory, although additional studies would be needed to be certain. Later, using the Triple Test Cross (TTC), a breeding design in which individuals from the F_2 are crossed to two extreme tester lines and their F_1 (Jinks et al., 1969), it was established by Valerie Owen, a student at Birmingham University, that this crossover effect was controlled by gene interactions in which homozygous combinations were deleterious and heterozygosity raised performance not simply by dominance but by breaking up excessive homozygosity. The TTC data were also analysed using an F_2 and backcross approach and additional data. This analysis also indicated the same form of gene-action.

In the diallel cross technique, which uses only F_1 hybrids, these homozygous: homozygous interactions, or i-type interactions as they are termed in the nomenclature of Mather and Jinks (1971), are difficult to distinguish from simple dominance, completely mimicking it. Thus the results of the TTC, the classical F_2 and backcross design and the diallel cross appear quite consistent.

Subsequently, at the Institute of Psychiatry, John Hewitt

and I repeated the Triple Test Cross using the same tester strains
but now, instead of using F_2 rats, we used a sample of 22 wild
male rats obtained from a refuse disposal centre in Birmingham.
These rats were pups obtained by digging out nests and were not
trapped, as is usually the case with wild rats. We felt, therefore, that they probably represented a reasonably good sample of
genotypes.

What we were interested in knowing was whether gene complexes
from a natural population combined with those from laboratory
strains would reveal similar genetic control to our previous
laboratory studies, or whether they would reveal control typical
of non-co-adapted complexes. Our finding was that in almost every
respect the results were the same as those obtained using only
laboratory rats. That is, the results of the 8 x 8 diallel cross,
the laboratory TTC, the classical design and the wild rat TTC were
in very good agreement, showing similar levels of heritability
and the same gene-action changing in the same way over trials.
This agreement suggests not only that the biometrical designs in
common use are quite robust, but also that the inferences we make
concerning the adaptive significance of behaviour following an
analysis of gene-action are probably reasonably valid, too, even
though we seldom use inbred lines from a common origin.

(iv) Gene action and genotype-environment interaction

Where a cross-breeding design, such as the TTC, or a large
diallel cross is combined with control of an environmental variable, information can be obtained regarding the adaptive significance of quite complex behavioural responses. For example, in the
helplessness study previously described, had we used a crossbreeding design we would have been able to tell whether or not the
helpless response was maladaptive, as one would guess, and develop
an evolutionary view of the phenomenon as well as investigate its
immediate causes.

The scope of this interactive approach may be illustrated by
reference to another aspect of the 8 x 8 diallel cross study
previously cited (Fulker et al., 1972). In this study, two
replications of rat pups were subjected to infantile stimulation
by two minutes' daily handling during the pre-weaning period and
two replications were reared under undisturbed control conditions.
At 100 days, rats were tested in the open-field for four consecu-
tive days and their defecation scores recorded. For the sake of
simplicity, the adaptive significance of the rat's response both
to infantile stimulation and the effect of repeated experience
in the open-field was assessed by comparing habituation curves
for average parental strains and average F_1s as shown in Figure 4.

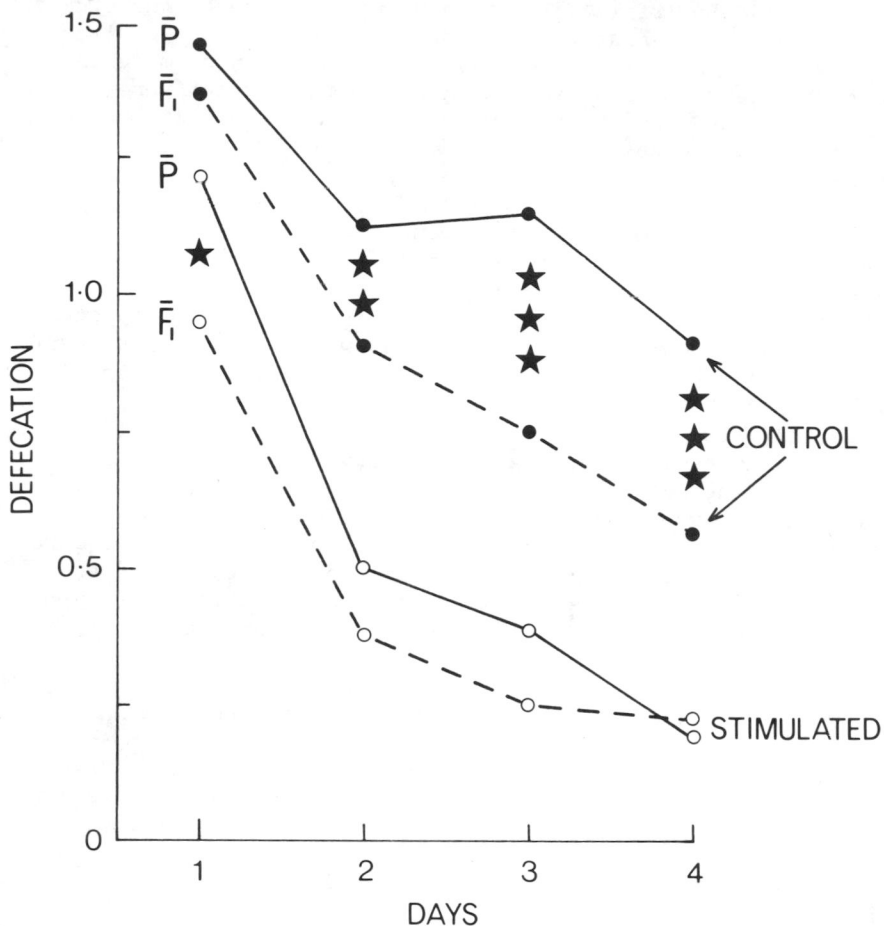

Figure 4. Parental means ($\overline{P}$) and F_1 means ($\overline{F}_1$) for defecation (square root transformed) in open field for rats in an 8 x 8 diallel cross.

The control group was reared according to the normal husbandry procedures and the stimulated group was subjected to daily handling for 2 minutes during the 21 days pre-weaning period. The habituation curves over 4 days of testing indicate directional dominance for rapid habituation.

$\overline{P}$ vs $\overline{F}_1$ significance levels are

*	$p < .05$
**	$p < .01$
***	$p < .001$

The following pattern of genetic control was apparent. On Day 1 in the control group the fear response was at its highest. However, there was no dominance, only additive gene-action controlling the phenotypic variation. A high uniform response would appear to be the adaptive norm, phenotypes either more or less extreme being maladaptive for rats bred under control conditions. Thereafter, on the days following initial exposure, when the rats had had the opportunity of reality testing what is, in fact, not a dangerous situation, rapid habituation of fearfulness appeared to be the optimal response. For the stimulated group who, overall, were much less fearful initially, dominance for a low level of defecation appeared straightaway on Day 1. Thereafter some degree of dominance appeared to remain but was increasingly obscured by a floor effect. Incidentally, the Day 1 effect of no dominance cannot have been due to a similar ceiling effect since genetic variation was at its highest for this group.

The above analysis lends support to the widely held theory that the effects of infantile stimulation are adaptive in character, a view that has little by way of direct support (Daly, 1973). Figure 4 shows that stimulation produces more rapid habituation than standard laboratory control conditions. The genetic analysis shows that rapid habituation is the adaptively superior response. It seems reasonable, therefore, to conclude that infantile stimulation, at least with respect to fear in novel situations, is also adaptive and therefore generally beneficial in its effects.

(v) Social interactions

Clearly interactive studies of this kind, in which genotypes are cross-classified with environments, can provide quite detailed information concerning the adaptive significance of complex behaviour. In modified form they are also capable of exploring the more complex problem of the genetic control of social interactions where the phenotype of an individual provides the environment of another. An understanding of the genetic consequences of social interactions is seen as central to an understanding of the evolutionary process in Edward Wilson's socio-biological synthesis (Wilson, 1975), social interactions comprising a primary mechanism in evolution. These interactions reach their most complex form in the case of Man, and Wilson suggests that the competing pressures of altruism, which promotes genotypes through co-operation and unselfishness, and the selfishness of individual selection provide a biological basis for man's uncertainty and doubt in moral situations. It is therefore of great interest to study the genetic control of social interactions to gain some insight into their mode of operation. This information, in turn, may serve a heuristic function when thinking about Man.

Fuller and Hahn (1976) have also recently discussed the evolutionary implications of social interactions having a genetic basis and suggest appropriate biometrical designs for their investigation. One experimental design they suggest is that of combining different pairs of genotypes in balanced fashion and observing social interaction. Blizard and Fulker (in press) carried out such a study, matching all possible combinations of strains in a mating situation. They found that interactions were predominantly male-genotype determined early on in a sequence of copulations, becoming increasingly jointly male-female determined as the sequence progressed.

More recently in our laboratory Sarah Wilson and I have started to look at genetic factors in mother-pup interactions using the natural combinations of genotypes generated by systematic cross-breeding, rather than putting together different combinations unnaturally after birth. This study, we are hoping, will shed some light on the genetic control of one simple form of altruism.

We wanted the interactive behaviour chosen for the model to conform to the requirements of being both simple to record on a continuous basis and of biological importance to the rat and other mammals. Time spent with litter, which has been shown by Grota and Ader (1969) to correlate highly with suckling and ratings of a number of other aspects of maternal care using the Seitz scale (1954, 1958) was chosen.

The material from the study fell into 8 genetic groups, two strains (RHA and RLA) two reciprocal F_1s and four kinds of backcrosses. These groups have been shown to be sufficient to allow a simple additive-dominance model of both pup and maternal effects to be evaluated without the necessity of unsatisfactory manipulations such as cross fostering (Fulker, 1970). The model has been further elaborated to take account of interaction between the main effects in the model (see Mather and Jinks, 1971). The eight groups used, together with the basic model, are shown in Table 3.

Preliminary analysis indicated that genetic differences in time spent with litter interacted with days, the most marked change occurring around Day 5. Consequently, the data were divided into two halves, Days 1-5 and Days 6-15. The average percentage time with the litter was analysed using the model in Table 3 for each of the two blocks of days, the results being shown in Table 4.

Considerable mother-pup interaction is indicated in the first 5 days. The analysis shows both significant mother and pup additive genetic influences of -22% and +15% respectively. The RHA genotype reduces the time spent with the litter by 22% when expressing itself through the mother, but increases the time

Table 3

Genetic model for offspring and maternal effects for 8 breeding groups

mother x father	mean	maternal genotypic effect	offspring genotypic effect
P_1 x P_1	m	$+dm$	$+do$
P_2 x P_2	m	$-dm$	$-do$
P_1 x P_2	m	$+dm$	$+ho$
P_2 x P_1	m	$-dm$	$+ho$
P_1 x (P_1 x P_2)	m	$+dm$	$+\frac{1}{2}do + \frac{1}{2}ho$
(P_1 x P_2) x P_1	m	$+hm$	$+\frac{1}{2}do + \frac{1}{2}ho$
P_2 x (P_1 x P_2)	m	$-dm$	$-\frac{1}{2}do + \frac{1}{2}ho$
(P_1 x P_2) x P_2	m	$+hm$	$-\frac{1}{2}do + \frac{1}{2}ho$

m is the mean of the two inbred lines
do is offspring additive effect
ho is offspring dominance effect
dm is mother's additive effect
hm is mother's dominance effect

P_1 = RHA strain

P_2 = RLA strain

352

Table 4

Percentage time spent with litters for 8 genetic groups for days 1-5 and days 6-15 with parameter estimates of maternal and pup effects

% Time with Litter

Genetic groups (mother x father)	Days 1 - 5 Observed	Days 1 - 5 Expected	Days 6 - 15 Observed	Days 6 - 15 Expected
P_1 x P_1	74.9	67.5	52.4	45.8
P_2 x P_2	72.8	81.7	44.6	63.9
P_1 x P_2	41.4	41.8	38.5	38.5
P_2 x P_1	87.1	85.9	61.4	66.1
P_1 x (P_1 x P_2)	49.3	54.3	37.2	42.1
(P_1 x P_2) x P_1	71.3	76.9	35.3	40.2
P_2 x (P_1 x P_2)	86.9	83.8	79.4	65.0
(P_1 x P_2) x P_2	73.3	61.9	45.4	35.5

Parameters				
m	74.6±5.1	p<.01	54.8±4.9	p<.01
do	15.0±6.8	p<.05	4.7±6.6	ns
ho	-10.8±8.6	ns	-2.5±8.2	ns
dm	-22.0±4.8	p<.01	-13.8±4.6	p<.01
hm	0.2±6.0	ns	-15.7±5.7	p<.05

by 15% when expressing itself through the pups. Thus there appear to be opposite, counterbalancing influences when pups are reared by mothers of their own strain. The absence of maternal dominance indicates that in a typical free mating situation, where additive effects also cancel, a high uniform level of maternal care would operate. A similar genetical picture of counterbalancing maternal and offspring influences has been found for offspring responses to prenatal stress by Joffe (1969) and by Fulker (1967, 1970) using the same model.

For Days 6-15 the picture is quite different. Offspring effects diminish, leaving only maternal ones. These are in the same direction as before, with RHA mothers spending less time with their litters than RLA mothers, but now we have a strong maternal dominance component ensuring that hybrid mothers also spend less time with their pups. We can see the development of maternal dominance quite clearly in Figure 5, where data for three kinds of mothers, RHA, RLA and hybrids are averaged and plotted over days. These effects would result in a minimum of time being spent with pups in a free mating situation after the first few days. This marked change in pattern of genetical control may represent a change in the adaptive needs of the pups and their mother from parturition to weaning. Initially the pups almost certainly need a consistent and fairly high level of maternal attention. Later the more normal demands of the environment on the mother take over, resulting in increased activity as she returns to exploring and foraging for food, an activity also necessary for the welfare of the pups.

Developing theories of animal behaviour within the context of biometrical genetics would appear to offer a number of advantages. Firstly, a substantial part of variation in individual difference is removed from error variance and made a systematic feature of the study as genotypic variation. Secondly, by controlling genetic variation in this way it can be combined with situational and other environmental stimuli to bring more complex behaviour under control. Thirdly, the inter-relationships among constitutional elements can be explored by multivariate analysis and, fourthly, the analysis of gene-action enables us to place the behaviour within the wider context of evolutionary theory.

II. GENETIC AND ENVIRONMENTAL ARCHITECTURE OF HUMAN PERSONALITY

(i) General model

In contrast, the study of human behaviour within a biometrical framework is still at a rudimentary stage, the limitations being both methodological and conceptual. However, in spite of these

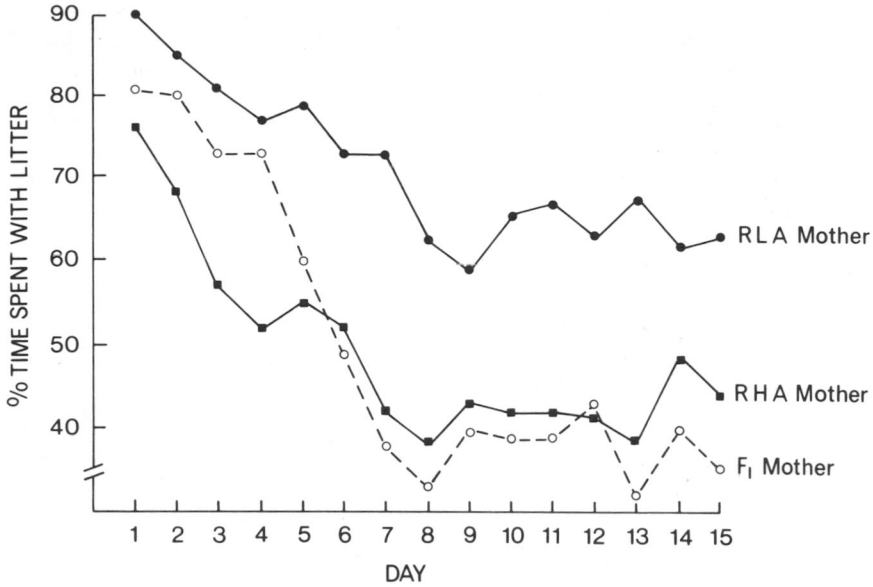

Figure 5. Percentage time spent by mother with litter.

   The three curves represent time spent with litter for
   mothers of three genotypes, irrespective of genotype
   of pups. The strains are Roman High Avoidance (RHA),
   Roman Low Avoidance (RLA) and their F_1 hybrid. The F_1
   curve gradually comes to resemble that of the RHA, indicating the development of maternal dominance for a
   low frequency of time spent with litter.

limitations, the approach does have a great deal to offer simply
at the level of focussing attention in appropriate directions,
particularly if combined with multivariate analysis.

     The basic biometrical approach outlined by Jinks and Fùlker
(1970) recognised two environmental components of variation, that
between families, designated E_2, and that within families, E_1.
These components refer respectively to shared family influences
causing sibling resemblance and those unique to the individual
tending to differentiate one sibling from another. These two components correspond broadly to factors in the social environment
compared to those operating within the family. In addition, two
genetic components were recognised analogous to the environmental
ones, G_2 and G_1. The first component reflects sibling genetic
covariance caused by their common genes and the second sibling
variance caused by the genetic segregation that takes place during
the reproductive process. Under conditions of random mating and

additive gene-action, G_1 is expected to equal G_2. In the absence of social influences, E_2 is expected to be zero. This model can be considerably elaborated but is useful even in this simple form.

(ii) Normal personality traits

A model in which $G_1 = G_2 = \frac{1}{2}G$ (where G is the total genetic variance) and $E_2 = 0$ appeared to be appropriate for a measure of neuroticism in data on MZ and DZ twins in a study by Shields (1962) which is used to illustrate the approach. The ANOVA on which the analysis is based is shown in Table 5. Parameter estimates are obtained by minimising the log likelihood ratio given at the foot of the table, subject to the condition that components are positive. In large samples this statistic approximates to χ^2 and provides a test of goodness of fit of the model. Clearly the model chosen here provides an adequate account of the variation between and within twin pairs. E_2, the shared environment component, is not required, pushing to its boundary condition of zero, and since we assume $G_1 = G_2$ only simple additive genetic variation is indicated.

Subsequent twin studies (Eaves & Eysenck, 1975, 1977) indicate a similar picture is appropriate for the major personality dimensions of Extraversion, Neuroticism and Psychoticism. Of course, since these studies are based only on MZ and DZ twins reared together, a fairly weak test of the adequacy of this simple model is provided. However, the consistency of the results across a number of studies is quite striking and is receiving stronger support from studies involving additional groups of subjects (Young & Eaves, personal communication).

Taken at face value, recent biometrical analyses suggest that the major personality dimensions are controlled by additive genes, that mating is at random, which is borne out directly by studies of assortative mating (Vandenberg, 1972) and that the social environment plays little or no part in their development. As a result of these analyses, those theories of personality development that involve general influences in the home or in the social environment are rendered quite implausible. In the wider evolutionary context, stabilising selection for an intermediate optimum is clearly indicated for these traits, suggesting extremes of personality are maladaptive relative to intermediate expression. Random mating, which reduces the frequency of extreme genotypes compared with the effects of assortative mating, also contributes to the maintenance of an intermediate optimum.

(iii) Schizophrenia

Liability to schizophrenia appears to follow a similar

Table 5

ANOVA and simple biometrical model of
Shields' (1962) neuroticism data

Twin		Item	Mean Square (MS$_i$)	df	Expected Mean Square (EMS)		
					G	E$_1$	E$_2$
MZ together	1	Between	22.16	42	2	0	2
	2	Within	8.12	43	0	1	0
MZ apart	3	Between	29.29	39	2	0	0
	4	Within	7.53	40	0	1	0
DZ together	5	Between	23.57	15	1½	0	2
	6	Within	13.86	16	½	1	0

$\hat{G} = 11.2 \pm 2.5$

$\hat{E}_1 = 7.7 \pm 1.3$

$\hat{E}_2 = 0$

$h^2 = 54\% \pm 9\%$

Estimates obtained by minimising the log likelihood ratio subject to the condition that variance components are positive.

$$\chi_3^2 = \sum_{i=1}^{6} df_i \left\{ \log_e (EMSi/MSi) + (MSi/EMSi) - 1 \right\}$$

$$= 1.3 \text{ ns.}$$

pattern. Foster studies (Heston, 1966; Kety et al., 1971) provide little direct support for any E_2 variation and compilations of data made according to reasonably uniform diagnoses and subjected to biometrical analysis quite strongly suggest the adequacy of the same very simple model that is applicable to the major personality dimensions (Fulker, 1974).

For traits like schizophrenia, diagnosed in an all-or-none fashion, it is assumed that a threshold operates such that the individual must accumulate a sufficient number of adverse influences (liabilities) in order to develop the disorder (Falconer, 1965). A simple demonstration of how such a model allows us to convert concordance rates into correlations or regressions is shown in Figure 6. Incidences and concordances are first converted to normal deviates and when compared define appropriate regression coefficients. In fact, more sophisticated methods are generally employed for calculating tetrachoric correlations and the development of multiple-threshold analysis now permits the investigation of traits with different incidences in men and women, for example, or in parents and offspring (Reich et al., 1965; Cloninger et al., in press).

One example of a biometrical model fitted to tetrachoric correlations is shown in Table 6 (Fulker, 1974). Once again a simple genetical system with no E_2 environmental effect is indicated for a major personality dimension. If this model is correct, how much time and effort has been wasted developing theories of schizophrenia in terms of social and general family environmental influences?

(iv) Genetic and environmental factor structure

The absence of E_2 may have additional implication for psychological theory in that it might well indicate that the remaining E environmental variation is not environmental at all in the usual sense of the word but similar in origin to genetic variation. Recent developments in genetic multivariate analysis (Martin & Eaves, 1977; Fulker, 1978) indicate how relevant information may be gathered on this point through the comparison of genetic and environmental covariance structures. These developments involve an extension of maximum likelihood factor analysis and offer a solution to the statistical problems inherent in additive decomposition of twin and other covariance matrices in order to explore their component structures (Loehlin & Vandenberg, 1968). This additive procedure often results in ill-conditioned or even negative definite component matrices that can neither be meaningfully factor analysed nor evaluated in any reasonable statistical manner.

The procedure consists of extending the parameters of the

Table 6

Concordance rates for recent schizophrenia studies,
together with simple biometrical model

Source	Concordance		
	MZ_T	DZ_T	PO_A
Gottesman and Shields (1966)	10/24	3/33	–
Harvald and Hauge (1965)	2/7	3/59	–
Tienari (1963)*	1/16	–	–
Kringlen (1966)	17/55	14/178	–
Heston (1966)	–	–	5/47
Rosenthal et al. (1968)	–	–	3/54
Heterogeneity χ^2	3.64 (ns)	0.57 (ns)	0.77 (ns)
df	3	2	1
% Concordance	29.41	7.41	7.92
Tetrachoric correlation based on p = 1.14%	0.76±0.04	0.35±0.01	0.37±0.02

*Given in Slater & Cowie (1971)

Biometrical model

Type of Family	Correlation	S.E.	Model		
			Additive variance	Dominance variance	Common environment variance
MZ_T	0.76	0.04	1	1	1
DZ_T	0.35	0.01	½	¼	1
PO_A	0.37	0.02	½	0	0

Estimates for full model

Additive variance = 0.74±0.07
Dominance variance = 0.05±0.12
Common environment =-0.03±0.03
Residual environment = 0.24±0.06

Estimates for reduced model

Additive variance = 0.73±0.06
Residual environment= 0.27±0.06
Model fit χ^2 = 1.64 ns

Taken from Fulker (1974)

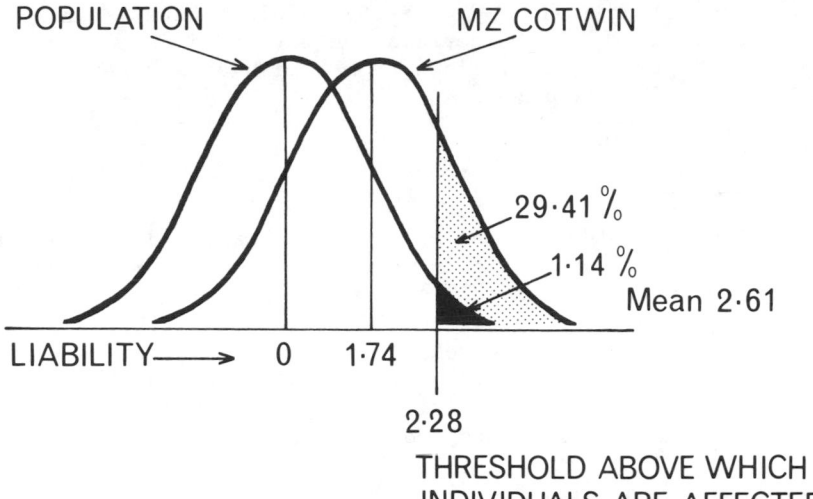

POPULATION   MZ COTWIN

29·41 %

1·14 %

Mean 2·61

LIABILITY ——⟶   0   1·74

2·28

THRESHOLD ABOVE WHICH
INDIVIDUALS ARE AFFECTED

REGRESSION OF COTWIN ON PROBAND

$$MZ = 1·74 / 2·61 = ·67$$

$$FOR\ DZ\ (7·41\%) = ·84 / 2·61 = ·32$$

THESE ARE ESTIMATES OF MZ, DZ CORRELATIONS

$$THUS\ h^2 = 2(·67 - ·32) = ·70$$

$$E_2 = ·67 - ·70 = -·03$$

Figure 6. Threshold model of schizophrenia.

This model is in terms of a hypothetical normally distributed variable liability. The disorder results when
sufficient liabilities are accumulated. With 1.14%
incidence of schizophrenia in the general population a
threshold of 2.28 is implied, this being the normal
deviate that cuts off 1.14% of the normal curve. The
mean liability of the 1.14% cut off by the threshold
is a normal deviate of 2.61. This figure is the ratio
of the ordinate at the threshold and the area it cuts
off. Given a proband sample of schizophrenics with
monozygotic brothers, 29.41% of whom are also affected,
the normal curve shifted to the right is obtained.
The mean of this curve, 1.74, is the mean liability of
MZ co-twins. Consequently the regression of co-twin

on proband is 1.74/2.61 = .67. This figure is an
estimate of the MZ correlation for liability. The
DZ figure of .32 follows from a similar argument based
on 7.41% concordance.

---

simple G, E_1 and E_2 model to the multivariate case and then equat-
ing them to the Between and Within mean cross product matrices of
twins or cross products derived from some other familial pairings.
These matrices take the place of the mean squares in the univariate
approach just outlined. Subsequently, factor models can be written on to the G and E component covariance matrices and their loadings and specific variance estimated directly as parameters in the
model by minimising the log likelihood ratio statistic

$$\chi^2 = \sum_{i=1}^{n} df_i \left\{ \log_e |\underline{ES}_i| - \log_e |\underline{S}_i| + \text{trace } \underline{S}_i \ \underline{ES}_i^{-1} - P \right\}$$

(Where $\underline{S}$ and $\underline{ES}$ are the observed and expected mean cross product
matrices and P the number of variates)

subject to the side condition that specific variances are non-
negative. Since E_1 specific variation is inevitable in psychological traits, arising from error of measurement, the expected cross
product matrices will almost always be positive definite and the
method work satisfactorily. This procedure provides maximum likelihood estimates of the parameters in the factor model and a goodness of fit test for the purpose of comparing different models, a
matter of key importance in the present context.

The example outlined here involves the Extraversion and
Neuroticism scales of Eysenck's Personality Questionnaire (PQ)
and four scales from Zuckerman's (1974) Sensation Seeking (SS)
questionnaire. There are four sub-scales in the SS questionnaire,
each measuring a different aspect of Sensation Seeking. One, Dis-
inhibition (Dis), is concerned with seeking release through activities such as party going, social drinking and sexual behaviour.
Another, Thrill and Adventure Seeking (TAS) is concerned with a
liking for dangerous and exciting sports. Experience Seeking (ES)
involves novel sensations and unconventional experiences, mainly
in the social context, while Boredom Susceptibility (BS) is concerned with intolerance of routine activities and dull, predictable
people. 422 pairs of male and female twins in the age range 18
to 52 were mailed the questionnaire and scores were age corrected
by analysis of covariance. Subscale variances were standardised
to unity across the whole sample. Preliminary univariate analysis
of same sex pairs established that the familiar additive genetic
variance and E_1 model adequately accounted for the mean score

variation, there being no suggestion at all of E$_2$, the shared environment component. A multivariate analysis was therefore attempted to explore the covariance structure of these genetic and environmental components.

The factor model was chosen with two purposes in mind; firstly to see how extraversion and neuroticism related to sensation seeking. For this purpose two uncorrelated factors were fitted, each loading on sensation seeking but only on one of the PQ traits. The second purpose was to see if the genetic and environmental covariance structures were the same. For this purpose genetic loadings were first constrained to be a constant multiple, b, of the environmental ones, and then freed of this constraint so that the two models could be compared statistically. At the same time, different environmental and genetic specific variance components were fitted, these all being constrained to be non-negative. The constrained model and its parameter estimates are shown in Table 7.

Several points emerge from the analysis. Firstly, there is more specific variance in the environmental structure than in the genetic. Since the environment includes unreliability variance this difference is to be expected and it is the reason we must fit different specifics to the two structures. The environmental factor loadings indicate that sensation seeking is more associated with extraversion than neuroticism, again as we might expect from the nature of the test. Loadings on extraversion are all positive, indicating a general factor. The weaker neuroticism loadings indicate a bi-polar factor, which seems reasonable, Dis and BS, on the face of it, reflecting a certain amount of social disorganization, with TAS and ES reflecting more organised and socially acceptable behaviour.

The most interesting feature of the analysis, however, is the finding that the same factor structure exists at genotypic and environmental levels, loadings merely being scaled up a factor of 2.55 in one case and 4.74 in the other to take account of an overall difference in genetic and environmental variation. Relaxing the constraint failed to improve the fit of the model, providing the necessary statistical test for this equality of the factor structures.

Sensation seeking appears to be organised in precisely the same way by genetic and environmental influences, suggesting that the same mechanisms, presumably constitutional ones since they must be for the genotypic component, underlie the two kinds of variation. From a theoretical point of view the explanation of individual differences in sensation seeking would therefore be better couched in terms of constitutional differences than different life experiences, an approach Zuckerman (1974) is increasingly adopting.

Table 7

Four Sensation Seeking scales and Extraversion (E) and
Neuroticism (N); genetic and environmental factors

	Genetic structure			Environmental structure		
	$b_i f_i$	$b_2 f_2$	s_g^2	f_i	f_2	s_e^2
E	1.37	–	3.53	.54	–	3.59
N	–	1.52	2.36	–	.32	4.17
Dis	4.33	2.25	.00	1.70	.47	2.15
TAS	2.76	−3.20	.46	1.08	−.68	5.61
ES	2.12	− .65	1.91	.83	−.14	2.31
BS	1.92	.78	2.06	.75	.17	3.51
b	<u>2.55</u>	<u>4.74</u>				

The factor model written on genetic (G_{ij}) and environmental (E_{ij})
component covariance matrices

$$G_{ij} = f_{1_i} f_{1_j} b_1^2 + f_{2_i} f_{2_j} b_2^2 + s_{gi}^2 \quad \text{when } i = j$$

$$E_{ij} = f_{1_i} f_{2_j} + f_{2_i} f_{2_j} + s_{ei}^2 \quad \text{when } i = j$$

Model fit $\chi^2_{145} = 173.46 \qquad p > .05$

All parameters highly significant except b_2 ($\chi^2_1 = 1.70$ ns)

Full model without b_i or b_2 $\chi^2_{134} = 159.33 \qquad p > .05$

Difference $\chi^2_9 = 14.13 \qquad p < .05$

The multivariate approach used with these data provides an optimal strategy for exploring Royce's factor-gene hypothesis (Royce, 1971) since all the loadings and specific variances have standard errors and appropriate comparison can be made reliably and with precision. In this context the relatively large specific variances suggest considerable specificity of gene action.

(v) Sex x genotype interaction

The same study illustrates an interesting form of genotype x sex interaction and suggests a relatively straightforward paradigm for investigating other environmental interactions using twins. The previous analysis was carried out omitting opposite sex DZ twins because on some of the sensation seeking scales they showed less pair resemblance than same-sex pairs, suggesting a form of sex interaction. A univariate interaction model was devised to explore the situation further.

In this model, which is shown in Table 8, random genetic effects (g_1 and g_1) and within family environmental ones (e_1) are allowed to interact with sex (s) as a fixed effect, generating interaction parameters sg_1, sg_2 and se_1 respectively. In the expected mean squares based on this model and shown in the table, the variance of these effects are in corresponding upper-case letters, as SG_1, SG_2 and SE_1. In addition to the variance components, covariance terms appear, involving possible associations between e_1 and its interaction se_1, and g_1 and g_2 with their corresponding interactions sg_1 and sg_2. In effect, these covariances allow an interpretation of the different phenotypic covariances of males and females that can arise in the presence of interaction. The derivation of the expectations in Table 8 is given in the Appendix.

The model was applied to the repeated measures univariate ANOVA of the four subscales of the sensation seeking questionnaire shown in Table 9. For the total sensation seeking score the simple additive genetic and E_1 model was perfectly adequate, as expected. However, for the scales x subjects interaction analysis it failed quite badly, due to the complete lack of DZ opposite-sex pair resemblance on subscale profiles. The χ^2_8 goodness of fit test for the simple model was 29.56 p<.001. When the sex interaction model was fitted, with the results shown in Table 10, χ^2_5 was reduced to a non-significant 2.28, indicating a satisfactory fit and a highly significant improvement over the simple model (χ^2_3 = 29.56 - 2.28 = 27.28 p<.001). Formally, this model represents two indistinguishable situations; either that the same genes determine sensation seeking profiles in the two sexes but that they express themselves differently, or that profiles are under two different forms of genetic control. Possibly the large interaction item and a small non-significant main genetic effect suggest the

Table 8

Sex interaction model for twins

MZ male	B	$2G + 2SG + E_1 + SE_1 + 2\text{ Cov }(e_1, se_1) + 4\text{ Cov }(g, sg)$
	W	$E_1 + SE_1 + 2\text{ Cov }(e_1, se_1)$
MZ female	B	$2G + 2SG + E_1 + SE_1 - 2\text{ Cov }(e_1, se_1) - 4\text{ Cov }(g, sg)$
	W	$E_1 + SE_1 - 2\text{ Cov }(e_1, se_1)$
DZ male	B	$1\tfrac{1}{2}G + 1\tfrac{1}{2}SG + E_1 + SE_1 + 2\text{ Cov }(e_1, se_1) + 3\text{ Cov }(g, sg)$
	W	$\tfrac{1}{2}G + \tfrac{1}{2}SG + E_1 + SE_1 + 2\text{ Cov }(e_1, se_1) + \text{Cov }(g, sg)$
DZ female	B	$1\tfrac{1}{2}G + 1\tfrac{1}{2}SG + E_1 + SE_1 - 2\text{ Cov }(e_1, se_1) - 3\text{ Cov }(g, sg)$
	W	$\tfrac{1}{2}G + \tfrac{1}{2}SG + E_1 + SE_1 - 2\text{ Cov }(e_1, se_1) - \text{Cov }(g, sg)$
DZ male/ female	B	$1\tfrac{1}{2}G + \tfrac{1}{2}SG + E_1 + SE_1$
	W*	$\tfrac{1}{2}G + 1\tfrac{1}{2}SG + E_1 + SE_1$

Parameters for estimation:
1. G
2. SG
3. $\text{Cov }(g, sg)$
4. $(E_1 + SE_1)$

*Mean effect of sex removed
5. $\text{Cov }(e_1, se_1)$

Table 9

Profile ANOVA of 4 sensation seeking sub-scales
for MZ and DZ Twins (age corrected by ANCOVA)

			df	MS	ε MS
MZ male	Between pairs	(B)	171	1.1653	1.0713
	Within pairs	(W)	177	.4694	.4503
MZ female		B	516	.9107	.9669
		W	522	.3651	.3587
DZ male		B	72	.9919	.9161
		W	78	.5179	.6024
DZ female		B	330	.7968	.8149
		W	336	.4694	.5140
DZ male/female		B	147	.6397	.6497
		Sex	3	1.8376	–
		SxB	150	.7601	.7740

Table 10

Result of fitting sex interaction model in Table 8 to data
on sensation seeking subscale profile in Table 9

Parameter	Estimate	P
G	.0915±.0558	.10
SG	.2158±.0571	<.001
E_1+SE_1	.4045±.0243	<.001
Cov (g_1, sg_1)	.0016±.0015	.30
Cov (e_1, se_1)	.0229±.0122	.03

Residual χ_5^2 = 2.28   p = .80

latter. In either case, a strong constitutional element in sensation seeking is again suggested, hormonal sex differences suggesting themselves as a possibility.

The plausibility of the sex interaction model was further explored, multivariately, and found to reside largely in the neuroticism contrast, Dis + BS versus TAS + ES, the former two involving sensation seeking through somewhat socially disapproved of means; the latter two by means socially more acceptable. The contrast also involves a like or dislike for dangerous sports. Clearly, sex differences would not be surprising for such a contrast, but a complete absence of E_2 makes an explanation in terms of social pressures seem unlikely.

A greater attention to opposite-sex DZ twins, often omitted from studies because they are a nuisance, would clearly be desirable in developing theories of sexual development. More generally, however, the paradigm could be developed to investigate other forms of genotype-environmental interaction if one member of a twin pair can be, or has been, exposed to differential experience. In this case the model could also be given a more thorough test, since the additional groups could be included where both twins either had or had not received the experience in question.

Biometrical analyses of personality measures suggest a simple form of gene-action and little or no E_2 effects, which it is suggested may well mean that constitutional factors account for most of the phenotypic variation. This picture, if correct, provides an appropriate starting point for the personality theorist. In addition, simple univariate and multivariate paradigms are available for exploring the complexities of environmental variables relevant to personality development.

III. GENETIC AND ENVIRONMENTAL ARCHITECTURE OF HUMAN COGNITION

(i) Additional complexities in the general model

When we turn from personality to cognition a different, much more complex picture emerges. So far as IQ is concerned there is evidence from numerous sources that common environment (E_2) is an important source of variation, an estimate of about 20% of phenotypic variation not being unreasonable. When we go on to consider specific cognitive skills and educational achievement, a much higher figure appears likely, somewhere in the region of 40% - 50% (Fulker & Eysenck, in press). In marked contrast to the development of personality traits, social environment appears very important in cognitive development. In addition, this environmental component appears likely to be correlated positively with the

genetic one (Gourlay, 1978; Loehlin, 1978; Rao et al., 1974) although for IQ it is difficult to detect with any certainty, since
it only accounts for a small proportion of the variation. For
educational achievement, however, this covariance may be quite
marked (Fulker, 1974; Fulker & Eysenck, in press). Much of this
covariance probably stems from the genotype of the parents making
a contribution to E_2 through their own phenotype and to their
children's phenotype through direct genetic transmission.

In addition to a complex relationship between the gene pool
and the social environment, the structure of the gene pool itself
appears to be more complex for cognitive ability than it does
for personality traits. In the first place there is marked associative disequilibrium caused by assortative mating and accentu-
ating individual differences. This assortative mating also increases GE covariance by means of an increase in the genotypic correlation between parents and their children and the increased phenotypic resemblance of the parents through its effect on E_2. This
picture of appreciable E_2, coupled with covariance between G and
E originating in the parent-child relationship and accentuated by
strong assortative mating points to traits regarded as, socially,
of some importance. In the second place, studies of inbreeding
(Schull & Neel, 1965; Bashi, 1977) show marked directional dominance
for cognitive ability, suggesting that natural selection has also
recognised cognitive ability is important. These findings, which
stem largely from the application of biometrical models to cognitive abilities, provide the psychologist with a complex sociobiological framework within which to develop cognitive theory.

This complexity also leads to problems of analysis, there
being as yet no entirely satisfactory biometrical model that can
encompass all its aspects (Loehlin, 1978). However, this complexity need not deter us from employing simplified models that probably involve a satisfactory degree of approximation for investigating
particular aspects of cognitive development. For example, the biometrical analysis of twin data has much to offer the social scientist concerned with the effects of the environment which can only
be satisfactorily studied if there is some degree of control over
genotype.

(ii) Multivariate analysis of environmental influences

Two simple examples of multivariate analysis that investigate
the structure of E_2 may serve to illustrate the point. The first
involves an analysis of Loehlin and Nichols' large twin study of
the National Merit Scholarship Qualifying Test (NMSQT). Altogether, over 1000 pairs of twins were examined in five subjects:
English Usage, Mathematics, Social Studies, Natural Science and
Vocabulary. Phenotypic, MZ and DZ cross-correlations are shown
in Table 11. These correlation matrices may be partitioned

Table 11

NMSQT phenotypic correlation and MZ and DZ cross
correlations taken from Loehlin & Nichols (1976)

Phenotypic correlation (P_{ij})

1	2	3	4	5
1.00	.50	.63	.55	.69
	1.00	.53	.58	.52
		1.00	.65	.75
			1.00	.62
				1.00

MZ cross correlations (MZ_{ij})

.72	.45	.57	.49	.65
	.72	.48	.54	.48
		.68	.57	.69
			.64	.57
				.88

DZ cross correlations (DZ_{ij})

.52	.35	.44	.33	.50
	.50	.37	.40	.39
		.53	.42	.52
			.44	.42
				.61

Key

1. English Usage
2. Mathematics
3. Social studies
4. Natural Science
5. Vocabulary

Table 12

Genetic (G_{ij}) and environmental ($E_{2_{ij}}$ and $E_{1_{ij}}$) covariance and

correlation matrices for the NMSQT data in Table 11

$G_{ij}=2(MZ_{ij}-DZ_{ij})$ $\qquad\qquad$ Correlation Matrices

1	2	3	4	5	1	2	3	4	5
.40	.20	.26	.32	.30	1.00	.48	.75	.80	.65
	.44	.22	.28	.18		1.00	.61	.67	.37
		.30	.30	.34			1.00	.87	.84
			.40	.30				1.00	.65
				.54					1.00

$E_{1_{ij}} = P_{ij}-MZ_{ij}$

.28	.05	.06	.06	.04	1.00	.18	.20	.19	.22
	.28	.05	.04	.04		1.00	.17	.13	.22
		.32	.08	.06			1.00	.24	.31
			.36	.05				1.00	.24
				.12					1.00

$E_{2_{ij}}=2DZ_{ij}-MZ_{ij}$

.32	.25	.31	.17	.35	1.00	.84	.89	.61	1.06
	.28	.26	.26	.30		1.00	.80	1.00	.97
		.38	.27	.35			1.00	.89	.97
			.24	.27				1.00	.97
				.34					1.00

Key

1. English Usage
2. Mathematics
3. Social Studies
4. Natural Science
5. Vocabulary

additively into environmental and genetic covariance components on the assumption that G_1 and G_2 are the same, which is likely to be approximately true, with the result shown in Table 12. Interesting differences appear between these component matrices when we convert them into correlations. Whereas the genetic correlation matrix indicates both general and specific genetic effects, many of the correlations in the E_2 matrix approach unity, indicating a strong general factor and very little specific variation. This unusual picture suggests that E_2 influences are of a similar nature whatever the cognitive skills involved. That this E_2 matrix is of single rank was tested by fitting just one single factor with no specific variation, the model providing a very good fit to the data and effecting no improvement over the full rank model. In contrast, the E_1 matrix shows a great deal of specific variation, suggesting that within family environment which, of course, includes many chance factors, exerts very little general effect.

Thus, so far as cognitive development is concerned, family environmental influences must involve a very simple mechanism, quite general in effect. One would guess this effect is the general intellectual and economic quality of the home. Other information would be needed to identify this factor but from a theoretical point of view the interesting thing is that no complex explanation of the home environment is called for in the light of such an analysis. In contrast, the within family environment is apparently quite complex and varied and may require a more detailed explanation.

What general effect there is in the E_1 matrix, some 4% to 8% of variation at most, has an interesting implication for Zajonc's (Zajonc & Markus, 1975) confluence theory of birth order effects on cognitive development, suggesting that at most it could account for the same very small amount of variation. A recent large study of birth order confirms this impression (Belmont, Stein, & Susser, 1975). This study involved about a quarter of a million subjects who had taken Raven's Progressive Matrices test of intelligence. Scores, z-transformed, are shown in Figure 7, taken from their paper. The effects appear quite marked and have led to exaggerated claims of the importance of birth order. However, if we calculate the proportion of variance accounted for by the effect it is less than 2%. A covariance analysis of E_1 variation twin studies, such as that of Loehlin and Nichols, clearly indicates that Zajonc's theory is most unlikely to account for more than 4% to 8% of variation even if it is the sole influence operating within the family. On the other hand, the E_2 matrix, accounting for some 30% of variation and due to a single cause, strongly suggests that the theoretical psychologist's efforts would be better employed in this direction.

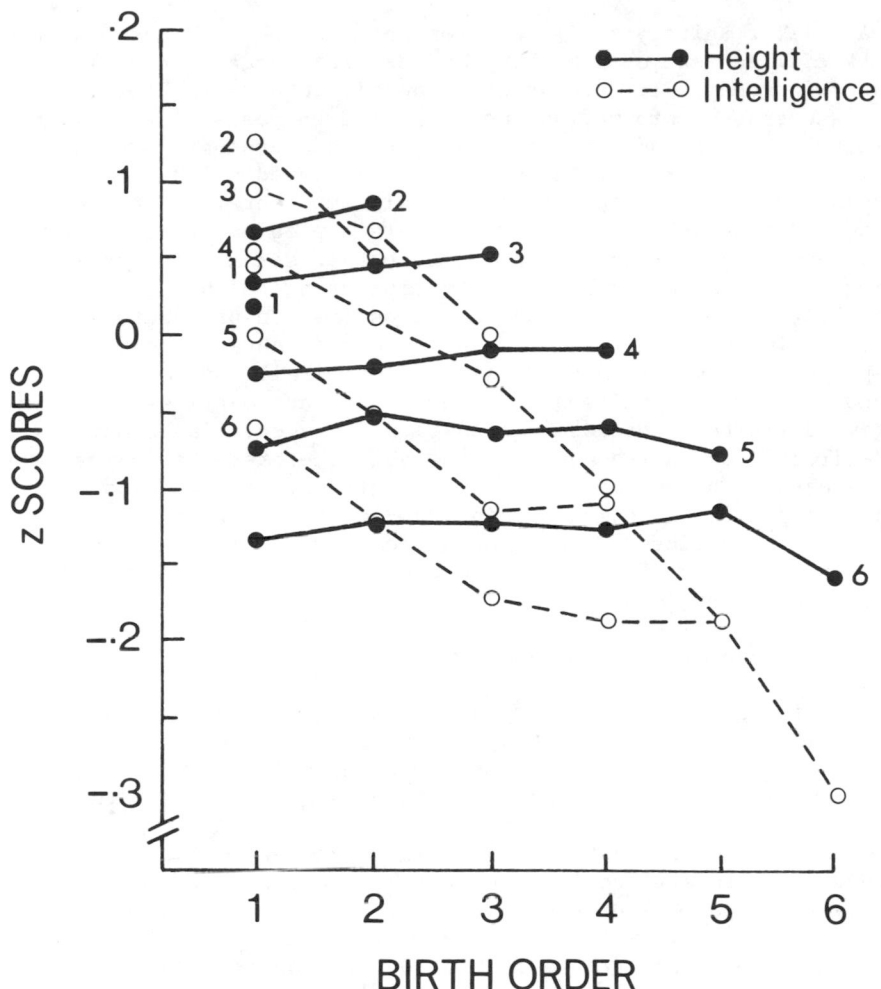

Figure 7. Birth order effects of IQ and birth weight taken from Belmont, Stein and Susser (1975).

The curves are obtained from averaged within family data, thus controlling for between family effects. When this procedure is followed, birth order has no effect on birth weight, but does have an effect on IQ. The curves are parallel, suggesting a similar mechanism for each size of family. The variance accounted for by the regression of IQ on birth order is less than 2%.

(iii) Longitudinal analysis of genetic and environmental
       determinants of SES

A similar unitary family environmental effect emerges in the
wider social context of schooling and SES in Taubman's (1977)
recent twin study. In this study of nearly 2000 pairs of white
US Army veterans, information was collected ōn years of schooling,
initial occupation and current occupation and earnings. Phenotypic and cross-pair correlations were calculated which allow partitioning into genetic and environmental components, as in the
previous example. However, in these data a problem arose in that
the E_2 covariance matrix produced a number of estimated correlations greater than unity and one negative variance on the leading
diagonal. Consequently, a constrained estimation procedure was
used to estimate the genetic and environmental covariance matrices.
This procedure involved minimising the log likelihood ratio statistic subject to the condition that the covariance matrices were non-
negative definite, a necessary condition for a covariance matrix
based directly on paired observations and, therefore, a desirable
feature of a component matrix. This constraint was achieved by
means of a penalty function forcing non-negative latent roots of
the component matrices. The results are shown in Table 13 in the
form of proportions of variance and component correlation matrices.
Clearly the procedure has forced a rank one E_2 matrix again, indicating a single unitary factor underlying variation in E exactly
as in the case of the NMSQT data.

In this example the unitary nature of E_2 is even more important to the social scientist than in the previous one, since it
suggests a very simple structure for the whole of the social environment relevant to education and status some 30 years later.

With longitudinal data of this kind a variety of models may
be constructed to explore its structure in more detail. One such
model, a modified form of path analysis, is shown in Figure 8.

In this model only three of the four variables have been
selected for analysis since they can be plausibly related longi-
tudinally. These are Schooling (S) and the two measures relating
to the individual some 30 years later, namely Occupational Status
(Oc2) and Income (Inc). On the left of the figure are the three
influences, G, E_1 and E_2 that affect schooling. These influences
are also assumed to affect income and status some thirty years
later. However, in addition, income and status are assumed to be
influenced by the residual genetic and environmental effects shown
in the right of the figure. No residual common environment is
needed in view of the rank one structure of this component. Following the conventions of path analysis (Wright, 1954) the causal
influences of the seven latent variables on the three measures,
S, Inc and Oc2 are represented by straight arrows bearing the path

Table 13

Constrained parameter estimates:
Taubman's Twin Study (1977)

	Correlations				Variances(%)
	Specific Environment $(E_{1_{ij}})$				
Schooling (S)	1.00	.17	.24	.10	23
Occupation 1 (O_1)		1.00	.17	.07*	48
Occupation 2 (O_2)			1.00	.14	64
Income (I)				1.00	45

	Genetic (G_{ij})				
	1.00	.60	.62	.55	46
		1.00	.63	.52	33
			1.00	.44	28
				1.00	47

	Common Environment $(E_{2_{ij}})$				
	1.00	1.00	1.00	1.00	31
		1.00	1.00	1.00	19
			1.00	1.00	8*
				1.00	8*

Resid $\chi^2_{16} = 24.99$ $p<.1$

*params $p<.01$

Rest $p<.001$

374

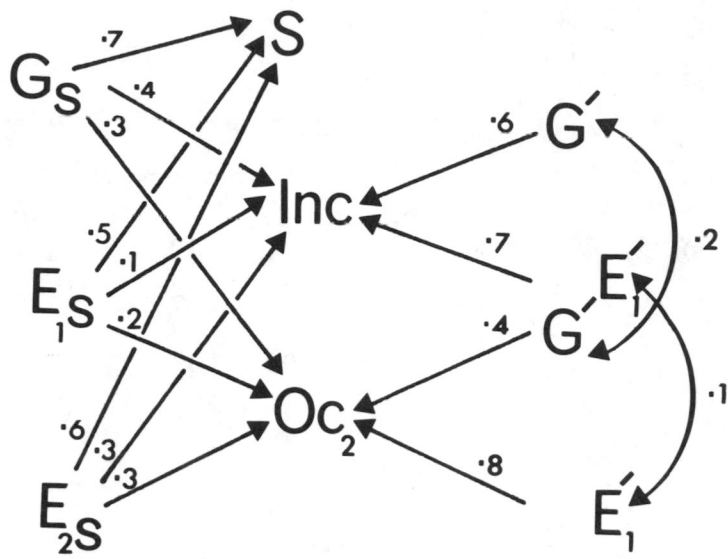

Figure 8. Path Analysis of Taubman's (1977) twin study.

Genetic and environmental influences are defined as follows:
Latent variables
G_s = genetic influences on schooling
$E1_s$ = specific environmental effect on schooling
$E2_s$ = common environmental effect on schooling
G_1^1 = residual genetic influences
E_1^1 = specific environmental influences

Observed variables
S   = schooling (years)
Inc = adult income (log $)
Oc2 = adult occupational status (Duncan scale)

The figure is fully explained in the final section of the text.

co-efficients that indicate their relative influence when all the other factors in the system are held constant. The relationships between the residual effects are represented by curved arrows simply indicating the existence of a correlation. Coefficients have been rounded to one decimal place for simplicity.

This diagram indicates aspects of the genetic and environmental influences on adult status and income, not all of which are obvious from simple inspection of the correlations and variances given in Table 13. Most of these conclusions follow from Taubman's analysis too, but the path diagram has the advantage of providing a convenient summary.

Firstly, both genes and E_2 for schooling subsequently influence adult status and income, roughly to the same extent, all four paths being between .3 and .4. Secondly, specific E_1 effects on schooling, that is chance and accidental factors, exert an almost trivial influence later, their paths being between .1 and .2. Thirdly, by far the greatest influences on adult income and status are residual genetic and specific E_1 environmental factors. Fourthly, these strong residual factors are largely independent of each other with respect to the two adult measures, their correlations being merely .1 and .2.

The analysis suggests, then, that insofar as schooling influences adult status, home environment is almost as important as genetic endowment, but that large independent genetic and environmental influences unrelated to home environment play the major role. One could hazard a guess that these later genetic influences are related more to temperament and special skills rather than to IQ, which we know has a powerful influence on schooling. The environmental factors probably relate to market imperfections and luck.

Summary

In the present chapter I have tried to give some idea of the range of behaviour genetic studies involving biometrical methods that are capable of shedding some light on wider, more general aspects of psychological theory. These studies range from simple strain studies with <u>Drosophila</u>, rats and mice that allow us to study genotype-environment interactions with implications for the generality of psychological theories, to crossbreeding studies that allow us to assess the general adaptive significance of the behaviour in question by investigating the genetic architecture. The study of genetic correlations using this material can help identify the network of constitutional or situational factors needed to explain the behaviour.

In human populations even simple twin studies allow us to
identify the major sources of variation needed for a theoretical
explanation of the behaviour, in particular whether or not shared
environment, which may broadly be equated with the social environment, is important. Studies of normal and abnormal personality
traits suggested social environment to be unimportant. The suggestion is made that individual differences in personality may
have an entirely constitutional basis. Studies of sex interaction
in trait profiles also lent support to this idea. In the cognitive domain a much richer, more complex picture emerges of both
social and within family environmental factors in addition to
constitutional factors. The relevance of multivariate methods to
these studies is discussed and their social and evolutionary implications.

References

Bashi, J. Effects of inbreeding on cognitive performance of
    Israeli Arab children. Nature, 1977, 266, 440-442.
Belmont, L., Stein, Z. A., & Susser, M. W. Comparison of associ-
    ations of birth order with intelligence test score and height.
    Nature, 1975, 255, 54-56.
Blizard, R. A., & Fulker, D. W. Interactions of strain of male
    and female on the mating behavior of the rat. Behavioral
    Biology (in press, 1978).
Breese, E. L., & Mather, K. The organisation of polygenic acti-
    vity within a chromosome in Drosophila. II. Viability.
    Heredity, 1960, 14, 375-399.
Broadhurst, P. L., & Bignami, G. Correlative effects of psycho-
    genetic selection: A study of the Roman high and low avoid-
    ance strains of rats. Behavior Research and Therapy, 1965,
    2, 273-280.
Broadhurst, P. L., & Jinks, J. L. Stability and change in the
    inheritance of behaviour in rats: A further analysis of
    statistics from a diallel cross. Proceedings of the Royal
    Society, London, 1966, B, 165, 450-472.
Cloninger, C. R., Reich, T., & Buze, S. B. The multifactorial
    model of disease transmission: II. Sex differences in the
    familial transmission of sociopathy (Antisocial personality).
    British Journal of Psychiatry, 1975, 127, 11-22.
Cloninger, C. R., Christiansen, K. O., Reigh, T., & Gottesman,
    I. I. Implications of sex differences in the prevalences of
    antisocial personality, alcoholism and criminality for
    familial transmission. Archives of General Psychiatry
    (in press, 1977/78).
Daly, M. Early stimulation of rodents: A critical review of
    present interpretations. British Journal of Psychology,
    1972, 64, 435-460.

Eaves, L., & Eysenck, H. The nature of extraversion: A genetical analysis. Journal of Personality and Social Psychology, 1975, 32(1), 102-112.

Eaves, L. J., & Eysenck, H. J. A genotype-environmental model for psychotism. Advances in Behavioural Research and Therapy, 1977, 1, 5-26.

Falconer, D. S. The inheritance of liability to certain diseases estimated from the incidence in relatives. Annals of Human Genetics, 1965, 29, 51-76.

Fulker, D. W. Mating speed in male Drosophila melanogaster. A psycho-genetic analysis. Science, 1966, 153, 203-205.

Fulker, D. W. Maternal buffering of rodent genotypic responses to stress: A complex genotype-environment interaction. Behavior Genetics, 1970, 1(2).

Fulker, D. W. A biometrical genetic approach to intelligence and schizophrenia. Social Biology, 1973, 20, 266-275.

Fulker, D. W. Applications of biometrical genetics to human behaviour. In J. H. F. van Abeelen (Ed.), The genetics of behaviour. Amsterdam: North Holland Publishing Co., 1974.

Fulker, D. W. Multivariate extensions of a biometrical model of twin data. Proceedings of the Second International Congress on Twin Studies, 1977. New York: Alan R. Liss, 1978.

Fulker, D. W., & Eysenck, H. J. Heredity and intelligence. In H. J. Eysenck (Ed.), The structure and measurement of intelligence. Berlin: Springer Verlag (in press, 1978).

Fulker, D. W., Wilcock, J., & Broadhurst, P. L. Studies in genotype-environment interaction. 1. Methodology and preliminary multivariate analysis of a diallel cross of eight strains of rat. Behavior Genetics, 1972, 2, 261-87.

Fulker, D. W., Zuckerman, M., & Eysenck, S. B. C. A genetic and environmental analysis of sensation seeking. Journal of Research in Personality (in press, 1978).

Fuller, J. L., & Hahn, M. E. Issues in the genetics of social behavior. Behavior Genetics, 1976, 6, 391-406.

Gaitonde, M. K., & Festing, M. F. W. Brain glutamic acid decarboxylase and open field activity in ten inbred strains of mice. Brain Research, 1976, 103, 617-621.

Gourlay, N. Heredity vs. environment: The effects of genetic variation with age. British Journal of Educational Psychology, 1978, 48, 1-21.

Grota, L. J., & Ader, R. Continuous recording of maternal behaviour in Rattus norvegicus. Animal Behaviour, 1969, 17, 722-729.

Henderson, N. D. The confounding effects of genetic variables in early experience research: Can we ignore them? Developmental Psychobiology, 1968, 1, 146-152.

Henderson, N. D. Genetic influences on the behaviour of mice can be obscured by laboratory rearing. Journal of Comparative and Physiological Psychology, 1970b, 72, 505-511.

378

Henderson, N. D. Brain weight increases resulting from environmental enrichment: A directional dominance in mice. Science, 1970a, 169, 776-778.

Heston, L. L. Psychiatric disorders in foster home reared children of schizophrenic mothers. British Journal of Psychiatry, 1966, 112, 819-825.

Jinks, J. L., & Fulker, D. W. Comparison of the biometrical genetical, MAVA, and classical approaches to the analysis of human behaviour. Psychological Bulletin, 1970, 73, 311-349.

Jinks, J. L., Perkins, J. M., & Breese, E. L. A general method of detecting additive, dominance and epistatic variation for metrical traits. Heredity, 1969, 24, 45-57.

Joffe, J. M. (Ed.). Prenatal determinants of behaviour. Oxford: Pergamon Press, 1969.

Kearsey, M. J., & Barnes, B. W. Variation for metrical characters in Drosophila populations. II. Natural Selection. Heredity, 1970, 25, 11-21.

Kety, S. S., Rosenthal, D., Wender, P. H., & Schulsinger, F. Mental illness in the biological and adoptive families of adopted schizophrenics. American Journal of Psychiatry, 1971, 128, 302-306.

Linney, R., Barnes, B. W., & Krarsey, M. J. Variation for metrical characters in Drosophila populations. III. The nature of selection. Heredity, 1975, 27, 163-174.

Loehlin, J. C. Heredity-environment analyses of Jencks' IQ correlations. Mimeo, 1978.

Loehlin, J. C., & Nichols, R. C. Heredity, environment and personality. Austin and London: University of Texas Press, 1976.

Loehlin, J. C., & Vandenberg, S. G. Genetic and environmental components in the covariation of cognitive abilities: An additive model. In S. G. Vandenberg (Ed.), Progress in human behavior genetics. Baltimore: Johns Hopkins Press, 1968.

Martin, N. G., & Eaves, L. J. The genetical analysis of covariance structure. Heredity, 1977, 38, 79-95.

Mather, K. The genetical structure of populations. Symposium of the Society for Experimental Biology, 1953, 7, 66-95.

Mather, K., & Jinks, J. L. Biometrical genetics (2nd ed.). London: Chapman and Hall, 1971.

Quinn, W. G., Harris, W. A., & Benzer, S. Conditioned behavior in Drosophila melanogaster. Proceedings of the National Academy of Science, U.S.A., 1974, 71, 708-712.

Rao, D. C., Morton, N. E., & Yee, S. Analysis of family resemblance. II. A linear model for familial correlation. American Journal of Human Genetics, 1974, 26, 331-359.

Reich, T., Cloninger, C. R., & Guze, S. B. The multifactorial model of disease transmission: I. Description of the model and its use in Psychiatry. British Journal of Psychiatry, 1975, 127, 1-10.

Rick, J. T., Tunnicliff, G., Kerkut, G. H., Fulker, D. W., Wilcock, J., & Broadhurst, P. L. GABA production in brain cortex related to activity and avoidance behaviour in eight strains of rat. Brain Research, 1971, 32, 234-238.

Royce, J. R. The conceptual framework for a multi-factor theory of individuality. Third Banff Conference on Theoretical Psychology, Banff, September, 1971.

Schull, W. J., & Neel, J. V. The effects of inbreeding on Japanese children. New York: Harper and Row, 1965.

Seitz, P. F. D. The effects of infantile experiences upon adult behavior in animal subjects: I. Effects of litter size during infancy upon adult behavior in the rat. American Journal of Psychiatry, 1954, 110:916.

Seitz, P. F. C. The maternal instinct in animal subjects: I. Psychosomatic Medicine, 1958, XX, 3.

Seligman, M. E. P. Helplessness. San Francisco: W. H. Freeman & Co., 1975.

Seligman, M. E. P., & Beagley, G. Learned helplessness in the rat. Journal of Comparative and Physiological Psychology, 1975, 88, 534-541.

Shields, J. Monozygotic twins. Oxford: Oxford University Press, 1962.

Taubman, P. The determinants of earnings: Genetic, Family and other environments; a study of white male twins. The American Economic Review, 1976, 66, 858-870.

Vandenberg, S. G. Assortative mating, or Who marries Whom? Behavior Genetics, 1972, 2, 127-157.

Weiss, J. M., & Glazer, H. I. Effects of acute exposure to stress on subsequent avoidance-escape behavior and on brain norepinephrine. Psychosomatic Medicine, 1975, 37, 499-521.

Wilcock, J., & Fulker, D. W. Avoidance learning in rats: genetic evidence for two distinct behavioral processes in the shuttlebox. Journal of Comparative and Physiological Psychology, 1973, 82, 247-53.

Wilson, E. O. Sociobiology: The new synthesis. Cambridge, Mass.: Belknap Press, 1975.

Wright, S. The interpretation of multivariate systems. In O. Kempthorne, T. A. Bancroft, J. W. Gowen, and J. L. Lush (Eds.), Statistics and mathematics in biology. Ames, Iowa: State College Press, 1954.

Zajonc, R. B., & Marcus, G. B. Birth order and intellectual development. Psychological Review, 1975, 82, 74-88.

Zuckerman, M. The sensation seeking motive. In B. Maher (Ed.), Progress in experimental personality research (Vol. 7). New York: Academic Press, 1974.

Appendix

A Model for Assessing Sex Interactions in Twin Studies

An individual's phenotype, X, is made up of the following eight effects:

m	population mean
g_1	segregating genetic effect (random)
g_2	family or shared genetic effect (random)
e_1	within family environmental effect (random)
e_2	shared family environmental effect (random)
$\pm s$	sex effect (fixed)

$$\left.\begin{array}{l} sg_1 \\ sg_2 \\ se_1 \\ se_2 \end{array}\right\} \text{ sex interactions with the above effects}$$

The variances of these effects are represented by corresponding upper case letters.

A pair of male MZ twins (X_1 and X_2) will be

$$X_1 = m + g_1 + g_2 + s + sg_1 + sg_2 + e_{11} + se_{11}$$

$$X_2 = m + g_1 + g_2 + s + sg_1 + sg_2 + e_{12} + se_{12}$$

The Sum $= 2m + 2g_1 + 2g_2 + 2s + 2sg_1 + 2sg_2 + (e_{11} + e_{12}) + (se_{11} + se_{12})$ and the corresponding mean square between pairs (MSB) obtained as

$$MSB = \tfrac{1}{2} \varepsilon\, Sum^2 \text{ about its mean of } 2m + 2s$$
$$= 2G_1 + 2G_2 + 2SG_1 + 2SG_2 + E_1 + SE_1 + 4\, Cov\,(g_1, sg_1)$$
$$+ 4\, Cov\,(g_2, sg_2)$$
$$+ 2\, Cov\,(e_1, se_1)$$

The Difference $= (e_{11} - e_{12}) + (se_{11} - se_{12})$ and the corresponding mean square within (MSW) obtained as

$$MSW = \tfrac{1}{2} \varepsilon\, diff^2 \text{ about zero}$$
$$= E_1 + SE_1 + 2\, Cov\,(e_1, se_1)$$

Pairs of female MZ twins will have the same expectations, except the covariances will take a negative sign.

COMMENT BY J. C. DeFRIES

Being the official discussant for a paper by Dr. David Fulker is both an honor and a challenge. I have known Dr. Fulker personally for almost a decade and have the highest regard for the quality of his research. During the last few years, Dr. Fulker has become an authority on multivariate-genetic analysis, a topic which he addresses at some length in this paper. Since I am only a neophyte in this area this makes my task rather difficult.

Dr. Fulker does an excellent job in his paper of sampling the literature of biometrical behavioral genetics. This is not surprising considering the fact that he has been a major contributor to this literature. However, because his coverage is so diverse, I will not attempt any comprehensive critique. Instead, I have chosen to comment upon only three of the many issues that he raises.

Dr. Fulker begins his paper by discussing the concept of genotype-environment interaction. As he points out, any theory regarding environmental influence which omits consideration of genetic predisposition may have limited generality. However, with regard to this issue of generality, it is very important to distinguish statistical significance from practical significance. Consider, for example, a recent paper by Taylor and Condra (1978). In this paper, an experiment is described in which the authors tested for the presence of genotype-environment interactions in several fitness characters of Drosophila pseudoobscura: percent emergence, mean development time for males and females, and wing length for males and females. Eggs from 12 strains were placed in vials which had been assigned to one of 20 different environmental conditions (10 different food media by 2 rearing temperatures). Five replicates were included for each strain-by-environment condition, resulting in a total of 1,200 culture vials. When two genotype-environment interactions (strain by temperature, and strain by food) were tested for each of the five fitness characters, eight of these ten interactions were found to be statistically significant. The authors summarized their results as follows: "These results support the belief that heritability studies of human IQ, which assume such interactions to be absent, are of dubious worth" (Taylor & Condra, 1978, p. 64). However, inspection of their tabulated mean squares suggested to me that the significant genotype-environment interactions may not really be very important. In fact, only one of the eight significant interactions accounted for as much as 2% of the total variance. I have no idea if this finding will turn out to be typical for studies of genotype-environment interaction. Nevertheless, the point remains clear: Merely finding a significant genotype-environment interaction by no means implies that some generality concerning hereditary and environmental main effects may not be possible.

In the next section of his paper Dr. Fulker discusses the
power of multivariate analysis to shed light on mechanisms which
underlie behavioral variation. A paper by Rick et al. (1971),
which involves an 8 x 8 diallel cross of rat strains, is cited.
The variables measured in this study were avoidances and inter-
trial crossings during escape-avoidance conditioning, activity
and defecation in an open field, and GABA production in brain cortex. The analysis employed in this study was elegantly simple.
Additive genetic values for the five variables were estimated for
each of the eight strains from their array means. The means for
the different variables were then intercorrelated across the
strains, yielding an additive genetic correlation matrix. This
matrix was subjected to principal component analysis with rotation
of two major dimensions: The first dimension was related positively to the learning measures and negatively to GABA production,
whereas the second dimension was related primarily to the open-
field defecation measure. To my knowledge, this is the first
study in which behavior genetic and biochemical data were subjected
to a combined multivariate analysis.

For several years, my colleague, G. E. McClearn, has independently advocated the use of multivariate analysis to study the
nature of drug tolerance and addiction. Such a study is currently
in progress at the University of Colorado, using a heterogeneous
population of mice. One problem with such a study, however, has
to do with experimentally dependent variables. For example, tests
of alcohol preference and alcohol-induced sleep time may invalidate
subsequent measures of liver-enzyme activity. With a diallel
cross, however, this problem can be circumvented. Since animals
representing a given cell in the diallel table are genetic replicates, it is not necessary to obtain more than one measure per
subject. Cell means corresponding to the different variables
may be intercorrelated across the various cells, resulting in a
genotypic correlation matrix which may subsequently be subjected
to multivariate analysis. (Obtaining cell means would be especially
important for measures with low reliability.) Such an approach
could be of considerable value to the budding tri-hybrid discipline
of behavioral pharmacogenetics.

The third and final issue which I wish to discuss concerns
recent developments in multivariate-genetic analysis cited by
Dr. Fulker. My question again pertains to the matter of practical
significance: How much better are these methods than the standard
methods currently in use? As a case in point, Meredith and Zonderman (in preparation) have recently derived some very complicated
expressions for obtaining maximum likelihood estimates of familial
correlations. For illustrative purposes, their methods were applied to data for one of the variables measured in the Hawaii
Family Study of Cognition (Raven's Progressive Matrices). At the
University of Colorado we have independently obtained estimates

of these parameters using standard Pearson product-moment and intra-class correlations for approximately the same data set. Although both the methods of age adjustment and the actual samples differed somewhat, the resulting familial correlations were almost identical. Is this just a coincidence, or may this often be the case? If it is often the case, is the extra effort required to obtain maximum likelihood estimates really worth it? I know that Dr. Fulker has considered these matters and hope that he will share his thoughts with us.

REPLY TO J. G. DeFRIES

D. W. Fulker

I would like to thank Dr. John DeFries for his kind remarks about my paper and for raising a number of interesting questions.

The first concerns the argument that the existence of genetic variation has serious implications for the generality of environmental theories. The argument depends on the expectation of substantial interaction between genotype and environment and if, as the discussant feels likely, these interactions are of negligible importance compared with the main genotypic and environmental effects, then environmental theories may still be quite valid.

My own experience in the animal laboratory is that for very many phenotypes interactions are, in fact, of modest importance. However, where they do appear to be important is in situations involving extremes of genotype and environment. Bi-directionally selected lines, for example, often differ quite markedly in their responses to environmental manipulations. Similarly, drugs that modify behaviour markedly often show strong interactions with strain as well. And, finally, when behaviour is changing substantially over time, as in the learning process, interactions with genotype are often quite powerful.

Thus I would suggest that the genotype-environmental interactions are most likely to be of importance in human behaviour when we are dealing with these kinds of extremes; that is, in the clinical or abnormal field and in education (e.g., in trying to understand the learning process, especially in relation to exceptionally bright or dull children). They may also be of considerable importance in response to many everyday situations. However, for stable phenotypes in the normal range, as in the case of typical twin studies of intelligence and personality, I would agree with Dr. DeFries that genotype-environment interactions are probably of minor importance. On the other hand it is worth noting that even in less extreme situations interactions may still be of considerable theoretical importance, since they allow us to relate behavioural processes to adaptation and the evolutionary process, as I tried to show in my discussion of open field behavior in rats.

I was pleased Dr. DeFries found the Rick et al. (1971) paper, in which we used a diallel cross to relate behaviour to brain biochemistry, of such methodological interest. The use of non-segregating generations does offer a much simpler and more power-ful approach to multivariate genetic analysis than that offered by segregating generations.

On the final question concerning the desirability of employing complex and time consuming techniques for genetic and environmental multivariate analysis when many simpler approaches give similar results, I am not entirely sure where I stand in the matter, but I think it goes like this. For exploratory purposes the simpler techniques probably suffice and, in fact, we all use them. However, when we need precise parameter estimates or, more importantly perhaps, we require a statistical test to decide between competing hypotheses, the more complex procedures seem to me to be preferable. The Meredith and Zonderman approach to estimating familial correlations illustrates the point. This procedure provides maximum likelihood parameter estimates and allows maximum likelihood tests of significance concerning specific relationships among the parameters (that is, of particular hypotheses; e.g., whether or not some subsets of correlations are equal to each other). A simpler approach is quite inadequate for this purpose since it ignores the correlated errors among the separate parameter estimates. Also, much depends on the nature and circumstance of the study. In large studies, such as the one carried out in Hawaii (for which the Meredith and Zonderman approach was devised and where many people have spent many years and quite a few dol-lars to collect the data), anything other than optimal estimation procedures, even using minutes of computer time, seems unthinkable.

COMMENT BY D. A. HAY

Dr. Fulker has done an excellent job of summarising some of the advantages of a biometrical approach to analysing behaviour. I would like to emphasise only one additional advantage of studying animal behaviour in this way, namely the ability to provide unambiguous controls. As an example I shall take Drosophila learn-ing because Dudai (1977) has pointed out that, at least in the case of their mutant studies, with the same learning task as Dr. Fulker used, it is impossible to attribute deficits in performance to learning or memory to the exclusion of other aspects of be-haviour, such as general activity, phototaxis, and shock sensitivity.

Can a biometrical approach unravel these factors? Firstly, if one has sufficient strains, one can demonstrate that the differences

in learning ability are uncorrelated with strain differences in
the other possible behaviours that might explain the results.
This we have done (Hay, 1975) for a different measure of learning
from that used by Dr. Fulker. Secondly, if, unlike Dr. Fulker, one
considers that learning can be adaptive to Drosophila--and I would
argue that the extensive work on honeybees (Wells, 1973), on
mating preference in Drosophila pseuodoobscura (Pruzen, Applewhite,
& Bucci, 1977) and on alcohol avoidance in D. melanogaster and
D. simulans (Soliman, unpublished data), two species which differ
greatly in their sensitivity to alcohol (McKenzie & Parsons,
1972), make this a distinct possibility--then one should be able
to demonstrate directional dominance for learning. If this happens, and dominance is not found for the other behaviours that
might be implicated in the task, then one can be sure, not only
that learning may be adaptive, but also that one has separated
learning from the other behaviours. This too we have managed to
do (Hay, in press, Experientia). I would emphasize that behaviours cannot be distinguished simply by comparing means--we
have examples from Drosophila activity where the means on different measures are very similar, but crossbreeding revealed very
different genetic architectures, presumably indicating different
behavioural traits (Hay, 1972).

Such an approach is, of course, not confined to Drosophila.
The paper by Henderson, at this conference, indicates, using
second-degree statistics, how many of the same points can be made
about the relationships among measures of learning in mice.

COMMENT BY J. C. LOEHLIN

I will comment briefly on three points. First, the suggestion that the social environment plays little or no part in the
development of the major personality dimensions is consistent
with the twin data reported, but it is clearly not a necessary
conclusion from them. An alternative view might be that the social and interpersonal environment is important for personality,
but acts to differentiate twins as much as to make them alike.

Secondly, in the multivariate analysis of the National Merit
test sub-scales, it is suggested that the within-family matrix
E_1 is largely specific, showing little general effect. An alternative analysis would have removed error variance from the diagonal
of the E_1 covariance matrix before converting it to correlations.
(Error variance ranges from .04 to .17 for the various subtests.)
The off-diagonal elements would then range from .23 to .53 in the
E_1 correlation matrix, suggesting a fairly substantial general
factor plus specifics.

Finally, I have some reservations about the use of a

386

constrained estimation procedure in analyzing the data of the U.S. veterans' sample. With a small sample size, one might be justified in supposing that the peculiarities in the results were just due to sampling error, and therefore in circumventing them in this manner. However, with this large a sample, shouldn't one suspect instead that the anomalous results warn of an unsatisfactory model?

REPLY TO J. C. LOEHLIN

D. W. Fulker

In reply to Dr. Loehlin's comments, briefly, it is indeed possible that social environment acts to differentiate twins, but there seems to be very little evidence of this when we try to fit appropriate models. As I understand it, such a process would lead to a negative covariance between genotype and environment, as Cattell suggested some time ago, and there does not appear to be much evidence for this process. However, I can fully believe that the dynamics of personality development are more complex than our current models would suggest, but I favour the principle of parsimony.

As to my analysis of the National Merit Test data, I fully accept Dr. Loehlin's criticism, providing one removes error variation from other within family environmental effects. However, I am not altogether happy about doing so because repeat performances vary for a good reason, presumably relating to environmental circumstances and possibly the genetic make-up of the individual (that is, what we call error may equally have a genetic component and be a form of genotype x environment interaction).

Concerning the reservations about the use of a constrained estimation procedure in analysing Taubman's data, I would accept Dr. Loehlin's general criticism, but in this particular case it is inappropriate since constrained and unconstrained estimations did not differ significantly regarding their fit to the data. In other words, so far as the E_2 matrix is concerned, in this data we are dealing with a "small sample" problem.

References

Dudai, Y. Properties of learning and memory in Drosophila melanogaster. Journal of Comparative Physiology, 1977, 114, 69-89.
Hay, D. A. Genetical and maternal determinants of the activity and preening behaviour of Drosophila melanogaster reared in different environments. Heredity, 1972, 28, 311-336.
Hay, D. A. Strain differences in the maze-learning ability of Drosophila melanogaster. Nature, 1975, 257, 44-46.

McKenzie, J. A., & Parsons, P. A.   Alcohol tolerance: an ecologi-
    cal parameter in the relative success of Drosophila melano-
    gaster and Drosophila simulans.   Oecologia, 1972, 10, 373–388.
Meredith, W., & Zonderman, A. B.   Maximum likelihood estimation
    of the parameters of familial resemblance given variable
    numbers of offspring, in preparation.
Pruzan, A., Applewhite, P. B., & Bucci, M. J.   Protein synthesis
    inhibition alters Drosophila mating behavior.   Pharmacology,
    Biochemistry and Behavior, 1977, 6, 355–357.
Rick, J. T., Tunnicliff, G., Kerkut, G. A., Fulker, D. W., Wilcock,
    J., & Broadhurst, P. L.   GABA production in brain cortex re-
    lated to activity and avoidance behaviour in eight strains
    of rat.   Brain Research, 1971, 32, 234–238.
Taylor, C. E., & Condra, C.   Genetic and environmental interaction
    in Drosophila pseudoobscura.   Journal of Heredity, 1978, 69,
    63–64.
Wells, P. H.   Honey bees.   In W. C. Corning & J. A. Dyal (Eds.),
    Invertebrate learning.   New York: Plenum, 1973, Vol. 2,
    pp. 173–185.

GENETIC CORRELATIONS, ENVIRONMENTAL CORRELATIONS, AND BEHAVIOR

J. C. DeFries, A. R. Kuse, and S. G. Vandenberg

Institute for Behavioral Genetics,
University of Colorado, Boulder, Colorado

The idea that an observed correlation between two characters may
be due in part to heritable causes clearly predates Mendelian
genetic theory. Darwin, for example, discussed the importance of
"correlated variation" as follows:

> Hence if man goes on selecting, and thus augmenting,
> any peculiarity, he will almost certainly modify un-
> intentionally other parts of the structure, owing to
> the mysterious laws of correlation. (Darwin, 1859,
> p. 35)

These "laws of correlation" are no longer so mysterious. We
now know that the observed (phenotypic) correlation between two
characters has both genetic and environmental causes. Pleiotropy
(influence of the same gene[s] on more than one character) is the
chief genetic cause of phenotypic correlations, although linkage
and non-random mating may have transient effects (Falconer, 1960;
Hazel, 1943). Environmental influences, of course, may also be
manifold.

1. QUANTITATIVE GENETIC MODEL

In elementary quantitative genetic theory, the phenotypic value
for a character measured on an individual is assumed to be due to
an additive genetic value (sum of the average effects of the
genes) plus the combined effects of environmental, dominance, and
epistatic interaction deviations, i.e.,

$$P = A + E, \qquad (1)$$

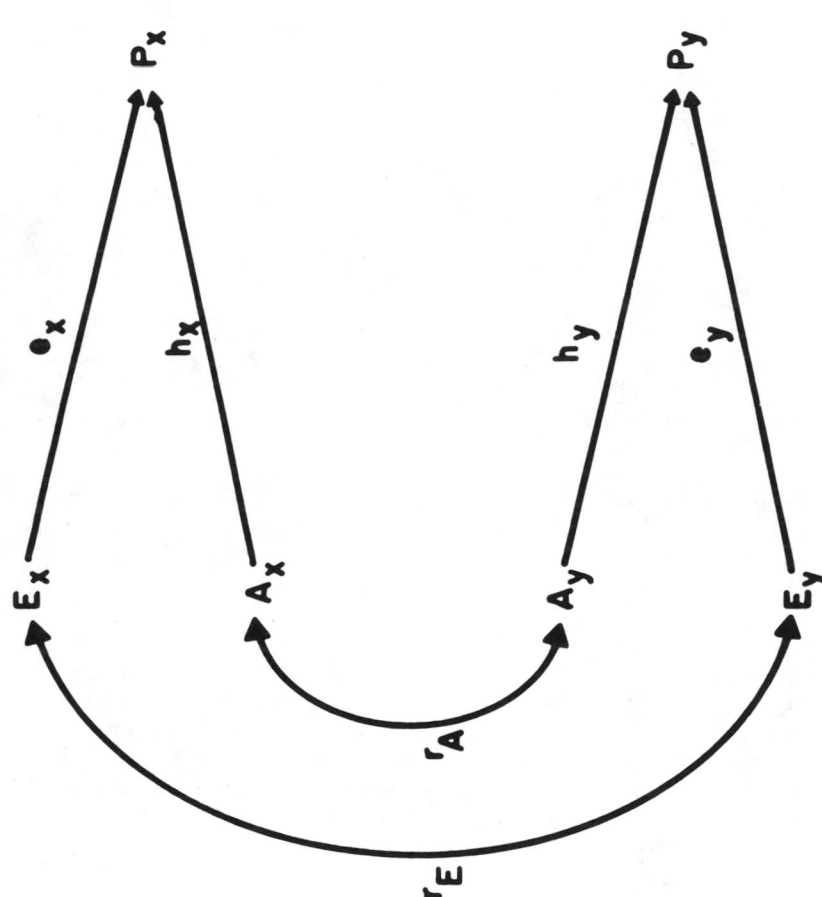

Figure 1. Path diagram of the phenotypic correlation between two characters (P_x and P_y) measured on an individual as a function of the genetic correlation (r_A) and the environmental correlation (r_E).

where P is the phenotypic value, A is the additive genetic value, and E is due to environmental plus non-additive genetic deviations.

When A and E are uncorrelated,

$$V_P = V_A + V_E, \qquad (2)$$

where V_P, V_A, and V_E symbolize phenotypic, additive genetic, and environmental (plus non-additive genetic) variances, respectively. Heritability in its "narrow sense" (h^2) is defined as the fraction of the observed variance in a population attributable to individual differences in additive genetic values, i.e., $h^2 = V_A/V_P$. (Like all population parameters, including the mean and the variance, heritability is a function of the population in which it is measured.) By dividing both sides of Equation 2 by V_P, it may be seen that

$$1 = h^2 + e^2, \qquad (3)$$

where $e^2 = V_E/V_P$. More complex models, which incorporate genotype-environment interaction and correlation, have recently been discussed by Plomin, DeFries, and Loehlin (1977).

Univariate quantitative genetic models, such as Equation 1, may be easily generalized to two or more characters. Initially, we shall consider only the bivariate case.

Assume that two characters which have been measured on a sample of individuals have phenotypic values symbolized as P_x and P_y. From the path diagram depicted in Figure 1, it may be seen that the observed correlation between P_x and P_y is a function of a genetic correlation (correlation between the additive genetic values for the two characters, symbolized r_A) and a corresponding environmental (plus non-additive genetic) correlation, symbolized r_E. It may also be seen that the total phenotypic correlation (r_P) is actually composed of a genetic and an environmental "chain" of paths as follows:

$$r_P = h_x h_y r_A + e_x e_y r_E. \qquad (4)$$

These genetic and environmental chains are equivalent to phenotypically standardized genetic and environmental covariances, i.e.,

$$h_x h_y r_A = \frac{\sigma_{A_x}}{\sigma_{P_x}} \frac{\sigma_{A_y}}{\sigma_{P_y}} \frac{CovA_{xy}}{\sigma_{A_x} \sigma_{A_y}} = \frac{CovA_{xy}}{\sigma_{P_x} \sigma_{P_y}}$$

and $\qquad (5)$

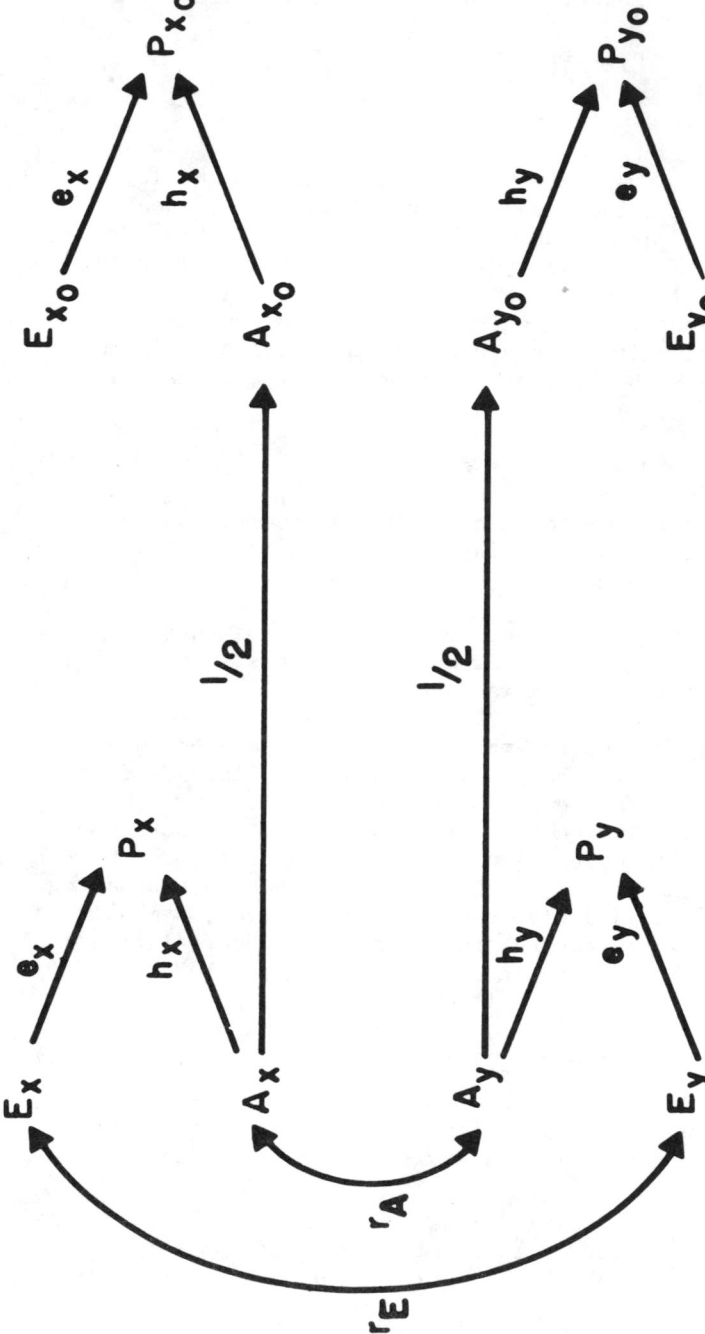

Figure 2. Path diagram of bivariate resemblance between parental phenotypes (P_x and P_y) and offspring phenotypes (P_{x_0} and P_{y_0}).

$$e_x e_y r_E = \frac{\sigma_{E_x} \sigma_{E_y} \text{CovE}_{xy}}{\sigma_{P_x} \sigma_{P_y} \sigma_{E_x} \sigma_{E_y}} = \frac{\text{CovE}_{xy}}{\sigma_{P_x} \sigma_{P_y}}.$$

Thus, phenotypically standardized genetic and environmental co-variances sum to yield r_p, a phenotypically standardized pheno-typic covariance.

Equation 4 may be generalized to the multivariate case as follows:

$$R_P = D_h R_A D_h + D_e R_E D_e, \tag{6}$$

where R_P is a matrix of phenotypic correlations among $\underline{m}$ variables, D_h is a diagonal matrix with the square roots of the heritabilities as diagonal elements, R_A is a matrix of genetic correlations among the $\underline{m}$ variables, R_E is a corresponding matrix of environmental cor-relations, and D_e is a diagonal matrix of square roots of $e^2 = 1 - h^2$. When R_P is expressed in terms of phenotypically stand-ardized covariance matrices, the relationship is simpler yet, i.e.,

$$R_P = C_P = C_A + C_E, \tag{7}$$

where C_P, C_A, and C_E are phenotypically standardized phenotypic, additive genetic, and environmental (plus non-additive genetic) covariance matrices, respectively.

2. ESTIMATION OF GENETIC AND ENVIRONMENTAL CORRELATIONS

Hazel (1943) proposed the first method for estimating genetic correlations. After noting that the genetic correlation is a function of the phenotypic correlation (or covariance) between one character of an individual (P_x) and another character of a relative (P_y'), he formulated the well-known "cross covariance" expression:

$$r_A = \left[\frac{(\text{CovP}_x P_y')(\text{CovP}_y P_x')}{(\text{CovP}_x P_x')(\text{CovP}_y P_y')} \right]^{\frac{1}{2}}. \tag{8}$$

Correlations or regressions may be substituted for the covariances in the above expression, since the variances cancel to yield Equation 8. In addition, when the two terms in the numerator dif-fer in sign, the arithmetic average may be used in place of their geometric mean.

Consider the path diagram in Figure 2, which is a model of

parent-offspring bivariate resemblance. Such a model would be appropriate for well-controlled animal studies in which there is no common environmental influence shared by parents and offspring or for human adoption studies in which little or no selective placement has occurred. Examination of Figure 2 reveals the following relationships:

$$r_{P_x P_{y_o}} = \tfrac{1}{2} h_x h_y r_A,$$

$$r_{P_y P_{x_o}} = \tfrac{1}{2} h_x h_y r_A,$$

$$r_{P_x P_{x_o}} = \tfrac{1}{2} h_x^2,$$

$$\tag{9}$$

and

$$r_{P_y P_{y_o}} = \tfrac{1}{2} h_y^2.$$

When the above expressions are substituted into Equation 8, an estimate of r_A is obtained, i.e.,

$$\left[\frac{(\tfrac{1}{2} h_x h_y r_A)(\tfrac{1}{2} h_x h_y r_A)}{(\tfrac{1}{2} h_x^2)(\tfrac{1}{2} h_y^2)} \right]^{\tfrac{1}{2}} = r_A. \tag{10}$$

It may be noted that genetic correlation estimation is merely a bivariate generalization of heritability estimation. For example, when $P_x = P_y$, Equation 4 reduces to Equation 3. Thus, whenever a data set is sufficient for estimation of h^2, r_A may also be estimated if more than one variable has been measured. As a consequence, r_A may be estimated from data on isogenic and segregating generations of laboratory organisms; diallel crosses of inbred strains; parent-offspring, sibling, and twin resemblances; the correlated response to selection; and so on. Once estimates of h_x^2, h_y^2, r_p, and r_A are available, they may be substituted into Equation 4 (recall that $e^2 = 1 - h^2$) to yield estimates of r_E.

In the case of human behavioral characters, where environmental influences are likely to be shared by relatives, adoption data could be especially valuable. Covariances (or correlations) between biological parents and their adopted children could be obtained and substituted into Equation 8 to provide estimates of r_A. Alternatively, a cross-regression approach could be utilized to estimate the genetic chain as follows:

$$h_x h_y r_A = 2 \left[(b_{P_{x_o} P_y})(b_{P_{y_o} P_x}) \right]^{\frac{1}{2}}. \tag{11}$$

When P_x and P_y are mid-parent values $(\overline{P})$, the bracketed term would not be doubled. Note that if $P_x = P_y$, Equation 11 reduces to $h^2 = 2b_{P_o P}$ or $b_{P_o}\overline{P}$, two well-known expressions for estimating heritability (Falconer, 1960). If data were also available on adoptive parents, Equation 8 could be utilized to estimate r_{E_c}, a correlation due to environmental influences shared by adoptive parents and their adopted children.

Because of its practical application for the simultaneous selection of economically important quantitative characters, the estimation of genetic correlations and covariances is an important aspect of quantitative genetic theory (Falconer, 1960; Pollak, Kempthorne, & Bailey, 1977). Although the partitioning of phenotypic correlation matrices into genetic and environmental components is conceptually important for the behavioral sciences (Crawford & DeFries, 1978), the empirical data base is woefully inadequate. In the next section, several multivariate twin analyses and two animal studies will be reviewed, and a multivariate analysis of data from the Hawaii Family Study of Cognition will be reported.

3. BEHAVIORAL EXAMPLES

3.1 Twin studies

Vandenberg (1965) and Loehlin (1965) conducted the first multivariate, behavioral genetic analyses of twin data. In his Michigan Twin Study, Vandenberg found that the variance within fraternal (DZ) twin pairs was significantly greater than that within identical (MZ) pairs for so many variables that he was asked: "Do you really think that all of these variables are different with independent hereditary control for each?" (Vandenberg, 1965, p. 35). Although the terminology used in this chapter was not employed, Vandenberg was essentially being asked whether or not there were genetic correlations among the variables. In order to answer this question, he invented a method for the multivariate analysis of the covariances of twin differences. Differences between members of a given pair of MZ twins should reflect only within-family environmental influences, whereas those between members of a pair of DZ twins are a function of both within-family environmental and genetic influences. The difference between members of a given pair for character X may be correlated with that for character Y. A matrix of such correlations or covariances obtained from MZ twin data would be due to within-family environmental influences which affect both characters, while such a matrix for DZ twins would reflect both within-family environmental and genetic sources of covariation.

Vandenberg considered subtracting the MZ covariance matrix from the DZ matrix to obtain a matrix which represents only the genetic covariance. He rejected this approach, however, because the difference matrix may not be Gramian. Instead, he solved the following determinantal equation:

$$|D - \lambda M| = 0, \qquad (12)$$

in which D is the covariance matrix of DZ twin differences, M is the corresponding MZ covariance matrix, and λ is the latent root of the characteristic equation. He reasoned that the number of significant roots would equal the number of independent sources of hereditary influence.

Vandenberg applied this method in an analysis of scores obtained on six Primary Mental Abilities (PMA) scales by 45 pairs of MZ and 37 pairs of DZ twins tested in the Michigan study. Solution of Equation 12 yielded four significant roots, leading Vandenberg to conclude that there are at least four independent hereditary components in the six PMA scores. He suggested that these components are rather similar to the number, verbal, space, and word fluency abilities.

In the same volume, Loehlin (1965) utilized a different analytical approach. He factor analyzed 35 small clusters of items from the Thurstone Temperament Survey and the Cattell Junior Personality Quiz. The clusters were ranked for genetic variance by using data from the Michigan Twin Study, and 15 "high heredity" and 14 "low heredity" clusters were identified. Scores on these clusters were then obtained for each of 231 eleventh and twelfth grade boys in two high schools in Lincoln, Nebraska. Items were combined with unit weights and then intercorrelated within the high- and low-heredity clusters and factor analyzed. Four factors were extracted from each matrix and were rotated to oblique simple structure. Similarities between the factors obtained from the two matrices were apparent. Factor I for both high- and low-heredity clusters appeared to concern extraversion-introversion, and there were an emotionality or adjustment factor and a factor involving physical activities in each set. However, there were also some differences. Loehlin concluded that the factors obtained from the high-heredity clusters were more focused on the individual, whereas those from the low-heredity clusters were more related to the individual's reaction to the environment.

Although the approaches of Vandenberg (1965) and Loehlin (1965) may appear at first glance to be similar, they were really quite different. Vandenberg sought to estimate the number of independent sources of genetic influence. When this number is less than the number of variables, at least some non-zero genetic correlations are indicated. In contrast, Loehlin analyzed phenotypic correlations among sets of variables that were of either high or low heritability. As may be seen from Equation 4, a phenotypic correlation among two highly heritable characters does not necessarily imply that r_A is large. Thus, no strong conclusions may be drawn regarding genetic correlations among the measures obtained by Loehlin.

In 1966, Thompson reviewed the multivariate, behavioral genetic literature and summarized the methods available for estimating genetic and environmental correlations. He concluded his review as follows:

> To the knowledge of the writer, no worker has attempted
> so far to compare the psychological composition of fac-
> tors from such different sets of correlations. Such a
> project would be of importance in at least two ways.
> In the first place, it would represent a crucial step
> in defining the heritable limits of different behavioral
> traits. Second, it would also initiate a closer liaison
> between the rather abstract methods of factor analysis
> and manipulable empirical variables. (Thompson, 1966,
> p. 724)

Two years later, Bock and Vandenberg (1968) formalized Vandenberg's test for the number of independent dimensions of hereditary influence and applied it to Differential Aptitude Test data on 50 MZ and 25 DZ boy twin pairs and 56 MZ and 54 DZ girl twin pairs in the Louisville Twin Study. Utilization of Bartlett's criterion for statistical significance indicated three dimensions of heritable variation for the boys' data and two for the girls' data.

Bock and Vandenberg (1968) also applied an algebraic solution to obtain unbiased positive semi-definite estimates of within-family genetic correlation matrices. Principal component analyses of these matrices revealed that a general component accounted for 44% and 63% of the heritable variation in the boys' and girls' data, respectively. The authors concluded that these results indicated that the general factor obtained in conventional factor analyses of mental test data is not due primarily to cultural and educational differences among subjects.

In the same volume, Loehlin and Vandenberg (1968) addressed the issue previously raised by Thompson (1966) by examining the dimensionality of genetic and environmental correlation matrices based on PMA data from the Michigan and Louisville twin studies. Intercorrelations of MZ and DZ pair sums (between-pair) and differences (within-pair) on the 15 PMA scales were subjected to principal component analysis, and the first five factors were retained for Varimax rotation. Resulting factors from the between-pair covariation for both MZ and DZ twin data were found to correspond to Thurstone's five primary mental abilities. At least four of these factors were also represented in the MZ and DZ within-pair data.

Loehlin and Vandenberg (1968) noted that the correlations of MZ twin within-pair differences must reflect only within-family environmental influences. In order to obtain a matrix which reflected within-family genetic sources of variation, the within-pair MZ covariance matrix (corrected for differences in reliability among PMA scales) was subtracted from the corresponding DZ matrix. It was noted that this procedure may not eliminate the environmental sources of covariance completely, but that it should at least markedly reduce them. The difference matrix was then transformed to a correlation matrix and factor analyzed. Resulting rotated factor loadings were similar to those obtained from the within-pair MZ correlation matrix. These results, plus those of a reanalysis of a small data set from Thurstone's Chicago Study, suggested to the authors that the environmental and genetic components of cognitive abilities have similar dimensions. In a discussion of this observation, they stated:

> On general grounds findings such as these are perhaps not unreasonable. Presumably the development of cultural institutions is to some extent influenced by the human biological tendencies they control or exploit. A sex factor, for example, might emerge either from purely sociological or from purely biological data. The case is perhaps less obvious for cognitive traits, but it is at least conceivable that the biological capacities of the human organism have historically had some bearing on what society has tended to recognize, name, and educate as a unit. (Loehlin & Vandenberg, 1968, p. 275)

A somewhat similar approach was taken more recently by Loehlin and Nichols (1976) in their National Merit Study of specific cognitive abilities and personality in 850 pairs of twins. Although difference matrices representing genetic covariances were not obtained, a similar pattern of MZ and DZ total correlations, between-pair correlations, and within-pair correlations was observed.

During the last several years, a methodologically sophisticated series of multivariate, behavioral genetic analyses has been reported by Eaves and his colleagues. Eaves and Gale (1974) extended multivariate twin analyses to estimate additive genetic, dominance, and between- and within-family environmental covariances. Reanalyses of Loehlin and Vandenberg's PMA twin data again demonstrated that a large proportion of the genetic variance may be accounted for by a single general factor.

More recently, Martin and Eaves (1977) adapted Jöreskog's (1973) analysis of covariance structures to the simultaneous maximum likelihood estimation of genetic and environmental factor loadings and specific variances. Their method facilitates formulation of both a biometrical-genetical model and a model for the structure of trait covariation. Goodness of fit is tested by chi square, and standard errors of estimated parameters are obtained. Application of this method to Loehlin and Vandenberg's PMA twin data indicated that the multivariate structure of the five ability measures is consistent with a causal model of additive gene action and both within- and between-family environmental influences.

3.2 Animal studies

In contrast to the analyses of twin data reviewed in the previous section, estimates of r_A and r_E have been explicitly reported in animal studies. Hegmann and DeFries (1970a) obtained open-field behavioral data on members of two inbred mouse strains (BALB/cJ and C57BL/6J) and their derived F_1, backcross, F_2, and F_3 generations (total N = 2,641). Heritabilities of single-day activity and defecation scores and genetic correlations among them were estimated from parent-offspring comparisons in the F_2 and F_3 generations. These estimates, as well as pooled estimates of phenotypic correlations for these generations, are presented in Table 1.

Environmental correlations among the single-day measures (see Table 2) were estimated in two different ways: (1) from phenotypic correlations within the isogenic inbred and F_1 generations; and (2) from substitution of the values in Table 1 into Equation 4. Environmental correlations estimated from the data on the isogenic generations (above diagonal) are functions of environmental deviations only, whereas those estimated from the data on the segregating F_2 and F_3 generations (below diagonal) are due to environmental plus non-additive genetic deviations. A comparison of corresponding estimates above and below the diagonal in Table 2 indicates remarkable agreement, especially considering that entirely different data sets and methods of estimation were used.

A comparison of the values of r_E in Table 2 with those of r_A in Table 1 also reveals considerable congruence. Note that this

Table 1

Genetic Correlations (Above Diagonal), Phenotypic Correlations
(Below Diagonal), and Heritabilities (Main Diagonal) of Single-Day
Open-Field Behavioral Scores of Mice in F_2 and F_3 Generations

	Day 1 activity	Day 2 activity	Day 1 defecation	Day 2 defecation
Day 1 activity	(.28)	.94	-.51	-.89
Day 2 activity	.63	(.09)	-.10	-.76
Day 1 defecation	-.34	-.23	(.14)	.20
Day 2 defecation	-.29	-.47	.32	(.07)

Note. From Hegmann and DeFries (1970a).

Table 2

Environmental Correlations Among Single-Day
Open-Field Behavioral Scores

	Day 1 activity	Day 2 activity	Day 1 defecation	Day 2 defecation
Day 1 activity	---	.35	-.23	-.15
Day 2 activity	.59	---	-.13	-.25
Day 1 defecation	-.30	-.25	---	.29
Day 2 defecation	-.21	-.44	.34	---

Note. From Hegmann and DeFries (1970a). Estimates above diagonal were calculated from pooled phenotypic correlations within
isogenic generations, whereas those below diagonal were obtained
from solution of Equation 4.

is the same pattern of association observed by Loehlin and Vandenberg (1968) in their study of human cognitive abilities. This
similarity prompted Hegmann and DeFries (1970a) to entitle their
paper, "Are Genetic Correlations and Environmental Correlations
Correlated?"

The cultural hypothesis of Loehlin and Vandenberg (1968) did

not seem appropriate for explaining the pattern of association between r_A and r_E in the mouse data. Instead, Hegmann and DeFries
(1970a) proposed the following explanation: "From the standpoint
of biological efficiency, it would seem most reasonable that correlated characters should respond similarly to both genetic effects
and environmental deviations" (p. 285).

As a purely heuristic exercise, consider the metabolic path-
way/path diagram illustrated in Figure 3. Each of the three steps
in the pathway from tyrosine to norepinephrine is mediated by an
enzyme and, thus, is under genetic control. Dopamine and norepinephrine are brain amines which rodent studies have shown to be
related positively to wheel-running activity (Kempf, Greilsamer,
Mack, & Mandel, 1974) and negatively to feeding (Hoebel, 1977).
As a consequence, a gene substitution which increases the activity
of tyrosine hydroxylase (TH) or dopa decarboxylase (DD) will result
in more wheel-running and less feeding behavior. Conversely, a
mutation which results in reduced activity of TH or DD will increase feeding and reduce wheel running. Thus, mutations which
affect TH or DD activity will have pleiotropic effects on wheel
running and feeding which will result in a negative correlation
between the two behaviors. But how would environmental influences
be manifested? A higher dietary intake of tyrosine, for example,
would presumably result in greater wheel running and reduced feeding. Lower room temperature, on the other hand, could increase
feeding and reduce wheel running. Thus, at least at the biochemical level, it seems to make sense that there should be an element-
by-element association between r_A and r_E matrices. Perhaps the
congruence between such matrices could be employed as an index of
the extent to which genetic and environmental influences are mediated by the same physiological systems.

Hegmann and DeFries (1970b) subsequently subjected phenotypically standardized genetic, phenotypic, and environmental covariance matrices (Equation 7) to principal component analysis in
order to obtain linear composites with maximum genetic, phenotypic,
and environmental variances, respectively. Predicted rank order of
heritabilities was realized; however, the differences were relatively small, presumably due to the similar structures of the r_A
and r_E matrices.

An example of r_A estimation utilizing diallel analysis is provided by Henderson's (1972) study of the relative effects of early
rearing environment and genotype on discrimination learning by
mice. A total of 768 mice from six inbred strains and their F_1
hybrid generations were reared in either enriched or standard cages
for the first six weeks of life and then tested for discrimination
learning on several tasks. For all tasks, early enrichment
accounted for a relatively small proportion of the variance. From
the r_A estimates presented in Table 3, it may be seen that there is

402

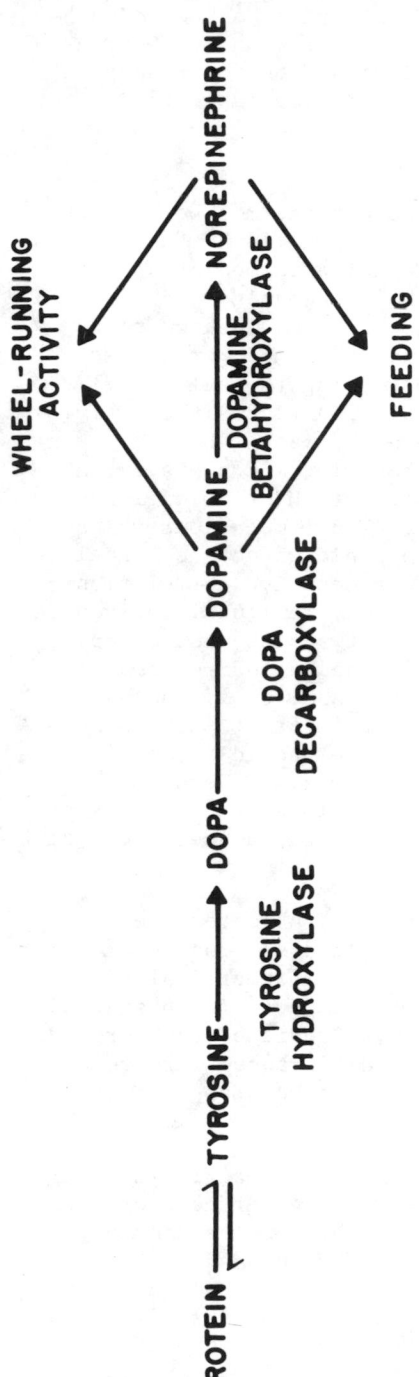

Figure 3. Metabolic pathway/path diagram of the relationship between brain amines and rodent behavior.

Table 3

Genetic Correlations Between Discrimination Tasks

	Vertical-horizontal	Improvement	T-maze (initial)	T-maze (reversal)
Black-white	.99	.52	-.34	.44
Vertical-horizontal		.58	-.19	.39
Improvement			-.93	-.80
T-maze (initial)				.84

Note. From Henderson (1972).

a high genetic relationship between performances on the two visual discrimination tasks and a moderately large relationship between performance on these problems and both improvement on the second task and T-maze reversal. In contrast, initial T-maze learning was negatively related to the two visual discrimination tasks and to improvement. These findings led Henderson (1972) to conclude that genotypes which do well on visual discrimination tasks tend to do poorly on the nonvisual T-maze problem and that no single learning factor could account for the results of this experiment.

3.3 Hawaii Family Study of Cognition

"Familiality" has been defined as familial resemblance due to genetic factors, environmental factors, or both (DeFries, Johnson, Kuse, McClearn, Polovina, Vandenberg, & Wilson, 1979). It is necessary, but not sufficient, evidence for the presence of heritable variation. Measures of familiality (regressions of offspring on mid-parent, single-parent/single-child correlations, and sibling correlations) for individual tests of specific cognitive abilities and principal component scores obtained in our Hawaii Family Study of Cognition have been reported elsewhere (DeFries, Ashton, Johnson, Kuse, McClearn, Mi, Rashad, Vandenberg, & Wilson, 1976; DeFries et al., 1979). In the remainder of this chapter, we shall report evidence of "cross familiality" in the Hawaii study.

A battery of 15 tests of specific cognitive abilities (see Table 4) was administered to members of 1,816 intact nuclear families (total N = 6,581) living on the island of Oahu. Both biological parents and one or more children 13 years of age or older were tested in each family. Due to the presence of marked age effects (Wilson, DeFries, McClearn, Vandenberg, Johnson, & Rashad,

Table 4

Cognitive Tests in the Hawaii Family Study

Test/Abbreviation	Test time	Relia-bility
Primary Mental Abilities (PMA) Vocabulary/VOC	3 min	.96
Visual Memory (immediate)/VMI	1-min exposure/ 1-min recall	.58
Things (a fluency test)/TH	2 parts/3 min each	.74
Shepard-Metzler Mental Rotations (modified for group testing by Vandenberg)/MR	10 min	.88
Subtraction and Multiplication/S&M	2 parts/2 min each	.96
Elithorn Mazes ("lines and dots"), shortened form/L&D	5 min	.89
Educational Testing Service (ETS) Word Beginnings and Endings/WB&E	2 parts/3 min each	.71
ETS Card Rotations/CR	2 parts/3 min each	.88
Visual Memory (delayed)/VMD	1 min	.62
PMA Pedigrees (a reasoning test)/PED	4 min	.72
ETS Hidden Patterns/HP	2 parts/2 min each	.92
Paper Form Board/PFB	3 min	.84
ETS Number Comparisons/NC	2 parts/1½ min each	.81
Whiteman Test of Social Perception (verbal)/SPV	10 min	.69
Raven's Progressive Matrices, modified form/PM	20 min	.86

Note. Reliabilities from Wilson et al. (1975). Details concerning testing procedure are available in this source.

1975), scores were age-adjusted using a z-score banding technique which eliminates both linear and non-linear differences among age bands (see DeFries et al., 1979).

Phenotypic correlations among the 15 cognitive variables were subjected to principal component analysis with Varimax rotation.

Communalities of one were used, and the number of factors retained for rotation was equal to the number of eigenvalues greater than one. The two largest ethnic groups in our sample are Americans of European ancestry (AEA) and Americans of Japanese ancestry (AJA). The same four readily interpretable factors (spatial visualization, verbal, perceptual [numeric] speed and accuracy, and visual memory) emerged when data were analyzed within each ethnic group (DeFries, Vandenberg, McClearn, Kuse, Wilson, Ashton, & Johnson, 1974). When these analyses were subsequently applied separately for males and females and for members of different age groups (Wilson et al., 1975), the same factor structure was found.

Parameter estimates reported in this chapter were obtained by means of the Kuse CROSS-COR program. This program provides estimates of phenotypic correlations among variables separately by sex and generation, as well as providing pooled estimates. Genetic correlations are calculated by cross-covariance and then substituted into Equation 6 to yield estimates of r_E. Regressions of offspring on mid-parent are employed as estimates of $h^2 = 1 - e^2$.

In the absence of common (between-family) environmental influences, the regression of offspring on mid-parent provides a direct estimate of h^2. Members of intact nuclear families, however, share environmental experiences which may have important effects on mental ability. Thus, for measures of cognitive abilities, the regression of offspring on mid-parent should be regarded as an index of phenotypic (genetic and/or environmental) similarity and not as a direct estimate of h^2. The same problem, of course, applies to estimation of r_A. Environmental deviations shared by family members for character X may be correlated to those shared for character Y. To the extent that this occurs, cross-correlation (or covariance) estimates of r_A may be inflated. Thus, in this chapter, estimates of genetic correlations obtained from the Hawaii data will be symbolized "r_A" to indicate that they serve as estimates of cross familiality, not direct estimates of r_A. Corresponding estimates of environmental correlations (due to within-family environmental and non-additive genetic influences) will be symbolized "r_E."

Data from a total of 830 AEA families in which both parents and at least one child (total of 655 sons and 670 daughters) completed all tests were subjected to cross-covariance analyses. Resulting estimates of "r_A" and "r_E" among the 15 test scores are shown in Table 5. Regressions of offspring on mid-parent are reported on the main diagonal. Corresponding phenotypic correlations (pooled across sex and generation) obtained from this data set are presented in Table 6.

Principal component analysis with Varimax rotation was employed in an initial investigation of the structures of the

Table 5

"R_A" (Above Diagonal), "R_E" (Below Diagonal) and Regression of Offspring
on Mid-Parent (Main Diagonal) for AEA Cognitive Test Scores

	VOC	VMI	TH	MR	S&M	L&D	WB&E	CR	VMD	PED	HP	PFB	NC	SPV	PM
VOC	(.64)	.32	.55	.50	.38	.57	.74	.41	.33	.77	.53	.51	.42	.88	.66
VMI	.11	(.15)	.26	.46	.03	.55	.36	.74	1.00	.49	.58	.52	.31	.47	.39
TH	.24	.06	(.41)	.45	.15	.42	.57	.34	.19	.46	.48	.58	.19	.58	.52
MR	.01	.03	.02	(.43)	.05	.82	.48	.84	.22	.63	.75	.77	.32	.64	.75
S&M	.30	.09	.24	.14	(.38)	.34	.42	.18	.00	.35	.31	.17	.73	.36	.21
L&D	-.12	-.03	.04	-.02	.12	(.24)	.47	.78	.37	.71	.82	.76	.54	.68	.77
WB&E	.27	.05	.27	.11	.24	.05	(.39)	.42	.14	.58	.48	.52	.36	.73	.64
CR	.05	-.10	.12	.27	.28	.06	.18	(.46)	.27	.51	.73	.69	.43	.53	.64
VMD	.01	.35	.03	.08	.12	-.03	.12	.01	(.31)	.41	.39	.31	.20	.18	.32
PED	.27	.11	.25	.15	.37	.05	.29	.24	.06	(.52)	.55	.46	.38	.89	.76
HP	.17	-.01	.13	.16	.27	.09	.21	.17	.01	.34	(.45)	.68	.47	.59	.73
PFB	.07	-.04	.10	.13	.16	.04	.13	.24	.01	.26	.28	(.51)	.36	.68	.68
NC	.21	.09	.15	.15	.48	.05	.23	.22	.10	.42	.26	.19	(.38)	.33	.31
SPV	.22	.10	.15	.11	.13	-.02	.15	.09	.12	.17	.16	.08	.17	(.26)	.90
PM	.10	.07	.08	.21	.27	.00	.17	.11	.01	.26	.22	.20	.26	.15	(.52)

Note. Parent-offspring regressions from DeFries et al. (1979). AEA = Americans of European ancestry.

Table 6

R_p Among AEA Cognitive Test Scores, Pooled Across Sex and Generation

	VOC	VMI	TH	MR	S&M	L&D	WB&E	CR	VMD	PED	HP	PFB	NC	SPV	PM
VOC	1.00	.16	.39	.27	.33	.16	.49	.25	.15	.56	.36	.32	.31	.47	.42
VMI	.16	1.00	.11	.14	.07	.08	.13	.13	.49	.21	.15	.12	.14	.17	.15
TH	.39	.11	1.00	.20	.20	.16	.39	.22	.09	.35	.28	.32	.16	.29	.28
MR	.27	.14	.20	1.00	.10	.25	.26	.52	.13	.38	.42	.43	.22	.28	.47
S&M	.33	.07	.20	.10	1.00	.19	.31	.24	.08	.36	.29	.16	.57	.20	.24
L&D	.16	.08	.16	.25	.19	1.00	.18	.30	.08	.28	.33	.29	.19	.15	.28
WB&E	.49	.13	.39	.26	.31	.18	1.00	.28	.12	.42	.32	.30	.28	.33	.38
CR	.25	.13	.22	.52	.24	.30	.28	1.00	.11	.37	.43	.46	.31	.24	.37
VMD	.15	.49	.09	.13	.08	.08	.12	.11	1.00	.20	.15	.13	.14	.14	.14
PED	.56	.21	.35	.38	.36	.28	.42	.37	.20	1.00	.44	.37	.40	.43	.52
HP	.36	.15	.28	.42	.29	.33	.32	.43	.15	.44	1.00	.48	.35	.30	.47
PFB	.32	.12	.32	.43	.16	.29	.30	.46	.13	.37	.48	1.00	.26	.30	.44
NC	.31	.14	.16	.22	.57	.19	.28	.31	.14	.40	.35	.26	1.00	.22	.28
SPV	.47	.17	.29	.28	.20	.15	.33	.24	.14	.43	.30	.30	.22	1.00	.42
PM	.42	.15	.28	.47	.24	.28	.38	.37	.14	.52	.47	.44	.28	.42	1.00

Note. AEA = Americans of European Ancestry.

Table 7

Varimax Rotated Factor Loadings Obtained from AEA Phenotypic,
"Genetic" and "Environmental" Correlation Matrices

Variables	Phenotypic factors				"Genetic" factors				"Environmental" factors			
	1	2	3	4	1	2	3	4	1	2	3	4
VOC	.13	.77	.22	.08	.18	.85	.26	.17	-.04	.69	-.36	-.02
VMI	.08	.11	.03	.85	.42	.16	.05	.91	-.10	.12	-.06	.78
TH	.13	.66	.01	-.01	.28	.68	-.06	.03	-.03	.64	.03	-.03
MR	.75	.20	-.07	.09	.88	.37	-.02	.06	.66	-.19	-.20	.15
S&M	.08	.22	.85	.00	.00	.25	.92	-.07	.39	.54	.20	.17
L&D	.56	.01	.20	.02	.78	.37	.29	.21	.06	.08	.85	.02
WB&E	.16	.67	.21	.03	.21	.78	.25	.05	.18	.55	.01	.07
CR	.74	.11	.16	.05	.87	.17	.15	.25	.60	.09	.10	-.11
VMD	.07	.08	.06	.85	.11	.14	.01	.99	.05	.00	.01	.81
PED	.36	.59	.30	.16	.32	.74	.21	.29	.44	.53	.04	.08
HP	.63	.29	.23	.07	.74	.33	.25	.24	.49	.32	.07	-.08
PFB	.67	.30	.01	.04	.75	.41	.05	.14	.55	.11	.04	-.12
NC	.25	.14	.81	.10	.31	.11	.87	.14	.45	.44	.10	.18
SPV	.19	.67	.01	.12	.39	.87	.14	.09	.18	.31	-.36	.18
PM	.54	.50	.08	.07	.59	.68	.06	.11	.53	.14	.14	.10

Note. AEA = Americans of European ancestry. Relatively high loadings (.40 or greater) on each factor
are underlined.

Rp, "R$_A$," and "R$_E$" matrices. For each matrix, there were four eigenvalues greater than one. From the Varimax rotated factor loadings given in Table 7, it may be seen that Factors 1 through 4 obtained from the Rp matrix correspond to spatial visualization, verbal ability, perceptual speed and accuracy, and visual memory, respectively. In the case of the "R$_A$" matrix, two small negative eigenvalues (-.01 and -.23) were found. Nevertheless, the factors obtained from "R$_A$" correspond relatively closely to those obtained from Rp. Principal component analysis of "R$_E$" yielded no negative eigenvalues, but the pattern of factor loadings differs somewhat from those of the other two matrices. Although the first two factors again correspond to spatial visualization and verbal ability, they also load on tests of perceptual speed (Subtraction and Multiplication, and Number Comparisons). Factor 4 again corresponds to visual memory, but Factor 3 is specific to Elithorn Mazes ("lines and dots"). Thus, the factor structures of "R$_A$" and "R$_E$" are similar, but they are by no means identical.

In order to quantify this subjective evaluation, the factor structure comparison method of Kaiser, Hunka, and Bianchini (1971) was utilized. This method yields measures of relationships among factors which may be interpreted as correlation coefficients. Resulting correlations among the principal components extracted from "R$_A$" and "R$_E$" are shown in Table 8. Inspection of the main diagonal of this table reveals considerable congruence among the factors. A more detailed analysis of the structures of "R$_A$" and "R$_E$," which employed confirmatory factor analysis of the phenotypically standardized "genetic" and "environmental" covariance matrices, is discussed elsewhere (Zonderman, Meredith, DeFries, & Vandenberg, 1979).

4. FACTOR-GENE MODEL

Royce (1957, 1977) has discussed the relationship between the multifactor theory of psychology and the multiple-factor theory of genetics. As may be noted in Figure 4, Royce suggests that sets of gene pairs influence specific group factors of intelligence. For example, genes at the A, B, C, and D loci influence spatial ability; those at the E, F, G, and H loci influence memory; etc. The model thus clearly implies genetic correlations among various measures of spatial ability and among various measures of memory. Evidence for the existence of such correlations was presented in Table 5. But to what extent may genetic correlations exist among the group factors?

Data from the Hawaii study were utilized to address this question. A finding of zero or near-zero "r$_A$" estimates among phenotypic principal component scores would indicate that genetic correlations among group factors are unimportant. On the other

410

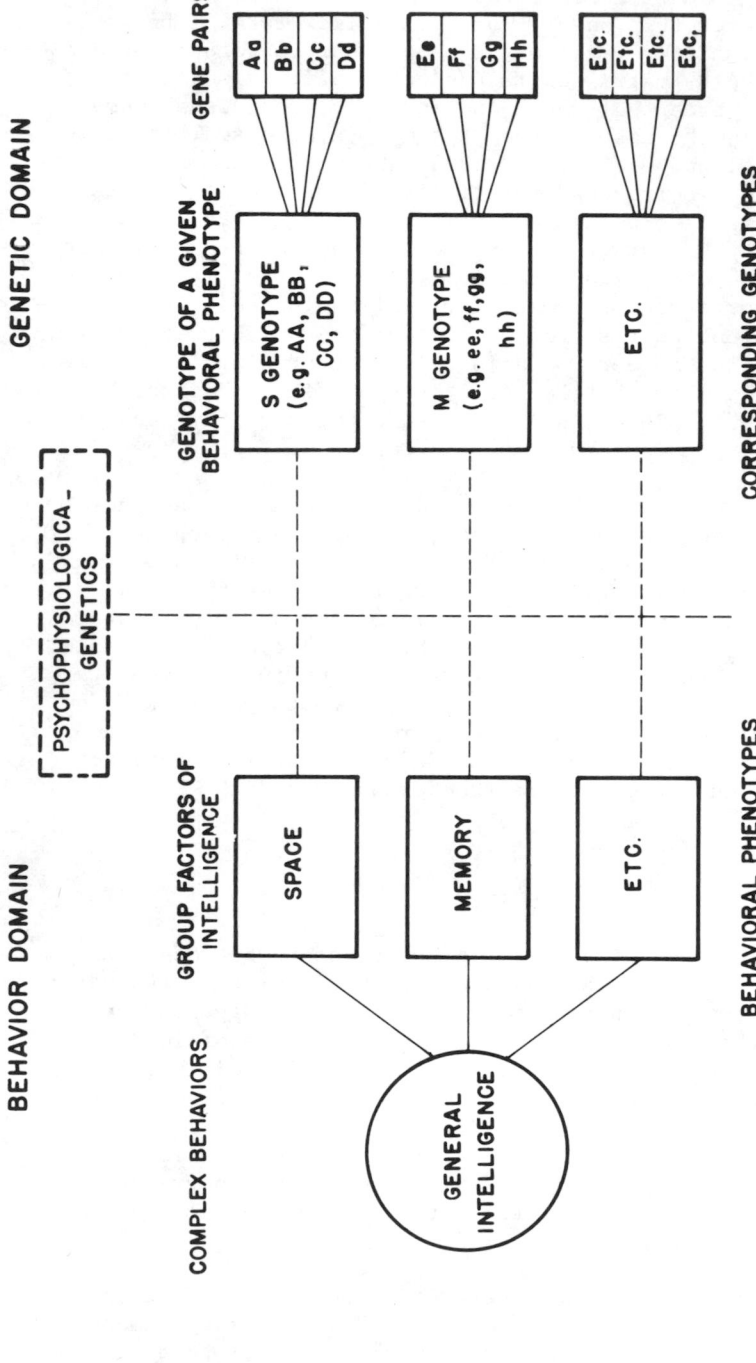

Figure 4. Royce's factor-gene model of the possible relationship between the multifactor theory of psychology and the multiple-factor theory of genetics. (Redrawn from Royce, 1977.)

Table 8

Factor Structure Comparisons Between "R_A" and "R_E"

"Environmental" factors	"Genetic" factors			
	1	2	3	4
1	.99	.17	-.01	.04
2	-.14	.82	.55	-.01
3	.10	-.54	.84	-.01
4	-.05	.01	.02	1.00

hand, values significantly different from zero would suggest that such correlations may exist among factors.

Cross-covariance analysis of AEA principal component scores resulted in the estimates of "r_A" and "r_E" presented in Table 9. The estimates of "r_A" between verbal and spatial abilities and between spatial ability and visual memory are both significantly different from zero ($p < .01$). These results suggest that some of the genes which influence spatial ability may also influence verbal ability and visual memory.

Table 9

"R_A" (Above Diagonal), "R_E" (Below Diagonal),
and Regression of Offspring on Mid-Parent (Main Diagonal)
for Varimax Rotated Principal Component Scores

	Verbal	Spatial	Perceptual speed	Visual memory
Verbal	(.54)	.26	-.04	.04
Spatial	-.30	(.60)	-.03	.31
Perceptual speed	-.05	.15	(.41)	-.06
Visual memory	-.04	-.14	-.03	(.31)

Note. Score coefficients obtained from total Hawaii sample. Regressions of offspring on mid-parent from DeFries et al. (1979).

For the benefit of those who, like the senior author, are neophytes in multivariate analysis, it is instructive to note that r_A and r_E among linear composites may be computed directly from r_A and r_E among the variables, i.e., it is not necessary to calculate principal component scores for each individual and then subject them to cross-covariance analysis. Matrices of phenotypically standardized genetic and environmental covariances among factors may be estimated from factor score coefficients and the variable matrices as follows:

$$C_{A_f} = F'C_A F$$

and   (13)

$$C_{E_f} = F'C_E F,$$

where C_{A_f} and C_{E_f} are $\underline{p}$ x $\underline{p}$ matrices of phenotypically standard-ized genetic and environmental covariances among $\underline{p}$ factors, C_A and C_E are $\underline{m}$ x $\underline{m}$ matrices of phenotypically standardized genetic and environmental covariances among variables (see Equation 7), F is an $\underline{m}$ x $\underline{p}$ matrix of factor score coefficients (estimated from R_p), and F' is its transpose. Genetic and environmental correlations among the factors may then be estimated by pre- and post-multiply-ing C_{A_f} and C_{E_f} by the inverse of D_h and D_e, respectively (cf. Equations 6 and 7). In order to test this method, factor score coefficients estimated from the Hawaii data (total sample) were substituted into Equation 13. The results shown in Table 9 (with-in rounding error) were again obtained.

When an orthogonal rotation of factors is employed, it would seem that r_A and r_E among the factors would be at a minimum. If so, estimates of r_A and r_E should tend to increase when oblique rotations are used. In order to test this hypothesis, phenotypic correlations obtained from the AEA sample (Table 6) were subjected to principal component analysis with oblique rotations (direct oblimin solutions) for a range of delta values from -5.00 to +.25, i.e., solutions ranging from relatively uncorrelated to highly correlated (Nie, Hull, Jenkins, Steinbrenner, & Bent, 1975, pp. 485-486). As may be seen in Table 10, phenotypic correlations among factors tend to increase as delta increases. Corresponding factor score coefficients were then utilized (Equation 13) to obtain estimates of "r_A" and "r_E" among factors. From the results presented in Tables 11 and 12, it may be seen that "genetic" and "environmental" correlations among factors also increase as the rotation becomes more oblique.

It should be recalled that the values shown in Tables 9 and 11 are not direct estimates of r_A. Nevertheless, the size of the

Table 10

r_p Among AEA Principal Component Scores,
Oblique (Direct Oblimin) Rotation

Delta	Spatial-verbal	Spatial-speed	Spatial-memory	Verbal-speed	Verbal-memory	Speed-memory
-5.00	.00	.06	-.02	.28	.18	.09
-4.00	.09	.09	.02	.31	.19	.11
-3.00	.24	.17	.09	.30	.19	.12
-2.00	.30	.23	.14	.24	.16	.11
-1.00	.32	.24	.14	.23	.16	.10
- .50	.35	.24	.15	.24	.16	.10
- .25	.38	.25	.16	.25	.18	.10
.00	.43	.28	.20	.26	.21	.11
+ .25	.56	.42	.37	.39	.38	.27

Note. Score coefficients obtained from R_p matrix (Table 6).
AEA = Americans of European ancestry.

coefficients certainly suggests that genetic correlations may
exist among group factors of intelligence, especially when oblique
rotations are employed. Adoption studies of specific cognitive
abilities, such as one currently being conducted by DeFries,
Plomin, and Vandenberg, should allow more definitive conclusions
to be drawn.

5. SUMMARY AND CONCLUSIONS

The theory and estimation of genetic correlations (correlation
between the additive genetic values for two characters measured on
the same individual) and environmental correlations are outlined
in this chapter, and behavioral examples are selectively reviewed.
Results of twin studies of cognition and personality and mouse
studies of open-field behavior suggest that genetic correlations
and environmental correlations are correlated. Evidence of "cross
familiality" consistent with this hypothesis was obtained from
data of the Hawaii Family Study of Cognition.

Data from the Hawaii study were also used to test Royce's
(1957, 1977) "factor-gene model" of the relationship between the

Table 11

"r_A" Among AEA Principal Component Scores,
Oblique (Direct Oblimin) Rotation

Delta	Spatial–verbal	Spatial–speed	Spatial–memory	Verbal–speed	Verbal–memory	Speed–memory
−5.00	.13	.09	.19	.32	.40	.25
−4.00	.25	.14	.28	.36	.40	.27
−3.00	.44	.20	.42	.35	.37	.24
−2.00	.49	.22	.45	.28	.30	.16
−1.00	.51	.21	.44	.26	.27	.13
− .50	.54	.21	.44	.25	.28	.13
− .25	.56	.22	.45	.25	.29	.13
.00	.60	.24	.48	.27	.33	.15
+ .25	.69	.40	.63	.41	.52	.33

Note. Score coefficients obtained from R_P matrix (Table 6).
AEA = Americans of European ancestry.

Table 12

"r_E" Among AEA Principal Component Scores,
Oblique (Direct Oblimin) Rotation

Delta	Spatial–verbal	Spatial–speed	Spatial–memory	Verbal–speed	Verbal–memory	Speed–memory
−5.00	−.20	.03	−.15	.25	−.01	.00
−4.00	−.16	.06	−.16	.26	.01	.02
−3.00	−.07	.14	−.16	.25	.04	.05
−2.00	−.02	.25	−.12	.22	.06	.08
−1.00	.01	.28	−.10	.22	.08	.08
− .50	.05	.30	−.09	.23	.09	.08
− .25	.08	.31	−.07	.24	.10	.09
.00	.14	.35	−.04	.27	.13	.10
+ .25	.31	.47	.14	.39	.28	.23

Note. Score coefficients obtained from R_P matrix (Table 6).
AEA = Americans of European ancestry.

multifactor theory of psychology and the multiple-factor theory of genetics. Results obtained from cross-covariance analysis of principal component scores suggest that genetic correlations may exist among group factors of intelligence, especially when oblique rotations are utilized. Adoption studies of specific cognitive abilities should provide more definitive results.

ACKNOWLEDGMENTS

The results reported here are made possible by collaboration of a group of investigators (G. C. Ashton, R. C. Johnson, M. P. Mi and M. N. Rashad at the University of Hawaii, and J. C. DeFries, G. E. McClearn, S. G. Vandenberg and J. R. Wilson at the University of Colorado) supported by National Science Foundation Grant GB-34720 and Grant HD-06669 from the National Institute of Child Health and Human Development. This report was also supported in part by NICHD Grant HD-10333.

We thank A. C. Collins and G. P. Horowitz for suggestions pertaining to Figure 3. We also thank Rebecca G. Miles for typing the manuscript and for her superb editorial assistance.

REFERENCES

Bock, R. D., & Vandenberg, S. G. Components of heritable variation in mental test scores. In S. G. Vandenberg (Ed.), Progress in human behavior genetics. Baltimore: Johns Hopkins University Press, 1968.

Crawford, C. B., & DeFries, J. C. Factor analysis of genetic and environmental correlation matrices. Multivariate Behavioral Research, 1978, 13, 297-318.

Darwin, C. The origin of species by means of natural selection or the preservation of favoured races in the struggle for life. New York: The New American Library of World Literature, 1958. (Originally published, 1859.)

DeFries, J. C., Ashton, G. C., Johnson, R. C., Kuse, A. R., McClearn, G. E., Mi, M. P., Rashad, M. N., Vandenberg, S. G., & Wilson, J. R. Parent-offspring resemblance for specific cognitive abilities in two ethnic groups. Nature, 1976, 261, 131-133.

DeFries, J. C., Johnson, R. C., Kuse, A. R., McClearn, G. E., Polovina, J., Vandenberg, S. G., & Wilson, J. R. Familial resemblance for specific cognitive abilities. Behavior Genetics, 1979, in press.

DeFries, J. C., Vandenberg, S. G., McClearn, G. E., Kuse, A. R., Wilson, J. R., Ashton, G. C., & Johnson, R. C. Near identity of cognitive structure in two ethnic groups. Science, 1974, 183, 338-339.

Eaves, L. J., & Gale, J. S. A method for analyzing the genetic basis of covariation. Behavior Genetics, 1974, 4, 253-267.

Falconer, D. S. Introduction to quantitative genetics. New York: Ronald Press, 1960.

Hazel, L. N. The genetic basis for constructing selection indexes. Genetics, 1943, 28, 476-490.

Hegmann, J. P., & DeFries, J. C. Are genetic correlations and environmental correlations correlated? Nature, 1970, 226, 284-286. (a)

Hegmann, J. P., & DeFries, J. C. Maximum variance linear combinations from phenotypic, genetic, and environmental covariance matrices. Multivariate Behavioral Research, 1970, 5, 9-18. (b)

Henderson, N. D. Relative effects of early rearing environment and genotype on discrimination learning in house mice. Journal of Comparative and Physiological Psychology, 1972, 79, 243-253.

Hoebel, B. G. The psychopharmacology of feeding. In L. L. Iversen, S. D. Iversen & S. H. Snyder (Eds.), Handbook of psychopharmacology, Vol. 8, Drugs, neurotransmitters, and behavior. New York: Plenum, 1977.

Jöreskog, K. G. Analysis of covariance structures. In P. R. Krishnaiah (Ed.), Multivariate analysis III. New York: Academic Press, 1973.

Kaiser, H. F., Hunka, S., & Bianchini, J. C. Relating factors between studies based upon different individuals. Multivariate Behavioral Research, 1971, 6, 409-422.

Kempf, E., Greilsamer, J., Mack, G., & Mandel, P. Correlation of behavioural differences in three strains of mice with differences in brain amines. Nature, 1974, 247, 483-485.

Loehlin, J. C. A heredity-environment analysis of personality inventory data. In S. G. Vandenberg (Ed.), Methods and goals in human behavior genetics. New York: Academic Press, 1965.

Loehlin, J. C., & Nichols, R. C. Heredity, environment and personality. Austin: University of Texas Press, 1976.

Loehlin, J. C., & Vandenberg, S. G. Genetic and environmental components in the covariation of cognitive abilities: An additive model. In S. G. Vandenberg (Ed.), Progress in human behavior genetics. Baltimore: Johns Hopkins University Press, 1968.

Martin, N. G., & Eaves, L. J. The genetical analysis of covariance structure. Heredity, 1977, 38, 79-95.

Nie, N. H., Hull, C. H., Jenkins, J. G., Steinbrenner, K., & Bent, D. H. Statistical package for the social sciences (2nd ed.). New York: McGraw-Hill, 1975.

Plomin, R., DeFries, J. C., & Loehlin, J. C. Genotype-environment interaction and correlation in the analysis of human behavior. Psychological Bulletin, 1977, 84, 309-322.

Pollak, E., Kempthorne, O., & Bailey, T. B. Proceedings of the International Conference on Quantitative Genetics. Ames: Iowa State University Press, 1977.

Royce, J. R.   Factor theory and genetics.   Educational and Psycho-
    logical Measurement, 1957, 17, 361–376.
Royce, J. R.   Genetics, environment and intelligence: A theoret-
    ical synthesis.   In A. Oliverio (Ed.), Genetics, environment,
    and intelligence.   Amsterdam: North-Holland, 1977.
Thompson, W. R.   Multivariate experiment in behavior genetics.   In
    R. B. Cattell (Ed.), Handbook of multivariate experimental
    psychology.   Chicago: Rand McNally, 1966.
Vandenberg, S. G.   Multivariate analysis of twin differences.   In
    S. G. Vandenberg (Ed.), Methods and goals in human behavior
    genetics.   New York: Academic Press, 1965.
Wilson, J. R., DeFries, J. C., McClearn, G. E., Vandenberg, S. G.,
    Johnson, R. C., & Rashad, M. N.   Cognitive abilities: Use of
    family data as a control to assess sex and age differences in
    two ethnic groups.   International Journal of Aging and Human
    Development, 1975, 6, 261–276.
Zonderman, A. B., Meredith, W., DeFries, J. C., & Vandenberg, S. G.
    Confirmatory factor analysis of phenotypically standardized
    "genetic" and "environmental" covariance matrices.   Behavior
    Genetics, 1979, in press.

COMMENT BY J. C. LOEHLIN

I am in substantial agreement with nearly all that DeFries and his colleagues say in their excellent chapter, but I might amplify one or two points.

The authors note of their equation (8) that if the numerator terms differ in sign, the arithmetic mean may be used in place of the geometric mean. But if this is other than a trivial difference due to both terms being near zero, better advice might be not to compute r_A at all, but to find out what has gone wrong instead.

It is an interesting consequence of equation (8) and Figure 2 that one can sometimes estimate genetic correlations from data that do not permit estimating heritabilities. To estimate heritabilities one must know what the genetic relationship is among the relatives being compared. To estimate genetic correlations, one need not. In Figure 2, to estimate h_x and h_y it is necessary to know the value of the paths from A to A_0. To estimate r_A one need only know that these two paths are the same.

In Table 9 it may be worth noting that if these are truly orthogonal factors, correlating zero phenotypically, any given r_A must be matched by an opposite-signed r_E whose size is governed by the relative weights of the h^2s and e^2s. The values in Table 9 approach but do not quite meet this condition, suggesting only approximate orthogonality. Observe that Table 9 provides--if the values are not all due to artifact and sampling error--a counterexample to the major thesis of the chapter, a case where genetic and environmental correlations are not alike in pattern, indeed are directly opposite.

Nevertheless, the vast majority of available data clearly support the authors' conclusion of similar genetic and environmental correlation matrices. Why should this be the case? The authors mention some possibilities. One is that (in the case of human traits) cultural pressures may be to some extent shaped by the biological facts which they attempt to control or exploit. Another is that biochemical systems that act in opposite ways on two traits will tend to produce negative correlations between them regardless of whether the influences affecting the control systems themselves are genetic or environmental. One might consider still other possibilities. Certain behaviors are inherently related via part-whole or common element relationships. The ability to add, for example, is a component part of the ability to multiply three-digit numbers, and every genetic or environmental event that affects the former skill ipso facto will have an impact on the latter, producing both genetic and environmental correlations between the two abilities. Time constraints can have the same effect. Average daily hours of sleeping and of waking should have a perfect negative correlation across individuals, and again, any influence, genetic or environmental, that increases waking decreases sleeping and vice versa, yielding negative correlations r_A and r_E. Such a constraint might be a factor in the negative feeding and wheel-running correlations in the DeFries example--when a mouse is feeding he isn't running in the wheel, and vice versa. In still other cases, several traits may have in common some underlying structure--performance on a variety of cognitive tasks may be affected by (say) density of brain interconnections. Any influence, genetic or environmental, that pushes the underlying structural feature in one direction or the other in different individuals will produce correlations among the cognitive tasks, and positive r_A's and r_E's. Finally, testing artifacts can produce correlations among behaviors irrespective of their causal origins.

So there are a number of reasons why genetic and environmental correlations might often show similar patterns. Still, in the case of humans at any rate, it is difficult to believe that arbitrary patterns are not <u>sometimes</u> imposed on behavior from without. If this is so, we should be able to find--once in a while--distinctively different patterns in r_A and r_E matrices. Let's keep looking.

COMMENT BY A. OLIVERIO

DeFries gives a good example of how genetic and environmental influences may be mediated by the same physiological system. It involves dopamine and norepinephrine, which are positively related to wheel running and negatively to feeding. A gene substitution (which increases the activity of tyrosine hydroxylase) results in more wheel running and less feeding behavior. Conversely, a higher dietary (environmental) intake of tyrosine also results in greater wheel running and reduced feeding. Thus, at the biochemical level correlated characters should respond similarly to both genetic and environmental effects.

While this is true for simple phenomena, such as wheel running activity and catecholamine metabolism in mice, it may also explain more complex behavioral events and the idea that the environment does not act on a "vacuum" but is mediated by biological systems. For example, take the case of environmental pressures and stress--the emerging behaviors are a reaction to environmental forces but they are also modulated by hormones. Similarly, isolation produces depression, and sometimes aggression, in both animals and human beings (consider people in jail or the isolated aged people). There is evidence that depression is accompanied or followed by a turnover of brain amines. The point is that both nature and nurture are needed to understand behavior.

COMMENT BY J. R. ROYCE

The main point of the Royce (1957) statement of the factor-gene model was that there are multi-factors at both the behavioral and genetic levels. It should be kept in mind that this point, which is now generally accepted, was not at all clear twenty years ago. This bit of history can serve as a reminder of the wide variety of ways theory and experiment interact in the advancement of science (Kuhn, 1970; Royce, 1978). In advanced stages there is a continuing interaction between theory construction and experimental observation. This occurs because of a high degree of, formalism (rationalism) combined with a high degree of perceptual acuity (empiricism) (Royce, 1970). However, in earlier stages of scientific development, it is not unusual for either theory construction or experimental observation to outstrip its counterpart. In general, theory construction has lagged behind experimental observation in the domain of behavior genetics. This is primarily due to the empiricistic ethos of both experimental psychology and biology in the 20th century (Royce, 1970; Royce, Kearsley, & Mos, 1975). This state of affairs is also attributable to delays in the development of quantitative theory in genetics and differential theory in psychology.

However, the factor-gene model is an example of theory construction preceding experimental observation. And, although the model was testable in principle, it was not tested in fact until after the methods of biometrical genetics were introduced to psychology (Royce, in preparation; Royce, Poley, & Yeudall, 1973; Royce, Holmes, & Poley, 1975). It is to be hoped that DeFries, Kuse, and Vandenberg's analytic-empirical contribution is a sign of maturity concerning the factor-gene model. They have provided a simultaneous demonstration of formal analysis and empirical observation which is characteristic of more advanced forms of science. If we can continue to sharpen our theoretical structures and our perceptual acuity, the factor-gene model will take on more and more substantive content, thereby providing the basis for evolving into a scientific theory with true explanatory power (Royce, 1978).

REPLY TO LOEHLIN

J. C. DeFries, A. R. Kuse, S. G. Vandenberg

We are in substantial agreement with nearly all that Professor Loehlin says in his kind review of our paper, but a rejoinder to one or two points is required.

In his paragraph four, Loehlin correctly points out that the values in Table 9 indicate only approximate orthogonality among the AEA principal component scores. Exact orthogonality was not obtained because the factor score coefficients utilized to calculate the AEA principal component scores were derived from the total data set, i.e., not just the AEA subsample. Nevertheless, AEA principal component scores are nearly orthogonal, with correlations between factors ranging only from -.05 to +.06.

In his paragraph four, Loehlin also notes that the genetic and environmental correlations among the principal component scores (Table 9) are not alike in pattern. This, of course, is artifactual, a necessary consequence of the zero or near zero phenotypic correlations between the principal component scores.

Finally, we completely agree with Loehlin's conclusion that distinctively different patterns in r_A and r_E matrices for human behavioral characters may sometimes be found and that we should keep looking for them.

REFERENCES

Kuhn, T. S. The structure of scientific revolutions (2nd ed.). Chicago: Chicago University Press, 1970.

Royce, J. R. Factor theory and genetics. Educational and Psychological Measurement, 1957, 17, 361-376.

Royce, J. R. The present situation in theoretical psychology. In J. R. Royce (Ed.), Toward unification in psychology. Toronto: University of Toronto Press, 1970, pp. 10-52.

Royce, J. R. How we can best advance the construction of theory in psychology. Canadian Psychological Review, 1978, in press.

Royce, J. R. The genetic correlates of emotionality, in preparation.

Royce, J. R., Poley, W., & Yeudall, L. Behavior-genetic analysis of mouse emotionality: I. Factor analysis. Journal of Comparative and Physiological Psychology, 1973, 83(1), 36-47.

Royce, J. R., Holmes, T. M., & Poley, W. Behavior-genetic analysis of mouse emotionality: III. The diallel analysis. Behavior Genetics, 1975, 5(4), 351-372.

Royce, J. R., Kearsley, G. P., & Mos, L. P. Psycho-epistemological profile manual. Center for Advanced Study in Theoretical Psychology, University of Alberta, 1975.

A Critique of the Concepts of Heritability and
Heredity in Behavioral Genetics

D. Wahlsten

The Taxonomy of Psychophenes

J. L. Fuller

A CRITIQUE OF THE CONCEPTS OF HERITABILITY AND HEREDITY IN BEHAVIORAL GENETICS*

Douglas Wahlsten

Department of Psychology, University of Waterloo,
Waterloo, Ontario, Canada

1. INTRODUCTION

The conceptual foundations of a scientific discipline have a pervasive influence on the kinds of experiments that are performed, how results are interpreted and how the findings are applied to social problems.

When these conceptual foundations are not strictly in accordance with the phenomena of nature themselves, experimental results will eventually compel a reassessment of the basic concepts, because the results directly contradict established hypotheses, or, as will be demonstrated in this essay, the results are quite consistent with a number of radically different hypotheses. In this latter case, social applications of experimental findings may be proposed which have absolutely no scientific basis and which encourage the most inhumane treatment of the dispossessed members of our species. These points are readily apparent in behavioral genetics.

In the laboratory where the heredity and environment of animal subjects are easily controlled, the most sophisticated experiments are yielding data which demand a re-examination of the basic concepts of behavioral genetics, especially the tenets of quantitative genetics. Large experiments on heredity-environment interaction are forcing a reconsideration of the assumption of additive effects of genotype and environment, and hence of the concept of heritability

---

* This work supported in part by grant A0398 from the National Research Council of Canada

itself. Results from the broader disciplines of genetics and developmental biology are calling into question the supposition that all heredity is comprised of Mendelian genes. Consequently, a brief review of these recent findings is in order.

The social applications of behavioral genetics also call for a most rigorous examination of the tenets of the discipline, especially in view of the notorious and pernicious proposals advanced by some individuals for compulsory sterilization on the basis of high "heritability" coefficients. Less controversial applications of these tenets are already being made on rather dubious grounds.

Many professionals in the life sciences maintain that disease with a genetic cause is incurable. Although it may be true that severe mental disorders cannot really be cured using available techniques, a belief that a disorder is incurable in principle necessarily impedes serious attempts to discover a cure or a means of prevention. This seems to have happened in research on psychoses, where studies of biological therapy to suppress symptoms outnumber studies of social etiology by about 30 to one (Brodie and Sabshin, 1973).

Others assert, on genetic grounds, that human aggression is innate and that war has its roots in human nature itself, not in the world social and economic system. It is apparent that violence is an everyday occurrence and that a new world war is a very real threat, but a belief that neither murder nor war can ever be eliminated from human society because of instincts inherent in the species necessarily directs thinking away from social changes which could potentially ameliorate the human condition.

2. THE CURRENT CONCEPTION OF HEREDITY AND HERITABILITY

Heredity is a property of an individual organism in relation to its parents and its offspring. Heritability is a property of a population of organisms. Heritability expresses the extent to which variability of some measurable characteristic of individuals comprising a population is attributable to variation in the heredities of the organisms.

It is almost always the case that a property of an organism which can be measured accurately and represented as a real number varies among organisms. It is also true that the heredities of individuals are rarely identical and that their environments are never identical. In order to study the inter-relationships among the measured property, the heredity and the environment of an organism, statistical models have been developed which are part of the field of quantitative genetics.

The model most commonly employed in behavioral genetics has been clearly presented by Falconer (1960). It consists of ten essential features.

A. The physical property of the organism which is actually measured, such as weight, speed or IQ, is termed the <u>phenotype</u> and is symbolized as P.

B. Heredity consists of the set of <u>genes</u> comprising the <u>chromosomes</u> of the individual which are obtained from the two parents. Inheritance of the <u>alleles</u> occurring at a single <u>locus</u> is Mendelian, whereas inheritance of several Mendelian genes is termed <u>polygenic inheritance</u>. The individual's entire set of genes pertinent to a particular phenotype is called the <u>genotype</u>, G. In most situations it cannot be observed directly.

C. The <u>environment</u> of the individual, E, is every influence on the phenotype which is not a result of the genotype. It includes the environment external to the organism proper (food, temperature, etc.) as well as factors inside the organism (e.g., cytoplasm) other than the chromosomes.

D. The effects of genotype and environment on the phenotype are <u>additive</u>. This is summed up in a fundamental passage from Falconer (1960):

> "The <u>genotype</u> is the particular assemblage of genes possessed by the individual, and the <u>environment</u> is all the non-genetic circumstances that influence the phenotypic value. Inclusion of all non-genetic circumstances under the term environment means that the genotype and the environment are by definition the only determinants of phenotypic value. The two components of value associated with genotype and environment are the <u>genotypic value</u> and the environmental <u>deviation</u>. We may think of the genotype conferring a certain value on the individual and the environment causing a deviation from this, in one direction or the other. Or, symbolically,
>
> P = G + E " (p. 112)

E. If for an individual, i, the relation is $P_i = G_i + E_i$, then E is defined such that for all N individuals in the population,

$$\sum_{i=1}^{N} E_i = 0, \text{ and } \overline{P} = \frac{\sum_{i=1}^{N} G_i}{N} + \frac{\sum_{i=1}^{N} E_i}{N} = \overline{G}.$$

When G and E are uncorrelated, their variances (V) are additive, and $V_P = V_G + V_E$. From this relationship, heritability <u>in the broad sense</u> is taken to be the ratio V_G/V_P, and it is symbolized by h_B^2.

G. The genotype is further subdivided into three components:

A = average effects of the genes of an individual, or the breeding value of the individual when mated to a wide range of genotypes (which averages out dominance and epistasis);

D = dominance deviation, the effect of interaction between alleles within a single locus;

I = interaction deviation, the effect of epistatic interaction between loci.

These are additive, G=A+D+I, and their variances are regarded as additive, $V_G = V_A + V_D + V_I$. Heritability <u>in the narrow sense</u> reflects only the population variation in the <u>average</u> effects of genes, $h_A^2 = V_A/V_P$.

The distinction between h_B^2 and h_A^2 is important, because the parameters are measured and interpreted differently.

H. Expected resemblances between different kinds of relatives are <u>deduced</u> from a simple single-locus model summed across several segregating loci that influence the phenotype.

For example, in animal research a large number of male-female pairs and their offspring can be measured where the father impregnated the mother but never lived with the family. The model predicts that the regression of the mean score of the offspring (0) on the father's score (P) will be $b_{OP} = \frac{1}{2} h_A^2$ or $\frac{1}{2} V_A/V_P$.

I. The resemblances between relatives actually observed in an experiment are used to estimate the heritability of the phenotype in the particular population.

For the case of offspring - father regression, the result is $h_A^2 = 2b_{OP}$.

Using monozygotic (MZ) and dizygotic (DZ) human twins, and <u>assuming</u> that the environmental difference between co-twins is the same for both MZ and DZ pairs,

$h_B^2 \doteq 2(r_{MZ} - r_{DZ})$, where r is the intra-class correlation coefficient. There is no way to estimate h_A^2 from twin data.

Estimates of heritability from numerous other kinds of relatives are given by Falconer (1960) and McClearn and DeFries (1973).

J. The estimates of heritability are then applied in one of two ways.

a. Broad-sense heritability indicates the proportion of the phenotypic variance which is attributable to variation in genotype in the population. As will be discussed in detail in this paper, the main use of h_B^2 has been in polemics. For example, Jensen (1969) used published twin correlations to conclude that broad sense heritability of human IQ is about .8. Others have questioned whether more recent data are sufficient to reject the null hypothesis that $h_B^2 = 0$ for human IQ. Recommendations for government policy are sometimes based upon measured h_B^2.

b. Narrow-sense heritability is used to predict the initial response of a population to selective breeding for high or low values of the phenotype. If h_A^2 is measured for the population in question, and if the difference between the population mean and the mean of the selected parents is S, the selection differential, then the response to selection is R, the difference between the population mean and the mean of the offspring of the selected parents. The polygenic model predicts that $R = h_A^2 S$ for one generation of selection.

In most laboratory and farm experiments where environment is held constant over generations, eventually a limit to selection is reached where all V_A in the particular phenotype is exhausted and $h_A^2 = 0$. The model cannot predict what the selection limit will be or how rapidly it will be approached. Nonetheless, selection acts on variation in average effects of genes, and it tends to exhaust this variation.

This in a nutshell is the current conception of heredity and heritability in behavioral genetics. Heredity consists of Mendelian genes, and heritability reflects the additive actions of genotype and environment.

3. A CRITIQUE OF HERITABILITY

The majority of published articles and books in the field of behavioral genetics upholds a view of heredity and heritability very similar to the one outlined above. An accummulation of many experimental findings, with both animal and human subjects, however, is compelling a re-examination and reformulation of this view.

The paragraphs below will analyse some difficulties that have appeared in recent experiments that attempted to measure heritability. The problems can be broadly categorized as confounding, covariance and interaction of heredity and environment. The experimental findings challenge the fundamental assumption that the effects of heredity and environment are additive, and they raise grave doubts about many previous attempts to draw simple conclusions from estimates of heritability in human populations.

3.1 Confounding of heredity and environment

In order to separate experimentally the effects of heredity and environment on a particular phenotype, individuals with the same heredities must be subjected to different environments, and individuals with different heredities must be tested in the same environment. If two strains of mice with different heredities, H_1 and H_2, are reared in different environments, E_1 and E_2, according to this design

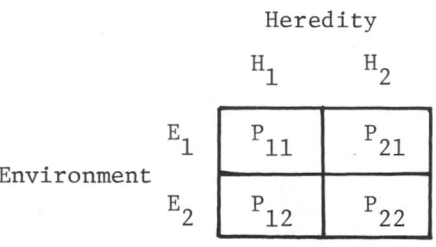

Fig. 1. Factorial design.

then definite conclusions about the influences of different heredities and environments on the phenotypes can be drawn.

A confounded experiment has the following design:

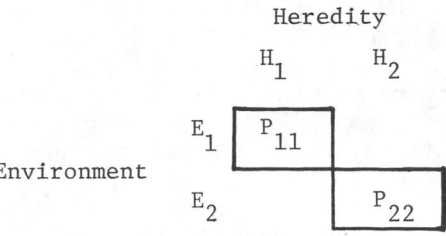

Fig. 2. Confounded design.

In this case it is impossible to ascertain whether $P_{11} - P_{22}$ is attributable to $H_1 - H_2$, $E_1 - E_2$ or both. This may seem like an elementary point, but it is precisely this point which is often ignored in behavioral genetics when human problems are the issue.

This problem is especially apparent in racial comparisons of behaviour. Drawing conclusions about a genetic basis for phenotypic IQ difference between people with "white" and "black" skin in the United States is generally not acceptable in scientific circles these days, mainly because of the obvious confounding of skin colour and income, education, etc. Consequently, some investigators have undertaken more complicated experiments in order to find some way out of this dilemma.

Both Vandenberg (1970) and Scarr-Salapatek (1971) combined racial comparisons of mental test performance with the MZ, DZ twin method. Vandenberg predicted that because of the widespread environmental deprivation of "Negro" children in Kentucky and Georgia, the expression of their genotypic variation would be suppressed, and hence heritability of mental performance as well as mean test scores would be lower than those of "white" children reared in more favourable environments. He observed that indeed among "Negro" children, MZ twins were not more similar than DZ twins, which indicated very low heritability. For the "White" children, DZ twin pairs differed more than MZ pairs. He concluded "...there is good evidence for the thesis that the ratio between hereditary potential and realized ability was generally lower for Negroes than Whites...".

Scarr-Salapatek (1971) conducted a similar study with many more twin pairs (N = 786) among black and white children of various social classes in Philadelphia. She observed the usual black-white mean difference on aptitude test scores, which proved nothing, but she also presented evidence that broad-sense heritability was higher among white children.

Furthermore, heritability of aptitude test scores was higher among the economically advantaged children than the disadvantaged, regardless of race. She concluded: "Since most blacks are socially disadvantaged, the proportion of genetic variation in the aptitude scores of black children is considerably less than that of the white children, as predicted by Model 1", the environmental disadvantage hypothesis.

There are two serious errors in these experiments, however.

1) Although the environmental deprivation hypothesis is consistent with the observed results of both Vandenberg and Scarr-Salapatek, a hypothesis of genetic causation is also consistent with their findings. Consider two models that are polar opposites.

Model I - The average genotypes for aptitude scores of black and white children are the same, but black children are reared in poor environments which impede the expression of genetic potential. Prediction: Mean score of whites will exceed that of blacks, and heritability of aptitude among whites will exceed that of blacks.

Model II - Early environment does not affect the expression of G; G and E are strictly additive. At one time long ago the genotypes of black and white people were similar, but many generations of selection against high mental ability in black people led to a decline in their genotypic values. Prediction: Because selection exhausts V_A, heritability of aptitude in blacks will be lower than heritability in whites, and mean aptitude test scores will also be lower.

Hence, two diametrically opposed models predict the same outcome of the twin study.

2) The environmental disadvantage model accepted by Scarr-Salapatek entails gene-environment interaction or non-additive effects. Nevertheless, the formula which she used to calculate broad-sense heritability was the familiar

$$h_B^2 \doteq 2(r_{MZ} - r_{DZ}),$$ which is based on strictly additive effects of genotype and environment.

How can we find a way out of this morass? There is no way out! The heredity and environment of the experimental subjects are confounded, and there is no statistical tour de force which can remedy this. When the two variables are confounded it is utterly impossible to discriminate between a host of alternative hypotheses concerning cause of phenotypic differences.

The trouble with the heritability coefficient is that the real conditions of the experiment may violate every assumption of the polygenic model (section 2. B-G), and yet an impetuous investigator can take the correlations r_{MZ} and r_{DZ}, insert them into $2(r_{MZ} - r_{DZ})$ and obtain a number which simply is <u>not</u> the heritability of the phenotype under investigation. This mystery coefficient can then be published in a journal, reprinted in popular textbooks, cited in the Congress and the parliaments, etc. Wild flights of speculation about a genetic basis for racial differences have taken off from a swamp of inconclusive research of precisely this kind.

This problem has existed from the earliest period of research on heredity and behaviour, long before quantitative genetics and the heritability coefficient were developed.

In his well-known <u>Hereditary Genius</u>, first published in 1869, Francis Galton (1892) stated:

"The arguments by which I endeavour to prove that genius is hereditary, consist in showing how large is the number of instances in which men who are more or less illustrious have eminent kinsfolk." (p.5)

Today this seems incredibly naive, because, of course, most of Galton's eminent men grew up in the family of their biological parents, thereby confounding the physical substance of heredity and the environment. He found that not simply genius but even the specific profession of his subjects was familial.

As primitive as this research design may appear, there are numerous modern studies which have not progressed beyond this humble beginning. For example, a study of heritability of neuroticism in twins employed a "postal personality questionnaire" that was mailed to twins who were reared in the <u>same</u> <u>home</u> (Eaves and Eysenck, 1976).

The same authors concluded that social attitudes on a "radicalism-conservatism" scale had a heritability of .65 (Eaves and Eysenck, 1974). The statistical methods may be more advanced today, but the actual experimental design differs little from that of Galton over 100 years ago. A cogent argument can be made that the mathematics serves mainly to obscure the simple fact that heredity and environment are hopelessly confounded.

434

3.2 Confounding of heredity and environment

Confounding of heredity and environment is just an extreme instance of <u>covariance</u> of heredity and environment. Recall that heritability is

$h_B^2 = V_G/V_P$ only when G and E are uncorrelated as well as additive. If the relation P = G + E holds, but G and E are correlated in the real world, variances are no longer additive. Instead,

$V_P = V_G + V_E + 2\ COV_{GE}$, where the last term is covariance of genotype and environment. Covariance can be either positive or negative, and it can be either less than or greater than V_G. When heredity and environment are hopelessly confounded, it means that they are perfectly correlated. This is represented in Fig. 3a. When G and E are uncorrelated, Fig. 3b obtains. Finally, when several levels of E occur at each value of G but COV_{GE} is non-zero, the situation resembles Fig. 3c. In this latter case, it is possible in principle to disentangle the contributions of V_G, V_E and COV_{GE}.

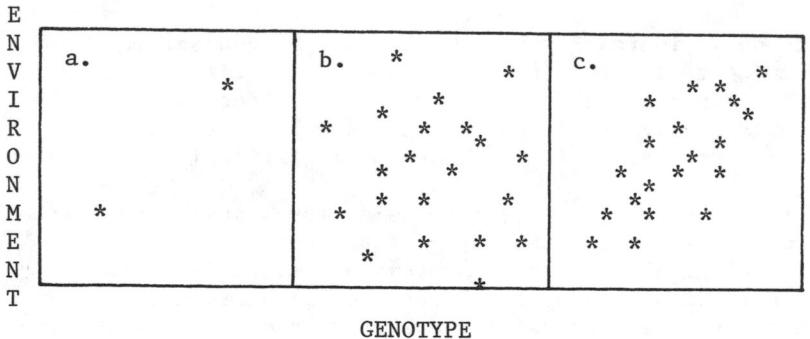

GENOTYPE

Fig. 3. Three types of Genotype-Environment Covariance

The real difficulty, of course, is that the genotypes cannot be measured directly and must be inferred from the observable phenotype. Because of this, the covariance of heredity and environment acquires special importance when heritability of some phenotype is to be calculated.

It is common practice in behavioural genetics to assert dogmatically that COV_{GE} should be lumped together with V_G. For example, Roberts (1967) asserted: "... the environment is defined as that which affects the phenotype independently of the genotype. If an effect stems from the genes, it is genetic; any other effect is an environmental one." (p. 218). This may look good on paper, and it certainly does simplify the algebra, but in the real world the covariance term goes where it pleases. It can act to reduce or augment the magnitude of measured "heritability" in comparison to h_B^2 when heredity and environment are independent.

Stafford (1970) approached this problem by assessing both the musical aptitude and amount of prior musical training in MZ and DZ twins. When the members of a twin pair had different amounts of training, the tendency was for the difference between DZ twins to increase more than the difference between MZ twins, thereby inflating "heritability" compared to cases where the members of a twin pair received similar training.

It is possible that the opposite phenomenon could occur. The twin with lower ability might receive special help in a society where the emphasis is on remedial training as opposed to special training for children of high ability. Provided that the remedial help was negatively correlated with genotype, it would tend to reduce "heritability" in comparison with a society where training was either equal for all genotypes or randomly distributed across genotypes.

Assortative mating is another culture-dependent social phenomenon which affects the magnitude of heritability. If the husband-wife correlation for a certain phenotype is positive, the additive genetic variance and hence heritability will be increased (Cavalli-Sforza and Bodmer, 1971; Wright, 1969), whereas a negative correlation between parents will act to reduce heritability relative to a population with no assortative mating. Of course, knowledge of phenotypic correlation between parents allows the contribution of assortative mating to be calculated according to the usual genetic models.

Heredity-environment covariance may also intrude if a society is afflicted by discrimination in education, employment, housing, etc., purely on the basis of overt physical features such as skin colour, nose shape, hair texture, voice quality, etc. Take a case where heritabilities of physical features themselves are high and heritability of mental performance without effects of social discrimination is low. If social discrimination has a substantial effect on mental performance, then the genotype (physical feature) – environment (discrimination) correlation will make the heritability of mental performance appear to be relatively large, compared to a population of similar genotypes raised in a society without such discrimination.

"Heritability" is supposed to represent the proportion of phenotypic variation in a population which is <u>attributable to</u> variation in heredity; that is, $h_B^2 = V_G/V_P$. It is true that when there is very little variation in heredity, as in a highly inbred strain, covariance will be nearly zero, because two things cannot covary if one of them does not vary. Nevertheless, covariance itself is no more attributable to variation in heredity than to variation in environment. If environment is uniform, covariance will also be zero. Covariance, and therefore the measured value of heritability, is as much a measure of the environment of a population as of variability in heredity. Heritability does not indicate the extent to which phenotypic variation is "determined" by genes.

Now let us turn this entire argument around. Genotypes cannot be measured directly; they are inferred from phenotypes. Environment can be measured in many situations, but the experimenter may not know <u>which</u> of the multitudinous attributes of the environment are the crucial ones that covary with the unseen genotypes. If a particular environmental characteristic, e.g., family income, does not correlate significantly with the phenotype under investigation, one <u>cannot</u> conclude that heritability of the phenotype is free from effects of heredity-environment covariance. There may be unmeasured features which play a large role. A really comprehensive study which collects information on many, many features of the environment has the power to exclude a host of environmental variables as contributors to significant covariance effects, but it cannot prove the complete <u>absence</u> of covariance effects.

Consequently, in human populations where direct measures of genotypes are lacking and environment cannot be controlled experimentally, it is impossible to discriminate perfectly between the contributions of variation in heredity and the covariance of heredity and environment to measured heritability. It is possible to demonstrate the presence of covariance when it exists, but the failure to detect significant covariance does not prove its absence.

3.3   Interaction of heredity and environment

The <u>interaction</u> of heredity and environment has both physiological and statistical aspects which contradict the supposition
that genotype and environment are additive (P = G + E).
Physiologically, interaction means that the expression of the
genotype depends upon the environment, and that the response to
a change in environment depends upon the genotype. Statistically,
interaction means that the two variables are not confounded and
do not covary, yet neither are their effects additive. Statistical interaction indicates the present of physiological interaction.

This phenomenon is most apparent in carefully controlled
laboratory research on animals using a factorial design where
each level of heredity, such as strain, is tested at each level
of environment, such as drug, early experience, etc.

Sometimes effects actually are additive, For example, Chen
and Fuller (1975) administered three dosages of thyroxine as
well as placebo to neonatal mice from lines selected for either
high, medium or low brain weight. Brain weight 22 days after
birth showed comparable effects of thyroxine for all three lines
(See Fig. 4).

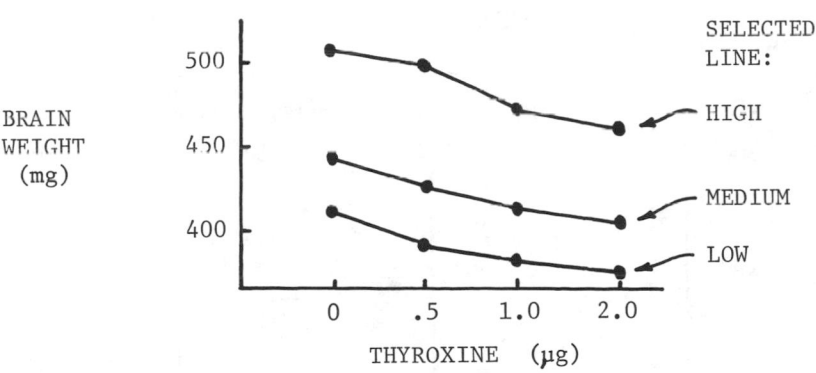

Fig. 4. Brain weight of mice, reported by Chen and Fuller (1975).

438

On the other hand, large interactions are commonplace. Anisman, et al. (1975) assessed the motor activity of three inbred strains of mice before and after a single electric shock. Half of the animals received saline injections and half received d-amphetamine prior to testing. As shown in Fig. 5, the effects of shock on activity depended not only upon strain and drug conditions, but also upon the specific strain-drug combination. Amphetamine caused the rank ordering of the three strains to be reversed.

Many phenotypes studied in behavioral genetics are exquisitly sensitive to experiences early in life and show large interactions with heredity, to the extent that the mode of inheritance in a particular experiment depends upon the early experience of the subjects.

Audiogenic seizures in mice normally occur only in susceptible strains such as DBA/2, but they can be induced in resistant strains such as C57BL/6 by a single brief exposure to a loud bell at about two weeks after birth (priming). Henry and Bowman (1970) primed the two strains and their F_1 hybrid at several different ages, and found that the degree of strain difference as well as F_1 mode of inheritance depended strongly on the day of priming, as shown in Table 1. This phenomenon may help to explain how one group of researchers studying the same strains found no clear evidence of single-locus control of seizure susceptibility (Schlesinger et al., 1966) whereas Collins and Fuller (1968), using slightly different rearing and assessment conditions with the same strains and crosses detected a Mendelian gene effect.

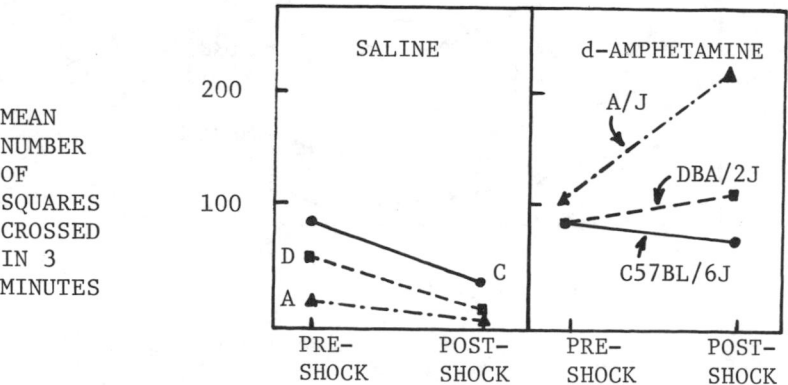

Fig. 5. Motor activity of mice, reported by Anisman, et al. (1975)

AGE AT PRIMING	STRAIN		
	C57BL/6J	F_1	DBA/2J
12 days	3.8	17.2	40.3
16 days	67.8	60.6	67.8
20 days	48.1	25.9	68.1
24 days	9.1	48.8	46.9

Table 1 Seizure severity score, obtained by linear interpolation from Fig. 1, p.238 of Henry and Bowman (1970)

Clearly, interaction effects can be very large and theoretically profound. There is simply no way to incorporate the results shown in Fig. 5 or Table 1 into the additive model where P = G + E. A separate term for G X E interaction must be introduced, making the analysis of variance model P = G + E + GE.

The problem is also evident in the results of Henderson (1970), who tested complex exploratory behaviour in mice from a diallel cross of six inbred strains which were reared either in standard plastic mouse cages or an enriched environment. The effects of rearing condition depended heavily upon genotype. As a result, heritability (h_A^2) was only .04 in the standard cages but increased to .37 in the enriched cages. In other words, rearing in standard cages (deprived environment) suppressed the expression of strain differences in heredity. The environments did not affect heritability merely by changing the environmental variance. On the contrary, estimated V_E was slightly decreased by enrichment. Just as in the case of heredity-environment covariance, heredity-environment interaction cannot be attributed exclusively to either heredity or environment. Whether interaction serves to increase or decrease measured heritability, compared to a situation with strictly additive effects, depends exclusively upon the relevant physiological functions of the organisms and the specific environments under investigation.

In a situation where neither heredity nor environment is under strict control of the experimenter, as in all human research, we should expect a priori to find heredity-environment covariance and interaction acting simultaneously, neither of which can be measured directly. To draw simple, unqualified conclusions about "genetic determination" of some characteristic from a measure of its "heritability" is therefore an act of blind faith, not a rigorous inference.

This problem was addressed by Falconer (1960), who concluded that in "normal circumstances" where the range of environments is not so wide, and where genotypically homogeneous groups such as inbred and F_1 mice are used, "... the variance due to genotype-environment interaction, since it cannot be separately measured, is best regarded as part of the environmental variance." (p. 134). But as Henderson has shown experimentally, this does not even hold true for a diallel cross. Having paid lip service to G X E interaction, Falconer then proceeds to derive expressions for relations between relatives and heritabiltty by assuming the irrelevance of G X E interaction. This may make for easy mathematics, but the conscious decision of a human being to include interaction with environmental variance need not correspond with the objective phenomena of nature that exist independent of human will. The whole edifice of this particular brand of quantitative genetics is built on a foundation of sand which is now being jeopardized by a rising tide of contradictory findings.

3.4 Heritability versus plasticity

Heredity-environment interaction can be viewed from a more molar perspective by examining the relationship between the heritability of a characteristic in a population and its plasticity within an individual in response to environmental change. There are two schools of thinking on this question.

Some individuals maintain that heritability and plasticity are inversely related, such that a phenotype which exhibits high heritability is therefore resistant to modification by the environment. For example, Jensen (1969) asserted that heritability of human intelligence was about .8 and on this basis speculated about the "genetic enslavement" of people on welfare which might result unless aided by "eugenic foresight" (selective breeding, or sterilization of welfare recipients). Thus, a large measured "heritability" is held to be indicative of "genetic" determination. "Enslavement" means that plasticity is very low for the phenotype "welfare recipient", and hence selective breeding is the only recourse.

Conversely, the adherents of this view regard evidence of the great resistance of a phenotype to modification as evidence that it is "genetic" or "innate". Lorenz (1965) gave this view in his interpretation of the results of the deprivation experiment in animal research:

> "If the information which is clearly contained in the behavioral adaptation to an environmental given is made inaccessible to the individual's experience and if, under these circumstances, the adaptedness in question remains unimpaired, we can assert that the information is contained in the genome." (p. 107)

Others maintain that heritability and plasticity are independent, in the sense that a phenotype with high heritability in a particular environment may nonetheless be easy to modify by changing the environment of an individual, and that a character may be resistant to short-term modification without being heritable at all.

Hirsch (1970) has made this point in unmistakable terms:

"High or low heritability tells us absolutely nothing about how a given individual might have developed under conditions different from those in which he actually did develop. Heritability provides no information about norm of reaction." (p. 101)

Applying this notion to the controversy surrounding human mental ability McGuire and Hirsch stated (1977):

"Since heritability is not a nature-nurture ratio, it says absolutely nothing about how much an individual can profit by education. Heritability deals solely with variances and is independent of the mean. That is, the heritability could remain constant for a population even if the mean IQ were raised from 100 to 120. High heritability sets no limits on what educational opportunity can do for individuals." (p. 68).

Data which confirm this view exist in great abundance in the literature. Take the case of height and body weight in humans. Newman, et al. (1937) measured phenotypic correlations in MZ and DZ twins, and their results (Table 2) demonstrated that broad-sense heritability was the same for the two phenotypes. Nonetheless, it is common knowledge that when a person goes on a starvation diet, weight plummets but height does not. Blubber is more plastic than bone. The relationship between heritability and plasticity of any particular characteristic is matter to be investigated, not a dogma to be asserted a priori.

	MZ TWINS	DZ TWINS	$h_B^2 \doteq 2(r_{MZ} - r_{DZ})$
HEIGHT	r = .93	r = .64	.58
WEIGHT	r = .92	r = .63	.58

Table 2 Newman, et al (from Stern, 1960, p. 556)

Within behavioral genetics proper there are many studies which prove that substantial heritability does not necessarily indicate low plasticity. For instance, Lagerspetz and Lagerspetz (1971) reported that by the 19th generation of selection for and against aggressiveness in male mice, there was almost no overlap between the aggressiveness scores of the non-aggressive (TNA) and aggressive (TA) lines. These results occurred when male mice were reared in isolation for at least eight weeks prior to testing. However, rearing male siblings together completely eliminated tail rattling and biting behavior for both selected lines. From previous studies it is also known that mouse aggression scores can be completely reversed by training (Lagerspetz, 1969).

The opposite phenomenon is apparent for human hand preference. Collins (1977) reviewed a large bulk of data for hand preferences (R or L) of twins, the results of which are summarized in Table 3. Thus, the twin data demonstrate a very low "heritability" of hand preference. This is an important finding, because hand preference is very difficult to modify in adults, yet its heritability is low.

To conclude this argument, let us refer back to Fig. 5. The behavioral response to the drug-shock combination depends upon the strain of mouse. Likewise, Table 1 shows that the pattern of response to priming on different days depends upon the strain of mouse. Therefore, the response to the environment depends upon the heredity (G X E interaction), and plasticity is heritable. From Table 1 we can also see that the extent of between-strain difference depends upon the day of priming. Henderson's (1970) study shows that rearing environment influences the heritability of exploratory behavior. Therefore, the expression of the organism's heredity depends upon its environment (G X E interaction), and heritability is plastic.

NUMBER OF TWIN PAIRS
OF EACH TYPE

	R-R	R-L	L-L	Phi Coefficient
MZ TWINS	782	244	37	.072
DZ TWINS	812	224	18	.002

Table 3 Number of twins pairs where both twins are right-handed (R-R), both are left-handed (L-L) or there is one of each type (R-L). Data from Collins (1977).

3.5 Conclusion

The supposition that heredity and environment are additive is untenable. Heredity-environment interaction is a property of real, living organisms. Heredity and environment interact in the physiological sense from conception throughout the life of an organism, and the moment that this interaction ceases, life ceases, and the organism drops into its grave. Heredity-environment interaction may give rise to wonderous and varied forms of life, but it means the death of the modern concept of heritability. "Heritability" is a creation of the human mind, and lacking a life of its own, its stillbirth has not caused it to decay and disappear.

It is becoming almost a ritual in modern behavioral genetics to speak with reverence of heredity-environment interaction and call for a restructuring of the basic model P = G + E. For example, there have been formulations proposed such as

"Phenotype = genotype + environment + genotype X environment interaction" (Manosevitz, 1969, p. 1101)

"P = G + E + (G X E)" (McClearn and Defries, 1973, p. 185)

"$\overline{P}_{ij} = \mu + (d)_i + e_j + g_{dij}$" (Jinks and Broadhurst, 1974, p. 29)

Nevertheless, the implications of tacking this interaction term onto the end of a moribund model have not been elaborated and tested in practice.

As has been shown above, interaction makes it impossible to interpret "Heritability" in the usual way in anything other than a carefully controlled laboratory or agricultural setting. It is not at all apparent how simply adding a term "GE" or "G X E" onto an already discredited "G + E" is going to save the day. Perhaps a more general formulation is needed such as P: (H$\longleftrightarrow$E); phenotype is the manifestation of the joint action and mutual interaction of heredity and environment. This formulation may not be readily amenable to deductive inference, but given the present situation in science, it possesses three outstanding advantages over the additive model: 1) It is not known to be false. 2) It cannot be used to derive coefficients such as "heritability" which are so far removed from their conceptual foundations that they seem to acquire an existence and meaning of their own. 3) It cannot be abused by racists.

Additivity makes a model mathematically convenient, and a model with additivity may describe a phenomenon with a high degree of accuracy, but accurate <u>description</u> in one situation is not tantamount to correct <u>explanation</u> of a phenomenon. It is well known that finite values of almost any functional relationship can be closely approximated by a convergent power series of the general form:

$$y = f(x) = a_0 + a_1 x + a_2 x^2 + a_3 x^3 + \ldots\ldots + a_n x^n$$

Take a situation where the rate of decline of a magnitude x over time t is directly proportional to its present magnitude, for example, depth of wine (x) in a cask that is being drained through a spigot. We have the explanatory model

$$\frac{dx}{dt} = -kx, \text{ where k is a constant. Hence,}$$

$$\int_{x_o}^{x} \frac{1}{x} \, dx = -k \int_{0}^{t} dt \,, \text{ which gives the result}$$

$$x = f(t) = x_0 e^{-kt} \,, \text{ exponential decay.}$$

It turns out that e^y can be approximated by

$$e^y = 1 + y + y^2/2! + y^3/3! + y^4/4! + \ldots\ldots y^n/n!$$

Thus,

$$x = x_0 \left[1 - kt + k^2 t^2/2! - k^3 t^3/3! + k^4 t^4/4! + \ldots \right].$$

These sorts of additive functions are extremely useful in hand calculators for computing non-additive functions such as exponential decay, but getting drunk on numbers and actually getting drunk on wine are two different things.

A model such as P = G + E + GE is perfectly adequate for analysis of an entire experiment with a factorial combination of strain and treatment using independent groups of animal subjects, but it is not necessarily a valid representation of the physiological processes of the developing organism or of the situation in a human population in everyday life.

At a time when abundant evidence from animal research demonstrates the pervasive and powerful nature of heredity-environment interaction, simple models which assume additivity of effects serve to impede theoretical advance. Given what is already known about the tremendous modifiability of human behavior,

it is unwarranted to think that heredity-environment interaction
will be any less important for humans than it is for laboratory
animals.

4. A CRITIQUE OF THE GENE THEORY OF HEREDITY

In modern behavioral genetics, the vast majority of published
articles are based on the idea that all heredity consists of
Mendelian genes which reside on chromosomes. From this theoretical
foundation, a continuous phenotype is dichtomized into genotype,
the set of an individual's genes, and environment, all non-
genetic influences. As Falconer (1960) maintains: "Quantitative
differences, in so far as they are inherited, depend on gene
differences at many loci, the effects of which are not individually distinguishable...Quantitative genetics is therefore an
extension of Mendelian genetics, resting squarely on Mendelian
principles as its foundation." (p. 1-2)

As shown in the previous section, the idea that genotype and
environment act additively is untenable. In this section, it
will be argued that a major source or erroneous thinking on this
question is the supposition that all heredity is Mendelian
genetic. It will be shown that there is much more to heredity
than just the chromosomes, and that most experiments in behavioral
genetics are incapable of distinguishing between chromosomal and
non-chromosomal mechanisms of heredity. Many kinds of evidence
compel a re-examination of the conclusions drawn from a vast
array of studies, and they illustrate unequivocally the need for
theoretical advance in order to pave the way for experimental
and methodological advances.

4.1 Historical overview

The modern conception of heredity evolved rapidly into its
present form over a period of roughly one hundred years. It
went from a stage where the laws and mechanisms of heredity were
quite unknown to one where textbooks and advanced treatises on
the topic are extremely abundant and where most high school
students can recite the basic doctrines. It developed in the
course of a vigorous and prolonged struggle between different
theories of heredity, eventually culminating in the nearly
universal acceptance in the Western world of the gene theory of
heredity.

When Darwin published his masterful Origin of Species, he
quite frankly acknowledged the limitations of existing information
about heredity:

"The laws governing inheritance are for the most part unknown. No-one can say why the same peculiarity in different individuals of the same species, or in different species, is sometimes inherited and some-times not so; why the child often reverts in certain characters to its grandfather or grandmother or more remote ancestor; why a peculiarity is often transmitted from one sex to both sexes, or to one sex alone, more commonly but not exclusively to the like sex." (1958, p.36).

The following passage shows the extent to which Darwin anti-cipated the experiments of Mendel:

"The offspring from the first cross between two pure breeds is tolerably and sometimes (as I have found with pigeons) quite uniform in character, and every-thing seems simple enough; but when these mongrels are crossed one with another for several generations, hardly two of them are alike, and then the difficulty of the task becomes manifest." (1958, p. 41)

As is well-known today, Mendel surmounted the "difficulty of the task" for certain characteristics of the garden pea in a classic paper published in 1865 (see Mendel, 1965, p. 7ff). He demonstrated a number of principles which are today considered to be the hallmarks of Mendelian inheritance.

1) Heredity functions via discrete units of heredity, or "constant differentiating characters".

2) These units possess integrity and constancy over gener-ations.

3) They exist in pairs, one from each parent.

4) The pairs segregate in the process of forming egg and pollen (or sperm) cells.

5) Units recombine randomly at the time of fertilization.

6) Qualitatively different pairs of "constant differenti-ating characters" are inherited independently.

From his remarks on the transformation of one species into another by artificial fertilisation and selection, it is apparent that Mendel also believed that all differences in heredity between species could be ascribed to his "constant differentiating characters".

Approaching these same problems from the realm of cell biology was August Weismann, who developed the theory that heredity is a property exclusively of a substance within the nucleus of the germ cells. In 1885 he wrote:

> "I propose to call it the theory of 'The Continuity of the Germ-Plasm,' for it is founded upon the idea that heredity is brought about by the transference from one generation to another of a substance with a de-finite chemical, and above all, molecular constitution. I have called this substance 'germ-plasm,' and have assumed that it possesses a highly complex structure, conferring upon it the power of developing into a com-plex organism." (Weismann, 1977, p. 168) "We cannot, it is true, directly see the ancestral germ-plasms, nor do we even know the parts of the nucleus which are to be looked upon as constituting ancestral germ plasm..." (p. 359).

He simply termed the germ-plasm "nuclear thread". He clearly saw the necessity for this substance to be reduced by half in the reduction division of reproductive cells prior to sexual mating, and he saw that as a consequence "..no two eggs can be exactly alike as regards their hereditary tendencies: they must all differ." (p. 379) However, Weismann did not follow his theory to its statistical conclusions about the laws of heredity which today bear Mendel's name.

After the turn of the century, Morgan and others demonstrated the phenomenon of linked loci and identified the chromosomes as the "nuclear threads" or "germ-plasm" of Weismann. Fisher and others proposed that all resemblances between relatives, even on continuous measures, could be deduced from multiple genes acting in concert. Finally, in 1953 Watson and Crick proposed that the deoxyribonucleic acid (DNA) molecule was the gene which alone possessed the property of heredity. Subsequent research led to the current formulation that DNA contains a code in the sequence of nucleotide bases which is transcribed by ribonucleic acid (RNA) and translated at the ribosome to yield a protein with a specific sequence of amino acids. The protein then acts as an enzyme, a hormone or a structural protein, guiding the metabolism and growth of a cell.

This theory denies that the physical substance of heredity can be modified in a desired direction by changing the environ-ment of an organism (inheritance of acquired characters). Rather, the source of all variation in heredity is believed to be random mutations in nuclear DNA, and the sole directing force of evolution is thought to be selection or differential reproduction of the fittest genotypes.

448

It is precisely this theory of heredity which is the conceptual foundation of the formulation P = G + E, additivity of genotype and environment. The roots of this theory can be traced directly to the ideas of Mendel and Weismann. Their ideas are the basis for the view advanced by numerous quantitative geneticists that the cytoplasm of the zygote counts as environment of the genes in the nucleus, not as an integral part of the organism's heredity.

To sum up, the gene theory states that all heredity consists of allelic pairs of genes which comprise the nuclear chromosomes, and that these genes are DNA molecules. The "central dogma" holds that DNA is the only self-replicating molecule and that it determines the structure of protein via an intermediary, messenger RNA. Symbolically,

Heredity = Chromosomes = Genes = DNA

4.2. Non-Mendelian inheritance

Although the chromosome theory of heredity went almost unchallenged in the West for many years, a large number of facts have accumulated in the past 25 years that demonstrate non-Mendelian or non-chromosomal inheritance in many species. Prior to 1950 there were a few classic cases of cytoplasmic heredity that appeared in many textbooks, but today there are new reports in the literature every week that cannot be accounted for by Mendelian mechanisms. Many introductory textbooks now devote at least a chapter to non-Mendelian inheritance, and there are even entire monographs available on this topic.

As one recent genetics text put it:

"If a strict, classical geneticist were transported through time and launched into the midst of non-Mendelian heredity, he might conclude that either genetics had gone mad or that geneticists had... Perhaps what is needed is a new point of view." (Pratt and Pratt, 1975, p. 315).

Because the topic has been well-reviewed elsewhere, simply outlining the diverse categories of non-Mendelian inheritance will suffice for the present purposes.

Several instances of non-chromosomal inheritance are

particularly relevant to this essay because they were originally
believed to have a Mendelian genetic basis. Belief that all
heredity was Mendelian led to uncritical acceptance of inconclusive results from experimental designs that lacked sufficient
power to discriminate between Mendelian and non-Mendelian
patterns.

A. The examples of non-chromosomal inheritance can be
roughly divided into those which apparently involve transmission
of nucleic acid molecules (germ plasm) from parent to offspring,
and those which apparently do not involve specific nucleic acids.
The former category has been well documented recently by
Grun (1976), although his review included a few examples of the
latter as well.

Many cases of cytoplasmic inheritance involve non-nuclear
structures which are endogenous to the cell and are permanent
over many generations. Mitochondria are classic examples of
this type, as are plastids in plants. These organelles possess
their own DNA and produce specific enzymes for important aspects
of cell metabolism. Inheritance follows a maternal pattern via
the cytoplasm of the egg. There are also many cases where
heredity follows this maternal cytoplasmic pattern, but the responsible cellular organelle cannot be identified. In this case
the hereditary factor is sometimes designated as a "plasmon".
Cytoplasmic inheritance is not wholly independent of the nuclear
chromosomes. On the contrary, phenotypes such as sterility in
mosquitoes (French, 1978) and fruit flies (Bucheton and Picard,
1978) have been shown to reflect the interacting effects of
cytoplasmic and nuclear heredity. In certain instances the
sterility results only when the cytoplasm and nucleus are made
incompatible by crossing two different strains.

Other possible mechanisms dependent in part on nucleic acids
entail infections with bacteria or viruses. The distinction between genuine parent-offspring transmission that counts as
heredity and simple infection is not always easy to draw. It
is well known that bacterial diseases such as syphillis and
viral diseases such as hepatitis in the mother can infect the
fetus (Brent and Harris, 1976) and are therefore hereditary, although many of these diseases can be cured readily through
chemotherapy. Grun (1976) points out that transmission of
bacteria from parent to offspring is extremely important for
viability in most species, and that acquisition of symbiotic
bacteria plays an important role in evolution. In humans the
intestinal bacterium Escherichia coli is a good example of
this phenomenon. In one study it was shown that intestinal
bacteria of chickens developed tolerance to the antibiotic
tetracycline and that these drug-resistant organisms spread

throughout a flock. But more startling was the observation that the tetracycline-resistant E. coli began to appear in the farmers and their families (Levy, 1978). Thus, chicken to human transmissions can occur by a similar pathway as parent to off-spring transmission, but only the latter could be regarded as real inheritance.

In between the categories of permanent cytoplasmic organelles and the transitory bacterial and viral infections are certain virus-mediated disorders which appear to be transmitted from parent to offspring over many generations and are not highly in-fective of non-relatives. Certain of these slow viruses have been incorrectly ascribed to the actions of Mendelian genes. One prominent example is Creutzfeldt-Jakob disease, a rare degener-ative disorder of the human nervous system, which was previously suspected of being caused by one or more genes (Pratt, 1967). Further research showed that the disorder could infect other organisms, and it was shown to bear many similarities to scrapie virus of sheep. (Gadjusek, 1977). Gadjusek has hypothesized that the disease was originally contracted by humans from sheep and then transmitted within families. Scrapie, too, was once be-lieved to be a Mendelian genetic disorder, and in Ontario it was customary to destroy all the immediate blood relatives of an affected animal in a flock. However, when its viral nature was confirmed, it became official policy to destroy the entire flock ("Disease", 1977).

Leukemia is now known to be induced in mice by a number of transmissible viruses, as are several other types of cancer such as mammary gland tumors. These viruses can be transmitted for many generations within an inbred line (Gross, 1970). Although several of these hereditary viruses have been well-characterized, the physiological basis of cancer is even more complicated because susceptibility to induction of leukemia is itself subject to in-fluence of Mendelian genes (Meredith and Okunewick, 1976).

It cannot be said that all phenotypes reflect either Mendelian, viral or cytoplasmic mechanisms. Rather, complex phenotypes reflect the concurrent and intertwined activities of nuclear chromosomes, cytoplasmic organelles and infective agents. By suitably complex experiments, the contributions of these different mechanisms to disease can be sorted out and understood, and this knowledge can then be applied to cure or even prevent scourges such as cancer.

The fact that many hereditary disorders may reflect the action of the slow viruses and not just chromosomes opens the door to potential cures for diseases which heretofore had been considered incurable because they were believed to be caused by Mendelian genes.

The relative importance of chromosomal and cytoplasmic inheritance for individual differences in brain and behavior is impossible to estimate at the present time. Obviously the vast majority of experiments in behavioral genetics deal with Mendelian inheritance, whereas reports of cytoplasmic effects are quite exceptional. The real problem is that most experiments cannot distinguish one source of variation from the other.

B. There are also cases of inheritance where specific DNA molecules do not appear to be the basis of individual differences. These are roughly divisible into a) inheritance of cell morphology, b) transmission of chemical substances other than nucleic acids, and c) "cultural" inheritance.

1) A cell with its characteristic shape and intricate structure does not arise de novo from a liquid pool of intermediate metabolites into which some chromosomes are plunged. On the contrary, a cell arises from a parent cell which possesses definite internal and external structure. The primitive idea that cytoplasm was like some sort of jelly cannot endure the astounding revelations of cell structure made with the electron microscope. The fertilized egg already possesses a rich complement of cytoplasmic structures, and these are an integral part of heredity.

There are certain well-documented cases where the structure of an organism is passed directly from parent to offspring. For example, the pond duckweed, Lemna perpusilla, reproduces by budding, and the first daughter frond emerges from either the right or the left of mother's midline (Doss, 1978). Within any one clone, "handedness" of first frond emergence persists for many generations, but the pattern can be disrupted and reversed by inducing a plant to bear two flowers through exposure to 8 hours of light and 16 hours of darkness instead of the usual continuous light. The new pattern is then perpetuated.

Even more astounding are the investigations of Sonneborn and others with protozoa, including the inheritance of doublet Paramecia and Tetrahymena. These doublet forms can be induced suddenly by treatment of dividing organisms with formaldehyde or an immobilizing anti-serum, and the doublet pattern can be inherited for many generations. Reviewing these and other experiments with protozoa, Nanney (1977) arrived at three fundamental principles:

    i) "Cells with the same genes and the same molecular composition may neverthesess have different hereditary patterns." (p. 27)

ii) "Genes and the molecules they specify determine the
permissible modes of pattern per mutation and the
states of greatest stability." (p. 30)

iii) Cells with essentially the same hereditary patterns
may have entirely different genes and molecular
compositions." (p. 30)

To what extent these principles operate in mammalian reproduction is not yet known, but their implications are profound
indeed.

2) Many diffusable substances can be transmitted from
mother to offspring across the placenta or via the milk, and these
substances can affect behavior and presumably parent-offspring
resemblance.

Mothers addicted to heroin give birth to addicted babies
(Brent and Harris, 1976), and mothers exposed to a polluted environment can transmit deadly poisons to their unborn children
(Zetterlund, et al., 1977). Antibodies can also be transmitted
across the placenta and confer immunity on the offspring
(Krakowka, et al., 1978). Stress on the mother can influence the
fetus (Beck and Gavin, 1976). A mother with a disorder such as
phenylketonuria or diabetes can exert a deleterious effect on
offspring development, even though the child is not afflicted
with the same disorder itself (Hornchen, et al., 1977; Kalhan,
et al., 1977). Offspring of some wild species show a preference
for the specific food substance eaten by the parent (Martin, 1956).
This has been demonstrated recently with controlled studies using
laboratory rats (Bronstein, et al., 1975) where the young rats
suckled on a mother which ingests a specific food later prefer
that food.

Most of these examples pertain to transitory effects, or
what Martin (1956) terms "lingering modifications", but they are
nonetheless sources of parent-offspring resemblance which must
be considered when designing and interpreting experiments in
behavioral genetics.

3) "Cultural" inheritance is important for studies of
heredity when offspring acquire specific information from their
parents via their sensory apparatus or other route instead of
through a direct physiological link.

Offspring learn many things from their parents by observation and interaction, for example, language. Many species of
birds can learn a unique dialect of song and even transmit it
across generations (Becker, 1978; Dittus and Lemon, 1969), and

laboratory animals are capable of acquiring knowledge of sophisticated tasks by observing conspecifics (Savage-Rumbaugh, 1978).
In one study with cats it was shown that kittens learn better
while watching their own mother as opposed to a stranger
(Chesler, 1969).

In human society it is generally the case that wealth and
poverty are hereditary. Complex legal structures are established
to guarantee the transmission of private property rights from
parent to offspring. Low income, poor diet, and many diseases
are also known to run in families. This fact was used by certain
unscrupulous individuals to justify their claim that pellagra
occurred in many poor white families in the southern United
States because of a hereditary defect and hence there was no
point in raising the wages of the workers so that they could
afford a better diet (Chase, 1977).

In most species the offspring inherit the environment of
their parents. Oak trees drop their acorns into soil favourable
for the growth of the particular species. The black oak grows in
dry soils, whereas the swamp oak thrives in moist bottomlands.
The offspring of each species are not spread randomly over the
countryside, but rather they are deposited into the environment.
which favored the growth and maturation of their parents in the
first place. Likewise, mice of a particular inbred strain begin
their lives deep within the body of a mother of that strain. They
inherit the maternal environment of that strain and no other.

All of the phenomena mentioned in this section can give
rise to parent-offspring resemblance. None of them depend upon
allelic differences in Mendelian genes that reside on chromosomes.
Some may not possess the durability of chromosomal inheritance,
but they can intrude into behavioral genetic experiments nonetheless.

4.3. Distinguishing Mendelian from non-Mendelian inheritance

At this point it is fruitful to consider a number of experimental designs commonly employed in behavioral genetics in order
to determine whether they are capable of distinguishing
Mendelian from non-Mendelian inheritance.

A. Comparison of inbred strains is probably the most common
design to be found in the literature. Almost every investigator
interprets a significant difference between two inbred strains
reared in the same lab as indicative of a "genetic" difference.
Indeed, the author of the present essay behaved this way until
1976.

However, two inbred strains may differ not only in the composition of their chromosomes but also in every one of the non-Mendelian mechanisms mentioned in Section 4.2. They can have different mitochondria and carry different viruses. The uterine environments and care provided by their mothers may be different. Inbred strains purchased from the Jackson Laboratory have been maintained for many generations on strain-specific diets (see Table 4).

Thus, simple comparisons of inbred strains are altogether incapable of distinguishing between Mendelian and non-Mendelian inheritance. It is a mistake to consider significant strain differences as proof of the importance of "genetic" variation. At best, they indicate variation in heredity. Reports should not be entitled "Genetic variation in behavior" but rather should appear as "Differences in behavior of inbred strains" or "Variation in behavior associated with variation in heredity".

STRAIN:	A/J	BALB/cJ C57BL/6J	DBA/2J Week 1	Week 2[*]
DIET[**]:	96WA	911A	96WA	234A
SUBSTANCE:				
Ground Milling Wheat	33.4%	51.5%	33.4%	46.8%
Skim Milk, Milk Protein	12.0	20.0	12.0	7.5
Edible Corn Oil	3.4	10.2	3.4	3.0
Dried Beet Pulp, Oat Feed, Alfalfa Meal, Fish Meal	None	None	None	25.0
Edible Wheat Germ	40.0	None	40.0	None
Other Substances	11.2	18.3	11.2	17.7

Table 4   Diets fed to different inbred mouse strains at the Jackson Laboratory, Bar Harbor, Maine

Source: E. P. Les, Staff Supervisor of Animal Health, March 20, 1975, personal communication.

[*] Diets given on alternating weeks.

[**] Diets prepared for The Jackson Laboratory by The Emory Morse Company of Guilford, Connecticut.

B. All of the points made about comparisons of inbred strains apply equally to selection experiments. High and low selection lines can diverge from control lines because of many mechanisms that are extra-chromosomal. The high line can rise above controls for a reason which is qualitatively unlike the reason for the low line declining. Increase in magnitude could be associated with Mendelian mechanisms, whereas decrease could be cytoplasmic. In either case, a selection experiment itself cannot discern chromosomal from non-chromosomal mechanisms.

C. Cross-breeding experiments have the potential to discriminate different mechanisms of heredity, but many complex crosses are necessary to accomplish this. The diallel cross which assesses only inbred strains and their F_1 hybrids is of limited utility in this regard. Reciprocal backcrosses and F_2 crosses are necessary, as will be described in detail in Section 5 of this essay. Crossing experiments can be used to separate various causes of a difference between inbred strains or between selected lines.

D. Sib analysis has limitations similar to those for the diallel cross. The between-sire component is a relatively good measure of additive chromosomal variation, just like the between-male component in the diallel cross. It is not a flawless estimate of V_A, because viruses, for example, can be transmitted by the male in some sexually-reproducing species (Thompson and Beaty, 1977). On the other hand, the differences between dams within sires may reflect non-chromosomal as well as chromosomal variation. Cytoplasmic and maternal phenomena in aggregate will tend to be reflected in the "common environment" term of the analysis. Further analysis of the components of "common environment" of full-sibs can be done only by crossing members of different families and breeding systematically within families.

E. Parent-offspring regression is afflicted with all of the perplexities of inbred strain and selection methods, whenever regression is done between score of the offspring and mean score of the two parents. If the male impregnates the female but does not live with the family, as in many farm and lab situations, regression of offspring mean on father's score may reflect mainly

additive Mendelian inheritance. Sophisticated regression analyses
can also be employed to distinguish between sex-linkage and autosomal Mendelian inheritance (DeFries and Kuse, 1978), but the
difficulties are multiplied in human research when the children
are reared with both biological parents.

In general, cytoplasmic inheritance and other maternal
effects should enhance mother-offspring resemblance, with mother-
son and mother-daughter correlations being increased similarly
in comparison with father-son and father-daughter correlations,
respectively. On the other hand, it is conceivable that mother-
offspring correlation can actually be smaller than father-offspring
correlation because of cytoplasmic inheritance, provided that the
cytoplasmic factors interact with chromosomal factors. Cytoplasm-
chromosome interactions have been demonstrated in insects
(French, 1978), and persistent maternal effects on gene expression
in mice are also known (Wolff, 1978).

The main conclusion from this discussion is that parent-
offspring regression by itself cannot be used to distinguish reliably among the different mechanisms of inheritance. It has been
shown that the most powerful design for assessing "heritability"
from a parent-offspring study is identical to the first stage of
a selective breeding study (Hill, 1970), and therefore selection
followed by crossing analysis appears to be a more promising
approach in animal research.

F. The twin method is the most commonly employed design for
the study of "genetics" and human behavior. In addition to
serious problems of heredity-environment co-variance in twin
research (e.g. Fabsitz, et al., 1978), the method is incapable of
discriminating precisely between chromosomal and other mechanisms
of inheritance. In comparison with dizgotic twins derived from
two separate eggs fertilized by different sperm, monozygotic
twins derived from mitosis of a single fertilized egg will tend
to have more similar cytoplasm and uterine environment as well
as chromosomes. The two eggs that form DZ twins can be derived
from separate ovaries and implant in different regions of the
uterus. The exact times of their ovulation and their maturities
at fertilization can also differ, whereas these things are
necessarily the same for MZ twins. The chorions of DZ twins are
always separate, whereas MZ twins frequently occupy a common
chorion, and they generally share a single placenta, although
DZ twins may also share one placenta (Stern, 1960). Thus, there
are many non-chromosomal factors in embryogenesis which may act
to make dizygotic twins less similar than monozygotic twins. At
the same time, cytoplasmic factors may operate to decrease the
concordance of MZ twins (Giroud, 1975).

There do not appear to be any feasible modifications of the twin method in humans that can separate the effects of the various mechanisms of inheritance. There are good reasons to believe that non-chromosomal effects exercise less influence on twin similarities in adult behavior than do chromosomal effects, but the precise degree of their relative effects is not known. We must conclude that, in circumstances where heredity-environment correlation is very low, the twin method can be used to explore the effects of differences in heredity in the broad sense, but that statements about the effects Mendelian genes based solely upon comparison of monozygotic and dizygotic twins are proscribed.

4.4. Genes and additivity of heredity and environment

From the above discussion as well as the ubiquity of strain comparisons, selection experiments and twin studies in behavioral "genetics", the conclusion is inescapable that belief in the Mendelian genetic nature of all inheritance generally leads to the conduct of experiments which are incapable of detecting non-Mendelian heredity or discerning one kind of inheritance from another. It leads to unwarranted conclusions about the effects of "genes" on behavior when in fact no "genes" have been observed at all. It leads to easy acceptance of evidence purporting to demonstrate the effects of a major locus on behavior, to the extent that a gene effect on learning can be named, published and catalogued on the basis of a single inconclusive experiment (Sprott, 1974).

Belief that chromosomes ("germ-plasm") are the exclusive wellspring of heredity also leads to a neat dichotomy of heredity and environment in biological theories and then to $P = G + E$. In the additive model "G" is held to be a definite numerical magnitude of a characteristic which emanates from a particular set of genes of an individual. Differences in environment among members of the population supposedly do not modify "G" itself but only act on the phenotype through the "E" term.

However, when the multitude of mechanisms which can influence parent-offspring comparisons is considered, the isolation of heredity from environment is not at all apparent. Where does a cancer-inducing virus or a slow virus belong, in G or E? And what about the mitochondria? The additive model elaborated by Falconer clearly includes these cytoplasmic organelles as "environment", yet they have been an integral part of our heredity for innumerable millenia. Perhaps quantitative geneticists would have us include these phenomena under the rubric of "common environment", but those who are not dyed-in-the-wool Mendelians ought to

recognize that mitochondria, plasmons and slow viruses are part
of heredity, and they should proclaim this conclusion under the
banner of "common sense".

Even the work of scientists who accept the gene theory of
heredity contra-indicates the assumption of isolation and additivity of heredity and environment. It is generally recognized
that all portions of the chromosomes are not metabolically active
throughout the life of an organism. On the contrary, chemical
events in the cytoplasm, which themselves may be consequences of
changes either internal or external to the cell, regulate the
activities of the nucleic acids and protein synthesis. It has
been proven beyond any doubt that the expression of the genotype
itself is regulated by factors external to the chromosomes and
that all gene action is not free-running and self-regulating
(Davidson, 1968; Hamburgh, 1971).

The metabolic interactions of nucleus and cytoplasm are
sufficiently complex that no clear distinction can be drawn about
what parts of the cell are "heredity" and what parts are
"environment". In order to metabolize carbohydrates, for example,
enzymes of both nuclear and mitochondrial origin are absolutely
necessary. At the same time, the metabolic products resulting
from the activity of the nucleus serve as the local environment
of the mitochondria, and vice versa. The products of one segment
of DNA can likewise regulate the activity of another segment,
making one gene the "environment" of another. Considering the
relationships between adjacent cells of different types, it is
known that the expression of the genes of one cell can serve as
an environmental stimulus to its neighbor cell, as in the case of
the interrelations of melanocyte and follicle cell in the mouse
hair bulb (Wolfe and Coleman, 1966).

The antiquated notion of Weismann that one particular molecule in the cell possesses heredity and exercises sovereign
control over the subordinate molecules cannot survive the mountain
of contrary evidence accumulating at an accelerating rate. When
it collapses, the familiar models of quantitative genetics will
also collapse.

4.5. An alternative formulation of heredity

Having criticized the theory that all heredity consists of
Mendelian genes on chromosomes, it is worthwhile to propose an
alternative view.

Heredity is everything that is obtained by the organism from
the parents. It includes the physical substance of heredity con-

tained in the sperm and the egg; that is, the entire metabolic system and intricate morphology of the zygote. It includes things such as viruses and chemicals which are incorporated from the parental environment, and it may also include experiences provided by the parents which change the internal state of the organism through sensory transduction. In many human cultures, even wealth and social position are, strictly speaking, hereditary.

The different components of heredity vary in their modifiability during the lifetime of the individual and their permanence over generations. A fool and his money may be parted with relative ease, whereas his chromosomes may possess a high degree of permanence. A chronic bacterial infection may be much easier to cure than a slow virus infection.

The causes of parent-offspring resemblance in some characteristic and the degree of modifiability of the components of heredity underlying any particular phenotype must be investigated for each population.

5.   THE ANALYSIS OF HEREDITY AND BEHAVIOR

In the final section of this essay it will be shown that criticisms of the current conceptions of heritability and heredity do not merely lay waste to ideas and thereby leave the field devoid of guides to experimentation. Quite the opposite is true. This essay does not challenge the existence of chromosomes or Mendelian inheritance but rather puts them in their place alongside other mechanisms of inheritance. Rather, it attempts to expand the field of investigation and counteract the faddish pursuit of "genes" at all costs and the concommitant neglect of potentially valuable discoveries of a non-Mendelian character.

Many of the familiar research methods can still be employed fruitfully, although the conclusions drawn from them need to be restricted. There is definite knowledge which can be gleaned from each type of experiment, and by performing these experiments in a logical sequence, hereditary mechanisms underlying variation in behavior can be discovered and manipulated in beneficial ways.

5.1 Detecting variation in heredity

The first step is to choose some behavior which is of interest to the investigator and then conduct a search for organisms with differing heredities which also differ in the behavior. In lab animals, comparisons of many inbred strains or selection in a heterogeous population for high and low expression of the behavior is a good starting point. In humans, the twin method may prove useful in this regard. Great care must be taken in all cases to insure that there is no confounding of the heredities of the experimental subjects and their environments.

Only if relatively substantial differences in behavior are observed is it then worthwhile to proceed with further analysis of the variation in heredity.

5.2. The dissection of heredity

The next step is to dissect the various components of heredity and determine their relative contributions to the original strain or line difference. In laboratory animals reared on the same food, bedding, etc., the major factors that can be disentangled by crossing the strains are:

A. The autosomes, and in some cases the X chromosome;
B. The Y chromosome;
C. Permanent cytoplasmic organelles;
D. Maternal environment.

If it is assumed that the male inseminates the female but does not live with the family, and if the sperm contribute mainly a haploid set of chromosomes but no cytoplasm, then the crosses listed in Table 5 can detect effects of each factor.

Given this set of crosses, the contributions of each factor can be measured by comparing two groups which are equated for three of the four factors. It is best to do this for more than one pair of groups in order to detect strain-specific effects and avoid spurious findings. From Table 5 it can be seen that each factor is measured by the following comparisons.

A. Autosomes

1) Females of Group 1 vs Females of Group 3 (also X chromosome)
2) Females of Group 2 vs. Females of Group 4 (also X chromosome)
3) Group 1 vs. Group 6
4) Group 2 vs. Group 7
5) Group 3 vs. Group 5
6) Group 4 vs. Group 8
7) Group 9 vs. Group 14
8) Group 10 vs. Group 16
9) Group 11 vs. Group 13
10) Group 12 vs. Group 15

CROSS NUMBER	MOTHER	FATHER	MATERNAL ENVIRONMENT	CYTOPLASMIC ORGANELLES	AUTOSOMES	Y CHROMOSOME
Inbred Strains						
1.	C57 X	C57	C57	C57	C57	C57
2.	DBA X	DBA	DBA	DBA	DBA	DBA
Reciprocal F_1 Hybrids						
3.	C57 X	DBA	C57	C57	F_1	DBA
4.	DBA X	C57	DBA	DBA	F_1	C57
Reciprocal Backcrosses						
5.	C57 X	(CxD)	C57	C57	B_C	DBA
6.	C57 X	(DxC)	C57	C57	B_C	C57
7.	DBA X	(CxD)	DBA	DBA	B_D	DBA
8.	DBA X	(DxC)	DBA	DBA	B_D	C57
9.	(CxD) X	C57	F_1	C57	B_C	C57
10.	(DxC) X	C57	F_1	DBA	B_C	C57
11.	(CxD) X	DBA	F_1	C57	B_D	DBA
12.	(DxC) X	DBA	F_1	DBA	B_D	DBA
Reciprocal F_2 Hybrids						
13.	(CxD) X	(CxD)	F_1	C57	F_2	DBA
14.	(CxD) X	(DxC)	F_1	C57	F_2	C57
15.	(DxC) X	(CxD)	F_1	DBA	F_2	DBA
16.	(DxC) X	(DxC)	F_1	DBA	F_2	C57

Table 5 Crosses of two inbred strains and their F_1 hybrids necessary in order to dissect their heredities into their components

(Note: C57 = C57BL/6J, DBA = DBA/2J, F_1, F_2, B_C and B_D indicate the distributions of chromosomes and maternal environment characteristic of a F_1 hybrid, F_2 hybrid, backcross to C57 and backcross to DBA, respectively.)

B.   Y chromosome (males only)

1)   Group 5 vs. Group 6
2)   Group 7 vs. Group 8
3)   Group 13 vs. Group 14
4)   Group 15 vs. Group 16

C.   Permanent cytoplasmic organelles

1)   Group 9 vs. Group 10
2)   Group 11 vs. Group 12
3)   Group 13 vs. Group 15
4)   Group 14 vs. Group 16

D.   Maternal environment

1)   Group 6 vs. Group 9
2)   Group 7 vs. Group 12

These comparisons are not statistically orthogonal, so it would not be wise to take any one comparison too seriously. However, the pattern of results for each factor should give a good estimate of its relative contribution to the original strain or line difference. The four major components of variation will not account for the entire inbred strain difference whenever there is interaction between mechanisms.

These comparisons by no means exhaust all possibilities for dissecting heredity. For example, ovarian transplantation can be used to study maternal environment, and cross-fostering can be employed to separate pre-natal and post-natal maternal factors. Successive backcrossing can potentially separate the contributions of cytoplasmic organelles and nuclear chromosomes to the effect of maternal environment. Further crossing can also detect semi-permanent cytoplasmic or maternal effects which dissipate over generations (Resslar and Emery, 1978).

Complex and systematic crosses of the type outlined in Table 5 have for many years been used to dissect hereditary factors. Recent examples can be seen in flax (Tyson, et al. 1978), fruit flies (Bucheton and Picard, 1978), mice (Wainwright, 1979) and many other organisms. Large numbers of subjects are necessary for experiments like these, but they are worthwhile if done well, because definite conclusions can be reached. When modest experiments are performed, modest conclusions are generally the outcome.

5.3. Mendelian analysis

If dissection of heredity reveals the importance of chromosomal mechanisms, then the familiar Mendelian analysis of segregating units can be undertaken. If there are no statistically
significant effects of permanent cytoplasmic factors or maternal
environment, then many of the groups in Table 5 can be pooled
for genetic analysis. On the other hand, Mendelian analysis must
be done only within a group when significant cytoplasmic and maternal environment effects are present, because the non-chromosomal
factors may very well affect the expression of chromosomal genes
and modify the observed mode of inheritance.

There is also a possibility that cytoplasmic factors may act
by influencing the metabolic activity of chromosomes. Thus,
observation of a significant difference between Groups 13 and 15,
for example, would not necessarily mean that the phenotype under
investigation is a direct product of a cytoplasmic organelle.
The phenotype itself could be strongly dependent on some chromosomal factor, but the origin of the phenotypic difference between
groups would be the cytoplasm, even if it were mediated by
nuclear-dependent enzymes differentially expressed in a segregating
population.

5.4. Salvaging heritability

What about heritability? Can anything be salvaged to make
this concept serviceable? Collins (1977) has approached this
question by developing a non-parametric measure of realized
heritability which makes no assumption about the specific
causes of parent-offspring resemblance. If c_j is the proportion
of members of a population who are selectively bred because they
possess a specific phenotype which other individuals lack (e.g.,
left-handedness), c_{j+1} is the new proportion of individuals
showing the phenotype among their offspring, then heritability of
left-handedness is given by

$$h_c^2 = \frac{c_{j+1} - c_j}{1 - c_j}$$

which is simply the ratio of the actual increase in the proportion
of individuals with that characteristic to the total possible increase, the proportion which lack the characteristic. According
to Collins:

"The observation of heritable forms makes, in general,
no necessary statements or proper predictions about the

genetic regulation of phenotypic variation. Similarly, the observation of genetic regulation of phenotypic variation makes, in general, no necessary statements or proper predictions concerning the heritability of phenotypic forms. Heritability should be considered to be a concept distinct and orthogonal to that of 'genetic inheritance.'" (p.287)

By following this approach, the experimenter can measure h_c^2 through one generation of selection. If progress occurs and heritability has a moderate value, continued selection may lead to substantial divergence of high and low lines. Once the lines have become well separated and asymptotic, then the crossing scheme outlined in Table 5 can be employed to dissect the heredities of the lines and discover the physiological bases for the response to selection.

REFERENCES

Anisman, H., Wahlsten, D., and Kokkinidis, L. Effects of d-amphetamine and scopolamine on activity before and after shock in three mouse strains. Pharmacology, Biochemistry and Behavior, 1975, 3, 819-824.

Beck, S.L., and Gavin, D.L. Susceptibility of mice to audiogenic seizures is increased by handling their dams during gestation. Science, 1976, 193, 427-428.

Becker, P.H. Sumpfmeise lernt kunstliche Gesangsstrophe vom Tonband und tradiert sie. Naturwissenschaften, 1978, 65, 338.

Brent, R.L., and Harris, M.I. Prevention of embryonic, fetal and perinatal disease, Bethesda, Maryland: National Institutes of Health, 1976.

Brodie, H.K.H., and Sabshin, M. An overview of trends in psychiatric research: 1963-1972. American Journal of Psychiatry, 1973, 130, 1309-1318.

Bronstein, P.M., Levine, M.J., and Marcus, M. A rat's first bite: The nongenetic, cross generational transfer of information. Journal of Comparative and Physiological Psychology, 1975, 89, 295-298.

Bucheton, A., and Picard, G. Non-Mendelian female sterility in Drosophila melanogaster: Herditary transmission of reactivity levels. Heredity, 1978, 40, 207-223.

Cavalli-Sforza, L.L., and Bodmer, W.F. The genetics of human populations. San Francisco: Freeman, 1971.

Chase, A. The legacy of Malthus. The social costs of the new scientific racism. New York: Knopf, 1977.

Chen, C-S., and Fuller, J.L. Neonatal thyroxine administration, behavioral maturation, and brain growth in mice of different brain weight. Developmental Psychobiology, 1975, 8, 355-361.

Chesler, P. Maternal influence in learning by observation in kittens. Science, 1969, 166, 901-903.

Collins, R.L. Origins of the sense of asymmetry: Mendelian and non-Mendelian models of inheritance. Annals of the New York Academy of Sciences, 1977, 299, 283-305.

Collins, R.L., and Fuller, J.L. Audiogenic seizure prone (asp): a gene affecting behavior in linkage group VIII of the mouse. Science, 1968, 162, 113-139.

Darwin, C. The origin of species. New York: Mentor, 1958. (from Sixth Edition, January, 1872).

Davidson, E.H. Gene activity in early development. New York: Academic, 1968.

DeFries, J.C., and Kuse, A.R. Sex linkage: An alternative test. Paper presented at the Behavior Genetics Association meeting, Davis, California, June, 1978.

Disease forcing destruction of flocks of purebred sheep. Kitchener-Waterloo Record (Ontario), June 4, 1977, p. 29.

Dittus, W.P.J., and Lemon, R.E. Effects of song tutoring and acoustic isolation on the song repertoires of cardinals. Animal Behaviour, 1969, 17, 523-533.

Doss, R.P. Handedness in duckweed: Double flowering fronds produce right and left-handed lineages. Science, 1978, 199, 1465-1466.

Eaves, L.J., and Eysenck, H.J. Genetics and the development of social attitudes. Nature, 1974, 249, 288-289.

Eaves, L., and Eysenck, H. Genetic and environmental components of inconsistency and unrepeatability in twins' responses to a neuroticism questionnaire. Behavior Genetics, 1976, 6, 145-160.

Fabsitz, R.R., Garrison, R.J., Feinleib, M., and Hjortland, M. A twin analysis of dietary intake: Evidence for a need to control for possible environmental differences in MZ and DZ twins. Behavior Genetics, 1978, 8, 15-26.

Falconer, D.S. Introduction to quantitative genetics. New York: Ronald, 1960.

French, W.L. Genetic and phenogenetic studies on the dynamic nature of the cytoplasmic inheritance system in Culex pipiens. Genetics, 1978, 88, 447-455.

Gajdusek, D.C. Unconventional viruses and the origin and disappearance of kuru. Science, 1977, 197, 943-960.

Galton, F. Hereditary genius. An inquiry into its laws and consequences. London: Macmillan, 1892. (First Edition 1869).

Giroud, A.   Role possible du cytoplasme au cours de la morpho-
genese notamment dans le cas de la gemellite.   Acta Geneticae
Medicae et Gemellologiae, 1975, 24, 251-259.

Gross, L.   Oncogenic viruses.   Oxford: Pergamon, 1970.

Grun, P.   Cytoplasmic genetics and evolution.   New York: Columbia
University Press, 1976.

Hamburgh, M.   Theories of differentiation.   London: Arnold, 1971.

Henderson, N.D.   Genetic influences on the behavior of mice can
be obscured by laboratory rearing.   Journal of Comparative and
Physiological Psychology, 1970, 72, 505-511.

Henry, K.R.,   and Bowman, R.E.   Behavior-genetic analysis of the
ontogeny of acoustically primed audiogenic seizures in mice.
Journal of Comparative and Physiological Psychology, 1979, 70,
235-241.

Hill, W.G.   Design of experiments to estimate heritability by regression of offspring on selected parents.   Biometrics, 1970, 26,
565-571.

Hirsch, J.   Behavior-genetic analysis and its biosocial consequences.   Seminars in Psychiatry, 1970, 2, 89-105.

Hornchen, H., Stuhlsatz, H.W., Plagemann, L., Eberle, P., and
Habedank, M.   Kinder phenylketonurischer Mutter.   Deutsche
Medizinische Wochenschrift, 1977, 102, 308-312.

Jensen, A.R.   How much can we boost IQ and scholastic achievement?
Environment, heredity, and intelligence.   Harvard Educational
Review, 1969, Reprint Series No. 2, 1-123.

Jinks, J.L., and Broadhurst, P.L.   How to analyse the inheritance
of behavior in animals - the biometrical approach.   In J.H.F.
van Abeelen (Ed.), The genetics of behaviour.   Amsterdam: North
Holland, 1974, 1-41.

Kalhan, S.C., Savin, S., and Adam, P.A.   Attenuated glucose production rate in newborn infants of insulin-dependent diabetic
mothers.   New England Journal of Medicine, 1977, 296, 375-376.

Krakowka, S., Long, D., and Koestner, A.   Influence of transpla-
centally acquired antibody on neonatal susceptibility to canine
distemper virus in gnotobiotic dogs.   Journal of Infectious
Diseases, 1978, 137, 605-608.

468

Lagerspetz, K.M.J. Aggression and aggressiveness in laboratory mice. In S. Garattini and E.G. Sigg (Eds.), Aggressive Behavior, Proceedings of the Symposium on the Biology of Aggressive Behaviour, Milan, May, 1968. Amsterdam: Excerpta Medica, 1969, 77-85.

Lagerspetz, K.M.J., and Lagerspetz, K.Y.H. Changes in the aggressiveness of mice resulting from selective breeding, learning and social isolation. Scandanavian Journal of Psychology, 1971, 12, 241-248.

Levy, S.B. Emergence of antibiotic-resistant bacteria in the intestinal flora of farm inhabitants. Journal of Infectious Diseases, 1978, 137, 688-690.

Lorenz, K. Evolution and modification of behavior. Chicago: University of Chicago Press, 1965.

Manosevitz, M. A note on genotype x environment interaction. Texas Reports on Biology and Medicine, 1969, 27, 1089-1103.

Martin, C.P. Psychology, evolution and sex. Springfield, Illinois: Thomas, 1956.

McClearn, G.E., and DeFries, J.C. Introduction to behavioral genetics. San Francisco: Freeman, 1973.

McGuire, T.R., and Hirsch, J. General intelligence (g) and heritability (H^2, h^2). In I.C. Uzgiris and F. Weizmann (Eds.), The structuring of experience. New York: Plenum, 1977, 25-72.

Mendel, G. Experiments in plant hybridisation. (J.H. Bennett, Ed.) London: Oliver and Boyd, 1965. (Original 1865).

Meredith, R.F., and Okunewick, J.P. Genetic influence in murine viral leukemogenesis. Biomedicine, 1976, 24, 374-380.

Nanney, D.L. Molecules and morphologies: The perpetuation of pattern in the ciliated protozoa. Journal of Protozoology, 1977, 24, 27-35.

Newman, H.H., Freeman, F.N., and Holzinger, K.J. Twins: A study of heredity and environment. Chicago: University of Chicago Press, 1937. (Cited in C. Stern, Principles of Human Genetics, Second Edition).

Pratt, R.T.C. The genetics of neurological disorders. London: Oxford University Press, 1967.

Pratt, D.I., and Pratt, G.R. An introduction to modern genetics.
Don Mills, Ontario: Addison-Wesley, 1975.

Resslar, P.M., and Emery, D.A. Inheritance of growth habit in
peanuts: cytoplasmic or maternal modifications? Journal of
Heredity, 1978, 69, 101-106.

Roberts, R.C. Some concepts and methods in quantitative genetics.
In J. Hirsch (Ed.), Behavior-genetic analysis. New York:
McGraw-Hill, 1967, 214-257.

Savage-Rumbaugh, E.S., Rumbaugh, D.M., and Boysen, S. Symbolic
communication between two chimpanzees (Pan troglodytes).
Science, 1978, 201, 641-644.

Scarr-Salapatek, S. Race, social class, and IQ. Science, 1971,
174, 1285-1295.

Schlesinger, K., Elston, R.C., and Boggan, W. The genetics of
sound-induced seizure in inbred mice. Genetics, 1966, 54,
95-102.

Sprott, R.L. Passive-avoidance performance in mice: Evidence
for single-locus inheritance. Behavioral Biology, 1974, 11,
231-237.

Stafford, R.E. Estimation of the interaction between heredity
and environment for musical aptitude of twins. Human Heredity,
1970, 20, 356-360.

Stern, C. Principles of Human Genetics, Second Edition.
San Francisco: Freeman, 1960.

Thompson, W.H., and Beaty, B.J. Venereal transmission of La
Crosse (California encpehalitis) arbovirus in Aedes triseriatus
mosquitoes. Science, 1977, 196, 530-531.

Tyson, H., Taylor, S.A., and Fieldes, M.A. Segregation of the
environmentally induced relative mobility shifts in flax geno-
troph peroxidase isozymes. Heredity, 1978, 40, 281-290.

Vandenberg, S.G. A comparison of heritability estimates of US
Negro and white high school students. Acta Geneticae Medicae
et Gemellologiae, 1970, 19, 280284.

Wainwright, P. The relative effects of maternal and pup heredity
on postnatal mouse development. Developmental Psychobiology,
1979, in press.

Weismann, A. Essays upon heredity and kindred biological problems. Oceanside, New York: Dabor Science Publications, 1977. Reprint of 1889 English edition published by Clarendon Press, Oxford, England.

Wolfe, H.G., and Coleman, D.L. Pigmentation. In E.L. Green (Ed.), Biology of the laboratory mouse. New York: McGraw-Hill, 1966, 405-426.

Wolff, G.L. Influence of maternal phenotype on metabolic differentiation of agouti locus mutants in the mouse. Genetics, 1978, 88, 529-539.

Wright, S. Evolution and the genetics of populations. Vol. 2. The theory of gene frequencies. Chicago: University of Chicago Press, 1969, pp 273-289.

Zetterlund, B., Winberg, J., Lundgren, G., and Johansson, G. Lead in umbilical cord blood correlated with the blood lead of the mother in areas with low, medium or high atmospheric pollution. Acta Paediatrica Scandanavia, 1977, 66, 169-175.

COMMENT BY J. L. FULLER

Wahlsten's purpose, a critique of some basic concepts of behavioral genetics is commendable. Any science must continuously examine its postulates and practices. To this appraisal of technical matters he has added comments on the social significance of our field of interest. He implies that behavior genetics has on the whole had a negative effect on attempts to better the human condition because its spokesmen, at least some of them, espouse a form of genetic determinism that is scientifically invalid. I shall comment first on this second theme which has important political and ethical implications.

In my opinion behavior geneticists as a group have abandoned genetic determinism without turning to its opposite, environmental determinism, a view that seems more prevalent among sociologists and cultural anthropologists. Nevertheless there are exceptions and Wahlsten fears that public policy has been adversely affected by statements such as he quotes in his text. I am less impressed than he by the ability of scientists to alter public policy by their statements. Science is seldom univocal, and partisans on either side will find authority to support their views.

Wahlsten seems to have accepted Rousseau's concept of natural man who, if uncontaminated by society's prejudices would dwell in earthly paradise. It follows that the belief in innateness of violence and inequity is a major barrier to social betterment. He is right in emphasizing the role of held beliefs in determining social action, but societies are the creations of their members, and their dynamics are the function of a human biological heritage reacting to available resources. I see little likelihood, given our mammalian nature, that social problems will ever be "solved" in a final sense. The assumption that a change of views regarding the heritability of behavior could eliminate violence and social injustice is unlikely to be true. It rests upon the inappropriate application of the problem solving paradigm of the physical sciences to social problems (Sarason, 1978).

I join with Wahlsten in his distaste for extremism on the issue of genetic determinism, but I wish he had similarly rejected genetic nihilism, which regards heredity as unimportant for individual differences. In fact, his own research yields fine examples of interactions between genotype and environment that argue for a middle point of view.

Turning to more technical matters, the main themes of his chapter are genotype-environment correlations and genotype-environment interactions. Wahlsten defines environment (E) as "every influence on the phenotype not included in the genotype" (G). This may seem straightforward, but it is not. Organisms free to move

from one environment to another may create G-E correlations because individuals of different genotypes differ in choice behavior. Thus, environment may be considered as a proximate cause
of observed behavioral variation but genotype may have an equal
claim as an ultimate cause. This matter does not simply relate
to partitioning variance, but to the way we think about the joint
action of genes and environment upon behavioral development. A
similar caution should be placed on Wahlsten's assumption that
special training of one member of a DZ twin pair will decrease r_{DZ}
and thus increase estimates of $\underline{h}^2$. This is a possible outcome,
but it is equally plausible that the less adept co-twin receives
more help than the already proficient sibling so that r_{DZ} increases. These are empirical problems that are devilishly difficult to investigate. Perhaps one situation is much more common
than the other, but I am unaware of any good data on the matter.

There are, of course, G-E covariances that are imposed upon
organisms from the outside. We may do this deliberately in the
laboratory as part of an experimental design. In our human societies discriminatory practices are often based upon superficial
physical characteristics or upon cultural stereotypes. In these
instances a G-E correlation will result if, and only if, the criterion for discrimination is heritable in a genetic sense. If
the criterion character is a superficial physical trait (skin
pigmentation, for example) it is of trivial behavioral interest.
Any correlation between it and behavior is logically attributable
to environmental influences. However G-E correlation could be
based upon differences in genes influencing neural functions and
hence selection of environments. Such correlations seem inevitable
if good genotypes are defined as those that guide organisms to find
good environments. Since most subtle neural characteristics are
ascertained primarily by their behavioral manifestations it may be
difficult to establish either the presence or absence of this type
of correlation.

Genotype-environment interaction is a second major topic discussed by Wahlsten. Treatments may have different effects depending upon the genotype of the individual being treated. For me
this is one of the most interesting and important aspects of behavior-genetic research. I regard it as an opportunity rather
than a difficulty. So apparently does Wahlsten, although he seems
worried about the fact that the heritability of a character often
changes when conditions of rearing or testing are altered. I
consider changes in genetic parameters as signals that interaction
has occurred and as encouragement for a search for physiological
and psychological explanations. Because biometric approaches are
not the whole story, and because they can be misunderstood or
even misused, is not a valid reason for discarding them completely.

In the real world the intensive behavioral analysis of G-E

correlation and G-E interaction may be possible only with animal material. However, though I share Wahlsten's doubts regarding the assumption of G and E additivity in the analysis of human data, on the whole it seems unlikely that disordinal interactions will be common. Instead I believe that "good" environments will be similar for all individual members of a species with a similar history of natural selection. Similar environments will not ensure equal performance; "better" environments may help some to achieve above the average. Rarely will a "bad" environment be good for any individual. G-E interactions are most likely to reflect quantitative variation in threshold of stimulation, persistence in problem solving, and slope of learning curves.

Space does not permit detailed discussion of Wahlsten's criticism of the general assumption that heredity is primarily Mendelian. There are other modes of transmission of behavioral characteristics from parents to offspring. In particular, maternal factors have been widely sought and often found. My impression is that they are somewhat less influential than genes except, perhaps, in the area of human personality. In discussions of these matters I urge that we do not become confused over semantic issues associated with the words heredity and heritability. Although "cultural heritage" and "inheritance of property" are common terms in our language, heredity in scientific discourse has come to mean that which is transmitted by DNA and heritability to mean the ratio of genetic to total phenotypic variance. It is possible to use other terms to distinguish other postulated modes of transmission of physical and psychological characteristics.

In conclusion, I found much of interest in this paper that combines a critique of genetic methodology with concern for the social implications of behavior genetics. Fortunately most persons working in this area are aware of its sensitive aspects, and know the complexities of G-E correlations and interactions. It is good to be reminded that overlooking their existence may lead to faulty conclusions and premature generalization. But behavior genetics is an area that will continue to generate controversy, and its practitioners cannot escape from criticism by both the left and the right. We can only continue to present and interpret our data with honesty, clarity, and modesty.

COMMENT BY D. D. THIESSEN

I have never been sanguine about the value and use of heritability scores, hence I see several points of agreement with Dr. Wahlsten. h^2 is occasionally overused, tells us little about an individual, and suggests almost nothing about physiology.

However, I do not think that the concept need be thrown out altogether and all previous conclusions based on h^2 dismissed. I see h^2 as similar to the Hardy-Weinberg law of genetic equilibrium, which is based on the erroneous assumptions of panmixia, absence of directional or stabilizing selection, and the lack of random drift. Nevertheless, the Hardy-Weinberg law has acted as a valuable null-hypothesis against which deviations can be assessed. Furthermore, as a population measure it allows us to work from heuristic generalities to specific experiments. For example, we are attempting correlations between the extent of h^2 for a number of traits and the degree of assortative mating, assuming that there is some association between h^2 and Darwinian fitness which couples may attend to.

In addition, heritability estimates must be seen in the context of other studies, and evaluated in terms of their overall consistency as well as the degree of fit with theoretical models.

Dr. Wahlsten may have taken an extreme negative position based on selected experimental results. The dramatic examples used to show the interaction between genotype and environment among inbred strains of mice should not be used to illustrate the uselessness of computing h^2. Since the stocks are not heterogeneous, striking interaction effects would be expected. It is more proper to calculate and assess h^2 scores in heterogeneous populations, in situations where h^2 values are normally obtained.

Finally, I object to the inference that investigators interested in h^2 estimates have questionable motives, or are guilty of social errors by association. I would only agree that we must continue to refine our measures, attempt to characterize the interactions between genes and environment, and carefully define the so-called "non-genetic" factors of inheritance.

COMMENT BY J. C. LOEHLIN

Wahlsten correctly points out that heredity and environment are often not perfectly discriminable in research with humans, but does it follow from this that because we cannot discriminate perfectly, we should not attempt to discriminate at all? Wahlsten seems to argue so. Unfortunately, his critique of heritability studies is itself sometimes vulnerable to criticism. Two brief examples: The fact that the twins were reared in the same home is not critical, since the heritability estimate depends only on the assumption that the environments were equally similar for two types of twin; Statistical interaction does not necessarily indicate the presence of physiological interaction—for example, it may reflect the characteristics of the scale on which the trait is measured.

COMMENT BY E. CASPARI

Since I have done some work on cytoplasmic and infectious inheritance I would like to amplify some aspects of Dr. Wahlsten's paper. Cytoplasmic inheritance has been known since 1908 (Correns, 1908) and has been generally accepted in Germany since 1920. In the U.S.A. its existence was acknowledged only after the appearance of my review in 1948 (Caspari, 1948). Mitochondria contain their own chromosomes, but their phenotypic effects depend on an interaction between nuclear and mitochrondrial genes since most mitochondrial enzymes are coded by nuclear DNA. The reproductive ability of infectious agents is frequently influenced by host genes resulting in a different type of interaction. Mitochondrial inheritance has been most thoroughly studied in yeast; in mice, mitochondria are transmitted maternally (Caspari & Blomstrand, 1956). Models incorporating interaction between nuclear genes and cytoplasmic constituents or infectious agents show that in populations no stable equilibrium between two cytoplasms can exist. Cytoplasm does not, therefore, contribute to individual variation within natural populations but may differ between non-interbreeding populations, inbred strains and species (Caspari & Watson, 1959; Watson & Caspari, 1960; Watson, 1960). Thus, cytoplasmic transmission is usually irrelevant to Behavior Genetics. Transmission by learning and sociocultural transmission are formally similar and more important. The crossing schemes described by Dr. Wahlsten for the analysis of nuclear and non-Mendelian heredity have been widely used for investigating cytoplasmic effects. For the distinction of permanent cytoplasmic components from the transmission of chemicals many generations of backcrosses are needed.

COMMENT BY P. L. BROADHURST

I will concentrate on one aspect of this paper, its treatment of maternal effects. Wahlsten states that diseases with which the mother can infect the fetus are hereditary. Such effects may be "innate", in the sense that they are inborn, or even "constitutional" in the sense that they are part of the physical make-up of the organism, but they are certainly not "hereditary" in the normal scientific sense of the word. Genic inheritance is fixed at the moment of conception and any effects transmitted via the maternal route are by definition environmental in origin. They may be of two kinds, pre- and post-natal, and appropriate methodologies for investigating and isolating such effects are extant in the literature (Broadhurst, 1961). Briefly, the latter may be investigated by the technique of cross-fostering litters between strains differing phenotypically, and pre-natal effects by using the method of reciprocal crosses between inbred strain. Care may be needed to exclude the possibilities of sex-linkage or delayed inheritance before the reality of a genuine maternal effect mediated by differences in the intra-uterine environment can be concluded, and the further possibility, extensively discussed by Wahlsten, relates to extrachromosomal or cytoplasmic inheritance (Jinks, 1964). Here again, however, analytic techniques are available, the method of ova transplantation being the most appropriate. As it happens, very little evidence of the importance of such perturbations of maternal effects is available in the behavioral literature. As for cytoplasmic inheritance, I know of only one study in which it is invoked as an explanatory mechanism (Eleftheriou, Bailey, & Denenberg, 1974), and the data presented do not support it.

COMMENT BY J. H. F. van ABEELEN

My brief comment on Wahlsten's contribution is brought to the fore in the form of a question: If, for some extraneous reason (e.g., winning in a lottery), a sudden change occurs in somebody's wealth, would you call such a sudden change a mutation?

COMMENT BY J. R. ROYCE

As co-editor of this volume it was my hope that Professor Wahlsten's contribution would provide the kind of conceptual analysis which would move behavior genetics in the direction of conceptual-linguistic precision and theoretical power (see the Prologue). What has emerged, however, is a paper which, unhappily, cannot be characterized as responsible metatheory, but rather, as a mixture of sophistry and polemics which, if taken seriously, can only lead to conceptual confusion and theoretical chaos.

Because of space limitations I can only cite one example. Professor Wahlsten develops a section on "cultural" inheritance which includes such sentences and phrases as "'cultural' inheritance is important for studies of heredity when offspring acquire information from their parents . . . In human society it is generally the case that wealth and poverty are hereditary . . . . In most species the offspring inherit the environment of their parents." (underlining mine) I submit that usage of the term inheritance for what is clearly cultural transmission does not constitute conceptual clarification. To my knowledge there is no evidence that acquired characteristics are inherited in the sense meant by geneticists.

Serious metatheoretic analysis is both important and difficult. However, it involves more than the sophomoric questioning of the conceptual foundations of a discipline. The responsible metatheorist also demonstrates how to move the discipline ahead.

It is my guess that my colleagues share Professor Wahlsten's concerns about the shortcomings of the contemporary conceptual foundations of behavior genetics, but that they must reject his subsequent recommendations because they are so flagrantly inadequate.

REPLY TO COMMENTS
D. Wahlsten

The comments of the discussants are, in the main, directed at five important issues.

1) <u>The nature of heredity</u>. Semantics is the study of the meaning of words. What meaning is ascribed to words in a scientific discipline is in turn a reflection of the conceptual foundations of that discipline. Hence, the scientific issues pertaining to the nature of heredity and the semantic issues are intimately related, and disagreement over semantics in the present dispute reflects disagreement over theory itself.

The phrases "cultural heritage" and "inheritance of property" are commonly used in the English language because culture and wealth do in fact contribute substantially to familial resemblance in many human phenotypes, just as cytoplasmic organelles and viruses contribute to differences between inbred strains of other organisms and are part of heredity. Some geneticists have singled out a tiny fraction of the whole organism, the set of DNA molecules in the chromosomes of the germ cells, and dogmatically asserted that this genotype is the sole physical basis for heredity. This assertion is not a valid scientific generalization. It is contradicted by numerous facts cited in my paper.

The usage of "cultural inheritance" in my paper is not at all new. For example, Cavalli-Sforza (1974), in discussing phenotypic plasticity, says: ". . . the problem is complicated by the existence of two mechanisms of transmission, a biological and a cultural one, which are highly confounded." He proceeds to use "cultural transmission" and "cultural inheritance" interchangeably. And why not? <u>Transmission</u> of a characteristic from one generation to the next is what we mean by inheritance. If one mechanism of transmission does not correspond to rules of Mendelian transmission, it does not follow that the mechanism is not part of heredity. It is simply non-Mendelian inheritance.

Cultural inheritance certainly functions much differently than Mendelian inheritance. Goldschmidt (1976) suggests that "Cultural evolution is Lamarckian; that is, unlike biological evolution, acquired elements are inherited." Whether his view of biological evolution is correct remains debatable, but his point about cultural inheritance is clear. Acquired wealth, for example, can be inherited. If it is acquired through windfall such as a lottery win, it would be <u>analogous</u> to a genetic mutation. Actually, the concept of random genetic mutation unrelated to the organism's environment is quite a good analogy with a lottery win, but this is not a shortcoming of the concept of cultural inheritance. It reveals a feature of the concept of genetic mutation which borders on the mystical.

Any individuals who stubbornly assert that "genic inheritance is fixed at the moment of conception and any effects transmitted by the maternal route are by definition environmental in origin" have <u>absolutely no right</u> to speak of a difference between inbred strains or selected lines as indicative even of a difference in heredity. After all, it could be what they wish to call "environmental".

I maintain that when inbred strains or selected lines of animals are raised for many generations on identical diets in the same laboratory setting, it is legitimate to ascribe differences in their behaviors to differences in heredity. Whether the difference is the result of Mendelian (genetic) or non-Mendelian inheritance must then be assessed using the appropriate crosses, etc. Unless the role of non-Mendelian inheritance is demonstrably insignificant, the familiar techniques of quantitative genetics propounded by Falconer (1960) and McClearn and DeFries (1973) should not be foisted upon the readers of scientific literature.

2) <u>The prevalence of maternal effects</u>. There is no doubt that few instances of maternal effects have been reported in the literature of behavioral genetics. The issue, however, is whether such effects are generally investigated. Belief that maternal effects are insubstantial "perturbations" leads to neglect of these phenomena. For instance, in the first five issues of <u>Behavior Genetics</u> in 1978, only two of 18 studies of non-human animals seriously examined maternal effects at all, and these used only reciprocal F_1 hybrids, a very weak method compared to reciprocal backcrosses. A study of olfaction in <u>Drosophila</u> found no reciprocal hybrid effects (Fuyama, 1978), whereas a diallel analysis with mice revealed significant maternal effects for both body weight and brain weight (Hahn & Haber, 1978).

Sometimes maternal effects are observed, and sometimes they are not. Therefore, it is wrong to exclude such effects without first testing for them. Unless maternal effects are proven to be insignificant, it is incorrect to attribute a strain difference to additive genetic variation.

3) <u>The dissection of heredity</u>. The scheme for dissecting heredity which is outlined in my paper is neither new nor exhaustive, and it is not represented as such. However, it is very

rarely put into practice in behavioral genetics. It is presented
in this paper as an alternative to the more common analyses of
quantitative genetics. The analysis employed by Hay (1972) is a
radical departure from the methods outlined by Falconer (1960)
and McClearn and DeFries (1973), and instead it provides an excellent example of the kind of research which is advocated in
the present paper.

It should be obvious that I do not deal with the intricacies
of estimating additive, dominance and epistasis components of
variation. Rather, I say that: "If dissection of heredity reveals the importance of chromosomal mechanisms, then the familiar
Mendelian analysis of segregating units can be undertaken." This
"familiar" analysis includes methods of quantitative genetics in
the case of polygenic inheritance.

Concerning the set of crosses in Table 5, it is explicitly
stated that: "these comparisons by no means exhaust all possibilities for dissecting heredity", and other procedures are indicated. The proposed analysis is not intended to stultify the
analysis of heredity by confining future experiments to a specific
set of crosses. This approach needs to be elaborated further,
but not in a discussion of the more general theoretical issues in
behavioral genetics.

4) <u>Heredity x environment interaction</u>. Studies which demonstrate dramatic heredity x environment interaction virtually always use inbred strains and their F_1 hybrids, and for good reason.
To measure the effects of interaction, organisms having the <u>same</u>
heredity must be subjected to different environments, and vice
versa. In a heterogeneous population, heredities vary widely and
cannot be measured accurately. Using a within-subject design, it
would be possible to show that two individuals differ significantly
in their response to some drug, for example, but the effect could
not be readily attributed to heredity or environment. When variation in early experiences is involved the difficulty becomes
magnified. The difficulty of measuring heredity-environment
interaction in a heterogeneous population in no way allows such
an effect to be dismissed from consideration. On the contrary,
it means that heterogeneous populations pose the greatest risks of
incorrectly interpreting "heritability" estimates.

Can interaction be eliminated by changing the scale of measurement? Statistically, yes. If depth of wine in a draining
wine cask is considered as the natural logarithm of depth, the relationship with time becomes linear. But anyone who seriously
looks at drinking in this way in the real world, physiologically,
will end up under the table for sure. The fact that mathematical
transformations can make interactions appear or disappear like
apparitions does not in any way minimize the importance of

480

heredity x environment interaction in behavioral genetics. Rather, it provides good reason to keep a closer eye on the statistical shenanigans of many of our colleagues.

5) Who has plunged behavioral genetics into "conceptual confusion and theoretical chaos"? There are two kinds of "confusion" afield in behavioral genetics today. Some people are confused because different investigators advocate different conceptual foundations for the discipline. Different things are meant by the word "heredity", and differing degrees of respect exist for the concept of "heritability". This kind of disorder is inevitable whenever old ideas are challenged. It is absolutely necessary for progress in scientific theory, and the existence of confusion at this time is a sign that theoretical advance in behavioral genetics is taking place.

The other kind of confusion arises when predictions from an established theory do not correspond to experimental results. This problem is apparent in many published studies wherein heredity is conceptualized as the exclusive provenance of Mendelian genes. Studies which observe whopping reciprocal F_1 hybrid differences or strain-by-treatment interactions provide an impetus for revision of the fundamental tenets of behavioral genetics.

In the history of a scientific discipline, as well as in the history of a species, it seems that necessity is the mother of invention.

References

Broadhurst, P. L. Analysis of maternal effects in the inheritance of behaviour. Animal Behaviour, 1961, 9, 129-141.
Caspari, Adv. Genet., 2, 1, 1948.
Caspari & Blomstrand, Cold Spring Harbor Symp. Quant. Biol., 21, 291, 1956.
Caspari & Watson, Evolution, 13, 568, 1959.
Cavalli-Sforza, L. L. The role of plasticity in biological and cultural evolution. Annals of the New York Academy of Sciences, 1974, 231, 43-59.
Correns, Ber. Dtsch. Bot. Ges., 36, 686, 1908.
Eleftheriou, B. E., Bailey, D. W., & Denenberg, V. H. Genetic analysis of fighting behavior in mice. Physiology and Behavior, 1974, 13, 773-777.
Fuyama, Y. Behavior genetics of olfactory responses in Drosophila. II. An odorant-specific variant in a natural population of Drosophila melanogaster. Behavior Genetics, 1978, 8, 399-414.
Goldschmidt, W. Reply to D. T. Campbell. American Psychologist, 1976 (May), 355-357.

Hahn, M. E., & Haber, S. B. A diallel analysis of brain and body weight in male inbred laboratory mice (<u>mus</u> <u>musculus</u>). <u>Behavior Genetics</u>, 1978, <u>8</u>, 251-260.

Jinks, J. L. <u>Extrachromosomal inheritance</u>. Englewood Cliffs, N.J. Prentice Hall, 1964.

Sarason, S. B. The nature of problem solving in social action. <u>American Psychologist</u>, 1978, <u>33</u>, 370-380.

Watson, <u>Evolution</u>, <u>14</u>, 256, 1960.

Watson & Caspari, Evolution, <u>14</u>, 56, 1960.

THE TAXONOMY OF PSYCHOPHENES

J.L. Fuller

Department of Psychology, State University of New York at Binghamton

1. CLASSIFICATION IN THE BEHAVIORAL SCIENCES

Behavior genetics is characterized by the phenotypes with which it deals. The objective of most workers in the field is to gain a deeper understanding of behavior rather than to elucidate genetic mechanisms. There are exceptions. The motor behavior of simple organisms such as Paramecium aurelia (Kung, 1971) and Caenorhabditis elegans (Brenner, 1974) provides a quick and easy method of screening large populations for mutants affecting basic cellular processes. Genetically influenced differences in mating behavior are possibly the most potent force directing the evolutionary process (Mayr, 1970), and may be studied mainly because of their effects on the genetic structure of populations. The heritability of social behavior is central to the current interest in sociobiology (Wilson, 1975). Despite these possible exceptions a perusal of literature in the field will confirm the statement that behavior geneticists, as a group, find unity in their concern with a special class of phenotypes rather than in a particular branch of genetics. I propose in this paper to discuss the problems associated with the selection of phenotypes and the ways in which the choice of a phenotype can affect the form of genetic analysis. To begin with I shall consider some general problems in the classification of behavior.

To make a science of behavior manageable there must be some system of classifying its subject matter based on objective criteria. In contrast with biology, psychology has no tradition of classification based on lines of descent. It does have a long history of tension between structural and functional approaches to its material. The functionalist approach as exemplified by Skinnerian behaviorism plays down individual variability as a determinant of behavior. Individuality is not denied, but it is not considered relevant to the control of behavior through contigencies of reinforcement (Skinner, 1953). In contrast, structuralist approaches stress individual variations in personality traits, perceptual processes and learning ability. These variations become attributes of individuals that are significant predictors of behavior. In many ways the structuralist approach to the science of behavior seems more congenial than the functionalist approach for behavior genetics. Yet it has many problems. Not the least of these is the fact that psychological structures are not structures in the same sense as are the majority of phenotypes studied by geneticists. Behavior is a process, not a substance. The structures of psychology are patterns of organization, not things.

Nevertheless, processes as well as structures can be classified for scientific purposes. Before attempting this let us consider some properties of a good classification system. Deese (1969) describes two steps in the process of producing such a system. Most fundamental and general is the grouping of objects, events and ideas that have something in common. A second step is class-ification into a hierarchial branching arrangement with a niche for every item in the inventory to be classified. Deese gives as examples the classification of animals and plants by the Linnean system and the classification of words (ideas) in Roget's Thesaurus. The two are not really comparable. In biological taxonomy each species has an unique position. None can appear on more than one branch of the tree. In Roget a word may appear in several places. Thus give is found under: ideas related to motion, to the hardness of matter, to prospective volition, and to moral affections. This demonstrates that the meaning of give varies according to the context in which it is used. The only way we can give it an unique position is by alphabetization; certainly a trivial attribute for the useful classification of word meanings. The situation for the classification of behavior is very much the same. Raised eyebrows may indicate disbelief, tension, or visual concentration.

Classification can be useful even if it does not conform to the model of biological taxonomy. The hierarchial, branching structure of systematic biology is possible and valid only because a species or an individual can have only one line of descent. For some purposes a classification by habitat or behavior is as useful as classification in the Linnean system. Animals may be aquatic or terrestrial, carnivorous or herbivorous, monogamous or poly-gamous. Grouping by such criteria may have more relevance to the theoretical formulations of ecologists and sociobiologists than grouping by phylum down to genus and species. Similarly it is useful to categorize behavior according to a number of criteria. Nissen (1958) suggested three axes of behavioral comparison.

Along the _functional_ axis behaviors are grouped with respect to
common types of biological utility (e.g., food getting, mating,
rearing of offspring). His descriptive axis is concerned with the
mechanics of behavior including locomotion, manipulative skills
and sensory capacities. The _explanatory_ axis goes beyond the
immediately observable behavior into its antecedents including
phylogenetic history, physiological and biochemical correlates,
the influence of individual life history, and genetic variability.
Nissen's axes are more a schema for the investigation of a specific
form of behavior in depth than a guide for its formal classification. They do, however, provide a basis for developing a number
of behavioral taxonomies. More recently Purton (1978) has called
attention to the distinction between classification of behavior by
function, form and causation, and to the implications of employing
three different conceptual schemes in ethology. Each is valid
and useful but failure to recognize conflation of two systems can
lead to serious misunderstandings.

1.1. A classification of phenotypes

Fuller and Wimer (1973) divided phenotypes into two broad
categories, somatophenes and psychophenes. Here I shall extend
their classification by subdividing each of the two main categories,
and adding a third that cuts across the other two because it is
actually a composite.
1. _Somatophenes_ are defined by structural criteria.
   A. Chemophenes are defined by their molecular configur-
      ation. e.g. hemoglobin A.
   B. Morphenes are defined by structural arrangements that
      include more than one molecular species e.g. pigment
      distribution patterns, body size.
2. _Psychophenes_ are defined by behavioral criteria, that is
   by a process rather than a structure.
   A. _Ostensible_ _psychophenes_ are acts that are recognizable
      by all qualified observers and are measurable in such
      units as frequency, latency and force. e.g. meters
      traversed by a rat in an open field.
   B. _Inferred_ _psychophenes_ are more general attributes of
      states of organisms that are manifested in a variety
      of related situations. e.g. anxiety level, aggres-
      sivity.
3. _Syndromes_ are groups of psychophenes, and usually also
   somatophenes that occur together regularly. Some are
   associated with a mutant gene (e.g. phenylketonuria) or
   chromosomal anomaly (e.g. Down syndrome). Other syndromes
   (using the term in a broad sense) are less stereotyped
   in their manifestations and are not associated with a
   known genotype (e.g., schizophrenia).

The division between psychophenes and somatophenes does not imply that the former are independent of a physical substrate. Even the most cerebral forms of behavior require a neural substrate with input and output. It is also true that the boundary between the two kinds of phenes is a bit indistinct. Consider a study of the genetics of alpha activity in the electroencephalogram, an ostensible psychophene in my terminology. Most psychologists would consider such a study to belong to physiology rather than to behavior. It would be possible to establish a more complex classification scheme to meet this problem but I see little value in doing so at present.

Regardless of an investigators choice of psychophene it is very unlikely that there will be precise correspondence between units of heredity and units of behavior. In fact it is difficult to separate behavior into units suitable for genetic analysis. Behavior is continuous and although transitions can be found between different types of activities the exact boundaries may be indefinite. Behavior is complex. Many effectors and sensory inputs, each with its own regulatory system, are involved in an act like food getting. Counting bar presses or meters traveled in an open field gives an incomplete picture of total activity. Behavior is plastic. Some response patterns may be precisely determined by genotype, but even Drosophila alters its response characteristics depending upon experience (Pruzan and Ehrman, 1974). Although genes, like neurons, may be active or inactive at various stages of development, they certainly do not vary in activity in time with the rapid shifts of minute to minute behaving.

1.2. What makes a good psychophene?

It is not difficult to find psychophenes for behavior-genetic analysis. There is, in fact, an embarrassment of riches in the behavioral repertoire of most species. For behavior genetics the following criteria are most important.
1. The chosen psychophene should be relatable to important issues of psychological or evolutionary theory. This criterion may be so general that it excludes nothing. Probably all behavior has some psychological implications and is the product of natural selection. But when there are so many kinds of behavior that could be studied it is advisable to concentrate on those whose relation to some general scientific or practical issue is clear.
2. The psychophene should have appreciable genetic variance. That is, it should be significantly heritable. Since heritability is a property of populations rather than of phenotypes, this stipulation deals primarily with the choice of subjects rather than the specific measurements to be taken. Because there is general consensus that characteristics with major significance for biological fitness have low heritabilities, there may be some

conflict between this criterion and the first one. It is probably
not serious. Few characteristics of behavior fail to show genetic
variance when it is looked for. Also, over the long run even low
heritabilities are sufficient for selection to change gene
frequencies.

3. The psychophene should be one that can be measured reliably.
This requirement, of course, is central to all behavioral research
and I shall not develop it in detail. The point to be made is
that reliability of measurement is secondary to the two previous
criteria.

4. The psychophene should be one that can be ascertained with
relative ease and economy. Again, this desideratum applies to
many kinds of research. It is particularly important for behavior-
genetic analysis since the testing of most genetic hypotheses
requires large numbers of subjects with controlled breeding.
Procedures requiring extensive training or in depth psychological
examination of human subjects at different stages of life are
seldom feasible even though they might yield important information.

2. OSTENSIBLE PSYCHOPHENES

As defined previously ostensible psychophenes are the raw
stuff of behavior. Except for the inherent error of human and
instrumental observers the experimental record is an accurate
description of the subject's actions. It is not a complete record.
Human observers preferentially note those items they are looking
for; a machine is programmed only to record prescribed physical
events such as the interruption of a light beam or the heart rate.
Such psychophenes are in the behavioristic tradition and are also
dominant in ethological studies. The difference between the two
approaches is that experimental psychologists have tended to
concentrate on a few standard responses which are used as indicators of the effects of environmental manipulations. Ethologists
have looked at a wider range of responses in less structured
situations. Both groups have generally paid scant attention to
individual differences except those resulting from unlike histories
of reinforcement or exposure to particular classes of stimuli.
Thus Skinner (1953), after acknowledging the innateness of much
behavior, writes, "among members of a species, the extensive
differences are less likely to be due to hereditary endowment, and
to that extent may be traced to circumstances in the history of
the individual". He assumes that organisms inherit capacities
that can be reinforced by particular events, but this knowledge
is of little help in predicting the effect of an untried stimulus.
Skinner handles the problem of individual differences in a behavioral character by ranking organisms relative to their position
in the distribution of that character in the species as a whole.
He shows little interest in seeking an explanation for high or
low position in the distribution. "The most that can be said is
that knowledge of the genetic factor in producing limitations of

capacity may enable us to use our techniques of control more intelligently". For Skinner, genotype, like age, may have some relevance for the application of psychological principles, but for fundamental theory testing, genetic variance is unwelcome noise.

Clearly, if one's purpose is the modification of an individual's behavior it is impossible to do so by altering that individual's genotype. Also it is plausible that the laws of reinforcement are the same for a genetic retardate and for his normal sibling. Although the retardate will not progress as quickly or as far in a programmed learning situation, he can be taught in fundamentally y the same manner as his sibling. In the Skinnerian view situations are more decisive than individuality in shaping behavior.

2.1. Genetic variability of ostensible psychophenes.

Skinner's judgment of the unprofitability of considering genetic individuality is debatable, but its existence with respect to ostensible psychophenes is well documented. I will discuss briefly two examples. van Abeelen (1963 a,b,c) observed four types of mutant mice in a chamber and recorded the occurrence of each of a set of carefully defined acts (the ethogram of the species). The mutants included a neurological defect (jerker), an endocrine anomaly (yellow), a coat-color variety without other obvious phenotypic correlates (brown), and a color variant with unpigmented eyes (pink-eyed dilution). Each mutant type was compared with appropriate wild-type controls from its own line. No quantitative or qualitative differences between yellow and control mice were observed. For each of the other three mutants significant effects were detected. Not surprisingly these were most apparent for the jerkers. In my opinion the author's most important finding is that feeding, fighting and sexual behavior were affected hardly at all from a quantitative point of view. Those aspects of behavior most relevant to fitness were resistant to disruption by peripheral or central defects of the sensory and nervous systems. The differences that were found were not obviously related to evolutionary or psychological theory.

My second example is McGill's (1962, 1970) genetic analysis of male sexual behavior in mice. His subjects were 6-8 week males of three inbred strains who were tested with females of their own strains that had been brought into estrus by hormonal injections. Observations were made in a circular glass chamber. Strain differences were found on many quantitative aspects of mating (e.g. number of mounts, latency to ejaculation) and crosses were made to learn the mode of inheritance. As a result of these studies McGill (1970) enunciated two principles.
1. Conclusions regarding such genetic parameters as mode of inheritance, heritability and degree of genetic determination are

specific to the population or strains studied. This statement was
based on the fact that various objective indices that were purported
to measure sexual vigor were uncorrelated; hence no general statement regarding the inheritance of a general trait of sexual vigor
could be made.

2. Genetic conclusions reached in any particular experiment
are specific to the total environmental conditions of that experiment. This statement was based on the finding that C57BL males
tested in the glass observation chamber had an extraordinarily
long post-ejaculatory refractory period compared with DBA males.
When the behavioral observations were shifted to the animals' home
cages the strain difference in length of the refractory period
was abolished.

It is apparent that well defined behavioral criteria combined
with rigorous environmental controls do not necessarily lead to
fundamental understanding of the relationship between genes and
behavior. There was no difficulty in the van Abeelen and McGill
experiments in finding behavioral variation associated with genotype. But one reads their papers with a sense of disappointment.
Both experiments yielded a vast number of particulars bound together
only by negative conclusions, van Abeelen's finding that feeding,
fighting and mating were not impaired in his mutants, and McGill's
conclusion that tests in a strange environment do not predict
behavior in a home cage. Is much of the data gathered in such
experiments "genetic junk" (Thiessen, 1972)? Are behavior
geneticists guilty of the sin of "overparticularization" (Thiessen
and Rodgers, 1967)? These questions are not intended to depreciate
the value of the contributions of van Abeelen and McGill. Quite
the contrary. They, themselves, recognized the problems and called
them to the attention of others. The answer is not to abandon
quantitative measures in a controlled setting but to look more
closely at the relationships between settings, genotypes and
behavior.

2.2. Situational and temporal variability of ostensible psycho-
      phenes

In the van Abeelen experiments an attempt was made to keep
the test situation as similar as possible to the subject's natural
habitat. Artificiality entered only to the degree necessary to
restrain the animals sufficiently for accurate recording of their
behavior. The subjects themselves determined the particular
aspects of their behavior that would be included in the data. The
observer's function was to make this data as complete and accurate
as possible. More common are experiments in which animals are
compared on one or a few behavioral parameters in apparatus designed
to elicit a particular response. Mazes, shuttle boxes, open fields,
running wheels and many other devices are too well known to require
description here. In behavior genetics their use implies that a

prior decision has been made regarding the characteristics of the subjects that are of interest and the appropriateness of the apparatus for their elicitation and measurement. The primary data, however, come out in the same form as those derived from more ethologically oriented investigations. Thus one obtains sets of latencies, frequencies, durations and the like from each of several genetic groups and uses them to test a genetic hypothesis. The simplest hypothesis, that genetic differences exist, can usually be supported. More complex hypotheses related to heritability, dominance and maternal effects can also be tested though today there is growing realization that the parameters found in one study are not necessarily generalizable to different situations or to a different collection of genotypes.

Thus, today there is great interest in genotypic effects on phenotypic stability and in the demonstration of genotype-phenotype interactions. In the former case, given character X, we are interested not only in its mean, $\bar{X}$, but in its standard deviation, s. Low values of s indicate efficient developmental homeostasis, that is resistance of the character to uncontrolled fluctuations in a relatively constant environment. Discussions of the concept of developmental homeostasis as related to behavior may be found in Caspari (1958), Mordkoff and Fuller, (1959), Fuller and Thompson (1960), Fulker, Wilcock and Broadhurst (1972) and Hyde (1973). As generally defined, developmental homeostasis deals only with phenotypic variability associated with random environmental perturbations. This is important but there is greater interest in the interactions of genotypes with specific features of the environment.

Given psychophene X we can measure it repeatedly in a number of genotypes and compare them with respect to the function, dX / dT, where T is time. The time scale may be as short as the interval between successive trials of a test or as long as the life span of the subjects. One could also compare genotypes with respect to the function ds / dT, though I am unaware of any examples of this procedure. An example of the functional approach to defining psychophenes is the experiment of Tyler and McClearn (1970) on runway learning in mice. Each individual's acquisition of the running response (expressed as $X = \log 10\ y$ where y is time in seconds) was determined by fitting its scores to the polynomial $X_t = a + bt + ct^2$, where X_t is expected score on trial t. The coefficients are interpreted as: a, initial level; b, amount learned previously; and c, approach to asymptote. The t in this equation is not linearly related to clock time though in principle it could be. X_t is also not strictly an ostensible psychophene though it has the dimensions of one and might be considered as an adjusted value of a particular observation. The constants a, b and c are, in a sense, inferred psychophenes, but they can stand on their own as descriptions of the data without any psychological interpretation.

Differences between genotypes in behavioral response to environmental change are as important as differences in rate of learning. Two types of environmental variation may be distinguished: those related to the immediate situation in which the behavioral observations are made and those related to the subject's life history. We can denote the first function as dX / dS and the second as dX / dH. The quantitative analysis of these relationships involves complications not found when behavior is compared over time. In a developmental or learning experiment it is relatively simple to define a metric relating a behavioral measure to a point in time defined by a clock or by number of trials. It is not as simple to be sure that one has equal intervals or even a correct ordinal ranking on a scale of situational complexity or stressfulness. Consider, for example, Henderson's (1967) experiment on the effect of prior experience on open field behavior in four inbred strains of mice and their F_1 hybrids. Henderson measured ambulation and defecation in an open field after three prior treatments. Group U was undisturbed prior to the test; group B was placed individually in an exploratory maze where they were stimulated by a loud buzzer; group S was exposed to the buzzer which was followed by foot shock. The main points of Henderson's conclusion are: 1) six different patterns of relationship between intensity of prior stimulation and emotionality (defined by the defecation score) were found among the sixteen genetic groups in the study; 2) not one of these corresponded to the pattern produced by averaging the responses of all the F_1 hybrids in the experiment. Depending upon one's choice of subjects one could conclude: a) prior experience of the types employed had no effect upon emotionality; b) highest emotionality follows shock treatment; c) the undisturbed groups are the most emotional; d) an intermediate amount of stress maximizes emotionality. If these data had come from a number of independent experiments a protracted and fruitless controversy over the validity of each conclusion might have developed.

One lesson of the Henderson experiment is obvious. We must be very cautious in generalizing from an experiment with one genotype to a species as a whole. Even if principles are derived from averages of a heterogeneous population we may end up with rules that do not apply to many of the individuals comprising the group. There is an additional problem of interpretation. Henderson is probably right in assuming that exposure to a loud buzzer is more stressful than remaining undisturbed and that being shocked is still more stressful. However, there is no independent physical way of determining whether the stress of the B treatment falls midway between U and S or at some other point. One might work backward and estimate the stressfulness of each treatment by its effects on emotionality, reasoning that stress is a physiological and psychological construct that is better measured by an organism's response than by a sound meter or a volt meter. But how does one decide on the genotype and the response that will serve as the stress meter?

Another point can be made concerning the investigation of genotype- environment interactions. In some experimental settings the same individual may be observed under each condition. Order effects can be controlled by varying the sequence of exposure. This is not possible for investigations of genotype-life history interactions. A subject can have only one life history. We can get around this problem in animal experiments since inbred strains and their F_1 hybrids are made up of genetically identical individuals who can be reared under various controlled conditions during development. In human studies one encounters not only extreme genetic heterogeneity, but environments that can be grouped as similar only with respect to general characteristics that may or may not be relevant to behavioral development.

3. INFERRED PSYCHOPHENES

It is evident that a variety of problems in behavior genetics have been attacked using ostensible psychophenes and simple functions based on their variance, changes over time and changes related to present environment or to past experience. For a hardcore behaviorist this may be sufficient for all research needs. Scientists should confine themselves to determining the relations between genetic and environmental inputs and objectively measured behavioral outputs. But it is not enough for all investigators in the field. Particularly in the areas of human personality and intelligence there are many attempts to define traits that influence and predict behavior in a wide range of situations. Traits can be measured by objective criteria but they are something more than the raw data. On one side they have predictive value; on another their characterization and naming are indicative of the proposer's views on the organization of behavior.

Allport (1966) is representative of those students of personality who believe that the trait concept is valid and useful for psychological research. He is well aware of problems in the trait approach and decries their reification and references to them as causative agents. But in his opinion the rejection of the trait concept leads to rejection of all intervening variables and the creation of the "empty organism". More serious is the tendency of those denying the validity of traits (many sociologists, anthropologists and radical behaviorists) to concentrate on situational determinants of behavior while neglecting the inner structure of the behaving organism. As behavior geneticists we are all concerned with these internal determinants and must postulate their existence whether we deal with psychological dispositions (traits), with physiological characteristics or with latencies, frequencies and intensities of specific acts. Allport espouses a "heuristic realism" that postulates generalized action tendencies which are not directly observable. Although factor analysis "should provide eventually a satisfactory taxonomy of personality and its hierarchial structure", he has some misgivings regarding exclusive dependence upon it. The more important thing is to develop testable hypotheses within the framework of trait theory and submit them to critical analysis. Factoring is often but not always helpful.

As one would expect, Skinner (1953) takes a dim view of the usefulness of the trait concept. They may predict but the prediction is from effect to effect, not from cause to effect. The advantages of functional analysis are lost when behavior is viewed as controlled through traits, and the possibilities of control are not enhanced by such analysis; it is easier to predict and control a response than a trait. According to Skinner trait names may begin as adjectives but they become nouns which are then taken to be the active causes of observed behavior. Factor analysis does detect entities that appear to have different dimensions than the behaviors from which they are inferred and the patterns of covariance indicate varying degrees of common causation. Still the mathematical procedures are based upon observations of dependent variables only; prediction is always from effect to effect. He is not apparently familiar with Eysenck's (1950) criterion analysis.

Despite such reasoned arguments the concept of traits is alive and well. I suspect that even hard-nosed Skinnerians employ common trait concepts in their descriptions of students whom they are recommending for a position. But researchers in personality and intelligence have attempted to go beyond a common-sense classification in order to develop a logical, hierarchial arrangement of these domains. Cattell's (1953) multiple abstract variance analysis (MAVA) is well known for its genetic implications. His methods of factor analysis are designed to detect specific, group and general factors. A distinction is made between surface traits (clusters of associated manifest behaviors) and source traits with broader influence. The latter are the real structural influences and correspond to physiological dispositions, major tempermental sets, and to the pervasive influences of the social and physical environment. Ideally a source trait, since it is presumed to be related to one independent source of variance, should turn out to be predominantly based upon either a biological characteristic (hereditary) or a specific type of environmental influence. Cattell recognizes, however, that in the real world correlation between genotype and environment may complicate matters. Cattell's work is of interest to behavior genetics because he, more than most personality theorists, has devoted much time and effort to the analysis of the interactions between genetic and environmental determinants. The MAVA analysis was designed to distinguish between surface and source traits. The former are expected to be factorially complex with both genetic and environmental variance of substantial proportions. Source traits should be more factor pure with one or the other source of variance predominating. Cattell has not been particularly interested in the nature of gene action (dominance, heterosis, etc.) but he favors polygenic over simple Mendelian models of inheritance for his factors. His major objective has been to use a genetic analysis of behavior to test general hypotheses about behavioral development. For example, Cattell believes it is likely that hereditary influences upon behavior increase with age; thus highly heritable factors will be more prominent in adults than in young children. Through proper design and suitable observations it might be possible to explore the causal direction of heredity-environment co-relations. For example, does a bright child seek out and create a more stimulating environment or does a stimulating environment make a bright child? These alternatives are not mutually exclusive and positive feedback may make both of them true. Another of Cattell's intriguing hypotheses is that of "cultural coercion to the bio-social norm". This idea was deduced from the common finding of negative correlations between hereditary and environmental factors for highly heritable traits. Such relationships would be produced when parents try to suppress the rough play of a boisterous, noisy child and try to encourage outgoing behavior in a shy and introverted child. The empirical evidence for these hypotheses (Cattell, Blewett and Beloff, 1955; Cattell, Stice and Kristy, 1957) is not as good as one would like. Nevertheless Cattell's interest in looking at the joint effects of nature and nurture as applied to major issues in human development is commendable.

3.1. Factor analysis

Factor analysis has been used more in the genetic analysis of human than of animal behavior. Nevertheless it has been applied to the behavior of mice, rats and dogs. The most fully developed theory is that of Royce (1957, 1977). Royce's model is based primarily on human intelligence but he presents it as a general scheme applicable to other domains and other species. Its main points are: 1) intelligence is a multidimensional rather than a single entity; 2) factor analysis is the best available approach to the identification of its components; 3) both heredity and environment contribute to individual differences in the level of each factor; 4) factors differ in the relative degree in which their variation is produced by genetic or by environmental causes. Royce writes of <u>heredity</u> <u>dominant</u> and <u>environment</u> <u>dominant</u> factors. I have applied the terms <u>phenostable</u> and <u>phenolabile</u> to behavioral characteristics with much the same meaning. He also assumes that each genotype is characterized by a <u>performance</u> <u>level</u> <u>limit</u>, the phenotype that might be attained under optimal environmental conditions. This limit seems to be equivalent to the top of the reaction range, the whole gamut of phenotypes that might conceivably result from the development of a specified genotype. Determining the optimal level of any factor may be difficult since factors interact with each other and different environments make different demands. An investigator's evaluation of the best phenotype need not necessarily coincide with that of the impersonal forces that regulate fitness and determine the eventual fate of all organisms.

3.2. Rating scales

Rating scales are common in clinical evaluation of treatment effects. They are subject to criticism on the basis of subjectivity and the difficulty of equalizing scale intervals. Despite these problems they have been successfully employed in behavior genetic investigations. Two examples will suffice. Fuller and Clark (1966) measured the effects of isolation on the behavior of two dog breeds in an arena where their responses to a human, another dog of the same age and breed, and two toys were measured. Responses were classified as: no directed response (0); turn away (1); orient toward (2); approach (3); contact (4); and manipulate or mouth (5). Records were made at fixed uniform intervals. The sums of the numerical values were used as measures of general strength of response to each type of stimulus. This number varied with latency of responding and with the duration, frequency and intensity of the response. The authors concluded that the system yielded data that accurately reflected breed differences, but they did not test any formal genetic hypotheses.

Lagerspetz (1961) selected aggressive and nonaggressive lines of mice with a 7-point rating scale. The lowest category contained mice that tried to escape from a partner and squeaked if attacked. The highest rating was assigned to a mouse that wrestled vigorously and bit hard enough to draw blood. From a starting point of 3.5 her aggressive line reached an average score of 5.5, and her non-aggressive line fell to a mean of 2.7.

The rating scale procedure differs from factor analysis in having a predetermined definition of the trait to be measured, a selection of the acts that are diagnostic of the trait, and an empirical judgment of their relative position on a scale of intensity.

4. SYNDROMES

A syndrome is defined as the collection of characteristic symptoms of a disease. The association of these symptoms implies that they derive from some common cause. Phenylketonuria and Down syndrome are common examples with a known genetic basis. I shall broaden the definition of syndromes to include any form of deviant behavior that is given a distinguishing name (e.g. schizophrenia). Syndromes play a greater role in psychiatry than in psychology. Two classifications of psychopathology are commonly encountered (Sahakian, 1970). The World Health Organization recognizes three major categories: 1) psychoses; 2) neuroses, personality disorders, other nonpsychotic mental disorders; and 3) mental retardation. Its classification is empirical and symptomatic and not related to etiology. Thus, category 303, alcoholism, specifically excludes alcoholic psychosis (category 291). The American Psychiatric Association has adopted a scheme based on etiology, one that could change as more is learned of the causes of psychological disorders. Their three classes are: 1) disorders caused by or associated with impairment of brain tissue function; 2) primary mental deficiency without demonstrated brain disease or known prenatal cause; and 3) diseases without clearly defined physical cause or structural change in the brain. The two taxonomies are very different. Thus the American Psychiatric Association separates primary mental deficiency from PKU at the level of a major category; the World Health Organization places them both under mental deficiency.

Behavior geneticists seem to have their own tripartite classifications: 1) mental disorders attributable to chromosomal anomalies or inherited in clear Mendelian fashion; 2) disorders that are concentrated in families without sufficient evidence to place them in category 1; 3) disorders in which genetic variation appears to play little part in determining risk. Syndromes are encountered most frequently in the human literature but some work has been done with animals. Thiessen (1965) reported a very detailed study of physical and behavioral development in the wabbler-lethal mouse. The more subtle neurological and behavioral correlates of the albino gene are of current interest (Guillery, 1974; Henry and Haythorn, 1975).

5. CHOICE OF PSYCHOPHENE AND GENETIC ANALYSIS

Demonstrably there is a wide choice of psychophenes for genetic analysis. It might seem that a structural approach to determination of behavioral units is more readily conformable to the particulate organization of genetics than is a functionalist approach, but, on reflection, there is no necessary reason that this should be true. Either approach can generate an array of numbers that can be inserted into equations to yield estimates of correlation, variance and Chi-square evaluation of goodness to fit to a particular hypothesis. Does it make any difference, then, as to whether one opts for an ostensible or an inferred psychophene or for a complex syndrome? None of these restricts the choice of admissible genetic models.

5.1. Monogenic and polygenic regulation

I will argue that both ostensible and inferred psychophenes are determined essentially polygenically. It is impossible to

conceive of a way in which a protein molecule by itself could be
the structure underlying a spatial relations factor in a human
subject or emotionality in a rodent. Polygenic determination of
even very specific acts that are parts of a more complex pattern
also seem logically necessary. It is misleading to name genes in
a manner that suggests that one locus controls a complex process,
be it a fixed action pattern or a particular type of learning.
Obviously, alternate alleles at a locus can produce major effects
upon behavior. It is more consistent, however, to consider such
a locus as the site of a critical part of an organized portion of
the genome rather than as the address of master gene. As an example, Rothenbuhler (1964) has described a behavior pattern in honey
bees that he calls hygienic behavior. The pattern has two distinct
components, uncapping the cell which contains a diseased larva and
removing the larva from the hive. As commonly described each of
the processes is controlled at a separate locus; the complete pattern requires homozygosity for a recessive allele at both (thus
uurr, where u is the uncapping locus and r the removal locus).
It is more logical to assume that both uncapping and removal involve
the coordination of structures that develop under polygenic influences. Under this hypothesis the dominant genes, U and R, produce
products that disrupt the development of different parts of the
system. Nonhygienic behavior can then be classified as an apiar-
ian syndrome of genetic etiology. The same reasoning can be
applied to other cases in which a single locus is named after a
specific psychophene which it modifies.

There is evidence that even the most simple components of
complex, highly heritable behavior are polygenically regulated.
An instructive example is the work of Bentley and Hoy (1974) on
two species of crickets, Teleogryllus oceanicus and T. commodus.
In their elegant studies of genetic control of the male calling
song no evidence was found that any detail of the song was controlled by segregation at a single locus.

These remarks must not be interpreted as deprecating all
research aimed to detect behavioral effects of gene substitution
at a single locus. Such a substitution may be a form of treatment
that is not duplicable by any other method. A fine example is the
work of Coleman and Hummel (1969) and Coleman (1973) on the control
of food intake in obese and diabetes mutant mice. Their studies
provide new insights into the physiological basis of satiety.
Discovery of the physical basis of a single locus effect upon a
psychological disorder could have important implications for
treatment and prevention, even though that locus is only part of
a complex system. Take schizophrenia for example. Statistical
analysis of its familial distribution appears unable to receive
the question of whether a monogenic or polygenic model fits the
data better (Kidd and Cavalli-Sforza, 1973). Confirmation of a
monogenic basis for some underlying physiological or biochemical

correlate of the disorder would hold promise for early treatment and for the detection of unaffected carriers. But even if there should turn out to be an unique schizophrenia gene the disorder itself might continue to be protean at the phenotypic level.

We may tend to think of single-locus effects as related to Garrodian errors of metabolism; metabolic anomalies attributable to faulty enzymes. However, it is well known that a large proportion of the genome of eukaryotes, the creatures that most interest us, is devoted to intragenomic regulation. That regulator rather than structural genes might play the major part in the fine-tuning of behavioral development has been suggested by Fuller (1964) and by Thiessen (1972). The physiological genetics of such regulatory systems must be very difficult to investigate, but an experiment by Thiessen and Yahr (1970) suggests that it is possible.

It is clear that a change at a single locus can influence a great range of complex behavior. It seems also true that variation in a polygenic system may affect only a small part of the behavioral repertory. Our choice of a psychophene for investigation is not, therefore, influenced by the genetical requirements of our science. Decisions must be based on psychological issues.

5.2.   Are inferred psychophenes real?

If we are willing to put aside the philosophical issues of phenomonalism and empiricism and accept the idea that sensory input as processed by the human brain tells us something about the true world, there is no doubt that ostensible psychophenes are real events that could, if we wished, be expressed in terms of dimension, mass and time. Since psychophenes are dynamic fluxes of energy rather than static structures, and since they involve whole organisms rather than the product of one or a few cistrons, they cannot be matched congruently with the units of the genome. But there seems to be no logical barrier to investigating the relationships between two kinds of reals, ostensible psychophenes and genes. In fact, if we were discussing this issue in the early days of genetics we would consider ostensible psychophenes as real and genes as hypothetical factors.

Inferred psychophenes, traits or factors, have a somewhat different status. They are not fluxes of energy but overlapping systems of control that are organized to deal with a variety of generally similar situations. In Royce's gene-factor model there is a terra incognita named psychophysiological genetics lying between groups of genes and groups of factors. I would add developmental to the name of this area for much of the genetic effect is attributable to the way in which the genome controls growth and differentiation long before mature behavior patterns are expressed. Although it is accessible with difficulty there again seems to be no logical barrier to the investigation of genic effects upon developmental-psychophysiological-genetics. The technical problems are horrendous but much of the data is conceivably measurable in CGS units.

It is not, I believe, possible to quantify Cattell's human and Royce's mouse factors in physical units. They are designations for groups of actions based on empirical physical data, but they also involve a human judgment regarding what belongs in the group. It is claimed that factor analysis determines the nature of a domain by objective criteria independent of preconceived ideas, but the observations that are included in the original correlation matrix must always represent a selected portion of the organism's repertory. No matter how traits, factors, or rating scales are derived they are essentially descriptive terms for associations of acts that are grouped by some criterion of similar appearance or function.

5.3. Factors, genetic communalities and environments

I disagree with Skinner's contention that traits or factors imply only a relationship between one effect and another. True, their existence is postulated on observations of nonrandom association of certain effects. However, association implies some common component or components in the network of causation underlying the behaviors deemed characteristic of the trait. How do such associations come to be? Fuller and Thompson (1960, 1978) postulated four kinds of communality of antecedents that could lead to correlations between actions: genic, chromosomal, gametic and environmental. Individuals carrying the same allele at a locus have genic communality; closely related individuals may demonstrate chromosomal communality for a set of linked genes; gametic communality arises from assortative mating and sexual isolation so that the members of each subgroup share a restricted portion of the gene pool of their species. Finally, environmental communalities may be divided into two classes: effects attributable to defined similarities in the environment of individuals and unexplained (error ?) communality based on nonrandom association of unspecified environmental influences.

Most factor analyses of animal behavior have paid little attention to the various types of communality (an exception is McClearn and Meredith, 1964). Yet, their interpretation is different. Chromosomal communality is probably not important in most studies and is of more interest to geneticists looking for linkages than to behaviorists. Genic communality can be interpreted as indicating that alternative forms of a gene product (or alternative kinds of gene regulation) are responsible for a phenotypic difference. The implications for further exploration in psychophysiological genetics are clear. Gametic communality could result from a past history of selection for assemblies of genes that maximize the fitness of those members of a species who are exposed to a particular environment. It can also result from nonrandom mating, from inbreeding and from artificial selection for prescribed sets of characteristics. Thus assortative mating and natural or artificial selection could lead to genetic-dominant second-and third-order factors through their effect on gene distribution within in a population. As for environmental communalities their analysis seems so far to be restricted to a separation of within-family and between-family influences (Cattell, 1960; Eaves and Eysenck, 1974; Jinks and Fulker, 1970). These are useful separations but they are relatively crude. Perhaps we can do no more with humans without undue intrusion upon privacy, but more rigorous analysis should be possible in animal experiments.

If my speculations are valid there should be merit in comparing factorial structure in populations of diverse genetic composition. The one animal study of this nature with which I am familiar (Poley and Royce, 1973) reported similar factorial structure in three populations, a mix of three inbred strains, a mix of their F_1 hybrids, and a mix of the three possible F_2s. The inbred strain and the F_1 populations can each be considered as composed of three genetically homogeneous subgroups. Within each subgroup the pheno-typic correlations upon which the factor analysis was based must have been of environmental origin. Any genetic contribution to the matrix would have to come from genetic differences between the subgroups arising from their past histories. Between subgroup correlations could also arise if strain of mother exerts differ-ential influence on specific factors. The F_2 correlation matrix is still more complex. Because of segregation of alleles both within and between subgroup variation reflect a mix of genic, chromosomal, gametic and environmental communalities. The Poley and Royce analysis did not separate these genetic and environmental components, but there is no theoretical barrier to doing so in future experiments. Such research would be relevant to Royce's (1957, 1977) factor-gene hypothesis.

A twin study of personality by Loehlin (1965) is relevant to the issue of the relative role of genetic and environmental influ-ences on factor structure. Loehlin made separate factor analyses of test items showing maximal MZ-DZ differences (presumably attri-butable to genetic variance) and on items with minimal MZ-DZ differences (presumably low in genetic variance). The two sets of factors obtained were very similar. However, Loehlin suggested that the items with high loadings in the first set seemed to reflect what a person brings to a situation; those in the second set were related to what a person gets from an activity. This is a rather subtle distinction which should be verified by additional research.

6. SUMMARY

The choice of psychophenes for behavior-genetic analysis is crucial. Both ostensible and inferred psychophenes have found a place in research programs with both animal and human subjects. There is no logical reason to expect that one or the other type of psychophene is more amenable to genetic analysis, or more likely to vary in a manner compatible with a simple Mendelian pattern of transmission. The choice of a psychophene should be based primarily on its significance for problems of general psychological, psychiatric or evolutionary interest.

This line of reasoning leads to the conclusion that traits and factors are real in the sense that a pattern of organization is real. We judge an organization in terms of the effective integration of its components--not by its total energy expenditure but by the ratio of work performed to energy expended. For our purposes we might rephrase this criterion as the ratio of energy devoted to acts that increase fitness to total energy expended. The ramifying pleiotropic effects of a gene substitution upon behavior are based on communication of that gene with other genes and their products. The potential for organization, however, goes far beyond the one-way influence of a single gene. Messages go back and forth; negative and positive feedback are involved in effective regulation. The patterns of interaction are subject to natural selection; the result is the coadapted genotype of Dobzhansky (1962). In one sense all factors and traits in all species are genetically determined since the patterns of organization that underlay them is dependent upon the genotype of the individual. But in another sense the coadapted genotype is the product of environmental demands and is thus molded by them. Whether there is enough genetic variance left in any species to generate reliable genetic correlations that will lead to a complete understanding of the pattern of organization is doubtful. We will come closer to our goal by looking at the widest possible diversity of genotypes, preferably those that have evolved through natural selection. The more varied the environment inhabited and the more varied the social roles of individuals, the more likely it is that genetic diversity will be maintained within a species. If our interest is to understand the genetic basis of individual differences, this is where we should look.

BIBLIOGRAPHY

Allport, G.W. 1966. Traits revisited. American Psychologist, 21: 1-10.
Brenner, S. 1974. The genetics of Caenorhabditis elegans. Genetics, 77: 71-94.

502

Caspari, E. 1958. Genetic basis of behavior. In A. Roe and G.G. Simpson (eds.) Behavior and Evolution, pp. 103-127. New Haven: Yale University Press.

Cattell, R.B. 1953. Research designs in psychological genetics with special reference to the multiple variable analysis method. American Journal of Human Genetics, 5: 76-93.

Cattell, R.B. 1960. The multple abstract variance analysis equations and solutions: for nature-nurture research on continuous variables. Psychological Review, 67: 353-372.

Cattell, R.B., Blewett, D.B. and Beloff, J.R. 1955. The inheritance of personality. A multiple variance analysis determination of approximate nature-nurture ratios for primary personality factors in Q-data. American Journal of Human Genetics, 7: 122-146.

Cattell, R.B., Stice, G.F. and Kristy, N.F. 1957. A first approximation to nature-nurture ratios for eleven primary personality factors in objective tests. Journal of Abnormal and Social Psychology, 54: 143-159.

Coleman, D.L. 1973. Effects of parabiosis of obese with diabetes and normal mice. Diabetologia, 9: 294-296.

Coleman, D.L. and Hummel, K.P. 1969. Effects of parabiosis of normal with genetically obese mice. American Journal of Physiology, 217: 1298-1304.

Deese, J. 1969. Behavior and fact. American Psychologist, 24: 515-522.

Dobzhansky, T. 1962. Mankind evolving. New Haven: Yale University Press.

Eaves, L.J. and Eysenck, H.J. 1974. Genetics and the development of social attitudes. Nature, 249: 288-289.

Eysenck, H.J. 1950. Criterion analysis- an application of the hypotheticodeductive method to factor analysis. Psychological Review, 57: 38-53.

Fulker, D.W., Wilcock, J. and Broadhurst, P.L. 1972. Studies in genotype-environment interaction. I. Methodology and preliminary multivariate analysis of a diallel cross of eight strains of rat. Behavior Genetics, 2: 261-287.

Fuller, J.L. 1964. Physiological and population aspects of behavior genetics. American Zoologist, 4: 101-109.

Fuller, J.L. and Clark, L.D. 1966. Genetic and treatment factors modifying the postisolation syndrome in dogs. Journal of Comparative and Physiological Psychology, 61: 251-257.

Fuller, J.L. and Thompson, W.R. 1960. Behavior genetics. New York: John Wiley.

Fuller, J.L. and Thompson, W.R. 1978. Foundations of behavior genetics. St. Louis: Mosby.

Fuller, J.L. and Wimer, R.E. 1973. Behavior genetics. In D. A. Dewsbury and D. A. Rethlingshafer (eds.) Comparative Psychology. New York: McGraw-Hill. Pp. 197-237.

Guillery, R.W. 1974. Visual pathways in albinos. Scientific American, 230 (5): 44-54.

Henderson, N.D. 1967. Prior treatment effect on open field behaviour: a genetic analysis. Animal Behaviour, 15: 364-376.

Henry, K.R. and Haythorn, M.M. 1975. Albinism and auditory function in the laboratory mouse. I. Effects of single gene substitutions on auditory physiology, audiogenic seizures and developmental processes. Behavior Genetics, 5: 137-149.

Hyde, J.S. 1973. Genetic homeostasis and behavior: analysis, data, and theory. Behavior Genetics, 3: 233-245.

Jinks, J.L. and Fulker, D.W. 1970. Comparison of the biometrical genetical, MAVA and classical approaches to the analysis of human behavior. Psychological Bulletin, 73: 311-349.

Kidd, K.K. and Cavalli-Sforza, L. 1973. An analysis of the genetics of schizophrenia. Social Biology, 20: 254-265.

Kung, C. 1971. Genic mutants with altered system of excitation. I. Phenotypes of the behavioral mutants. Zeitschrift für vergleichende Physiologie, 71: 142-164.

Lagerspetz, K.M.J. 1961. Genetic and social causes of aggressive behavior in mice. Scandinavian Journal of Psychology, 2: 167-173.

Loehlin, J.C. 1965. A heredity-environment analysis of personality inventory data. In S.G. Vandenberg, (ed.) Methods and goals in human behavior genetics. New York: Academic Press.

McClearn, G.E. and Meredith, W. 1964. Dimensional analysis of activity and elimination in a genetically heterogeneous group of mice. Animal Behaviour, 12: 1-10.

McGill, T.E. 1962. Sexual behavior in three inbred strains of mice. Behaviour, 19: 341-350.

McGill, T.E. 1970. Genetic analysis of male sexual behavior. In G. Lindzey and D.D. Thiessen (eds.), Contributions to behavior-genetic analysis: the mouse as a prototype. Appleton-Century-Crofts: New York. Pp. 57-88.

Mordkoff, A.M. and Fuller, J.L. 1959. Variability in activity within inbred and crossbred mice. Journal of Heredity, 50: 6-8.

Nissen, H.W. 1958. Axes of behavioral comparison. In A. Roe and G.G. Simpson (eds.), Behavior and evolution. New Haven: Yale University Press. Pp. 183-205.

Poley, W. and Royce, J.R. 1973. Behavior-genetic analysis of mouse emotionality. II. Stability of factors across genotype. Animal Learning and Behavior, 1: 116-120.

Pruzan, A. and Ehrman, L. 1974. Age, experience and rare-male mating advantage in Drosophila pseudoobscura. Behavior Genetics, 4: 159-165.

Purton, A.C. 1978. Ethological categories of behaviour and some consequences of their conflation. Animal Behaviour, 26: 653-670.

Rothenbuhler, W.C. 1964. Behavior genetics of nest clearning in honey bees. IV. Responses of F_1 and backcross generations to disease-killed brood. American Zoologist, 4: 111-123.

Royce, J.R. 1957. Factor theory and genetics. Educational and Psychological Measurement, 17: 361-376.

Royce, J.R. 1977. Genetics, environment and intelligence: a theoretical synthesis. In A. Oliverio (ed.), Genetics, environment and intelligence. Amsterdam/New York: Elsevier North Holland. Pp. 239-268.

Sahakian, W.S. 1970. Psychopathology today. Itasca, Illinois: Peacock.

Skinner, B.F. 1953. Science and human behavior. New York: The Free Press.

Thiessen, D.D. 1965. The wabbler-lethal mouse: a study in development. Animal Behaviour, 13: 87-100.

Thiessen, D.D. 1972. A move towards species-specific analyses in behavior genetics. Behavior Genetics, 2: 115-126.

Thiessen, D.D. and Rodgers, D.A. 1967. Behavior genetics as the study of mechanism-specific behavior. In J.N. Spuhler (ed.), Genetic diversity and human behavior. Chicago: Aldine.

Thiessen, D.D. and Yahr, P. 1970. Central control of territorial marking in the Mongolian gerbil. Physiology and Behavior, 5: 275-278.

Tyler, P.A. and McClearn, G.E. 1970. A quantitative genetic analysis of runway learning in mice. Behavior Genetics, 1: 57-70.

van Abeelen, J.H.F. 1963. Mouse mutants studied by means of ethological methods. I. Ethogram. Genetica 34: 79-94. II. Mutant and methods. ibid. 34: 95-101. III. Results with yellow, pink-eyed dilution, brown and jerker. ibid. 34: 270-286.

Wilson, E.O. 1975. Sociobiology. Cambridge, Mass.: Harvard University Press.

COMMENT BY J. R. ROYCE

Fuller's paper is central to the theme of this institute, for it deals with the problem of identifying basic theoretical constructs. And the epistemic correlation between data and constructs combined with the relationships among constructs in a nomological network are keys to the development of explanatory theory (Royce, 1978b). Furthermore, by focusing on behavioral phenotypes, Fuller has put his finger on the critical link in the chain of gene-behavior causal analysis.

The psychophene is critical because it constitutes the conceptual bridge to psychology, and it is at the psychological level that extant theory is weakest--that is, theory of individual differences is less developed than either gene theory or evolutionary theory.

Despite this inadequacy, there are relevant developments in psychology--and they point to Fuller's "inferred psychophene" category as the one most pertinent to psychological theory construction. Why? Because inferred psychophenes are the psychological equivalents of genetic phenotypes--that is, they refer to psychological characteristics or traits. Ostensible psychophenes, on the other hand, refer to observable behaviors, not psychobiological properties. The point is that behavior is a manifestation of a trait, not a trait per se. Furthermore, behavior per se constitutes the raw data of psychological science and, as such, it cannot provide a theoretical structure. Thus, the mere accumulation of behavior genetic findings (i.e., raw empiricism) is an endless, and possibly a fruitless, task. It will give us something that looks more like a telephone book rather than a rational science. In short, some form of conceptual framework which codifies observables as "for instances" of underlying principles and regularities is what we're after in science, not endless inventories of unrelated observables.

What about syndromes? Are they better than raw behavior? Probably, but not much. The problem with syndromes is that they are composites, not unities. And, as with all composites, there is an assumption that we know the elements of which the composite is made. I personally know of no viable psychological syndromes. These include the widely used psychopathological syndromes, such as schizophrenia. What I'm saying is that psychological syndromes have not provided us with a viable taxonomy of behavioral variation. Rather, they constitute clinically evolved (translate as "completely uncontrolled") observations which are, at best, unusual or strange manifestations of the mind/brain. In short, there is little basis, on either conceptual or empirical grounds, for turning to syndromes as the basic units on which to build an explanatory theory of behavior genetics.

Let me now move on to factor analysis as one of the most powerful approaches available for identifying underlying psychological traits or psychophenes. However, before elaborating on this point there are several old saws about factor analysis that must be reiterated in order to clear up misunderstandings. They have to do with test sampling, preconceived ideas regarding the interpretation of a factor, and objectivity. Yes, any one factor analysis can only get at a selected portion of the organism's behavioral repertoire. This is, of course, true of any investigation, particularly the typical bivariate experiments. The remedy is clear--we get at the organism's total repertoire via a well conceived series of factor studies. Cumulative investigation is characteristic of all effective science, including the factor analytic paradigm. And yes, any investigator worth his salt has some preconceived ideas about the variables he intends to use in his research, including factor analysts. However, it doesn't follow that he necessarily has preconceptions about what factors will emerge from a given study, nor does it follow that preconceived factors will necessarily emerge when the data are factor analyzed.

All of these points, about which there is persistent misunderstanding, can be clarified if we understand factor invariance. And the critical requirement of factor invariance is that we must specify the boundary conditions of a factor--that is, the conditions of its replicability. In its deepest sense this means that the functional characteristics of a factor eventually become so well established that no further investigation is necessary concerning factor interpretation (i.e., we have identified an "unknown"). A brief summary of the present state of affairs regarding factor invariance is that it is empirically demonstrable despite inadequacies in the extant mathematical formulations of the problem,[1] but that much more research along these lines is required.

There are two categories of factor invariance--internal and external (Royce, 1976). Invariance of the first kind involves construct replication across several factor analyses. Examples of this approach include the Air Force Aviation Psychology Program (see the 21 volumes from World War II and the post-war

---

[1] The dozen or so quantitative solutions which are available deal with the relatively easy classes of invariance which involves the same subjects or/and the same measures. However, the most interesting form of invariance, namely the case involving both different subjects and different tests, may not be amenable to mathematical formalization (i.e., due to insufficient information concerning the functioning of each unknown).

reports), and the massive research programs carried out by Cattell
(1965, 1973) in the affective (personality) domain and Guilford
(1967) in the cognitive (intelligence) domain. External invariance
refers to the experimental or laboratory manipulation of previously
identified factors. The most convincing and extensive research
programs in this category include Fleishman's (1967) analyses of
the learning dynamics of psychomotor dimensions, Eysenck's (1967)
massive laboratory extensions of his third order personality constructs, and Royce's (see chapter in this book, and 1978; Royce,
Yeudall, & Bock, 1976; Mos, Lukaweski, & Royce, 1977) identification of the genetic and brain site correlates of affective and cognitive factors.

COMMENT BY J. H. F. van ABEELEN

In his thought-provoking contribution, Fuller proposes a
classification of phenotypes, dividing them into somatophenes,
psychophenes, and syndromes. This prompts me to ask the following
question: Are stress induced electroencephalographic patterns or
changes in blood pressure to be considered as somatophenes or psychophenes? These are processes but not acts. Where do you place
these? Or should there be a fourth category?

I might add that I entirely agree with Fuller's opinion that
the choice of a psychophene should be based primarily on its significance for problems of general psychological, psychiatric, or
evolutionary interest.

On the issue of the role of theoretical constructs, I feel
that much of the discussion hinges on the distinction between
percepts and concepts. Objectivistic scientists tend to believe
in percepts, but they distruct concepts. Wouldn't this viewpoint
reconcile some of the disagreements?

COMMENT BY D. D. THIESSEN

For most behaviors of great interest to behavior geneticists
there seems to be little hope that they will yield to systematic
classification. As pointed out by Dr. Fuller, such behaviors are
extremely complex, fluid, highly modifiable within the stream of
an ever changing environment, and almost without definable boundaries. A classical taxonomist schooled in biological systematics
would throw up his hands in despair if faced with such a task. In
contrast to the artifacts of the taxonomist, there do not seem to
be units for complex behaviors. Behavior geneticists lack the
equivalent of a cell, a DNA molecule, fossil dentition or a pattern of pigmentation.

Nevertheless we recognize the pressing need for some way to organize and describe behavior. As long as behavioralists deal with complex concepts like learning, motivation, emotion, or anxiety some broad form of classification and measurement is essential. John Fuller's use of the concept of psychophenes, and his distinction between <u>ostensible</u> and <u>inferred</u> psychophenes is a potentially important first step. At the very least it allows us to conceptually separate those things we can see from those things that are not directly visible. Within the current context of behavior genetics the distinction is not trivial.

But as a discipline have we really done our homework? Perhaps we are still riveted to notions of the past. Historically, behavior genetics grew out of a long tradition of preoccupation with man's destiny. The problems of interest then, and now, are those dealing with learning, motivation, and perception. It could be argued that we have simply taken over these arcane issues (with the exception of perception) and have added a little genetic style. Unfortunately, in the process we have neglected perception, an area of investigation where psychophysical units of behavior are more evident, and where we stand a chance of defining the underlying genetic architecture. My guess is that overall we have not profited by this long association with tradition and our anthropomorphic stance with regard to animal behavior.

Accepting the most complex of human traits for study, we may be guilty of over-particularizing our behaviors in the search for stable units and of prying into every genetic nook and cranny. It is nearly impossible, for example, to explain the nuances of anxiety at any level when we can neither define their structures not stipulate their functions. Focusing on characteristics of great variability and high heritability may do little more than suggest nature's disinterest in these characteristics. And, repetitively emphasizing gene-environmental interactions does little to help us understand behaviors.

If these are not the tracks we should be following, what should we be doing? Well, this conference is a healthy start, where we can freely probe our empirical hypotheses and test the strength of our theories. Let me now throw caution to the winds, and offer several more extreme suggestions. Let's forget much of what we know and begin anew. We might even consider dropping our open fields, mazes, intelligence tests, and personality inventories. Let's learn more biochemistry, molecular biology, embryology, information theory, and sociobiology. Let's concentrate on simple behaviors of obvious value to reproduction - mating strategies, assortative mating, parental investment, and social communication processes. Finally, I believe that we should at least occasionally step out of our laboratories and view behavior in the natural environment, be it on the slopes of the Canadian

Rockies or in the ghettos of San Francisco. In short, let's plug
into the scientific zeitgeist and absorb biology to its fullest.

While Dr. Fuller has not suggested such a revolutionary approach, he does seem to agree that we can begin to make progress
by narrowing our fences of classification and moving toward a
study of significant problems, including those handed us by
natural selection. I heartily agree.

COMMENT BY P. L. BROADHURST

Dr. Fuller's delineation of the psychophene is an attractive
concept, but I remain to be convinced of the necessity for it. To
speak of a psychophene is a special way of referring to the behavioral aspects of the phenotype: indeed, it is essentially a
behavioral phenotype. However, perhaps even in referring to "behavioral phenotypes" in this way we already do violence to genetic
terminology. After all, the phenotype is the whole complex of
characters in respect of which individual organisms differ from
each other and the behavioral are merely a subset of those differences. In the early days of biometrical genetics there was controversy (Mather, 1952; Woolf, 1952) about the reality of phenotypic differences which were mathematical derivations of actual
data. Indeed, Woolf referred to one such usage as "a biological
monstrosity" (p. 93). Biological monstrosities are familiar cur-
rency among psychologists, witness variance as such, which has
been successfully used as a phenotype (Broadhurst & Jinks, 1966).
The problem may have contemporary relevance in the use of factors
and factor scores in the search for the "units of behavior" which
might be tied to genetic substrates.

Another point which may be raised in this connection would
be the status of the phenotype in the psychopharmacogenetic experiment. It is ostensible in the sense defined by Fuller, but
it has some of the attributes of the inferred psychophene since
"stimulation" or "depression" may be a characteristic action of
the drug concerned and hence of a more general property.

COMMENT BY D. WAHLSTEN

Dr. Fuller categorizes phenotypes into somatophenes, psychophenes, and syndromes. However, when these things are considered
from a developmental or historical point of view, their interrelations become most apparent. Three points can be argued:

1)   All structure is the outcome of process.
2)   A behavioral process takes place by virtue of organic and
      molecular structure.

3)   Considered developmentally, every behavior appears as part
      of a syndrome.

      Consider the spider's web. It is the result of the spinning
process, and the web itself could be termed a "behavioral somatophene". Either the structure or the process may stand out because
of a perspective imposed by a measuring technique, but they are
both features of what might be termed a "web-weaving spider syndrome", the life history of an animal that captures food in a web
of its own making. If the webs (somatophenes) of two individuals
of the same species are substantially different, the only way to
determine whether this reflects perhaps a difference in body size
(somatophene) or weaving strategies (psychophenes) in animals of
equal size is to measure the spiders, their weaving behavior, and
their finished products.

      Likewise, the process of neural transmission occurs because
of the topographical structure of the nervous system as well as
the molecular structure of the neurotransmitter molecules and
their corresponding receptors. Brain structure is itself a product
of the dynamic processes of neural ontogeny.

      The conclusion is that a very serious investigation of be-
havior and its physiological substrates should be undertaken prior
to embarking on a genetic analysis of specific psychophenes.
Otherwise the investigator will not know the significance of the
measured phenotypes for the life of the individual and consequently
will be unable to conclude much about their significance for the
offspring of the individual or the evolution of the species.

                    COMMENT BY D. A. HAY

      I was pleased to be able to chair this session as I share
Professor Fuller's concern over the behaviors that we study, and
agree that the selection of phenotypes is a crucial question.
However, I must confess to being a little breathless after reading his paper. In these few pages he covers organisms from Paramecium to man, techniques from single mutant genes to the more
elaborate polygenic models such as Cattell's MAVA, the influences
of behaviorism, ethology, and individual difference psychology, and
just about every possible way of measuring behavior.

      At the end of it all we are left without a sense of direc-
tion - 'no one behavior is any better for research than any other,
but we should study it in as many environments and genotypes as
possible' is my over-simplification and paraphrase of Professor
Fuller's conclusions. Perhaps he did not want to let his own personal views intrude, but I am sorry that he brought up all these
research possibilities, without giving us a clue as to which

directions he would favour.

Otherwise, by highlighting all the potential points of contention rather than unifying themes in behavior genetics, is he not just encouraging the "overparticularization" to which he refers in the earlier part of his paper? Elias (1973) makes the point that many disciplines, such as psychology as a whole, are suffering an information overload rather than a lack of synthesis and organisation of existing data. Behavior genetics has a long way to go, but, despite my criticism of Fuller, I must admit that the goal of unification must include the diversity to which he points.

REPLY TO COMMENTS

J. L. Fuller

I concur strongly with Royce's comments on the importance of inferred psychophenes as the bases for relating genetic and psychological theory. Raw behavioral data provide an objective means for comparing individuals and groups, but something more is needed to make a theoretical science. It may turn out that the term psychogenetics reflects our theoretical interests better than behavior or behavioral genetics. The genetics of inferred psychophenes may be more interesting and profitable than the genetics of ostensible psychophenes. We must always ask about the latter, "why are you interested in this behavior?"

Factor analysis is an important way by which one transforms data on ostensible psychophenes to estimates of inferred psychophenes. I do not intend to depreciate the value of the methodology for behavior genetics. Nevertheless the choice of tests, method of analysis and interpretation of factors are matters of judgment. Hence subjectivity may to a degree enter into the design of such studies and the conclusions drawn from them. But this is also true of other methodologies and competent experimenters often recognize that their data runs contrary to their preconceived ideas. I anticipate that factor analysis will continue to make important contributions to our branch of science.

I reacted to van Abeelen's first comment on the place for physiological characters in my classification by a revision of my text. There I consider them as a subclass of ostensible psychophenes. However, an argument could be made for a separate class of physiophenes. Although van Abeelen's distinction between percept and concept was challenged during the open discussion I believe that it is valid and useful. (See, for example, Noble, 1974). It is true that scientists are admonished to retain an intelligent skepticism regarding the hypotheses and theories of their specialties. Nevertheless many concepts have stood up well for decades or centuries and most of us act as though they were true. I doubt that even extreme pragmatists can completely dispense with them.

Thiessen is kind in commending my classification of phenotypes, particularly those I have called psychophenes. I claim little originality for the classification but hope that the new words will be helpful in developing general concepts in behavior genetics. Thiessen's challenge to traditional choices of phenotypes also makes sense. I like his suggestion that we look for genetic variability in the regulation of physiological processes that could influence a wide range of behavior. Also we should note that the bold ideas of sociobiology mostly lack the kind of empirical foundation that can be provided by ethology on one hand and behavior genetics on the other. I hope for a rapprochement between these three specialties.

I am not sure that I wholly understand Broadhurst's comments. King (1974) defines phenotype as "the observable properties of an organism; produced by the organism in conjunction with the environment", and phene as "a phenotypic character controlled by genes". In common usage phenotype sometimes is used inclusively to refer to all properties, sometimes specifically as to name a red-cell antigen. Broadhurst's definition, "characters in respect of which individual organisms differ from each other", is inaccurate since a character that appears universally in a species is still part of its phenotype. The point I make in my paper is that only the subset of phenes that I call chemophenes are congruent point by point with portions of the genotype. Psychophenes, and also morphenes, are products of patterns of genes operating in an appropriate environment. Identical psychophenes, as viewed externally, may be associated with different but functionally equivalent genotypes. The distinction between ostensible and inferred psychophenes falls in the purview of psychology rather than genetics. Both kinds of psychophenes are "monstrosities" in Woolf's sense unless they are based on a suitable theory of behavior. I certainly would not refer to Broadhurst's and Jinks' use of variance as a character as perpetuation of a monstrosity. On the contrary I hope that their type of analysis will be adopted more widely.

Wahlsten's points, like van Abeelen's and Broadhurst's are partially covered by the addition to my original draft in which I emphasize the dependence of psychophenes upon somatophenes. Whether behavior genetics should give priority to investigation of the physiological substrates of psychophenes (as Wahlsten argues) or to the role of psychophenes in enhancing individual fitness (as Thiessen suggests) is a personal judgment. Both kinds of research are valid endeavors. In my own research career I have gradually become more interested in the systems (e.g., see the chapter by Royce) than in the reductionist approach.

References

Broadhurst, P. L., & Jinks, J. L.   Stability and change in the inheritance of behaviour in rats: A further analysis of statistics from a diallel cross.   Proceedings of the Royal Society, B, 1966, 165, 450–472.

Cattell, R. B.   The scientific analysis of personality.   London: Penguin, 1965.

Cattell, R. B.   Personality and mood by questionnaire.   San Francisco: Jossey-Bass, 1973.

Elias, M. F.   Disciplinary barriers to progress in behavior genetics: defensive reactions to bits and pieces.   Human Development, 1973, 16, 119–132.

Eysenck, H. J.   The biological basis of personality.   Springfield, Illinois: Charles C. Thomas, 1967.

Fleishman, E. A.   Toward a taxonomy of human performance.   American Psychologist, 1975, 30, 1127–1149.

Guilford, J. P.   The nature of human intelligence.   New York: McGraw-Hill, 1967.

King, R. C.   A dictionary of genetics, (2nd. ed.) New York: Oxford University Press.

Mather, K.   Comment on Dr. B. Woolf's paper.   In E. C. R. Reeve, and C. M. Waddington (Eds.), Quantitative inheritance, London: HMSO, 1952.

Mos, L. P., Lukaweski, R., & Royce, J. R.   Effects of septal lesions on factors of mouse emotionality.   Journal of Comparative and Physiological Psychology, 1977, 91, 523–532.

Noble, C. E.   Philosophy of science in psychology.   Psychological Reports, 1974, 35, 1239–1246.

Royce, J. R.   Psychology is multi: Methodological, variate, epistemic, world-view, systemic, paradigmatic, theoretic, and disciplinary.   In W. J. Arnold (Ed.), Nebraska Symposium on the Conceptual Foundations of Psychology.   Lincoln, Nebraska: University of Nebraska Press, 1976, pp. 1–63.

Royce, J. R.   The genetic correlates of emotionality.   Center Paper in Progress, 1978a.

Royce, J. R.   How we can best advance the construction of theory in psychology.   Canadian Psychological Review, 1978b, in press.

Royce, J. R., Yeudall, L. T., & Bock, C.   Factor analytic studies of human brain damage: I.   First and second-order factors and their brain correlates.   Multivariate Behavioral Research, 1976, 4, 381–418.

Woolf, B.   Environmental effects in quantitative inheritance.   In E. C. R. Reeve & C. M. Waddington (Eds.), Quantitative inheritance, London: HMSO, 1952.

PSYCHOLOGICAL THEORY

Genetic Models, Theory of Personality and
the Unification of Psychology

H. J. Eysenck

The Genetics of Information Processing

G. E. McClearn

The Factor-Gene Basis of Individuality

J. R. Royce

GENETIC MODELS, THEORY OF PERSONALITY AND THE UNIFICATION OF PSYCHOLOGY.

H. J. Eysenck

Institute of Psychiatry, University of London.

1. PSYCHOLOGY AS THE STUDY OF ORGANISMS

The natural sciences share certain characteristics, certain ways of increasing knowledge, and certain ways of judging evidence. Philosophers of science have attempted to categorize these ways and characteristics, with some degree of success, but total agreement is still far from being achieved (Suppe, 1974). What we can say is that scientists have worked out invariances, laws, and generalizations which cover a broad field; within each field we find certain *paradigms* which are widely if not universally accepted. Viewed from this perspective, psychology is still no better than that "hope of a science" which William James spoke of; we have certainly not reached any more advanced stage of development. Wolfgang Köhler once complained that psychology was nothing better than a series of chapter headings, strung together haphazardly on the spine of a text-book; it lacked altogether the unifying principles which alone would make it into a science. Similarly lacking are paradigms, or even the will and the desire to achieve such paradigms; most psychologists seem content either to accept Freudian revelations without reservation, without proof, and without criticism, or else to carry out small-scale experiments, technically perfect but without any larger relevance.

Put in another way, natural science as we know it builds up its imposing edifice brick by brick, each scientist adding to the overall structure. Psychology looks more like a large field into which each contributor throws his bricks higgledipiggledi, without attention to any larger plan, with the result that we have no building but rather a desert full of bricks! Much time has gone by since Köhler made his complaint, but things have not

improved. We have had the unreasonable sanctification of Hul-
lian learning theory, followed by the equally unreasoning
anathematization of the same learning theory; one fad following
another, rather than experiment-based criticism sharpening and
improving theory. In this sad and pessimistic situation it may
be useful to say a few words about the conditions which make this
failure inevitable, and to suggest ways and means of improving
the position in which we find ourselves.

It is not, I think, necessary to adopt a position which
states that psychology is so different from physics that we cannot hope to adopt the methods of investigation which have made
physics so influential and powerful. Farrel (1978) has given a
good discussion on this point, and his major conclusions are I
think justified, namely that sceptics of scientific objectivity in
psychology, like Koch (1974), are not in a strong position. But
of course there are differences between physics and psychology,
and these lead us directly into the reasons for the apparent
sterility of much psychological research. Above all, psychology
deals with the behavior of *organisms*, whereas physics deals with
aggregates which are (almost) infinitely divisible. This fact
immediately renders impossible the search for meaningful atoms of
behaviour; we must look for laws applying to the organism as a
whole, not attempt to destroy the organism by (almost) unlimited
subdivision.

Early behaviourism failed to recognize the importance or even
the very existence of organisms; it attempted to phrase its laws
in terms of stimulus-response bonds or connections which were
looked upon as the equivalent of the physicist's atoms. But
stimuli and responses do not exist in and of themselves; it is
the organism which makes a stimulus out of simple physical change,
and it is the organism which unifies physical movements into responses. The very terms "stimulus" and "response" have an adver-
bial quality; it is always the stimulation or the response of
something - the nouns should not really be used in an intransi-
tive sense, even though grammatically this is permissible. The
lack of concern for the organism which characterized Watson has
been developed into a battle-cry by Skinner and his followers;
the doctrine of what Boring called the "empty organism" has been
widely adopted, in spite of its essentially nonsensical character.

This denial of the very existence of the organism as a
psychological reality has escalated into a denial of the existence
of concepts like "personality" as meaningful scientific hypotheses.
Thus E. L. Thorndike, one of the founders of the S - R theory of
behaviour, wrote almost 70 years ago that "there are no broad,
general traits of personality, no general and consistent forms of
conduct which, if they existed, would make for consistency of

behaviour and stability of personality, but only independent and
specific stimulus-response bonds or habits." (Thorndike, 1903).
And in recent years, Mischel (1968, 1973) has published views
which, although not quite so extreme, essentially mediate the
same message; the organism is devalued, and changing patterns
of stimulation are considered as more useful for the purpose of
explicating human behaviour. The modern substitution of "social"
or "cognitive" stimulation for the more old-fashioned type of
sensory stimulation has done nothing to make this devaluation of
the organism more acceptable.

What is the non-empty organism full of? We are not as ignorant of this as Skinner often suggests; we know about cells,
and synapses, axons and dendrites, the C.N.S. and the A.N.S., the
brain stem, the limbic system, the paleocortex and the neocortex,
the hippocampus and the amygdala, the thalamus and the septum;
above all, we know something about the chromosomes and the genes
which are responsible for the very existence of the organism as a
functioning unit. To write books and articles about personality,
as Mischel does, without mention of the genetic contribution is
truly to play Hamlet without the Prince; even Thorndike recognized
the importance of genetic factors, but modern psychology has
purposefully repressed this knowledge.

2. GENERAL LAWS AND INDIVIDUAL DIFFERENCES

We thus have the curious position that psychologists - experimental, social, clinical, industrial - operate in their search
for general laws, or even for small-scale generalizations as if
human beings were all MZ twins, identical in all relevant aspects,
and completely interchangeable. How else can we justify the
practice of basing our laws of learning, memory, perception or
social behaviour on completely non-representative samples of
students, pressed into service by threat or bribery? Some psychologists have gone even further than this, using any mammal
as equivalent of any other; thus Hull based some of the constants
in his formulae on rat experiments, no doubt in the hope that rats
and humans were sufficiently similar to make extrapolation possible! All this is very much as if physicists, instead of specifying most carefully the nature of the metals, alloys, gases, rare
earths, or plasmas they were studying in their laboratories, were
to throw together any old rubbish, and claim triumphantly that
they had determined the constants of nature from this unanalyzed
and irreproducible compound. The degree of care needed in specifying the nature of the material analyzed is illustrated by the
study of the physicist who was awarded the Nobel price for increasing by an order of magnitude the accuracy of measuring the
weight of atoms - just before the discovery of isotopes showed
this whole process to be illusory, because different isotopes

have different atomic weights.

Experimentalists might answer that general laws apply to all organisms, or perhaps to all human beings, and that students are as good a sample as any. Thus Cofer (1967), in denying the importance of recognizing personality differences in the study of memory, stated: "I remain to be convinced . . . that there are but a few basic processes underlying individual differences in learning, and that the interactions of specific task character- istics with highly specific individual propensities are not the basis of the enormous individual differences which everyone finds in most learning tasks." (p. 139) M. W. Eysenck (1977) has sur- veyed the field of human memory from this point of view, and has shown that such optimism is unjustified; there are widespread, lawful, replicable differences in learning and forgetting, re- lating to fundamental properties of the organism; personality is inextricably linked with memory, to such an extent that averating results over introverts and extraverts, stable and labile subjects simply makes no sense at all.

What happens as a consequence of this neglect of individual differences? The answer is of course well known. In our experi- mental designs the variance contributed by main effects remains derisory; the variance properly attributable to personality and interaction effects is relegated to the error term; and the error term assumes frighteningly large proportions - so large that it usually outweighs every other part of the analysis! Unless the main effects are so obvious in prospect that no experiment is really necessary, this is the typical picture presented by article after article in our experimental literature. Physicists and chemists avoid similar humiliation by controlling their experi- ments properly; such control in psychology is lacking unless we admit the existence of powerful organismic variables whose existence can create and obscure main effects of the kind looked for by experimentalists.

Recent publications in the fields of perception, memory, learning, psychophysiology, social psychology, and many others make it abundantly clear how widespread are the effects of per- sonality differences (Eysenck, 1976b). It is less widely known that even the rat is not the homogeneous organism suggested by its position as the test bed of modern psychology. Wide-ranging theoretical disputes, such as that between Hull and Spence on the one side, Tolman on the other, may have originated and been con- tinued largely because the former were working with descendants of Hall's non-emotional strains, while the latter was working with descendants of his emotional strains (Eysenck, 1967). The mechanical regularity of the former, adding their quotas of habit strength with each repetition of the learning paradigm, contrasts with the emotion-induced V.T.E. behaviour of the latter; there is no need to adduce different types of learning in order to predict and understand the differential patterns of reaction of emotional and non-emotional animals. Thousands of experiments may have been wasted because the experimenters neglected to look into the question of systematic individual and strain dife in their animals. No wonder it became the rule rather than the exception to find results "non-replicable". We would not expect results of experiments on gold to be replicable in experiments using mercury, or agreement between workers, one of whom used hydrogen, the other helium!

In the applied field also there is a tradition which makes many practitioners assume the quite unrealistic role of egalitarianism; methods of treatment are judged on an overall basis, as if each individual reacted in precisely the same manner to the changes proposed. In education, to take but one example, Cronbach & Snow (1969) have amply documented the fact that for most proposed innovations, the main effects are minimal or nonexistent; the new method, looked at from an overall point of view, does no better and no worse than the old method or methods. Eysenck (1978c) has surveyed the field from the point of view of treatment x personality interaction, and has shown that this general failure to disconfirm the null hypothesis arises from the simple fact that extraverts and introverts, stable and neurotic subjects react in diverse and often contradictory ways to the changes introduced, with effects cancelling out overall. "Discovery" methods are likely to improve the performance of extraverts, worsen that of introverts, leading to an overall verdict of "no change"; all the significant variance is in the interaction term - or in the error term when personality is not explicitly introduced into the design.

There is some evidence that the same is true of psychotherapy. Di Loreto (1971) has shown that Rogers's client-centered therapy and Ellis's rational psychotherapy give similar results, exceeding those of "no treatment", when applied to groups of monosymptomatic patients; he also found, however, that this similarity in outcome disappeared completely when the patients were divided into extraverts and introverts. Client-centered therapy worked very well with extraverts, but not at all with introverts, whereas rational psychotherapy worked very well with introverts, but not at all with extraverts. The mean reductions in (maladapted) behaviour ratings from pre-therapy to follow-up condition are given in Table 1 for introverts and extraverts respectively, for the client-centered, rational psychotherapy, and no treatment conditions. It will be seen that the treatments inappropriate to each personality type were identical in effectiveness with no treatment, while the treatments appropriate to each personality type were highly successful, and very significantly different from no treatment. Thus without the interaction term the results of the statistical analysis would have been very misleading, grossly underestimating the possibilities of effective action. Much the same is true in the field of criminology (Eysenck, 1977).

	Introverts:	Extraverts:
C.C.T.	7	22
R.T.	20	9
N.T.	7	9

Table 1. Mean reduction in appropriate behaviour ratings for introverts and extraverts respectively after client-centered therapy, rational psychotherapy, and no therapy.

These are of course only examples of a very general position; in theoretical psychology, experimental psychology, and applied psychology it is universally true that individual differences are vitally important if correct conclusions are to be drawn from empirical data, when theories are to be tested or assessed, and when practical proposals for the application of psychological methods to education, psychiatry, criminology, or social work generally are to be implemented. All this is not perhaps new; to many readers it may appear but a gloss on Cronbach's famous 1957 paper on "The two disciplines of scientific psychology". Much evidence has been accumulating since that paper was published, and all of it illustrates the simple truth that a house divided against itself, setting the experimental against the correlational approach, cannot succeed.

3. PERSONALITY AS A NATURAL SCIENCE CONCEPT

So far we have argued that the experimentalist requires the help of the personality theorist, if he is ever to carry through a programme of scientific analysis of human behaviour; we shall now turn the argument around and suggest that equally the personality theorist requires the help of the experimentalist (and the general theoretician) if he is ever to carry through a programme of scientific analysis of differential human behaviour. This reciprocity principle was recognized early on by Hull (1945), when he wrote that "the natural science approach to behaviour theory presents two major tasks. The first is to make a satisfactory working analysis of the various behaviour processes; this consists in deriving, i.e., deducing, from the primary laws of the system the characteristic observable phenomena of the behaviour process in question, as displayed by the modal or

average organism under given conditions . . . The second major
task of the natural science approach to behaviour theory concerns
the problem of innate behavioural differences under identical
conditions between different species and different individuals
within given species . . . Both types of tasks cry out loudly
for completion. But most neglected of all is the relationship
between the two approaches."

Hull's last postulate in his system (Hull, 1951, Postulate
XVIII; Hull, 1952, Postulate XVII) is in fact a postulate of
individual differences, and reads as follows: "The 'constant'
numerical values appearing in equations representing primary
moral behavioural laws vary from species to species, from individuals to individuals, and from some physiological states to others
in the same individuals at different times, all quite apart from
the factor of behavioural oscillation (sO_R)." Thus what Hull is
clearly suggesting is that the principles of description of individual differences in human conduct should be derived from
general psychological theory, rather than being worked out independently and ideosyncratically in isolation from the major
findings of experimental psychology and behaviour theory.
Eysenck (1957) made an attempt to translate this programme into
reality, with results which were only partly encouraging; in
particular, the attempt to make use of Hull's own principles failed
in part because these principles were too insecurely grounded.
Later efforts to use concepts more securely grounded in physiological knowledge rather than in psychological theory were more
successful (Eysenck, 1967); it clearly is possible to build
bridges between physiological and experimental psychology, on the
one side, and social and personality psychology, on the other,
using the laws and concepts of the former to explain and deduce
the observations of the latter. This is an important beginning
to a unification of psychology.

It is an interesting and encouraging fact that the major
dimensions of personality, discovered by factor analysis in
innumerable studies of young and old, male and female, European,
American and non-Caucasian subjects, and even of animals, should
find an explanation in the major physiological systems that have
come to interest experimental and physiological psychologists.
The link between extraversion-introversion and the reticular
formation - cortical arousal system, and that between neuroticism
and the limbic system - visceral brain, has been subjected to a
good deal of experimental study, and the outcome has for the most
part been quite encouraging (Eysenck, 1976b). The link between
psychoticism and masculinity, although not researched in sufficient detail to allow of any definitive conclusions, appears
well supported (Eysenck & Eysenck, 1976). It would be absurd
to suggest that the type of work which Hull considered the most
neglected of all, namely that on the relationship between his two

approaches, had been successfully completed; what can be said is
that a promising beginning has been made.

Before turning to a consideration of the importance of
genetic factors in this whole development, we may perhaps briefly
deal with the extensions of this rudimentary unified system of
behaviour to social and other forms of conduct which are usually
considered outside the field of experimental psychology, and
which are rarely integrated with a system of personality description. Individual differences in cortical arousal and autonomic
activation, in this system, are responsible for differences in
conditioning, habituation, extinction, perception, vigilance,
sensory thresholds and j.n.d.s., reactions to pain and sensory
deprivation, psychomotor behaviour, learning, memory and recall,
cognitive styles, creativity, and many more (Eysenck, 1976b);
through some of these, notably conditioning, causal links are
forged with patterns of social behaviour, such as antisocial and
criminal behaviour (Eysenck, 1977), sexual behaviour (Eysenck,
1976c), neurotic and psychotic behaviour (Eysenck & Eysenck,
1976; Eysenck & Rachman, 1965), drug addiction and smoking
(Eysenck, 1965; Teasdale, 1973). In this way there is created a
causal chain from the fundamental biological sciences (physiology,
anatomy, biochemistry) through experimental psychology and personality study to the social sciences (social psychology, sociology, anthropology). In this chain the major connecting link is
personality; without it the chain would break into two disjointed
and entirely separate parts, the biological and the social. Man's
inherent position as a biosocial organism makes it impossible to
understand his behaviour in terms either of biological variables
alone, or of social variables alone; the integration of the biological and the social components of Man is an essential prerequisite to the building up of a unified science of psychology.

4. THEORY OF GENETICS

In this attempt, genetics plays an indispensable part. Pos-
tulating as we do both biological and social antecedents to human
behaviour, we must inevitably ask, in connection with each type
of behaviour, to what extent it is indebted to the one set of
causes or to the other; to what extent it is determined by
genetic causes, to what by environmental ones. Many psychologists
consider such questions as being impossible to answer, but in
principle this objection is not valid; Fisher originated the
scientific search for an answer to this problem in 1918, and
other workers have built upon his brilliant generalization of the
Mendelian system to incorporate polygenic variation in a manner
to make possible the quantitative precision which now character-
ises our work (Mather & Jinks, 1971). Assessments of heritability
are of course not the only, or even the main, problem thrown up

by attempts to make real the conception of Man as a biosocial organism; we shall discuss other problems later. Nor is it true that assessments of heritability have universal validity; they are clearly circumscribed in many ways. Heritability is a population statistic; it describes a given population, at a given moment of time. Such statistics are not scientific constants, like the speed of light; this does not make them useless, although of course the precise manner in which they can be used has to be thoroughly understood. Population statistics do not apply to individuals; because in our type of society the variance of intellectual differences between people is accounted for by heredity to the extent of 80% approximately does not mean that the intelligence of any given individual is due 80% to heredity, 20% to environment. There are ways and means of getting information on the genotypic and phenotypic contributions in individuals, but these require us to go beyond simple heritability assessments (Eysenck, 1978b). Finally, heritability does not refer to a property of the organism, fixed for ever, and limiting its development under all conditions; unknown environments of the future may create quite different conditions to which our past calculations do not apply - although of course this possibility should not encourage us to imagine that such environments are easy to create, or prevent us from realising that they might not exist at all.

The facts of heritability of personality are easy to summarize (Eysenck, 1976a); they completely contradict the picture usually painted in our textbooks of an almost entire absence of genetic determination. Using the a-theoretical, purely psychometric devices constructed by the traditional producers of questionnaires and inventories, we find that approximately half of the variance is accounted for by genetic factors when MZ and DZ twins are studied, and when traditional indices of heritability are used. Using measures of the major personality dimensions P, E and N, and calculating heritabilities along the lines of modern biometrical genetical analysis, we get figures more in the band from 60% to 80% when test unreliability has been allowed for (Eaves & Eysenck, 1975, 1976a, 1976b, 1977). The figures certainly suggest a strong genetic component for variation along the major dimensions of personality, a component not noticeably weaker than that found in connection with intelligence (Eysenck, 1978b). Equally strong are genetic components in relation to psychiatric abnormality (Eysenck, 1978a), and even in relation to criminality the evidence for partial genetic determination is strong (Eysenck, 1977). These facts are of the utmost importance from the point of view of creating a unified science of psychology.

There are several reasons for holding this view. The first reason is that as entropy provides physicists with the possibility of determining the direction of the arrow of time, and hence creates the opportunity for causal analysis, so the genetic determination of personality, intellect and abnormality provides for us the possibility of analysis in terms of causation. It is clearly not sufficient to demonstrate that Thorndike and Mischel are wrong in denying the existence of "general traits of personality" and "general and consistent forms of conduct"; the existence of such generalities does not eo ipso prove the importance of genetic factors. The generalities could have been generated by ante-natal environmental factors, or more plausibly by different histories of reinforcement; it is clearly wrong to think that even a psychology of S-R bonds is confined to postulates of specificity of conduct (Eysenck, 1970). Consistent reinforcements along one direction or another could create consistencies of conduct which would show themselves as personality traits or even types; we would then have an environmental arrow of causation pointing in the opposite direction to that postulated by genetic hypotheses. Instead of starting with an organism whose genetic potentialities select and shape alternative environments, we would have an organism being entirely shaped by environments selected for him, or on a random basis. Clearly this is a vital question for psychologists to answer, and the current lack of interest in this problem is difficult to understand other than in ideological terms. Even more difficult to understand is of course the usual assumption that the question has no meaning, or that it has already been answered in the environmentalist direction. Both these positions, prominent though they be in current textbooks, are untenable.

As an extension of this argument, it may be stated quite without circumlocution that the current failure to take this problem seriously renders much of psychological research in the social field, and most of sociological research, meaningless. The present position is that simple correlational designs are interpreted as giving rise to causal interpretations, a misunderstanding of elementary statistical principles so widespread as to have been given the name "the sociological fallacy". Quite typically sociologists will argue that because working class children have lower scores than middle class children on IQ tests, therefore class-related environmental factors are responsible for the observed difference. Similarly, it has been stated that because criminals come more frequently from broken homes, therefore broken homes cause criminality. Again, because divorced men and women frequently have a history of divorce in the family, it is argued that the environment to which they were exposed as children caused their later divorce. It has even been suggested that because proportions of different classes and races are unequally represented at University, or in Educationally subnormal classes, therefore there must have been some degree of racial and social prejudice. It will be clear that all these causal interpretations are only acceptable if we also accept as a major premise that genetic factors are completely ineffectual in causing individual differences in personality, intelligence, psychiatric abnormality, etc. In view of the fact that the evidence contraindicates such a premise, we must reject all such experimental designs as incapable of giving an answer, even a suggestive answer, to the causal question, thus ruling out of court the major part of sociological and social psychological work in the fields covered.

5. GENETIC MODELS IN PERSONALITY RESEARCH

What is being suggested here, to put it in a more positive form, is simply that research designs in psychology, in order to be acceptable, must embody estimates of the major genetic and environmental variables likely to influence the outcome of the experiment. This is particularly so in the field of social psychology and sociology, but it may also affect many areas of experimental psychology – unless we are willing to relegate the greater part of the variance to the error term, a willingness which, as we have already seen, seems to be endemic among experimental psychologists. It is fortunate that the necessary designs are already available; geneticists have always been ready and willing to take into account both genetic and environmental variables, and to design their analyses in such a way as to partition the total phenotypic variance out among the various causal determinants recognized, such as additive genetic and environmental variance, assortative mating, epistatis, dominance, correlated environments, genetic-environmental interaction, error, etc. In other words, it is the geneticists who have worked out a comprehensive formulation for the causal analysis of genetic and environmental contributions to human behaviour, while psychologists and sociologists persist in the use of patently inadequate and scientifically meaningless designs which in the nature of things cannot give us the kind of information which is required (Mather & Jinks, 1971; Rao et al., 1974, 1976).

Psychologists do not always realize the extent to which these designs are able to furnish us with invaluable information against which to test our theories. As an example, let us take the Freudian theory of schizophrenia, according to which it is the early behaviour of the mother which is responsible in large part for the later psychosis of her sons. Or, as an alternative from much the same stable, let us consider Laing's theory of schizophrenia, which also is bound up closely with the parental behaviour patterns vis-a-vis the growing child. Both theories have been found extremely difficult to test directly; indeed, such a test is demonstrably impossible because it must confound genetic and environmental causes. Even if we could demonstrate a correlation between parental and filial behaviour (ice-box mother - schizophrenic son), this correlation would not be proof of the causal nature of the parental behaviour; equally possible would be a genetic hypothesis in which the behaviour of the parents was determined by the same genes which later on produced schizophrenia in the children. Thus the typical psychiatric methods of investigation would at best result in a quite inconclusive correlation between parental behaviour and child psychosis, without throwing any light on the causal determinants.

We may contrast this type of research with research planned along the more comprehensive lines of biometrical behavioural genetics. In this design, there is an important distinction between within family and between family environmental variance; clearly the Freudian and Laingian theories require for their support that a large portion of the variance should be produced by the between family term. Eysenck & Eysenck (1976), Eaves & Eysenck (1977), and Fulker (1973) have shown that for schizophrenia and also for psychoticism, a continuous personality variable hypothesized to underlie psychotic and particularly schizophrenic behaviour, a simple model incorporating D_R (additive genetic variance) and E_1 (within family environmental variance) is sufficient to account for the phenotypic variance; there is no evidence for E_2 (between family environmental variance) in the data. The model gives much greater weight to genetic variance, but insofar as it does require environmental variance, this is exclusively within rather than between family, thus throwing great doubt on the Freudian and Laingian hypotheses.

This finding, namely that personality differences can be accounted for largely in terms of D_R and E_1, applies equally to extraversion and neuroticism, as to psychoticism; in all this it is doubtful if E_2 has much of a contribution to make. This finding is of great importance to psychology; it suggests, on the theoretical level, that explanations involving familial influences (i.e., the great majority of environmental theories) are effectively ruled out of court, and that insofar as the environment has an influence on personality, this must be exerted through fairly random, unsystematic events affecting different members of the family differently, rather than through behaviours of fathers, mothers, and other members of the family which affect all the children equally. On the practical and empirical level, the findings suggest that if we wish to search for causal environmental factors, this search will be difficult (because of the small extent of the total environmental influence), and they also suggest the direction which such a search should take, by ruling out familial and other similar influences. The statistical reasoning on which these comparisons are based has been explicated elsewhere (Eaves & Eysenck, 1975, 1977); it would not be in line with the aims of this paper to go into any detail here.

Not all human behaviours follow this simple model; it is equally important to be aware of the exceptions. Thus in the field of social attitudes, Eaves & Eysenck (1974) would fit the model: D_R, E_1, and E_2. Here, in other words, between family influences appear to exert a powerful influence, and this finding of course is in good agreement with expectation. Note, however, that hitherto the stress on between family variance so common among social psychologists and sociologists was based entirely on assumption; there was no evidence, and indeed no attempt at proof. Note also that although we now have evidence of the relevance of between family factors, these are no more important than within family factors (not usually much noticed by writers on the subject), and above all additive genetic factors, usually passed over completely as theoretically inadmissible. Thus even when empirical studies verifying certain assumptions traditionally maintained by social psychologists, the precise quantitative statement goes well beyond the vague predictions made by these environmental models.

In thus referring to empirical studies, it should be emphasized that the intention was merely to illustrate the argument. These are pioneering studies, and obviously replication, preferably in different countries, and by different authors, must be a requisite before we can accept the conclusions as firm fact. Quite possibly the major substantive conclusions to which we have come may require modification, possibly drastic modification. This, however, is immaterial as far as the main argument is concerned, to wit, that it is by the formulations and designs of biometrical behavioural genetics, and by these alone, that we can get a proper foothold on the vexed, complex and difficult question of psychological causation in the fields of personality, intelligence and mental disease. If psychology is ever to become a unified science, this can only be accomplished by an acceptance of the paradigms outlined above; the intentional or accidental failure to take into account genetic factors in our research designs and paradigms automatically ensures that we end up with correlations, not with causally valid conclusions. No science can be built on such shifting quicksands.

6. GENETICS AND PSYCHOLOGICAL RESEARCH

Genetical paradigms can be of use to psychological research in general, not only to research involving personality. The distinction, as we have tried to indicate, is less clear-cut than is usually assumed, but it has nevertheless some basis, and in this section an attempt will be made to illustrate the point made. Again only one or two illustrations will be offered, but of course many other applications of the principle in question could be envisaged. We shall begin with a demonstration by A.

Jensen (personal communication) which is relevant to the long dispute over the "existence" of a general factor of intelligence (Eysenck, 1978b). British authors, following Spearman, have usually posited a general factor of intelligence, together with a small number of less important "group" factors; American authors have usually followed Thurstone and laid main emphasis on various "primary" factors (usually identical with the English "group" factors), and only admitting general intelligence as a less important second-order factor, derived from the intercorrelations between the primaries. Others, like Guilford, deny the existence of even such a general factor, and split up the total variance into over a hundred separate factors. Given that mathematically there is no reason why we cannot split up the observed variance in any way we choose, is there any method which would enable us to decide between these various theories? Here again we see the opposition between the psychometric and the experimental type of psychologist; although the problem is clearly not soluble by purely psychometric methods, nevertheless psychometricians have made no effort to carry out experiments which might help.

Jensen has suggested the following method, which is essentially based on the acceptance of the well-known facts that differences in intelligence are largely inherited, and that some of the genetic variance (V_G) is non-additive, with both dominance and assortative mating being implicated. Schull and Neel (1965) have shown that "inbreeding depression" occurs in the offspring of married relatives (mainly first and second cousins in Japan), as has Bashi (1977) for Arab children. Schull and Neel used the sub-tests of the Wechsler, and give the degree of "inbreeding depression" for each test. Jensen argued that the degree of depression shown in the scores on each subtest should be proportional to the general factor loading of these tests when their intercorrelations are factor analysed. The factor loadings of the tests are in fact very similar for American and Japanese populations, and Jensen argued that this proportionality should occur if and only if general intelligence had a genuine biological existence as a unitary trait. He was able to show that indeed there was a very strong statistical evidence for the existence of such proportionality, tests having high loadings on general intelligence showing marked inbreeding depression, and tests having low loadings showing little inbreeding depression. Thus reference to genetic arguments makes it possible to settle a long-standing argument in psychology, indicating how closely the two sciences are related, and how important training in genetic methods and findings can be for the psychologist.

The second example is taken from Eysenck's theory of neurosis and criminality (Eysenck, 1976d, 1977), which postulates that neurotic and criminal behaviour is largely mediated by Pavlovian conditioning. This view has been criticized quite cogently on

the grounds that typical laboratory experiments on conditioning
are very closely circumscribed by time relations between the CS
and the UCS, with periods of 500 to 1,500 milliseconds constituting the optimal ISI, and with periods longer than 2,500 milliseconds hardly producing any conditioning at all in such paradigms
as that of the eye-blink CR. In life situations such find adjustment of the ISI is clearly impossible, and very unlikely to
occur naturally; consequently it seems very unlikely that a conditioning paradigm can be made to account for the development of
behaviour patterns related to crime and neurosis.

The answer seems to lie in the concept of "preparedness."
Seligman (1970, 1971) has pointed out that "phobias comprise a
nonarbitrary and limited set of objects, whereas fear conditioning
is thought to occur to an unlimited range of conditioned stimuli.
Furthermore, phobias, unlike laboratory fear conditioning, are
often acquired in one trial and seem quite resistant to change by
'cognitive' means" (1971, p. 307). He goes on to argue that
"phobias are highly prepared to be learned by humans, and, like
other highly prepared relationships, they are selective and resistant to extinction, learned even with degraded input, and
probably non-cognitive" (Ibid, p. 312). In other words, through
the history of evolution certain types of fear become "instinctive", i.e., either inherited directly (as in many animal fears
studied by ethologists), or else easily conditioned even with degraded input. It is this "degrading" of the input which gets us
out of the theoretical difficulty of having to use laboratory-
determined ISI intervals for an explanation of non-laboratory,
every-day life conditioning; the evidence shows quite clearly
that where the CS is biologically appropriate and "prepared", such
rules as those pertaining to the ISI become much more relaxed, and
can accommodate periods as long as 1 hour, even for rat conditioning. Thus here again genetic factors point the way to the
solution of a problem in general psychology which, without this
help, would have been quite insoluble.

We believe that what has been illustrated here by reference
to just two examples is in fact quite general in psychological
theory. Many of our theories have become hag-ridden by our entirely environmentalist outlook, which makes it in fact impossible
to accommodate instinctive and other inherited modes of behaviour,
or their interaction with conditioning and learning. The work of
Breland and Breland (1966), of the ethologists, and much else
could be cited in support of this view; the elimination by the
early behaviourists, and their later followers, of all biological
and evolutionary concepts, of all genetic and constitutional factors in human and even animal behaviour, has been one of the most
constricting and sterile theoretical straitjackets ever to be
imposed on a growing science. No wonder that all possibility of
genuine unification within that science, or between that science

and other, biological sciences, was lost at the same time. It
is only by retracing our steps, and avoiding this particular pit-
fall, that we will regain our position in the company of other
biological sciences.

7. FUTURE USES OF GENETIC MODELS

There are many other aspects of human behaviour which can be
clarified by reference to the principles of genetic model making;
only two will be mentioned here as examples. Thus Eaves &
Eysenck (1976a) showed that variation in the trait of neuroticism
itself, and in the inconsistency of measurement, accorded with a
simple model assuming random mating, additive genetic variation,
and within family environmental effects; these points have already
been mentioned. The focus of interest, however, was variation
between subjects' responses on two occasions separated by an interval of 2 years; this showed no genetic component and reflected
only environmental experiences unique to individuals. This finding is of importance in its own right, but also with respect to an
important statistical problem, namely the correction of observed
heritability estimates for unreliability in the measure chosen.
Such correction would not be admissible if the lack of reliability
were itself due to genetic causes. The fact that it is not enables
us to make the requisite corrections.

In another paper, Eaves and Eysenck (1976b) again looked at
the age variable in the measurement of neuroticism, but this time
from the point of view of the different ages of the participant
twins, rather than that of test-retest changes in score. The
analysis suggested that long-term changes in neurotic behaviour
are under genetic control, i.e., that genetic differences in N
become more pronounced with advancing age. There are two possible
interpretations of this finding. One suggests that additional
genes become operative later in life and contribute to greater
variability. Alternatively the same genes may operate all the
time but developmentally significant environmental experiences
are not randomly distributed over genotypes so that neurotics tend
to seek or create less therapeutic environments than normals, resulting in a slower decline in N scores for neurotics than normals.

It would not be appropriate to spell out here the many ways
in which behavioural genetical analysis could help psychologists
test important theories relating to personality, abnormality, or
social behaviour generally, or even to experimental laboratory
studies; one word must however be said about the design of such
studies. In the past there has been a tendency to restrict psychological work in genetics to twins, usually twins reared together, to use samples too small by a large factor to give meaningful results, and to use formulae for the calculation of

heritability which had no assignable genetical meaning. In the
future it seems likely that more inventive designs will be used
(e.g., married twins, their spouses, and their children; this
design has been employed by Nance and Corey (1976) as making
better use of the numbers tested than most others); that much
larger numbers will be used in order to reduce the fiduciary limits
within which generalizations can be made; and that more informative and genetically meaningful methods of analysis will be used.
Last but not least, it is hoped that recourse will be had to
sources of information other than twins; adopted children are
perhaps the most likely untapped source of genetic data easily
available. The more quantitative methods now available, not only
for analysis but also for estimating optimal selection of subjects, ensure that in future much more incisive questions can be
asked, and much more decisive answers be given (Eaves, 1969, 1976,
1977; Martin et al., 1978). Among the questions that have already
been looked at, even if only in a preliminary way, are the causes
of covariation between temperamental traits (Martin & Eaves, 1977;
Eaves & Eysenck, 1975; Eaves, Martin, & Eysenck, 1977), and sibling effects in man (Eaves, 1976b; Eysenck, 1976c). The former
question relates to the problem of whether the observed correlation between two traits, e.g., sociability and impulsiveness, is
due mainly to genetic causes, to environmental causes, or to both.
The latter question relates to the problem which arises because in
the human family one sibling constitutes part of the environment
in which the other develops; if the phenotype of one sibling influences the behaviour of the other, we may be said to have a
"sibling effect". Siblings, for example, may "compete" or "cooperate", depending on whether the presence in the family of a
high-scoring sibling inhibits or facilitates the development of
the other sibling. Evidence for the existence of such effects is
contained in some of the references cited above.

Some of the assumptions made in the genetical model can be
tested, not only by seeing how well the empirical data fit the
model, but also by independent research. Thus for personality
(though not for intelligence) we are assuming a state of panmixia,
and numerous studies have shown that when husbands and wives are
correlated for personality variables, the correlations tend to be
small or non-existent, thus giving support to the assumption
(Eysenck, 1976a). For intelligence, of course, the evidence
suggests a sizeable additional component due to assortative
mating, and indeed most direct studies of this effect have found
correlations between spouses of between 0.40 and 0.60.

Of interest in relating psychological variables to the wider
horizon on biological and evolutionary studies is the problem of
dominance. Here too personality study has shown little evidence
of non-additive genetic factors, suggesting that there is no directional dominance attached to P, E or N; in the case of

intelligence again the position is different. Inbreeding is
shown to depress intelligence in inbred progeny, a demonstration,
in agreement with other types of evidence, that intelligence is
dominant over dullness. Mather (1973) summarizes evidence suggesting that directional dominance is produced by a history of
directional selection, and for intelligence this evidence for
directional selection makes good sense; in our ancestors clearly
intelligence would have been a useful tool for survival and pro-
creation.

8. DIVERSITY & INEQUALITY

Just as the stress on dividing lines within psychology has
been overdone in the past, and has prevented a unified theory or
set of theories from emerging, so also with respect to the dividing lines between disciplines. Attention has already been drawn
to the links which connect genetics, physiology, anatomy and the
other biological sciences to psychology on the one hand, and the
equally strong links which connect it with sociology, anthropology,
economics and history on the other. History teaches us that all
societies (other than perhaps the smallest and most primitive)
have some form of class system, but that castes are relatively
rare, and have to be maintained by legislative ukase and by force.
It seems clear that both these widespread principles of organization have a psychological, and indeed a genetic cause. The wide
differences in mental ability between individuals in all societies
are largely genetically determined; they form the basis of class
systems, i.e., systems which officially recognize such differences
and put them on an institutionalized basis. On the other hand,
regression effects ensure that these class differences do not become enshrined in castes; within some five generations the
original differences in intelligence between high-grade and low-
grade families are likely to be reduced to an absolute minimum,
or to disappear completely. The whole debate on egalitarianism
or inequality has been largely based on philosophical, ethical,
ideological and political arguments; the truth of course is that
such a debate must rest firmly on the factual basis of empirical
research, and the facts of genetic determination, regression,
etc. (Eysenck, 1973).

This general statement applies not only to the measurement
of intelligence; it equally applies to differences in personality
and psychiatric characteristics which are known to be determined
largely by genetic factors. Rutter and Madge (1976), reviewing
a large body of data related to the hypothesis of "cycles of
disadvantage", came to the conclusion that "undoubtedly there are
continuities over time. However, only some of these involve
familial continuity . . . With respect to intelligence, educational attainment, occupational status, crime, psychiatric

disorder and 'problem-family' status there are moderate continuities over two generations . . . Even with forms of disadvantage
where (intergenerational continuities) are strong, discontinui-
ties are striking. At least half of the children born into a
disadvantaged home do not repeat the pattern of disadvantage in
the next generation. Over half of all forms of disadvantage arise
anew each generation . . . In short, familial cycles are a most
important element in the perpetuation of disadvantage but they
account for only a part of the overall pattern" (p. 303-304).
This pattern is exactly what we would expect from a combination
of genetically produced similarity within the family, plus a
strong regression to the mean effect; the more widely held environmentalistic theories are quite unable to account for the
facts summarized by Rutter and Madge. Thus sociology and history
require the psychological and genetic type of theory on which we
have laid so much stress throughout this chapter.

Few writers have accepted this general view; there is an
overwhelming stress on environmental theories, and a complete
dearth as far as genetic approaches to this theme are concerned.
Darlington's "Evolution of Man and Society" (1969) is an honour-
able exception, in which an attempt has been made to look at
history from the genetic point of view; Wilson's (1975) "Sociobiology" has achieved much fame in recent years because of the
attempt to account for human social behaviour in terms of biological principles. Baker (1974) and Hebert (1978) have attempted
to look at the intractable problem of race from the biological
point of view, taking into account not only psychological differences but also the differences in cultural level achieved. We
thus have a beginning of what will in due course amount to a unification of the social and biological sciences, but clearly such
a beginning is at best extremely tentative, and in need of a much
wider factual basis before we can rest content with what has been
achieved. The problems are formidable, and so are the difficulties presented by the Zeitgeist; as Cicero said: "Eaque enim
quae aequabilitas appellatur, iniquissima est", but a recognition
of the truth of these words is no more widespread now than when
he pronounced them 2,000 years ago. Ideological arguments have
taken precedence over factual ones, and in many countries empirical research into these problems is all but impossible for
reasons of political and social censorship.* Egalitarianism and

---

*It is sometimes argued that this ideology of egalitarianism
is founded on Marxist theories; such a belief is obviously erroneous. Not only did Marx and Engels implicitly deny that human
beings are innately equal with respect to their abilities and
their needs ("From each according to his abilities, to each according to his needs"), but publications from communist countries
make it quite clear that interactionist beliefs are accepted there

environmentalism are still so strongly entrenched that, to take
but one telling example, the great majority of students of psychology achieve their degrees, even advanced degrees, without
any tuition in the principles of genetics, and without any appreciation of the important role which genetic factors play in
human life, and in causing human diversity.

It is the major theme of this chapter that this is an impossible situation, and that no unification of psychology, as
a bio-social science, can be possible without the recognition
that genetic factors are absolutely fundamental to any understanding of human behaviour, to the formulation of any testable
theories of human conduct, and to the integration of the many
diverse aspects of psychology. An attempt has been made to illustrate some of the many ways in which genetic models can help
the psychologist test his theories, relate apparently divergent
concepts, and judge the relevance of different causal factors.
Genetics is relevant even to sociological, historical and anthropological investigations where at first sight it might have nothing
important to say; the work on "cycles of disadvantage", for instance, or Darlington's contribution to the study of history
spring to mind. Much of this influence is exerted through the
causation, by genetic factors, of diversity in personality, in
intelligence, in psychiatric abnormality, in criminality, and in
other social modes of conduct. The dominant mode of research and
theorising which completely excludes genetic factors is doomed to
sterility and failure; no research paradigms which leave out
genetic factors can have any validity, or produce meaningful results. It would of course be equally true to say that no research
paradigm which excludes social and other environmental factors
could give scientifically valid and meaningful results, but it is
hardly necessary to make such a statement because geneticists always begin with the distinction between genotype and phenotype,
and hence recognize the importance of both heredity and

---

without hesitation. Thus Guthke (1978), in a recent textbook on
the measurement of intelligence published in the D.D.R. (East-
German Republic) states: "Marxist psychology does not by any means
deny the importance of genetic factors in producing differences in
intellectual ability, as is sometimes objected in criticisms by
poorly informed observers who rely on extremist views of a small
number of Marxist scientists. Marx and Lenin already emphasized
the biological and psychological inequality of men" (My translation
and emphases. p. 69.) Given slight differences in emphasis,
Guthke's book clearly brings out the same points I made in my own
(Eysenck, 1973a). The whole association alleged to exist between
right-wing politics and hereditarian beliefs, left-wing politics
and environmentalism, is illusory (Eysenck, 1973b).

environment from the beginning. All genetic models in use at
present incorporate environmentalist and non-additive genetic
contributions to the variance as well as simple additive genetic
contributions; it is this comprehensiveness that makes them the
only models acceptable for research in these fields. Psychology
will cease to be the "hope of a science", and become a true science
in its own right, once it accepts the inevitability of genetic
influences, and incorporates genetics in its structure. Academic
boundary lines should not prevent us from realising that psychology
without genetics is but a pseudo-science, and that we must cease
to feed our students on the customary diet of social pap, while
depriving them of the proper nourishment to be found in biological reality.

References

Baker, J. R. Race. London: Oxford University Press, 1974.
Bashi, J. Effects of inbreeding on cognitive performance.
    Nature, 1977, 31st March, 440–442.
Breland, K., & Breland, M. Animal behavior. New York: Mac-
    millan, 1966.
Cofer, C. N. The specificity of individual differences in learn-
    ing. In R. M. Gagne (Ed.), Learning and individual differ-
    ences. Columbus: Merrill, 1967.
Cronbach, L. J. The two disciplines of scientific psychology.
    The American Psychologist, 1957, 12, 671–684.
Cronbach, L. J., & Snow, R. E. Individual differences in learning
    ability as a function of instructional variables. Stanford:
    Research Report, Stanford University, 1969.
Darlington, C. D. The evolution of man and society. London:
    Allen & Unwin, 1969.
DiLoreto, A. O. Comparative psychotherapy. London: Aldine-
    Atherton, 1971.
Eaves, L. J. The genetic analysis of continuous variation: a
    comparison of experimental designs applicable to human
    data. British Journal of Mathematical and Statistical
    Psychology, 1969, 22, 131–147.
Eaves, L. J. The effect of cultural transmission on continuous
    variation. Heredity, 1976a, 37, 41–57.
Eaves, L. J. A model for sibling effects in man. Heredity,
    1976b, 36, 205–214.
Eaves, L. J. Inferring the causes of human variation. Journal
    of the Royal Statistical Society: A., 1977, 140, Part 3,
    324–355.
Eaves, L. J., & Eysenck, H. J. Genetics and the development of
    social attitudes. Nature, 1934, 249, 288–289.
Eaves, L. J., & Eysenck, H. J. The nature of extraversion: A
    genetical analysis. Journal of Personality and Social
    Psychology, 1975, 32, 102–112.

538

Eaves, L. J., & Eysenck, H. J.   Genetical and environmental com-
    ponents of inconsistency and unrepeatability in twins'
    responses to a neuroticism questionnaire. Behavior
    Genetics, 1976a, 6, 145-160.
Eaves, L. J., & Eysenck, H. J.   Genotype x age interaction for
    neuroticism. Behavior Genetics, 1976b, 6, 359-362.
Eaves, L. J., & Eysenck, H. J.   Genotype-environmental model for
    psychoticism. Advances in Behaviour Research & Therapy,
    1977, 1, 5-26.
Eaves, L. J., Martin, N. G., & Eysenck, S. B. G.   An application
    of the analysis of covariance structures to the psycho-
    genetical study of impulsiveness. British Journal of
    Mathematical and Statistical Psychology, 1977, 30, 185-197.
Eysenck, H. J.   The dynamics of anxiety and hysteria. London:
    Routledge & Kegan Paul, 1957.
Eysenck, H. J.   Smoking, health and personality. London:
    Weidenfeld & Nicolson, 1965.
Eysenck, H. J.   The biological basis of personality. Springfield:
    C. C. Thomas, 1967.
Eysenck, H. J.   The structure of human personality (3rd ed.).
    Methuen, 1970.
Eysenck, H. J.   The inequality of man. London: Maurice Temple-
    Smith, 1973a.
Eysenck, H. J.   The measurement of intelligence. Lancaster:
    Medical & Technical Publisher, 1973b.
Eysenck, H. J.   Genetic factors in personality development. In
    A. R. Kaplan (Ed.), Human behavior genetics. Springfield:
    C. C. Thomas, 1976a.
Eysenck, H. J.   The measurement of personality. Lancaster:
    Medical and Technical Publishers, 1976b.
Eysenck, H. J.   Sex and personality. London: Open Books, 1976c.
Eysenck, H. J.   The learning theory model of neurosis - a new
    approach. Behavior Research & Therapy, 1976d, 14, 251-267.
Eysenck, H. J.   Crime and personality (3rd ed.). London: Rout-
    ledge & Kegan Paul, 1977.
Eysenck, H. J.   Genetische Faktoren bei psychischer Abnormalitat.
    In L. J. Pongratz (Ed.), Handbuch der Klinischen Psychologie,
    2. Halbband. 3039-3073. Toronto: Verlag fur Psychology,
    1978a.
Eysenck, H. J.   The nature and measurement of intelligence.
    London: Springer, 1978b.
Eysenck, H. J.   The development of personality and its relation
    to learning. Melbourne: Melbourne University Studies in
    Education, 1978c.
Eysenck, H. J., & Eysenck, S. B. G.   Psychoticism as a dimension
    of personality. London: Hodder & Stoughton, 1976.
Eysenck, H. J., & Rachman, S.   Causes and cures of neurosis.
    London: Routledge & Kegan Paul, 1965.
Eysenck, M. W.   Human memory. London: Pergamon Press, 1977.

Farrell, B. A. The progress of psychology. British Journal of Psychology, 1978, 69, 1-8.

Fulker, D. W. A biometrical-genetic approach to intelligence and schizophrenia. Social Biology, 1973, 20, 266-272.

Guthke, J. 1st Intelligenz Messbar? Berlin: Deutscher Verlag der Wissenschaften, 1978.

Hebert, J. P. Race et intelligence. Paris: Copernic, 1978.

Hull, C. L. The place of innate individual and species differences in a natural-science theory of behavior. Psychological Review, 1945, 52, 55-60.

Hull, C. L. Essentials of behavior. New Haven: Yale University Press, 1951.

Hull, C. L. A behavior system. New Haven: Yale University Press, 1952.

Koch, S. Psychology as science. In S. C. Brown (Ed.), Philosophy of psychology. London: Macmillan, 1974.

Martin, N. G., & Eaves, L. J. The genetical analysis of covariance structure. Heredity, 1977, 38, 79-95.

Martin, N. G., Eaves, L. J., Kearsey, M. J., & Davies, P. The power of the classical twin study. Heredity, 1978, 40, 97-116.

Mather, K. Genetical structure of populations. London: Chapman & Hall, 1973.

Mather, K., & Jinks, J. L. Biometrical Genetics (2nd ed.). London: Chapman & Hall, 1971.

Mischel, W. Personality and assessment. New York: Wiley, 1968.

Mischel, W. Toward a cognitive social learning reconceptualization of personality. Psychological Review, 1973, 80, 252-283.

Nance, W. E., & Corey, L. Genetic models for the analysis of twin data from the families of identical twins. Genetics, 1976, 83, 811-826.

Rao, D. C., Morton, N. E., & Yee, S. Analysis of family resemblance: 2. A linear model for familial correlation. American Journal of Human Genetics, 1974, 26, 331-359.

Rao, D. C., Morton, N. E., & Yee, S. Resolution of cultural and biological inheritance by path analysis. American Journal of Human Genetics, 1976, 28, 228-242.

Rutter, M., & Madge, N. Cycles of disadvantage. London: Heineman, 1976.

Schull, W. J., & Neel, J. R. The effects of inbreeding on Japanese children. New York: Harper & Row, 1965.

Seligman, M. E. P. On the generality of the laws of learning. Psychological Review, 1970, 37, 405-418.

Seligman, M. E. P. Phobias and preparedness. Behavior Therapy, 1971, 2, 303-320.

Suppe, F. (Ed.). The structure of scientific theories. Chicago: University of Illinois Press, 1974.

Teasdale, J. D. Drug dependence. In H. J. Eysenck (Ed.),
    Handbook of Abnormal Psychology (2nd ed.). London:
    Pitman, 1973.
Thorndike, E. L. _Educational psychology_. New York: Teachers'
    College, 1903.
Wilson, E. O. _Sociobiology_. Cambridge: Belknap, 1975.

COMMENT BY W. J. BAKER

Basically, Professor Eysenck's paper points out that we cannot hope to have a complete science of psychology if we ignore the role of genetic factors in influencing behavior. I doubt if anyone at this conference would want to argue that point. Actually, I doubt if any serious psychologist would want to, in principle. And yet, Professor Eysenck is correct in suggesting that a great deal of psychological research, otherwise reasonably well thought out and carefully conducted, seems to be done as if we could ignore these factors.

It would seem that behavioral geneticists have not yet convinced the rest of the world to take them seriously. Really, then, the issue Professor Eysenck is raising is how do you escape the apparent insularity of your field? How do you have some impact on researchers outside of your specialty? Dr. Thiessen was leading in that direction when he was asking for the study of "more obviously important behaviors" to give more substance to the field. He illustrated rather clearly what he meant by this in his presentation on assortative mating. That kind of work, and Dr. Eysenck's work with human subjects, is bound to have more impact on mainstream psychology than work on the species usually employed by geneticists, for rather obvious reasons within their discipline, unless real connections for the latter are made much more obvious.

We've seen a reasonable growth in recent years in the sophistication of thinking in psychology. (I don't accept Professor Eysenck's rather grim view that we haven't progressed since William James in developing any broad paradigms, and I'm not the least bit inclined to apologize for being a psychologist.) From unsuccessful attempts to characterize behavior in rather simplistic S-R terms (the empty organism view), we have progressed to the point where most psychologists will grant that behavior is a function of an organism whose properties and states critically determine the effective stimulus (i.e., the information selected from the stimulus array) and which critically modify the nature, range, and intensity of the responses to be made to the information taken in.

I don't know if he intended it that way or not, but Gibson put the organism in this privileged position with respect to the stimulus in his text, "The Senses Considered as Perceptual Systems" (1966), and Miller, Galanter, and Pribram provided the same service on the response side in their "Plans and the Structure of Behavior" (1960). The organism is very clearly present and anything but empty in today's behaviorism, and it is essential in all current theories of information processing.

Having gotten that far, the next step is for us to push (as

Professor Eysenck suggests) for an adequate description of the
states and properties of the organism which will enable us to
account for the differential salience of various stimulus parameters and response patterns. The majority of psychologists, for
perfectly good reasons, are clearly committed to an over-riding
concern with environmental rather than genetic or, more generally,
organismic factors. They do prefer to treat subjects as homogeneous or, at least, randomly amorphous, null instruments against
which environmental factors can be assessed. They have to be
brought to a clearer understanding of the fact that the effects of
environmental factors are critically dependent upon the genetic
constitutions of the particular organisms being studied.

It is precisely this point which is behind Professor Eysenck's
concern with the cavalier disregard to subject-by-treatment interactions. This was the basis for part of our discussion on drug
studies and interaction terms. Geneticists run into this interaction all the time, but even their results are often reported in
strictly genetic terms--as if the environment were not all that
critical! Clearly, the ubiquitous nature of gene-environment interaction has not been adequately articulated.

The message is bound to be difficult to sell on either side,
because, if the premise is accepted, all research will become considerably more complex. The demands on sample sizes and experimental sophistication will increase dramatically. The cost of
doing research will escalate. The counterargument, of course, must
be that anything less is fundamentally inadequate and, therefore,
a waste of time, effort, and money to begin with. I'm sure you
see the nature of the problem and can then appreciate how robust
a case you will have to make if you expect to have an impact.

The root of the problem would appear to be the old dilemma
about the proper focus of our concerns--is it general trends or
individual differences? Even more basically, though, do we really
have a choice? This issue has arisen here on a couple of occasions
in questions about intraspecies variation which, if present, would
undercut general claims for a species. It seems fairly evident
that the question of individual differences has a logical priority
over statements about groups, that groups can be called groups only
to the extent that we are willing to claim, at least implicitly,
that any remaining individual differences are of no practical significance for the kind of group being described. Since one of the
basic points of breeding controls is to produce groups that are
as homogeneous as possible with respect to some critical traits or
properties, a concern with the direct measurement of residual individual differences ought to be an over-riding concern for
geneticists, but reports on group trends seem much more prominent,
and often the exclusive concern. Again, it seems to me that much
of the intent of Professor Eysenck's paper is to draw attention

back to the more fundamental question, but not exclusively, of course.

Now how is it, you really ought to ask, if this ubiquitous interaction is so important, that so many of us have gotten away with ignoring it all these years? The answer is, we really haven't. The proof is not in our inability to find significant main effects (as Professor Eysenck's paper would seem to suggest), but in our incredible inability to replicate each other's results. Independent replicability is one of the crucial tests for the scientific validity of any claim.

The kinds of main effects we usually study on the restricted kinds of subject samples usually employed are sufficiently robust so that they can be detected against the <u>residual</u> noise of the interaction. The noise of the interaction is muted because the particular sample available to a particular investigator is preselected, more homogeneous than the general population to which claims are to be made. But shifting samples from one study to the next often produces apparently <u>different</u> main effect values as a consequence of sample differences, specifically the selection of a different line of the interaction pattern.

Our inability to replicate is what is at the basis of our inability to build on each other's findings, to construct the broad paradigms Professor Eysenck is looking for. If we are to detect these interactions within rather than between studies, our samples must be less selected. Since this is generally impractical, the alternative must be that individual restricted samples must be accompanied by appropriate standardized measures to allow cross-study adjustment for broader compilations.

REPLY TO BAKER

H. J. Eysenck

The characteristic of a paradigm is that it is universally accepted and taught. I wish I could agree with Professor Baker that we have succeeded in developing any broad paradigms in psychology. There is certainly agreement on certain rather narrow points, particularly in physiological psychology, but broad paradigms? I hope Professor Baker is right, although I have my doubts.

COMMENT BY S. G. VANDENBERG

Because my comments have to be so brief, I will concentrate on only two thoughts.

I share Professor Eysenck's dismay that a century of psychological research has resulted in so much public expectation yet so little scientific substance. But I am (1) more lenient and (2) more optimistic. Even though we have in Professor Eysenck's and my lifetimes seen more changes, particularly more rapid changes than any generation before us, we can see that some things change much slower than others. Thoughts about human behavior are amongst those changing at the slowest rate. While Descartes or Hobbes would not understand TV or black holes, they could follow most psychological papers written today because few new concepts have been introduced. There are only new names for old ideas.

In retrospect it seems that it was probably necessary for Wundt to continue largely in the 18th and 19th century tradition of speculating about the nature of consciousness rather than to start precise experiments about thought processes, even though Galton and Donders suggested and performed experiments on reaction time and the partitioning of mental processes by timing increases in response time as new aspects were added to a task. Later, the detours of Gestalt demonstrations of the hopeless complexity of perception (and thought) and the countervailing optimism of Behaviorism that everything is due to simple S-R connections had to be gone through at a rather agonizingly slow pace, given the delay caused by two world wars.

Of course Wundt's major error, in spite of his great gifts, was that he took physics rather than biology as a model for the new science. This is understandable because the former had so much more status and because Helmholtz, Wundt's teacher, was as much a physicist as a physiologist. Fortunately Darwin changed all that. Wundt's choice of a model led him to consider individual differences as theoretically useless. This caused the unfortunate split-off of differential psychology from experimental psychology (rather like the split between engineering and physics), in spite of efforts by Spearman, Thurstone, and others.

So much for my reasons to be lenient, or at least understanding. Now about optimism. As I see it, cognitive psychologists (and I regard the adjective as redundant) are finally starting to eliminate the nearly century-old split by investigating, or at least allowing for, individual differences. Shepard's beautiful studies of mental rotation and Sternberg's componential analysis, as well as the work of Lunneborg and Hunt, are examples. Soon Professor Eysenck will no longer be alone.

REPLY TO VANDENBERG

H. J. Eysenck

Professor Vandenberg is more lenient, which does credit to
his heart, and more optimistic, which does credit to his personality. I think optimism is not the right attitude when the past
10 years have seen a devastating attack on the role of behavioural
genetics by politically motivated psychologists and geneticists,
when the study of these issues has been very actively discouraged,
and proponents attacked savagely, not only in print but also in
person. The skies may be clearing a little now, but I don't think
that optimism is really applicable to our situation at the moment.

COMMENT BY D. WAHLSTEN

I would like to point out two factual errors and then raise
one question.

The author suggests that "heritability" and other population
parameters "are not scientific constants, like the speed light
. . ." However, in 1690 Christian Huygens showed that the refraction of light by water could be explained if the speed of the light
wave is less in water than in air. This fact was demonstrated experimentally by Foucault in 1862. The speed of light, v, in a
medium with index of refraction, n, is given by $v = c/n$, where c
is the speed of light in a vacuum, 3.00×10^8 m/sec. In water, v
$= 2.25 \times 10^8$ m/sec; and in diamond, $v = 1.24 \times 10^8$ m/sec; all values
being at 20°c for yellow light of wavelength 589 millicrons. Furthermore, Einstein (1952) showed that the speed of light is not even
constant in a vacuum, because light itself can be refracted by a
gravitational field. No physical phenomenon has properties which
exist eternally and in isolation from its surroundings. It is
precisely its development and its interaction with its surroundings
which gives a thing the properties which we observe.

The author also suggests that all but "the smallest and most
primitive" societies "have some form of class system", and that
genes are partly responsible for this. However, there is one
country in Europe without a class system of this nature, namely
the People's Socialist Republic of Albania. There are no exploit-
ing classes in Albania (1977), and neither is society divided into
rich and poor. The ratio of the highest paid employee to lowest
paid worker within an enterprise is 1.7:1, and the ratio of the
wage of a director of a government ministry and the average wage
of a factory worker is 2:1. This modest inequality in wages is
being slowly but steadily reduced. Albania is the only country
in the world with advanced industry which is not beset by unemploy-
ment and inflation. The people pay no taxes of any kind, and the
entire country is free from foreign indebtedness. Thus, it

certainly does not qualify as a "primitive" society. Assuming that the Albanian people still possess chromosomes like other mortals, their example contradicts the theory that genetic variation causes a class structure to exist.

Finally, what are the implications of the recent demonstration by Dorfman (1978) that Cyril Burt fabricated his data on IQ and social class? How does the exposure of yet another fraud by Burt affect the author's present discussion of genes and social structure?

REPLY TO WAHLSTEN

H. J. Eysenck

It is arguable whether Albania is or is not a primitive society; it cannot be argued that it is very definitely an example of a class society. It is governed by a ruthless non-elected autocracy, which, together with police and military forces constitutes a well-defined upper class, sharply distinguished from the rest of the population. To quote ratios in pay between the highest and the lowest paid is obviously nonsensical in a Communist country where privileges rather than money are the important considerations. In any case, the 2:1 ratio in earnings quoted by Wahlsten is almost exactly the ratio between middle-class and working-class people in England, often quoted as the most class-ridden country in the world!

It is difficult to see what relevance Cyril Burt's alleged malfeasances have to the discussion, even if Dorfman's one-sided and factually erroneous "demonstration" had been more to the point. Burt's data are entirely in line with those of the large majority of investigators in the field, and omitting them completely makes no difference to the verdict as I have shown in the recent reanalysis of existing data other than Burt's (Eysenck, 1979). If Dr. Wahlsten wishes to indict fraudulent practices in this field, one would have thought that Lysenko, who, in addition to falsifying data, murdered his opponents by having them tortured and finally starved in labour camps, would be a better example.

I take it that Dr. Wahlsten's references to the speed of light are meant as a joke; light can indeed be slowed down, but it is accepted in physics as a constant when measured in a vacuum. No human population could be used in a similar way as a reference point for genetic investigation.

COMMENT BY J. R. ROYCE

I disagree with the statement that psychology is non-paradigmatic, but developing an adequate argument requires space. All I can do, therefore, is refer the reader to my Nebraska symposium paper (Royce, 1976), where I develop the thesis that psychology is multi, including multi-paradigmatic. Psychology's many paradigms include behaviorism, psychoanalysis, gestalt psychology, and factor theory. Furthermore, I develop the thesis that structuralism-functionalism is the paradigmatic combination which comes closest to capturing the entire discipline throughout psychology's 100 year history as a science.

My second point has to do with the claim that Jensen's research on inbreeding depression settles the issue concerning the existence of "g". That strikes me as too strong a claim. As I see it Jensen's argument hinges on having assumed the existence of some kind of general construct in the first place. Furthermore, it is extremely doubtful that a general construct based on the 10 subtests of the Wechsler constitutes an adequate empirical test for "g" (since Spearman's factor must load on all measures in the cognitive universe). Finally, one wonders about the evidence for the claim that now "general intelligence has a genuine biological existence as a unitary trait". A high correlation between EEG and I.Q. is hardly a sufficient basis for claims about either Spearman's "g" (I.Q. is not equivalent to "g") or its neurology (EEG measures are gross indices of brain function).

My final point has to do with Professor Eysenck's belief that physics provides the best model for the construction of psychological theory. I don't think this argument is convincing for a variety of reasons, a major one being the significantly greater complexity of psychological phenomena. I should have thought that biology and evolutionary theory would be more germane models, particularly since Professor Eysenck turns to biology rather than physics for explanatory constructs in his own theorizing.

REPLY TO ROYCE

H. J. Eysenck

In my paper I suggested that psychology might with advantage adopt the methods of physics, and this suggestion has received a good deal of criticism. It may be useful to state briefly the intent of this suggestion. Psychologists without acquaintance of modern research approaches in physics often have an altogether erroneous view of what physicists actually do when they approach a novel and difficult problem; in this psychologists usually base themselves on views presented in elementary "philosophy of science" books or recollections of school courses in science. As an example of what I have in mind, let us look at the massive contribution of several renowned physicists (e.g., Erwin Schrödinger, Leo Szilard, Max Delbrück) to the discovery of the Watson-Crick model of DNA. Consider the reluctance of professional biologists (e.g., Avery) "to extrapolate decisively from the role of DNA in a single bacterium to the role of DNA in general" (Fleming, 1969, p. 161). Fleming convincingly describes the different approaches of biologists and physicists, best exemplified by the statement of Szilard that what he had brought to biology was "not any skills acquired in physics, but rather an attitude: the conviction which few biologists had at that time, that mysteries can be solved." This attitude, which is often linked with a reductionist point of view, is even less commonly found in psychologists than in biologists; psychologists seem to prefer to preserve the secrets of nature, and to become guardians of prestigious myths! It was in this sense, i.e., of approaching problems head-on and with the intention of solving them, that I advocated the methodology of physics.

Delbrück (1949) remarked that biology as he found it was a "depressing" subject to a physicist, because "analysis seems to have stalled around in a semidescriptive manner without noticeably progressing towards a radical physical explanation." As Fleming comments, "physicists, clearly, did not believe in stalling around. They had come into biology to put a stop to these ineffectual motions leading nowhere . . . It was not simply that the physicists believed in themselves. They heartily disbelieved in the biologists. They thought that nobody had even been trying to make biology less trivial" (p. 163). This is the major point I am trying to make; too many psychologists are not even trying to make psychology less trivial. In suggesting that we adopt the approach of the physicist, I am suggesting a different outlook, not a slavish imitation of a particular method.

This failure to make psychology less trivial is intimately connected with the lack of paradigmatic research I deplored. Like Royce, I believe that there are indeed paradigms in psychology (the Spearman-Thurstone model of intelligence is one), but it is clear that there is a resolute resistance among many psychologists to accept these paradigms, and work on them. The examples Royce cites are not paradigms in Kuhn's sense; they are philosophies (Behaviorism), or research methodologies (factor theory). Psychoanalysis might be considered an exception, but typically it is not a scientific paradigm but a literary one (Popper, 1959; Eysenck & Wilson, 1973).

My references to Jensen's work on inbreeding depression, and our own work on evoked potentials, were meant to indicate the direction in which the paradigm might lead if we wanted to make research less trivial, and more causally meaningful; these studies cannot at the moment provide decisive proof. They may do so in the future. Such at least would be my hope and my confident expectation.

References

Albania. General Information. Toronto: Norman Bethune Institute, 1977.

Delbrück, M. A physicist looks at biology. Transactions, Connecticut: Academy of Arts and Sciences, 1949.

Dorfman, D. D. The Cyril Burt question: New findings. Science, 1978, 201, 1177–1186.

Einstein, A. On the influence of gravitation on the propagation of light. Reprinted in The Principle of Relativity by H. A. Lorentz, A. Einstein, H. Minkowski, & H. Weyl. New York: Dover, 1952. (Translated from "Über den Einfluss der Schwerkraft auf die Ausbreitung des Lichtes", Annalen der Physik, 1911, 35.)

Eysenck, H. J. The structure and measurement of intelligence. New York: Springer, 1979.

Eysenck, H. J., & Wilson, G. D. The experimental study of Freudian theories. London: Methuen, 1973.

Fleming, D. Émegré physicists and the biological revolution. In D. Fleming & B. Bailyn (Eds.), The intellectual migration. Cambridge: Harvard University Press, 1969.

THE GENETICS OF INFORMATION PROCESSING

Gerald E. McClearn

Institute for Behavioral Genetics,
University of Colorado, Boulder, Colorado

Some years ago, by virtue of a committee membership, I was given
an assignment to make some comments on human behavioral genetics.
My research at the time was concerned with activity, alcohol
preference, aggression, and learning phenotypes in mice. To be
candid, I had given little previous thought to the state of affairs
on the human research side of the discipline. I began by trying
to abstract from the more useful and successfully investigated
phenotypes in human genetics some principles that might guide
human behavioral geneticists in their choice of subject matters
for study. In the main, I decided, it was most important to be
lucky. There were a few consistencies that appeared to offer
some guidance--e.g., typically "good" phenotypes in human genetics
had been minimally subject to environmental influence, and most
of them had been qualitative categories rather than quantitative
measures. As I noted at the time (McClearn, 1967), however,
these attributes really offer little counsel to the geneticist
interested in behavior, which is so often continuously distributed
and so manifestly subject to modification by environment.

To date at least, investigators appear to specialize in
behavioral genetics more because of an expectation that genetics
can illuminate behavior than the converse. Therefore, the
behaviors chosen for assay will be, in the first instance, those
interesting to the investigator, and these will often be those
phenotypes that are the focus of attention in the behavioral
science disciplines themselves. This is advantageous because the
richer the empirical and theoretical context of a phenotype, the
more will be known about correlated characters, and the more
methods and techniques will be available for application in the
genetic context.

In surveying the array of human behaviors then being investigated from this genetic perspective, I concluded that only a very constrained sample of that wide and diverse array of phenomena psychologists had learned to define and measure was represented in the behavioral genetic literature. I then made so bold as to suggest some areas that appeared to me to offer particular promise. One area especially impressed me:

> It is with respect to amount of related material, however, that the behaviors studied in experimental psychology are particularly to be recommended. Many behavior domains have become centers of theoretical controversy, and the experimental information yielded in some cases is almost overwhelming. The area of verbal learning is a prime example. Research output in this area is so voluminous that a separate journal (now also overflowing) was initiated a few years ago. Replete with theoretical issues, dealing with material of the highest ultimate importance for education, and characterized by a wealth of highly sophisticated techniques and instrumentation, the field of verbal learning offers a cornucopia of phenotypes virtually untapped for genetic study. While verbal learning is admittedly an extraordinarily popular field of research and therefore not entirely representative, similar advantages may be expected from many other dependent variables of experimental psychology.

> It is also possible that many such traits will be relatively free of problems of environmental confounding. For traits of personality and intelligence, the social values assigned lead almost inevitably to direct attempts to educate or discipline and thus to the serious complications of genetic analysis mentioned earlier. For many of the behavioral characteristics studied in experimental psychology, no strong relationship to the socially valued traits is evident, and no direct environmental pressures are brought to bear. It is true that such traits may be related to others which are in fact subject to educational efforts and other environmental forces. However, some may be found to be comparatively free of features of environmental confusion and thus particularly valuable for certain types of inquiry. (McClearn, 1967, pp. 39-40)

Had I really been knowledgeable about the theoretical developments swirling around the issues of human learning and memory, I should have been even more enthusiastic. The old verbal learning was undergoing anastomosis with the old perception and with information theory and various other disciplines and metamorphosing into the information processing area, which occupies so dominant a position in psychology today.

This highly articulated area, replete with ingenious techniques (and the phenotypes defined by those techniques), has still not been discovered by many behavioral geneticists. I would like to draw the attention of my colleagues to this domain by outlining briefly some of its salient characteristics and by examining some of the early individual differences and behavioral genetic research that seems to offer promise. Regrettably, I cannot claim expert status as an information processing researcher or theorist, and this account may therefore be somewhat idiosyncratic.

1. INFORMATION PROCESSING THEORIES AND METHODS

As is true of most identifiable areas of investigation, developing as they do out of preceding areas, it is rather difficult to pinpoint the beginning of the information processing approach. Certainly, Miller (1956) and Broadbent (1958) figure prominently in almost all discussions of the early history of the area. The basic ideas have been amplified and extended by a number of workers (e.g., Brown, 1958; Neisser, 1967; Peterson & Peterson, 1959; Posner, 1967; Sperling, 1960; Sternberg, 1966; Waugh & Norman, 1965; and many others). One type of model that has emerged from this research distinguishes various stages, or stores, of memory and characterizes them in terms of distinct structures with connecting communication channels. Typically, these structural models involve a sensory store, a short-term memory (STM) or short-term store (STS), and a long-term memory (LTM) or long-term store (LTS). The sensory stores are usually regarded as being specific to sensory modes; the most frequently investigated ones are often termed "iconic" (visual) or "echoic" (auditory). These sensory stores are seen as having a large capacity, but rapid decay. For example, information from the iconic store is gone within 1 sec--and, perhaps, within 250 msec in many situations. Some information from the sensory store is transferred to STM. In this store, there is a much more limited capacity, but a very much slower decay (or forgetting) rate--perhaps as long as 30 sec. However, there is a possibility of rehearsal in STM, so that material can be "held" essentially by recycling. Some information in STM can be transferred to LTM, where there is no demonstrated capacity limit and where decay either does not occur at all or is very slow. (For concise examination of some of these mechanisms and processes, see Craik & Lockhart, 1972; Klatzky, 1975; and Loftus & Loftus, 1976.)

The circumstances that determine which material is transferred from the sensory store to STM and from STM to LTM are obviously crucial and have been the topics of much research and much debate.

"Control processes" (such as attention, rehearsal, coding strategies, and so on), which have been invoked to explain the dynamics
of the transfer, have assumed increasingly important roles in
model considerations.

In recent years, an alternative type of model for the conceptualization of human memory has been receiving a great deal of
attention. This approach (Craik & Lockhart, 1972) eschews the
idea of distinct structural entities and seeks to account for the
phenomena of memory by positing different levels of processing.
Analyses of physical attributes of the stimulus (such as length
of lines, angular relationships, brightness, loudness, etc.) are
regarded as preliminary or "shallow" processing levels, while
matching the stimulus against stored information to accomplish
recognition of patterns and to extract meaning represents much
"deeper" processing. The persistence of the information in memory
is a function of the depth of processing that has been performed
upon it. Therefore, that information upon which complex cognitive
and semantic analyses have been performed will be retained longer
than information based on the brief identification of physical
attributes.

The attributes of the structural entities or of the processing
levels are made real, of course, by the operations that generate
the data upon which the concepts are based. Thus, the phenotypes
we might employ are defined by the experimental operations, and
it must be said that the information processing researchers
have provided us with a wealth of ingenious and elegant methods.
A now classic procedure was devised by Sperling (1960). Traditionally regarded as a method of exploring the parameters of the
visual sensory store, it can also be regarded as pertinent to the
description of preliminary levels of processing. Sperling presented
arrays of letters tachistoscopically and asked the subjects to
report as many of the displayed letters as possible. An upper
limit of about four reported letters was found, regardless of the
size of the stimulus array. In a subsequent variation of this
procedure, an auditory stimulus presented at the time of offset
of the visual array designated by its pitch whether the top,
middle, or bottom row was to be reported. The fact that the
subjects were able to report back letters from any one of the three
rows suggests that all rows were present in the icon under this
condition. However, the finding of an upper limit of about four
reported letters when the subject was asked for as complete a
report as possible suggests that the act of "reading out" was so
time consuming that the icon had disappeared before the report
could be completed. These results, and the results of other, more
detailed investigations by Sperling, led to the description of the
iconic store as being almost photographically complete, but of
very short duration.

Another example, pertinent to retrieval of information from STM, is provided by the paradigm of Sternberg (1966). The subject is presented with a list of digits of a specified length (say, from one to six), which is studied until the subject indicates that he or she is confident of mastery. A single test item then appears, and the subject's task is simply to report whether or not the test item was included in the set just learned. The response is to press one button if the item was included and another button if it was not; the principal measure is the reaction time. The basic discovery was that the relationship between the length of the learned (or positive) set and the reaction time was positive and essentially linear. For each item added to the set, an increment of approximately 38 msec was added to the mean response time. The fact that the slope of the curve was non-zero suggests that the searching process is serial rather than parallel, with each item being examined in turn. It is of special interest that the slope was the same whether the test stimulus was or was not a member of the initially presented set. If the search through the memorial representation of the positive set were terminated when the matching item were found, it would be terminated on the average half way through the scanning of the memory set. On the other hand, under circumstances where the test stimulus is not a member of the set, it would be necessary to scan all the way through in order to be certain it was not. Thus, if the search were terminated upon positive identification, the slope for the positive trials should be only half that of the negative trials. The fact that they have the same slope suggests that the search is exhaustive rather than self-terminating.

Another interesting aspect concerning the relationship of reaction time to size of the positive set is that the Y-intercept is at about 400 msec. After subtracting time required for input and output (see Sternberg, 1975), about 200 msec are left over. Sternberg posits the existence of stages of stimulus encoding, serial comparison, binary decision, and translation and response organization--which together account for those 200 msec. This basic method has been expanded, elaborated, and applied to a diversity of situations. (For a recent review, see Sternberg, 1975.)

The relative adequacy of the structural and the levels of processing conceptualizations is a matter of vigorous theoretical and empirical contention at the present time. Almost any phenotype that might be selected by the unsuspecting behavioral geneticist might be identified with one particular school of thought and therefore be judged by some of the adversaries in the debate to be dated, or wrong, or at least off target. What, then, shall we do? Two points seem pertinent. In the first place, resolution of the contention in the field certainly does not appear to be just around the corner. Even if the levels of processing proponents carry the day and the supporters of structural models surrender completely (or vice versa), it is unlikely that will be the end. From the history of psychology in particular and science in general, we may expect that new schools of thought will emerge and that the successful innovators of one wave of thought will become the embattled defenders of the status quo in the next. Therefore, to advise the behavioral geneticist to wait until the issue is clarified is not to be very helpful. The second point is that it might not make that much difference after all, for the purposes of behavioral genetic analysis, exactly which conceptualization is superior, providing that one of them is not shown to be utterly ridiculous. That is to say, a method that began or developed in one theoretical context is unlikely to yield no information about another model in the same domain. Thus, if we select for research some phenomenon that is interpretable by both current theoretical models and that makes some sense in both camps, then we are probably pretty safe in launching investigations. This is not to say that we might not wish to tune our phenotypes more finely as we progress, in response both to our own findings and to developments in the field of information processing. However, it is unlikely that our early efforts will be wasted.

Finally, it is not at all impossible (indeed, my intuition is that it is highly likely) that the individual differences, behavioral genetic approach will aid very substantially the attempts at theory refinement. In other words, I do not see us behavioral geneticists as passive recipients of the wisdom generated by more purely psychological research. The information we obtain in our studies of family relationships, correlated characters, and so on may very well make substantial contributions to theory development in information processing itself.

I suppose that one of the reasons I am attracted by the information processing domain is that it offers a level of discourse and data intermediate to the traditional psychometric paper-and-pencil measures of cognitive ability and aptitude and the more molecular explanations of memory provided by the biopsychologists (see, for example, the articles by Barondes, Gold and McGaugh, Isaacson, and Nakamura and Gazzaniga in a collection of papers prepared by Deutsch and Deutsch in 1975). These information processing concepts, therefore, appear to me to occupy a most strategic location that will permit the communication of ideas from one level to another. I do not say this as a reductionistic chauvinist; I am quite as convinced that the more molecular approaches can be enriched by attending to the psychometric as I am convinced that the converse is true. If, indeed, the trade routes between the psychometricists and the biopsychologists do cross in the land of information processing, we may expect a flourishing ideational metropolis to develop there.

However, it is not just these prospects and promises that recommend information processing phenotypes. Quite apart from whatever theoretical developments may occur in the future, it is already becoming clear that measures of information processing are excellent, sensitive indicators in a variety of other theoretically interesting and socially important areas. I shall illustrate by providing a few examples of the usefulness of information processing research in several diverse phenotypic domains in which I have an interest--reading disability, aging, and sensitivity to the effects of alcohol.

2. INFORMATION PROCESSING AND READING DISABILITY

Because reading requires integration of sequential stimuli (letters within words, words within sentences, etc.), some sort of memory processing seems likely to be involved, and the possibility that memory disturbances might be characteristic of reading disorders has long been considered. In 1906, for example, Claiborne (cited in Critchley, 1970) suggested that reading disability is due to "imperfect development and tardy reaction of the word- and letter-memory cells." In 1917, Hinshelwood (cited in Ingram 1970) proposed that it resulted from a failure of normal development of brain centers concerned with visual (but not auditory) memory of words, letters, or figures. A substantial body of literature based on paper-and-pencil tests has since strengthened the evidence for the involvement of memory disturbances in reading disability. In recent years, investigators in this area have begun to apply the strong theories and powerful methods of information processing research.

Stanley (1975) compared reading-disabled children to a group of age-matched controls on a measure of the duration of iconic store. He reported that the reading-disabled children retained a stimulus object in the iconic store for durations 30% to 50% longer than did controls. One implication of this persistence is that the transfer of information from immediate memory to subsequent phases in the memory process may be impeded. Furthermore, Stanley and co-workers (1975) have found that reading-disabled children display sequential memory deficits in both auditory and visual processing modes when compared to a group of control children. No difference in performance was noted, however, for a tactual serial matching task.

Rudel and Denckla (1976) addressed the methodological problem which arises from the fact that auditory tests of memory are by necessity of a sequential nature, whereas visual memory stimuli are more often presented simultaneously so that there is an emphasis on memory for spatial qualities. It is the opinion of these authors that this sequential-spatial dimension is more relevant to performance deficits in reading-disabled children than the distinction between auditory and visual modes. They reported that both reading-disabled and control subjects found it relatively easy to perform spatial memory tasks and that there was no significant difference between the scores of the two groups. However, performance of the reading-disabled children was significantly lower than that of the controls on all tasks which involved memory for sequential material, presented in either the auditory or the visual mode.

Vellutino and co-workers (1975) investigated another aspect of visual information processing in reading-disabled children and controls. In this investigation, subjects were presented with tachistoscopic displays of verbal and nonverbal materials. Two response conditions were incorporated into the design: (1) The child was asked to reproduce the stimulus presentations (both verbal and nonverbal) on paper. (2) In the case of certain letter and word presentations, the child was asked to pronounce each letter or word. Results showed that poor readers performed as well as control children when asked to draw the stimulus items, but that their performance was severely handicapped when they were asked to identify the item verbally. This finding suggests that a verbal recoding deficit may be present, at least in certain forms of reading disability.

Morrison, Giordani and Nagy (1977) used a variant of the Sperling procedure for assessing visual information storage parameters in 12-year-old children with reading disability and in normal control subjects. Their evidence suggested that the reading-disabled children showed no perceptual deficit, but that they demonstrated a significant deficit during a 300- to 2,000-msec interval after stimulus presentation. This finding indicates that reading disability may be accompanied by a deficit in coding, organizing, or retrieving information.

Taken together, the results of these studies encourage us to believe that the investigation of memory function in reading disability based upon an information processing approach is both feasible and potentially of great value.

3. INFORMATION PROCESSING AND AGING

The search for differential consequences of aging also has extended beyond the domains sampled by psychometric devices into that of information processing. Particularly important has been the work of Birren (1965), who contends that slowing of behavioral responses is a major attribute of aging and proposes that this slowing of responses is a function of central processes. Various research paradigms assessing simple reaction time, differential reaction time, and movement time have explored the basis of behavioral

slowing. The recent review by Botwinick (1973) of data in this
area suggests that changes in the central nervous system are the
antecedents of slowing with age, but that implications for higher
level functioning are equivocal. Factors of exercise, practice,
and motivation have been shown to influence the rate of aging, and,
a topic to be explored in greater detail later, there exist very
large individual differences.

As an example of a finding contrary to this general conclusion,
Waugh, Fozard, Talland and Erwin (1973) studied two-choice reaction
times of male volunteers from 20 to 70 years of age and concluded
that the longer latencies of the older subjects reflected impaired
psychomotor function rather than deficiency in decision making.
Spirduso (1975) also studied reaction and movement time in active
and inactive men in older and younger groups. The data were
interpreted as a repudiation of the hypothesis that central
processing decrements account for slowing of responses in the aged.

That central processing is influenced by age is clearly
illustrated by a somewhat different line of experimentation. For
example, Brinley, Jovick and McLaughlin (1974) administered concept
identification problems to subjects ranging from 21 to 80 years
of age. Age differences in efficiency of reasoning performance,
specifically associated with the encoding, storing, and utilizing
of information, were found beginning with the 36- through 50-year-
old group. Elias and Kinsbourne (1974) required groups of older
and younger subjects to match verbal and nonverbal visual stimuli
on the basis of membership in binary sets. In both sexes, the
older group was significantly slower than the younger, and there
was a strong interaction of age with sex. Botwinick and Storandt
(1974) found no sex difference in the slowing of reaction time
with age.

As we have seen, memory or memories lie at the heart of information processing. In both folklore and the established literature, memory is reputed to decline with age. In a classic work,
Gilbert (1941) matched 174 sensecents with 174 young persons in
their 20's on vocabulary level. A greater loss on the part of the
senescents was found for retention than for immediate recall. In
particular, age deficits for auditory and visual digit span were
very small. However, others have found short-term memory deficits.
Talland (1968) has reviewed this literature and concludes that
the capacity to transmit information, as measured by the span of
immediate recall, diminishes between the ages 20 and 70, and that
loss appears to occur at critical stages--especially at about 40
and again at about 60 years of age. Craik (1968) reviews research
suggesting that age-related deficits in short-term memory are due
to changes in retrieval mechanisms.

The evidence is not unambiguous, however. Keevil-Rogers and Schnore (1969) studied auditory digit span in individuals from 17 to 78 years of age using three retention intervals. It was found that digit recall was related to length of interval and to required activity during the interval, but was not related to age. It is speculated that the discrepancy of these results from others in the literature can be explained in terms of the relatively high level of intelligence of the subjects examined. Another study inconsistent with earlier literature is that of Erber (1974), who found an older group to be deficient relative to a younger group on recognition memory tasks. This older group, in keeping with the earlier results, was also relatively deficient in word recall. Adamowicz (1976) found age-related deficits at the encoding and post-encoding stages, but not in retrieval functions. A particularly interesting analysis by Wickelgren (1975), in a study of recognition memory, revealed that the form and rate of the retention function were the same for three groups with mean ages of 9.5, 21, and 68 years. Young adults were superior to elderly adults, who were superior to children in acquisition, but the similarity of the form and rate led to the conclusion that storage dynamics appear to be invariant with age.

It would seem likely that continuing application of the information processing procedures will contribute strongly to the elucidation of individual differences in the effects of aging upon memory.

4.   INFORMATION PROCESSING AND ALCOHOL SENSITIVITY

The field of pharmacogenetics has experienced a phenomenal recent growth. Much of the evidence regarding human pharmacological responses has been concerned principally with complications after medical administration of drugs. There is, however, a growing awareness that genes might contribute importantly to individual differences in response to the entire gamut of drugs--used commonly or infrequently, legally or not. Of particular interest from the social perspective are those commonly used drugs (such as alcohol, tobacco, coffee and tea, or tranquilizers) that may have beneficial or detrimental effects on mood or on psychomotor performance. Most intensively studied has been the effect of alcohol on perceptual and cognitive processes.

In recent years, there has been a pronounced increase in the utilization of information processing paradigms in investigations of the effects of alcohol upon human memory. Several examples may be cited. Moskowitz and Burns (1973) required subjects to name as quickly as possible a presented digit or digits. Uncertainty was varied by increasing the number of digits in the presented set. The task therefore makes no demands on STM, but does involve central processing of information. Male university students, 21 to 39 years of age, displayed lower performance levels under the influence of alcohol. Moskowitz and DePry (1968) found that alcohol disrupted the ability of the brain to monitor two separate channels of information. In related studies, Moskowitz and Murray (1976a, 1976b), using a backward masking task in one study and a Sperling partial report approach in the other, found alcohol to impair the rate of transfer of information from the sensory store to STM. They also found that alcohol does not significantly alter the rate of decay of information in iconic store, although it does impair either the data acquisition or extraction stage. In 1974, Tharp and co-workers, using a Sternberg probe and an auditory modification of it, found alcohol consistently to impair information outputting (response selection-organization) rather than information inputting (stimulus pre-processing and encoding). They also discovered that subjects under the influence of alcohol made more errors on positive trials; that is, they were more likely to say that the test item was not a member of the positive set when in fact it was.

Further work of this sort should contribute to the more precise definition of the nature of the effect of alcohol upon behavior. Such studies, and similar applications of an information-processing approach in research on the effects of other drugs, should yield information of practical as well as of basic scientific import.

5. AN INDIVIDUAL DIFFERENCES PERSPECTIVE ON INFORMATION PROCESSING

Despite the elegance of the experimental techniques devised and used by information processing researchers, certain inadequacies become apparent when the techniques are examined for possible use in behavioral genetic research. In the context of the experimental psychology tradition in which the basic research was conducted, it is typical to obtain measures on relatively few subjects, and these subjects are often highly educated, situation-docile, and test-wise individuals. For example, Sperling's original report (1960) was based upon five subjects, four of whom were obtained through a student employment service (presumably of Harvard University), with the fifth being a faculty member. Sternberg's early (1966) results were based upon eight undergraduate students at the University of Pennsylvania. These individuals could be given any reasonable amount of pretraining in order to reach some plateau or asymptote of performance, and they could be tested for an extended number of trials.

In many respects, the design requirements of behavioral genetic research are those of research on individual differences. Relatively large numbers of subjects are needed for many purposes; a wide age range might be required, particularly in two-generation family studies; and subjects may be available for only brief test periods,

permitting no time for exhaustive pretraining. Thus, the procedures employed should yield highly reliable results from brief
tests administered to unsophisticated individuals (in the sense of
test wisdom) who vary widely in age. Regrettably, data on psychometric attributes of information processing measures (their reliabilities, validities, factor structures, population norms, age
trends, etc.) are lacking for the most part.

Recently, however, there have been several encouraging attempts
to relate individuality in information processing functions to traditional psychometric indicators of cognitive ability. For example,
Hunt, Frost and Lunneborg (1973) compared individuals of high quantitative ability to those of high verbal ability. The former were
found to be characterized by less loss of retrievable information
from intermediate-term memory, less susceptibility to interference
while consolidating information in STM, less responsiveness to
blocking of material in free recall, and faster memory search. A
later study by Hunt, Lunneborg and Lewis (1975), again using a mean
comparison design with 8 to 25 subjects per group, showed individuals high in verbal ability to be superior to those low in verbal
ability in speed of conversion of a physical pattern to conceptual
meaning, in retention in STM of information concerning order of
stimulus presentation, and in speed of manipulation of data in STM.
They also concluded, on the basis of discriminant analysis, that
information processing tasks can be used to distinguish between high
and low verbal ability individuals and that, to a degree, information processing and paper-and-pencil psychometric tasks measure the
same abilities. More recently, Chiang and Atkinson (1976), using
34 Stanford undergraduates as subjects, obtained substantial reliabilities for several indices of short-term memory processing and
visual searching, and found significant correlations between these
measures and verbal and quantitative scores on the Scholastic
Aptitude Test.

A correlational approach was used by Lunneborg (1978), who
administered a variety of information processing and psychometric
measures to 63 University of Washington freshmen. Very substantial
correlations were reported between the two types of tasks. Speeded
tests, both nonverbal (WAIS performance IQ) and verbal (vocabulary),
were most highly predictable. Multiple correlations with the information processing tasks "accounted for" about 35% of the test variance for these measures. Particularly interesting in this study
was the negative correlation between verbal comprehension and performance on a task measuring difficulty in overcoming conventions
of the language (substituting R's for L's in reading visually presented words). This correlation (r = -.43) was interpreted as
demonstrating that the ability to overcome linguistic convention is
a major determinant of high vocabulary scores. Another highly
salient outcome was the observed relationship between WAIS performance IQ and ability to detect the prior arrival (by 30 or 45 msec)

of non-speech sounds to the left ear. The fact that performance on the Raven Progressive Matrices Test was generally less predictable, with the only significant correlate being ability to perceive prior arrival of speech sounds to the right ear, is a particularly interesting outcome. It suggests that further research might distinguish information processing differences between verbal and nonverbal reasoning abilities.

An especially ambitious assessment of the memory domain by multivariate procedures has recently been reported by Masson (1977). Some 30 tests of memory, drawing from both psychometric and information processing traditions, were administered to 243 male University of Colorado students. Five first-order factors were identified as associative memory ability, ability to derive information from brief visual displays, meaningful memory, short-term visual memory (geometric figures), and span memory. Second order factoring produced two factors which were interpreted as representing strategic and nonstrategic memory processing abilities. That is to say, the first second order factor--including associative, meaningful, and visual memory--involved tests which had the common property of permitting utilization of strategic processing. Less opportunity for the utilization of processing strategies is apparent in the span memory and short-term visual memory tests that characterized the other second order factor. When Masson applied a subject clustering procedure to his data, he found that the subjects were grouped into five categories. One group was quite poor on all five factors, one group was generally superior on all five, and a third group was average across all factors. The remaining two groups scored relatively higher on the nonstrategic factors (short-term visual and span memory) than they did on the strategic factors. These results supported the second-order factor analysis and provided additional evidence for the validity of a general distinction between the strategic and nonstrategic memory abilities and tasks.

The findings of these studies strongly suggest the importance, both with respect to basic theory and for educational application, of examining information processing parameters from the perspective of individual differences.

6. THE HAWAII STUDY OF THE GENETICS OF INFORMATION PROCESSING

Recently, with a number of colleagues, I have been engaged in some research that has offered the opportunity to begin an investigation of the genetics of information processing parameters. The context for this work is the Hawaii Family Study of Cognition (HFSC), in which over 1,800 families have been tested on a variety of paper-and-pencil cognitive measures. Although data from this study are still being analyzed, some reports have appeared (DeFries et al., 1974, 1976; Wilson et al., 1975; Johnson et al., 1976) which provide detailed descriptions of the test battery, testing conditions, and early results pertaining to cognitive structure, sex and age differences, assortative mating, and parent-offspring resemblance.

During the summer of 1975, 118 families from this sample were retested on the main battery and, in addition, were administered a variety of new tasks to test various hypotheses and clarify issues raised by our early analyses. Included in this new battery were an adaptation of Sperling's procedure for assessing short-term visual memory and an auditory analog of that procedure.

In the measurement of short-term visual memory, subjects were asked to attend to a small dot in the center of a grid which was back-projected on a screen 6 feet in front of them. One-half second after an audiotaped voice said, "ready," three rows of three letters appeared for 500 msec. Three visual information processing tasks were employed. In the first task (VIS 1), subjects were asked to write down as many letters as they could recall on a response sheet ruled into blocks corresponding to the three rows of three letters. Two practice trials and six actual trials were given to each subject. For this analysis, a letter was scored as correct only if it was placed in exactly the position where it appeared in the stimulus. For the second task (VIS 2), subjects were asked to attend to all nine letters as they were presented, but then were required to report only one row of three. On each trial, the row to be reported was unknown to the subject until it was denoted by an arrow which appeared immediately after the offset of the stimulus array. One practice and six actual trials were given. The third task (VIS 3) was similar to the second, except that there was a delay of .5 sec before specification of the row to be reported.

The short-term auditory memory tasks were similar to the visual tasks. In this case, sequences of letters were recorded on audiotape and presented to the subject binaurally through earphones. In the first task (AUD 1), a sequence of nine letters was given, in three-letter groups, and the subject was asked to write down as many letters as possible. In the second task (AUD 2), using the same type of stimulus, the subject was asked to write down the first, second, or third three-letter group. The group to be reported was unknown to the subject until verbal instructions were given immediately after stimulus presentation. The third task (AUD 3) required the subject to perform subtraction mentally (e.g., 100 minus 3; 97 minus 3; etc.) for 5 sec after stimulus presentation before reporting one of the three-letter groups. For each task, the score was the number of letters reproduced correctly with respect to identity and position. After two practice trials at the beginning of auditory testing, each subject received six actual trials on each task. It should be noted that the visual and auditory tasks involved simultaneous and successive presentations, respectively.

Also included in the new battery was a paper-and-pencil test of figure memory. Subjects were asked to scan for 1 min an array of 40 line drawings of geometric figures displayed on a page of a test booklet. They were then asked to turn the page to a second (test) array, in which 20 of the items were identical to those scanned in the stimulus array and 20 were different, and to circle the items which were exactly like those seen previously. One minute was allowed for completion of this task. The number of figures chosen correctly constituted the score for figure memory--immediate (FMI). About 5 min later, after the interpolation of another task, subjects were presented with a test array consisting of the 20 original stimuli not presented in the first test plus 20 new distractors. The number chosen correctly was the score for figure memory--delayed (FMD). These tests were adapted from material provided by I. G. Ord (personal communication). They were designed to parallel the visual memory tasks (VMI and VMD) of the HFSC battery, which utilized line drawings of everyday objects rather than geometric figures.

In addition to these three sets of memory tasks, several other measures were included in the new battery administered during the retesting session. Among these was the Wechsler Adult Intelligence Scale (WAIS). Digit span (DS) performance and total score on the WAIS were included in the analyses reported here.

One of the first questions to be addressed was the factor structure of that part of the memory domain we had sampled. The significant intercorrelations (and the reliabilities) of the various memory measures are shown in Table 1. First, a comment with respect to the reliability estimates is in order. In general, in the context of psychometric tests, these estimates must be regarded as modest. However, given the origin of many of the procedures in the experimental psychology tradition, and the relatively small amount of attention given to their psychometric niceties, the results are encouraging. They certainly lead us to believe that further refinements will generate highly reliable test procedures that can be administered quickly to a broad range of subjects. Intercorrelations among the memory tasks are also only low to moderate. Even considering that the modest reliabilities must impose upper limits on the magnitude of the intercorrelations, this result suggests the complexity of the memory domain. It is of particular interest that only moderate correlations exist between parts within a given test. It seems possible that this outcome reflects the independence of different levels or stages of memorial processing related to the delay intervals in the VMI or FMI versus the VMD or FMD tests and to various tasks in the AUD and VIS series.

The oblique factor pattern after quartamin rotation of a principal component solution is shown in Table 2. Four factors had eigenvalues greater than one. These were interpreted as <u>auditory</u>

Table 1

Significant Intercorrelations and Reliabilities of Memory Task Scores

	FMI	FMD	VMI	VMD	DS	AUD 1	AUD 2	AUD 3	VIS 1	VIS 2	VIS 3
FMI	.66[a]	.48	.18	.17	.11	---	.11	---	.12	.16	.10
FMD		.63[a]	.19	.19	.09	---	---	---	---	---	---
VMI			.45[a]	.51	.10	.10	---	---	---	---	.10
VMD				.51[a]	---	---	---	---	---	---	---
DS					.71[b]	.49	.46	.32	.10	---	---
AUD 1						.74[c]	.49	.30	.18	.16	.10
AUD 2							.46[c]	.24	.16	.12	.13
AUD 3								.38[c]	---	---	---
VIS 1									.72[c]	.48	.43
VIS 2										.63[c]	.38
VIS 3											.60[c]

Note. FMI, FMD, VMI, VMD, and DS are paper-and-pencil tests; the three AUD and VIS measures are apparatus-presented tasks.

[a]Test-retest reliability.

[b]From test manual.

[c]Coefficient alpha estimates from the present data.

Table 2

Oblique Factor Structure Matrix of Memory Tests

Task	Factor I	Factor II	Factor III	Factor IV
FMI	.04	-.01	.04	.85
FMD	-.03	.03	-.03	.86
VMI	.02	.86	.02	.01
VMD	-.01	.87	.00	.01
DS	.80	-.02	-.08	.08
AUD 1	.78	-.01	.11	-.05
AUD 2	.74	-.05	.10	.03
AUD 3	.59	.07	-.08	-.04
VIS 1	.06	.03	.81	-.05
VIS 2	-.05	.04	.78	.06
VIS 3	-.01	-.05	.76	.00

sequential memory, visual memory, figure memory, and a factor identified by the three VIS scores. A second order analysis provided two factors--one representing the paper-and-pencil memory tests, and the other representing the auditory and visual information processing measures (the apparatus-presented tasks).

Another interesting question concerns the relationship of the memory measures to performance on more conventional paper-and-pencil tests of cognitive ability. Correlations of the AUD and VIS measures with factor scores derived for these subjects from the HFSC battery are presented in Table 3. The factors identified in previous analyses (DeFries et al., 1974) were verbal, spatial, perceptual speed, and visual memory. Correlations with the first principal component of the HFSC data and with WAIS total score are also shown in the table. Although none of the correlations is large, the AUD tasks have more significant associations with the other measures than do the VIS tasks. The difference is especially pronounced with respect to the measures of general cognitive ability (the first principal component of the HFSC data and the WAIS total score). Whether this finding can be attributed to the particular modality or to the difference between simultaneous and successive presentation remains to be determined by further investigation.

Table 3

Significant Correlations of Memory Tasks with Cognitive Factors
and with WAIS Total Score

Task	Verbal	Spatial	Perceptual Speed	Visual Memory	First Principal Component	WAIS
FMI	---	.08	.13	.18	.15	---
FMD	---	.09	.11	.19	.18	---
VMI	.09	.09	.10	.84	.35	.11
VMD	---	---	.12	.86	.23	.08
DS	.32	.16	.14	---	.38	.48
AUD 1	.21	.16	.10	.10	.23	.36
AUD 2	.22	.15	.16	.11	.24	.39
AUD 3	.15	---	---	---	.13	.27
VIS 1	.18	---	.18	---	.17	.13
VIS 2	---	---	---	---	---	.13
VIS 3	.10	---	.14	.11	.12	---

Our primary concern, of course, is with respect to measures
of familial resemblance. Acknowledging that such resemblances
might be due to environmental sources of variation as well as to
genetic ones, it is nonetheless of interest to examine the upper-
limit estimates of heritability provided by regressions of offspring on midparent for the information processing measures and to
compare them to the regressions obtained from the HFSC paper-and-
pencil tests.

Table 4 gives the results for the present sample for selected
AUD and VIS tasks. Results for the factors obtained from analyses
of the HFSC data (DeFries et al., 1976) are presented separately
for two ethnic groups in that study (AEA = Americans of European
ancestry; AJA = Americans of Japanese ancestry). Clearly, the
parent-offspring resemblances for these information processing
memory phenotypes are of the same order of magnitude as those for
the paper-and-pencil measures of cognitive ability. Given that
the parent-offspring regressions for the apparatus-presented memory
tasks may be limited by the reliabilities of the tasks, there would
appear to be much promise for research with tools suitably polished
and honed with respect to psychometric considerations.

Table 4

Significant Regressions of Midchild on Midparent
for Selected Measures

Task/Factor	Present Sample	HFSC Samples	
		AEA	AJA
AUD 1	--		
AUD 2	31		
AUD 3	53		
VIS 1	33		
VIS 2	--		
VIS 3	43		
Verbal		57	51
Spatial		57	41
Perceptual speed		41	29
Visual memory		32	22
First principal component		61	42

Furthermore, the evidence that the information processing tasks are tapping some of the same processes as the paper-and-pencil variety, but that they are substantially independent, suggests that this domain merits further exploration by behavioral geneticists. The results of this study are reported in greater detail by Cole et al. (1979).

At the beginning of this chapter, I cautioned that the account of information processing to be presented herein might be idiosyncratic because of the special interests and outlooks that I have brought to the area. This caveat should be underscored in closing by repeating that I am not a native guide in this terrain. Rather, I could perhaps be characterized as an excited prospector who has found some terrain features of great interest, suggestive of a rich mine and maybe (who knows-?) even of the mother lode.

7. SUMMARY AND CONCLUSIONS

From a theoretical point of view, the domain of information processing appears attractive for individual differences and

behavioral genetic analyses because it occupies an explanatory
stratum intermediate to the physiological and molecular levels of
explanation of memory on the one hand and the traditional psychometric levels on the other hand. Furthermore, individual differences in information processing functions appear to be related to
a wide range of theoretically important and socially relevant
matters such as reading disability, aging, and sensitivity to
alcohol.

Special problems inhere in the utilization of information
processing methods in research with an individual differences perspective. In general, this sort of research requires tests that
provide reliable results when briefly presented with little or no
pretraining to subjects of widely varying age. A prelusive study
is encouraging in suggesting that, with development, information
processing tasks may meet these criteria satisfactorily. Data
also reveal interesting relationships of the information processing parameters to more traditional factors and indicate that
the degree of familial resemblance for the former tasks is of the
same order of magnitude as that for the latter.

ACKNOWLEDGMENTS

The results of the Hawaii research on the genetics of information
processing are made possible by collaboration of a group of investigators (G. C. Ashton, R. C. Johnson, M. P. Mi and M. N. Rashad
at the University of Hawaii, and J. C. DeFries, G. E. McClearn,
S. G. Vandenberg and J. R. Wilson at the University of Colorado)
supported by NSF Grant GB-34720 and Grant HD-06669 from the
National Institute of Child Health and Human Development.

I also wish to acknowledge the support of a faculty fellow-
ship from the University of Colorado Council on Research and
Creative Work and to thank Rebecca G. Miles for her expert assistance in the preparation of the manuscript.

REFERENCES

Adamowicz, J. K. Visual short-term memory and aging. Journal of
    Gerontology, 1976, 31, 39-46.
Barondes, S. H. Protein-synthesis dependent and protein-synthesis
    independent memory storage processes. In D. Deutsch & J. A.
    Deutsch (Eds.), Short-term memory. New York: Academic
    Press, 1975.
Birren, J. E. Age changes in speed of behavior: Its central
    nature and physiological correlates. In A. T. Welford &
    J. E. Birren (Eds.), Behavior, aging and the nervous system.
    Springfield, Ill.: Charles C. Thomas, 1965.

Botwinick, J. Aging and behavior. New York: Springer, 1973.

Botwinick, J., & Storandt, M. Cardiovascular status, depressive affect, and other factors in reaction time. Journal of Gerontology, 1974, 29, 543-548.

Brinley, J. F., Jovick, T. J., & McLaughlin, L. M. Age, reasoning, and memory in adults. Journal of Gerontology, 1974, 29, 182-189.

Broadbent, D. E. Perception and communication. London: Pergamon Press, 1958.

Brown, J. A. Some tests of the decay theory of intermediate memory. Quarterly Journal of Experimental Psychology, 1958, 10, 12-21.

Chiang, A., & Atkinson, R. C. Individual differences and inter-relationships among a select set of cognitive skills. Memory and Cognition, 1976, 4, 661-672.

Cole, R. E., Johnson, R. C., Ahern, F. M., Kuse, A. R., McClearn, G. E., Vandenberg, S. G., & Wilson, J. R. A family study of memory processes and their relations to cognitive test scores. Intelligence, 1979, in press.

Craik, F. I. M. Short-term memory and the aging process. In G. A. Talland (Ed.), Human aging and behavior. New York: Academic Press, 1968.

Craik, F. I. M., & Lockhart, R. S. Levels of processing: A framework for memory research. Journal of Verbal Learning and Verbal Behavior, 1972, 11, 671-684.

Critchley, M. Developmental dyslexia. London: William Heinemann Medical Books, 1970.

DeFries, J. C., Vandenberg, S. G., & McClearn, G. E. Genetics of specific cognitive abilities. Annual Review of Genetics, 1976, 10, 179-207.

DeFries, J. C., Vandenberg, S. G., McClearn, G. E., Kuse, A. R., Wilson, J. R., Ashton, G. C., & Johnson, R. C. Near identity of cognitive structure in two ethnic groups. Science, 1974, 183, 338-339.

Deutsch, D., & Deutsch, J. A. Short-term memory. New York: Academic Press, 1975.

Elias, M. F., & Kinsbourne, M. Age and sex differences in the processing of verbal and nonverbal stimuli. Journal of Gerontology, 1974, 29, 162-171.

Erber, J. T. Age differences in recognition. Journal of Gerontology, 1974, 29, 177-181.

Gilbert, J. G. Memory loss in senescence. Journal of Abnormal and Social Psychology, 1941, 36, 73-86.

Gold, P. E., & McGaugh, J. L. A single-trace, two-process view of memory storage processes. In D. Deutsch & J. A. Deutsch (Eds.), Short-term memory. New York: Academic Press, 1975.

Hunt, E., Frost, N., & Lunneborg, C. Individual differences in cognition: A new approach to intelligence. In G. H. Bower (Ed.), The psychology of learning and motivation (Vol. 7). New York: Academic Press, 1973.

Hunt, E., Lunneborg, C., & Lewis, J. What does it mean to be high verbal? Cognitive Psychology, 1975, 7, 194-227.

Ingram, T. T. S. The nature of dyslexia. In F. A. Young & D. B. Lindsley (Eds.), Early experience and visual information processing in perceptual and reading disorders. Washington: National Academy of Sciences, 1970.

Isaacson, R. L. Memory processes and the hippocampus. In D. Deutsch & J. A. Deutsch (Eds.), Short-term memory. New York: Academic Press, 1975.

Johnson, R. C., DeFries, J. C., Wilson, J. R., McClearn, G. E., Vandenberg, S. G., Ashton, G. C., Mi, M. P., & Rashad, M. N. Assortative marriage for specific cognitive abilities in two ethnic groups. Human Biology, 1976, 23, 311-316.

Keevil-Rogers, P., & Schnore, M. M. Short-term memory as a function of age in persons of above average intelligence. Journal of Gerontology, 1969, 24, 184-188.

Klatzky, R. L. Human memory: Structures and processes. San Francisco: Freeman, 1975.

Loftus, G. R., & Loftus, E. F. Human memory. Hillsdale: Lawrence Erlbaum Associates, 1976.

Lunneborg, C. E. Some information-processing correlates of measures of intelligence. Multivariate Behavioral Research, 1978, 13, 153-161.

Masson, M. E. J. A multivariate approach to the study of memory and problem solving. Unpublished M. A. thesis, University of Colorado, 1977.

McClearn, G. E. Psychological research and behavioral phenotypes. In J. N. Spuhler (Ed.), Genetic diversity and human behavior. Chicago: Aldine, 1967.

Miller, G. A. The magical number seven, plus or minus two: Some limits on our capacity for processing information. Psychological Review, 1956, 63, 81-97.

Morrison, F. J., Giordani, B., & Nagy, J. Reading disability: An information-processing analysis. Science, 1977, 196, 77-79.

Moskowitz, H., & Burns, M. Alcohol effects on information processing time with an overlearned task. Perceptual and Motor Skills, 1973, 37, 835-839.

Moskowitz, H., & DePry, D. Differential effect of alcohol on auditory vigilance and divided-attention tasks. Quarterly Journal of Studies on Alcohol, 1968, 29, 54-63.

Moskowitz, H., & Murray, J. T. Alcohol and backward masking of visual information. Journal of Studies on Alcohol, 1976, 37, 40-45. (a)

Moskowitz, H., & Murray, J. T. Decrease of iconic memory after alcohol. Journal of Studies on Alcohol, 1976, 37, 278-283. (b)

Nakamura, R. K., & Gazzaniga, M. S. Comparative aspects of short-term memory mechanisms. In D. Deutsch & J. A. Deutsch (Eds.), Short-term memory. New York: Academic Press, 1975.

Neisser, U. Cognitive psychology. New York: Appleton-Century-Crofts, 1967.

Peterson, L. R., & Peterson, M. J.   Short-term retention of individual verbal items. *Journal of Experimental Psychology*, 1959, 58, 193-198.

Posner, M. I.   Short-term memory systems in human information processing. *Acta Psychologica* (Amsterdam), 1967, 27, 267-284.

Rudel, R. G., & Denckla, M. B.   Relationship of IQ and reading score to visual, spatial, and temporal matching tasks. *Journal of Learning Disabilities*, 1976, 9, 169-178.

Sperling, G.   The information available in brief visual presentations. *Psychological Monographs*, 1960, 74(Whole No. 498).

Spirduso, W. W.   Reaction and movement time as a function of age and physical activity level. *Journal of Gerontology*, 1975, 30, 435-440.

Stanley, G.   Visual memory processes in dyslexia. In D. Deutsch & J. A. Deutsch (Eds.), *Short-term memory*. New York: Academic Press, 1975.

Stanley, G., Kaplan, I., & Poole, C.   Cognitive and nonverbal perceptual processing in dyslexics. *Journal of General Psychology*, 1975, 93, 67-72.

Sternberg, S.   High-speed scanning in human memory. *Science*, 1966, 153, 652-654.

Sternberg, S.   Memory scanning: New findings and current controversies. In D. Deutsch & J. A. Deutsch (Eds.), *Short-term memory*. New York: Academic Press, 1975.

Talland, G. A.   Age and the span of immediate recall. In G. A. Talland (Ed.), *Human aging and behavior*. New York: Academic Press, 1968.

Tharp, V. K., Jr., Rundell, O. H., Jr., Lester, B. K., & Williams, H. L.   Alcohol and information processing. *Psychopharmacologia* (Berlin), 1974, 40, 33-52.

Vellutino, F. R., Smith, H., Steger, J. A., & Kaman, M.   Reading disability: Age differences and the perceptual-deficit hypothesis. *Child Development*, 1975, 46, 487-493.

Waugh, N. C., Fozard, J. L., Talland, G. A., & Erwin, D. E.   Effects of age and stimulus repetition on two-choice reaction time. *Journal of Gerontology*, 1973, 28, 466-470.

Waugh, N. C., & Norman, D. A.   Primary memory. *Psychological Review*, 1965, 72, 89-104.

Wickelgren, W. A.   Age and storage dynamics in continuous recognition memory. *Developmental Psychology*, 1975, 11, 165-169.

Wilson, J. R., DeFries, J. C., McClearn, G. E., Vandenberg, S. G., Johnson, R. C., & Rashad, M. N.   Cognitive abilities: Use of family data as a control to assess sex and age differences in two ethnic groups. *International Journal of Aging and Human Development*, 1975, 6, 261-276.

COMMENT BY K. V. WILSON

McClearn's paper is essentially a proposal that behavior geneticists should consider the forms of information processing which may be basic to various types of psychometric test performance and disability. In my comments, I would like to first spell out what is meant by "information processing" and mention some allied areas which could be involved in the "bridge building" McClearn proposes. Second, I would like to show how information processing concepts could be used in an area other than those discussed by McClearn - namely, the controversy over the inheritance of intelligence.

Information Processing and Related Fields

In psychology, the term "information processing" can refer to any or all of the extremely complex chain of events between reception of information (i.e., stimuli) by the receptors and the organization of motor behavior (i.e., responses). In both visual perception and in language processing, there appears to be considerable use of abstractions which are quite far removed from uninterpreted sensory information. Thus, information processing has a very substantial area of common concern with cognitive psychology - an area of considerable recent ferment. Also, information processing is closely related to the concerns of the more "macroscopic" theorists of physiological psychology who are working towards an account of how the brain functions as a system (e.g., Karl Pribram, 1971, and E. Roy John, 1967). For example, the processing of visual information would include both the processing in the retina and the thalamus (i.e., relatively physiological and non-cognitive events) and also the analysis of the visual information into the identification of objects, events and their relations to each other (i.e., cognitive events whose physiological details are not yet known). Thus, McClearn's proposal that behavior geneticists be concerned with information processing virtually entails that they also be concerned with both cognitive processes and at least the more macroscopic aspects of physiological psychology. Of course, all this kind of concern is a tall order and I can only offer the meager consolation that the work will have to be shared by a large number of people over a long period of time. Another problem is the active controversy among information processing - cognitive psychologists over very basic issues - a virtually inevitable feature of a developing scientific field. The willing behavior geneticist can well be left with the impression that he is trying to build a "bridge" to a land plagued by earthquakes. Still, there are some substantial areas where progress has been made and which should be utilized if behavior genetics is to come to grips with many important questions. To support that conclusion, I would like to offer a somewhat speculative discussion of how the heated controversy

over the role of heredity in the determination of intelligence
might be more fruitfully examined by the kind of analysis McClearn
proposes than by the kinds of polemics which have been offered
by some.

Information Processing and the Development of Intelligence

I need not remind the reader that there has been a controversy
raging concerning the relations of heredity to intelligence and
involving claims regarding the relative intelligence of various
racial groups. The critics of intelligence tests can make an
apparently strong case. Briefly, their argument is that the
items of many intelligence tests reflect the results of learning
in particular environments and so cannot reflect the effects of
heredity. It is not hard to find items for which this could be
the case and it is also worth recalling the common failure of infant intelligence tests in predicting performance in later life.
The best defense which defenders of conventional intelligence
testing can make is to claim that the individual differences in
performance within such groups reflect differences in learning
abilities of some sort. While I believe this to be the case, I
find such a defense not very convincing since there is an uncom-
fortable vagueness regarding the nature of these abilities. Given
the importance of the memory systems for cognition (e.g., Hunt,
1973), this looks like a very good place to look for links between the psychometric and biopsychological domains of the sort
that McClearn advocates.

It is fairly generally agreed that there are three somewhat
distinct memory systems. Sensory information enters the iconic
memory where it is stored for about a second (probably less) in
a relatively unanalyzed form. This information is then analyzed
under the control of the contents of long term memory (i.e.,
"knowledge") and stored in short term memory for a period of
minutes to hours. Finally, some of this information is lost but
some is eventually consolidated into long term memory under the
control of processes about which there is relatively little knowledge or agreement. Since the brain is a neuronal network capable
of differential arousal, it seems possible that the analysis of
the material in iconic memory will more effectively utilize present
long term memory contents to the degree that there is effective
and general arousal associated with iconic memory processes.
Following the more effective analysis (i.e., recoding) of sensory
information into short term memory, it would follow that the
material encoded into long term memory would be more effectively
and, hopefully, more abstractly analyzed as well. Hence, the efficiency of iconic memory may be related to the differential acquisition of the behaviors tapped by intelligence tests. There
may also be relations to the presently not very well understood
processes through which short term memory is converted into long

term memory. Further, it is plausible that individual differences in either or both of these processes could reflect inheritable structural or biochemical differences.

Some interesting data relevant to the above speculations has been reported by Eysenck (1973, pp. 72-73). In a sample of 93 adults, the latency of cortical evoked potentials to auditory stimuli correlated about -.4 with measured I.Q. while the amplitude of these potentials correlated about +.4. Since amplitude and latency are independent, the net multiple correlation would be about .6. Moreover, the correlations with verbal I.Q. were higher than for performance I.Q. which is reasonable since skills tapped by verbal items would be based heavily on early learning involving the auditory modality.[1] Hendrickson and Hendrickson (1978) report further empirical work in which an even higher correlation is found with the length of the evoked potential wave (which is a composite of the number of maxima and their amplitude) occurring during 0.25 seconds following stimulation - well within the range of iconic memory.[2] While further research is obviously needed, it seems plausible that measured I.Q. has a substantial relationship to the effectiveness of arousal associated with auditory iconic memory processes. Further, Hendrickson and Hendrickson (1978) offer an at least plausible hypothesis (supported by some evidence) as to why this might be the case, although their analysis is stated in rather different terms from that above. If it could then be shown that auditory evoked potential, or other indices of iconic memory efficiency, are inherited to a substantial degree, it would then be possible to explain how the acquisition of the largely environmentally acquired skills measured by intelligence tests can be controlled by hereditary mechanisms.

However, a final note of caution is in order. Callaway (1975, pp. 134-136) correctly points out that evoked potentials, and other biological measures, could well reflect environmental events[3] even though they appear to be more "culture fair" than

---

[1]In his paper, McClearn reports higher correlations of digit span and measures of auditory memory with the WAIS total score than he obtained for any of his other measures (Table 3).

[2]See Callaway (1975) for a review of earlier work on the relations of evoked potential to intelligence. He has a cogent discussion of the earlier and quite controversial work of Ertl who obtained visual rather than auditory evoked potentials.

[3]John (1974, Chap. 11) reports changes in evoked potentials in animals which are associated with learning.

many verbal intelligence test items. Thus, while the argument
over the contribution of heredity to intelligence could and
probably will continue,[4] an examination of the intervening phenomena should be rewarding since the role of heredity in determining
intelligence is, at best, a very indirect one.

COMMENT BY J. R. ROYCE

This paper is important because of the relevance of the
information processing approach to the advancement of psychology.
However, McClearn's presentation is limited to traditional experimental psychology. And, while I agree that this is a good place
to begin, I see no reason to limit ourselves to such areas as
verbal learning, memory, and sensory processes (i.e., I am not
only in sympathy with McClearn's recommendations, I don't think
he goes far enough in his survey of potentially relevant information processing variables). On the assumption that Professor Mc-
Clearn agrees with this, I will now put forward several related
questions.

It has been said that there is little to be gained by further
demonstrations that a given behavior or trait is heritable.
Given that assumption, why should behavior geneticists now focus
their attention on information processing variables? In particular, I get the impression you view such variables as more critical
or fundamental than the variables we've been focused on for the
past 25 years. Why? And in what sense of "critical" or "fundamental"? Finally, can you extend the argument (or at least allude to the possibilities) concerning the relevance of information
processing variables which come from areas (such as personality,
emotion, psychopathology, social, etc.) other than experimental
psychology?

---

[4]Of course, hereditary determination of intelligence need
not imply the validity of racial differences. However, there has
been one racial comparison which yielded (perhaps happily) confusing results. Callaway (1975, pp. 48-50, 134, 136, 172-175)
discusses results in which black U.S. naval recruits displayed
lower intelligence test performance than white recruits but had
evoked potentials which are associated with higher intelligence.
Both groups showed the same direction of correlation between the
two measures. Such results have a variety of interpretations
but they do illustrate the potential complexities of research in
this area.

COMMENT BY J. H. F. van ABEELEN

I do not think this comment detracts from the significance
of McClearn's stimulating paper if I observe that a point of
central importance in his contribution is the question: What
makes a stimulus a stimulus? Wavelength, vibration, presence of
certain molecules, or pressure are physicochemical factors;
color, sound, odor, or touch are stimuli. It is self-evident
that those two categories cannot be equated. The stimulus is
already a function of the organism and hence of its gene-controlled
physiological machinery. That is why McClearn, in my opinion, is
drawing attention to a most important point when he discusses information processing and its relevance to behavior genetics or,
more specifically here, the phenogenetics of behavior.

COMMENT BY D. WAHLSTEN

Dr. McClearn first acknowledges that parent-offspring resemblances in the Hawaii study "might be due to environmental
sources of variation as well as to genetic ones", and then he asserts that regressions of offspring mean on mid-parent score will
provide "upper-limit estimates of heritability".

Should not the environmental and genetic sources be at least
appended by gene-environment covariance and gene-environment interaction sources as well? If this is done, then there is no
longer any basis for asserting that parent-offspring regression
imposes an upper limit on heritability. Either covariance or
interaction could act to reduce parent-offspring resemblance
relative to what it would be with strictly additive effects.

"Heritability" refers explicitly to the relative magnitude
of genetic variation. If a design is incapable of yielding a
proper measure of heritability, then there is no solid scientific
basis for using the word at all. Why not simply report regression
coefficients as in Table 4 and conclude nothing about heritability? This would avoid a futile crossing of swords with "environmentalists" who could just as legitimately assert that parent-
offspring regression in a simple family study imposes an upper
limit on "plasticity" of information processing.

The study employs a design in which heredity and environment
are confounded, and hence there is no way to separate their effects. Nobody can cut the Gordian knot of heredity and environment with a dull sword.

The really puzzling thing about the results reported by Dr.
McClearn is the low regression coefficient for the "AUD 1" task
whose reliability is relatively high. If both heredity and

environment contribute to familial resemblance, then what might
be causing the individual differences in this particular measure
of information processing? If it is something outside of the
family, perhaps in the schools, then a "mother lode" may be found
which can be exploited rapidly to improve education. If, on the
other hand, it is a complex intertwining of heredity-environment
covariance and interaction, then Dr. McClearn may have come upon
an immense Gordian knot.

References

Callaway, E. Brain electrical potentials and individual psycho-
    logical differences. New York: Grune and Stratton, 1975.
Eysenck, H. J. The inequality of man. Glasgow: Fontana-
    Collins, 1975.
Hendrickson, A. E., & Henrickson, D. E. The biological basis and
    measurement of intelligence. Paper read at the XIX'th In-
    ternational Congress of Applied Psychology, Munich, August,
    1978. For reprints, write the authors at the Department of
    Psychology, Institute of Psychiatry, De Crespigny Park, Lon-
    don SE5, England.
Hunt, E. The memory we must have. In Schank, R., & Colby, K.
    (Eds.), Computer models of memory and thought. San Francisco:
    W. H. Freeman, 1973.
John, E. R. Mechanisms of memory. New York: Academic Press,
    1967.
Pribram, K. H. The languages of the brain. Englewood Cliffs,
    N.J.: Prentice Hall, 1971.

THE FACTOR-GENE BASIS OF INDIVIDUALITY

Joseph R. Royce[1]

The Center for Advanced Study in Theoretical Psychology,
University of Alberta, Edmonton, Alberta, Canada

I. INDIVIDUALITY THEORY

A Brief Overview

Multifactor-systems theory is a general theory of individual
differences and integrated personality in which the interacting
components are identified via factor analysis, and the principles
of integrated functioning are derived from general system and
information processing theory (Royce, 1973, 1978a; Royce & Buss,
1976; Royce & Powell, 1978). The total personality, or the
suprasystem, is postulated to be composed of six interacting
systems. The cognitive (Diamond & Royce, 1978; Powell & Royce,
1978) and affective (Royce & McDermott, 1977) systems are conceptualized as central processing units which function as information transformers. The style (Wardell & Royce, 1975, 1978) and
value (Schopflocher, Royce, & Meehan, 1979) systems are also central processing units, but they function more as personality integrators. Finally, the sensory (Kearsley & Royce, 1977) and
motor (Powell, Katzko, & Royce, 1978) systems are more peripheral
processing units which function as input/output transducers and
encoders and decoders. These six systems are organized as a
multilevel, hierarchical, system (Mesarovic, Macko, & Takahara,
1970) in which there is a controlled-process layer or stratum
(sensory, motor), a learning-adaptive layer (cognitive, affective),
and an integrative layer (styles, values). In turn, each of the
individual systems is conceptualized as a multilevel, hierarchical,
system, where the elements of the hierarchies are identified via
factor analysis.

The individual systems and major system interactions that are postulated to constitute integrated personality are diagrammed in Figure 1. The major subsystems within each of the six personality systems are also depicted in this figure (for example, the cognitive system is composed of the perceiving, conceptualizing, and symbolizing subsystems, while the subsystems of the motor system are spatiality and temporality). These subsystems can also be described as higher-order factors or dimensions of individual differences. To be more specific, the various subsystems depicted in Figure 1 are identified via third-order factos which subsume a variety of second and first-order (or primary) factors. To date in our research on the structure and dynamics of the various systems of integrated personality, approximately 150 factors have been identified as reliable dimensions of individual differences.[2] The system interpretation of these factors emphasizes their role as psychological processors (cf. Royce, 1963; Royce, Kearsley, & Klare, 1978) which transduce, transform, and integrate psychological information.

Integrated personality has been conceptualized as being hierarchically organized since there are systems which intervene in the functioning of other, lower-level, systems. For example, there are control-decision units, such as cognition or value, which provide coordinating inputs (Mesarovic, Macko, & Takahara, 1970; Royce, 1977) into lower-level systems, such as motor and affective. Such coordinating inputs are depicted in Figure 1 as arrows pointing from higher to lower-level systems, while feedback and other inputs (e.g., feedforward) are represented by the arrows that point toward the higher-level systems. The level of integrated personality, or the supra-system, is regarded as the supremal control unit; the two levels immediately below this one are treated as infimal control units; and the sensory-motor level represents a controlled process. The overall system goal is coordinable only in the event that the supremal and infimal systems' goals can be coordinated by a family of coordination principles (e.g., interaction balance; interaction prediction; and interaction estimation--cf. Mesarovic, Macko, & Takahara, 1970). That is, the overall system goal can be achieved only if there are appropriate coordinating inputs which correctly predict, estimate, or balance intra-level interaction inputs, or if a change in the coordination mode will provide such inputs. Alternatively, the system will fail to attain its goals when there are no appropriate inputs which will coordinate the lower-level systems with respect to the overall system goal.

In general, the lowest level systems (i.e., the sensory and motor) define the boundary structure (Miller, 1973; Berrien, 1968) which transduces and codes information, while the higher levels define the characteristic structures (Cortes, Sprague, & Pzrezowski, 1974) which determine how information is to be

Table 1

System Interactions and Integrations (Royce & Powell, 1978)

	Sensory	Motor	Cognitive	Affective	Style	Value
Sensory						
Motor	Sensory Motor Coordination					
Cognitive	Meaningful Information (Perception)	Ideo-motor Coordination				
Affective	Affective Information (Feelings)	Affect Laden Movement	Cognitive-Affective Interaction			
Style	Sensory Style	Motor Style	Cognitive Style (World View)	Affective Style		
Value	Value Laden Information	Value Laden Movement	Value Laden Cognition (Ideology)	Affect Laden Value (Life Style)	Self Concept	

transformed. This distinction is not without psychological implications. For example, the sensory and motor systems represent "boundaries" to the kinds of information that can be directly admitted to, or output by, the total system. They set the limits of supra-systemic reception or production of information. The characteristic structure of the supra-system, on the other hand, sets limits on the mode or manner of transformation of information processed by the boundary structure. For example, cognitive abilities set limits upon the organism's capacity for the abstract transformation of sensory inputs as well as the capacity for skilled performances.

One final point needs to be made with respect to the postulated structure of integrated personality. That is, the supra-system, as well as its component central processing systems, are construed as goal-seeking systems (Mesarovic, Macko, & Takahara, 1970; Sommerhof, 1969; Bertalanffy, 1955) with internal norms for evaluating positive and negative feedback information. Furthermore, the goals of the system are hierarchically decomposable, as for example when plans can be decomposed into strategies, and strategies into tactics, etc. (Miller, Galanter, & Pribram, 1960; Royce, 1977; Royce & Powell, 1978; Singer, 1975). At the highest level of personality the system goal is to optimize personal meaning, which involves such sub-total goals as establishing a satisfactory life style and evolving an adequate world view (see Figure 1). But life style entails coordination of the value and affective systems (Powell & Royce, 1978) and world-view involves coordination of the style and cognitive systems (Royce, 1973, 1975).

The Structure of Individuality

The basic units of analysis in individuality theory are the dimensions of individual differences which have been identified via the theory and methodology of factor analysis. More precisely, a factor is conceived as a theoretical construct which (1) accounts for observed covariation when viewed in the context of the factor model (Royce, 1963), and (2) is a processor when embedded in the conceptual framework of system-information theory (Royce & Buss, 1976; Royce, Kearsley, & Klare, 1978). In either case the conceptual focus is on factors as O variables rather than S or R variables. Thus, at the dimensional level, we are attempting to describe the trait or behavior phenotypic properties of organisms.

The identification of traits inevitably leads to the issue of how such traits or dimensions are organized, and further, how such elemental parts are organized into larger sub-wholes of the total system. These questions have to do with both structure

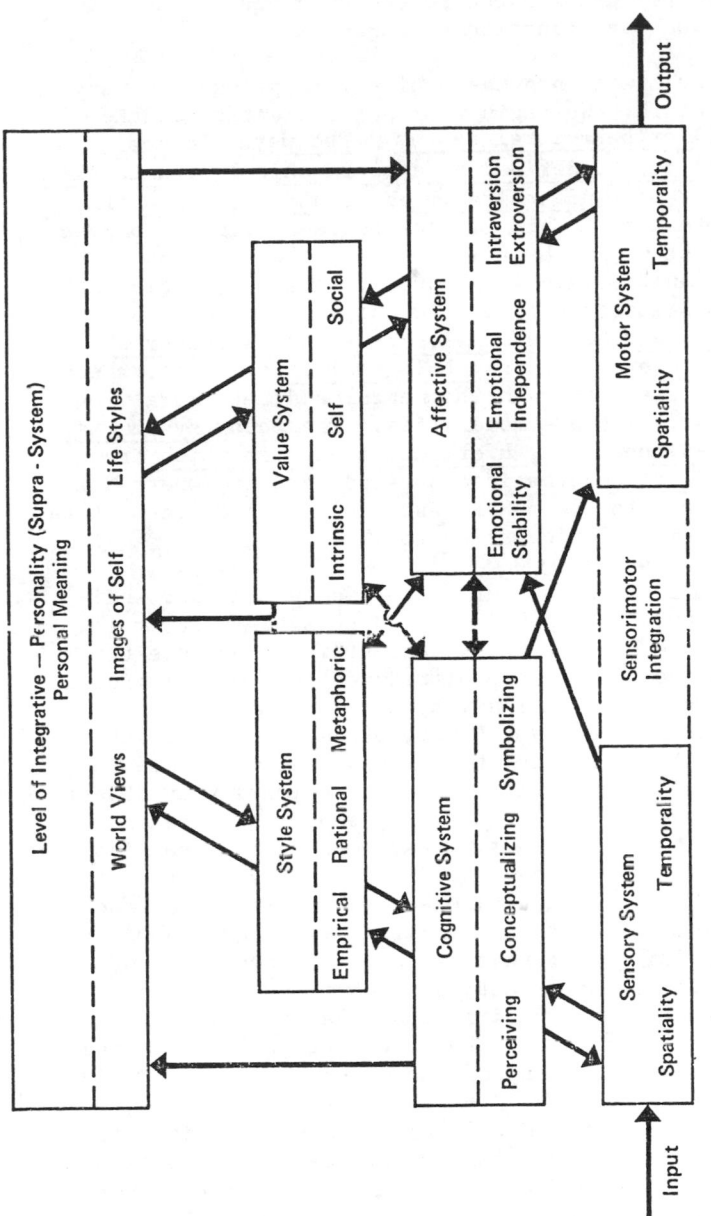

Figure 1. Integrated personality and system interactions (a modified version of Powell & Royce, 1978).

and function--that is, not only with how parts and wholes are organized, but how they provide the necessary coordination and integration of the unitary functioning organism.

In this section I will provide a highly compressed summary of individuality structure. We begin with our conception of the **total psychological or behavioral system**. The psychological system (or personality) is defined as a hierarchical organization of systems, sub-systems, and traits which transduce, transform, and integrate information. This complex supra-system is composed of six major sub-systems, each of which is further decomposed into multi-leveled multi-dimensional sub-systems. We begin with the two boundary systems, the input and output transducers. The sensory system is a multi-dimensional, hierarchical system which transduces physical energy into psychological information, where the term sensation refers to both the mental and behavioral phenomena of the various sense modalities. The motor system is defined as a multi-dimensional, hierarchical system which trans-duces psychological information into physical energy, where the term motor refers to both the mental and behavioral aspects of the organism's skeletal-muscular constitution.

The hierarchical structures of these two systems are indi-cated as Figures 2 and 3, respectively. Both systems carry the same constructs at the highest two strata--this is because these constructs were imposed onto these structures on a priori grounds. The construct at the apex of all six systems, for example, is a type construct by definition (see Royce, 1978a). However, the third-order constructs of spatiality and temporality (indicated via the roman numeral at the left), although primarily hypothetical constructions, are based on the cumulative empirical research on sensory and motor processes. Thus, these constructs were hypo-thesized on the basis of the lower level constructs and the relevant non-factor analytic literature. The primaries of these two systems, on the other hand, are empirically based. However, the empirical basis for factor invariance is stronger for motor factors than it is for sensory factors. But first order motor factors also tend to be more specific than the primaries of the other domains. This accounts for the fact that this system has more levels (i.e., five) than any of the others.

Let us now look at the middle level systems (see Fig. 1), the level which is focused on transformation processes. This level involves the cognitive and affective systems, whose hierarchical structures are shown in Figures 4 and 5 respectively. The cog-nitive system is a multi-dimensional, hierarchical system which transforms information in order to detect environmental in-variants, where the term cognition refers to both the mental and behavioral phenomena of the perceptual, conceptual, and symbolizing sub-systems. Similarly, the affective system is a multi-dimensional,

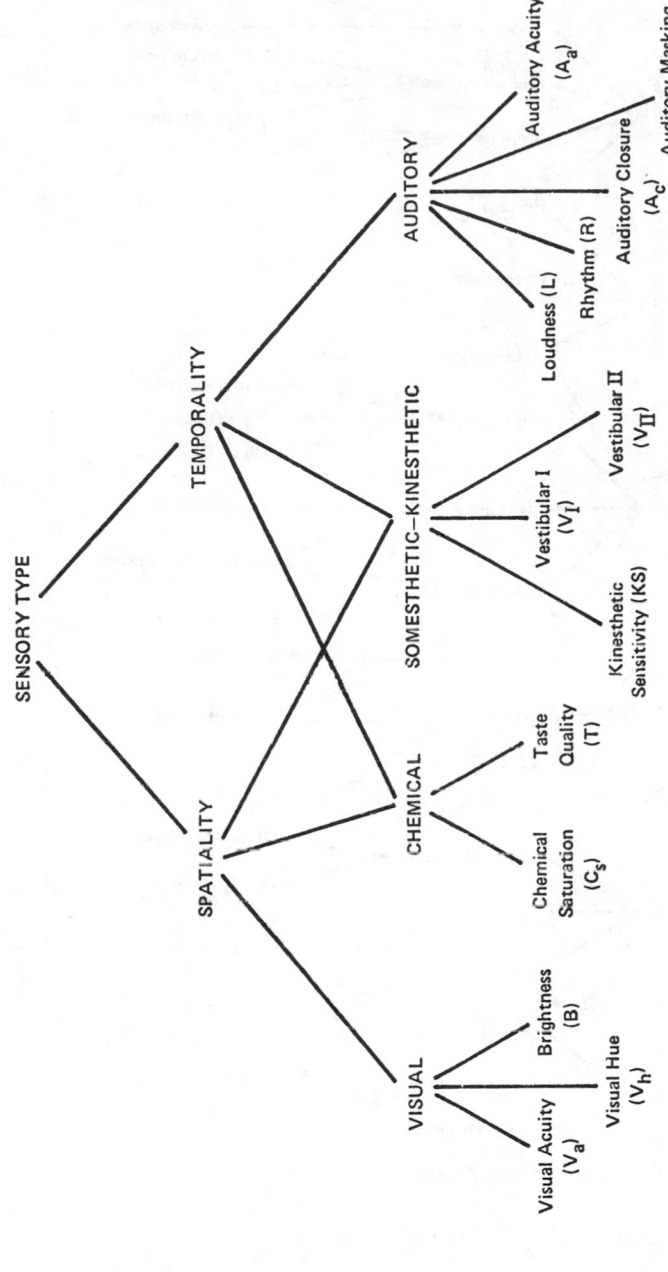

Figure 2. The hierarchical factor structure of the sensory system (Kearsley & Royce, 1977).

586

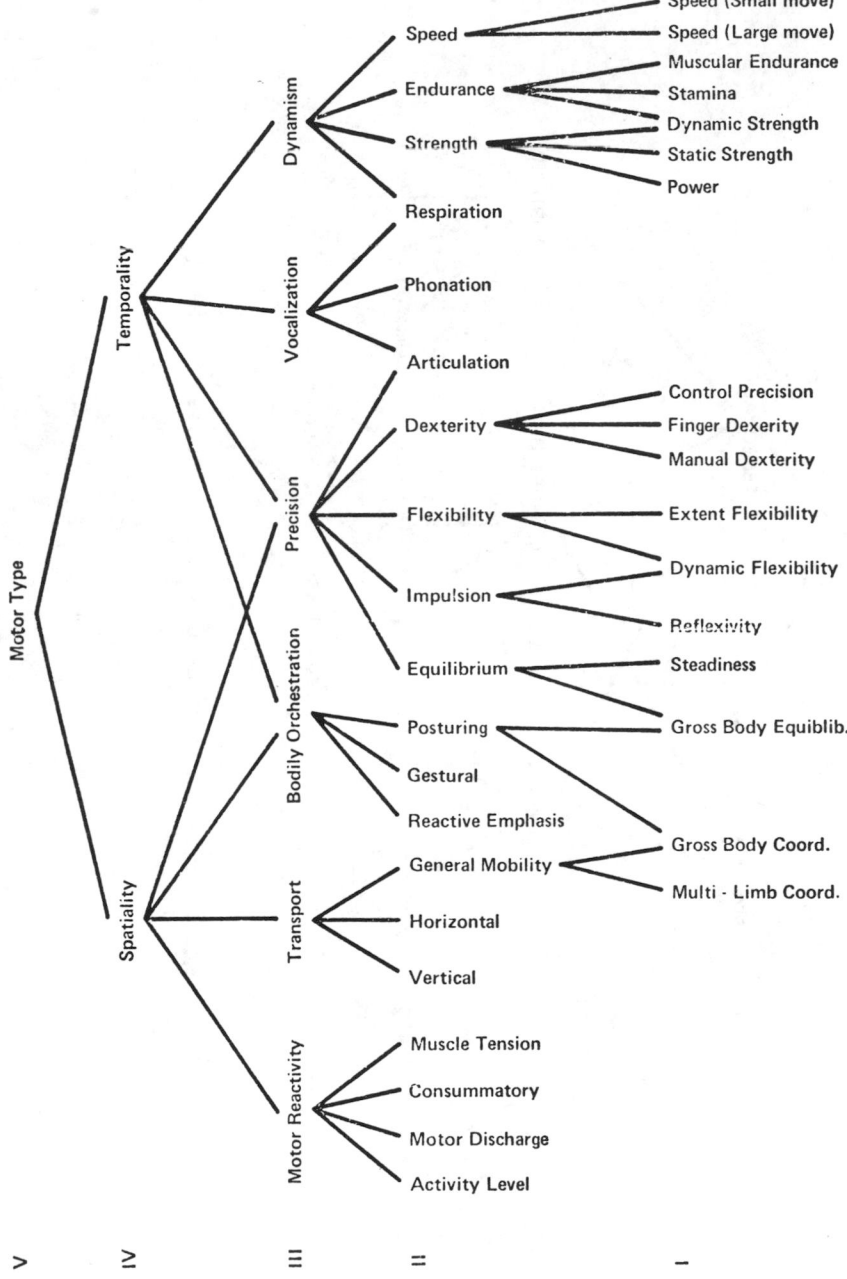

Figure 3. The hierarchical factor structure of the motor system (Powell, Katzko, & Royce, 1978).

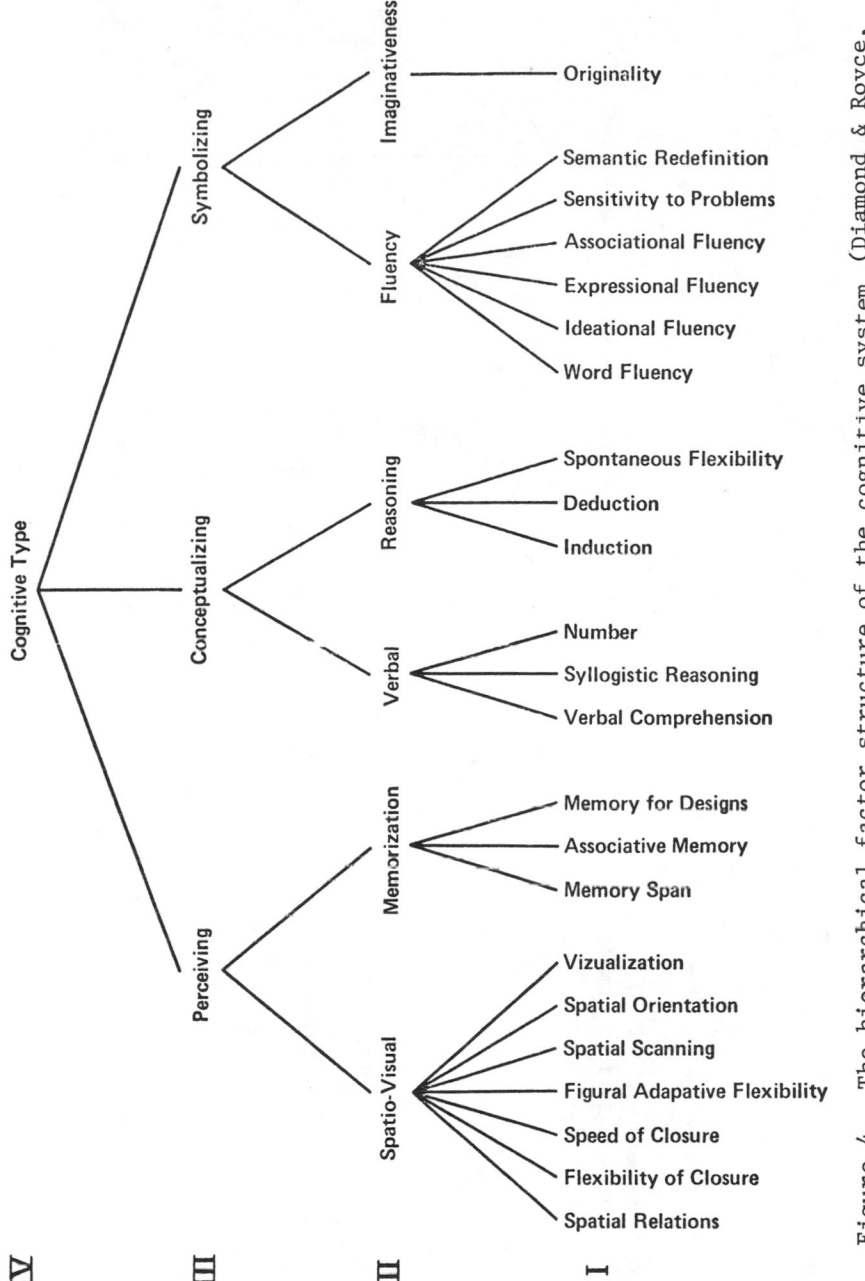

Figure 4. The hierarchical factor structure of the cognitive system (Diamond & Royce, 1978).

588

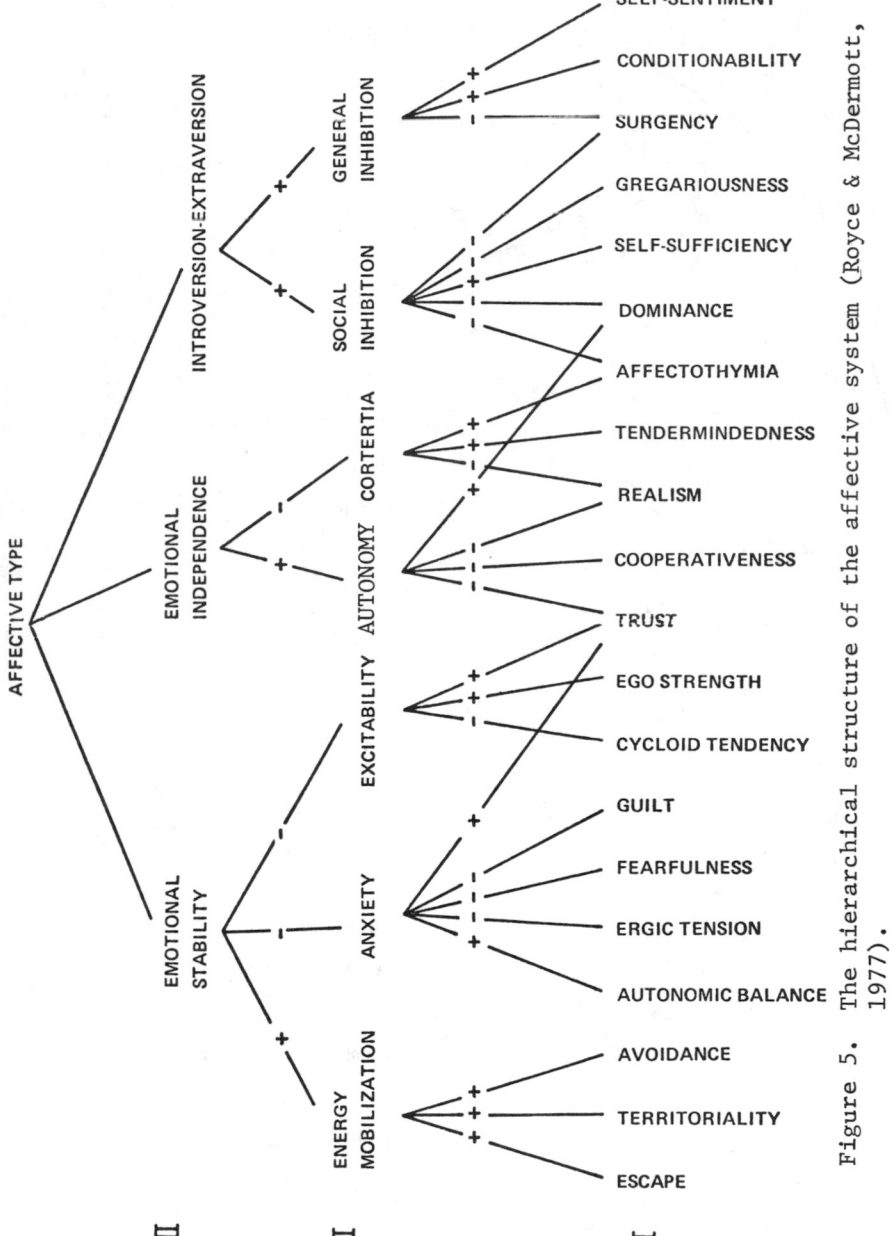

Figure 5. The hierarchical structure of the affective system (Royce & McDermott, 1977).

hierarchical system which transforms information into arousal states, where the term affective refers to both the mental and behavioral phenomena of the emotional stability, emotional independence, and introversion-extraversion sub-systems.

Individual differences in these two domains are the most thoroughly researched of the six systems. This means, for example, that the case for factor invariance is stronger for these two systems than it is for the remaining four, particularly at the primary level. However, the case for invariance is equally strong at the third order of the affective system, primarily because of the extensive experimental research of Eysenck. There is also less extensive confirmation of the second order factors of the cognitive domain. On the other hand, the factorial evidence for third order cognitive constructs is minimal. However, in spite of this deficiency, the cumulative, non-factorial, experimental literature provides a compelling empirico-inductive basis for these higher order constructs (Royce et al., 1978), and there is now one empirical study which provides factorial confirmation of these constructs (Schopflocher & Royce, 1978). The second order constructs of the affective domain, on the other hand, are much less secure. Although there is weak empirical evidence for each of them, it would be very surprising if all of these factors are eventually confirmed. Factorial clarification of the second stratum of the affective domain is the most critical structural deficiency of these two systems.

Finally, we come to the two integrative systems--style and value. The integrative property of these two systems has to do with their role in providing linkages between the cognitive and affective systems. We have defined the style system as a multi-dimensional, hierarchical system which integrates and modulates information by coordinating cognition and affect, and by selecting particular modes of processing. When a style construct is limited primarily to cognitive phenomena we refer to it as a cognitive style. When a style construct is limited primarily to affective phenomena we refer to it as an affective style. And when a style construct links across both cognition and affect we refer to it as a cognitive-affective style. Because of the complexity of stylistic linkages it is impossible to visualize the style hierarchy via a single figure. The basic idea, however, can be conveyed via the following two figures. The two figures combined show the double-barreled nature of the style hierarchy. It should be noted that the same three styles are common to the cognitive styles depicted in Figure 6 and the affective styles depicted in Figure 7. Furthermore, it should also be noted that there are no primary styles. This is the case because style constructs are defined as higher level constructs which subsume cognitive or/and affective constructs. Figures 8 and 9 illustrate such linkages in the case of rational style.[3] Figure 8 shows the

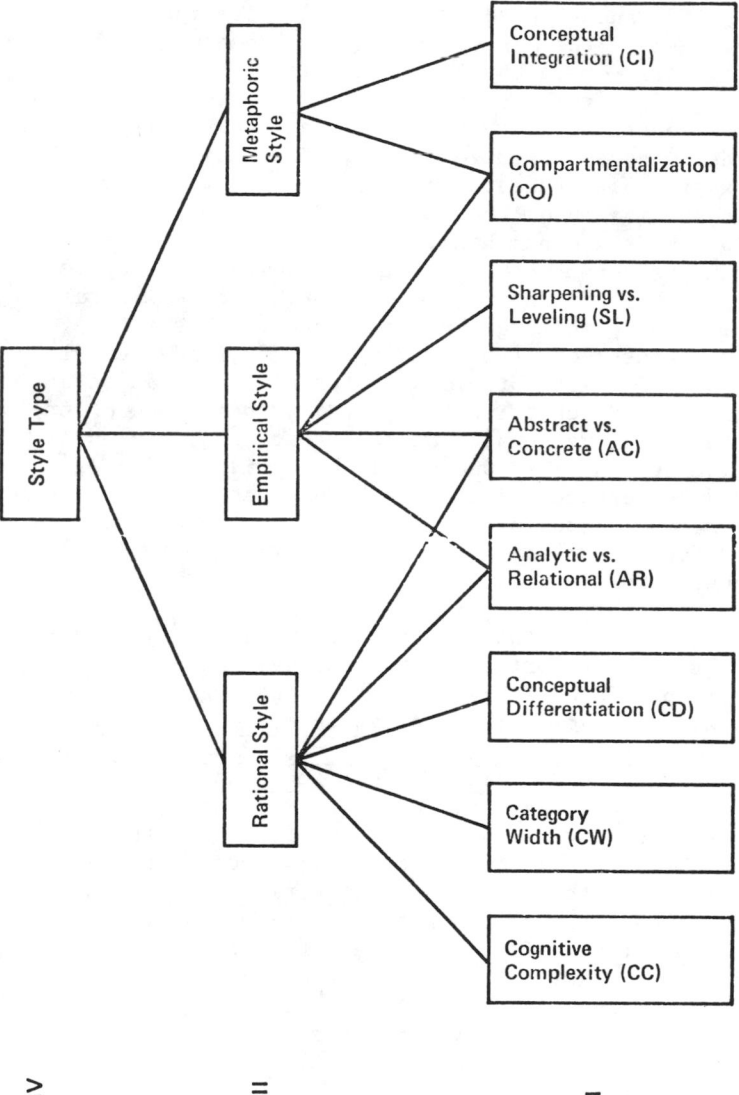

Figure 6. Relationships of higher-order styles and cognitive styles (Wardell & Royce, 1978).

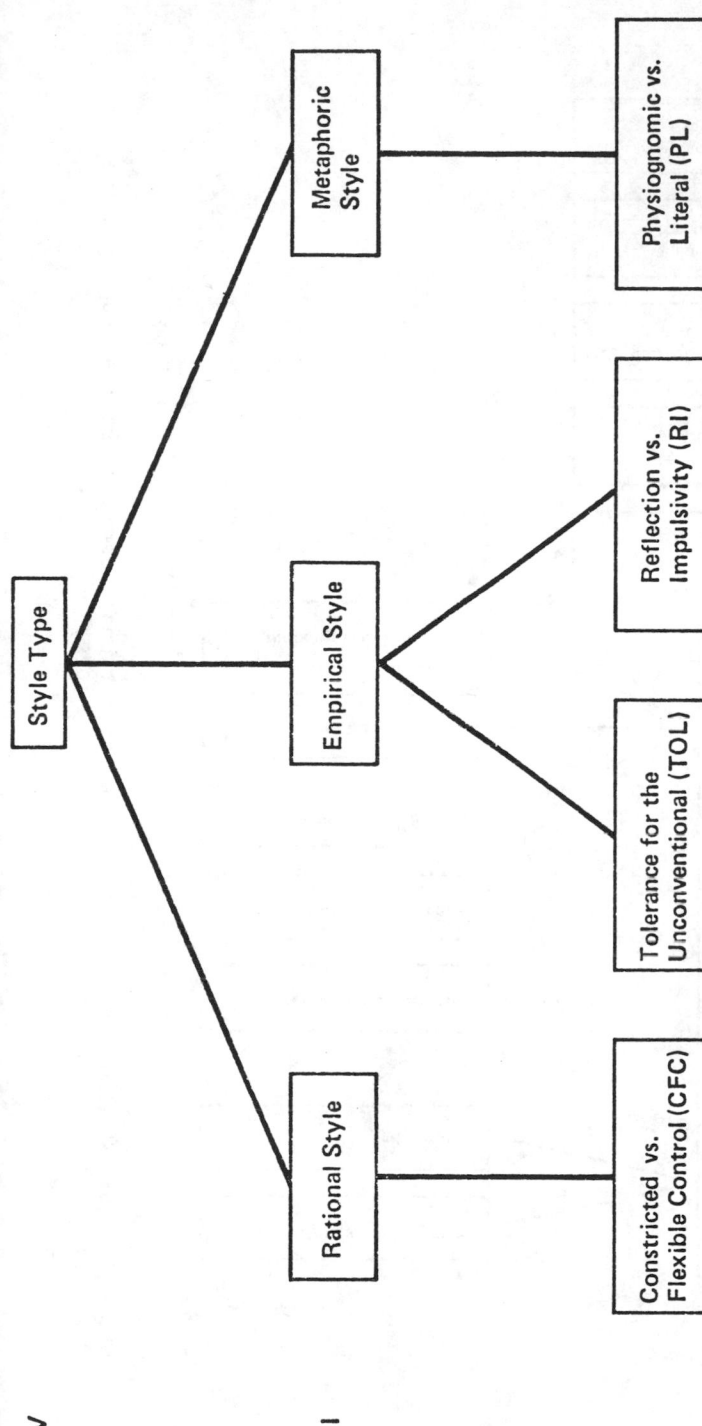

Figure 7. Relationships of higher-order styles and affective styles (Wardell & Royce, 1978).

592

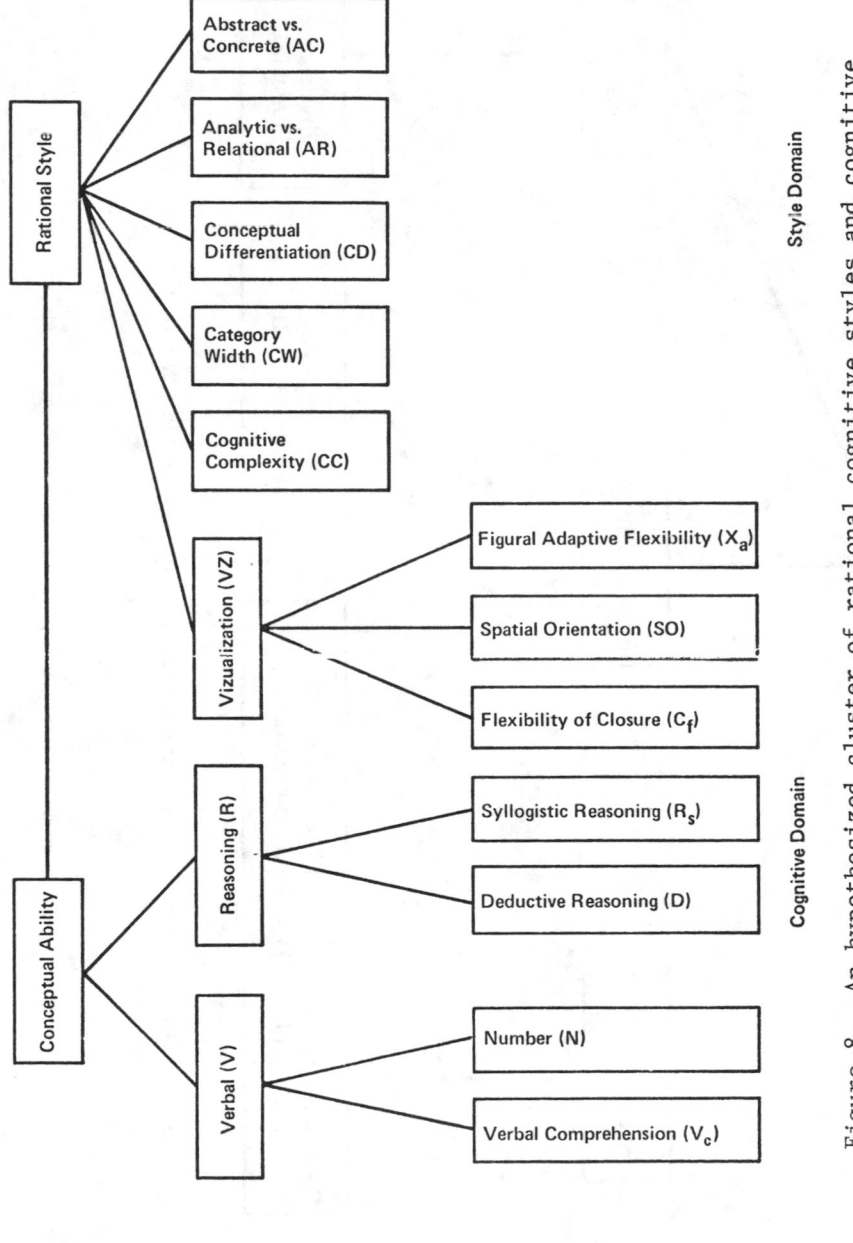

Figure 8. An hypothesized cluster of rational cognitive styles and cognitive abilities (Wardell & Royce, 1978).

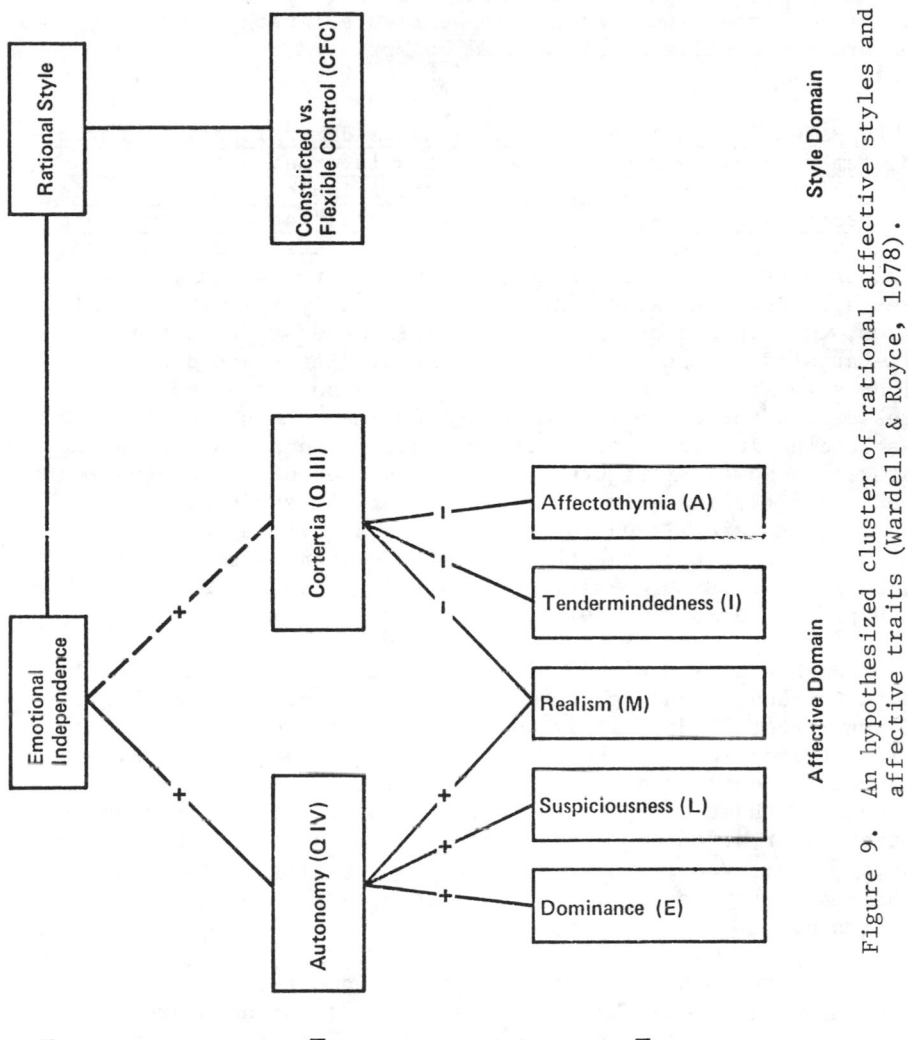

Figure 9. An hypothesized cluster of rational affective styles and affective traits (Wardell & Royce, 1978).

linkages of the third order construct of rational style to the
cognitive system via the third order as well as a direct linkage
to the second order visualization factor and four second order
cognitive styles. Figure 9 shows the linkage of rational style
to the relevant affective factors via the third order affective
factor of emotional independence as well as a linkage to the
second order affective style labeled constricted vs. flexible
control.

The value system is defined as a multi-dimensional, hierarchical system which integrates and modulates information by coordinating cognition and affect to achieve specifiable goals, by satisfying specifiable needs, or by selecting specifiable informational
content, where normative refers to both the mental and behavioral
aspects of affective (i.e., needs) and cognitive values (i.e.,
interests). Because value linkages are formally similar to style
linkages, two figures are also required in order to show the
double-barreled nature of the value system. These are depicted
in Figures 10 and 11. Once again, it should be noted that these
figures depict three sub-systems--in this case the higher order
values labeled intrinsic orientation, self orientation, and social
orientation. However, Figure 10 shows linkages of these constructs
to needs or affective values, whereas Figure 11 shows how these
same constructs are linked to interests or cognitive values. Although not shown, it is hypothesized that the value system has
conceptual linkages to cognition and affect which are similar to
those depicted for styles (e.g., see Figures 8 and 9).

Although both style and value constructs are critical for
our eventual understanding of personality integration (see Figure
1 and see Royce, 1978a), it is unfortunately the case that the
empirical foundation for these constructs is relatively weak.
While there is considerable empirical literature for all the
constructs in these domains, there is a critical need for factor
analytic confirmation of these constructs. Many of the style
constructs, for example, have not been factorially identified,
and the claims for factor invariance are generally weak in the
value domain.

The fact that there is one less level in the style domain
than in the value domain suggests that style constructs are
broader, in general, than value constructs. The greater content-
laden aspect of values is probably the major reason for the greater
specificity of value constructs. That is, both needs (affective
values) and interests (cognitive values) have to do with what
humans commit themselves to, whereas styles are focused on how
commitments are made.

Finally, it should be noted that while both styles and values
are linkage constructs, individuality theory holds that styles

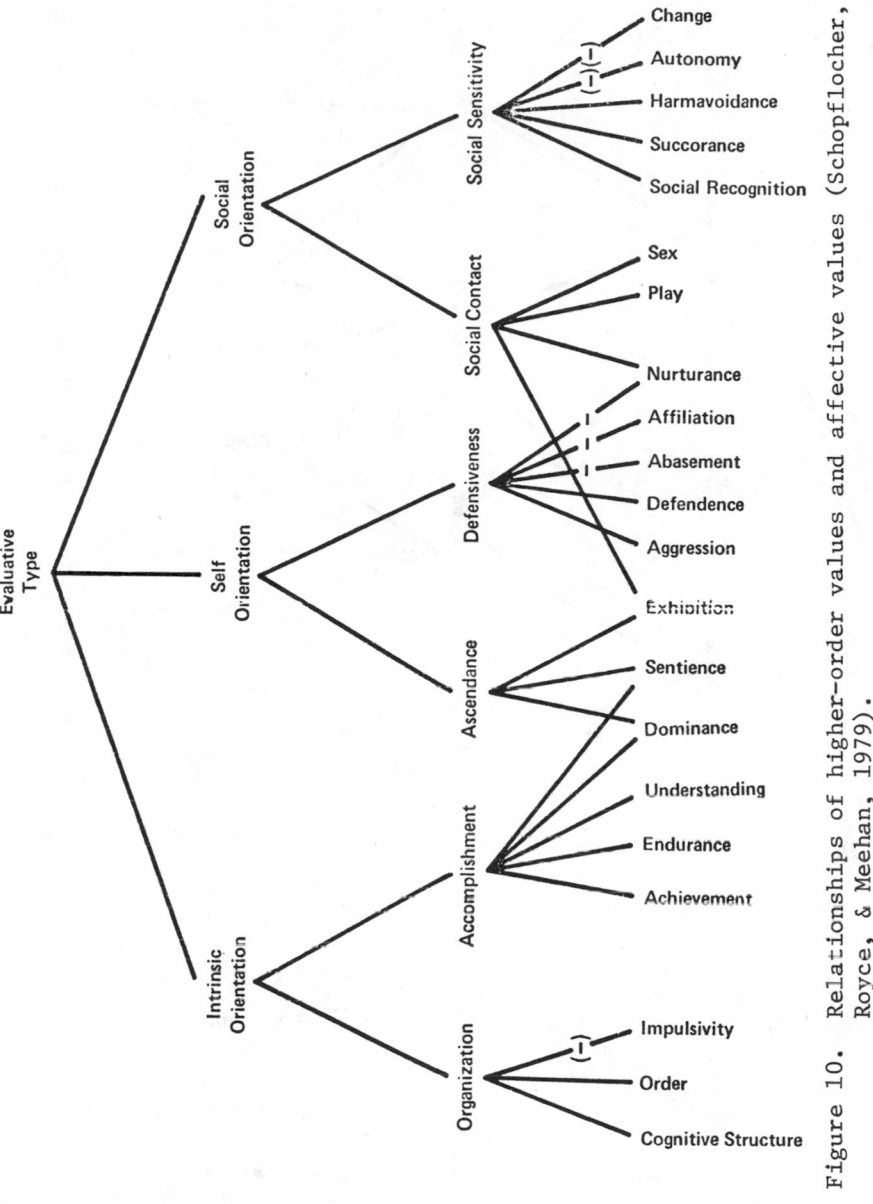

Figure 10. Relationships of higher-order values and affective values (Schopflocher, Royce, & Meehan, 1979).

596

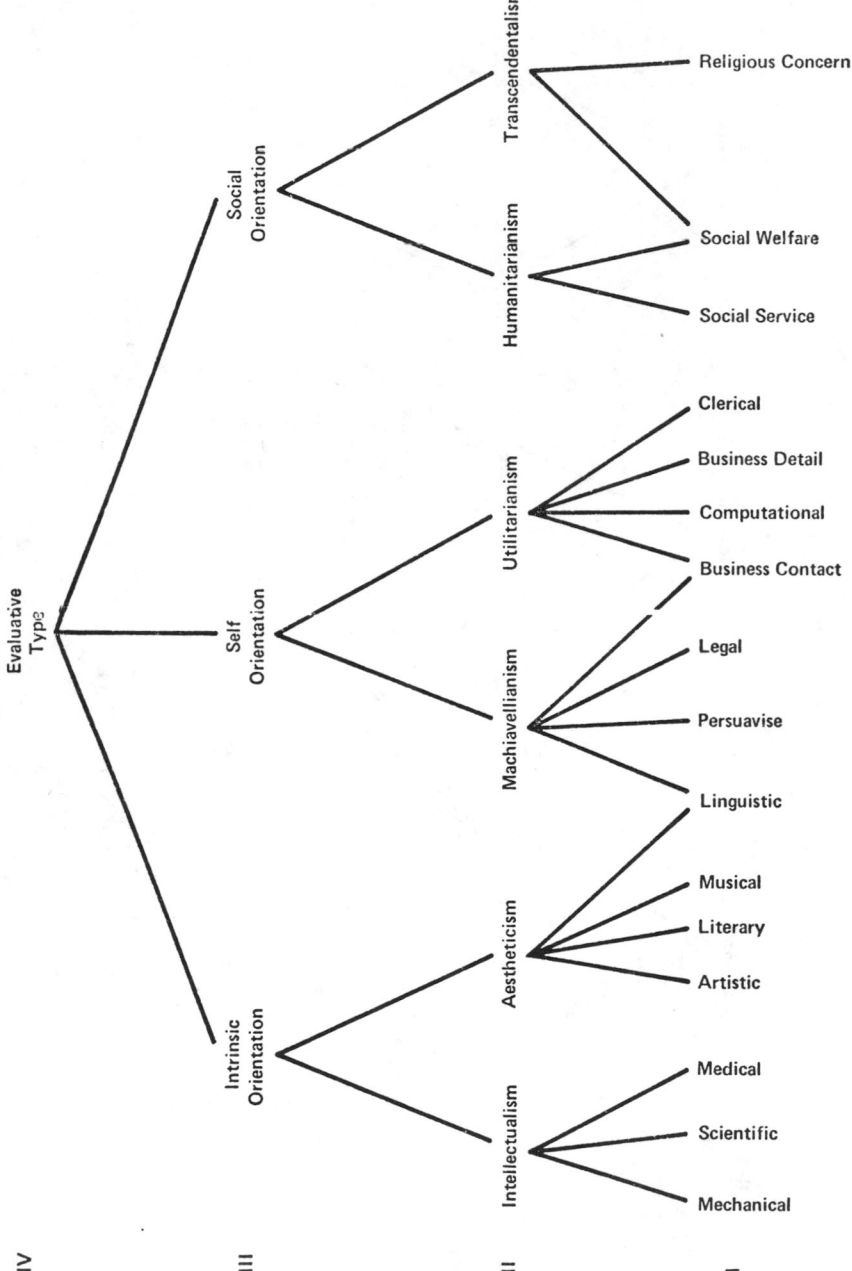

Figure 11. Relationships of higher-order values and cognitive values (Schopflocher, Royce, & Meehan, 1979).

are more closely aligned with the cognitive system, whereas values
are more closely linked to the affective system. Elaborations of
this point are provided in accounts of world view (Royce, 1964,
1974, 1975), which is analyzed as an output of the style and cognitive systems, and accounts of life style (Royce, 1977; Powell
& Royce, 1978), which is viewed as an output of the value and affective systems. Considerations such as these take us in the
direction of process or dynamics, the topic of the next section.

Individuality Dynamics

The system dynamics aspect of individuality theory is dealt
with via a comprehensive description of functional interactions
of relevant dimensions at different phases of information processing. This approach is based on the biological principle
that function is dependent upon structure. Thus, whereas the
figures above indicate the structural inter-relationships between
the dimensions, what follows will focus on their functional interactions. The point is that complete understanding of the dynamics of individuality requires a detailed information flow account of both factor interactions and the temporal sequentiality
of these interactions. Thus, factors are construed as organismic
processors which transmit, transform, and integrate information
as it proceeds from S inputs to R outputs (Royce, 1963; Royce,
Kearsley, & Klare, 1978). This kind of analysis involves details
of simultaneous, sequential, and recursive processing for specified situations. For example, if the task at hand involves a
highly complex visual display, such as a pilot is confronted
with, the implication is that many of the perceptual dimensions
will be processing simultaneously. On the other hand, the involvement of various conceptual and sensory-motor factors is dependent upon the psychobiological idiosyncrasies of that particular pilot (i.e., his multi-dimensional profile), and when these
mediational processors are needed as the pilot proceeds through
take-off, ascent, level flight, descent, and landing. While the
multi-dimensional model of factor analysis has been applied to a
wide range of pure and applied problems, research to date has
been essentially of a static nature. Thus, the typical investigation identifies the relative weights (i.e., factor loadings)
to be assigned to a given predictor variable, but these beta
weight equivalents do not shift with the changing requirements of
the situation.

Although we have provided process analyses for each of the
six systems, one example should suffice to illustrate what is
involved. The example I have selected comes from the affective
domain. It involves a situation where some fear-arousing stimulus is introduced to the individual. While such a situation
does not exclude the other systems, especially the cognitive and

motor systems, affective processing is primary. And, although the entire affective system would be activated, the Royce and McDermott (1977) analysis indicates that a fear-arousing situation is primarily mediated by the emotional stability sub-system. This aspect of the analysis is indicated on both the left and right sides of Figure 12. While the left side is concerned with the present moment activation of the three sub-systems, the right side is similarly focused on memorial reactivation (via the emotional stability activation of the memory component). Let us now provide further elaboration of the functioning of emotional stability, the dominant sub-system in this situation. Activation of this sub-system, presumably via the limbic system (see Royce & McDermott, 1977; and Mos, Lukaweski, & Royce, 1977), involves activation of the second order factors of energy mobilization, excitability, and anxiety. Thus, manifestations of energy mobilization and excitability would tend toward avoidance and escape, while anxiety would manifest itself via the first order factors of autonomic balance, ergic tension, and fearfulness.

Secondary processing via the introversion-extraversion and emotional independence sub-hierarchies are also shown in Figure 12. What is not shown are the pre-affective, non-memorial cognitive aspects of the process, and the post-affective motor outputs. It should also be pointed out that the current state of knowledge does not permit us to specify the temporal details of information processing. Thus, the detailed specification of sequential, parallel, and recursive processing remains as a challenge for the future. However, specification of the functional relationships among factor identified dimensions, which is what we have accomplished to date, is a necessary prior step in any event.

The Current Status, Prospects, and Limitations of the Theory

While the analysis above is focused on the structural-functional aspects of the six systems of individuality, the extended theory involves much more. Some idea of the total effort can be grasped from inspection of Figure 13.

The long range goal is to offer an account of the entire psychological system (indicated as project #1 in Figure 13; this will eventually appear in book form, see Royce & Powell, in preparation). But this involves embedding factor theory (project #2) in the broader conceptual framework of system-information theory (project #3). Although a preliminary overview statement of the extended theory was put forward at the Third Banff Conference (Royce, 1973), that statement did not include the needed amalgamation with system and information theory (Royce & Buss,

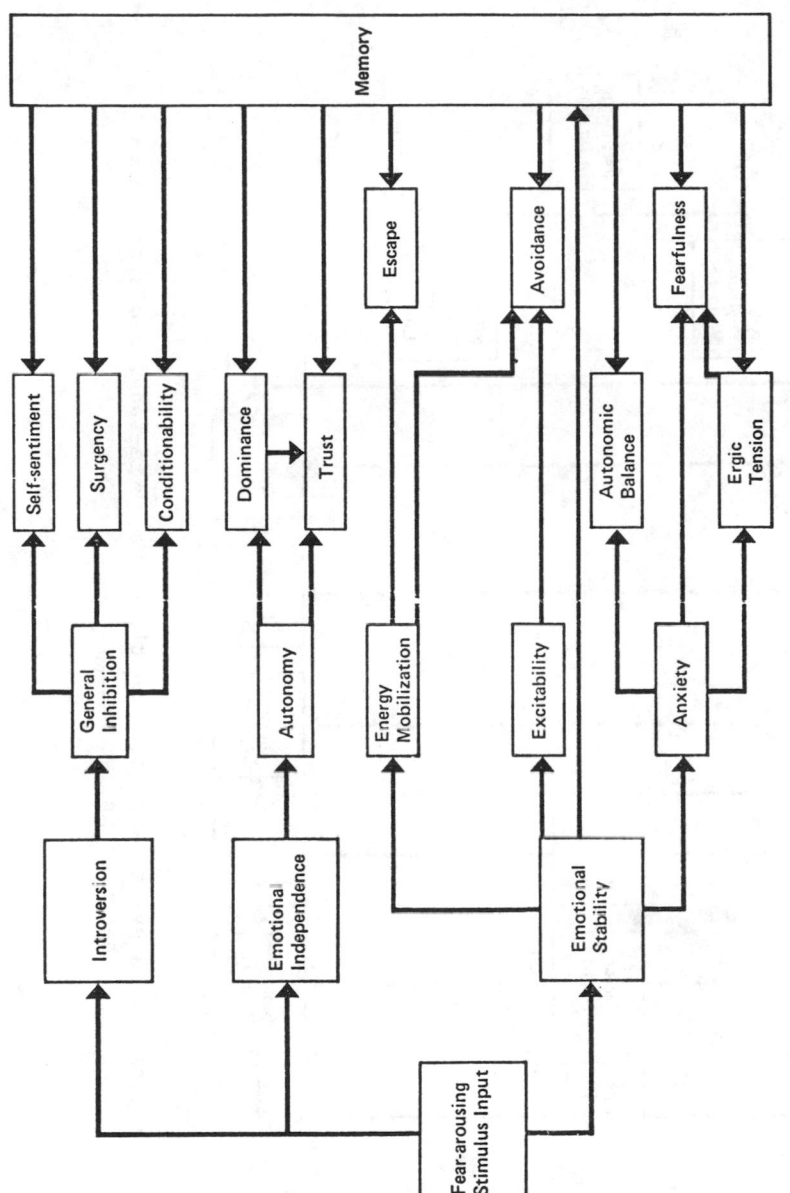

Figure 12. Orienting-adapting-emotive relationships in response to a fear-arousing situation (Royce & McDermott, 1977).

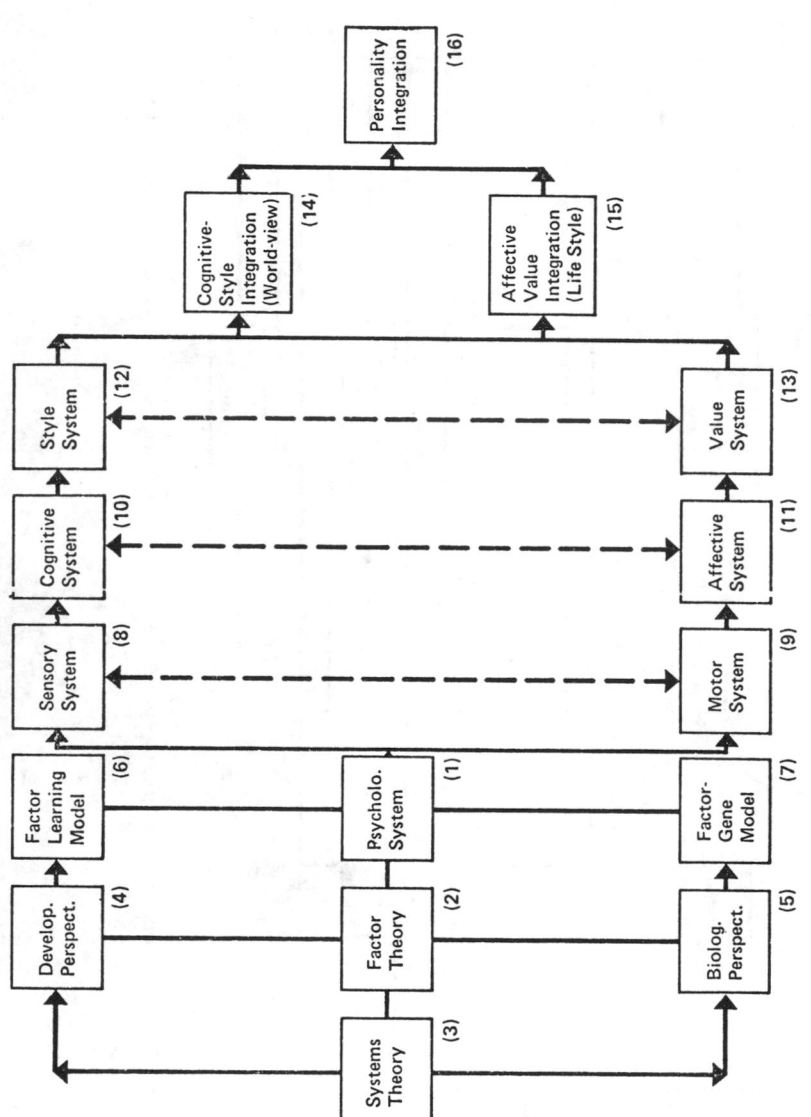

Figure 13. A system-analytic, multivariate, life-span, biopsychological theory of individuality.

1976). However, the subsequent mini-theories of each of the six systems (i.e., projects 8-13 in Figure 13) do incorporate the beginnings of such an amalgamation. (See Kearsley & Royce, 1977, for the sensory system; Powell, Katzko, & Royce, 1978, for the motor system; Diamond & Royce, 1978, and Powell & Royce, 1978, for the cognitive system; Royce & McDermott, 1977, for the affective system; Wardell & Royce, 1975, 1978, for the style system; and Schopflocher, Royce, & Meehan, 1979, for the value system.) That is, in each case we have interdigitated relevant system-information and factor analytic concepts and principles. Examples include the realization that higher order factors lie at the apex of sub-systems, and further, that specifiable principles of hierarchy theory apply with equal force to both factor theory and system theory.[4]

However, we have just begun to look at the complications of system interactions and integrations. Although we have already provided insights in our efforts at the system level, the more molar level of system interaction holds the prospect of providing conceptual breakthroughs. The reason is that, in spite of many gaps within any one system, the amalgamation of factor theory and system-information processing provides analytic power for getting at the major stumbling block in psychological theorizing--the part-whole problem (i.e., project #16; see Royce, 1978a). In an effort to account for complex behavior, we have been able to show, for example, that the model can accommodate such outputs as world-view and life style. These are very molar-holistic notions, but, because of the rich part-whole structure of the multi-dimensional, system dynamics model, it is possible to offer an account of behavioral complexes. We have demonstrated, for example, that individual differences in world-view (project #14 in Figure 13) are primarily a function of the style and cognitive systems (Royce, 1964, 1974, 1975). We have also offered an account of variations in life style (project #15) as due primarily to the functioning of the value and affective systems (Royce, 1977; Powell & Royce, 1978). It is anticipated that additional molar complexities of similar significance will emerge from a more complete analysis of system interactions and integrations. Fifteen such system interaction outputs are summarized in Table 1. These were derived by a consideration of all possible paired combinations of the six systems. In addition to the already completed elaborations of world-view and life style, we are currently working on analyses of sensory-motor coordination (Powell, Katzko, & Royce, 1979), self concept (Powell, Schopflocher, & Royce, 1979), and cognitive-affective interaction (Royce & Diamond, 1979). It is anticipated that each of these paired system outputs will receive further elaboration in the context of subsequent analyses of the parts and wholes of integrated personality (Royce, 1978a).

Returning to Figure 13, we see that, in addition to the

centrality of the factor-system conceptual framework, the approach
we have adopted also includes a developmental perspective
(project #4), a biological perspective (project #5), the factor-
learning model (project #6), and the factor-gene model (project
#7). I have withheld these projects for last as they are directly
germane to the major task at hand--to offer a factor-gene account
of individuality. Although all of these perspectives are required for a full account of individual differences, in this
paper attention will be focused on the developmental perspective
and the factor-gene model. Although we have initiated the inquiry concerning the factor-learning model (Royce, 1973; Buss,
1973), further developments along these lines will occur as part
of a general model of factor change (i.e., multivariate learning,
multivariate development, and multivariate behavior genetics).
We are also delaying a complete analysis of the biological correlates of factorially identified dimensions (i.e., project #5)
until we've concluded our analysis at the psychological level
(however, see Kearsley & Royce, 1976; and see Royce & McDermott,
1977, and Royce, 1978b, for the beginnings of a biological
analysis of affect). We have, however, made considerable headway with projects 4 (developmental perspective) and 7 (the factor-
gene model). Since both of these projects are crucial for what
follows, I will briefly summarize these efforts as a basis for
what follows.

A former student and colleague, Allan Buss, gave particular
attention to a variety of metatheoretic and methodological problems which are inherent to an understanding of multivariate development (Buss, 1974a,b,c). This was followed by more substantive theoretic efforts (Buss & Royce, 1975), including a first
statement of multivariate development (see Kearsley, Buss, &
Royce, 1977, concerning cognitive development, and Powell, Holt,
& Royce, 1979, concerning the development of all six systems).

The first version of the factor-gene model was put forward
over twenty years ago (Royce, 1957). It provided the conceptual
framework for a long range experimental research program (e.g.,
see Royce, 1978b). Fortunately, the findings which ensued confirmed the model. While previous theoretical-empirical syntheses
of the factor-gene model and multivariate developmental theory
have been confined to the affective (Royce, 1978b) and cognitive
(Royce, 1977) systems, the present effort will cover all six
systems.

II. THE FACTOR-GENE MODEL

Factors and the Problem of
Behavioral Phenotypes

Since the assessment of gene effects can only occur via observable phenotypes, it is clear that the identification of reliable and valid phenotypes is crucial to genetic analysis.
While this is a relatively minor problem in the case of physical
characteristics, such as height and eye color, it has been a
major stumbling block in research on behavior genetics, particularly when dealing with complex behaviors such as intelligence
and emotionality. And, although the power of factor analysis
lies in its ability to identify components of behavioral complexes, relatively little effort has been devoted to replicating
factor identified components.

The point is that invariant factors provide the behavior
geneticist with a convincing basis for the identification of
stable behavioral phenotypes. Failure to take this step, particularly when dealing with complex behavior, constitutes a
serious methodological deficiency (Royce, 1973). In particular,
it leads to contradictory data and conceptual confusion. The
major reason is that the same concept (e.g., emotionality) is
used for different subsets of variables which implicitly reflect
unknown, but different underlying dimensions of complex behaviors.
Since such a situation involves different dimensions masquerading
under the same, apparently univariate dimension, investigators
cannot help but (unknowingly) report apparently contradictory
findings. Unless bivariate studies are preceded by multivariate
studies which get at the dimensionality issue (Royce, 1950, 1977),
investigators will continue to be harassed in this way. Unfortunately, although behavior geneticists should not be subject to
this error (e.g., note the polemics which accompany the heritability of general intelligence, usually assessed by omnibus tests
such as the Binet or the Wechsler) because of their sophistication
about phenotypes, psychological testing, laboratory investigations,
and individual differences, the situation is unsatisfactory in
this field as well (e.g., see Royce, 1966). The factor-gene
model was developed as one way to deal with the issue of identifying stable behavioral phenotypes.

The Relationship Between Factors
and Genes

We take our point of departure from the basic factor equation,
which states that any behavior, indicated as a standard score
z_j (where $z = \frac{X}{\sigma}$) is equal to the product of the loading (a_{jm})

of the measurement j on factor one, times the amount of this factor possessed by individual i (F_{1i}), plus the product involving the loading of the variable on factor two ($a_{j2}F_{2i}$), plus the product involving the loading on factor three, etc., until all the common factor variance is accounted for. In simplified mathematical terms this has been expressed as follows:[5]

$$Z_{ji} = a_{j1}F_{1i} + a_{j2}F_{2i} + a_{j3}F_{3i} + \ldots\ldots + a_{jm}F_{mi} \tag{1}$$

If we now restate this in the more compact matrix form, we get

$$Z = AF \tag{2}$$

where Z is a matrix of standardized test scores, A is a matrix of factor loadings, and F is a matrix of factor scores. However, since the focus of our attention is on the underlying components rather than the original observations, we solve for F and get

$$F = A^{-1}Z \tag{3}$$

But, since this involves an impractical form of F because of the fact that there is no inverse for A, we turn to a variation of F (Harman, 1976), as follows:

$$F = A'R^{-1}Z \tag{4}$$

A major aspect of individual differences theory (or individuality theory) involves an elaboration of hereditary and environmental sources of variation. Thus, we must find a way to link heredity and environment to factors. One approach is to decompose the A matrix into its hereditary, environmental, and interaction and correlational components, as follows:

$$A = H + E + I + C \tag{5}$$

Substituting in (4), we get

$$F = H'R^{-1}Z + E'R^{-1}Z + I'R^{-1}Z + C'R^{-1}Z \tag{6}$$

Thus, the factor-gene model involves an elaboration of the first term of equation six:

$$F_H = H'R^{-1}Z \tag{7}$$

The second term is the basis for the factor-learning model:

$$F_E = E'R^{-1}Z \tag{8}$$

The third term deals with heredity-environment interaction effects:

$$F_I = I'R^{-1}Z \tag{9}$$

and the fourth term deals with heredity-environment correlation effects:

$$F_C = C'R^{-1}Z \tag{10}$$

The key terms for our purposes are F_H and H', where F_H refers to a matrix of factor scores and H' is based on the underlying genotype. A visual version of the proposed model, which is exemplified by intelligence and its components, is depicted in Figure 14.[6] The key concept is that there are multiple factors at both the behavioral and genetic levels, and that they are linked via a variety of unspecified, intervening psycho-biological mechanisms (labeled psychophysiological genetics). Note that in both the behavioral and genetic domains many elemental factors account for a complex. On the behavioral side many different factors (both first order factors such as space and memory, and higher order factors such as g_1 and g_2) or behavioral phenotypes account for the complex we call intelligence. On the genetic side, various combinations of many genes account for a particular behavior phenotype such as S or M. Thus, a person may inherit all of the capital letter forms of the gene pairs of the space factor (i.e., AA, BB, CC, DD, EE, FF, GG). Since this means that the individual has the maximum number (seven chosen arbitrarily) of capital letter genes for this particular genotype, and assuming optimal environmental conditions, we would expect him to perform at the highest possible level in tasks involving the perception of spatial relationships. If another person inherited genes f, g, h, i, j, k, and l from the available gene pairs of the M factor, we would expect a minimal performance on pure memory tasks.

Such profile differences are brought out most dramatically when the element or component aspect of factor analysis is contrasted with the component obfuscating results of more traditional psychometric approaches. For example, if we average the two profiles depicted in Figure 15, we get exactly the same value,

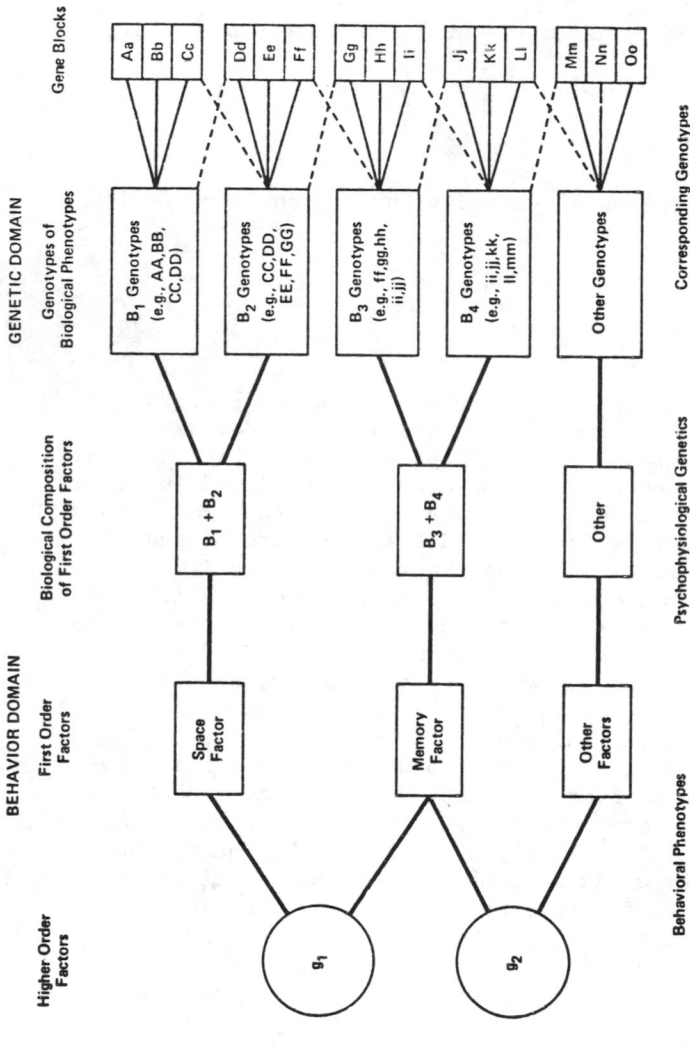

Figure 14. Showing the most probable linkage between the multifactor theory of psychology and the multiple-factor theory of genetics (A modified version of Royce, 1957a). The capital letters signify the presence of the trait or phenotype; the small letters mean the absence of the characteristic.

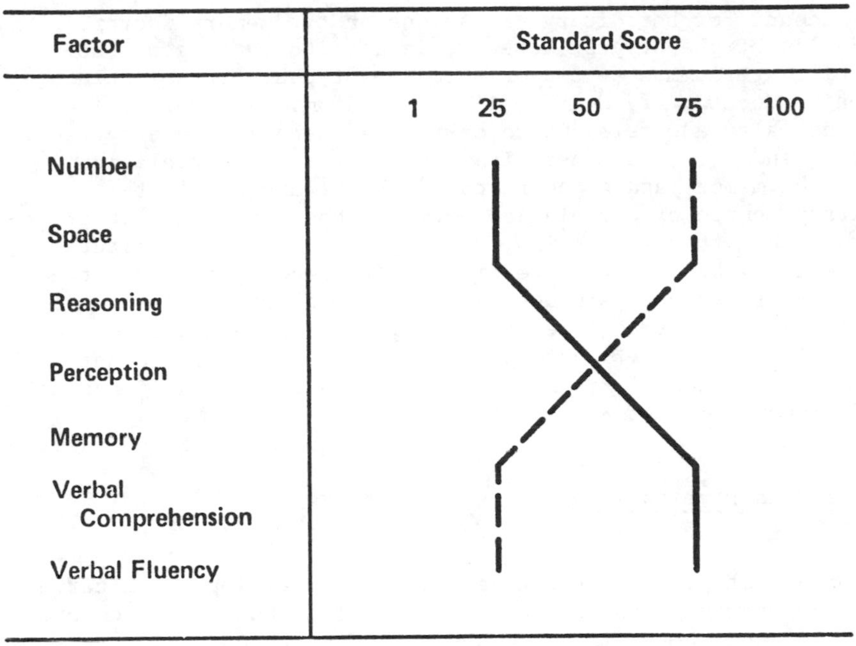

Factor	Standard Score				
	1	25	50	75	100
Number					
Space					
Reasoning					
Perception					
Memory					
Verbal Comprehension					
Verbal Fluency					

Fig. 15. Showing two persons, A (solid line) and B (dotted line) with the same IQ but with opposite mental ability profiles (Royce, 1957b).

50, or an I.Q. of 100. If the I.Q. was the only information available, we would conclude that these two individuals are intellectually identical. It is obvious, however, that they are identical only in their performance on the perception factor. Otherwise person A (solid line) is essentially verbal in his intellectual strength whereas person B (broken line) is essentially quantitative. These high and low peaks of mental ability profiles are, of course, well established in the psychological literature.

Note that the hereditary correlate for each factor is polygenic, and that the usual genetic mechanisms, such as dominance, epistasis, pleiotropy, and sex linkage, are operative, depending on the factor in question. It is important to note that the factor-gene model does not imply a one factor--one gene linkage, as erroneously claimed by Fuller and Thompson (1960). Nor does the model imply that there are mutually exclusive blocks of genes with corresponding uncorrelated factorial phenotypes. Rather, it implies that specifiable subsets of the gene pool account for the hereditary variation and covariation of factors. For example, gene pairs Aa through Gg combine, via biological phenotypes 1 and 2, to account for hereditary variation on the space factor, and gene pairs Ff through Ll combine, via biological phenotypes 3 and

4, to account for hereditary variations on the memory factor. Covariation of phenotypes, however, is attributed to gene subsets which are common to two or more phenotypes. These include gene pairs Cc, Dd, Ff, Gg, Ii, Jj, Ll, and Mm. However, only four gene pairs are relevant to correlated behavior phenotypes-- namely Ff and Gg, as the hereditary basis for the correlation between the memory and space factors, and Ll and Mm, as the hereditary source of correlation between the memory and "other" factors. The other gene pairs, Cc, Dd, Ii, and Jj, constitute the hereditary basis for those biological phenotypes (i.e., the full range of psychophysiology, such as brain function, hormone function, and biochemical mechanisms) which are relevant to specifiable first order factors (gene pairs Cc and Dd account for the covariation of B_1 and B_2 and gene pairs Ii and Jj account for the covariation of B_3 and B_4).

The Life-Span Development
of Factors

The prototypic, quantitative, life-span developmental curve for factor growth is shown in Figure 16. The abscissa is chronological age and the ordinate is the scaled score on a given factor. There are three parameters of psychological interest: K_1, K_2, and K_3. On the age dimension, maturity (M), or maximum performance, is indicated by K_2, and the onset of senility (S), or performance level before death, is indicated by K_3. The location of the y-intercept, K_1, indicates the extent of prenatal development, or the degree to which the factor is present at birth (B).

The value of the parameter K_2 indicates the maximum factor performance level (P) which occurs at maturity (M). If a factor does not reach optimal development in the life-span of an individual (i.e., continues to either increase or decline over the entire life-span), the value of K_1 will take the value of the factor score at birth or death (for a decrease or increase, respectively). The curve segment K_1-K_2 indicates the rate of developmental change during childhood, adolescence, and early adulthood.

The parameter K_3 represents the factor score at the onset of senescence (S) (or death if there is no senescent period). It is to be expected that factor scores will always decline in any post-senescence measurement. The segment of development represented by the K_2-K_3 portion of the curve is, of course, factor change over the major part of the life-span of the individual.

In Figure 16 we showed the prototypic factor as a function of age. The relationship between actual performance level and

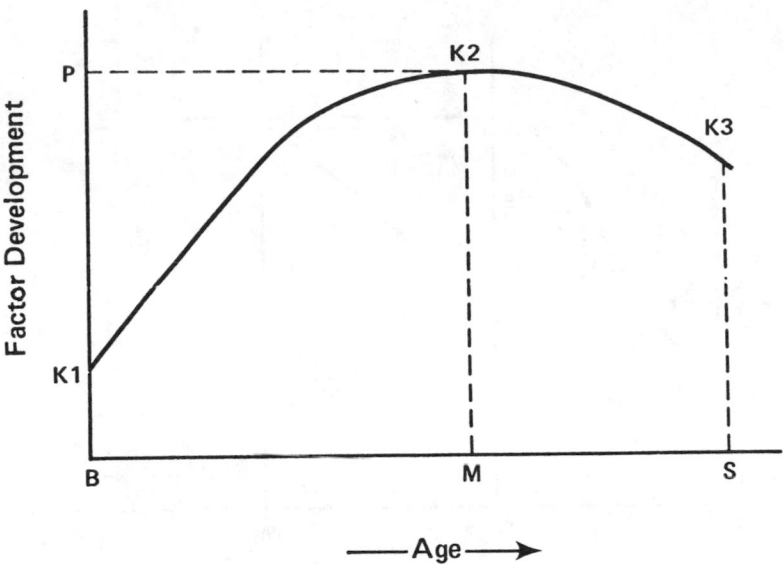

Fig. 16. The generalized life-span development curve (modified version, Royce, 1973).

performance level limit is brought out in Figure 17. Here we see a difference between actual and potential performance level for a given factor, where actual performance level refers to the observed score on a given factor, and potential performance level refers to a heredity-environment determined theoretical upper limit.

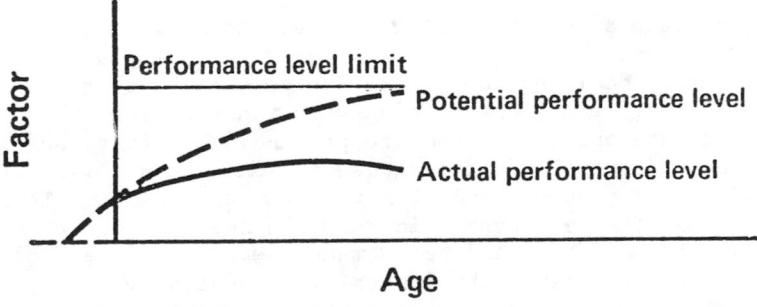

Fig. 17. The relationship between performance level and performance level limit (Royce, 1973).

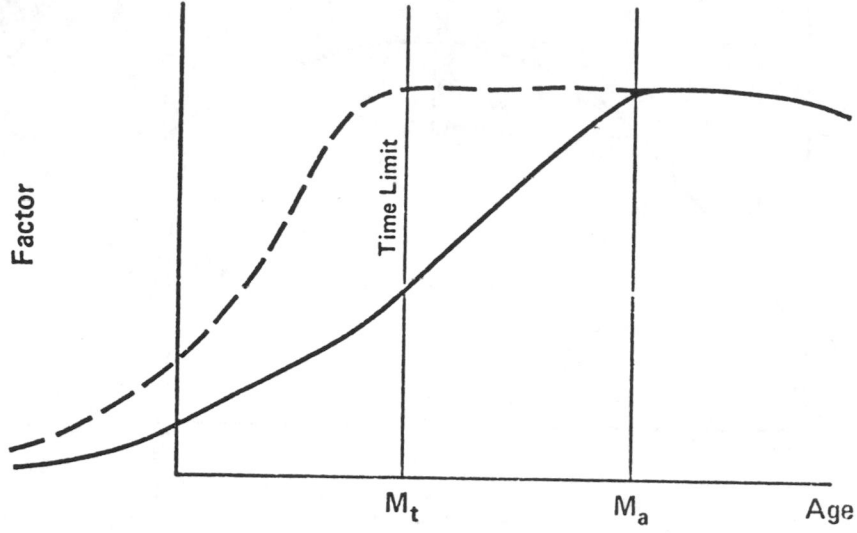

Figure 18. The relationship between performance and age of maturity (Royce, 1973).

A similar set of concepts is called for when we focus on age of maturity, the age at which maximum performance occurs. However, in this case (see Figure 18) the difference between actual (M_a) and potential (M_t) performance is a matter of timing rather than level of performance per se. M_t denotes the heredity-environment determined earliest possible age of maturity.

The Concepts of Heredity and
Environment Dominant Factors

Let us now take a closer look at the relationships between heredity, environment, and development. Note, for example, that actual performances depicted so far are due to both heredity and environment. Hence, it will be necessary to tease out exactly how such effects are operating. Before proceeding further, however, let me offer several additional definitions. I shall refer to the age of maturity performance limit as the time limit. This limit implies that the performance in question does not occur earlier for a given genotype and performance level regardless of amount of training or other environmental interventions. The performance level limit refers to the highest possible level of performance for a given genotype in interaction with the most optimal environment, independent of time (i.e., given infinite time). Furthermore, by hereditary effect I shall mean any observed variance due to the genotype. And, by environmental

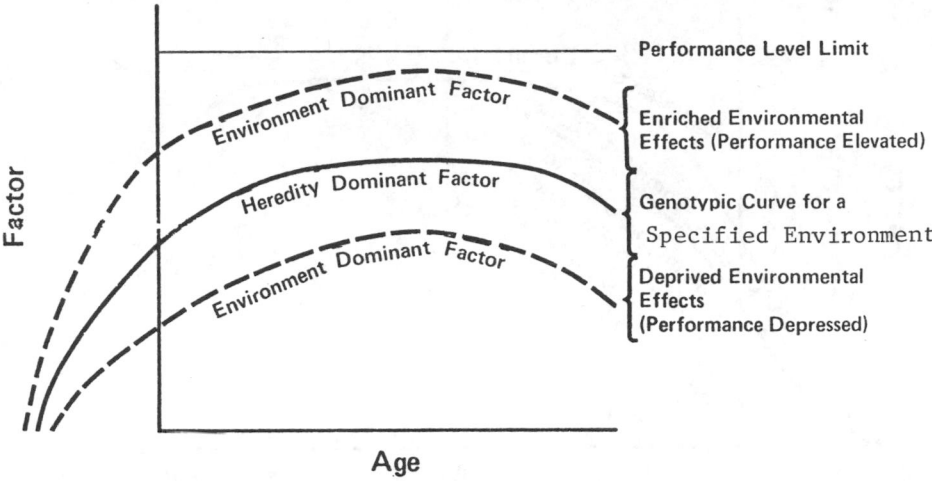

Fig. 19. Heredity and environment dominant factors in terms of performance (Royce, 1973).

effect I shall mean any observed variance due to differences in the environment. If we now combine the concepts of performance level and age of maturity curves with those of genetic and environmental effects we can characterize two classes of factors under the rubrics of heredity dominant factors and environment dominant factors. Elaboration of what is meant by these concepts can be implemented by reference to Figures 19 and 20. The solid line curve in Figure 19 shows the performance level for a particular genotype in interaction with a specified environment. To the extent performance can be shifted in either direction from this genetic base line we get environmental effects. If the effect of environment is severe, performance level will be drastically changed, as in the case of the two dotted line curves labeled environment dominant. If the effect is minimal, there will be no significant departure in observed performance; hence the solid line curve is labeled heredity dominant. Similar effects concerning age of maturity have been idealized in Figure 20. Environmental effects can either speed up, retard, or have no effect on age of maturity. Those factors (dotted line curves) which are highly susceptible to such effects have been labeled environment dominant, whereas the solid curve has been labeled heredity dominant.

Thus, a heredity dominant factor is a primarily genetically determined dimension with a developmental curve which is highly resistant to environmental effects. It is statistically definable in terms of relatively small deviations from the genotypic curve despite attempts to induce environmental effects. An environment

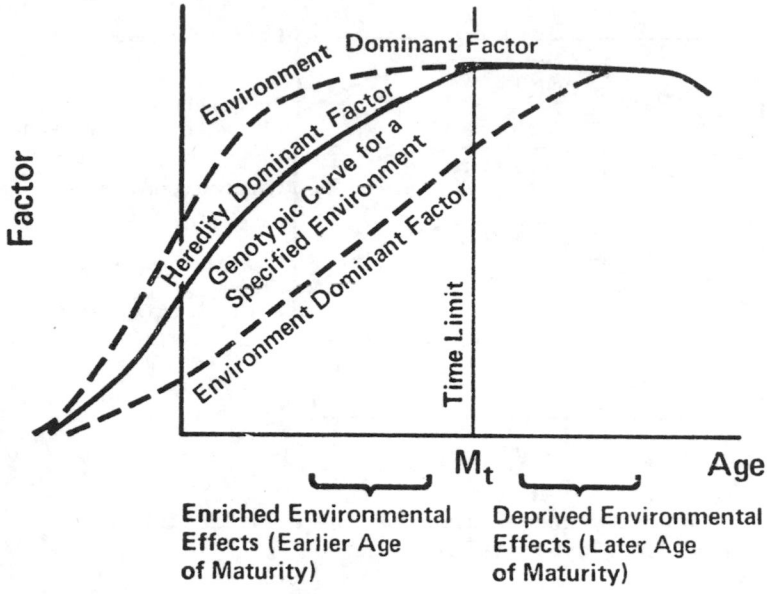

Fig. 20. Heredity and environment dominant factors in terms of age and maturity (Royce, 1973).

dominant factor is a dimension with a primarily environmentally determined developmental curve which is relatively uninfluenced by hereditary effects. It is statistically definable in terms of a relatively large deviation from the genotypic curve as a result of attempts to induce environmental effects.

It should be obvious that these are idealized extremes, and that most cases, being subject to both environmental and genetic influences, will fall in between. We will refer to such inter-action cases as partial heredity dominance or partial environmental dominance, in accordance with the direction of the major effect. Furthermore, it should be apparent that complete or partial hereditary or environmental dominance may occur in connection with either or both genetic-environment limits. The point of immediate importance is that this analysis provides a plausible theoretical basis for empirically finding out the extent to which performance on factors is due to hereditary and environmental causes.

The Empirical Findings for Each
    of the Six Systems

Since the focus of this paper is on the factor-gene basis

of individual differences, no attempt has been made to summarize
the effects of environmental manipulation of factors. Furthermore, while a taxonomy of behavioral phenotypes as heredity
dominant, environment dominant, and intermediate would carry
considerable theoretical and practical weight, it is clear that
the extant empirical work is not adequate to the task. Thus,
the present effort is put forward as a step in the desired direction. We will, therefore, focus our efforts on the primary target; namely, to summarize the evidence on the hereditary basis
of factor identified behavioral phenotypes. However, in those
cases where there is no such evidence, we will allude to the
most relevant non-factor analytic findings.

The available methods for estimating hereditary effects fall
into three categories: the classical methods of analysis, family
resemblance analysis, and biometric analysis. Investigators who
are identified with the classical methods include Holzinger
(1929), Neel and Schull (1954), Nichols (1965), and Vandenberg
(1966). The family resemblance methods include MAVA (Cattell,
1953, 1960), path analysis (Wright, 1934; Spuhler, 1976), and regression analysis (DeFries et al., 1976). Biometric analysis,
which was developed as an answer to the problem of quantitative
inheritance, evolved out of early contributions by Fisher (1918),
and has culminated in the recent contributions of Falconer (1960)
and Mather and Jinks (1971).

It is generally conceded that the biometric methods, such as
the Jinks-Mather diallel cross, are potent methods, particularly
when they are combined with good experimental controls. It is
also generally conceded that such controls can be more readily
implemented by employing animal rather than human populations.
Thus, studies which combine animal subjects with biometric analysis usually provide the most convincing evidence. On the other
hand, investigations which are limited to human populations and
the classical statistical methods (such as heritability coefficients) are particularly lacking in experimental controls, and
are evaluated accordingly. And family resemblance methods, which
were explicitly designed for investigations involving human subjects, are viewed as more satisfactory than the classical methods
but not as informative as the biometric methods.[7]

In order to deal with this broad range of findings we have
evolved a three category scheme for assessing the strength of
the evidence for claims of a hereditary effect. We will use the
terms strong, moderate, and minimal as arbitrary, qualitative
distinctions. For example, a laboratory investigation involving
a highly replicable behavioral phenotype (such as advoidance conditioning), highly inbred mouse strains, and a diallel cross
mating design, would be evaluated as a strong test of a hereditary
effect. Heritability coefficients obtained on human populations,

on the other hand, will usually be evaluated as weaker tests of a hereditary effect. However, in spite of the confounding effects of the heritability coefficient, it would also be inappropriate to ignore these findings, particularly when accompanied by careful investigation. We have, therefore, evolved the following general guide concerning the probability of a genetic influence for a specifiable heritability coefficient:

no hereditary effect - coefficients ranging from .00 - .10
minimal hereditary effect - coefficients ranging from .11 - .30
moderate hereditary effect - coefficients ranging from .31 - .50
strong hereditary effect - coefficients greater than .50

The findings will be presented in two categories--those for which there is factor-gene evidence, and those for which there is no such evidence. The first category includes the cognitive, affective, and style systems, and the second category includes the sensory, motor, and value systems.

The Cognitive System

The generally held view is that intelligence is the most heritable of the various facets of personality. In fact, it has been estimated that 60% to 80% of the observed variation in general intelligence (as measured by the I.Q. or its equivalent) is due to genetic variation. Estimates of this kind are typically based on heritability coefficients, twin studies, and global measures of intelligence such as the Binet or the Wechsler. Despite the limitations inherent in human studies (e.g., see Kamin, 1974), the impact of the cumulative evidence (e.g., see Figure 21), namely that there is strong evidence for hereditary sources of intellectual variability, is impressive. These data are impressive because of the consistency of the findings over such a wide range of observations (e.g., 56 studies involving 99 groups, covering a period of 50 years of investigation). The data involve correlations between paired individuals of varying degrees of genetic relationship (e.g., unrelated individuals reared apart at one extreme and identical twins reared together or apart at the other extreme). The overall conclusion is that intellectual similarity varies with genetic similarity.

If we turn our attention to factorially identified behavior phenotypes, on the other hand, it is surprising how few investigations have been carried out in the cognitive domain. In fact, direct evidence on the genetic correlates of cognitive factors is limited to the Primary Mental Abilities and a handful of studies. These are briefly summarized in Table 2.

Most of the studies summarized in Table 2 involve monozygotic

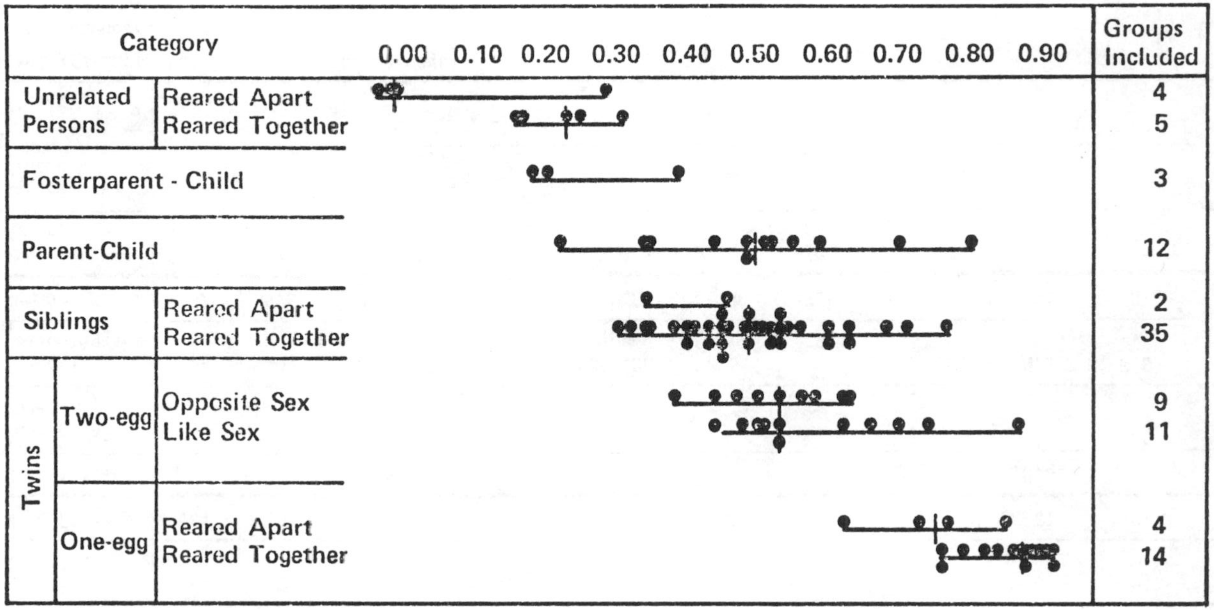

615

Figure 21. Correlations between IQs of paired individuals of genetic relations ranging from none to complete (Erlenmeyer-Kimling & Jarvik, 1963). Dots represent correlations from single studies; median is shown by short vertical lines.

Table 2

Factor Heritabilities In The Cognitive Domain

Relative Strength of Evidence	Factor	Blewett 1954		Thurstone-Strandskov 1955	Vandenberg 1961*	Vandenberg 1962		Vandenberg 1964*	Vandenberg 1965		Vandenberg 1966*
		HE†	SL†	SL	SL	HE	SL	SL	HE	SL	SL
Strong	Verbal Comprehension	.68	.01	.01	.01	.62	.01	N.S.	.43	.01	.05
	Spatial Relations	.51	.05	.01	N.S.	.59	.05	.01	.72	.01	.01
	Word Fluency	.64	.01	.01	N.S.	.61	.01		.55	.01	.01
	Memorization			N.S.		.20	N.S.			N.S.	
Moderate	Perceptual Speed										
	Inductive Reasoning	.64	.01	N.S.	N.S.	.28	N.S.	N.S.	.09	N.S.	
	Number	.07	N.S.	N.S.	N.S.	.61	.01	N.S.	.56	.01	.01
Minimal	Associate Memory										
	Associative Fluency										
	Ideational Fluency										

Classical Heritability Coefficient

†HE = Heritability Estimate; SL = Significance Level

*Reported in Vandenberg, 1968

Table 2 (Continued)

Relative Strength of Evidence	Factor	Multiple Abstract Variance Analysis Cattell, et al. 1955, 1957	Intraclass Correlation Coefficient Partanen, et al. 1966			Regression Analysis** DeFries, et al. 1976		Path Analysis Spuhler 1976	
		HE	MZ	DZ	SL	Sample 1	Sample 2	HE	SL
Strong	Verbal Comprehension	.65	.75	.51	.01	.65	.58	.77	.001
	Spatial Relations		.58	.33	.01	.61	.44	.86	.001
			.60	.39	.01				
	Word Fluency		.81	.54	.01				
	Memorization		.69	.35	.01	.44	.31	.83	.001
			.58	.29	.01				
	Perceptual Speed					.46	.32	.78	.001
Moderate	Inductive Reasoning	.80							
	Number	.65 to .80	.73	.55	.01				
			.72	.45	.01				
Minimal	Associative Memory	.80							
	Associative Fluency	.65							
	Ideational Fluency	.65							

** Upper bound estimate of heritability

and dizygotic twin samples and classical heritability estimates.
The findings typically take two forms, a statistical significance
level or a heritability ratio. These studies are summarized in
the left half of Table 2. The remaining studies, summarized in
the right half of the table, involve a wide range of strategies.
Intraclass correlation coefficients also involve monozygotic and
dizygotic twins, but all three of the remaining techniques include
a variety of family resemblance measures, such as those obtaining
between parents and offspring and between siblings. Such studies
are important because they extend the range of observations from
which to make inferences concerning heritability.

It should be noted that Table 2 is divided into three segments. The upper segment includes three factors (verbal comprehension, spatial relations,[8] and word fluency) with heritability
estimates that are both large and highly replicable (e.g., only
two negative findings).

The middle segment of Table 2 identifies a set of factors
(memorization, perceptual speed, inductive reasoning, and number)
for which the heritability estimates are not quite as high nor
are they as replicable. On the other hand, it should be pointed
out that the two studies in support of significant heritabilities
for the factors of memorization and perceptual speed are based on
the Colorado-Hawaii project--an investigation of mammoth proportions and considerable sophistication. For example, the exten-
siveness of the test battery (i.e., 15 tests and 4 factors for
both the Spuhler and the DeFries et al., studies) and the sample
sizes (e.g., 1,490 families and 5,077 individuals in the DeFries
et al., study) are impressive. In both studies the authors report significant hereditary effects for all four factors--with
the effects being greater for the verbal comprehension and spatial
relations factors than for memorization and perceptual speed.

Finally, the lower segment of Table 2 includes three factors
(associative meaning, associational fluency, and ideational
fluency) with heritability estimates which should be interpreted
with caution. They are based on early MAVA studies of Cattell
and associates (Cattell, Blewett, and Beloff, 1955; Cattell,
Stice, & Kristy, 1957; Cattell, 1971) and they provide only indirect evidence for the heritability of the factors indicated in
Table 2. The evidence is indirect because Cattell was investigating the genetic and environmental bases for individual differences on the second order constructs of crystallized (g_c) and
fluid (g_f) intelligence. Cattell concluded that about 80% of
the total variance is hereditary in the case of fluid (i.e., biological) intelligence, and that about 65% of the total variance
is hereditary in the case of crystallized (i.e., cultural) intelligence. From these findings I have made the inference that
factors subsumed under each of these second order umbrellas should

have similar heritability estimates. If we confine ourselves to those Cattell factors which have been incorporated in the cognitive hierarchy shown in Figure 4, there are two fluid intelligence primaries (associative memory, and inductive reasoning) and three crystallized intelligence primaries (verbal comprehension, associational fluency, and ideational fluency). The inference is that the "fluid" factors have heritabilities around .80 and that the heritabilities of the "crytallized" factors are around .65. In the case of the "mixed" or fluid-crystallized factors (e.g., the number factor from Figure 4) the implication is that these heritabilities should be greater than 65% but less than 80%.

By way of summary, there is direct evidence for a significant hereditary effect for seven (e.g., Thurstone's Primary Mental Abilities) of the thirty-two factors of the cognitive hierarchy (see Figure 4), and indirect evidence for three additional cognitive factors (i.e., a total of around 31% of the cognitive system). The combination of high replicability and high magnitudes of heritability estimates indicates that a hereditary effect is particularly strong for three factors--verbal comprehension, spatial relations, and word fluency. However, the evidence is only moderately strong in the case of the memorization, perceptual speed, inductive reasoning, and number factors, and the evidence is weakest in the case of the associative memory, associational fluency, and ideational fluency dimensions. The moderate-minimal distinctions are based primarily on the relative robustness of the findings in the moderate category (e.g., the Colorado-Hawaii study), and the fact that the findings in the minimal category are based on scientific inferences of a circuitous nature.

The Affective System

Research on the hereditary basis of factor identified behavioral phenotypes in the affective domain is extensive. Furthermore, it includes investigations at all levels of the affective hierarchy. For ease of presentation the findings will be presented separately for the lower and higher order factors. We begin with the lower order factors.

Most of the studies summarized in Table 3 involve twin samples and some form of either MAVA, the classical heritability ratio, or a combination of both. In most cases the evidence is presented as a heritability coefficient; in the remaining cases significance levels are indicated. It should be noted that the evidence indicated in the first column (Cattell, 1973) is actually a summary of some half dozen studies. Because of this the Cattell estimates constitute the primary basis for the three groupings indicated in

Table 3

Heritability Estimates For Primaries In The Affective Domain

Relative Strength of Evidence	Factor	Multiple Abstract Variance Analysis		Biometric Analysis		Classical Heritability Coefficient		
		Cattell 1973*	Cattell et al** 1957	Royce & Assoc. 1970,73a,73b,75	Royce & Assoc. 1960,71,72,74	Vandenberg 1962		Other Investigator
		HE†	SL†	SL	SL	HE	SL	HE
	Surgency	.60				.31	N.S.	
	Avoidance				very signifi-cant			
Strong	Fearfulness			very signifi-cant (.59)				
	Escape			very signifi-cant				
	Territoriality			very signifi-cant				
	Autonomic Balance			very signifi-cant				

Table 3 continued

Category	Trait	HE	MHVA		SL	Studies
Moderate	Tendermindedness	.50	moderate (MHVA)		.05	
	Trust	.50				
	Affectothymia	.50		.23	N.S.	
	Ego Strength	.40	minimal (MHVA)		.01	
	Self-Sentiment	.40		.47	.05	
	Realism	.40				
	Gregariousness	.40			N.S.	
	Dominance	.25		.20	N.S.	Eysenck & Prell 1951 .49(p=.01) Nichols 1966 .52 Gottesman1966 .42
Minimal	Self Suffering	.25				
	Guilt	.25				
	Ergic Tension	.10		.52	.01	

†HE = Heritability Estimate; SL = Significance Level

*Summarized heritability estimates based on research by Cattell, Blewett, & Beloff (1955), Canter (1969), Gottesman (1963), and Klein & Cattell (1972, 1973). Cattell indicated allowances were made for a wide range of variables, such as sample size and test reliability.

**MHVA, or Multiple Hypothetical Variance Analysis, refers to an early variant of MAVA.

Table 3. However, since the findings from two other investigators (Royce and Vandenberg) are also extensive, these results are summarized in detail. Furthermore, three additional studies each involve only one entry--these are, therefore, summarized under "Others" in the last column on the right.

Except for the surgency factor, the evidence in the strong category (indicated in the upper third of Table 3) is based on Royce's 25-year research program on the genetic correlates of mouse emotionality. This project involved the diallel crossing of six inbred mouse strains and a large scale testing program (e.g., 42 variables and 775 Ss, and close to 3,000 mice in the case of the avoidance phenotype). The biometric analysis included assessments of the mode of inheritance (e.g., dominance effects) in addition to the standard estimate of additive effects. The evidence indicated that there were significant polygenic effects for all 10 factors, and a variety of dominance effects, depending upon the factor in question. (N.B. Only 5 are shown in Table 3, since the other 5 are not included in the affective hierarchy). Figures 22 and 23 exemplify these findings. The inference that the genotype is polygenic is based on the wide range of F_1 entries (i.e., the small black and white circles showing magnitudes of 45 to 70) on the y axis of each figure. Dominance effects are assessed by comparing the average F_1 score with the average parental (i.e., mid-parent) score. For example, in the case of autonomic balance (Figure 22), the F_1 score is approximately equal to the mid-parent score, indicating an intermediate or blending form of inheritance (i.e., no dominance effects). On the other hand, since the F_1 score for territorial marking (Figure 23) lies outside the parental range, it exhibits over-dominance or heterotic effects. Furthermore, since these effects are consistent in their directionality (i.e., all but three of the overdominance effects are in the upward direction), territoriality also manifests directional dominance.[9] These findings are based on the only research available which combines factor analysis, diallel analysis, and animal behavior. This methodological combination constitutes an unusually rigorous and convincing test of heritability.

The middle segment of Table 3 identifies eight factors which fall in the moderate evidence category. Seven of these (all but dominance) have been estimated by Cattell to have heritability estimates of .40 or .50; furthermore, Vandenberg reports significant heritabilities for three of the seven (tendermindedness, ego strength, and self sentiment). Cattell et al. (1957) also provide moderate evidence for tendermindedness and minimal evidence for ego strength. Although Cattell and Vandenberg estimate the heritability of dominance as minimal (.25 and .20 respectively), we have categorized it as moderate because of the consistently higher estimates provided by Nichols (.52), Gottesman (.42), and

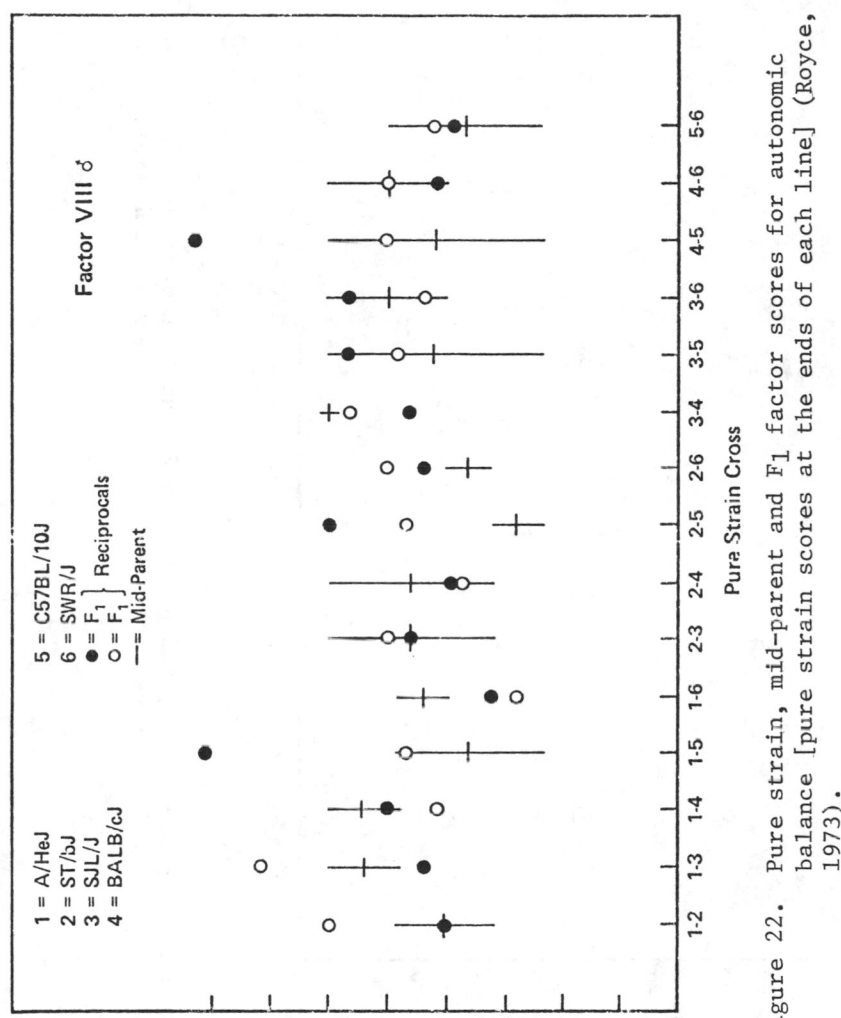

Figure 22. Pure strain, mid-parent and F₁ factor scores for autonomic balance [pure strain scores at the ends of each line] (Royce, 1973).

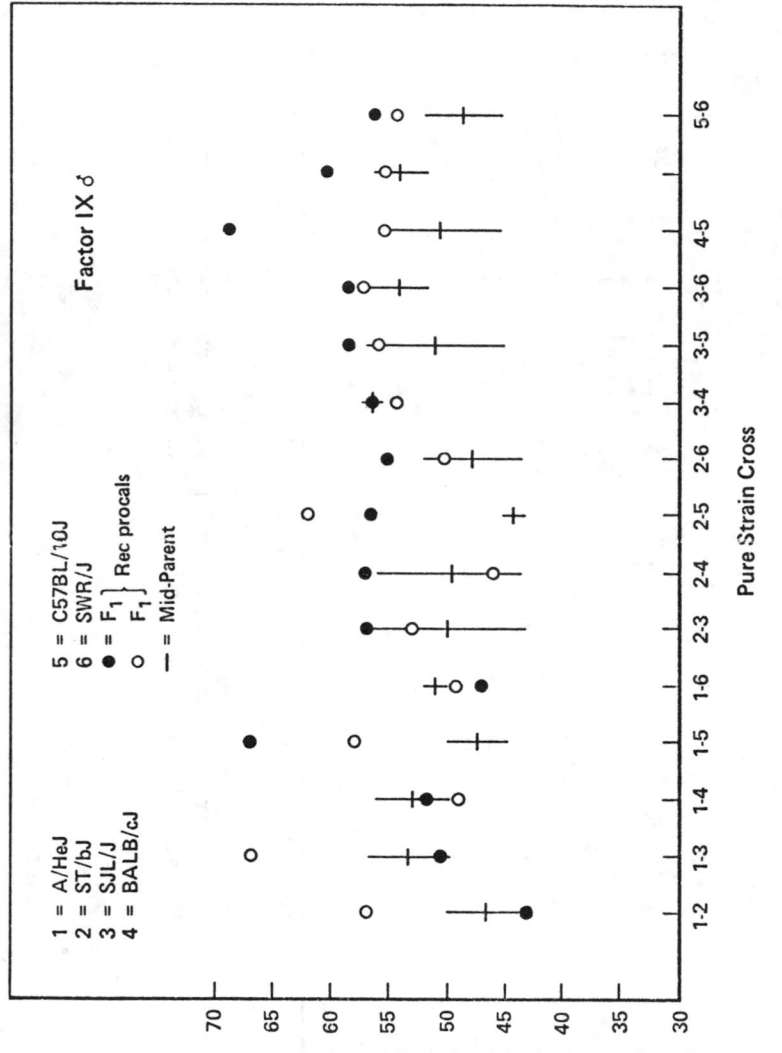

Figure 23. Pure strain, mid-parent and F₁ factor scores for territorial marking (Pure strain scores at the ends of each line. From Royce, 1973).

Eysenck and Prell (.49).

Finally, the lower segment of Table 3 includes three factors (self sufficiency, guilt, and ergic tension) for which the heritability estimates are relatively weak. Although Vandenberg reports a heritability estimate of .52 for ergic tension, it is our view that Cattell's multiply determined estimate should be given priority.

The evidence concerning higher order factors is summarized in Table 4. In all cases except two the data in this table take the form of a heritability coefficient.[10] In the case of the Cattell findings heritabilities were typically estimated via MAVA, and in the case of Eysenck heritabilities were estimated via biometric analysis. The remaining estimates were arrived at via the classical method. As in Table 3, the evidence summarized in the first column (Cattell, 1973) of Table 4 will be given greater weight because it is a summary of multiple findings. However, equivalent weight will be given to Eysenck (Eysenck & Eysenck, 1969; Eysenck, 1976) because his reports also summarize multiple findings.

The three factors in the strong category are based primarily on Eysenck's reports of heritabilities in the range of .70 to .80. The evidence in this category is particularly convincing in the case of introversion-extraversion, for we get confirmation from four other investigators (Vandenberg, Nichols, Scarr, and Gottesman) in addition to the replications reported by Eysenck. Despite the lack of replication for the emotional independence factor, we have placed it in the strong evidence category because of the analytic power of biometric analysis (Eaves & Eysenck, 1977) combined with the unusually high sample size reported in this study (544 pairs of twins).[11]

The middle segment of Table 4 identifies three factors which fall in the moderate evidence category. They all fall within the stipulated range for this category (i.e., .31 - .50) and, furthermore, two of them have been corroborated--anxiety with a higher estimate (i.e., 83), and cortertia with a lower one (i.e., a minimal heritability).

Two higher order factors, autonomy and excitability, have been placed in the minimal evidence category. The distinction between anxiety as moderate and autonomy and excitability as minimal is essentially an arbitrary decision based on the conventions indicated on page 26 (i.e., heritabilities ranging from .11 - .30 classified as minimal, and those ranging from .31 - .50 classified as moderate). This state of affairs points up the need for more convincing data on which to base conclusions concerning the role of heredity.

Table 4

Heritability Estimates For Higher Order Factors In The Affective Domain

Relative Strength of Evidence	Factor	Multiple Abstract Variance Analysis		Biometric Analysis		Classical Heritability			
		Cattell 1973*	Cattell, et al 1957**	Eysenck & Eysenck 1969; Eysenck, 1976	Eaves & Eysenck 1977	Gottesman 1963	Nichols 1966	Scarr 1966	Vandenberg 1966
Strong	Introversion-Extraversion			.70, .75		.71	.39		.83 (p = .05)
	Emotional Stability (Neuroticism)	.44		.75					
	Emotional Independence (Psychoticism)				.81				
	Social Inhibition	.45							
Moderate	Cortertia	.45	minimal (MHVA)						
Minimal	Anxiety	.35						.83	
	Autonomy	.26							
	Excitability	.25							

*Summary heritability estimates based on research by Eysenck & Prell (1951), Shields (1953, 1962), Canter (1969), and Klein & Cattell (1973). Cattell indicated allowances were made for a wide range of variables, such as sample size and test reliability.

**MHVA, or Multiple Hypothetical Variance Analysis, refers to an early variant of MAVA.

By way of summary, there is evidence for a significant
hereditary effect for twenty-five of the thirty factors (i.e.,
83%) of the affective system. The strong evidence factors include all three third order factors and six primaries (surgency,
fearfulness, escape, territoriality, avoidance, and autonomic
balance). The moderate evidence factors include three second
order factors (social inhibition, cortertia, and anxiety), and
eight primaries. And the minimal evidence factors include two
second order factors (autonomy and excitability) and three primaries. In general, the category distinctions blend into one
another, thereby highlighting the major value of such a classi-
ficatory scheme--to provide a means for summarizing findings.
However, there is one methodological implication which can be
drawn from inspection of Tables 3 and 4. It has to do with the
superiority of the biometric method, since it was prominently
involved in all cases except one (surgency) in the strong evidence category. In short, greater use of methods which can provide more stringent controls (via statistical analysis or/and
experimental techniques) is the best way to generate a more convincing data base.

The Style System

There is hereditary evidence for only one of the factor
identified styles in the style system, the rational or field
articulation style. Because of the persistent finding that males
are more field independent than females, Goodenough et al. (1977)
tested the hypothesis that field articulation is an x chromosome
(i.e., sex) linked characteristic. This involved a sample of 67
three-son families. Goodenough et al. tested for the possibility
of x chromosome linkage via two markers, red-green color blindness and $x_g(a)$ blood grouping, and they tested for field articulation via nine measures of cognitive style and ability. They
found that brothers who are identical in the $x_g(a)$ phenotype are
more like each other on the embedded figures and the rod and
frame tests than brothers who are different in the $x_g(a)$ phenotype. No significant findings were reported for the other field
articulation marker variables, nor did a significant difference
appear for brothers who differed in the red-green color blindness
marker. This constitutes evidence that an x-chromosome gene contributes to variation on the field articulation or rational style.

This finding raises many questions in a domain where the notion of a hereditary source of phenotypic variation appears to be
highly counter intuitive. Specifically, the argument is that it
makes good sense to argue that genes contribute to what organisms
can do (e.g., abilities) but not to how they do things (e.g.,
styles). Furthermore, there are a multitude of questions concerning the nature of Witkin's concept of field articulation.

For example, although it was originally called a cognitive style, it has gone through several terminological shifts (e.g., see Witkin, 1976), and it has been identified via both ability and affective markers (Wardell & Royce, 1978).

The problems surrounding the possible genetic basis for styles highlight the major reason for assembling this Institute—namely, the need to develop explanatory theory in psychology (e.g., see Royce, 1978c). What we are up against in the case of styles is, unfortunately, typical of most of psychology. What we have is a vast collection of wide ranging and often contradictory observations which are not bound together by either method or synthesizing thought. On the other hand, in the case of field articulation at least we are dealing with the best documented construct in the style domain.[12]

Let us see how individuality theory can provide insights for dealing with the questions raised by the Goodenough et al. research summarized above. It will be recalled that the style system is viewed as a hierarchical structure with three third order factors, twelve second order factors, and conceptual linkages to both the cognitive and affective systems (see Figures 6, 7, 8, and 9). It will also be recalled that there is evidence for the heritability of ten cognitive abilities and twenty five affective traits (see Tables 2, 3, and 4). Let us now focus our attention on those cognitive abilities and affective traits for which there is both evidence of heritability and a conceptual linkage to the construct of field articulation. These relationships are shown in Figure 24. What we have here is the third order rational style (field articulation) with double linkages to the cognitive system and a single linkage to the affective system. The cognitive linkages occur via the third order conceptual ability sub-hierarchy and the second order spatio-visual construct (the latter is subsumed under the third order perceptual sub-hierarchy, which is not shown in Figure 24). The relevant cognitive primaries are verbal comprehension, number, and spatial relations (three of Thurstone's primaries). The affective linkages involve emotional independence (or Eysenck's "psychoticism") at the third order, autonomy (or Cattell's "independence") at the second order, and three first order affective traits.

The major point to be noted here is that the rational style (or field articulation) is identifiable via a large number of lower order cognitive and affective markers. The Goodenough et al. investigation was focused on only one of these—the spatio-visual (e.g., spatial relations) abilities. Figure 24 indicates that if future hereditary analyses were to focus on the number and verbal comprehension cognitive primaries and the dominance, realism, and trust affective dimensions, they would also provide access to field articulation.

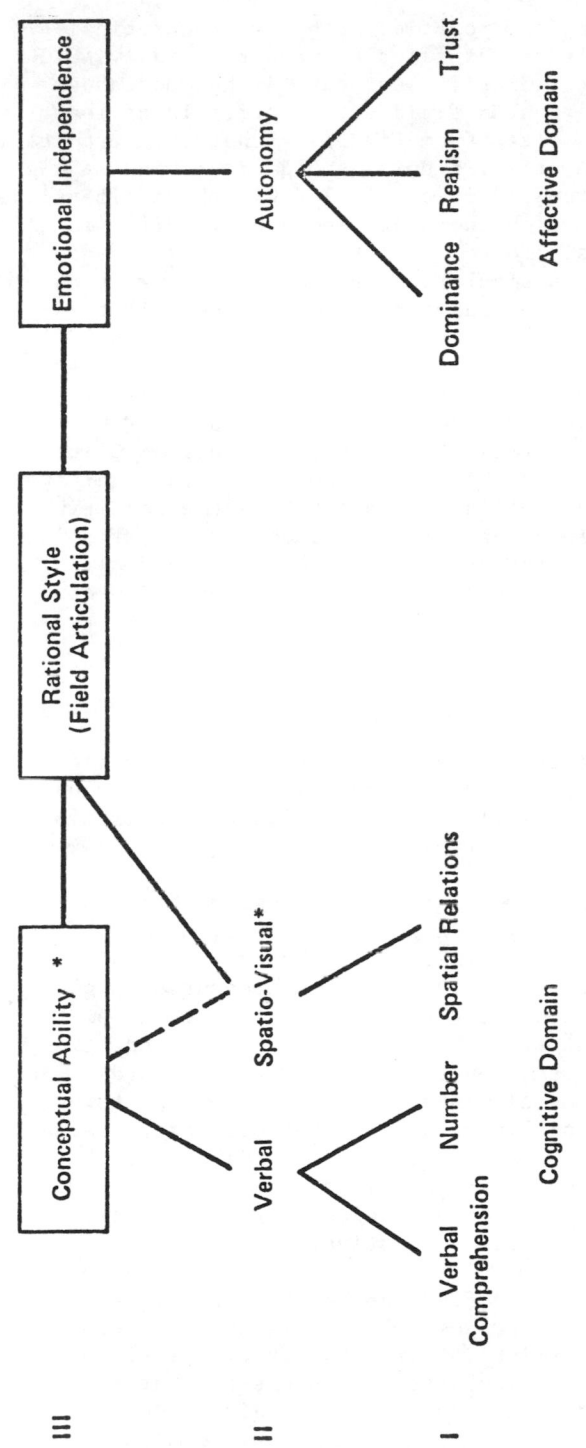

III   Emotional Independence

Autonomy

Dominance   Realism   Trust

Affective Domain

II   Rational Style
(Field Articulation)

Conceptual Ability *

Verbal   Spatio-Visual*

I   Verbal   Number   Spatial Relations
Comprehension

Cognitive Domain

*The Hereditary Evidence is Inferential in These Cases.

Figure 24.   The conceptual linkages between rational style (field articulation) and heritable cognitive and affective dimensions.

However, there is another point of much more theoretical import. It has to do with the conflict between the widely held intuition that styles are primarily learned and the Goodenough et al. finding that variation on field articulation is at least partly hereditary. It is clear from Figure 24 that the hereditary portion of the Goodenough et al. finding could occur via the cognitive and affective systems,[13] in particular via those dimensions (shown in Figure 24) for which there are known heritabilities and known conceptual linkages. There is little doubt of the conceptual confounding of field articulation as a style construct on the one hand and as a spatio-visualization cognitive ability on the other hand. This confounding raises difficult questions concerning exactly what aspect of personality (e.g., style per se, cognitive ability, and/or affect) is affected by heredity in the Goodenough et al. investigation. The Wardell-Royce (1978) analysis constitutes a significant step in the direction of teasing out the intricate relationships which hold between cognitive-affective styles (such as field articulation) and the cognitive and affective systems. This analysis, combined with the findings summarized in Figure 24, suggests that the Goodenough et al. hereditary effect is probably due to the cognitive ability of spatial relations.

The Value System

To our knowledge there have been no attempts to investigate the hereditary basis of factor identified values. This includes both the affective (i.e., needs) and the cognitive (i.e., interests) aspects of the value hierarchy.

There have been weak hints that the interest patterns of twins are more similar than sibs (e.g., Koch, 1966; Newman, Freeman, & Holzinger, 1937; Shields, 1962), but these studies typically involved psychometrically inadequate measures (e.g., a simple biographical rating sheet rather than the Strong or the Kuder). However, a recent study by Grotevant, Scarr, and Weinburg (1978) appears to measure up to contemporary standards. However, the genetic aspect merely involves the interest patterns between parents, natural siblings, and adopted siblings. Because of the genetic weakness of such studies, the finding that the interests among parents and their biological offspring are more similar than the interests of non-biologically related individuals must be regarded as merely suggestive.

Furthermore, even if these findings are confirmed, it will still be necessary to determine just what it is about interest patterns that is gene determined. Our analysis of the style system (see the previous section) strongly suggests that its heritability is traceable to the cognitive and affective dimensions to which it is linked. Because cognitive values (i.e., interests) are also cognitive-affective linkage constructs (see Figure 11), individuality theory indicates that heritability claims concerning interests are also traceable to the cognitive and affective systems.

The Sensory System

There is no research on the sensory system which is directed at factor-gene relationships. On the other hand, there is an extensive non-factor analytic literature.

Vision is probably the most thoroughly investigated of the sense modalities. The most obvious example is color blindness, which is due to a recessive, sex linked gene, and expresses itself in males (Pickford, 1951; Thiessen, 1972). A high degree of genetic determination has also been reported for accommodative convergence and extreme myopia (Hofstetter, 1948; Hofstetter & Rife, 1953), and Eysenck and Prell (1951) report a hereditary effect for performance on the critical flicker-fusion task.

Fuller and Thompson (1960) report that hereditary deafness of various sorts has been identified in man, mouse, and dogs. For example, MZ twins are distinguishable from less closely related subjects on tune deafness as measured by the Seashore tests. However, it is probable that the most extensive research related to audition has been conducted on audiogenic seizures. This research, which was initiated by Hall (1947), has since proliferated to include a wide range of biochemical findings which are associated with the seizure phenomenon. These include mellanin level (Henry & Haythorne, 1975), neurotransmitter levels (Schlesinger & Griek, 1970; Sze, 1970), corticosteroid levels (Ginsburg & Miller, 1963; Maxson & Sze, 1977) and auditory priming effects (Deckard, 1977; Fuller & Collins, 1968, and Itrevian & Fink, 1968). However, the most pertinent genetic analysis is that of Collins (1970), who has put forward a single locus model which attributes audiogenic seizure proneness to a recessive allele.

Although taste has not been extensively investigated, the data available on this sensory modality are highly convincing. A case in point is the early finding (Snyder, Blakeslee, & Salmon, 1931; Harris & Kalmus, 1949; and Barnicot, 1950) that individuals with a specifiable recessive allele are unable to detect PTC (phenylthiocarbomide). Other compounds which are associated with genetically-determined taste sensitivities include diphenyl guanadine (Snyder & Davidson, 1937), brucine (Barrows, 1945), and PROP (propylthiouracil) (Kaplan, Powell, Moorhouse, & Hinko, 1976). Strain differences in sensitivity to cyclohexamide have also been identified in rat populations (To-bach, Bellin, & Das, 1974).

Although there is evidence of hereditary effects in the remaining sense modalities (e.g., olfaction, proprioception, thermal, etc.), the findings are fragmentary. However, the overall impression which emerges from reviewing the research in the sensory domain is that a large genetic component is involved. The most convincing basis for this conclusion is the research on color and taste blindness, hereditary deafness, and susceptibility to audiogenic seizures.

The Motor System

There are no data on the genetic correlates of factors in the motor system. However, an educated guess is that heredity accounts for a significant portion of motor performance. The basis for such a statement comes from several sources. First, there is the fact that various species of animals can be bred for specifiable motor characteristics. On the basis of the phylogeny of motor behavior, there is little reason to suppose that man would be much different. Second, it is well established that human stature and weight have a large hereditary component (Mueller, 1976), and it is obvious that stature and weight would at least delimit the development of certain motor abilities. Third, the mildly mentally retarded can be differentiated from normals on a number of motor abilities, many of which share variables with the motor system factors (Eckert & Rarick, 1976; Dobbins & Rarick, 1975; Dobbins, 1976). There is evidence that at least a portion of such differences involve a genetic component. Fourth, Ahe and Perez (1974) argue cogently for a significant genetic component of cardiovascular and neurocirculatory individual differences that would obviously delimit the development of endurance factors. Fifth, there are a number of studies demonstrating a significant genetic component in such motor variables as reaction time (Surwillo, 1977), tapping speed (Eysenck & Prell, 1951), pursuit rotor and steadiness (McNemar, 1933; Vandenberg, 1962), and hand speed and dexterity (McNemar, 1933; Jarvick, Blum, & Varma, 1972). Although none of this evidence is particularly strong, it supports the contention of a significant genetic component in individual differences involving the motor system.

Heredity, Environment, and
Individuality

What conclusions can be drawn concerning the relative roles of heredity and environment as sources of observed psychological variation? If we confine ourselves to the factor-gene findings, it is clear that only two of the six systems have been adequately investigated--cognition and affect. The available factor-gene evidence appears to justify the conclusion that heredity contributes significantly to the functioning of these two systems. However, there is also suggestive evidence that there are indirect hereditary effects on the functioning of the style system. There have been no factor-gene studies in the value, sensory, and motor domains.

But what if we go beyond the factor-gene data and bring the total spectrum of findings to bear on the heredity-environment issue, then what conclusions appear to be justified?[14] It is my impression that the available evidence concerning sensory and motor processes is quite clear--namely, that the functioning of these two systems is primarily genetically determined.[15] The bulk of the available evidence makes it equally clear that styles and values are primarily learned. However, the situation concerning the two remaining systems, cognition and affect, suggests that heredity and environment are roughly equivalent sources of the observed variation.

What can be said from the perspective of individuality theory and the factor-gene model? It will be recalled that the theory includes the concepts of heredity and environment dominance (see pp. 25-27). Applying these concepts to the six systems, we hypothesize that the sensory and motor systems are heredity dominant, that the cognitive and affective systems are partially heredity dominant, and that the style and value systems are environment dominant. This simply means that genetic variation constitutes most of the variance in the case of sensory and motor phenotypes, that environmental variation constitutes most of the observed variation in the case of the style and value systems, and that genetic sources of variation are somewhat (the exact extent is not presently specifiable) greater than environmental sources of variation in the case of the cognitive and affective systems. These hypotheses receive support on both empirical and theoretical grounds. The factor-gene empirical grounds have been summarized in Part II of this paper. The theoretical grounds have to do with the evolutionary-adaptive significance of living information processing systems.

Elsewhere we have elaborated on the transductive information processing role of the sensory (Kearsley & Royce, 1977) and motor (Powell, Katzko, & Royce, 1978) systems. The transduction of information has to do with converting (decoding) physical inputs (e.g., wavelengths of light and sound) into psychologically meaningful units (e.g., color and pitch discrimination) at the input or the sensory end of the system, and converting (encoding) from psychologically meaningful forms (e.g., cognitions and affects) to action at the physical output or motor end of the system. This kind of information processing occurs at the interface between the organism (the psychological system) and the environment (the organism's supra-system), and is, therefore, critical to species survival. That is, organismic survival is presumed to be impossible without some kind of input-output structure (Miller, 1978). Evolutionary theory implies that species with ineffective input and output transducers are weeded out via natural selection. In short, since the sensory and motor systems are the most biologically primitive of the six systems it is not surprising that heredity should play a greater role than environment in the case of these two systems.

It is hypothesized, on the other hand, that the cognitive and affective systems are only partially heredity dominant. This means that heredity is more important than environment, but only slightly--perhaps in the neighborhood of 55%-60% of the variance attributable to heredity and the remainder attributable to environment. How does this square with the evolutionary-adaptive role of the organism? According to individuality theory, these two systems are information transformers. This means they take the transduced information provided by the sensory system and change it into some other psychologically meaningful form, such as cognitions (i.e., percepts, concepts, and symbols) and affects (i.e., the emotions). We have argued elsewhere that the major role of the cognitive system is to interpret or understand the environment. More specifically, this means identifying environmental invariants--that is, perceptual, conceptual, and symbolized invariants (Powell & Royce, 1978). Since such invariances constitute human constructions of "the way things are", they are also critical components of world-view (Royce, 1974, 1975). The affective system plays a similar role, but the transformational process is focused on preparing the organism for action via a variety of arousal mechanisms (Royce & McDermott, 1979). The affective system is organized for coping with the daily stresses of life (Royce & Diamond, 1979) as well as providing a basis for life style (Powell & Royce, 1978). In short, the argument is that the cognitive and affective systems have been selected for adaptive flexibility. Biologically, flexibility implies the capacity to adapt to the widest possible range of ecologies. Thus, such reactions as fixed action patterns and rigid perceptions would be inconsistent with optimizing flexibility. The implication is that behavior would be too rigid in the case of extreme genetic determination, too flexible in the case of extreme environmental determination, but optimally flexible in the case of near equivalent genetic-environment determination.

Finally, we come to the hypothesis that the functioning of the style and value systems is environment dominant. This means

that environment is more important than heredity in such cases.
Why should this be the case? According to individuality theory
these two systems are primarily concerned with integration--that
is, the coordination and synthesis of information and personality.
However, integration clearly requires prior informational inputs
and transformations. But it seems equally clear that there will
be a wide range of possible syntheses, depending upon what information has been previously stored, how it has been transformed,
and the particular styles and values which have guided the synthesizing process. The point is that nature has not evolved a
genetic-evolutionary mechanism for transmitting informational
content (an acquired characteristic) from one generation to the
next. Thus, biological evolution appears to be irrelevant in
the case of styles and values. But cultural evolution is critical, for cultural evolution has to do with those styles and values
which have been institutionalized. The institutionalization of
styles and values refers to "how and what commitments" that were
so adaptive in a given time and place that it was thought they
might be equally adaptive in another time or/and place. Thus,
styles and values are passed on from one generation to the next
via the culture. Furthermore, they constitute the major building
blocks for such molar behavioral complexities as world view, life
style, and self image. In short, styles and values are relevant
to the big questions of existence--the nature of reality, the
key to one's self identity, and how we should live our daily
lives. Psychological questions of this magnitude are clearly
beyond the ken of genes. The genes have enough burden to bear
in accounting for variations in the sensory, motor, cognitive,
and affective systems.

III. SUMMARY AND CONCLUSIONS

        Part I of this chapter provides a brief summary of a general
theory of individual differences. The theory involves a synthesis of factor analysis, information processing, and system
theory. Personality is conceptualized as a multi-level, hierarchical supra-system which is comprised of six systems with
differential roles, as follows: the sensory and motor systems
are information transducers, the cognitive and affective systems
are information transformers, and the style and value systems
are information integrators. Each of the six systems is also
hierarchically organized, with third order factors identifying
the major sub-system of each systemic unit, and the lower order
factors constituting the elements of each of the sub-systems.
The theory involves around 185 factors which have been empirically
identified as reliable dimensions of individual differences.
Further interactions and integrations account for such system
outputs as cognitions, affects, and styles, and system interactions and integrations account for such supra-system (i.e.,

personality) outputs as world-view, life style, and self image.

Part II provides an elaboration of the factor-gene model. This model regards invariant factors as behavioral phenotypes, and then proceeds to identify the genetic correlates for each factor. There is convincing evidence of hereditary causation for ten cognitive factors (i.e., 31% of the cognitive system). These factors are Thurstone's primaries (verbal comprehension, spatial relations, word fluency, memorization, perceptual speed, inductive reasoning, and number), and three other first order factors (associative meaning, associational fluency, and ideational fluency). There is also convincing evidence of hereditary effects for 25 of the 30 factors (i.e., 83%) of the affective system. These include all three of Eysenck's third order factors (i.e., introversion-extraversion, emotional stability, and emotional independence in our terminology), five of the seven second order factors (social inhibition, cortertia, anxiety, autonomy, and excitability), and 17 of the 20 affective primaries (i.e., surgency, avoidance, fearfulness, escape, territoriality, autonomic balance, tendermindedness, trust, affectothymia, ego strength, self-sentiment, realism, gregariousness, dominance, self sufficiency, guilt, and ergic tension). In addition, there is suggestive evidence for a partial hereditary effect in the case of one style factor (Witkin's field articulation construct, which is labeled rational style in individuality theory). There have been no factor-gene studies in the remaining three domains (sensory, motor, and value).

If we confine ourselves to the factor-gene evidence, it is clear that only two of the six systems have been adequately investigated--cognition and affect. Furthermore, the factor-gene evidence is more extensive in the affective domain than in the cognitive domain. However, if we go beyond the factor-gene data and bring the total spectrum of findings to bear on the heredity-environment issue, we are led to the hypothesis that the sensory and motor systems are heredity dominant (i.e., there is a greater proportion of genetic than environmental variance), that the cognitive and affective systems are partially heredity dominant, and that the style and value systems are environment dominant.

NOTES

[1]Preparation of this manuscript was partially supported by Canada Council Grant Number S76-0908-R1. In particular, the author wishes to acknowledge the assistance of John R. Wozny, who tracked down the empirical findings in the affective and sensory domains, Peter Holt, who checked out the motor domain, and Donald Schopflocher, who researched the relevant value and style literature. Requests for reprints should be sent to Joseph R. Royce, The Center for Advanced Study in Theoretical Psychology, University of Alberta, Edmonton, Alberta, Canada, T6G 2E9.

[2]There are an additional 35 dimensions for which the empirical evidence is less secure, giving us around 185 dimensions for the total psychological system. The breakdown by systems is as follows: Sensory = 19, Motor = 46, Cognitive = 32, Affective = 30, Style = 15, and Value = 43.

[3]There are, of course, similar linkages for the empirical and metaphoric styles as well. See Wardell and Royce (1978) for details.

[4]Examples include the three sub-systems or/and third order constructs of the cognitive hierarchy labeled conceptual, perceptual, and symbolizing (see Figure 4), and the three sub-systems or/and third order constructs of the affective hierarchy labeled emotional stability, emotional independence, and introversion-extraversion (see Figure 5). It is of considerable theoretical import to note that the notion of a hierarchical structure of complex systems (such as cognition and affect) arose independently in general system and factor theory. Furthermore, the concept of hierarchical structure is now so pervasive that there is a considerable cross-disciplinary literature on hierarchy theory. It is our view that hierarchy theory has untapped implications for the understanding of complex psychological systems, particularly in connection with control mechanisms and decision making.

[5]For the sake of simplicity this presentation is confined to orthogonal (i.e., uncorrelated) common factors; that is, the uniqueness and error components of each variable are omitted.

[6]This modification of the factor-gene model arose out of extended interaction between Royce and Fuller at the Banff Institute. We presume it is obvious that all possible factor-gene relationships are not shown in this figure. Because of the degree of complexity involved it would require a series of figures. Furthermore, because of the paucity of experimental research on factor-gene relationships, there are relatively few empirical constraints presently available as guidelines for complete specification of the model. However, now that the fundamentals of polygenicity (Royce and associates, 1960, 1970, 1971, 1972, 1973a, 1974, 1975) and correlated factors (DeFries et al., 1979) appear

to be well grounded empirically, we can anticipate further theoretical developments of the factor-gene model, preferably via close interaction with relevant experimental research. On the other hand, because of inadequacies in contemporary molecular psychobiology, it is anticipated that the terra incognita labeled psychophysiological genetics in Figure 14 will continue to be relatively refractory for at least the immediate future.

[7]There is a serious need for a thorough, critical review of the methods for investigating hereditary effects. Although the recent review by Jinks and Fulker (1970) is an important step in the right direction, it only covers three such methods, and it is focused on statistical considerations. Much of the current polemics on heredity vs. environment is due to ignorance concerning the assets and limitations of the burgeoning armamentarium of these methods. Since the methodological analysis provided in this paper is impressionistic rather than critical, it may be necessary to revise some of the conclusions stated herein if and when we are subsequently provided with the pragmatic guidance we need. It is my hope that the behavior genetics methodologists will accept this challenge by first providing the required technical analysis, and then communicating what it all means to the rest of the scientific community. For example, it is my bias that it is extremely difficult to draw strong scientific inferences from the typical **behavior genetic study which uses human subjects because** of the lack of experimental controls for both genetic and environmental variables. I doubt that it is possible to completely overcome inadequate experimental controls via the statistical methods that have been put forward. It is my impression, therefore, that the human behavior geneticist is more like an astute detective than a laboratory scientist, and I'm frankly concerned about the validity of the inferences that have been made in these investigations. To put my concern another way, I wonder how far genetics would have advanced if it had confined itself to human subjects? Stated more explicitly, exactly how have the studies on human genetics advanced our understanding of genetic principles? The answer to this question will largely determine how behavior geneticists can profit from the experience of one of its parental disciplines, genetics. It must, of course, be granted that psychology has a special need to turn to human subjects because of the general interest in human phenotypes. However, from the perspective of genetic methodology, this may be a relatively limited strategy.

[8]This factor has received extensive genetic investigation, particularly in the context of the well established sex difference (i.e., males score significantly higher). It has been suggested, for example, that this difference is sex-linked and due to a major gene effect. Despite the mixed evidence regarding this claim, Vandenberg and Kuse (1977) take the stance that the genetic influence is strong, and further, that environmental

effects are relatively weak.

[9]In general, factors related to escape and avoidance--that is, the avoidance, territorial marking, fearfulness, audiogenic reactivity, and escape components--are governed by complete or over (i.e., heterotic) dominance effects. Furthermore, in three of these cases--escape, audiogenic reactivity, and territorial marking--there is evidence of directional dominance. Factors related to undifferentiated arousal, such as autonomic balance, motor discharge, and activity level, showed either partial or no dominance effects (i.e., an intermediate or blending form of inheritance; see Royce, 1978b, for a more complete summary of these findings). In the context of individuality theory, the implication is that arousal effects of the emotional stability sub-system (a unit of the affective system) are generated via the fight/flight functioning of the limbic system in contrast to the reticular activation of one of the other sub-systems, introversion-extraversion (e.g., see Figure 12 and the relevant text, and see Royce & McDermott, 1977, for a more complete analysis). In the context of genetic-evolutionary theory the implication is that survival oriented behavioral phenotypes (e.g., the territoriality and escape factors), which are characterized by higher dominance than additive effects, have been subjected to directional selection effects, whereas the undifferentiated arousal factors (e.g., autonomic balance and activity level), which are characterized by additive genes and little or no dominance effects, have been subjected to a stabilizing form of natural selection.

[10]Vandenberg reports a probability value for introversion-extraversion, and Cattell offers a qualitative (i.e., a minimal hereditary effect) rather than a quantitative report.

[11]The typical twin study has involved around 50 to 100 pairs of twins. The following sample sizes are illustrative: Eysenck and Prell (1951), N = 50 twin pairs; Shields (1953), N = 62 twin pairs; Vandenberg (1962), N = 82 twin pairs; Shields (1962), N = 112 twin pairs; and Gottesman (1963), N = 68 twin pairs. Both MAVA and biometric analysis typically involve much larger samples. Cattell, Blewett, & Beloff (1955), for example, involved close to 1000 subjects, including 84 twin pairs.

[12]See, for example, Witkin and Goodenough's (1976) recent theoretical summary and Witkin et al's (1973) bibliography on field dependence, which lists over 1500 references.

[13]A more elaborate treatment of this point is currently in progress as part of a paper on multidimensional life span development (Powell, Holt, & Royce, 1979). The basic idea is that the cognitive and affective systems, which have a strong hereditary basis, develop prior to styles and values and strongly influence the subsequent development of the latter. However, styles per se are probably primarily learned. Furthermore, styles and values

become increasingly important in the second half of life.

[14]It should be noted that the speculations offered herein are impressionistic. Furthermore, since this paper is concerned with the genetic basis of behavior, the environmental evidence has not been explicitly reviewed. In short, revisions may be called for in the light of this evidence.

[15]Because of the biological characteristics of these two systems, the evidence concerning their phylogeny and neurology is particularly pertinent. The point for point localization of sensory and motor functioning constitutes the strongest evidence available concerning the phylogenetic evolution and pre-wiring of human psychological structures.

References

Ahe, K., & Perez de Francisco, C. Genetic aspects of psycho-
    physiological variables. Neurologia, Neurocirugia, Psi-
    quitria, 1974, 15, 5-18.
Barnicot, N. A. Taste deficiency for phenylthiourea in African
    Negroes and Chinese. Annals of Eugenics, 1950, 15, 248-254.
Barrows, S. L. The inheritance of the ability to taste brucine.
    M.A. Thesis, Stanford University, 1945.
Berrien, F. K. General and social systems. New Brunswick, N.J.:
    Rutgers University Press, 1968.
von Bertalanffy, L. General systems theory. Main Currents in
    Modern Thought, 1955, 11, 75-83.
Blewett, D. B. An experimental study of the inheritance of in-
    telligence. Journal of Mental Science, 1954, 100, 922-933.
Broadhurst, P. L. The inheritance of behavior. Science, 1965,
    29, 39-43.
Buss, A. R. A conceptual framework for learning effecting the
    development of ability factors. Human Development, 1973,
    16, 273-292.
Buss, A. R. A general developmental model for interindividual
    differences, intraindividual differences, and intraindivi-
    dual changes. Developmental Psychology, 1974, 10, 70-78. (a)
Buss, A. R. A multivariate model of quantitative, structural,
    and quantistructural ontogenetic change. Developmental Psy-
    chology, 1974, 10, 190-203. (b)
Buss, A. R. A recursive-nonrecursive factor model and develop-
    mental causal networks. Human Development, 1974, 17, 139-
    151. (c)
Buss, A. R., & Royce, J. R. Ontogenetic changes in cognitive
    structure from a multivariate perspective. Developmental
    Psychology, 1975, 11, 87-101.
Canter, S. 'Personality traits in twins'. Unpublished paper
    delivered to annual conference of the British Psychological
    Society, 1969. In P. Mittler (Ed.), The study of twins.
    Middlesex, England: Penguin Books, 1971.
Cattell, R. B. Research designs in psychological genetics with
    special reference to the Multiple Variance Method. Ameri-
    can Journal of Human Genetics, 1953, 5, 76-93.
Cattell, R. B. The multiple abstract variance analysis equations
    and solutions. Psychological Review, 1960, 67, 353-372.
Cattell, R. B. Abilities: Their structure, growth and action.
    Boston: Houghton-Mifflin, 1971.
Cattell, R. B. Personality and mood by questionnaire. San
    Francisco: Jossey-Bass, Publishers, 1973.
Cattell, R., Blewett, D., & Beloff, J. The inheritance of per-
    sonality. A multiple variance analysis determination of
    approximate nature-nurture ratios for primary personality
    factors in Q-data. American Journal of Human Genetics,
    1955, 7, 122-146.

642

Cattell, R. B., Stice, G., & Kristy, N. A first approximation
to nature-nurture ratios for eleven primary personality factors in objective tests. Journal of Abnormal and Social
Psychology, 1957, 54, 143-159.

Collins, R. B. A new genetic locus mapped for behavioral variation in mice. Behavior Genetics, 1970, 2, 99-109.

Cortes, F., Przeworski, A., & Sprague, D. Systems analysis for
social scientists. New York: Wiley, 1974.

Deckard, B. Genetic, biochemical and pharmacological correlates
of responses to priming in mice. Behavior Genetics, 1977,
7, 52-53.

DeFries, J., Ashton, G., Johnson, R., Kuse, A., McClearn, G., Mi,
M. P., Rashad, M., Vandenberg, S., & Wilson, J. Parent-offspring resemblance for specific cognitive abilities in two
ethnic groups. Nature, 1976, 261, 131-133.

Diamond, S., & Royce, J. R. Cognitive abilities as expressions
of three "ways of knowing". Center Paper in Progress, 1978.

Dobbins, D. A. Separation potential of educable and intellectually normal boys as function of motor performance. Research
Quarterly, 1976, 47, 346-357.

Dobbins, D. A., & Rarick, G. L. Structural similarity of the
motor domain of normal and educable retarded boys. Research
Quarterly, 1975, 46, 447-456.

Eaves, L. J., & Eysenck, H. A genotype-environmental model for
psychoticism. Advances in Behavior Research and Therapy,
1977, 1, 5-26.

Eckert, H. M., & Rarick, G. L. Stabilometer performance of educable mentally retarded and normal children. Research Quarterly, 1976, 47, 619-623.

Erlenmeyer-Kimling, L., & Jarvik, L. Genetics and intelligence:
A review. Science, 1963, 142, 1477-1479.

Eysenck, H. J. Genetic factors and personality development. In
A. R. Kaplan (Ed.), Human behavior genetics. Springfield:
C. C. Thomas, 1976, pp. 198-229.

Eysenck, H. J., & Eysenck, S. B. C. Personality structure and
measurement. San Diego: Knapp, 1969.

Eysenck, H. J., & Prell, D. B. The inheritance of neuroticism:
An experimental study. Journal of Mental Science, 1951,
97, 411-465.

Falconer, D. S. Introduction to quantitative genetics. Edinburgh and London: Oliver and Boyd, 1960.

Fisher, R. A. The correlation between relatives on the supposition of Mendelian inheritance. Transactions of the Royal
Society of Edinburgh, 1918, 52, 399-433.

Frings, H., & Frings, M. The production of stocks of albino
mice with predictable susceptibilities to audiogenic
seizures. Behavior, 1953, 5, 305-309.

Fuller, J. L., & Collins, R. L. Temporal parameters of sensitiza-
tion for audiogenic seizures in SJL/J Mice. Developmental
Psychobiology, 1968, 1, 185-188.

Fuller, J. L., & Thompson, W. R. Behavior genetics. New York:
    John Wiley & Sons, 1960.
Ginsburg, B. E., & Miller, D. S. Genetic factors in audiogenic
    seizures. Psychophysiologie neuropharmacologie et biochemie
    de la crise audiogene. Editions du Centre National de la
    Recherche Scientifique, 1963, 112, 217-225.
Goddenough, D. R., Gandini, E., Olkin, E., Pizzamiglio, L., Thayer,
    D., & Witkin, H. A study of x-chromosome linkage with field
    dependence and spatial visualization. Behavior Genetics,
    1977, 7, 373-387.
Gottesman, I. Heritability of personality. Psychological Mono-
    graphs, 1963, 77, 1-21.
Gottesman, I. I., & Shields, J. Schizophrenia in twins: 16 years
    consecutive admissions to a psychiatric clinic. Diseases
    of the Nervous System, 1966, 27, 11-19.
Grolevant, H., Scarr, S., & Weinberg, R. Are career interests in-
    heritable? Psychology Today, March 1978, pp. 88-90.
Hall, C. S. Genetic differences in fatal audiogenic seizures be-
    tween two inbred strains of house mice. Journal of Heredity,
    1947, 38, 2-6.
Harman, H. H. Modern factor analysis. Chicago: University of
    Chicago Press, 1976.
Harris, H. T., & Kalmus, H. Chemical specificity in genetical
    differences of taste sensitivity. Annals of Eugenics, 1949,
    15, 32-45.
Henry, K. R., & Haythorne, M. M. Albinism and auditory function
    in the laboratory mouse. 1. Effects of single-gene sub-
    stitutions on auditory physiology, audiogenic seizures, and
    developmental processes. Behavior Genetics, 1975, 5, 137-149.
Hirsch, J. (Ed.). Behavior-genetic analysis. New York: McGraw-
    Hill, 1967.
Hofstetter, H. W. Accommodative convergence in identical twins.
    American Journal of Optometry, 1948, 25, 480-491.
Hofstetter, H., & Rife, D. Miscellaneous optometric data on
    twins. American Journal of Optometry, 1953, 30, 139-150.
Holmes, T. M., Aksel, R., & Royce, J. R. Inheritance of avoid-
    ance behavior in mus musculus. Behavior Genetics, 1974, 4,
    357-371.
Holzinger, K. The relative effect of nature and nurture influences
    on twin differences. Journal of Educational Psychology, 1929,
    20, 241-248.
Itturian, W. B., & Fink, G. B. Conditioned convulsive reaction.
    Federation Proceedings, 1967, 26, 737.
Jackson, D. N. A sequential system for personality scale develop-
    ment. In C. D. Spielberger (Ed.), Current topics in clinical
    and community psychology (Vol 2). New York: Academic
    Press, 1970.
Jinks, J. L., & Fulker, D. W. A comparison of biometrical genetical,
    MAVA, and classical approaches to the analysis of human be-
    havior. Psychological Bulletin, 1970, 73, 311-349.

644

Kamin, L. J. The science and politics of IQ. Potomac, Maryland: Erlbaum, 1974.
Kaplan, A. R. (Ed.). Human behavior genetics. Springfield,
U.S.A.: C. Thomas, Publishers, 1976.
Kaplan, A., Powell, W., Moorhouse, A., and Hinko, E. Taste sensation and human variation. In A. Kaplan (Ed.), Human behavior genetics. Springfield: C. Thomas, 1976, pp. 401-
423.
Karp, S. A. Field dependence and overcoming embeddedness. Journal of Consulting Psychology, 1963, 27, 294-302.
Kearsley, G. P., Buss, A. R., & Royce, J. R. Developmental change
and the multi-dimensional cognitive system. Intelligence,
1977, 1, 257-273.
Kearsley, G. P., & Royce, J. R. A multifactor theory of sensation: Individuality in sensory structure and sensory processing. Perceptual and Motor Skills, 1977, 44, 1299-1316.
Klein, T. W., & Cattell, R. B. Heritabilities of HSPQ personality factors from intra-class correlations on twins and sibs.
Advance Publication #52, Institute for Research on Morality
and Adjustment. Boulder, Colorado, 1973.
Koch, H. L. Twins and twin relations. Chicago: University of
Chicago Press, 1966.
Mather, K., & Jinks, J. L. Biometrical genetics: The study of
continuous variation (2nd ed.). London: Chapman & Hall,
1971.
Maxson, S., & Sze, P. The role of GABA in the sensory and genetic
induction of AGS. Behavior Genetics, 1973, 3, 409.
Maxson, S. C., Sze, P. Y., & Deckard, B. Glucocorticoids and
development of AGS in DBA/1 Bg Mice. Behavior Genetics,
1977, 7, 323-326.
McClearn, G., & DeFries, J. Introduction to behavior genetics.
San Francisco: Freeman & Co., 1973.
McNemar, Q. Twin resemblances in motor skills and the effect of
practice thereon. Journal of Genetic Psychology, 1933,
42, 70-97.
Mesarovic, M. D., Macko, D., & Takahara, Y. Theory of hierarchical, multi-level, systems. New York: Academic Press, 1970.
Miller, G. A., Galanter, E., & Pribram, K. H. Plans and the structure of behavior. New York: Holt, Rinehart, & Winston,
1960.
Miller, J. G. Living systems: The organism. Quarterly Review
of Biology, 1973, 48, 92-276.
Miller, J. G. Living systems. New York: McGraw-Hill Book Company, 1978.
Mittler, P. The study of twins. Middlesex, England: Penguin,
1971.
Mos, L. P., Lukaweski, R., & Royce, J. R. The effect of septal
lesions on factors of mouse emotionality. Journal of Comparative and Physiological Psychology, 1977, 91, 523-532.

Mueller, W. H. Parent-child correlation for stature and weight among school aged children: A review of 24 studies. Human Biology, 1976, 48, 379-397.

Murray, H. A. Explorations in personality. New York: Oxford University Press, 1938.

Neel, J., & Schull, W. Human heredity. Chicago: University Press, 1954.

Newman, H. H., Freeman, F. N., & Holzinger, J. Twins, a study of heredity and environment. Chicago: University of Chicago Press, 1937.

Nichols, R. C. The national mint twin study. In S. G. Vandenberg (Ed.), Methods and goals in human behavior genetics. New York: Academic Press, 1965.

Partanen, J., Bruun, K., & Markkanenen, T. Inheritance of drinking behavior. A study on intelligence, personality and use of alcohol of adult twins. Helsinki: Finnish Foundation for Alcohol Studies, 1966.

Pickford, R. W. Individual differences in color vision. London: Routledge & Kegan Paul, 1951.

Powell, A., Holt, P., & Royce, J. R. The development of individuality. Center Paper in Progress, 1979.

Powell, A., Katzko, M., & Royce, J. R. A multifactor-systems theory of the structure and dynamics of motor function. Journal of Motor Behavior, 1978, 10(3), 191-210.

Powell, A., Katzko, M., & Royce, J. R. A multifactor systems theory of sensory-motor integration. Center Paper in Progress, 1979.

Powell, A., & Royce, J. R. Paths to being, life style and individuality. Psychological Reports, 1978, 42, 97-1005.

Royce, J. R. The factorial analysis of animal behavior. Psychological Bulletin, 1950, 47, 235-259.

Royce, J. R. Factor theory and genetics. Educational and Psychological Measurement, 1957a, 17, 361-376.

Royce, J. R. Psychology in mid-20th century. American Scientist, 1957b, 45, 53-57.

Royce, J. R. Factors as theoretical constructs. American Psychologist, 1963, 18, 522-528.

Royce, J. R. The encapsulated man: An interdisciplinary essay on the search for meaning. Princeton: D. Van Nostrand & Co., 1964.

Royce, J. R. Concepts generated from comparative and physiological psychological observations. In R. B. Cattell (Ed.), Handbook of multivariate experimental psychology. Chicago: Rand McNally, 1966, 642-683.

Royce, J. R. Avoidance conditioning in nine strains of inbred mice using optimal stimulus parameters. Behavior Genetics, 1972, 2, 107-110.

Royce, J. R. The conceptual framework for a multi-factor theory
    of individuality. In J. R. Royce (Ed.), Multivariate
    analysis and psychological theory: The Third Banff Conference
    on Theoretical Psychology. London: Academic Press, 1973,
    pp. 305-407.
Royce, J. R. Cognition and knowledge: Psychological epistemology.
    In E. C. Carterette & M. P. Friedman (Eds.), Handbook of per-
    ception. Vol. 1. Historical and philosophical roots to
    perception. New York: Academic Press, 1974, pp. 149-176.
Royce, J. R. Epistemic styles, individuality and world-view. In
    A. Debons & W. Cameron (Eds.), NATO Conference on Information
    Sciences. Leyden, The Netherlands: International Publish-
    ing, 1975, pp. 259-295.
Royce, J. R. Genetics, environment and intelligence: A theoreti-
    cal synthesis. In A. Oliverio (Ed.), Genetics, environment
    and intelligence. Amsterdam, The Netherlands: Elsevier/
    North-Holland, 1977, pp. 239-268.
Royce, J. R. Personality integration: A synthesis of the parts
    and wholes of individuality theory. Center Paper in Pro-
    gress, 1978a.
Royce, J. R. The genetic correlates of emotionality. Center
    Paper in Progress, 1978b.
Royce, J. R. How we can best advance the construction of theory
    in psychology. Canadian Psychological Review, 1978c, in
    press.
Royce, J. R., & Buss, A. R. The role of general systems and in-
    formation theory in multi-factor individuality theory.
    Canadian Psychological Review, 1976, 17, 1-21.
Royce, J. R., Carran, A. B., & Howarth, E. A factor analysis of
    emotionality in ten strains of inbred mice. Multivariate
    Behavioral Research, 1970, 5, 19-48.
Royce, J. R., & Covington, M. Genetic differences in the avoid-
    ance conditioning of mice. Journal of Comparative and
    Physiological Psychology, 1960, 53, 197-200.
Royce, J. R., Coward, H., Egan, E., Kessel, F., & Mos, L. Psy-
    chological epistemology: A critical review of the empiri-
    cal literature and the theoretical issues. Genetic Psy-
    chology Monographs, 1978, 97, 265-353.
Royce, J. R., & Diamond, S. Toward a multifactor-system theory
    of emotion: Cognitive-affective interaction. Center
    Paper in Progress, 1979.
Royce, J. R., Holmes, T. M., & Poley, W. Behavior genetic analy-
    sis of mouse emotionality. III. The diallel analysis. Be-
    havior Genetics, 1975, 5, 351-372.
Royce, J. R., Kearsley, G. P., & Klare, W. The relationship be-
    tween factors and psychological processes. In J. M. Scandura
    & C. J. Brainerd (Eds.), Structural/Process theories of com-
    plex human behavior, NATO Advanced Study Institute. Leiden,
    Holland: Sijthoff International Publishing Company, 1978.

Royce, J. R., & McDermott, J. A multi-dimensional system dynamics model of affect. Motivation and Emotion, 1977, 1, 193-224.

Royce, J. R., Poley, W., & Yeudall, L. T. Diallel analysis of avoidance conditioning in inbred strains of mice. Journal of Comparative and Physiological Psychology, 1971, 76, 353-358.

Royce, J. R., Poley, W., & Yeudall, L. T. Behavior-genetic analysis of mouse emotionality: I. Factor analysis. Journal of Comparative and Physiological Psychology, 1973a, 83, 36-47.

Royce, J. R., & Poley, W. Behavior genetic analysis of mouse emotionality: II. Stability of factors across genotypes. Animal Learning and Behavior, 1973b, 1, 116-120.

Royce, J. R., & Powell, A. An overview of a factor-system theory of individuality. Center Paper in Progress, 1978.

Royce, J. R., & Powell, A. A multifactor-system dynamics theory of individuality (book in preparation).

Scarr, S. Genetic factors in activity motivation. Child Development, 1966, 37, 663-674.

Schlesinger, K., Elston, R. C., & Boggan, W. The genetics of sound-induced seizures in mice. Genetics, 1966, 54, 95-103.

Schlesinger, K., & Griek, L. Genetics of audiogenic seizures. III. Time response relationships between drug administration and seizure susceptibility. Life Sciences, 1970, 9, 721-729.

Schopflocher, D., & Royce, J. R. The internal validity of the Psycho-Epistemological Profile. Center Paper in Progress, 1979.

Schopflocher, D., Royce, J. R., & Meehan, K. The structure of values: A multi-factor theory. Center Paper in Progress, 1979.

Shields, J. Personality differences and neurotic traits in normal twin schoolchildren. Eugenics Review, 1953, 45, 213-246.

Shields, J. Monozygotic twins: Brought up apart and brought up together. London: Oxford University Press, 1962.

Singer, R. N. Motor learning and human performance: An application to physical education skills (2nd ed.). New York: MacMillan, 1975.

Snyderk L. H. Inherited taste deficiency. Science, 1931, 74, 151-152.

Snyder, L., & Davidson, D. Studies in human inheritance. XVIII. The inheritance of taste deficiency to diphenylgranadine. Eugenics News, 1937, 22, 1-2.

Sommerhof, G. The abstract characteristics of living systems. In F. I. Emery (Ed.), Systems thinking: Selected readings. Middlesex, England: Penguin, 1969.

Spuhler, K. P. Family resemblance for cognitive performance. An assessment of genetic and environmental contributions to variation. Unpublished dissertation, University of Colorado, 1976.

Surwillo, W. W. Internal histograms of period of electroencephalogram and reaction time in twins. Behavior Genetics, 1977, 7,
161-169.

Sze, P. Y. Neurochemical factors in auditory stimulation and de-
velopment of susceptibility to audiogenic seizures. In B. L.
Welch & A. S. Welch (Eds.), Psychological effects of noise.
New York: Plenum Press, 1970, pp. 259-270.

Thiessen, D. D. Gene organization and behavior. New York: Random House, 1972.

Thurstone, T., Thurstone, L., & Strandskov, H. A psychological
study of twins. Chapel Hill: University of North Carolina,
Psychometric Lab., #4, 1953.

Tobach, E., Bellin, J. S., & Das, D. K. Differences in bitter
taste perception in three strains of rats. Behavior Genetics,
1974, 4, 405-410.

Vandenberg, S. G. The hereditary abilities study: Hereditary
components in a psychological test battery. American Journal
of Human Genetics, 1962, 14, 220-237.

Vandenberg, S. G. Multivariate analysis of twin differences. In
S. G. Vandenberg (Ed.), Methods and goals in human behavior
genetics. New York: Academic Press, 1965, pp. 29-44.

Vandenberg, S. G. Contributions of twin research to psychology.
Psychological Bulletin, 1966, 66, 327-352.

Vandenberg, S. G. The nature and nurture of intelligence. In
D. C. Glass (Ed.), Genetics. New York: Rockefeller University Press, 1968, pp. 3-58.

Vandenberg, S., & Kuse, A. R. Spatial ability: A critical review of the sex-linked major-gene hypothesis. In M. Wittig
& A. Peterson (Eds.), Determinants of sex-related differences
in cognitive functioning. New York: Academic Press, 1977.

Wachtel, P. L. Field dependence and psychological differentiation:
A re-examination. Perceptual and Motor Skills, 1972, 35,
179-189.

Wardell, D., & Royce, J. R. Relationships between cognitive and
temperament traits and the concept of "style". Journal of
Multivariate Experimental Personality and Clinical Psychology,
1975, 1, 244-266.

Wardell, D., & Royce, J. R. Toward a multi-factor theory of styles
and their relationships to cognition and affect. Journal of
Personality, 1978, 46(3), 474-505.

Witkin, H. A., Dyk, R. B., Faterson, H. F., Goodenough, D. R., &
Karp, S. A. Psychological differentiation. New York:
Wiley, 1962.

Witkin, H. A., & Goodenough, D. R. Field dependence revisited.
Research Bulletin. Princeton, New Jersey: Educational
Testing Service, 1976.

Witkin, H. A., Oltman, P. K., Cox, P. W., Ehrlichman, E., Hamm, R. M., & Ringler, R. W. Field-dependence-independence and psychological differentiation. A bibliography through 1972. Research Bulletin. Princeton, N.J.: Educational Testing Service, 1973.

Wright, S. The method of path coefficients. Annals of Mathematical Statistics, 1934, 5, 161-215.

COMMENT BY H. J. EYSENCK

I would think that the effort that has gone into this paper is very much worthwhile, and has been to some degree successful. I would think on the whole that the systematization attempted is impossible but useful, while the methods employed, particularly those of factor analysis, are necessary but not sufficient. Factor analysis has always been in the curious position of having many devoted friends and many determined enemies; I myself fall between these two chairs, a position which is undignified but scientifically perhaps more defensible. I agree with Royce that, contrary to the position taken by Mischel and others, trait and type concepts are essential in the psychology of personality, and that there is ample evidence to support the view of long-lasting structural concepts in personality; these concepts can be purified and localised best by means of factor analysis.

However, there are many difficulties in the use of this technique, particularly when large numbers of factors are involved. Some of these difficulties are as follows.

1. The analysis depends very much on the elements analysed. Thus factor analysts in the ability field usually work with test scores, but it is clear that a given test score can be arrived at in many different ways. People having identical scores may have the same number of items right, but they may differ in the number of items wrong, the number of items abandoned, the number of items omitted, or the particular difficulty level of the items scored right, wrong, abandoned, or omitted. When an analysis of latency scores on single items is carried out, the apparently univocal I.Q. or primary ability investigated breaks down into three independent variables, namely mental speed, persistence, and error checking; these could never have been discovered by means of factor analysis (Eysenck, 1973). The choice of elements analysed is usually subjective (and in the case of intelligence tests, erroneous) and this subjectivity renders the findings from factor analysis less acceptable than they would otherwise be.

2. It is usually assumed that primary factors are "unitary" in some way. I have taken a typical factorially "pure" measure of social shyness from the Guilford Scales and correlated the individual items with scales measuring the independent dimensions of neuroticism and extraversion (Eysenck, 1956). The results showed that half the items correlated with N but not with E, the others with E but not with N. In other words a scale which was claimed to be univocal on the basis of factorial analysis in fact broke up into two quite independent parts. This must make one doubtful about the reality of primary factors as "univocal".

3. Factors are often declared to be identical in terms of their content, or other subjective appreciations. Factors may be discovered to be more or less similar to each other, in terms of objective indices of factor comparison, but they are never identical, and such comparisons are inevitably subjective. For this reason any scheme based on factorial analysis alone is bound to lack sharp definitions, and also to lack objectivity to some extent.

4. Factors in order to be acceptable as building stones of a theory of personality must be replicable. Royce includes in his summary Cattell's factors of surgency, affectothymia, ego strength, cortertia, etc.; yet these factors have never been found to be replicable by workers outside the Cattell laboratories, although many have attempted to carry out such replications in different countries. Nonreplicable factors of this kind cannot form the foundation for a secure science of personality study.

5. Some of the terms used by factor analysts, which recur in Royce's paper, such as "memorization" are meaningless in terms of the experimental study of memory, which deals with such concepts as iconic memory, short-term memory, long-term memory, retrieval, etc. In order to make such terms meaningful there should be a close relationship between experimental psychology and factor analysis, which unfortunately is usually missing.

As a general critique, applying to most if not all factor analytic studies, and based on the existence of what Cronbach called the two disciplines of scientific psychology, no definitive conclusions are possible from purely correlational studies unsubstantiated by univariate, theoretically oriented experimental work, and similarly experimental studies need to include personality and other multivariate concepts in their design to obviate the overloading of the error term with variance attributable to individual differences (Eysenck, 1977). This unification of psychology is essential for any proper systematization, such as that attempted by Royce. Multivariate analyses are not enough; they require supplementation by experimental studies of the bivariate type.

REPLY TO H. J. EYSENCK

Joseph R. Royce

Professor Eysenck's major point is that the two psychologies (Cronbach, 1957) need each other—a point with which I'm in complete agreement (e.g., Royce, 1950, 1977a). Furthermore, my own experimental research has focused on the multivariate-bivariate strategy à la Eysenck's comment (Royce, 1978a, b). Finally, in my oral presentation and elsewhere (e.g., Royce, 1973; Royce & Powell, 1978) I have made the point that factor analysis merely gets at the dimensional basis of individuality. The total project, on the other hand, involves: (1) a theoretical synthesis—interdigitating concepts from factor theory, system theory, and information processing theory, (2) a methodological synthesis—accommodating the roles of the two psychologies, and (3) an empirical synthesis—explaining the relevant empirical findings.

As to Eysenck's critique of factor analysis, especially his first point concerning the composition of a test battery, I refer the reader to my comment on Fuller's paper, and I offer the following supplementary remarks. We certainly need more of the kind of investigation Eysenck calls for in his first point. For example, analysis of the relationships between factors and information processing has barely begun. [For more on this see our theoretical analyses (Royce & Buss, 1976; Royce, Kearsley, & Klare, 1978), and see the experimental research of Carroll (1976); Hunt (1974); Hunt, Frost, & Lunneborg, 1973), and Snow (1976a, b, 1978).]

My answer to point #2 is that tests are usually factorially complex, but that factors are functional unities. More specifically, Guilford's test was never put forward as a pure measure of social shyness (i.e., Guilford did not make that claim). The development of pure measures of a specifiable factor remains as a challenge for the future. In the meantime the standard procedure involves estimating the factor in question in terms of an appropriate subset of "marker variables" via the regression formula

$F = A'R^{-1}Z$ (Harman, 1976; where F refers to the matrix of factor scores, A refers to the factor loadings, R refers to the correlation matrix and Z refers to standardized scores). The unitary interpretation of first order factors seems to be fairly straightforward, but there are complications concerning the interpretation of higher order factors because they are identified via subsets of lower order factors. Individuality theory provides one possible answer to this conceptual dilemma—namely, the hypothesis that higher order constructs are molar systemic functional units (such as sub-systems) whereas the primaries constitute the elemental functional units of systems (Royce, 1979a).

In point #5 Professor Eysenck raises the issues of structural complexity and functional dynamics. I am in agreement with his point that our treatment of the memory aspects of cognitive processing is oversimplified. On the other hand, the reader is urged to compare our treatment of cognitive structure (Diamond & Royce, 1978) and dynamics (Powell & Royce, 1978) with the available alternatives. What we have found is that extant multivariate (i.e., individual differences) statements are long on structure and short on dynamics, and that the available bivariate (i.e., experimental)

statements are long on dynamics and short on structure. In short,
it is our view that no existing statement is adequate to the task,
but that the strategy of combining multivariate and bivariate
methodologies in an information processing context is more effective than either approach in isolation.

Points #3 and #4 have to do with the issue of factor invariance. Eysenck and I are in agreement on the relevance of the
principle of invariance--the disagreements occur when we get to
conceptual frameworks and the empirical findings. And there have
been long standing incompatibilities in the conceptual frameworks
of Eysenck, Cattell, and Guilford (e.g., see the recent exchange
between Eysenck, 1977, and Guilford, 1975, 1977, for an example
of this point). The "theory laden" view of science (see such
authors as Feyerabend, 1965, 1970; Radnitzky, 1970; and Wartofsky,
1968, for the philosophic perspective, and see Royce, 1976, 1977b,
1978c, for an elaboration of its implications for psychology) is
transparently relevant to this situation. The essence of the
theory laden view is that there is no such thing as a neutral observation. The implication is that observations are made via a
conceptual lens, and that scientific observations are carried out
in order to provide the empirical correlates of a theory's constructs. Thus, observations provide the substantive content of
the theoretician's abstraction. The relevance of this bit of
metatheory to the present analysis is that Eysenck's conceptual
framework is focused on a small number (three--introversion-
extraversion, neuroticism, and psychoticism) of broad theoretical
constructs, while both Guilford and Cattell are committed to a
large number of narrow range concepts. One of the virtues of individuality theory is that it accommodates the empirical findings
of Eysenck, Cattell, and Guilford (and others) as complementary
(see especially Royce & McDermott, 1977, and Royce, 1979b) rather
than viewing them as contradictory.

COMMENT BY S. G. VANDENBERG

I must confess first of all to a sense of awe. What Professor
Royce is attempting to do is more than I can fully encompass, so
my comments are to be taken as a rather personal reaction. It
seems a bit like Einstein's attempt to unify the physical sciences.
I sense two contradictory aims. One is to detect through all the
diversity and individual creativity of hundreds of psychologists
the underlying master plan of the nature of behavior. The other
is to give to the ideas of all those individuals their "due" respect, i.e., nearly equal weight. I am afraid that the two aims
conflict basically.

One cannot write a good review of past research and at the

same time propose a new, comprehensive theory. Or, at least, it would be <u>very</u>, <u>very</u> difficult to accomplish both purposes simultaneously. It has frequently been said that if a physicist of the caliber of Einstein or Bohr--or, better yet, Newton--would take the time, psychology would be set straight in no time at all. I suspect that Royce believes this. Although he is modest enough to disclaim that sort of genius, he does believe that if a bright and well-trained individual spends all his time on theorizing, he can bring more order to psychology than we now have.

I happen to disagree. Although we certainly need more full-time theorists, we still have not enough basic data to begin useful theorizing at that level. Most of the data available to us are incredibly sloppy, ad hoc, biased, and whatever bad word you like better. Most of our experiments do not ask the sort of basic questions that need to be asked, even if not answered, to permit strong theories about important issues that would start defining the field of psychology in as unified a way as Royce strives to do.

The demands on psychology are just too overwhelming. We are asked to take the place of religion and philosophy, as well as to find man's place among the other animals . . . perhaps even to justify our expansion into space. But I do not want to sound defeatist.

I do believe that things are changing and that we may be on the brink of a new science of human intelligence, its limits and potentials, which we have been looking for since religion lost its monopoly, say with Descartes, but which was sought by Aristotle and Indian philosophers. I just wish I could see what will be published 25 years from now, if we do not blow ourselves off the earth or succumb to some type of government which will lead us into a new type of Middle Ages.

Perhaps Royce's integration can show us how far we are from that ideal condition of science which we all desire. Perhaps we need more rather than less of the type of effort to which he has so single-mindedly devoted his time.

REPLY TO S. G. VANDENBERG

Joseph R. Royce

Professor Vandenberg makes a point of the massiveness of individuality theory. But such efforts are miniscule when placed alongside the mammoth commitments to laboratories, computers, and the other paraphernalia for gathering data. Unless we make comparable commitments to the advancement of theory psychology will continue on its present course of increasing its empirical tonnage at the expense of rational syntheses. Recent analyses of the present state of psychology make it abundantly clear that sophistication in theory construction has not kept pace with the technical advances in experimentation and statistical-methodological analysis (e.g., see the writings of Koch, 1959, 1964, 1974, 1976, and Royce, 1970, 1976, 1978, and the recent Nebraska symposium edited by Arnold, 1976). The major implication of this point is that advancement in psychology is being severely retarded because of theoretical inadequacies. And, contrary to the super-empiricistic myth (exemplified once again in Vandenberg's comment), theoretical advance cannot be accomplished by the mere gathering of more (or even better) data. On the contrary, such advances depend upon creative and insightful theoretical analysis and synthesis, and theory construction strategies which take the current state of the art into account. For example, in the case of highly advanced domains (i.e., where explanatory theory has been developed), the optimal strategy is to maximize theoretical comprehensiveness while simultaneously minimizing the number of theoretical principles (parsimony). The optimal strategy in the case of descriptive theory involves developing a tight nomological network of relatively limited scope, with the prospect of expanding toward an area theory. And, finally, the optimal strategy for programmatic theory is to get a heuristic handle on the domain in question by identifying and precising some of the relevant theoretical constructs and exploring their interrelationships (i.e., by getting a nomological network started).

In short, theory is a necessary part of science, not a luxury. Furthermore, scientific advancement is optimized if we develop differential strategies in the construction of theory. For example, individuality theory in its present form has been characterized as descriptive. Whether it will evolve into an explanatory theory will not be determined by Vandenberg's views or mine--it will be determined by the outcome of the continuing interplay between the rational reconstructions of theory builders and the empirical observations of data gatherers.

REFERENCES

Arnold, W. J. (Ed.) Nebraska Symposium on motivation: Conceptual foundations of psychology. Lincoln, Nebraska: University of Nebraska Press, 1976.
Carroll, J. B. Psychometric tests as cognitive tasks: A new "structure of intellect". In L. B. Resnick (Ed.), The nature of intelligence. Hillsdale, New Jersey: Lawrence Erlbaum Associates, 1976.

Cronbach, L. J. The two disciplines of scientific psychology. American Psychologist, 1957, 12, 671–684.

Diamond, S., & Royce, J. R. Cognitive abilities as expressions of three "ways of knowing". Center Paper in Progress, 1978.

Eysenck, H. J. The questionnaire measurement of neuroticism and extraversion. Revista di Psicologia, 1956, 50, 113–140.

Eysenck, H. J. The measurement of intelligence. Lancaster: Medical & Technical Publishers, 1973.

Eysenck, H. J. The measurement of personality. Lancaster: Medical & Technical Publishers, 1977.

Eysenck, H. J. Personality and factor analysis: A reply to Guilford. Psychological Bulletin, 1977, 84, 405–411.

Feyerabend, P. K. Problems of empiricism. In R. G. Colodny (Ed.), Beyond the edge of certainty. New York: Prentice Hall, 1965.

Feyerabend, P. K. Against method. In M. Radner & S. Winokur (Eds.), Minnesota studies in the philosophy of science (Vol. 4). Minneapolis: University of Minnesota Press, 1970.

Guilford, J. P. Factors and pactors of personality. Psychological Bulletin, 1975, 82, 802–814.

Guilford, J. P. Will the real factor of extraversion–introversion please stand up? A reply to Eysenck. Psychological Bulletin, 1977, 84, 412–416.

Harman, H. Modern factor analysis (3rd ed.). Chicago: University of Chicago Press, 1976.

Hunt, E. B. Quote the raven? Nevermore. In L. Gregg (Ed.), Knowledge and cognition. Potomac, Md.: Lawrence Erlbaum, 1974, pp. 129–157.

Hunt, E. B., Frost, N., & Lunneborg, C. Individual differences in cognition: A new approach to intelligence. In G. Bower (Ed.), Advances in learning and motivation (Vol. 7). New York: Academic Press, 1973, pp. 87–122.

Koch, S. (Ed.). Psychology: A study of a science. New York: McGraw-Hill, 1959.

Koch, S. Psychology and the emerging conceptions of knowledge as unitary. In T. N. Wann (Ed.), Behaviorism and phenomenology. Chicago: University of Chicago Press, 1964, pp. 1–81.

Koch, S. Psychology as science. In S. C. Brown (Ed.), Philosophy of psychology. London: Macmillan, 1974.

Koch, S. Language communities, search cells, and the psychological studies. In W. J. Arnold (Ed.), The Nebraska Symposium on Motivation: Conceptual foundations of psychology. Lincoln, Nebraska: University of Nebraska Press, 1976, pp. 580–665.

Powell, A., & Royce, J. R. Cognitive information processing: The role of individual differences in the search for invariants. Center Paper in Progress, 1978.

Radnitsky, G. Contemporary schools of metascience. Goteborg: Adademiforlaget, 1970.

Royce, J. R. A synthesis of experimental designs in program research. Journal of General Psychology, 1950, 43, 295–303.

Royce, J. R.   The present situation in theoretical psychology.   In
    J. R. Royce (Ed.), Toward unification in psychology. Toronto:
    University of Toronto Press, 1970, pp. 10-52.
Royce, J. R.   The conceptual framework for a multi-factor theory
    of individuality. In J. R. Royce (Ed.), Multivariate
    analysis and psychological theory. London: Academic Press,
    1973, pp. 305-407.
Royce, J. R.   Psychology is multi: methodological, variate, epis-
    temic, world-view, systemic, paradigmatic, theoretic, and
    disciplinary. In W. J. Arnold (Ed.), Nebraska Symposium on
    Motivation: Conceptual foundations of psychology. Lincoln,
    Nebraska: University of Nebraska Press, 1976, pp. 1-63.
Royce, J. R.   Guest Editorial: Have we lost sight of the original
    vision for SMEP and MBR? Multivariate Behavioral Research,
    1977a, 12, 135-141.
Royce, J. R.   Toward an indigenous philosophy for psychology. The
    Ontario Psychologist, 1977b, 9, 16-32.
Royce, J. R.   How we can best advance the construction of theory
    in psychology. Canadian Psychological Review, 1978, in press.
Royce, J. R.   The genetic correlates of emotionality. Center
    Paper in Progress, 1978a.
Royce, J. R.   The life style of a theory oriented generalist in
    a time of empirical specialists. In T. S. Krawiec (Ed.),
    The psychologists (Vol. III). Brandon, Vermont: Clinical
    Psychology Publishing Co. Inc., 1978b.
Royce, J. R.   How we can best advance the construction of theory
    in psychology. Canadian Psychological Review, 1978c, in
    press.
Royce, J. R.   Toward a viable theory of individual differences.
    Center Paper in Progress, 1979b.
Royce, J. R., & Buss, A. R.   The role of general systems and in-
    formation theory in multi-factor individuality theory.
    Canadian Psychological Review, 1976, 17, 1-21.
Royce, J. R., Kearsley, G. P., & Klare, W.   The relationship be-
    tween factors and psychological processes. In J. M. Scandura
    & C. J. Brainerd (Eds.), Structural/process theories of
    complex human behavior, NATO Advanced Study Institute.
    Leiden, Holland: Sijthoff International Publishing Company,
    1978.
Royce, J. R., & McDermott, J.   A multi-dimensional system dynamics
    model of affect. Motivation and Emotion, 1977, 1, 193-224.
Royce, J. R., & Powell, A.   An overview of multifactor-system
    theory. Center Paper in Progress, 1978.
Snow, R. E.   Research on aptitudes: A progress report. Technical
    Report No. 1., Aptitude Research Project, Stanford University,
    1976a.
Snow, R. E.   Theory and method for research on aptitude processes:
    A prospectus. Technical Report No. 2, Aptitude Research
    Project, Stanford University, 1976b.

658

Snow, R. E. Aptitude processes. To appear in R. E. Snow, P. A.
    Federico, & W. Montague (Eds.), Aptitude, learning, and
    instruction: Cognitive process analyses, 1978, in press.
Wartofsky, M. W. Conceptual foundations of scientific thought.
    London: Macmillan, 1968.

EPILOGUE: The Goals and Future of Behavior Genetics

E. W. Caspari

EPILOGUE: THE GOALS AND FUTURE OF BEHAVIOR GENETICS

Ernst W. Caspari

Department of Biology, University of Rochester,
Rochester, N.Y., U.S.A.

> Wenn eine Wissenschaft zu stocken und, ohn-
> erachtet der Bemühung vieler tätiger Menschen
> nicht vom Flecke zu rühren scheint, so lässt
> sich bemerken, dass die Schuld oft an einer
> gewissen Vorstellungsart, nach welcher die
> Gegenstände herkömmlich betrachtet werden,
> an einer einmal angenommenen Terminologie
> liege, welcher der grosse Haufe sich ohne
> weitere Bedingung unterwirft and nachfolgt,
> und welcher denkende Menschen selbst sich nur
> einzeln und nur in einzelnen Fallen schüchtern
> entziehen.

> Goethe

> When a science appears to progress haltingly
> and does not move ahead in spite of the toils
> of many active workers it may be noted that
> this is often due to a particular habitual
> way of thinking and to an accepted terminology
> to which the crowd submits and follows uncon-
> ditionally and from which even thoughtful men
> deviate only individually and diffidently and
> in isolated cases.

This quotation is the preamble to a fragment of a treatise on Comparative Anatomy which Goethe wrote in the 1790s and which he never finished. The quotation is applicable to the present state of Behavior Genetics as presented in the letter of Professor Royce inviting us to participate in the present Institute. There is certainly much activity in the field and a large amount of work of high quality is being produced. The number of competent workers in the field is increasing and the growing number of papers appearing has forced our journal "Behavior Genetics" to publish two additional issues per year.

Still Professor Royce indicated that in spite of the accumulation of this interesting and important material the field as a whole is not progressing sufficiently and he seems to feel that something may be amiss in the conceptual and methodological basis of the field, and this concern is shared by a number of other behavior geneticists. Contrary to the habits of the 18th century, to which Goethe alluded, Dr. Royce decided that a departure from commonly held but impeding assumptions could be accelerated if it is not left to the tentative initiative of individuals, but is discussed freely within a group of competent, experienced, and critical scholars. Thus it was the goal of our discussions to investigate the basic assumptions of the field, not to present additional material. The material presented, old and new, serves primarily the purpose of illustration.

In this concluding chapter I shall therefore try to summarize the opinions of the participants concerning the methods and ideas in behavior genetics and I shall try to formulate the goals towards which our discipline is moving. I also shall try to make some guesses on the directions in which the field is going to develop in the future.

1. THE BACKGROUND AND SCOPE OF BEHAVIOR GENETICS

I will start by recalling the intellectual background in which behavior genetics is developing. Genetics is in many respects a dead science. Its goals were formulated by Muller (1922): ". . . the question as to what the general principle of gene construction is, that permits this phenomenon of mutable autocatalysis, is the most fundamental question of genetics." This formulation was widely accepted by geneticists at the time and later. At present this problem has been solved. We know the chemical structure of the genetic material, DNA, and we understand in principle how this structure accounts for its main functions, identical reproduction, mutability and the control of phenotypes. There is still much work going on to elucidate the exact mechanisms of these functions, and the problem of recombination still remains unsolved. But in general genetics represents at present an integrated system

of well established facts and theory which can be used by other
branches of the life sciences as a basis for their own concerns.
In this way subfields of genetics have developed which apply
genetic concepts to other disciplines, such as immunogenetics,
pharmacogenetics, behavior genetics and others.

As I have pointed out recently (Caspari, 1975), behavior
genetics combines inputs from several disciplines: genetics, psychology, ethology, evolutionary biology and more recently theoretical ecology, and, to a lesser degree, neurophysiology and neurochemistry. Out of this wealth of material certain aspects have
been emphasized in this Institute while others have been neglected
or only peripherally mentioned. There has been little concern
with neurology, neurophysiology and biochemistry, except for
Oliverio's talk and for Spuhler's discussion of neural mechanisms
involved in human language. The work on the behavior of lower
organisms has been de-emphasized, though some of it is mentioned in
the papers by Thiessen, van Abeelen and Fuller, and the chemotaxis
of bacteria is fully discussed by Spuhler.

The primary emphasis in this Conference has been on psychology
and the use of genetics for the understanding of psychological
phenomena. Royce has stated the purpose of the Institute in the
following words: "The problems surrounding the possible genetic
basis of styles highlight the major reason for assembling this
Institute—namely the need to develop explanatory theory in psychology." Thus the goals of behavior genetics are conceived with
relevance to psychological theory.

The attitudes of psychologists and of biologists in dealing
with behavior are quite different. Ethology is primarily descriptive and as van Abeelen put it, naturalistic. Immelmann states in
addition that ethologists in the past have mostly concentrated on
interspecific differences, though he shows that the methods of
ethology can be used to demonstrate individual variation. Psychologists, on the other hand, are more analytical and, as indicated by Thompson and Fuller, try to express general rules of behavior in terms of input and output, considering the intervening
organismic structures as a "black box". Psychologists, contrary
to ethologists, are also very interested in the modification of
behavior. For this reason the fixed action patterns which constitute a large part of the ethological literature are of little
interest to psychologists. The goal of psychologists is, as
Thompson put it, not only to understand but also to modify and
influence behavior. It is significant that of the extensive work
of Benzer and collaborators on the behavior of Drosophila only
the work by Quinn et al. on avoidance learning has been described
thoroughly in this Institute. Fulker has discussed these experiments and applied to them the methods of quantitative genetics.
These methods are the main statistical tools used by behavior

geneticists, and it may be convenient to start by examining the conceptual basis of this field.

2. PROGRESS IN QUANTITATIVE GENETICS

Most behavioral differences between individuals or inbred strains which are based on genes turn out to have a polygenic basis even though van Abeelen and Fuller point out that differences due to single mappable Mendelian genes have occasionally been observed. It was therefore decided early that the methods appropriate for the analysis of polygenic systems are the appropriate means for the study of behavioral differences. The first experiments in behavior genetics, Tryon's classical study of maze learning in rats, employed the technique of selective breeding, one of the standard methods of quantitative genetics. The early applications of quantitative genetics could, however, not give much information of theoretical interest. They could show that a particular character was influenced by additive genes and could therefore be selected for. Henderson points out that the techniques of quantitative genetics were originally designed for purposes of breeding in agriculture, and for this purpose these early concepts were satisfactory and successful. But for behavior genetics these methods did not give much information: they could give a minimum estimate of the number of independently segregating genes involved in a cross, in Drosophila the contribution of the different chromosomes could be estimated, and that was about it. Thus, quantitative behavior genetic work in the 1950s and early 1960s caused considerable frustration because it did not seem to lead to results of theoretical importance. The results could be used to counteract the pervasive influence of behaviorism which at that time was predominant in Psychology. But the methods were not sufficiently powerful to analyze the architecture of a behavioral character.

This situation has changed since 1960. New methods for the study of polygenic systems were developed by Mather, Jinks and others and these methods were successfully applied to behavior genetics primarily by Broadhurst. Introduction of these methods has greatly expanded the information obtained on behavioral characters by means of quantitative genetics.

Wahlsten, Broadhurst and Henderson agree that the concept of heritability, $\underline{h}^2$, does not give much information on the genetic architecture of a character. It is useful for selective breeding particularly if applied to morphological and physiological characters which can be more reliably measured than behavioral characters. Heritability does not indicate the direction of dominance or the existence of epistasis. Its value is influenced by the breeding structure of the population. Wahlsten has emphasized in his critical analysis that in both human and animal material genetic and environmental influences will show covariance as well as interaction, and that genes and environment are sometimes confounded. Thus heritability does not permit us to clearly distinguish genetic and environmental factors influencing a character.

Loehlin, however, has shown that heritability determinations can be treated with greater sophistication and then give reliable and important information on behavioral characters. Heritability for a character in human data can be estimated in several ways and, if these estimates agree, they can be combined to provide superior estimates. The data can be fitted to models considering both genetic and environmental factors, using correlation and path coefficient methods for human biometric data. Eysenck emphasizes that methods based on analysis of variance are more powerful and informative than those based on correlations.

The great advance in animal experimentation is based on the demonstration by Mather and his collaborators that genes which are under selective pressure show dominance or overdominance in the direction of the fittest allele while stabilizing selection and neutrality will result in additivity, or ambidirectional dominance. Thus, the index of average dominance is a measure for the effects of a character on Darwinian fitness. Neutrality of a character may be an indication that it is "unnatural", i.e., that it is not involved as a character per se in the natural environment of the organism but is a laboratory artefact produced by traits affecting the behavioral measures used. Sensitivity to electric shock is an example. The most widely used genetic method is the diallel cross, a very powerful method for analyzing additive and non-additive genetic variance. Another powerful breeding method has been introduced more recently, the triple test cross. This test is more sensitive than the diallel cross to intergenic and allelic interactions and thus can distinguish dominance from "potence", as Broadhurst and Fulker explain. Thus, we have now much more powerful methods of quantitative genetic analysis, and Broadhurst, Fulker and Henderson give numerous examples of the application of these methods, the results obtained and the pitfalls to be avoided.

These methods constitute an important step forward in the analysis of fitness in populations. It has always been a difficult problem to decide whether a particular character is of selective significance or whether it is not. Common sense hunches, naturalistic considerations and ethograms have been of little value, except for extreme cases such as viability and fertility, and experimental results have been ambiguous in many cases. Thus, it is of great importance that we have here a quantitative objective measure to indicate whether a particular measured character is under the influence of selection in nature and in which direction higher fitness lies. I was surprised by the analysis reported by Fulker indicating that avoidance learning is in fact a component of fitness in adult Drosophila. I had also some doubts whether in human populations there is a Darwinian advantage for intelligence. It is well established that intelligence has an influence on social success, but social success and reproductive success in humans are not necessarily correlated. It is thus comforting to learn from Fulker's paper that inbreeding studies indicate directional dominance for human cognitive ability, indicating that it is under positive selective pressure.

There is a second approach to the study of behavior genetics as indicated by van Abeelen, the use of mutations of single "major" genes. This approach has been primarily used in simple organisms. Thiessen reports the work by Bonner on slime molds and by Adler and others on bacteria, and Spuhler reviews thoroughly the work on chemotaxis in bacteria. In lower organisms the mutational approach has been successful insofar as the chemical basis of certain behavioral changes could be analyzed. In the work on bacteria reported by Spuhler it is striking that most of the mutations affecting chemotaxis are actually mutations of genes specifying receptors, i.e., part of the sensory apparatus, or the structure and function of the flagellum. There are apparently only four gene loci involved in the transfer of information from the sensory to the motor structures. Thus, the information transfer system in these organisms seems to be relatively simple and a similar situation may prevail in other simple organisms. Parallel work on animals, such as Benzer's work on Drosophila and Brenner's work on nematodes, has been mentioned. This work is based on the expectation that by isolating the interacting genes influencing a particular behavior the gap between sensory stimulus and motor reaction can be closed. The procedure is certainly not practical for use with mice, rats or humans. But the two ways of approaching behavior genetics lead us to raise the question of the relation between Mendelian genes and polygenic inheritance.

The first two decades of this century saw a bitter controversy between two schools of genetics, Mendelians and Biometricians. According to the historian of this struggle, W. B. Provine (1971), the views were reconciled by the demonstration by R. A. Fisher in 1918 that the results of biometric research can be explained as the result of many Mendelian genes with small effect acting additively. This has remained the fundamental theory of quantitative genetics. But while Fisher's explanation has ended the controversy it has not resulted in mutual understanding: quantitative geneticists do not usually keep up with the progress in Mendelian and molecular genetics and molecular geneticists frequently have difficulty in understanding the methods and language of quantitative genetics.

The usual assumption of quantitative genetics is that ordinary Mendelian genes have pleiotropic effects on many other characters and that the sum of genes affecting a particular character represents its polygenic system. That Mendelian genes can have pleiotropic effects on behavioral characters has been known since 1915 when Sturtevant described the effect of the gene yellow in Drosophila on mating behavior. An instructive example for the pleiotropic effect of genes controlling the enzymes dopa decarboxylase and dopa hydroxylase on wheel running activity has been given at this Institute by De Fries et al.

There is, however, the possibility that polygenic systems are determined not only by the pleiotropic effects of "major" genes but also by a different type of genes, polygenes. This hypothesis was originally proposed by Mather, but dropped at the time in the absence of confirmatory evidence. It has recently been revived, for different reasons, by Carson, J. L. King and myself (Carson, 1975; King, 1976; Caspari, in press), and the reasons for this assumption should be briefly discussed.

The term "gene" has undergone changes of meaning in its history. When Fisher attributed the biometric results to Mendelian genes he meant only that they are units which recombine and segregate, i.e., which are situated on the chromosomes. Under the influence of biochemical and molecular genetics we believe now that many genes act as structural genes, i.e., that they are DNA sequences determining the amino acid sequence of a specific protein; the pleiotropic effects are mediated by the reaction products of the protein or other results of the activity of the structural gene, as explained in the example given by De Fries. Thiessen has, however, pointed out that in addition to structural genes, we must assume the existence of regulatory genes which govern the activity of structural genes. Thiessen also raises the question how one can distinguish regulatory from structural genes in a higher organism. This is indeed a difficult question. Paigen (1971) has proposed that regulatory genes should show dominance while structural genes, at least at the first step of activity, show codominance or additivity, a possibility which would raise difficulties for the interpretation of dominance in evolutionary terms. I would like to raise here the question whether the distinction between these two types of genes is possible in principle.

It is well known that hormones can influence behavior. Furthermore, particular hormones affect certain target organs and cells but not others. This is due to the fact that the target cells possess receptors which combine specifically with the hormone. The hormone-receptor complex is carried to the nucleus and initiates activity of certain specific genes. The receptors are proteins and there must be genes which specify the structure of these proteins. Thus, <u>Tfm</u>, testicular feminization is a gene which inhibits the receptor protein for testosterone. <u>Tfm</u> individuals thus have rudimentary testes, but are phenotypically females and do not react to injection with testosterone. <u>Tfm</u> is a structural gene for receptor protein, but with respect to the genes activated by testosterone it would be described as a regulatory gene.

This relation becomes even clearer in the work of Nebert (in press). Certain carcinogens induce the synthesis of a number of enzymes, aryl dehydrogenases, which have similar but not identical functions. In different mouse strains, differences in inductivity are found, and these differences may be inherited in a monogenic or in a polygenic fashion. In one case of a monogenic difference the gene in question controls the receptor protein for the inducer. Thus, a gene which seems to control the expression of several structural genes actually controls a single protein responsible for the availability of an environmental substance, a stimulus, for the cell. Whether this gene is called a structural or a regulatory gene depends on the point of view of the investigator; it is a regulatory gene for the aryl dehydrogenases, a structural gene for the receptor protein. Control of receptor proteins is not the only controlling mechanism for gene action in higher organisms; control of transcription according to the Jacob-Monod model quoted by Thiessen is possible though it has not been demonstrated in animals. There are several additional possibilities.

It has been repeatedly mentioned in this Institute that pleiotropic action of genes is one of the main ways in which we can explain correlations between different behavioral characters. Another explanation of equal importance is suggested by the model of Nebert described above: many different genes may be activated by the same stimulus. Nebert has introduced the term "pleiotypic" for the response of several independent genes to the same environmental stimulus. Pleiotypic effects of this type may be quite important in the control of development as well as in the control of behavior. Thus, some of the factors in Royce's factor model may be genetically interpreted as the action of pleiotypic systems. Thiessen seems to have a similar idea when he introduces Clever's observations on the activation of batteries of genes in Drosophila. Whether batteries of genes are activated by means of a sequential cascade reaction, as Clever assumes, or by a common pleiotypic reaction, as is postulated in the model of Britten and Davidson, cannot be decided.

Pleiotypic reactions are important to reconcile the one to one reaction of gene and character found in the action of structural genes with the generalized and frequently hierarchic type of gene activity necessary for the interpretation of polygenic effects. From molecular biological findings we know that structural genes, defined as genes which give rise to m-RNA, make up only about ten percent of the whole DNA. While the remaining DNA may contain some "junk" DNA, i.e., DNA without informational function, much of it is assumed to have functions different from structural genes. Part of it is transcribed but not transformed into m-RNA. The whole field of the study of gene action in higher organisms is in a state of rapid development. The results will certainly have a bearing on our interpretation of the control of quantitative characters and of behavior genetics.

I feel that a model of gene action that is based exclusively on the model of the behavior of structural genes is insufficient. While I agree that the effects of structural genes are involved in the effects studied by the methods of quantitative genetics I propose that in addition various types of control of gene action account for the genetic architecture of polygenic characters.

The increase in the power of analysis by quantitative genetic methods has been spectacular and beneficial to progress in behavior genetics. We can look forward to further improvement in these methods and to the resulting deeper insights into the structure of behavioral characters and the human mind and their evolution. The activities in the molecular biology of gene action promise a different type of knowledge. As Loehlin has pointed out, one of the characteristics of quantitative genetic analysis is that genetic and environmental factors remain largely unspecified: they can be partitioned into different groups but not further identified. An understanding of the structure and functioning of the animal genome will help in clarifying further aspects of polygenic systems.

3. BEHAVIORAL PHENOTYPES

A recurrent concern of the Institute has been the choice of appropriate phenotypes for behavior genetic studies. There was general agreement that the characters chosen should be meaningful either for psychological theory or for an understanding of the evolutionary implications of behavior.

Several speakers, particularly Fuller, Henderson, and Royce, have proposed taxonomies of usable phenotypes. Their taxonomies are not congruent in every respect but one important category of distinction are those traits which can be directly measured, "ostensible phenotypes" in Fuller's nomenclature. Behaviorist psychologists have chosen characters which can be modified by environmental manipulation but which are otherwise reliable and reproducible. Ethologists, on the other hand, have chosen phenotypes observed in nature under uncontrolled conditions. Many of the latter are rigid responses and van Abeelen suggests that such behavioral characters should be used more extensively because they are better defined and are clearly related to fitness. But Henderson points out that the results may be less directly applicable to psychological theory and that many characters chosen from an ethogram may give less reproducible results under laboratory conditions than those conventionally used in psychology laboratories. Immelmann presents, however, an example of aspects of imprinting which are variable within a species, suitable for genetic analysis and can be easily studied under laboratory conditions. The choice between characters meaningful for psychological theory, easily and reproducibly managed in the laboratory, and interesting from the point of view of evolutionary theory remains an inherent difficulty in behavior genetic research.

Fuller distinguishes "ostensible phenotypes" from "inferred phenotypes" which cannot be directly measured but are derived from measurements by statistical manipulations, particularly factor analysis. They are in general identical with what Henderson calls "supercharacters" and are of greater interest for psychological theory than the ostensible phenotypes, since they reflect the internal structure of the behaving, goal-seeking organism. Therefore, a further subdivision of inferred phenotypes into specific, group and general factors has been proposed. Henderson assigns his supercharacters to seven levels additional to the ostensible phenotypes which form a hierarchic structure.

Particular phenotypes are discussed in the contributions of McClearn and of Eysenck. McClearn is concerned with the structure of an inferred phenotype called information processing which can be subdivided into components at the structural and at the processing level. There are in this phenotype good and reliable methods for measuring observed phenotypes which contribute to our understanding of the structure of memory. The results have wide applications to psychological theory and practical problems. The inferred phenotype studied by Eysenck is called personality and is regarded as the basis for the constancy and stability of the behavioral responses of individual organisms. Several dimensions of personality, such as extra- and introversion and neuroticism can be studied by appropriate tests. In both McClearn's and Eysenck's presentations the reality and constancy of the inferred phenotypes is emphasized, and an attempt is made to identify them and their components with specific neurological structures.

The most comprehensive and ambitious attempt at a description of behavioral phenotypes and their organization into a model of interacting components of personality is the factor model of Royce. He describes the structure of individuality in terms of six interacting systems each of which is organized in its own way at different levels. All levels consist of inferred phenotypes obtained by factor analysis. The phenotypes discussed by Eysenck and McClearn are components of this more general scheme.

The relations of the six systems and their functional role in the survival of the individual can be simply described. The sensory system translates environmental stimuli into biologically meaningful forms which are in turn translated into cognition and emotions by the cognitive and affective systems, respectively. Cognition consists in an organization of the environment and identification of environmental constancies and changes while emotions plus cognitive inputs prepare the organism for action via the motor system. The style and value systems are regarded as controlling cognition and affect and in this way action. All systems together constitute the individual personality; they control what the organism will react on and how it will react. The factors together describe the psychological system. Thus, factor theory is conceived as a synthesizing theory of psychology which is able to organize the vast amount of material supplied by psychological experimentation and observation.

Royce asks the question whether, and how much, the factors are genetically determined, and in his paper he offers evidence for genetic influences on many factors in the cognitive and affective systems. There is, in addition, one factor of the style system which shows a genetic component. This factor has been identified with Witkin's "field articulation" which has been known for some time to be in part determined by genes linked to the X-chromosome. Each of the factors is polygenically controlled and some of the polygenes involved may affect more than one factor. This has been demonstrated by De Fries in his analysis of data from Hawaii which show that genes determining spatial ability overlap with those for verbal ability and for visual memory. Thus, factors, as defined by factor analysis, are not necessarily defined by separate sets of genes.

Nor are they independent of environment. Royce has postulated that the sensory and motor systems should be heredity-dominant, the style and value systems environment-dominant, and the cognitive and affective systems mixed. Actually, strong genetic influences have been demonstrated in the cognitive and affective domain, while the only style factor investigated turned out to possess a genetic component. This finding was unexpected from the assumed function and origin of style which was assumed to be determined environmentally and transmitted culturally. But it should be considered that it contains many low-level components some of which may be more directly influenced by genes.

Behavioral phenotypes are actions of whole organisms. Thus, they cannot be direct gene products in the sense that enzymes and even morphological structures are. There can, therefore, be

no units of behavioral phenotypes, but they must be described in
the form of interacting dynamic systems such as Royce's factor
model. There is good evidence that many of the factors are influenced by genes, but as Fuller emphasized, the factors and
their components cannot be controlled by separate sets of genetic
units. Rather they must be the result of complex gene interactions, coadapted gene systems possibly dependent on pleiotypic
reactions.

For a system of this kind we can ask for the mechanism, how
it works. This is a descriptive and naturalistic task. We can
also ask for causes, and here many speakers have distinguished
between proximate and ultimate causes, the origin in individual
development and in evolution of the species. Some remarks about
the evolutionary implications have been made in our discussion of
polygenic systems. It remains to speak about the development of
behavioral phenotypes. This is an interesting topic because it
may be assumed that, just as in morphological development, batteries of genes become activated, possibly by pleiotypic responses.

4. BEHAVIORAL PHENOGENETICS

One difficulty in the analysis of the development of behavior
has always been that it has been contrasted to the development of
morphological structures. Morphological structures have frequently
been conceived as mainly determined by genes whereas for behavioral
characters the role of environmental factors has been emphasized.
Neither of these two statements is completely correct. The view
of morphological structures as determined by genes is due to the
fact that most morphological traits in animals develop early in
development and therefore to a certain degree independently of
environmental variables. But this is not true for plants where
environmental factors greatly influence development. On the other
hand, in many animals rigid behavior patterns are observed and
their development may be just as independent of the environment as
any morphological trait.

Genes affect phenotypes other than their biochemical primary
effects by means of development. This applies to behavioral phenotypes just as well as to morphological or physiological ones, as
pointed out by Oliverio. Royce has incorporated the developmental
dimension into his factor theory: every factor has its own developmental curve during the lifetime of the individual, with
maximum performance defining maturity. Maturity, as defined, can
be reached by different individuals at different chronological
ages. The developmental curve for heredity-dominant factors is
less easily shifted by environmental influences than it is for
environment-dominant factors. Behavioral phenotypes measured at
different times in the life cycle may therefore not be compared.

The observations of Immelmann on individual variation in the onset and duration of the sensitive period for imprinting opens up an important perspective for the developmental problem. A further complication is introduced by the report of Henderson that high activity in adult mice tends to be dominant while in infants dominance is directed toward low activity. As Henderson points out, this makes sense ecologically. But it also means that activity in infants and in adults may be genetically different characters. One has to be careful, therefore, to make sure whether a phenotype scored at different developmental periods is actually the same, i.e., controlled by the same genes, or whether it is a different character altogether which is functionally analogous at a different stage of life. The same consideration applies to the two sexes.

Developmental methods can give us an improved handle to analyze inferred phenotypes. If Fuller states that inferred phenotypes may be real he means that they have a definite and independent functional and developmental origin. This would express itself by the fact that the development of the components of a factor should show parallel dependence on genes and on environmental influences.

A very important developmental approach has been proposed by Oliverio. It deals with the difference between rigid and plastic phenotypes. In earlier times it was assumed that rigid behavior is characteristic for lower animals and plastic behavior for higher animals. Some modification has to be introduced: conditioning has been demonstrated in insects. On the other hand, plastic behavior patterns are more prominent in mammals, particularly in Cetacea, Carnivora and Primates than in other animals. In humans the predominance of learned behavioral characters has progressed so far that one is at a loss to describe a clear fixed action pattern in adults. From an ecological point of view, Mayr (1974) has pointed out that it is advantageous for some types of behavior, such as feeding behavior, to be to a certain degree modifiable and variable, while behaviors serving as intraspecific or interspecific signals should be rigid so as to be unambiguous. Similarly, Oliverio points out that one should expect rigid behavior patterns in ecological specialists while generalists may be assumed to be more plastic.

Oliverio's most important point is the suggestion that the difference between rigid versus plastic behavior patterns may developmentally be a consequence of maturity at birth. Precocial animals which are born with a relatively developed nervous system will show predominantly fixed action patterns and may be modified by imprinting, while atricious species are born with an immature nervous system which during maturation will find itself exposed to a variety of environmental stimuli. He supports this concept by

very interesting observations on mouse strains with slightly different maturity at birth. I wonder how different related species
with drastically different degrees of maturity at birth, such as
rat and guinea pig, would compare in this respect.

Oliverio thus accounts for a very fundamental behavioral difference, rigid versus plastic behavior, by differences in the
maturity of the CNS at birth. He points out, in agreement with
several other speakers, that genes do not directly influence behavior but do it via control of the differentiation and rates of
development of different parts of the brain. He feels that neurophysiology and neurobiochemistry will ultimately give more insight
into behavior genetics than the quantitative genetic approach.

It appears to me that these two approaches are complementary
rather than opposed. Neurobiochemistry and neurobiology are the
most direct ways by which the "empty organism" can be filled with
structures which are meaningful from the point of view of behavior.
Polygenes are not, in principle, defined by individual functions.
On the other hand, neurophysiology can give little information on
the fundamental processes involved in the evolution of behavior.
All evolutionary information obtained from neurological studies is
of the phylogenetic kind and does not apply to mechanisms of evolution.

5. THE NATURE/NURTURE PROBLEM

I do not want to spend much time on the nature-nurture problem
since it has been implicitly discussed in the preceding sections.
The partitioning of variance in the quantitative genetic approach
and the interpretation of developmental rates of brain and behavior
are all approaches to the heredity-environment problem. But it
should be pointed out that this problem has been, and still is,
the central problem of behavior genetics.

Therefore, a few remarks dealing specifically with this problem seem to be appropriate. The nature-nurture problem has been
historically the first one dealt with in behavior genetics. At
present, behavior geneticists are often somewhat tired of it.
Moreover, the problem has political and emotional overtones, conditions which are not conducive to objective research. Therefore
one can see a tendency to sweep the problem under the rug with
statements like the following: "The problem is in principle
solved"; "the problem is not correctly stated"; "it does not exist",
or even the moralistic and obscurantist attitude, "the problem
should not be raised." Nevertheless, it keeps always cropping up,
and we have a responsibility to face it. This is particularly
important since behaviorist and Freudian dogmas still dominate not
only academic psychology but even more importantly the attitude of

the public. I personally find the social and ethical implications of mind control implied in Skinner's "Beyond Freedom and Dignity" much more frightening than the potentialities of genetic engineering and cloning. But behaviorist psychologists have always had a better publicity than geneticists.

The nature-nurture problem can easily be solved in plants and animals by using the Latin square design, and similar experimental designs suited for the study of behavior genetics of laboratory animals have been reported by several participants of this Institute. The difficulty is that the number of possible genotypes and environmental conditions and the number of parameters involved becomes very high. The problem is even more difficult for human behavioral phenotypes since neither the genotype nor the environment can be controlled. Nevertheless, the present discussions have indicated some progress in the treatment of environmental variables. The partitioning of the variance into within and between families constitutes progress above the earlier vague concepts such as "home environment". The Hawaii study which has been referred to by McClearn and by De Fries et al. shows how much information can be gained by the analysis of a well designed collection of data. It has been pointed out that the between families variance is that which is important for Freudian and socio-economic models of the determination of behavior. On within-family sources of variance, birth order has been discussed by Thompson and by Fuller, but they came to different conclusions.

Wahlsten points out that many non-Mendelian types of inheritance exist. He mentions cytoplasmic inheritance (mitochondria), infectious transmission, transmission of cell morphology, transmission of chemicals and cultural inheritance. He proposes that the different types of inheritance are difficult to distinguish conclusively. In some cases of animals and plants this can be done experimentally: transmission through genes can be distinguished by segregation and recombination. Cytoplasmic components, infectious agents and chemicals are frequently transmitted through one sex only, usually the mother, and methods to distinguish these non-Mendelian factors from each other also exist. Wahlsten describes some experimental setups which can be used for some of these purposes and points out that they are very laborious and expensive. Cavalli-Sforza and Feldman (1978) have proposed to distinguish between genetic, phenotypic and environmental transmission. Under the term phenotypic they understand any characters in which the phenotype of one or both parents is directly transmitted to the progeny, cytoplasmic components, infectious agents but also characters acquired by learning, such as language. Environmental transmission in this sense means the influence of the environment provided by the parents for the developing offspring. This includes food provided by the parents, maternally transmitted social status in Primates such as the Japanese macaque, and social

status, wealth and other socio-economic variables in humans. Of
course there may occur interactions between these different types
of transmission, such as an influence of the genotype on the environment provided by the parents for the offspring. This is an
example of the confounding effects between heredity and environment
discussed by Wahlsten. Cavalli-Sforza and Feldman apply their tri-
variate model to specific cases, amongst them behavioral characters
in humans, including IQ. The analysis is complex due to the large
number of parameters involved but it appears possible if simpli-
fying assumptions are made.

The question of analyzing environmental factors and cultural
transmission has been discussed, especially by Thompson. He
points out that for the analysis of the effect of cultural variables in humans specific models for possible transmission should
be set up which can be tested by observation. He points out that
in some cases cultural transmission in humans may be either maternal, or related to the same sex, i.e., paternal for sons. It
is important to realize, as Thompson has shown, that cultural
transmission is not limited to Man but occurs in many animals with
parental care. Here cultural transmission of Thompson becomes
similar to environmental transmission of Cavalli-Sforza and Feldman. For its analysis it is necessary to develop particular models
specifying quantitative expectations for particular cases of environmental transmission.

While the influence of genes and environment on specific behavioral characters can in principle be analyzed, the application
of these methods is in many cases very difficult. Particularly
for human behavior the difficulty appears large, as is shown by
the sharp differences in the interpretation of the data relating
to IQ which have been repeatedly mentioned in this Institute. It
could be objected that the political implications involved in IQ
studies make this character particularly hard to work with. But
the same uncertainty applies to the data on handedness in humans
which should at first sight appear to be less controversial, and
to a number of other human behavioral characters.

6.   RESUME

The Institute has demonstrated that major progress has been
made in the methods of analysis of polygenic inheritance, as applied to behavior genetics. This applies to both the genetic and
the environmental parts of the variance and their interactions.
The results are most important for the interpretation of behavioral
phenotypes in terms of their contribution to fitness. It is expected that further progress will be made in devising even more
sensitive and powerful methods of genetic analysis. It should be
added that one of the consequences of this increase in analytic

power is that work in behavior genetics, both animal experimentation and the collection of human data will require increasingly complex designs. The cost of research in time, labor and money will become much larger.

Great progress in our understanding of polygenic models may arise if polygenic systems can be described more fully in terms of molecular biology. It is one of the unsatisfactory aspects of quantitative genetics that neither the genes nor the environmental factors involved are specified. Still genes have very specific effects, and behavioral reactions involve specific structures and functions of the organism. The same may be assumed for environmental factors.

Progress has also been made in the clarification of phenotypes used in behavior genetics. Previously, they were derived from the methods of experimental psychology and sometimes from ethograms, but the desiderata for a character to be studied had not been specified. Behavioral phenotypes are at first sight activities and the actions of organisms. They constitute the raw measurements of behavioral phenotypes. The main theory of psychology assumes that underlying these actions there is an invariant behavioral organization. This invariant organization may differ between species and between individuals within a species, and it is the tenet of behavior genetics that part of the individual differences in this invariant organization has a genetic basis, as species differences certainly have. In this way behavior genetics can and does contribute to general psychological theory.

It has been mentioned that classical psychology prefers to work with an "empty organism", i.e., to measure input and output of the organismic system without trying to describe the intervening system. The models of personality discussed here counteract this tendency: they offer a description of the intervening system derived from observations and formulated in terms of hierarchic psychological systems. To make these descriptions even more concrete the genetic basis for components of these systems should be analyzed and their neurological correlates should be determined. In this way the historical development of psychology may parallel that of genetics which has consisted of an increasing degree of concreteness of the gene concept. The neurological aspect, though not particularly stressed in this Institute, seems to be important because neurology is developing fast and the structural and biochemical basis of activities of the nervous system has been much clarified recently. The connection of these findings to psychological variables is as yet not well understood, nor is their relation to genetic factors. The way that such a connection may be established has been exemplified in Spuhler's discussion of human language systems. These systems offer some formal analogies to Royce's model of personality.

Genes control phenotypes by providing a program for development. The development of behavioral phenotypes in Man and in some animals has been thoroughly investigated and has been repeatedly referred to. In some cases genes provide the whole program for the sequence of developmental events. In other cases environmental factors can modify developmental processes or may even be necessary to start a developmental process. But it is not correct to say that in the latter cases genes do not play a role: genes determine the conditions for environmental influences to act, the sensitive periods during which they are effective and the reactions which will develop as the result of an environmental input. This applies not only to behavioral characters but constitutes a general scheme of development. It serves in the present context to clarify the interaction between genes and environmental factors in determining phenotypes.

7. SUMMARY

Behavior genetics has two major goals: first of all it is expected that it will contribute to a general explanatory theory of psychology. We have seen that considerable progress has been made in this respect and that more may be expected if we proceed with the task of defining the genetic, developmental and neurological bases of psychological organization. The second major goal involves evolutionary questions. Both the evolution of behavioral characters and the influence of behavioral characters in evolution and adaptation are important biological problems. The discussions have shown that in this area much progress has been made, particularly due to the improved methods of quantitative genetic analysis.

References

Carson, H. L. The genetics of speciation at the diploid level. American Naturalist, 1975, 109, 83.
Caspari, E. Probleme der modernen Verhaltensgenetik. Verhandlungen der Deutschen Zoologischen Gesellschaft, 1975, 68, 13.
Caspari, E. Evolutionary theory and the evolution of the human brain. In M. Hahn (Ed.), Development and evolution of brain size: Behavioral implications. New York and London: Academic Press, in press.
Cavalli-Sforza, L. L. & Feldman, M. W. The evolution of continuous variation. III. Joint transmission of genotype, phenotype and environment. Genetics, 1978, 90, 391.
King, J. L. Progress in the neutral mutation – random drift controversy. Federation Proceedings, 1976, 35(3), 2087.
Mayr, E. Behavior programs and evolutionary strategies. American Scientist, 1974, 62, 650

Muller, H. J. Variation due to change in the individual gene. American Naturalist, 1922, 56, 32.

Nebert, D. W. Genetic aspects of enzyme induction by drugs and chemical carcinogens. In R. W. Estabrook & E. Lindenlaub (Eds.), The induction of drug metabolism, 14th Symposia Medica Hoechst. Stuttgart and New York: Schattauer, in press.

Paigen, K. The genetics of enzyme realisation. In M. Rechcigl (Ed.), Enzyme synthesis and degradation in mammalian systems. Basel: Karger, 1971.

Provine, W. B. The origins of theoretical population genetics. Chicago: University of Chicago Press, 1971.

PARTICIPANTS

Antonelli, P. L., University of Alberta, Edmonton, Canada
Anant, S. S., Lethbridge, Canada
Abeelen, J. H. F. van, Katholieke Universiteit, Nijmegen, Holland
Baker, W. J., University of Alberta, Edmonton, Canada
Broadhurst, P. L., University of Birmingham, Birmingham, England
Caspari, E. W., University of Rochester, Rochester, U.S.A.
Collins, R. A., Bangor, U.S.A.
Collins, R. L., The Jackson Laboratory, Bar Harbor, U.S.A.
Crawford, C., Simon Fraser University, Burnaby, Canada
Damste, P. H., Academisch Ziekenhuis, Utrecht, Holland
DeFries, J. C., University of Colorado, Boulder, U.S.A.
DeGroot, P., University of Alberta, Edmonton, Canada
Dow, M., University of Edinburgh, Edinburgh, U.K.
Dworkin, R. H., Cornell University, Ithaca, U.S.A.
Epling, W. F., University of Alberta, Edmonton, Canada
Eysenck, H. J., University of London, England
Frender, R., University of Alberta, Edmonton, Canada
Fulker, D. W., University of London, London, England
Fuller, J. L., State University of New York, Binghamton, U.S.A.
Haber, S. B., Brookhaven National Laboratory, Upton, U.S.A.
Harnad, S., Princeton, U.S.A.
Hay, D. A., La Trobe University, Bundoora, Australia
Henderson, N. D., Oberlin College, Oberlin, U.S.A.
Holmes, M., University of Alberta, Edmonton, Canada
Johnson, R. G., MacAlester College, St. Paul, U.S.A.
Kittrell, E. M., University of Texas, Austin, U.S.A.
Klippel, J. A., Hollins College, Roanoke, U.S.A.
Kuse, A., University of Colorado, Boulder, U.S.A.
Lock, G. S. H., University of Alberta, Edmonton, Canada
Loehlin, J. C., University of Texas, Austin, U.S.A.
Lytton, C., University of Calgary, Calgary, Canada
Marshal, M. L., University of Alberta, Edmonton, Canada
Maxson, S. C., University of Connecticut, Storrs, U.S.A.
McClearn, G. E., University of Colorado, Boulder, U.S.A.
Milton, G. A., University of Victoria, Victoria, Canada
Morgan, K., University of Alberta, Edmonton, Canada
Mos, L. P., University of Alberta, Edmonton, Canada
Nelson, T. M., University of Alberta, Edmonton, Canada
Nyborg, H., University of Aarhus, Risskov, Denmark
Oliverio, A., Laboratorio Di Psicobiologia, Rome, Italy
Pauls, D., University of Iowa, Iowa City, U.S.A.
Plomin, R., University of Colorado, Boulder, U.S.A.
Reed, T. E., University of Toronto, Toronto, Canada
Rick, J. T., University of Sheffield, Sheffield, England
Roach, E. G., Indiana University, Indianapolis, U.S.A.
Rose, R. J., Indiana University, Bloomington, U.S.A.
Royce, J. R., University of Alberta, Edmonton, Canada
Rozeboom, W. W., University of Alberta, Edmonton, Canada
Satinder, K. P., Lakehead University, Thunder Bay, Canada

Spanjaard, C. C., Free University, Amsterdam, Holland
Spuhler, J. N., University of New Mexico, Albuquerque, U.S.A.
Stafford, R. E., Bridgewater State College, Bridgewater, U.S.A.
Streng, J., Free University, Amsterdam, Holland
Tennessen, H., University of Alberta, Edmonton, Canada
Thauberger, P. C., Edmonton, Canada
Thiessen, D. D., University of Texas, Austin, U.S.A.
Thompson, J. N., Jr., University of Oklahoma, Norman, U.S.A.
Thompson, W. R., Queen's University, Kingston, Canada
Truax, S., University of Nebraska, Lincoln, U.S.A.
Uyeno, E. T., Stanford Research Institute, Menlo Park, U.S.A.
Vandenberg, S. G., University of Colorado, Boulder, U.S.A.
Voorhees, B. H., University of Alberta, Edmonton, Canada
Wahlsten, D., University of Waterloo, Waterloo, Canada
Ward, R., Université Du Québec, Trois Rivières, Canada
Whitney, G., Florida State University, Tallahassee, U.S.A.
Wilson, K. V., University of Alberta, Edmonton, Canada
Wimer, C., City of Hope National Medical Center, Dwarte, U.S.A.
Woods, E. J., University of Alberta, Edmonton, Canada
Wozny, J., University of Alberta, Edmonton, Canada
Zonderman, A. B., University of California, Berkeley, U.S.A.

AUTHOR INDEX

A

Abeelen, J.H.F. van, 4, 45, *94*, 98, 101, 105. 107, *108*, 114, 117, *119*, 213, 476, 488, 489, 504, 507, 511, 512, 577, 663, 664, 666, 670

Acland, H., 314, *333*

Adair, L. B., *206*

Adam, P. A., 452, *467*

Adamowicz, J. K., 559, *569*

Ader, R., 350, *377*

Adler, J., 14, *36*, 188, *206*

Ahe, K., 632, *641*

Ahern, F. M., 568, *570*

Aksel, R., 76, *90, 643*

Alcock, J., 122, *132*

Alleva, E., 152, *161*

Allport, G. W., 492, *501*

Altman, J., 139, 147, *161*

Anastasi, A., 102, *109*

Anderson, R. A., 15, *36*

Angus, J., 52, 57, *85*, 98, *100*

Anisman, H., 69, 77, *85*, 438, *465*

Annet, M., 235, *236*

Applewhite, 385, *387*

Arnold, W. J., 655, *655*

Aronson, L. R., 4, *8*, 104, *109*

Aschoff, J., 152, *161*

Ashton, G. C., 405, 415, *415*, 562, 566, *570, 571*, 613, 617, 618, 637, *642*

Ashworth, J. M., 187, *207*

Atkinson, R. C., 561, *570*

Ayad, G., *162*

B

Baerends, G. P., 103, *109*

Bailey, D. W., 476, *480*

Bailey, T. B., 395, *416*

Baker, J. R., 535, *537*

Baker, R., 196, *209*

Baker, W. J., 541, 543

Bane, M. J., 314, *333*

Barash, D. P., 192, *206*

Barchas, J. D., *161*

Barchas, R. *161*

Barlow, G. W., 115, *118*

Barnes, B. W., 50, 51, 58, *85*, *90*, 342, *378*

Barnett, S. A., 64, *85*

Barnicot, N. A., 631, *641*

Barondes, S. H., 555, *569*

Barrows, S. L., 631, *641*

Bashi, J., 225, *237*, 367, *376*, 530, *537*

Bateson, P.P.G., 123, 130, *132*, 152, *161*

Beardmore, J. A., 64, *94*

Beatty, B. J., 455, *469*

Beauchamp, G. K., 174, *206*

Beck, S. L., 452, *465*

Becker, P. H. 452, *465*

Beerman, W., 171, *206*

Bellin, J. S., 632, *648*

Belmont, L., 225, 226, *236*, 370, 371, *376*

Beloff, J. R., 494, *502*, 617, 618, 621, 639, *641*

Belyaev, D. K., 58, 72, 73, *85*

Bennet-Clark, H. C., 117, *118*

Bent, D. H., 412, *416*

Bentley, D., 106, *109*

Benzer, S., 106, *111*, 342, *378*

Berg, H. C., 14, 15, 17, *36*

Bergsma, D., 30, *36*

Beritashvilii, I. S., 143, *161*

Bermant, G., *206*

Bernstein, F., 32, *36*

Berrien, F. K., 580, *641*

Berry, R. J., 251, *284*

Bertalanffy, L. von, 582, *641*

Bianchini, J. C., 409, *416*

Bignami, G., 338, *376*

Birren, J. E., 557, *569*

Bitterman, M. E., 45, *85*, 143, *161*

Blewett, D. B., 494, *502*, 616, 618, 621, 639, *641*

Blight, W. C., 253, *286*

688

Harris, H. T., 631, *643*
Harris, M. I., 449, 452, *465*
Harris, W. A., 342, *378*
Harrison, B. J., 48, *92*
't Hart, M., 104, *112*, 117, *119*
Hay, D. A., 52, *89*, 98, 99, *100*, 116, 117, 292, 295, *299*, 384, 385, *386*, 479, 510
Hayman, B. I., 55, *89*, 254, *285*
Haythorn, M. M., 496, *503*, 631, *643*
Hazel, L. N., 389, 393, *416*
Hazelbauer, G. L., 14, *37*, 188, *206*
Hebb, D. O., 102, *110*
Hebert, J. P., 535, *539*
Hegmann, J. P., 64, 72, *89*, *91*, 250, 279, 282, *284*, *285*, 399, 400, 401, *416*
Heinze, W. J., 80, *89*
Henderson, N. D., 5, 57, 65, 68, 69, 70, 78, 80, *89*, *90*, 96, 243, 245, 257, 267, 272, 274, 276, 277, *285*, *286*, 293, 296, 339, *377*, *378*, 401, 403, *416*, 439, 440, *467*, 491, *503*, 664, 665, 669
Henderson, P. W., 174, *207*
Hendrick, P. W., 173, *208*
Hendrickson, A. E., 575, *578*
Hendrickson, D. E., 575, *578*
Henry, F. V., 31, *40*
Henry, K. R., 438, 439, *467*, 496, *503*, 631, *643*
Hermetet, J. C., *161*, *162*, *164*
Heston, L. L., 357, *378*
Hewitt, J. K., 72, 77, *90*, 346
Heyns, B., 314, *333*
Hill, W. G., 456, *467*
Hinde, R. A., 101, *110*
Hinkelman, K., 60, 79, *87*, *91*
Hinko, E., 631, *644*
Hirsch, J., 102, *110*, 275, *286*, 441, *467*, *468*

Hjortland, M., 456, *466*
Hochachka, P. W., 188, *208*
Hockett, C. F., 23, 34, *37*
Hoebel, B. G., 401, *416*
Hoffeditz, E. L., 235, *237*
Hofstetter, H. W., 631, *643*
Hogan, E., *161*
Holmes, T. M., 62, 64, 68, 74, 76, 83, *90*, *93*, 420, *421*, *620*, *640*
Holt, P., 602, 639, *645*
Holzinger, K. J., 311, *333*, 441, *468*, 613, 630, *643*, *645*
Homyk, T., 106, *110*
Hopson, J. A., 198, *208*
Hörmann-Heck, S. von, 104, *110*
Horn, J., *208*, 226, *237*, 303, *333*
Hornchen, H., 452, *467*
Hotta, 106, *111*
Howard, M., 312, 313, *332*
Howarth, E., 620, *646*
Hull, C. H., 412, *416*
Hull, C. L., 519, 522, 523, *539*
Hummel, K. P., 497, *502*
Humphrey, T., 28, *36*
Hunka, S., 409, *416*
Hunt, E., 227, *237*, 561, *571*, 574, *578*, 652, *656*
Hyde, J. S., 62, 78, *90*, 490, *503*

I

Iino, T., 14, 17, 19, *37*
Illmensee, K., 107, *111*
Immelmann, K., 99, 114, 115, *118*, 122, 123, 131, *133*, 673
Ingram, T.T.S., 556, *571*
Ingvar, D. H., 29, *37*
Inman, O., *162*
Insel, P., 235, *237*
Isaac, G. L., 28, *37*
Isaacson, R. L., 107, *111*, 555, *571*
Itani, J., 33, *38*
Itturian, W. B., 631, *643*
Izawa, K, 33, *38*

694

T

Takahara, Y., 579, 580, 582, 644
Talland, G. A., 28, 40, 558, 572
Tanner, J. M., 32, 40
Tata, J. R., 211
Tauber, C. A., 106, 112
Taubman, P., 373, 374, 379
Taylor, C. E., 381, 387
Taylor, S. A., 462, 469
Teasdale, J. D., 524, 540
Tharp, V. K., 560, 572
Thayer, D., 627, 630, 643
Thiessen, D. D., 5, 107, 112, 115, 144, 162, 166, 169, 187, 189, 210, 211, 250, 287, 473, 489, 496, 498, 504, 507, 512, 631, 648, 663, 667, 668
Thomas, K., 81, 94
Thomas, M., 235, 237
Thompson, J. N. Jr., 135, 215
Thompson, W. H., 455, 469
Thompson, W. R., 5, 54, 70, 89, 99, 100, 221, 227, 228, 230, 232, 233, 237, 238, 243, 285, 397, 417, 490, 499, 502, 607, 631, 643, 663
Thorndike, E. L., 518, 519, 526, 540
Thorpe, W. H., 114, 118
Thurstone, L., 616, 648
Thurstone, T., 616, 648
Tiplady, B., 146, 164
Tobach, E., 632, 648
Trivers, R. L., 198, 201, 211
Tryon, R. C., 78, 94
Tunnicliff, G., 146, 164, 340, 379, 382, 384, 387
Tutin, C. E. G., 32, 38
Tyeson, H., 462, 469
Tyler, P. A., 490, 504

U

Underwood, B. J., 278, 287
Ursprung, H., 107, 111

V

Valatx, J. L., 147, 149, 164
Vale, C. A., 60, 65, 94, 211
Vale, J. R., 60, 65, 94, 103, 112, 211, 283, 287
Vandenberg, S. G., 203, 208, 211, 241, 355, 357, 378, 379, 389, 395-400, 403-406, 409, 411, 413, 415, 416, 417, 420, 431, 432, 469, 544, 545, 562, 566, 567, 568, 570, 571, 572, 613, 616-618, 620, 622, 625, 626, 632, 637-639, 642, 648, 653, 654
Vellutino, F. R., 557, 572
Verplanck, W. S., 102, 112
Vesell, E. S., 66, 95
Vicari, E. M., 54, 78, 95
Von Neumann, J., 13, 40

W

Wada, J. A., 28, 40
Wahlsten, D., 5, 245, 263, 276, 287, 288, 425, 438, 465, 477, 509, 512, 545, 546, 577, 664, 675, 676
Wainwright, P. 465, 469
Wallace, P., 174, 211
Walters, D. E., 248, 287
Walton, P. D., 63, 95
Wardell, D., 579, 590-593, 601, 628, 630, 637, 648
Warden, D. J., 4, 8
Warner, L. H., 4, 8
Wartofsky, 653, 658
Washburn, S. L., 192, 211
Watson, J. B., 15, 40, 475, 480, 481
Watts, C. R., 200, 211
Waugh, N. C., 552, 558, 572
Weiler, M.G.W., 210
Weinberg, R., 630, 643
Weismann, A., 447, 470
Weiss, J. M., 339, 379
Wells, P. H., 385, 387
Wender, P. H., 357, 378
Westlake, J., 335, 336
Whitaker, H. A., 22, 23, 29, 40
White, J. E., 250, 285

SUBJECT INDEX

702

individual differences and,
129ff.
irreversible, 123ff.
late, 132
prenatal, 172
sensitive phases of, 124ff.
sexual, 121ff.
inbreeding, 205, 289
inbreeding depression, 205, 257,
530, 534, 547-548
inclusive fitness, 201-202
individual differences,
and information processing,
560ff.
inductor hormone, 186
infanticide, 216
infectious inheritance, 574
infectious transmission, 675
inferred phenotypes, 670
inferred psychophenes, 492ff.,
501, 505, 508
information processing, 227,
556ff., 597-598, 634ff.,
670
information theory, 550ff., 652
inheritance,
of acquired characteristics,
447
Mendelian vs. non-Mendelian,
453ff.
non-Mendelian, 448ff., 675
innate behavior mechanisms,
101ff., 115, 130ff., 142
instinct, 102ff., 531
instrumental learning, 272
integrated personality, 601
intelligence, 149, 312, 366,
370, 440, 525, 534-536,
576, 603, 605, 651, 654,
666, 676
factors of, 410
interactionalism, 11
inter-racial crosses, 56
introversion, 520ff., 589ff.,
598-599, 653, 670
introversion-extraversion, 396
I.Q., 381, 383, 651
and environment, 275
heritability of, 222, 226
and mental abilities, 605-607

plasticity of, 235
and socioeconomic status,
319ff.
isoallelic variation, 255
isolation, 113, 297, 419

K

karyotyping, 205

L

L-amino acid decarboxylase, 145
lactation, 198
language, 22ff., 452
language areas,
and emotion, 28
cytostructure of, 25ff.
laterality,
in duckweed, 451
lateralization,
of speech, 25
Latin-square design, 674
Law of least parental effort,
234ff.
learned helplessness, 229ff,
238ff.
learning, 453
appetitive, 267
avoidance, 340, 382, 663
detour, 79
discrimination 270ff.
drosophila in, 342ff.
escape, 267
factors of, 265
genetics of, 263
innate components of, 147
maze, 78
measures of, 264
neurochemistry of, 154
phylogeny of, 143
social, 229
strain differences and, 147,
148
verbal, 550ff.
lethal genes, 255
leukemia, 450
life,
definitions of, 12